31931002929374

REFERENCE

ROGER WILLIAMS UNIV. LIBRARY

The Philosophy of Law

Garland Reference Library of the Humanities (Vol. 1743)

The Philosophy of Law

REFERENCE

An Encyclopedia

Volume II
K–Z

Editor
Christopher Berry Gray

GARLAND PUBLISHING, INC.
A MEMBER OF THE TAYLOR & FRANCIS GROUP
New York & London
1999

ROGER WILLIAMS UNIV. LIBRARY

#40668107

Ref. K 204 .P49 1999 v.2

REF K204 .P49 1999
v.2
The philosophy of law : an
encyclopedia

Copyright © 1999 Christopher Berry Gray
All rights reserved.

Library of Congress Cataloging-in-Publication Data

The philosophy of law : an encyclopedia / editor, Christopher Berry Gray.
p. cm. — (Garland reference library of the humanities ; vol. 1743)
Includes bibliographical references and index.
ISBN 0-8153-1344-6 (alk. paper)
1. Law—Philosophy—Encyclopedias. I. Gray, Christopher B.
II. Series.
K204.p49 1999 99-11065
340′.1—dc21 CIP

Contents

Volume I

Volume II

K

Kant, Immanuel (1724–1804)

Immanuel Kant's philosophy of law constitutes an attempt at specifying the institutional conditions for the realization of the only innate right he thought human beings possess, namely the right to freedom. His most systematic account of law can be found in his *Doctrine of Right,* which comprises the first part of a larger work entitled *The Metaphysics of Morals* (1797). Briefer, but nonetheless important reflections can also be found in two essays published shortly before the *Doctrine of Right,* "Theory and Practice" (1793) and "Toward Perpetual Peace" (1795).

A necessary condition of an agent's freedom is, in Kant's view, his ability to control external resources. Kant's account of what he terms "Private Right" is thus largely taken up with the problem of specifying the conditions under which an agent can truly be said to possess an object of choice (a concept which Kant construes broadly as including external things, but also the actions of others which one controls through promise or contract, and the status of persons related in various ways to the agent). Kant argued that a person cannot truly be said to possess an object unless his possession extends to occasions in which he is not in physical control of the object in question. Real, "intelligible" possession requires that the agent be able to view himself as having been wronged by any interference with the objects he claims to possess, even when he is not in physical control of them. A conceptual requirement of the possibility of this kind of relationship between agents and things is that others tacitly consent to relinquish any claim they may have had over the object. We must therefore presuppose, as a condition of making sense of individual possession, that all people, prior to individual acts of appropriation, possess an equal prima facie right to all things. Kant refers to this conceptual presupposition as the idea of the "original community of land, and with it of things upon it."

Prior to the establishment of a lawful civil order, however, people's possessions can in fact not be held with the kind of certainty that is required as a condition of their freedom, for they can never be assured that their respect of other people's possessions will be reciprocated. Full property rights can therefore only exist when people agree to quit the unlawful condition of the state of nature by submitting their individual wills to "a collective general (common) and powerful will." It is thus a duty for human beings who cannot avoid living side by side, and who therefore represent potential threats to each other's freedom in the state of nature, to submit themselves to a civil, constitutional order. (Kant even thought that those persons who refused to quit the state of nature could legitimately be coerced into doing so.) Kant terms "Public Right" the set of institutional conditions which must be in place in order to secure full property rights, and thus, to realize the right to freedom.

The grounds for the establishment of the state are thus clearly individualistic: individual agents rationally consent to submit themselves to legal authority so that their ability to acquire objects of choice, and thus freedom, might be secured. It follows that the "united will of the people" is the only legitimate source of law. The idea of the original contract uniting the wills of all individuals subject to the authority of the state must therefore serve as the normative basis for all legislative bodies. (Kant was not, however, a proponent of universal suffrage: he thought that certain classes of people—women, servants, apprentices, minors—lacked the "independence" required to be full citizens.) The people united through the idea of the original contract as sovereign legislators cannot, however, also hold executive authority, as the latter is subject to the laws enacted by the former, and it would be a logical contradiction for the legislative authority to be both sovereign and subject. The ruler holding executive authority is meant to administer the law that the legislature makes. Kant believed that simplicity was a prime virtue for this function and thus favored constitutional monarchy. The constitutional structure of Kant's republic is completed by the judicial authority. Kant likens the relationship of sovereign, ruler, and judge to the three propositions of a practical syllogism.

The actual function which the idea of the social contract is meant to perform is made clear in "Theory and Practice." It is meant to serve as a counterfactual constraint on the decision making of members of legislative bodies: the legitimacy of laws in Kant's view depends upon it being possible for all citizens to consent to them. However, Kant opposed all eudaemonistic interpretations of this condition. Law ought in his view to be enacted not with a view to the happiness of citizens, but rather so as to preserve and protect the conditions of their freedom and autonomous agency. For this reason, Kant was particularly insistent about the importance of a vigorous sphere of public debate, protected by legal guarantees of freedom of the pen, as an aid to legislation. Only by listening to the complaints and suggestions of citizens might legislators overcome the epistemic limitations which their finite condition imposes upon them.

Although Kant therefore supported some form of indirect public input into the legislative process, he was firm in his opposition to any right of public resistance to legal authority. The overthrow of a constitutional order would risk plunging a society back into the legal vacuum of the state of nature, a graver threat to individual freedom in Kant's view than even fairly despotic regimes. Additionally, the very idea of a right to resistance involves a logical contradiction, in so far as it would involve recognizing an authority superior to that of the (by hypothesis) supreme authority of the sovereign. Kant was nonetheless an admirer of the French revolution, if not of its revolutionaries, and saw the enthusiasm it instilled in observers throughout Europe as a sign of the progress of mankind.

The stern authoritarian strand in Kant's legal philosophy can also be seen in his brief remarks on penal law. He was a defender of the principle of retribution in punishment, and was a particularly steadfast proponent of capital punishment, against eminent legal theorists of his time such as Cesare Beccaria.

Kant's thoughts on international law complete his philosophy of law. He viewed perpetual peace as the final, most encompassing condition which had to be fulfilled for freedom to be realized, and he wrote his principal essay on the subject in the form of a peace treaty. In it, he envisaged a federation of states bound together through the observance of a set of peace-promoting articles, notably a commitment to republicanism as the form of government of all participating states, and the extension by all member states of hospitality to foreign nationals.

After generations of scholarly neglect, Kant's legal philosophy has enjoyed a renaissance in recent years. Renewed interest has inevitably led to conflicting views about what Kant actually meant. One very important debate has to do with the interpretation of Kant's contractarianism. Leslie Mulholland's account of Kant's philosophy of law argues that Kant's contractarianism is actually a thinly veiled version of natural law theory. However, while it is true that actual consent plays no role in the argument leading up to the rational necessity of the republican state, Kant's view of legal and political activity within the state is too resolutely proceduralist and antieudaemonistic for this interpretation to be entirely satisfactory.

References

Goyard-Fabre, Simone. *Kant et le problème du droit* (Kant and the Problem of the Law). Paris: Vrin, 1975.

Kant, Immanuel. *The Doctrine of Right.* In *The Metaphysics of Morals,* ed. and trans. Mary Gregor. Cambridge: Cambridge University Press, 1991.

———. "Theory and Practice" and "Toward Perpetual Peace." In *Kant's Political Philosophy,* ed. Hans Reiss. Cambridge: Cambridge University Press, 1970.

Mulholland, Leslie A. *Kant's System of Rights.* New York: Columbia University Press, 1990.
Rosen, Allen D. *Kant's Theory of Justice.* Ithaca: Cornell University Press, 1993.
"Why Kant?" *Columbia Law Review,* 87 (special issue) (1987).

Daniel M. Weinstock

Kaufmann, Arthur (1923–)

Arthur Kaufmann, German jurist and legal philosopher, is one of the foremost exponents of a hermeneutical approach to philosophical foundations of law. Kaufmann's legal philosophy developed, first of all, from axiological neokantianism (G. Radbruch in his late period) and philosophical hermeneutics (Hans-Georg Gadamer). The roots of his work may also be found in the existentialism of Karl Jaspers and the anthropology of Karl Löwith.

Kaufmann's conception is one which aspires to pinpoint the ultimate foundations of law and addresses the problems of legal philosophy at the level of basic epistemological and ontological questions. As a result, he proposes *a procedural justice theory which is founded on the person (eine personal [sachlich] fundierte prozedurale Gerechtigkeitstheorie).*

In his view, law in the primary meaning of the word always pertains to concrete cases. Legal norms or principles are solely "potential" law and the entirely real law is that which is just in a given situation (*ipsa res iusta*). Justice belongs to the essence of law and "unjust law" constitutes a contradiction in terms. Kaufmann opposes all those theories which accept legal norms (*Gesetz*) as the only foundation for establishing just law (*Recht*). In Kaufmann's opinion, such theories are powerless in the face of all types of distortions of law. He suggests that the basic phenomenon which needs to be explained and which cannot be disregarded by a philosopher of law is so-called legal lawlessness *(gesetzliches Unrecht).* According to Kaufmann, the "legal lawlessness" of twentieth-century totalitarian states proved with the accuracy of scientific experiment that the reality of law consists of something more than bare conformity with legal norms. The existence of *lex corrupta* indicates that law contains something "nondispositive," which is not at the free disposal either of legislator or judge and which determines the content of law.

Kaufmann accepts a concept of truth and cognition based on the principle of convergency: "nondispositive" content, emerging as the conformity of a number of cognitive acts by different subjects, indicates the presence of being. Taking into account the nondispositiveness of law, the fundamental questions of philosophy of law (What is law? and What are the principles of a just solution?) lead directly to ontology, to the question about a being that provides foundations of law.

The determination of what is just takes place in a certain type of process. A question about the ontic foundations of law is a question about the ontic foundations of this process. In analyzing the process of determining legal judgment, Kaufmann rejects a model based on simple subsumption and proposes one based on inference by analogy in which concrete law ensues through a process of "bringing to conformity" that which is normative with that which is factual. The understanding of legal norms is determined in respect of the concrete data, and the concrete data are interpreted in the light of norms. In this process a single sense is established and equally expresses an understanding of given data and corresponding norms. The establishment of this "sense" appears to be "nondispositive" and controlled intersubjectively. So, in conformity with his convergent concept of truth, he accepts the existence of an entity corresponding to that sense and calls it the "nature of things." The "nature of things" is a real relation that occurs between being and obligation, between the conditions of life and normative quality. A question arises about the ontic bases corresponding to the nondispositiveness of "material" undergoing "treatment" in the process of determining both judgment and the process itself. In Kaufmann's conception this ontic basis is man, not "empirical man," but man as a "person" understood as a set of relations between man and other people and things. A "person" is that which is given and permanent in the process of the finding of just law (the "what" of the process). On one hand, it consists of those relations which undergo "treatment" in the process. On the other hand, a "person" determines the procedure of the process (the "how" of the process). A "person" being, at the same time, the "how" and the "what" of the process of realization of law, is also, to put it in another way, a structural unity of relation and that which constitutes this relation (unity of *relatio* and *relata*). According to this approach a "person" is neither an object nor a subject. A "person" exists only "in between." It is relational, dynamic, and historical. A "person" is not substance, is not a state, but an event which changes in every process of finding a just solution.

References

Kaufmann, Arthur. *Analogie und "Natur der Sache."* Karlsruhe: Müller, 1962; 2d rev. ed. Heidelberg: Decker und Müller, 1982. Trans. I. Tammelo as "Analogy and 'The Nature of Things'." *Journal of the Indian Law Institute* 8 (1966), 386–401.

———. *Beiträge zur Juristischen Hermeneutik* (Essays on Legal Hermeneutics). Köln: Heymann, 1984; 2d ed. 1993.

———. *Das Schuldprinzip* (The Matter of Guilt). Heidelberg: Winter 1962; 2d ed. 1976.

———. "Entre iusnaturalismo y positivismo hacia le hermeneutica juridica" (Toward a Hermeneutics of Law: Between Naturalism and Positivism). *Anales Catedra Suarez* 17 (1977), 351–362.

———. *Grundprobleme der Rechtsphilosophie* (Basic Problems of Legal Philosophy). Beck: München 1994.

———. "National Socialism and German Jurisprudence from 1933 to 1945." *Cardozo Law Review* 9 (1988), 1629-1649.

———. *Rechtsphilosophie im Wandel* (Changes in Philosophy of Law). Köln: Heymann, 1984.

———. "The Small-Coin Right of Resistance: An Admonition to Civil Courage." In *Prescriptive Formality and Normative Rationality in Modern Legal Systems: Festschrift for Robert S. Summers,* ed. W. Krawietz, N. MacCormick, and G.H. von Wright, 573–579. Berlin: Duncker und Humblot, 1994.

———. *Über Gerechtigkeit: Dreißig Kapitel praxisorientierter Rechtsphilosophie.* Köln: Heymann, 1993.

Savarese, Paolo. "Il diritto tra essere e storia nella prospettiva di Arthur Kaufmann." *Rivista internazionale di filosofia del diritto* 60 (1983), 407–438.

Marek Piechowiak

See also Existentialist Philosophy of Law; Hermeneutical Philosophy of Law; Persons, Identity of

Kaufmann, Felix (1895–1949)

Businessman and lawyer, Felix Kaufmann taught philosophy of law in the law faculty in Vienna; he also participated in the Vienna Circle, the only follower of Edmund Husserl to be associated with it. From 1939 onward, he taught philosophy at the New School for Social Research in New York. Although Kaufmann was always very interested in mathematics, he first studied law, in part, for practical reasons; he completed a doctorate in law under Hans Kelsen (1881–1973) in Vienna in 1920, and a doctorate in philosophy (with a thesis in philosophy of law) in 1922. He was then named a *Privatdozent* in Vienna on Kelsen's recommendation. Since his university position was unpaid, he worked in the private sector, eventually becoming manager of the Anglo-Iranian Oil Company for Austria; all the while, he continued to teach, to attend meetings of Moritz Schlick's (1882–1936) and Friedrich Waismann's (1896–1959) circle, and to publish. After arriving in the United States in 1939, Kaufmann participated in the International Phenomenological Society and edited the phenomenological movement's American journal, *Philosophy and Phenomenological Research.*

During his student days, Kaufmann became acquainted with the work of Edmund Husserl, particularly the *Logical Investigations,* and considered himself to be a phenomenologist during his career. He never thought of himself as a logical positivist, but did have high respect for that group's rigorous, clear, logical analyses. He had an extremely wide range of interests, publishing books on the philosophy of law, on the philosophy of mathematics, and on the logic and methodology of social sciences (including economics). He took concepts from, among other places, Husserl's more logical and mathematical earlier works, and applied them to questions dealing with legal theory in particular and with theory in the social sciences in general.

Kaufmann's first three books, in the 1920s, dealt with the philosophy of law. Drawing on Husserl's *Logical Investigations,* he attempted to work out a logic of procedural rules in order to establish the logical basis for Hans Kelsen's pure theory of law. According to Kelsen, legal theory must abstain from making any value judgments about its object, the norm. The norm is an ought statement, can be neither true nor false, cannot be reduced to or derived from an is, a statement of fact which can be either true or false. Kaufmann rejected Kelsen's kantianism in favor of a more phenomenological point of view. For Kaufmann, the norm has a dual aspect—the substantive norm itself, the is, and the sanction, the ought—and it is possible to reduce the norm to the factual human behavior which underlies it.

Kaufmann believed that anything in human experience is open to rational thought, and that if the use of value terms follows rules, then it is possible to treat them as objectively as we treat the use of any other terms. As he notes, arguments using norms are often elliptical because the norms are not explicitly stated; however, once normative statements are clarified, we can see that they suffered from ambiguity but not from being "subjective." In fact, just as David Hume showed that it is impossible to demonstrate the validity of induction in natural science, so there may be no ultimate justification for the norms we choose, but once the norm is given, rational analysis is just as possible as in any "objective" science.

Kaufmann felt it was important to examine the conditions under which human experience in its various realms becomes intelligible, and this means to examine the logical and methodological issues involved in ensuring that discourse about experience can be meaningful and that judgments about experience can become justified. He rejected simplified views on the distinction between natural science and social science, claiming that there was a unity to science. Philosophy is essentially a critique of knowledge; thus philosophers must deal with the logic of science, handling questions of the means of validation of belief implicit in the different sciences and clarifying the concepts used in sciences and in the very structure of the various sciences. All special sciences, such as jurisprudence, require a philosophical foundation that will work out the rules and methods of analysis and interpretation that can be used validly to produce justified beliefs.

Although Kaufmann always claimed to be a phenomenologist and not a logical positivist, some themes common to the early Husserl and the Vienna Circle can be seen in his work: the desire to make philosophy scientific, the view that there was a unity to science, the notion that we are to deal with the things themselves and not with something transcending all possible experience, and the accent on logic and on detailed analyses.

References

Albertazzi, Liliana. "The 'Open Texture' of Concepts—Kaufmann and the Brentanists." In *Phenomenologie und Logischer Empirismus. Zentenarium Felix Kaufmann (1895–1959),* ed. Friedrich Stadler. Wien-New York: Springer, 1997.

Kaufmann, Felix. *The Infinite in Mathematics: Logico-Mathematical Writings.* Trans. Paul Foulkes. Ed. Brian McGuinness. Intro. Ernest Nagel. Dordrecht: Reidel, 1978.

———. "The Issue of Ethical Neutrality in Political Science." *Social Research* 16 (1949), 344–352.

———. *Die Kriterien des Rechts. Eine Untersuchung über die Prinzipien der juristischen Methodenlehre* (The Criteria of Law: An Investigation of the Principles of Legal Methodology). Tübingen: Mohr, 1924. Reprint, Darmstadt: Scientia Verlag Aalen, 1966.

———. *Logik und Rechtswissenschaft. Grundriss eines Systems der reinen Rechtslehre* (Logic and Legal Science: Foundations for a System of Pure Theory of Law). Tübingen: Mohr, 1922. Reprint, Darmstadt: Scientia Verlag Aalen, 1966.

———. *Methodology of the Social Sciences.* London: Oxford University Press, 1944.

———. "Phenomenology and Logical Empiricism." In *Philosophical Essays in Memory of Edmund Husserl,* ed. M. Farber, 124–142. Cambridge MA: Harvard University Press, 1940.

Zilian, H.G. *Klarheit und Methode: Felix Kaufmanns Wissenschaftstheorie* (Clarity and Method: Felix Kaufmann's Theory of Science). Amsterdam: Rodopi, 1990.

Richard Hudson
Henri R. Pallard

See also PHENOMENOLOGY OF LAW

Kelsen, Hans (1881–1973)

Hans Kelsen was born in Prague on October 11, 1881, to Jewish parents. After studying law at the University of Vienna, he began teaching law in the Habsburg capital. Following World War I, he was asked to draft the constitution for the new Austrian Republic. He became professor of public law at the University of Vienna, judge of the Constitutional Court, and one of the leading figures in Austrian academic, legal, and political circles. In 1930, following the dismissal of the members of the Constitutional Court by the government, Kelsen left Austria and during the following decade taught in Cologne, Geneva, and Prague. In 1940, he emigrated to the United States. After lecturing at Harvard and Wellesley College, he accepted a position with the University of California at Berkeley, where he taught until his retirement in 1952. He died in Berkeley on April 19, 1973.

As a professor of law, he wrote important treatises on public law, Austrian constitutional law, and international law. He was also interested in political science and political theory, writing works on the state, socialism and marxism, the parliamentary system, and democracy. Throughout his career, he conducted an unrelenting polemic against natural law theory; this led to studies of various moral philosophers, as well as excursions into anthropology. His central claim to fame, however, is his theory of law, which he began developing during his Austrian years with two colleagues, Adolf Merkl and Alfred Verdross, and which came to be called the "Pure Theory of Law." The theory took shape in the writings of the first quarter-century of his career and was set out programmatically in 1934. Thereafter, he refined and revised it in a series of publications, notably in 1960 and posthumously in 1979.

Kelsen's goal was to apply empiricism and moral skepticism to the study of law, to make possible a value-free "science of law." Nineteenth-century German legal thought had created a "general theory of law" (*Allgemeine Rechtslehre*) as a field of study separate from the "philosophy of law" (*Rechtsphilosophie*, or moral considerations about law). Kelsen saw himself as continuing the project of a general theory of law, but in a way which would remove some of the errors that still infected this discipline. Hence, the need for a purified theory of law, a "Pure Theory of Law."

Norms

Law is a collection of norms—standards for behavior—and the science of law is the systematic exposition of these norms. To locate norms (and law) among the possible objects of study, Kelsen appeals to the German distinction between *Naturwissenschaften* (natural science) and *Geisteswissenschaften* (the humanities), and the concepts of "meaning" and "interpretation" attendant on the latter term. Norms allow us to interpret events as having certain meanings. (For instance, one homicide is "interpreted" as murder, while another is interpreted as a lawful execution.) These meanings are not discernible empirically: to a natural scientist, the two homicides mentioned above look the same. For this reason, following neo-kantian practice, Kelsen refuses to say that norms "exist"; instead they are "valid" or "in force" (*gelten*). They are not facts, but meanings: they belong on the ought side of the is/ought distinction, and therefore cannot be discovered by empirical research.

This immunity to empirical research would appear to make any discussion of norms unscientific. However, there is one class of norms which can be the object of science, namely those whose validity is conditioned by human events: "positive" norms. (For instance, murder can be interpreted as "wrong" either because of a legal norm enacted by a legislature or because of an absolute moral norm.) The legal norm is positive, because it is interpreted as arising from an empirical event, while the moral norm is not. Positive norms can be identified by identifying the acts which are interpreted as giving rise to them. A science of norms, then, has an empirical basis. There are therefore two kinds of science: causal sciences (describing facts) and normative sciences (describing positive norms).

Nevertheless, a science of positive norms is never a purely empirical exercise. Every interpretation of an event as giving rise to a norm has both an empirical and a nonempirical component: the empirical component is the identification of the event, the nonempirical is the reliance on the existence of a higher norm making this event a source of norms. (For instance, acts of the legislature are interpreted as creating norms, because of the belief in the existence of a higher norm giving norm-making power to the legislature.) Thus, normative interpretations always rely on other normative interpretations.

This leads to a problem of infinite regress. An appeal to facts alone cannot be the answer, since an ought cannot be derived only from an is. The best answer Kelsen could give was to say that there was an ultimate normative interpretation relying on no other normative interpretation, which he called "presupposing the basic norm." (For instance, an event is interpreted as creating a constitution because we presuppose a basic norm, making this event a source of norms.) In a sense, therefore, it is a matter of personal belief whether there are any norms at all, even positive norms. Kelsen's theory of basic norms has been the object of much controversy and criticism.

Law

All the norms whose validity rests on one basic norm form a system of norms. Norms whose object is the behavior of people toward one another are called social norms. All systems of social norms rely on sanctions as a motive for compliance. Law differs from the other systems of social norms in that it is the only one which relies on physical force as a sanction. Indeed, it is a characteristic feature of law that it prohibits all use of force except as a sanction for wrongdoing. Law is therefore a technique for getting people to act in certain ways through the threat of coercion.

All legal norms are positive norms: they come into force and pass out of force when certain human events occur, and never because of their moral desirability or undesirability. The two social facts which can create or repeal law in all legal systems are the acts of competent officials and desuetude or "negative" custom (the fact that a law is neither obeyed nor enforced). Some legal systems also allow "positive" custom to be a source of law; precedent as a source of law in common law countries is understood by Kelsen to be a form of positive custom.

According to Kelsen, traditional jurisprudence thought of law as the will of the state. This view created problems for the concepts of international law (since there is no higher state imposing its will on other states) and public law (since it is unclear how the state can impose its will on itself). The pure theory of law corrects this misunderstanding, by defining law as a system of norms and defining the state as simply another name for a legal system which has reached a certain level of centralization. This allows us to see that international law is indeed law; it is a system of norms which makes use of coercive sanctions (reprisals and war). However, international law is a decentralized legal system, as law is in primitive societies; its norms arise through custom and treaties, and its sanctions are matters of self-help, decided on and enforced by the subjects of the system, namely individual states.

Legal Systems

A legal system is a *Stufenbau,* a hierarchical structure of norms; norms at one level are addressed to officials at the next lower level and regulate the creation of norms by these officials. The norms of the constitution are addressed to legislators and regulate the legislative process; the norms in statutes are addressed to judges and regulate judicial decisions; and the individual norms in judicial decisions are addressed to enforcement officials and order them to use coercion against specific individuals. Higher norms are made more specific by lower ones: law flows down in a series of cascades from the most general provisions to issue in specific acts of coercion against specific individuals. All legal norms (except those at the lowest level) are about the creation of more specific norms, and so law has this feature of regulating its own creation.

Traditional jurisprudence, says Kelsen, was unable to see the unity of a legal system. The pure theory reveals the unity of the system. All law is about the creation of lower norms and is addressed to officials; so there is no distinction in kind between public and private law. All officials (except those at the lowest level) perform both functions: they create law for the next lower level, and in so doing they apply the law of the next higher level. There is only a difference of degree, and not of kind, then, between the various levels: all applying of norms involves a degree of discretion, but legislators have more of it than judges, and judges more of it than enforcement officials.

Where norms are defective (obscure, ambiguous, inconsistent), the consequence of systematic unity is to leave the judge free to decide as he wishes. There is no way internal to the law of resolving these difficulties. The standard rules of interpretation are of no use, and there is no scientific way of weighing interests or finding the "just" solution. While these cases are not covered by any specific legal norm, nevertheless there are no gaps in the law, that is, no cases for which the law does not provide a solution, since the law requires the judge to dismiss a case which cannot be brought under any existing norm.

In some of his writings, Kelsen suggests that whenever a legal system is effective (that is, generally obeyed and enforced), a basic norm is presupposed. (Thus, when a revolutionary regime ousts an existing one, legal scholars will recognize the decisions of the new regime as law, that is, presuppose a new basic norm, if the new regime can make itself obeyed.) At one time, Kelsen was thought to hold that legal scholars should recognize a new regime when it is effective. Kelsen's doctrine of the basic norm has been invoked in a number of court cases following a revolutionary change of government, but with inconsistent results, since much uncertainty still surrounds the doctrine.

Developments

The basic features of Kelsen's theory just described remained constant throughout the decades. A number of other tenets changed over the years. The most important of these concern his view of the role of the legal scholar and of logic in the law. The change occurred in two stages.

In the first stage, which is reflected in *Reine Rechtslehre* (Pure Theory of Law), kantian constructivism was abandoned. Legal norms are not declarative sentences produced by the legal scholar's reformulation of the legal material; they are imperative sentences and are already given in the legal material. The scholar's task is limited to producing propositions of law (*Rechtssätze*), declarative sentences asserting the existence of the legal norms. This about-face entailed the demise of the earlier theory of the individuation, structure, and function of norms. So, Kelsen came to acknowledge that legal norms were not all duty-imposing; some granted permissions, others conferred powers, and others repealed existing norms. This change of view meant that a higher norm's regulation of the creation of lower-level norms in a legal system could be explained in terms of the conferral of power on the lower official rather than as a directive to the lower official to impose a sanction.

In the second state of Kelsen's development, which is reflected in *Allgemeine Theorie der Normen* (General Theory of Norms), once he came to see norms as imperative sentences, he concluded that they could not stand in logical relations (since logical relations hold only between sentences with truth-value). If they could not stand in relations of contradiction, then the incompatibility of conflicting norms was no longer a logical truth. Conflicting norms could coexist, and the only way a conflict could be resolved was by the explicit repeal of one of the norms, and not by the legal scholar. The new position also undermined the earlier claim that national and international law must form a single system. As well, if norms could not stand in relations of entailment, then it was impossible to derive an individual norm from a general norm (and suitable factual premises); creation of the lower norm by an official did not involve any logical derivation from a higher norm, but only an act of will. To replace the relation of entailment, Kelsen posited a relation of "correspondence" between higher and lower norms: a lower norm is justified if it "corresponds" to a higher norm.

Kelsen is considered by many to have been the most important legal philosopher of the twentieth century. His influence was greatest in German-speaking countries, where he is still widely discussed, in Latin America, where he was hailed as the defender of a nonideological treatment of law against natural law theory, and in Japan and Korea, where he is considered to be the model of European legal theory. He is one of the few continental legal theorists to be widely known in the English-speaking world, where he influenced thinkers interested in conceptual issues, such as H.L.A. Hart and Joseph Raz. In the decades since his death, his star has waned in the Anglo-American jurisprudential world, now preoccupied mainly with normative issues.

References

Kelsen, Hans. *Allgemeine Theorie der Normen.* Vienna: Manz, 1979. Trans. Michael Hartney as *General Theory of Norms.* Oxford: Clarendon Press, 1991. Contains an introductory essay by Michael Hartney on later developments in the Pure Theory of Law, and a bibliography of Kelsen's publications in English.

———. *Reine Rechtslehre.* Leipzig and Vienna: Deuticke, 1934. Trans. Bonnie Litschewski Paulson and Stanley L. Paulson as *Introduction to the Problems of Legal Theory.* Oxford: Clarendon Press, 1992. Contains an introduction and an annotated bibliography of secondary literature in English.

———. *Reine Rechtslehre.* Vienna: Deuticke, 1960. Trans. Max Knight as *Pure Theory of Law.* Berkeley and Los Angeles: University of California Press, 1967.

Walter, Robert. *Hans Kelsen: Ein Leben im Dienste der Wissenschaft.* Vienna: Manz, 1985. Contains a bibliography of Kelsen's publications.

Michael Hartney

L

Lasswell/McDougal Collaboration: Configurative Philosophy of Law

Myres S. McDougal (1906–1998) and Harold D. Lasswell (1902–1979), scholars with very different disciplinary and intellectual backgrounds, divergent but complementary work habits, and characteristic personality profiles, collaborated for almost fifty years in the construction of a jurisprudence for a free society. Its emphasis is on law, science, and the policies of human dignity. Over the years it has been subject to various designations, such as jurisprudence of the policy sciences, policy-oriented jurisprudence, contemporary legal realism, and the New Haven school or approach. In this entry we designate their approach configurative jurisprudence, because the framework or configuration it recommends is so distinctive when compared to conventional jurisprudence that friendly critics have suggested that it constitutes an incipient "new paradigm."

Every jurisprudential school of thought incorporates a framework—usually implied or assumed—of "thinking" processes that sets the conceptual boundaries of discourse and defines the standards of professionalism to either confirm or challenge conventional jurisprudential wisdom. Configurative jurisprudence is explicit about its purpose. It is a theory for inquiry about law and includes a requirement that it facilitate not only our understanding of law in any context, but law's improvement as well. Improvement is appraised in terms of how well law contributes to the achievement of human dignity.

The general orientation of configurative philosophy of law exhibits five major emphases to further inquiry and attendant professional responsibility.

1. It distinguishes the observational standpoints of the scholar and decision maker and, in aid of enlightenment, as well as of decision (for improving law's impact on the achievement of human dignity), develops a theory about law, and not merely of law.

2. It establishes a focus of attention and creates a map of inquiry, both comprehensive and selective, for effectively relating authoritative decision (that is, law) to the larger social and community processes by which that law is affected and which it in turn affects.

3. It formulates problems in terms of events in social process, that is, in terms of disparities between aspiration and achievement in a community's shaping and sharing of values.

4. It postulates, and makes commitment to, a comprehensive set of human dignity values for the public order of particular communities (including the world community as a whole), which can be made explicit, in social process terms, in whatever degrees of abstraction and precision may be required in inquiry and decision.

5. It identifies the whole range of intellectual tasks relevant to the making of decisions and inquiry about and about the interrelations of law and social process. It specifies economic and effective procedures for the performance of each of these tasks.

The roots of configurative jurisprudence are tied to the revolt against formalism in social theory generally, and its particular expression in law as reflected in legal realism. It is also highly influenced by philosophical pragmatism's concern with pedagogy and cognition as reflected in John Dewey, especially his "How We Think," which forms the conceptual inspiration of a problem-oriented, solution-directed jurisprudence of decision making.

Vantage Point

Jurisprudence is conceived as a theory for inquiry about law. Effective and credible inquiry requires sensitivity to vantage point as well as attention to deeper levels of self-scrutiny, since what is "observed" itself involves a question of values reposing so to speak in the antechamber of legal theory. The intellectual product of inquiry about law influences what becomes operational law. Observation involves some commitments about preferred values for the public order—for the self and as recommended for others. Human dignity is the recommended "postulate" to guide inquiry as well as the normative dimensions of legal interventions. The establishment and maintenance of the observer's standpoint is therefore the starting point of inquiry about law.

Observing Context and Decision

Configurative jurisprudence emphasizes a focus on problems in context as well as decisional responses to them. The focus on context and problems requires intellectual tools of flexibility and dexterity so as to particularize problems in microdetail *and* relate those problems to the larger community context from which they emerge. The method for performing these tasks is termed "phase analysis," a procedure that permits context to be assayed at whatever level of abstraction is appropriate to the nature of the problem and the goal-values implicated. The procedure requires inquiry into participants, their perspectives, the assets or base values at their disposal, the situations in which they operate, the strategies they employ, and the results and outcomes generated. In short, phase analysis reveals that every social process consists of human beings pursuing values through institutions using resources.

A significant insight into the nature of social process is that its manageability for contextual inquiry about law is in some measure delimited by a relatively small number of what are conceived as value-institutional categories. No claim is made that these categories are a closed system regarding the identification of other potentially relevant or functionally equivalent value-institutional categories. The values are power, wealth, respect, enlightenment, skill, well-being, affection, and rectitude. These values refer generally to what all people want. The list of eight values is logically exhaustive in this regard but empirically empty. That is, even though all people want each of the eight values the ways in which or processes through which people give definition to and evaluate values are likely to differ from context to context.

Improving the outcomes of the processes through which values are shaped and shared is the central objective of configurative jurisprudence. Because law is to be used to achieve this objective (that is, to assist in securing a public order of human dignity), developing an empirical picture or mapping the complex interrelations among law, power, and social process in any context of concern is essential for scholar and decision maker. The phase analysis procedure can be and has been used for this purpose.

Formulating Particular Problems in Decision Context

From the map of community social process and its interrelated outcomes, the particular focus of configurative jurisprudence is inquiry about law, that is, authoritative and controlling decision. The focus on decision making puts an emphasis on delineating the activities that are engaged in decision making. In general, configurative jurisprudence identifies seven activities or functions that comprise any process of decision making and explores how each function may be used to improve the explicitly rational aspirations of legal decision making. (For further discussion of the functions of decision, see especially "The World Constitutive Process of Authoritative Decision.") This contrasts sharply with rule or precept-focused jurisprudence. The differences are illustrated as follows:

Rule	*Decision*
All or nothing	Intelligence
Logically incomplete	Promotion
Ambiguous	Prescription
Circular	Invocation
Comes in opposites or legal complementarities	Application
Gaps (legal vacuum)	Termination
Normative ambiguity	Appraisal

As a functional matter, precept-focused jurisprudence addresses the issue of decision in an astigmatic manner. There is, in consequence, no desire or need for a comprehensive concept of decision making, or for contextuality.

The Key Intellectual Tasks

In addition to delimiting the general context of law (that is, authoritative decision), the jurist must formulate particular problems for systematic and comprehensive inquiry. Here the "intellectual" tasks of the jurist come to grips with the core elements of policy or configurative thinking.

This involves goal thinking, trend thinking, conditioning/factor thinking, projective thinking, and alternative thinking. For elaboration of these intellectual tasks, see, in particular, *Jurisprudence for a Free Society, A Pre-View of Policy Sciences,* and "Theory About Law."

The central questions that configurative jurisprudence addresses are as follows: What is the public order, constitutive process, and civil society that law defends and promotes? What kind of order, process, and society should law promote and defend? How might this be achieved in a principled, fair, expeditious, and economically sensible manner? The focus on decision as the fulcrum of a realistic jurisprudence of human dignity stresses the dynamic element of legal theory and professional responsibility for the shaping and sharing of basic values. Jurisprudence in this view is neither value free nor neutral toward the ends it is meant to serve.

References

Ascher, William. "The Evolution of the Policy Sciences: Understanding the Rise and Avoiding the Fall." *Journal of Policy Analysis and Management* 5 (1986), 365.

Brunner, Ronald D. "The Policy Movement as a Policy Problem." *Policy Sciences* 24 (1991), 65.

Lasswell, Harold D. *A Pre-View of Policy Sciences.* New York: American Elsevier, 1971.

———. *Psychopathology and Politics.* Chicago: University of Chicago Press, 1930; New York: Viking Press, 1960.

Lasswell, Harold D., and Myres S. McDougal. *Jurisprudence for a Free Society: Studies in Law, Science and Policy.* 2 vols. New Haven: Yale University Press; The Hague: Martinus Nijhoff, 1992.

McDougal, Myres S., Harold D. Lasswell, and W. Michael Reisman. "The World Constitutive Process of Authoritative Decision." *Journal of Legal Education* 19 (1967), 253, 403. Reprinted in *The Future of the International Legal Order,* vol. 1. Ed. Cyril E. Black and Richard A. Falk. Princeton: Princeton University Press, 1969. (Reprinted in McDougal and Reisman, 1981.)

McDougal, Myres S., and W. Michael Reisman. *International Law Essays.* Westbury NY: Foundation Press, 1981.

Nagan, Winston P. "Conflict of Laws in Conflict: A Systematic Appraisal of Traditional and Contemporary Theory." *New York Journal of International and Comparative Law* 3 (1983).

Reisman, W. Michael. "Theory About Law: The New Haven School of Jurisprudence." *Jahrbuch* [of the Berlin Institute for Advanced Study] 228 (1989–90).

Reisman, W. Michael, and Aaron M. Schreiber. *Jurisprudence: Understanding and Shaping Law.* New Haven CT: New Haven Press, 1987.

Reisman, W. Michael, and Burns H. Weston, eds. *Toward World Order and Human Dignity: Essays in Honor of Myres S. McDougal.* New York: Free Press, 1976.

Winston P. Nagan
Andrew R. Willard

Latin American Philosophy of Law

Latin American philosophy is European in origin; it constitutes a chapter in the history of western philosophy. Latin American philosophy of law, in particular, exhibits this character quite clearly and has been heavily dependent on the thought of continental philosophers and jurists. The influence Anglo-American philosophy has exerted upon Latin American legal philosophy, with very few exceptions, is relatively recent and limited.

The history of Latin American legal philosophy may be broken down into four periods, each of which is dominated by the influence of one or more European philosophical movements.

Colonial Period (ca. 1550–1750)

In the years that followed the European landing on America, the greatest influence exerted upon Latin American thought in general came from scholasticism. The texts studied were those of the medieval scholastics, primarily

Thomas Aquinas (1225–1274) and John Duns Scotus (ca. 1265–1308), and of their Iberian commentators, Francisco de Vitoria (1492/1493–1546), Domingo de Soto (1494–1560), Pedro da Fonseca (1528–1597), and above all, Francisco Suárez (1548–1617). Latin American legal philosophers in this period were mainly concerned with elucidating issues dealing with the legitimacy of the conquest, the morality of the economic system of *encomiendas* (grants of natives to landowners), and, above all, the rights of Native Americans. The most important thinker who questioned the legitimacy of the conquest was Vitoria. The generally accepted view of peninsular authors was that the Spanish and Portuguese Crowns had rights of property over the goods found in the newly discovered lands. Vitoria used an argument based on analogy against this view. Suppose Native Americans had discovered the European continent; would the mere act of discovering it yield property rights for them? An affirmative answer would imply that Native Americans had property rights over the European continent, a fact which no Europeans would have accepted.

During the years immediately following the discovery, the peninsular Crowns instituted a political-economic system of "allotment of Indians," more widely known as the system of *encomiendas*. This system rested mainly upon the tenets of the traditional feudal organization of medieval Europe. Native Americans were forced to work for Spanish and Portuguese settlers; they had a status similar to that of serfs in feudal Europe. Colonists were granted a certain number of natives, on many occasions well over several hundred; the colonists then put the natives to work and reaped the benefits. The colonists in charge of these natives were obliged to provide for their general welfare. However, both the nature of such welfare and its enforcement were quite inadequate. This prompted a heated philosophical debate concerning the rights of Native Americans.

The most important figure in this debate on the side of the natives was Bartholomé de Las Casas (1474–1566). Las Casas devoted his life to the defense of the rights of Native Americans. Among the fiercest adversaries of Las Casas was Juan Ginés de Sepúlveda (1490–1571). Sepúlveda's view was that the spiritual mission of the Catholic church justified the political subjugation of Native Americans.

Independentist Period (ca. 1750–1850)

Around the middle of the eighteenth century, leading Latin American intellectuals began to lose interest in the philosophical issues that had concerned scholastics and became interested in social and gubernatorial questions related to the political independence of the colonies from the European Crowns. They did not completely abandon their scholastic sources, and the theories of natural law they had inherited from Vitoria and Suárez played a significant role in the formation of their ideas. During this period most Latin American countries gained their independence and produced their first political constitutions. These constitutions were, for the most part, copies of European ones. This spirit of imitation has not diminished much with the passing of time—not only do many contemporary Latin American constitutions exhibit this imitation, but many contemporary laws do as well.

The first Latin American treatise on international law was written in this period by Andrés Bello (1781–1865). Bello was a strong defender of the thesis that Latin America was in need of a second independence, an intellectual independence. Another philosopher of this period concerned with the "intellectual independence" of Latin America was Juan Bautista Alberdi (1810–1884). These authors, as well as most others at the time, were influenced by the ideas of the Enlightenment, the French encyclopedists, and the intellectual leaders of the French revolution.

The leaders of the independentist movement were men of action who used ideas for practical ends. As a result there is limited theoretical value and originality in their views. These thinkers made reason a measure of legitimacy in social and governmental matters, and found the justification for revolutionary ideas in natural law. Moreover, they criticized authority, and some of them regarded religion as superstitious and were opposed to ecclesiastical power. These views paved the way for positivism.

Positivist Period (ca. 1850–1910)

Positivism in Latin America was more than a philosophical view which rejected metaphysics and theology; it became an ideology, a way of life, that pervaded most aspects of society. The positivist slogan, "Order and progress," has been immortalized in the Brazilian flag. In the realm of legal philosophy, the positivist attack on metaphysics was transformed into an attack on the main tenets of natural law: under the positivist light, law needs to be understood as an ever-changing phenomenon, contingent upon historical and geographical factors.

The single most important influence on Latin American philosophy during this period was Auguste Comte (1875–1925), although many other thinkers, including some followers of Comte, exerted considerable influence as well. A list of such thinkers must include Emile Durkheim (1858–1917), Charles Darwin (1809–1882), and Herbert Spencer (1820–1903). Their views were spread throughout Latin America by the works of Enrique José Varona (1849–1933), José Ingenieros (1877–1925), Valentín Letelier (1852–1919), José María Luis Mora (1794–1850), and others.

Among the most important positivist legal philosophers in Latin America is Carlos Octavio Bunge (1875–1918), whose theory placed law within the realm of ethics. He separated ethics from metaphysics and related it to psychology and biology. Other important positivists who worked in the field of law in Latin America were Mariano Cornejo (1866–1942), Gabino Barreda (1818–1881), and José Enrique Rodó (1871–1917).

It is in Brazil where the positivist movement exerted the greatest influence. Among the most important positivist philosophers of law in Brazil are Tobias Barreto (1839–1889), Carlos Bevilaqua (1859–1944), and Sylvio Romero (1851–1914). Romero tried to combine the thought of Kant with standard positivist ideas.

Contemporary Period (ca. 1910–present)

Contemporary legal philosophy in Latin America begins with the demise of positivism, although in Brazil positivism never died completely. This accounts for some of the differences between Spanish-American and Brazilian legal philosophy. Disenchanted with the perspective afforded by positivism, Latin American philosophers and jurists moved away from French philosophy. Either in the form of the ideas of the French revolution (independentist period) or in the form of the positivism embraced by Comte and his followers (positivist period), French philosophy had held sway in Latin America since around the middle of the eighteenth century.

However, contemporary Latin American legal philosophy continues to follow European developments closely. Among the most important European philosophical movements which have influenced Latin America in this century are neo-thomism, neo-kantianism, phenomenology, and analytic philosophy.

A return to scholastic philosophy by Latin American philosophers was but natural, since Latin Americans are Catholic for the most part. The work of the neo-thomist Jacques Maritain (1882–1973) exerted considerable influence on them. Among the most important Latin American philosophers of law embracing neo-thomist views are Octavio Nicolas Derisi (1907–), Tomás D. Casares (1895–), and Oswaldo Robles (1905–).

Neo-kantianism also exerted considerable influence. Early in the century this influence was mainly due to the work of José Ortega y Gasset (1883–1955) and Manuel García Morente (1886–1942), who had a profound impact on Latin American philosophy. In addition, Luis Recaséns Siches (1903–), Eduardo García Máynez (1908–), and Carlos Cossio (1903–1987) disseminated German philosophy in Latin America. These philosophers were also greatly influenced by Rudolf Stammler (1856–1938), Giorgio Del Vecchio (1878–1970), and above all by Hans Kelsen (1881–1973). Kelsen's "pure theory of law" continues to play a leading role in the curriculum at most Latin American law schools. The Brazilian Miguel Reale (1910–) deserves special mention; his system is hard to classify but displays the influence of historicism. He describes it as "cultural realism."

The extreme formalism inherent in Kelsen's doctrine engendered a reaction which eventually culminated in a more general attack on the formalism of Marburg neo-kantianism. The attack on Hermann Cohen (1842–1918) and on Paul Natorp (1854–1924), in particular, paved the way for the introduction of phenomenological philosophy of law in Latin America. This was further facilitated by the fact that some of the philosophers already mentioned, such as Ortega y Gasset, had themselves undergone this transformation. Edmund Husserl (1859–1938) is the inspiring figure of the phenomenological movement, but the influence of Martin Heidegger (1889–1976), Max Scheler (1874–1928), Nikolai Hartmann (1882–1950), and others has also been considerable. Juan Llambías de Azevedo (1907–1972) is the most important Latin American philosopher of law influenced by phenomenology, although he was also influenced by Catholic philosophy in general.

Analytic philosophy has exerted some influence in recent Latin American legal philosophy. Initially this influence was limited to Argentina, Brazil, and Mexico, but it has slowly spread into other countries. The Anglo-American philosophers of law who have had the greatest influence in Latin America are H.L.A. Hart (1907–1992) and Lon Fuller (1902–1978). Among those Latin American legal philosophers who have shown an interest in analytic philosophy are Eduardo Rabossi (1930–), Roberto Vernengo (1926–), Genaro Carrió (1922–), and Carlos Santiago Nino (1943–). Carrió has translated into Spanish works by Alf Ross (1899–) and H.L.A. Hart, and has written numerous articles. Nino was a prolific writer who published regularly in Anglo-American journals and concentrated, like Rabossi, on issues concerning constitutional law and human rights violations in Latin America.

In each of its stages of development, Latin American legal philosophy has produced scholarly pieces of high quality. In order to appreciate fully its achievements, however, its close relationship to developments in Europe must be taken into account. Latin American legal philosophy has evolved around European figures. The rejection of positivism carried with it a rejection of French philosophy and brought German philosophy into a preeminent role, which continues unabated to this day. The influence of German philosophy can be felt not only on the philosophy of law in general but also on specific legal areas, such as criminal law.

References

Davis, Harold Eugene. *Latin American Thought: An Historical Introduction.* New York: Free Press, 1974.

García Máynez, Eduardo. *Positivismo jurídico, realismo jurídico y iusnaturalismo* (Legal Positivism, Legal Realism, and Natural Law). Mexico: Universidad Nacional Autónoma de México, 1968.

Gracia, Jorge J.E., ed. *Latin American Philosophy in the Twentieth Century: Man, Values, and the Search for Philosophical Identity.* Buffalo: Prometheus Books, 1986.

Gracia, Jorge J. E., Eduardo Rabossi, Enrique Villanueva, and Marcelo Dascal, eds. *Philosophical Analysis in Latin America.* Dordrecht: Kluwer Academic Publishers, 1984.

Höffner, Joseph. *La ética colonial española del Siglo de Oro* (Ethics in Spanish Colonies During the Golden Era). Trans. Francisco de Asís Caballero. Madrid: Ediciones Cultura Hispánica, 1957.

Kunz, Joseph L. *Latin American Philosophy of Law in the Twentieth Century.* New York: Inter American Law Institute, New York University School of Law, 1950.

Larroyo, Francisco, and Edmundo Escobar. *Doctrinas fiosóficas en Latinoamérica* (Philosophical Schools in Latin America). Mexico: Porrúa, 1968.

Recaséns Siches et al. *Latin American Legal Philosophy.* Trans. Gordon Ireland et al. Cambridge MA: Harvard University Press, 1948.

Leonardo A. Zaibert
Jorge J.E. Gracia

See also COSSIO, CARLOS

Law and Economics

See ECONOMICS AND LAW

Law and Society

See ROLE; SOCIOLOGY OF LAW

Lease

See HIRE

Legal Ethics

See ETHICS, LEGAL

Legalism

Legalism holds moral conduct to be a matter of rule following and the moral relationship of rights and duties. However, legalism is first and foremost a personal and social *attitude* rather than a philosophical or theoretical *concept* in law.

Various aspects are important: (1) the *cultural context* of legalism is not limited to western history and democracy; (2) legalism as an attitude concerns the relation between individual and state as an expression of the *psychosocial development* of human beings, their moral and legal consciousness; (3) there are major *implications* of the rule-governed character of conduct in law, legal semantics, philosophy and theory or argumentation, and the pragmatics of politics; a legalistic attitude does not stand on its own but is related to all these aspects.

Cultural Context

One of the schools in the ancient period of Chinese philosophy, named the period of the hundred schools and lasting until 221 B.C., was the Legalist school. The name did not appear until 90 B.C., but the ideas had been influential for nearly five hundred years. The concentration of power in the ruler was the central motive of the Legalist school, and the manner to achieve that goal threefold: law, statecraft, and power. Perfection of a system of reward and punishment, rigid manipulation of power, and strict ordering of social relationships to maintain the state brought these goals to realization. The implicit image of a human being was based on the assumption of the evil nature of human character. Only a rigid system of rule following could prevent the devastating results from that nature to develop in social life. Application of state-laws were instituted to balance the ineffectiveness of moral values in social conduct. This totalitarian approach was extremely pragmatic and ahistorical. The school brought feudalism to an end and ushered a new dynasty.

Our modern mind is still fascinated by the legalism of the seer Han Fei Tzu (?282–233 B.C.). Our contemporaries recognize his discontent with the king's lack of authority, his disregard of the laws of the state, and his absence of influence on the officials. Taoists affirm enlightened rulers have to act in accordance with nature but foremost according to the talents of the people. Legalists combine this taoist insight with legal control, violence, and superiority of the state. The latter outweigh similarities with taoism. Legalism stresses the technicalities and pragmatics of the semantic correspondences between names and things and occurrences: not the ethical, social, or logical but the pragmatic dimensions of semantics further human dignity and righteousness. Facts of nature seldom serve the human world, which is a world of *techne* and of artifacts. Skills cause culture; state and law are no exception here.

Legalist philosophy seems subtle and understandable in terms of our own personal philosophies. However, the rigid, radical, absolutist, and often inhumane political and legal practice is incomprehensible to us. This concern not only affects the difference between theory and practice, but shows how the legalist attitude is deeply attached to the foundations of society and culture.

Psychosocial Development

A primary tenet of Chinese legalism is that principles of law and state are conveyed through education. Moral and legal consciousness mold the individual in society; the legalist attitude is formatted in education. Contemporary theories and experiences confirm the importance of this observation. The legalistic attitude is also a basic issue in modern philosophical ethics and developmental psychology.

Legalism is aparent in L. Kohlberg's discussion of the second level of moral development in adolescents, called the preconventional stage: "[W]hat is right is following rules . . . is acting to meet one's own interests and needs and letting others do the same . . . is what is fair." More than one presupposition of that theory is interesting to philosophers. (1) Is moral development in western democracies toward autonomy and mutual respect on an individualistic basis? Legalism appears as an integrating element of the process. What role does adapting learning to development play? Does one develop mentally if one learns to follow rules? (2) C. Gilligan researched gender differences in moral reasoning. Can such differences be overlooked in a theory of moral development so that the legalist attitude appears independent of care- or justice-based conceptions, and is legalism the same to both sexes? What concerns gender differences could also relate to differences in culture: Kohlberg's identification of a level in which custom is superseded, or a postconventionalism stage of moral development, appears seldom in nonwestern societies. Interestingly, J.C. Gibbs' sociomoral "Reflection Objective Measure" also includes the legalist attitude as a developmental phase in western individuals. Is the legalist attitude a universal phenomenon? (3) Jürgen Habermas understands moral development in terms of creative reorganization of cognition. He stresses the importance of individuals being able to change their attitude. This is, in Habermas' view, important for communication-oriented practical discourses. Legalism could petrify that possibility during the conveyance of moral rule-patterns and thus counteract communication and democracy. The legalist attitude endangers the transition to postconventional patterns of thought at all levels of developmental theories.

Legal Implications

None of these considerations are overt in jurisprudence or legal theory. Yet legalism as an attitude is omnipresent in legal thinking of the western world. Its relation to legal training is obvious. The observation by J.A.G. Griffith that "[a] man who has legal training is never quite the same again . . ." is still effective. The conveyance of legal awareness, a matter of moral development, is stronger if combined with professional training. Recent publications involve legal training in legal scholarship.

The "connoisseur of law" (Anthony Kronman's expression) develops a professional attitude that *always* relates to a legalistic component, sometimes embodied in the good lawyer and more often in the doctrinalist. Kronman observes how changes in the legal profession correlate to losses in social homogeneity. The holistic ideal in legal advice is lost, and the lawyer as a statesman is transformed into a competitive advisor. In short, the dissolution of intrinsic values in the legalist approach causes the downfall of standards in legal practice. An interesting question comes to the fore: is legalism at its strongest where it is said to be in dissolution? Richard Posner refers to the many inadequacies of training in legal ethics. The inadequacies reinforce the inarticulate presence of legalist foundations of the profession. According to Posner, legal doctrinalists are law's Talmudists—this remark shows all the features of legalism. The fact that legal practice as a profession differs from doctrinal considerations does not change legal training. Despite deprofessionalization of legal scholarship, legal training remains a secure monopoly of legal studies and its implicit legalisms. Legal practice is not just the practice of legal theory, it has great epistemological importance. How does legal practice relate to legalism as an *attitude*?

The question is an excellent entree for legal theory. Judith Shklar's well-known and generally accepted definition of legalism ("the ethical attitude that holds moral conduct to be a matter of rule following, and moral relationships to consist of duties and rights determined by rules") accompanies her observation that legalism is "often an inarticulate, but nonetheless consistently followed, individual code of conduct" and "its most nearly complete expression is in the great legal systems of the European world."

Legalism is not defined as an ideology, since the attitude is not primarily *on* law but *in* law, and it would not be very meaningful to define law in its entirety as an ideology. Legalism is in law's rule-character, its institutional character, its relationship to legal theory and legal practice, its argumentation. It is as if understanding legalism leads to disentangling the fabric of law. Furthermore, legalist attitudes are not identical to any passive law-abiding style or an absolutist and authoritarian political view. Phenomena such as rule following, communication, consensus, the practice of legal ideals, or the exploitation of rights language are not legalistic in themselves. What, then, has legal theory to say? Is it possible at all to detect the legalist attitude within the field of legal theory, since it seems to be nowhere and everywhere? How can it be articulated? Three key notions could assist: (1) legalism's *attitude,* (2) legalism's urge to *differentiate,* and (3) legalism's *representationalist* philosophy.

1. Understanding legalism as an *attitude* leads to the essence of the phenomenon. It differs from the analytic attitude, namely, grasping the rules (of analysis) which make following the rules (of law) understandable. Attitudes create worldviews. A major feature of this view is its use of a rights language. The semantics of that language intertwine with legal language. This legal outlook upon reality is a presupposition, deeply rooted in the mind of the professional and in our juridificated life situation. The logic of that view does not consider law as an artifact of human creativity. Legalism holds that reality conforms to the syntax and thesaurus of rights language.

2. Legalism displays the genius of *differentiation.* It takes the distinction between the private and the public to be natural, it draws clear lines between law and nonlaw, it isolates law as specificity from other domains of social reality, it claims that legal theory differs from other scientific theories. That is the minimum content of positivism. For that reason, the legal *is* bears *rights* all its own. The grandeur of legal interpretation, application, argumentation, and judgment, both theoretical and practical, stems from those rights.

3. Legalism is fundamentally *representationalistic.* Legal thinking is impossible if it is not a representation of a nonlegal something and if it cannot refer to an external reality in order to create arguments and to legitimate its judgments and conclusions. The self-interpretation of law is founded on relationships between rules and the conduct they represent. Ludwig Wittgenstein demonstrated the paradox at hand: "[N]o course of action could be determined by a rule, because every course of action can be made out to accord with the rule." That paradox is abolished, however, in the legalistic attitude. The clear line drawn by legalism between theory and practice is effective. Paradoxes may be philosophically interesting, but they do not interrupt the course of legal practice.

References

Chan, Wing-Tsit. *A Source Book in Chinese Philosophy.* Princeton: Princeton University Press, 1961.

Gibbs, J.C. et al. *Moral Maturity: Measuring the Development of Sociomoral Reflection.* Hillsdale NJ: Erlbaum, 1992.

Gilligan, C. *In a Different Voice: Psychological Theory and Women's Development.* Cambridge MA: Harvard University Press, 1982.

Griffith, J.A.G. "The Law of Property." In *Law and Opinion in England in the 20th Century.* Ed. Morris Ginsberg. London: Stevens, 1959.

Habermas, J. *Moralbewußtsein und kommunikatives Handeln* (Moral Consciousness and Communicative Exchange). Frankfurt: Suhrkamp, 1983.

Kohlberg, L. *Child Psychology and Childhood Education: A Cognitive Developmental View.* New York: Longman, 1987.

———. *Essays on Moral Development. Vol. 1. The Philosophy of Moral Development.* San Francisco: Harper & Row, 1981.

Kronman, Anthony T. *The Lost Lawyer: Failing Ideals of the Legal Profession.* Cambridge MA: Harvard University Press, 1993.

Lan, Fung Yu. *The History of Chinese Philosophy.* Princeton: Princeton University Press, 1952.

MacCormick, Neil, and Ota Weinberger. *An Institutional Theory of Law: New Approaches to Legal Positivism.* Dordrecht: Kluwer, 1986.

Piaget, J., and B. Inhelder. *The Psychology of the Child.* New York: Basic Books, 1969.

Posner, Richard. *Overcoming Law.* Cambridge MA: Harvard University Press, 1995.

Searle, John. *The Construction of Social Reality.* London: Allen Lane, 1995.

Shklar, Judith. *Legalism: Law, Morals, and Political Trials.* Cambridge MA: Harvard University Press, 1964.

Watson, Burton. *Han Fei Tzu.* Bejing: Confucius, 1964.

Jan M. Broekman

See also CONSTITUTIONALISM; LEGALITY

Legality

A common use of the term "legality" refers to the actions of an *official* within a legal system. In yet another it refers to the universalizability of principles in the internal processes of a *trial*; thus, a trial that ignored the basic norms of fair procedure might be described as "of doubtful legality." The legality of formulations that purport to be *laws or statutes* may also be contested; here the issue is usually less the content of the law or statute than whether or not the law or statute has been properly adopted.

A rule that had been improperly adopted is not to be recognized; thus, H.L.A. Hart's "rule of recognition" enabling a judge to distinguish between what is and what is not a law within the jurisdiction is a criterion of legality. In 1809–1917, for example, when different attempts at Russification threatened Finland's legal autonomy, it was argued, according to Aulis Aarnio, that "the decrees of the Russian government were invalid and not to be obeyed if they violated statutory law that had been enacted in Finland."

Even when a statute is challenged as of doubtful legality, apparently because of its content, it is common to find that the challenge is based on the claim that the content of the new statute is at variance with an already established law superior to it. So the legality of a proposed new statute may be challenged as being, with respect to its content, at variance and incompatible with a higher or supervening law. Aristotle (384–322 B.C.), in the *Rhetoric,* takes the passage in Sophocles' *Antigone* where Antigone refuses to obey Creon to be an exemplary legal argument, based on the conflict between the content of Creon's decree—that she should not bury her brother—and the content of an older, unwritten, and higher law. More usually nowadays, a proposed, or already existing, statute may be challenged as being incompatible with a written constitution.

To challenge the legality of a trial is usually to claim either that the court was improperly constituted according to the norms or values of the legal system of which it purported to be a procedure or to claim that, although properly constituted, the court did not carry out its task according to the accepted norms of the system.

It is possible to challenge the legality of a trial or, indeed, legality more generally, with reference to norms unknown or unaccepted within a particular legal system. However, this is to challenge that system as a whole, and the illegality of a particular feature becomes a consequence of the claimed illegality of the system of which it is a part.

Definition

Through the different usages runs a common current that suggests a definition: the legality of a law or procedure is its conformity to, and coherence with, a containing legal context that will itself define limits of what is legal. So a court that hears one side of the dispute but refuses to hear the other can be convicted of illegality within a containing context that includes the maxim "Hear both sides" or its equivalent. The containing context is not necessarily completely articulated and may be unwritten, but it cannot be completely unknown. When the challenge to a particular procedure is within the norms, written or unwritten, of the system itself, the challenge is internal. When the challenge rests on norms other than those of the system, the challenge is external.

Procedure

Conformity to, and coherence within, a context must be established. Since any legal system is a means of associating different people in a common jural context within which they can carry on their mutual lives, it must be possible to establish the legality of laws and procedures. There will be, therefore, a demand for an authoritative interpreter, that is, an interpreter whose authority is accepted, or acquiesced in, by the members of the jurisdiction. If, for example, the constitutionality, and so legality, of a statute is questioned, there must be some interpreter whose judgment on the issue will prevail. The compatibility of a law with some other law is not, and cannot be, abstractly established. When unchallenged, compatibility is presumed, thus giving rise to the general principle that enacted laws are presumed legal. When challenged, the issue must be settled by the authoritative interpreter, usually the supreme court of the jurisdiction.

It is worth noticing that even if one holds that there are "natural laws" that form the basic and universal containing context of every legal system and with which every statute should be compatible, it remains the case that this context must be discovered and accepted and that, whenever a statute is challenged, there must be an authoritative interpreter to judge whether or not the proposed statute is compatible with it.

Unless, implausibly, one assumes the infallibility of supreme courts or other authoritative interpreters, a problem emerges. Suppose, for example, that a supreme court were to interpret a constitutional provision as permitting a given action and that a later supreme court were to interpret the same provision as forbidding that same action. For practical purposes—and these are important purposes in an institution whose fundamental purpose is to support the possibility of mutual living—one may claim simply that what at one stage was declared legal is, at another stage, declared illegal, that the interpretation (and so the legality) was, at one time, thus, and, at another time, not thus. However, this would seem to involve one or other of two presuppositions: that contradictory interpretations can both be true or that legality is no more than what the interpreter decides. Of these, the first is incoherent and the second takes the legal system to be, even in theory, no more than force. The way through this apparent impasse is, perhaps, to acknowledge in practice, and to work out in theoretical reflection, the uncertain character of human inquiry. So the legality of a law or procedure is its compatibility with the containing legal context. The determination of that legality, however, rests with the authoritative interpreter whose judgment is not the "truth" but is the best available opinion; and agreement with, or acquiescence in, a legal system should rest, not upon one's certainty of its truth, but is upon one's conviction that it is the best available opinion.

Context

"Legality" has been discussed in two complementary ways: first, with respect to the conditions under which the legality of laws and procedures is realized; second, with respect to the possibility of determining the legality of laws or procedures within a system. What of the legality of the system as a whole, the legality of the containing context itself? The legality of the containing context cannot be established with reference to a further containing context and so on indefinitely. There are two common solutions. The first, or naturalist, solution posits a given, naturally known, basic containing context. The second or positivist solution posits or, better, and following the Austrian jurist Hans Kelsen, presupposes a "basic norm" or "original constitution" that becomes, as it were, an axiom of the system. A third solution, according to Judith Shklar, would suggest that legality is an unknown, important but not unique, ideal, or goal, of legal inquiry: "[T]he principle of legality in criminal law is certainly a primary value of legalism—perhaps its greatest contribution to a decent political order." So, legal traditions express the cooperative wisdom (and, sometimes, folly) of jurists over centuries. Considered as given static systems, legal systems are well accounted for in Kelsen, and legality is relative to system. As dynamic systems, legal systems are worked on by successive generations of jurists, and legality is a value to be progressively realized through responsible inquiry and invention.

References

Aarnio, Aulis. "Statutory Interpretation in Finland." In *Interpreting Statutes: A Comparative Approach.* Ed. D.N. MacCormick and F.W. Summers. Aldershot: Dartmouth, 1991.

Aristotle. *Rhetoric.* In *The Complete Works of Aristotle.* Ed. Jonathan Barnes. Princeton: Princeton University Press, 1984.

Harris, J.W. *Law and Legal Science: An Enquiry into the Concepts of Legal Rule and Legal System.* Oxford: Clarendon Press, 1979.

Hart, H.L.A. *The Concept of Law.* Oxford: Clarendon Press, 1961.

Kelsen, Hans. *Pure Theory of Law.* Trans. Max Knight. Berkeley: University of California Press, 1967.

———. *Reine Rechtslehre* (The Pure Theory of Law). 1934. 2d ed., rev. and enl., Vienna: Deuticke, 1960.

Lucas, J.R. *On Justice.* Oxford: Clarendon Press, 1980.

Shklar, Judith. *Legalism: Law, Morals and Political Trials.* 1964. 2d ed. Cambridge MA: Harvard University Press, 1986.

Villey, Michel. *Critique de la pensée juridique moderne* (Critique of Modern Juridical Thinking). Paris: Dalloz, 1976.

Garrett Barden

See also LEGALISM; LEGITIMACY

Legislation and Codification

Legislation designates the process of making or giving written laws as well as a single enactment or the entire body of enactments resulting therefrom. The institution was known already in antiquity; the term "legislation" has the Latin term *lex* (law) in it. In modern democracies, the power to legislate is reserved to the representative assembly (parliament or the legislature) and may be contrasted with the executive power, vested in the administration, and the judicial power, exercised by the courts. The principle of the separation of these three powers, attributed to Montesquieu, is a cornerstone of the rule of law. The laws enacted by the legislature are also called statutes or acts (of Parliament or of Congress); the term "bill" is used for legislative proposals before they become law. Legislation may authorize the administration or a particular agent, within strict limits, to complement the broad provisions in an act by detailed provisions (e.g., forms to be used or specific measurements for a concept in the act) spelled out in regulations; this is called subordinate or delegated legislation.

Legislation is nowadays becoming the principal source of law. Even in common law systems, its importance is overshadowing that of case law, the law found in the accumulated decisions of the courts. Custom is no longer considered a major source of law; it enters the law by being acknowledged in legislation or court decisions.

The prominence of legislation is a recent phenomenon. In the middle ages and early modern times, the prevailing conception saw the supreme law as being given by a divine source or arising out of human nature, and hence as immutable, like the laws of nature. Customs and practices adopted by the citizenry in their dealings and generally considered to be binding upon them were regarded as local variations allowed by natural law. Legislation could merely declare or clarify the rules of natural law, but not modify them, let alone create new law. The common law of England, developed by the courts and incorporating much local custom, could only be changed exceptionally and in secondary aspects by statute. On the continent, unwritten law embodied in customs left considerable scope for arbitrariness on the part of feudal lords. It led to movements from the thirteenth to sixteenth centuries to write down the customs for greater certainty and accessibility. The movement received the support of the highest authorities as a means of checking the autonomy of the local lords.

With the progressive centralization of power, legislation came to be seen not merely as a means of declaring and clarifying the law, but as a tool for creating new law, implementing policies desired by the authorities. Statutes became the supreme source of law. The French revolution consecrated this conception by declaring laws to be the public and solemn declaration of the general will. From the nineteenth century on, laws were used to effect social change, in particular in the form of social security and welfare legislation.

This broadened function led to a changed conception of law. The validity of a legal rule was considered to depend not upon its accordance with common ideas of justice, natural law, or custom, but upon its being adopted by the proper authority in the proper form and hence ascertainable. Law became separated from morality; written law—statute or case law—became the exclusive source of law. This view is called legal positivism.

Legal positivism, while apparently simplifying the task of ascertaining the legal rules applicable to a dispute, creates difficulties with regard to the content of the law. On this view, the accordance of legislation with justice, morality, or natural law is not a legal question, important though it may be on other grounds for the legislator carefully to consider the matter. The experience of profoundly unjust, yet technically valid, legislation in modern tyrannies—Nazi Germany or the communist regimes—cast a doubt upon this conception. It triggered a revival of interest in natural law and gave prominence to open-ended constitutional rights restricting what can be enacted as law, mandating the courts to strike down legislation violating those restrictions. This development reinforces the role of courts in lawmaking and of cases as a source of law.

The role of legislation is called into question in yet another way. The proliferation of statutes creating new law and modifying or repealing earlier law, as well as massive recourse to delegated legislation, undermines the specific requirements for legislation under the rule of law: stability, certainty, clarity, "knowability," and accessibility. In representative democracies, legislation may be used to give effect to privileges sought by interest groups. This practice violates the requirement that laws be formulated as abstract rules, uniformly applicable to all citizens and to an indefinite number of cases. To some, these developments are eroding the legitimacy of legislation.

Codification refers to the process of gathering in a single document and in revised form the dispersed legal rules and provisions dealing with a given subject matter. It consolidates the law, making it easier for citizens to know and for officials to administer.

In the narrowest sense, codification is undertaken for administrative reasons, to put order in a statute text after numerous amendments by subsequent acts. Periodic revision of statutes in states and provinces in North America is of this kind. It maintains the substance of the law and effects only minor changes in form. Of similar ilk are recent codifications in France in such fields as housing, consumer protection, and protection of the environment. They bring together and systematize legal provisions in dispersed acts, without changing their substance (*à droit constant*).

A more encompassing form of codification is the multivolume Restatement of Law undertaken by the private American Law Institute. The Restatement codifies and simplifies the most important principles and doctrines developed by the courts in such areas as the law of torts. It goes some way toward reformulating the law. The Restatement, while not legally binding, has substantial moral authority and is often referred to by the courts.

In the broadest sense, codification refers to the codes, which are the backbone of civil law (as distinct from common law) systems. Codes consist of a structured set of concise abstract articles designed to form a seamless and logically coherent system of rules covering an entire branch of law. The preeminent examples of such codification in modern times are the French Civil Code of 1804 and the German Bürgerliches Gesetzbuch (BGB) of 1900. Other branches of law, such as criminal law, civil procedure, and commercial law, have their own codes. Like the common law, civil law originates partly in customs and practices adopted by citizens and in court decisions resolving conflicts; unlike the common law systems, it also draws on the Justinian Code, which during the sixth century codified the Roman law that had evolved piecemeal over the preceding centuries.

While codification in this broader sense need not break with the preexisting law—a break intended in the French Civil Code of 1804, but not, for instance, in the Civil Code of Lower Canada, in 1866—in practice it has generally led to such a break, in form as well as substance. In France, the codes were meant to create a uniform law of the land, equal for all citizens, supplanting a multitude of diverse regional laws. Once in force, a code is treated as the encompassing source of all rules within the field of law it governs; it is deemed to have no gaps or internal contradictions. This view may instill among its practitioners a sense that all answers to questions of law can be found by reading and interpreting the code. Some see the code as a logical system deducible from first principles, to be discovered in the deep structure of its articles. Such a view obscures the fact that much law originates piecemeal in custom and cases.

It would be a mistake to believe that a code imposes upon the law greater rigidity than does the common law, or that cases play no significant role in a code system. Rules consolidated in long lines of precedent may be stifling; the abstract provisions of the code provide substantial leeway to the courts. Civilian lawyers, moreover, need not be less policy oriented than are their common law, particularly American, counterparts. In practice, civilian courts have interpreted the codes so as to keep them in phase with the evolution of society. The law of a mature code system cannot be known through the code articles alone, but requires in addition knowledge of the cases applying them and of scholarly writings (*doctrine*) explaining the systematic structure of the code. Special legislation has eaten away at the ordinary law of the land, which is the proper domain of the common law and of the codes, in civil law.

References

Allen, C.K. *Law in the Making*. 7th ed. Oxford: Clarendon Press, 1964.

Epstein, Richard A. *Simple Rules for a Complex World.* Cambridge MA: Harvard University Press, 1995.

Fuller, Lon L. "Positivism and Fidelity to Law—A Reply to Professor Hart." *Harvard Law Review* 71 (1957), 630–672.

Hart, H.L.A. *The Concept of Law.* Oxford: Oxford University Press, 1961.

———. "Positivism and the Separation of Law and Morals." *Harvard Law Review* 71 (1957), 593–629.

Hayek, Friedrich A. *Law, Legislation and Liberty.* 3 vols. Chicago: University of Chicago Press, 1973–1979.

Lawson, Frederick H. *A Common Lawyer Looks at the Civil Law.* Ann Arbor: University of Michigan Press, 1953.

Merryman, John Henry, David S. Clark, and John O. Haley. *The Civil Law Tradition: Europe, Latin America, and East Asia.* Charlottesville VA: Michie, 1994.

van Caenegem, R.C. *An Historical Introduction to Private Law.* Cambridge: Cambridge University Press, 1992.

Watson, Alan. *The Making of the Civil Law.* Cambridge MA: Harvard University Press, 1981.

Ejan Mackaay

See also CODIFICATION

Legitimacy

The concept of legitimacy can be used in both an empirical and a normative sense, even in the context of the law. *Empirical legitimacy* denotes the factual acceptance of the law in general or individual legal norms. *Normative legitimacy,* instead, refers to their acceptability.

The law in general and legal norms individually can be accepted or rejected and their acceptability measured on different grounds. A distinction can be made between, for example, pragmatic, ethical, and moral grounds. In the examination of legitimacy, attention is paid merely to ethical and moral reasons for obeying or disobeying the law. The concept of legitimacy is closely related to that of *obligation.* The law enjoys empirical legitimacy, if among the relevant group there exists a sense of obligation to obey it. Normative legitimacy, in turn, can be equated with ethically and morally justified obligation to obedience.

Legitimacy, in both its meanings, is a relational concept. Both empirical and normative legitimacy can only be examined in relation to the audience to which the claim of legitimacy raised by the law is directed. Legitimacy signifies a certain relation between the claimant and the audience of legitimacy. The *audience* of legitimacy may consist in, for example, the population as a whole or in the officials applying the law. We may also speak of the *legal community in a large and in a narrow sense* as the audience of the claim of legitimacy.

As to the *claimant* of legitimacy, a distinction should be made between the legitimacy of the law as a whole and the legitimacy of individual legal norms. There are individual legal norms, for instance, traffic rules, which do not have a direct connection to ethical values or to moral principles and which as such do not raise a claim of legitimacy. The issue of legitimacy arises only when such legal norms are set into the context of the law as a whole. It may also be the case that those individual legal norms that are not ethically or morally accepted or acceptable receive an obligatory character from the legitimacy of the law as a whole.

In a modern society, where the main source of law lies in the explicit decisions of public authorities, such as the legislature and the courts, the legitimacy of law as a whole is intimately connected to the legitimacy of political power. However, these issues should be kept separate. Thus compliance with (legitimate) law can be regarded as one of the central factors that affects the empirical legitimacy of political power, as well as one of the central yardsticks by which its normative legitimacy is to be appraised.

The crucial problem in the assessment of normative legitimacy consists in the criteria to be applied. Strong reasons can be presented in support of the view that legitimacy is a relational concept also, in the sense that the yardsticks of acceptability are bound to the culture of the society in question, that is, to its values and moral principles. In this view, there are no eternal normative criteria of legitimacy, contrary to the claims of natural law theories. Under the conditions of modern law, the search for yardsticks of normative legitimacy can be further narrowed. If one of the main characteristics marking modern law lies in its positive nature, even the criteria of its normative legitimacy should be somehow inherent in it, and thus share its positivity. Following this line of reasoning, the derivation and justification of the criteria to be used in judgments on the normative legitimacy of modern law are tasks of reconstructing its normative deep-structure.

If the yardsticks of normative legitimacy are seen as culturally and historically located, a link can be established between empirical and normative legitimacy. It can be argued, namely, that the law cannot maintain its empirical legitimacy if it stands in flagrant and permanent contradiction with the ethical and normative beliefs of the audience to which its claim of legitimacy is directed. These beliefs, in turn, manifest the basic values and principles, which determine the criteria of normative legitimacy.

The relevance of the issue of normative legitimacy has not been unanimously conceded. Thus, in Niklas Luhmann's view, modern law has managed to solve its problems of empirical legitimacy through particular systems of procedure, which make no reference to ethical or moral reasons. His view is, however, contradicted by, for instance, the pertinent phenomenon of civil disobedience, which is justified by these very reasons. In legal philosophy, Hans Kelsen's *pure theory of law* provides us with an example of a view, which allows no independent place for the issue of normative legitimacy. In Kelsen's theory, the legitimacy of legal norms is reduced to their formal validity.

In fact, the concept of legitimacy is related to that of *validity*, which, in legal philosophy, has been used to denote the specific mode of existence characterizing legal norms. In their discussions, Jerzy Wróblewski and Aulis Aarnio, among others, have distinguished between three aspects in the validity or validity claims of legal norms: formal or systematic validity, efficacy, and axiological validity (Wróblewski) or acceptability (Aarnio). Normative legitimacy can be equated with the last aspect of validity. The examination of empirical legitimacy, instead, finds its locus in the context of efficacy.

References

Aarnio, Aulis. *The Rational as Reasonable.* Dordrecht: Reidel, 1987.

Alexy, Robert. *A Theory of Legal Argumentation.* Oxford: Clarendon Press, 1992.

Beetham, David. *The Legitimation of Power.* London: Macmillan, 1991.
Gérard, Philippe. *Droit et démocratie* (Law and Democracy). Bruxelles: Facultés universitaires Saint-Louis, 1995.
Habermas, Jürgen. *Faktizität und Geltung* (Between Facts and Norms). Frankfurt: Suhrkamp, 1992.
Kelsen, Hans. *The Pure Theory of Law.* Berkeley: University of California Press, 1967.
Luhmann, Niklas. *Legitimation durch Verfahren* (Procedural Legitimation). 2d ed. Frankfurt: Suhrkamp, 1983.
Tuori, Kaarlo. "Discourse Ethics and the Legitimacy of Law." *Ratio Juris* 2 (1989), 125–144.
Weber, Max. *Economy and Society.* Vols. 1–2. 2d ed. Berkeley: University of California Press, 1978.
Wróblewski, Jerzy. "Verification and Justification in the Legal Sciences." *Rechtstheorie* 1 (1979), 195–214.

Kaarlo Tuori

See also LEGALITY

Legitimate Authority

See SUPERIOR ORDERS AND LEGITIMATE AUTHORITY

Legitimate Object of Contract

The morally or legally permissible range of goods and services available for the promise of future delivery in exchange for a present consideration is called the legitimate object of contract. Questions about the potential breadth of contractual agreements became an independent subject of scrutiny as a consequence of John Locke's seventeenth-century analysis of property rights in his *Second Treatise on Government,* published in 1689, and the source of further controversy after Karl Marx and Friedrich Engels began to question liberal assumptions about the almost indefinite scope of contract rights in *The Communist Manifesto,* published in 1848.

In "Of Property," Chapter 5 of his *Second Treatise,* Locke defended a labor theory of property, which, in its rudimentary form, maintains that (1) your body is your property; therefore, (2) the labor that you do with your body is also your property; and, consequently, (3) since your labor is your property, the product of your labor should also be your property. The labor theory is at the heart of the classical liberal (or libertarian) conviction that property rights, and consequently contract rights, should be virtually unrestricted.

The only restriction which Locke imposes on contractual agreements first appears a chapter earlier, in his discussion "On Slavery." There Locke contends (contrary to Thomas Hobbes' *Leviathan*) that "a Man, not having the Power of his own Life, *cannot,* by Compact, or his own consent, *enslave himself* to anyone, nor put himself under the Absolute, Arbitrary Power of another, to take away his Life, when he pleases. No body can give more Power than he has himself; and he that cannot take away his own Life, cannot give another Power over it." This passage suggests that Locke may have had theological reasons for excluding voluntary commerce in human beings as possible objects of contracts, thus limiting the extent to which we have property rights in our own bodies. Contemporary libertarians, such as Robert Nozick, offer a secular rationale for the prohibition of contractual self-enslavement: if we take Locke's labor theory at face value, the ultimate point of contractual rights is to preserve individual liberty by enforcing respect for each individual's property rights in his own body (via recognition of his full entitlement to the fruits of the labor of his body). Self-enslavement, on the other hand, is the abnegation of the individual's property rights in his own body, so contracts must exclude that option if their function is to preserve individual autonomy.

For present purposes, the most important facet of Locke's refusal to countenance self-enslavement as a legitimate object of contract is the fact that he recognizes the possibility of at least some restrictions on the kinds of goods which may be exchanged through contractual agreements. For liberal contract theory typically permits an otherwise unrestricted domain for possible objects of contract. This attitude has been most dramatically illustrated in the late-nineteenth- and early-twentieth-century behavior of the U.S. Supreme Court, when the majority consistently embraced a philosophy of economic libertarianism by arguing that the contracts clause in Article I, Section 10 of the U.S. Constitution ("No State shall . . . pass any . . . law impairing the obligation of contracts") should be construed as a guarantee of unrestricted freedom of contract. See, for example, *Coppage v. Kansas,* 236 U.S. 1 (1915), in which the Court overturned a Kansas law prohibiting yellow-dog contracts (which make employment contingent on a promise of nonmembership in labor unions), ruling that such a prohibition violated employers' and employees' constitutional right to contract terms of employment however they saw fit. While the Court majority conceded that there was obvious inequality between workers and employers, it argued that bargaining inequalities were an inherent feature of contracts generally. In the Court's view, the concept of economic pressure did not enter into the definition of what constitutes a free contract. Duress could not be used as a legal excuse for nonperformance of yellow-dog contracts, because economic pressure does not constitute duress. Through this kind of reasoning, the Court repeatedly struck down economic reform legislation designed to protect workers against unscrupulous employers, until the practice generated a constitutional crisis by interfering with Franklin Roosevelt's New Deal legislation in the 1930s. In response to popular pressure and Roosevelt's threat to pack the Court, a 5–4 majority began the process of dismantling the previous libertarian judicial philosophy in *West Coast Hotel v. Parrish,* 300 U.S. 379 (1937). There the Court upheld a minimum wage law for women on the hitherto novel ground that "[t]he Constitution does not speak of freedom of contract. It speaks of liberty and prohibits the deprivation of liberty without due process of law. . . . Regulation which is reasonable in relation to its subject and is adopted in the interests of the community is due process. What can be closer to the public interest than the health of women and their protection from unscrupulous and overreaching employers?" In this decision the Court ratified Oliver Wendell Holmes' famous dissent in *Lochner v. New York,* 198 U.S. 45 (1905), as the foundation for a more cautious judicial approach to economic legislation. When the Court majority struck down a state law designed to protect bakers from inordinately long workdays, Holmes accused the majority of using the Fourteenth Amendment to enact Herbert Spencer's social darwinism and a libertarian economic ideology no longer supported by an electoral mandate.

Social utility is not the only reason which has come to be recognized as a legitimate justification for restricting the objects of contracts. Marx attacked the classical liberal ideal of freedom of contract through his analysis of the commodification of labor, in which he blamed workers' inability to contract freely with employers on the practice of permitting the means of production to be the object of private contracts. Marx's analysis of the effects of this kind of commodification suggests that gross inequities ensue in the exercise of both political and economic rights, including, for the proletariat at least, even the revocation of the purported property right in one's own body.

Finally, and especially in the twentieth century, legal moralism and communitarianism have engendered yet another locus of concern to limit the objects of contract. A good current example is the ongoing debate in the United States over the question of recognizing marriage contracts between partners of the same gender. This is legal moralism at work—the doctrine that a society's legal institutions, and particularly the institution of criminal law, may legitimately be employed for the purpose of forbidding (or not ratifying) various forms of behavior simply on the ground that such activities are seriously immoral, or construed to be seriously immoral under some prevailing social orthodoxy.

Gerald Postema offers a less tendentious version of this kind of approach by focusing on the concept of a "collective harm": any behavior which leads to the neglect of some valued community tradition by undermining some countervailing "collective good." These values, in turn, are ones which "express components of a conception of *the good society,* or *the common good* . . . states of affairs [which] are collectively valued. . . . What makes these states of affairs valuable *to me* is (in part at least) that *we* value them."

In *The Gift Relationship,* a comparative study of blood donation practices in England and the United States, Richard Titmuss provides us with a clear example of Postema's concept of a collective harm in the context of contract rights. In England, unlike the United States, all blood must be donated voluntarily. Titmuss argues that the commodification of blood undermines the opportunity for the effective exercise of altruistic sentiments, since blood donation merely reduces the cost of blood to potential recipients, rather than providing an unconditional opportunity to save lives. Therefore Titmuss recommends that blood ought not to be an object of contract, in order to promote a desirable moral "ambience" in society.

In a more dramatic example of a hypothetical contract restriction, motivated this time by a concern to maintain community values rather than to change them, Irving Kristol invites us to reflect on the spectacle of well-paid professional gladiators fighting to death before a throng of enthusiastic New Yorkers in Yankee Stadium. Kristol assumes that we would respond to this morally repulsive tableau by prohibiting such contracts simply because we do not choose to live in a society which tolerates voluntary abdication of life merely to satiate the voyeuristic interests of bloodthirsty citizens.

These three classes of restrictions on legitimate objects of contract can be differentiated by degree. The range of potential restrictions on the objects of contracts that may emerge from communitarian concerns is potentially much larger than those that might be envisioned by marxist or socialist concerns about economic justice, and these restrictions in turn are more expansive than those envisioned by classical liberals. However, the idea that there should be absolutely no restrictions on the objects of contracts has not been seriously entertained since Locke first raised the issue.

References

Elster, Jon. *Karl Marx: A Reader.* New York: Cambridge University Press, 1986.

Feinberg, Joel. *Harmless Wrongdoing.* New York: Oxford University Press, 1988.

Kristol, Irving. "Pornography, Obscenity, and the Case for Censorship." *New York Times Magazine* (March 28, 1971).

Postema, Gerald J. "Collective Evils, Harms, and the Law." *Ethics* 97 (1987), 414–440.

Titmuss, Richard. *The Gift Relationship.* London: Allen and Unwin, 1970.

Richard Nunan

See also ACQUISITION AND TRANSFER; GIFT; PATERNALISM

Leibniz, Gottfried Wilhelm (1646–1716)

Gottfried Wilhelm Leibniz is one of a handful of thinkers who have advanced our knowledge in virtually every major area of inquiry. In mathematics he codiscovered both the calculus and binary arithmetic; in physics he first correctly articulated the concept of force; he was also a noted philosopher, philologist, librarian, theologian, poet, and inventor. Throughout his productive life he earned his livelihood through the law. After taking his M.A. at the university of Leipzig with a dissertation on "Some Philosophical Questions in the Law," he earned his Ph.D. in 1666, at the age of twenty, from the University of Altdorf. That dissertation was entitled "De casibus perplexis in jure" (On Complex Cases in the Law). The titles of his two theses give an indication of the lifelong direction of his thought about the law, which involved its connection with questions of theology, metaphysics, and logic. True jurisprudence, he said, is inseparable from religion and philosophy.

Leibniz made such an impression on the faculty of Altdorf by his thesis defense that they immediately offered him a position. He refused it, however, because he had made up his mind to practice law, determined that he would be a judge. That ambition he realized at two periods of his life. While still in his early twenties Leibniz was appointed a judge in the High Court of Appeal in the Electorate of Mainz. He later functioned briefly in that capacity during his long service to the Electorate of Hanover (1676–1716). For most of his life, however, he was a legal consultant to many of the noble houses of Europe. During his last years he was simultaneously counsel to the house of Hanover (the Hanoverian George I then occupying the British throne), to the German Emperor in Vienna, and to Czar Peter I of Russia. The latter once said that emperors were like schoolchildren in the cabinet of Dr. Leibniz.

The thrust of Leibniz's legal thought was an attempt to develop a Christian conception of natural law which would form the basis of a *justitia universalis* (universal justice). In that respect his legal research complemented a lifelong ecumenical interest in peace between the warring Christian confessions and a philosophical doctrine of "universal harmony," according to which all creatures are predisposed by God to entertain harmonious relations with one another. His great ambition was to reconcile ancient with modern, and East with West, in a perennial Christian philosophy, on the basis of which earthly communities could be governed on the same principles that obtain in what Leibniz, following Augustine, called the "city of God."

As already noted, the law for Leibniz has three dimensions: theological, philosophical, and jurisprudential. Each of these also has both a subjective and an objective correlative. The appropriate subjective response to God's revealed law is through piety, which expresses itself objectively in probity of life. Only the attempt to live uprightly (*honeste vivere*) on the part of all citizens can assure that justice will be universal.

If some aspects of God's law depend on revelation, unprejudiced reflection is sufficient to discover others, especially those belonging to what tradition calls natural law. The proper subjective expression of this law is charity, which Leibniz defines as making our own happiness to depend on that of our neighbor. It is only to the extent that we are motivated by charity, Leibniz says, that its objective correlative, equity, can be shown. The legal phrase which expresses the principle of equity is *suum cuique tribuere* (to give to each his own). Without charity neither the giver nor the recipient can properly understand what is due to him. Without equity there can be no justice in communities (*justitia particularis*).

Finally, there is the jurisprudential aspect of the natural law, whose subjective expression is prudence. Its objective correlative is utility and it is guided by the maxim "Harm no one—help all" (*neminem laedere–omnes iuvare*). Only when this is realized does one have individual (or distributive) justice. The city of God, whose citizens we are called to be, is thus the only one in which universal, communitarian, and individual justice are harmonized and in which the innate desire for equitable human relations at all these levels is satisfied.

It is unfortunate that Leibniz's contributions to the history of jurisprudence have been studied less than they deserve. Earlier legal historians were limited by the unavailability of the philosopher's works. Now that these are at last appearing in critical editions, an able historian of the law is needed to give a definitive evaluation of the scope and influence of the legal thought of this remarkable man.

References

Grua, Gaston. *Jurisprudence universelle et théodicée selon Leibniz* (Universal Jurisprudence and Theodicy for Leibniz). Paris: Presses universitaires de France, 1953 .

Friedrich, Carl J. "Philosophical Reflections of Leibniz on Law, Politics and the State." In *Leibniz,* ed. Harry G. Frankfurt. New York: Doubleday, 1972.

Leibniz, G.W. *Le droit de la raison* (The Law of Reason). Ed. René Sève. Paris: Vrin, 1994.

Wolf, Erik. "Leibniz als Rechtsphilosoph" (Leibniz as Jurisprudent). In *Leibniz,* ed. Wilhelm Totok and Carl Haase. Hanover: Verlag für Literatur und Zeitgeschehen, 1966.

Graeme Hunter

Liability, Criminal

Fitzjames Stephen's claim that "the meaning of responsibility is liability to punishment," considered by H.L.A. Hart in *Punishment and Responsibility,* led Hart to stress "the bewilderingly many meanings of 'responsibility,'" for example, legal responsibility, moral responsibility, criminal responsibility, causal responsibility, vicarious responsibility, collective responsibility, and individual responsibility.

Conditions of Liability

Since responsibility and liability seem synonymous, we need a theory to explain why one is liable to be punished. Hart stresses three criteria of responsibility: (1) mental or psychological conditions, (2) causal or other forms of connection between act and harm, and (3) personal relationships rendering one liable to be punished or to pay for the acts of another.

Focusing on the first, legal systems from England to Israel have inherited an embarrassing doctrine of criminal responsibility, especially concerning the liability of the mentally abnormal. Hart says that "[l]awyers of the Anglo-American tradition use the Latin phrase *mens rea* as a comprehensive name for . . . necessary mental elements [of a crime]; and according to conventional ideas *mens rea* is a necessary element in liability to be established before a verdict." Yet he states: "Most English lawyers would however now agree with Sir James Fitzjames Stephen that the expression *mens rea* is unfortunate, though too firmly established to be expelled, just because it misleadingly suggests that, in general, moral culpability is essential to a crime." It is misleading, too, since there are strict liability crimes, which focus on only the second criterion, the *actus reus* (wrongful act), rather than the mind. (The *actus reus* can be any conduct, including an omission rather than an overt act.) However, with strict liability there are also embarrassing problems. First, Hart notes that the law is unclear as to how strict the strict liability is. Second, he suggests that some jurists consider strict liability crimes to be such petty matters as traffic offenses and business fines that they deem most of them scofflaw or costs of doing business rather than full-blooded crimes. Third, he notes arguments that punishing negligence is a type of strict liability. Fourth, how can strict liability be reasonable, given that it holds people responsible even though they have done all that any reasonable person would have done to avoid the *actus reus*?

Liability to Punishment

According to Hart's view, the three main theories offered to justify liability to punishment and to explain the various defenses to criminal liability are retributive justice, utilitarianism, and nonretributive fairness.

Retributive justice stresses *lex talionis,* "the law of talion," which requires a proportionality so that the punishment fits the crime. Utilitarianism requires each person to try to maximize net happiness for everyone in the long run. That we are all dead in the long run, as John Maynard Keynes observed, is not supposed to matter any more than that the theory of retributive justice leads to absurdities like raping rapists, if taken literally. The necessity of a nonliteral interpretation creates some room for compromise or for a synthesis among the views. Hart's view, for example, while admitting that "responsibility is a question not of science but of law," concedes that the difficult problem of proving mental states makes the strict liability that Hart often rejects a more efficient means of social hygiene, more utilitarian.

Proving Liability

There are two extremes on the issue of how provable the "guilty mind" is in court. One is summed up in the saying that even a dog knows the difference between being kicked and being tripped over. Similarly, some jurists suggest that the inner workings of the mind are in principle no more mysterious than the inner workings of the intestines.

The other extreme Hart summarizes by quoting Lady Wootton: one's "responsibility or capacity to resist temptation is something 'buried in consciousness, into which no human being can enter,' known if at all only to him and to God: it is not something which other men may ever know; and since 'it is not possible to get inside another man's skin' it is not something of which they can ever form a reasonable estimate as a matter of probability." Hart notes how difficult it is to consistently adopt this view, since Wootton fails to adopt it for the M'Naghten Rules determining the sanity and hence the liability of the accused.

The great concern over the *insanity defense* seems overblown because (1) even when one is found not guilty by reason of insanity, the average time the accused spends in a supervised environment isolated from the public is greater than when the accused is convicted, and (2) only a fraction of 1 percent of all criminal cases involve pleas of insanity. Even in Charles Manson's case there was no plea of insanity, for example. Even where it is a plea, (3) juries are quite skeptical of it, partially because of fear that it can be faked so easily.

Sanity at the time of the crime is fairly straightforward to show in many cases, under the M'Naghten Rules. For example, knowledge of the difference between right and wrong appears, in Manson family member Tex Watson's case, by Watson's wiping off his bloody fingerprints in an attempt to conceal them; this shows that he knew that society condemned his acts, and hence proved sanity. Similarly, something as mundane as running away when spotted by police or witnesses can show sanity under the M'Naghten Rules, which stress the accused's knowledge, at the time of the crime, that society condemns the *actus reus*. Also required is the knowledge of the nature of one's act. For example, if one were delirious with fever or the victim of a strong hallucinogen hidden in a party's punch bowl, then one's resultant violent acts can be excused as the product of temporary insanity.

Much more controversial than the M'Naghten rules are additions such as the American Law Institute's statement that there is no criminal liability when the *actus reus* was committed on an irresistible impulse. This seems even harder to prove and easier to fake than anything in the M'Naghten Rules. Hart presents the warning of Wootton and others against circular argument where "we infer the accused's lack of capacity to control his actions from his propensity to commit crimes and then both explain this propensity and excuse his crimes by his lack of capacity." We must guard against begging the question.

Recently, criminal liability has undergone a crisis in confidence, as the *abuse excuse* has blocked liability in several notorious cases. The abuse excuse aims to explain away the *actus reus* as the product of receiving physical abuse, usually years of abuse from the victim of the *actus reus*. The battered women's syndrome defense is an example. Other new defenses include the premenstrual syndrome defense, perhaps best understood as similar to the plea of diminished capacity, which traces back to Scots law, with its traditional dependence upon civilian law and, ultimately, the jurisdiction in conscience of the ecclesiastical courts.

Fairness

Defenses to proof of criminal liability, including provocation, duress, and necessity, seem to have fundamental fairness in common. Hart states that "in most western morality 'ought' implies 'can' and a person who could not help doing what he did is not morally guilty." Hart rejects Lord Denning's claim that "[i]n order that an act should be punishable, it must be morally blameworthy," to note that "[m]orality and criminality are far from coextensive." Further, "[t]he coincidence of legal responsibility with moral blameworthiness may be a laudable ideal, but it is not a necessary truth nor even an accomplished fact," although one can see *mens rea* and these various defenses and limits on liability as consistent attempts to morally improve the law.

As a statement of fairness, "'ought' implies 'can'" means "If Agent X ought to do act Y, then Agent X can do act Y." However, this seems obviously false in some routine cases. For example, I ought to repay my loans, and it does not limit my liability for me to point out simply that I cannot repay. That would be too easy. I could simply gamble away the money and hence make it so I cannot pay. So a fuller version would be "'ought' implies 'can' or 'could have except for some fault.'" This fails, too, since I ought to repay my loan even if I lost the money through no fault of my own. For example, suppose a tornado destroyed the money. Still, one could argue that the borrower should have insured the money against loss, and failing to do so was negligence and hence fault. Alternatively, one could see the agreement to borrow the money as a waiver of one's protection against liability normally provided by "'ought' implies 'can.'" Hart cites another alternative: "[P]erhaps there are still some who hold a modified form of the Platonic doctrine that Virtue is Knowledge and believe that the possession of knowledge (and muscular control) is *per se* a sufficient condition of the capacity to comply with the law." The borrower knew the risks of losing the money, yet accepted them. Hart states that "[a]ll legal systems temper their respect for the principle that persons should not be punished if they could not have done otherwise, i.e., had neither the capacity nor a fair opportunity to act otherwise."

Like the insanity defense, *determinism* as an apparent contrast to this principle of fairness has provoked overblown concern. The most plausible view seems to be David Hume's that self-determinism (self-control within determinism) is all we need for the relevant sense of freedom that allows moral and criminal liability for our voluntary acts. Our desires still cause our voluntary actions and our desires are still a crucial part of us, whatever their ultimate origin. So we have the freedom of control and the responsibility that goes along with it. By overlooking Hume's soft-determinism, Hart overstates the threat of determinism for liability.

References

Feinberg, Joel. *Doing and Deserving.* Princeton: Princeton University Press, 1970.

Fingarette, Herbert, and Ann Fingarette Hasse. *Mental Disabilities and Criminal Responsibility.* Berkeley: University of California, 1979.

Glover, Jonathan. *Responsibility.* New York: Humanities Press, 1970.

Gorr, Michael J., and Sterling Harwood, eds. *Controversies in Criminal Law: Philosophical Essays on Responsibility and Procedure.* Boulder CO: Westview Press, 1992.

Hart, H.L.A. *Punishment and Responsibility: Essays in the Philosophy of Law.* Oxford: Oxford University Press, 1968.

Honderich, Ted. *Punishment: The Supposed Justifications.* New York: Pelican, 1984.

Katz, Leo. *Bad Acts and Guilty Minds.* Chicago: University of Chicago Press, 1983.

Kenny, Anthony. *Freewill and Responsibility.* London: Routledge, 1978.
Schoeman, Ferdinand, ed. *Responsibility, Character, and the Emotions: New Essays in Moral Psychology.* Cambridge: Cambridge University Press, 1987.
Wootton, Barbara. *Crime and the Criminal Law.* London: Stevens and Sons, 1963.

Sterling Harwood

See also DEFENSES; MENS REA; RESPONSIBILITY

Liability, Protections from Civil

The common law imposes civil liability in tort where a wrongful act of one person causes harm to a protected interest of another. Excluded from this essay is a discussion of civil liability imposed under contract, restitution, or by fiduciary obligations implied by the relationship between the parties. This study is intended to describe how the law determines the domain of tort liability, thus providing an indication of protection from liability. The common law has developed by a system of precedent since the thirteenth and fourteenth centuries. Early liability turned on conforming claims to recognized forms of action. Revolutionary changes in society saw commensurate changes in the law. For example, the invention of the printing press changed the law of defamation designed to protect individual reputation, and the transport and industrial revolution in England eventually reformed the law of torts as the numbers, severity, and notoriety of injury-causing accidents increased. The courts during the late nineteenth and twentieth centuries have expanded the reach of liability. The most powerful avenue for this expansion has been the law of negligence. Once restrained by the perimeters of privity of contract, the common law courts fashioned a generalized duty of care in negligence. The formula possessed an internal momentum: a duty was owed where one person should have reasonably foreseen that by her actions she would physically injure another. Reasonable foreseeability was an expansive concept. Typical of the common law, doctrinal transformation took place without extensive reference to the philosophy of, or rationale for, the imposition of liability.

The foreseeability formula demanded a search for limits to liability. The interest protected was person or property, and accordingly, liability would not normally extend in negligence to protect purely economic interests. Some restrictions, too, were placed upon recovery of emotional distress suffered at the hands of a negligent actor. In the interests of liberty of action, the law did not impose liability for mere omissions to act in the absence of a relationship imposing a special duty to act.

Limits were also introduced through causation. A person would not be liable for every consequence of his negligence, but only for those consequences that were proximate and would not have occurred but for his negligence. Again, the common law eschewed philosophical insights about the nature of liability. Rather, the question was a pragmatic one: should these consequences be ascribed to the defendant's tortious act?

Limits to liability derived from either the concept of reasonable foreseeability in the duty of care, or from causation, in the end rested on policy. How is the line to be drawn? The rules were broad and open-textured, allowing a wide ambit of choice. In the process of reasoned elaboration, the courts in the maturing law of torts have searched for underlying policy reasons for liability. The most influential judges have been those who have recognized the policy base of tort liability rules. At the time of the emergence of negligence as a generalizing and potent principle, Lord Atkin in England and Benjamin Cardozo in the United States played the leading roles; at a later time, post–World War II, when the law of negligence had matured, Lord Denning in England and Roger Traynor in the United States were the doyens of tort liability.

The story of tort liability has been its expansion and the concomitant crumbling of doctrine that restricted its application. An obvious and prime example is the erosion of immunities to liability. Immunities included governmental, charitable, public officer, spousal, and parent/child. The status of a person protected that person from liability. Immunities based on status crumbled because they appeared inconsistent with modern ideas of responsibility, deterrence, and compensation. A combination of legislative and judicial action led to the decline of immunities. The onus is now on the defender of an immunizing rule to show that the immunity is justified. Justification turns on whether the immunity bestows a benefit outweighing the utility of the application of tort liability. For example, high officials in carriage of their duties should be immune lest they be chilled in the proper performance of their duties. In these instances, other nontort remedies may be available to fulfill the goals of compensation and deterrence.

The decline of immunity, first, demonstrates the ascendancy of the presumption of liability in modern tort law and, second, shows that the protection from liability is not to be garnered by invocation of doctrinal rules, but must be justified by the same policies that undergird the application of liability.

In measuring the application of an immunity, the calculus was pragmatic and consequentialist. What are the costs and benefits in protecting an actor from liability? The calculus was made explicit by Judge Learned Hand in *United States v. Carroll Towing Co.*, 159 F.2d 169 (2d Cir. 1947): in deciding whether the actor had been negligent in respect of an accident, the court should ask whether the burden of taking precautions is less than or greater than the probability of the accident occurring multiplied by the probability of the accident occurring. This formula was later to inspire the most influential philosophical trend in modern tort law that perceived the fundamental rationale of negligence to be economic efficiency. In a positive, or descriptive, sense, the rules encouraged actors to put resources to their highest valued use. Common law rules were prescribed to reduce the sum of social costs arising from the conflicting resource use by two interacting parties. Judge Guido Calabresi, formerly dean of Yale Law School, made a fundamental contribution by arguing for the application of strict liability, that is, liability without the necessity of proof of the defendant's fault. Calabresi's was a normative analysis that strict liability should be employed as to reduce the costs that arise from accidents in our society. The utilitarian roots of economic analysis were sympathetic with the pragmatic and consequentialist aspirations of the common law, explaining the influence of utilitarianism.

Where negligence rules were viewed as an obstacle to achieving the goals of liability, some courts altered the rules. This is seen most starkly in respect of liability for defective products. Some courts decided that the costs of accidents caused by defective products (which could not be proved to be negligently produced) ought to be borne by manufacturers rather than injured consumers. Given the stimulus of section 402A of the *Restatement of Torts, Second,* strict product liability swept the United States. Little thought was given to protection from this strict form of liability. The limits of liability, however, were met not only because strict liability that was absolute (that is, entirely without fault) failed to fulfill consequential goals of risk and loss distribution, but also because, if taken to absolute liability, it flouted a fundamental of justice. The law of torts was built on a notion of individual responsibility and the correlative of corrective justice. The nature of private law, including torts, embodies the notion that a person suffering wrongful harm can recover compensation from those who wronged him. Under a regime of absolute liability, a manufacturer may be liable even though his act may not be *wrongful.*

The expansion of liability in defective products has been checked. Expansive doctrines elsewhere have been retrenched in favor of protections from liability. The most obvious reason is the perceived impact of liability on distinguishable interested groups who have employed the political system to gain protection. More than this, however, the range of liability was problematical in terms of the goals of tort law or its philosophical base.

Analyzed as protections from civil liability, vast tracts of human activity are now subject to regulation by civil liability in tort. This has resulted in the need for express protection where the rationales of liability would not warrant liability. It has also resulted in express protection usually flowing from legislative action. Civil liability has become more overtly the subject of political concern.

For the future, the persuasiveness of liability will remain, with ideals of identified protection. Protection will be obtained, as in the past, by principled argumentation according to well-known, albeit controversial policy grounds. Increasingly, the political process will shape the borders of those islands as tort liability is perceived as a powerful engine for influencing behavior and shifting social resources.

References

Calabresi, Guido. *The Costs of Accidents: A Legal and Economic Analysis.* New Haven: Yale University Press, 1970.

Coase, Ronald. "The Problem of Social Cost." *Journal of Law and Economics* 3 (1960), 1–44.

Coleman, Jules L. *Markets, Morals and the Law.* New York: Cambridge University Press, 1988.

Hart, H.L.A., and A.M. Honoré. *Causation in the Law.* 2d ed. London: Oxford University Press, 1959.

Henderson, James A., and Theodore Eisenberg. "The Quiet Revolution in Products Liability: An Empirical Study of Legal Change." *University of California at Los Angeles Law Review* 37 (1990), 479–553.

Huber, Peter W. "Safety and the Second Best: The Hazards of Public Risk Management in the Courts." *Columbia Law Review* 85 (1985), 277–337.

Owen, David. "The Moral Foundations of Products Liability Law: Toward First Principles." *Notre Dame Law Review* 68 (1993), 427–506.

Posner, Richard. "A Theory of Negligence." *Journal of Legal Studies* 1 (1972), 29–96.

Rabin, Robert L. "The Historical Development of the Fault Principle: A Reinterpretation." *Georgia Law Review* 15 (1981), 925–961.

Schwartz, Gary T. "Tort Law and the Economy in Nineteenth Century America: A Reinterpretation." *Yale Law Journal* 90 (1981), 1717–1775.

Wade, John W. et al. *Prosser, Wade, and Schwartz's Torts: Cases and Materials.* 9th ed. Westbury NY: Foundation Press, 1994.

Weinrib, Ernest. "Corrective Justice." *Iowa Law Review* 77 (1992), 403–425.

David F. Partlett

See also DEFENSES; ECONOMIC LOSS; LIABILITY, CRIMINAL; PRODUCTS LIABILITY; TORTS

Liaison

The morality, legality, and social status of sexual relationships outside of marriage has been a topic of legal and philosophical interest periodically through the ages. With the increasing breakdown of marriages, it is a matter of growing interest in the contemporary world.

The definition of marriage, in a significant sense, is also the definition of nonmarital liaisons. There are, of course, many possible definitions of marriage. Marriage may be defined by particular groups within society in a different way than the state defines marriage in the law. A relationship may be defined as a marriage by the parties and the subgroup of society to which they are most responsive, even though it is not recognized as a valid marriage by the state in the law; or a relationship may be recognized as a marriage by the state but not by a particular subgroup of society. An example of the latter is a marriage of divorced persons that may not be recognized as a marriage by the Roman Catholic church or its faithful adherents. An example of the former from recent history is the example of Mormon polygamy.

Liaisons may be encouraged by avoidance of legal restrictions on entry to or exit from marriage, or of the burdensome legal and economic incidents to lawful marriage. Repudiation of the social institution and its formal expectations, or serving as a trial preparation for marriage, also are reasons encouraging liaisons.

Nonmarital cohabitation is now permitted, de facto if not de jure, in virtually all American jurisdictions, most of which also recognize the possibility of certain legally enforceable marriage-like economic incidents arising out of nonmarital cohabitation (in variations of the influential *Marvin v. Marvin,* Cal. 557P.2d, 106, palimony case). Ironically, the formal recognition of legal status of nonmarital relationships may undermine and frustrate the reason for entering them and the expectation of parties who form them.

It is conceivable for legal systems to ignore marriage altogether—to decline to define marriage or use marriage as a basis for any legal classification at all, leaving marriage entirely to the realm of private regulation (by clan, religion, and so forth). It has been argued, for example, that many of the incidents of marriage already have been separated from the legal status of marriage and essentially deregulated (such as marital name, conformity to a prescribed model of relationship such as fidelity and lifelong commitment, legitimacy of children, immunity for intrarelational torts, and economic claims among nonmarital cohabitants comparable to the economic claims of divorcing married parties that have been recognized, and so on). It is entirely conceivable to regulate economic relations of dependent or interdependent cohabitants (including property control, support, division of property upon breakup, and transmission of property upon death) without the use of the legal status of marriage. Whether that would be practical or prudent is the critical issue.

It also is conceivable that the state could define marriage or the benefits of marriage so broadly that virtually all cohabitational relationships are deemed "marriages" for legal purposes. That process has already begun with the adoption of functional equivalence notions in family law. One result is the obscuring of the boundary between marriage and nonmarital liaisons. As the definition of marriage has become increasingly obscure, the difference between marriage and nonmarital liaisons has become blurred, and the legal consequences of the relationships have become less distinct. Some assert that this reflects the emergence of a new commercialization of intimate relationships and the death of the romantic model of marriage. Others see this as manifestation of a new egalitarianism of all relationships, a partnership model replacing the old trust model of marriage. Others assert that this definitional confusion is the waning of commitment and the withering of social morality, the privatization of relationships of intimacy in lieu of public regulation.

Is there a "right" to enter into nonmarital liaisons? Perhaps the starting point for analysis is by analogy to marriage. A long and important line of Supreme Court cases recognizes a "right" to marry. It has been argued that a right to enter into certain alternative nonmarital liaisons, likewise, must be recognized. The right recognized in the marriage cases seems, however, to exclude, by definition, nonmarital liaisons. Moreover, the policy reasons underlying recognition of the right to marry apply uniquely to lawful marriages, not extramarital liaisons.

Equality arguments also have been asserted in support of a "right" to enter nonmarital liaisons. However, equal protection has never required that different things be given like treatment, and marriage has long been considered to serve important social functions (particularly relating not only to procreation, socialization, and child rearing, but also as to the status of women, regulation of sexual behavior, and social stability) that nonmarital liaisons do not fully serve.

On the other hand, it has been argued that the unwritten constitutional "right of privacy" encompasses a right of consenting adults to enter into nonmarital liaisons free from government restrictions. This concept is based on the presumption that adults should be free to make whatever consensual intimate relationships they choose to make unless there are compelling reasons against a particular arrangement. The Millian principle of liberty restricted only when necessary to protect others is invoked.

The question of social effects (benefits and harm) thereby becomes critical; any "right" to enter nonmarital liaisons is merely the beginning, not the end, of the analysis. Such a right must be weighed against the social interest in restricting nonmarital liaisons. Consideration of the social interest raises two questions: Will marriage or the family be endangered by recognition of nonmarital liaisons? If so, does it matter? Since marriage has long been regarded as the basic unit of society, the second question is practically indisputable. Article 12 of the European Convention on Human Rights, for example, protects "the right to marry and found a family," which could suggest that marriage is considered the necessary foundation for a family. There is widespread belief and significant social science data suggesting that children and mothers flourish best in families built upon marriage, though some suggest, however, that the child-centeredness of society may be a waning orientation.

The more hotly contested question is whether recognizing nonmarital liaisons would harm conventional marriage and family institutions. Empirical research reveals that when parties who have cohabited marry they have higher incidence of divorce than do married couples who never cohabited before marriage. There is clear evidence that problems of economic insecurity for children, and of child abuse, are notably greater in nonmarital liaisons than they are in marriages, as are incidents of violence against women and economic inequality. Detrimental social consequences from nonmarital liaisons (including decreased productivity, increased crime and juvenile delinquency, more health problems, more drug use, more stress, decreased educational achievement, lower income, greater demands on the public welfare, less quantity and lower quality parenting, and so forth) are well attested by a large body of social science literature. Likewise, the claims of wives and nonmarital cohabitants are plainly incompatible, and some feminists argue that the expansion of nonmarital liaisons comes at the expense of wives and mothers. Others, however, assert that the society will best be served by the elimination of all economic dependency of women, and promote nonmarital liaisons to that end.

The types of contemporary nonmarital liaisons that are of greatest interest to lawmakers and commentators today probably are heterosexual nonmarital cohabitation, and gay and lesbian partnerships. Modern nonmarital cohabitation has much in common with the Roman relationship of *concubinatus* (concubinage). Concubinage was a legal nonmarital union; it was distinct from marriage, and also from legal prostitution (*licentia sturpi*), and was not considered disreputable. The concubine had legal and social status, but not the dignity of a wife. The cohabitation of a freed slave woman and her patron was apparently the most common type of concubinage. A man could not have both a concubine and a wife, since Roman marriage was monogamous. Concubinage flourished because Roman marriage restrictions prevented many marriages across national, social, and economic class lines. For example, the Augustan laws to encourage marriage were limited to encouraging what were considered suitable unions: members of the Senatorial classes were barred from marrying actresses and freed women; governors of provinces were not allowed to marry women from the province they governed; and soldiers were subject to marriage restrictions.

The critical difference between marriage and concubinage was the presence (marriage) or absence (concubinage) of intent to marry, and the giving (marriage) or withholding (concubinage) of dowry. Under the Christian emperors, concubinage was discouraged and the presumption of marriage encouraged to the point that a written declaration of concubinage became necessary to rebut the presumption of marriage. Concubinage was abolished by the Emperor Leo in the ninth century: "Why should you prefer a muddy pool when you can drink at the pure fount?"

The drive for recognition of same-sex marriage or same-sex domestic partnerships has recently become a profoundly divisive social issue. At the core of the controversy is the question of whether society has a sufficient, rational interest in denying the social dignity of practical incidents of legal status to consensual homosexual relations between adults. Some argue that the law distinguishes between relationships and behaviors that are prohibited, tolerated, and preferred, and argue that even if homosexual relations should be tolerated, that does not mean that they should be given preferred status in law. Likewise, the distinction between private and public relationships has been invoked in the argument that private homosexual relations between consenting adults are acceptable, but society has a compelling interest in preventing them from being publicly recognized because they would compete against marriage and family to the detriment of the welfare of society in general.

References

Bumpass, L.L., and J.A. Sweet. "National Estimates of Cohabitation." *Demography* 26 (1989), 615–625.

Chadwick, Ruth F., ed. *Ethics, Reproduction and Genetic Control.* New York: Routledge, 1992.

Curry, Hayden, Denis Clifford, and Robin Leonard. *A Legal Guide for Lesbian and Gay Couples.* Berkeley CA: Nolo Press, 1994.

Eekelaar, John M., and Sanford N. Katz, eds. *Marriage and Cohabitation in Contemporary Societies, Areas of Legal, Social and Ethical Change.* Toronto: Butterworth, 1980.

Eskridge, W.N., Jr. "A History of Same-Sex Marriage." *Virginia Law Review* 79 (1993), 1419.

Finnis, J. "Law, Morality, and Sexual Orientation." *Notre Dame Law Review* 69 (1994), 1049–1076.

George, R.P., and G.V. Bradley. "Marriage and the Liberal Imagination." *Georgetown Law Journal* 84 (1996), 301–320.

Glendon, Mary Ann. *The New Marriage and the New Property.* Toronto: Butterworth, 1981.

Hafen, B. "The Constitutional Status of Marriage, Kinship, and Sexual Privacy—Balancing the Individual and Social Interests." *Michigan Law Review* 81 (1983), 463–574.

———. "Individualism and Autonomy in Family Law: The Waning of Belonging." *Brigham Young University Law Review* (1991), 197–257.

Macedo, S. "Homosexuality and the Conservative Mind." *Georgetown Law Journal* 84 (1996), 261–300.

Wardle, L.D. "A Critical Analysis of Constitutional Claims for Same-Sex Marriage."

Brigham Young University Law Review (1996), 1–101.

Lynn D. Wardle

See also DIVORCE AND MARRIAGE; FAMILY LAW; INSTITUTIONAL JURISPRUDENCE

Liberal Philosophy of Law

The liberal theory of law is a cluster of views about both the nature of law and the permissible limits to the use of law. At the heart of liberalism is the view that the state should not use its coercive power to impose conceptions of the good life upon individuals. John Stuart Mill's *On Liberty,* written in 1859, is the classic defense of the idea that (adult) individuals should be left free to choose the kinds of lives they want to lead, up to the point at which their actions harm others. In at least one of its significant modern forms, liberalism is also committed to equality. The state treats its citizens as equals only when it permits each person to develop and act on his or her own conceptions of the good.

The commitment to liberty has, historically, been manifest in a philosophical association between liberalism and legal positivism. More often than not, liberals are drawn to the positivist insistence on the separation between law and morals, from the level of basic theories of law, to the level of adjudication in particular cases. The liberal's understanding of liberty requires a rejection of legal moralism, that is, the view that the state is permitted to enjoin an act solely on the ground that it is immoral or that the community considers it immoral, independent of considerations of harm. Resistance to legal moralism renders the liberal suspicious of any attempt to build morality into law, as in natural law theories, since importing morality into the law allows the enforcement of the community's morality, independent of harm, at the cost of liberty.

The political theory of liberalism has its initial roots in the social contract theories of the seventeenth and eighteenth centuries, particularly in that of John Locke, who argued that government rests on the consent of its citizens and that there are basic human rights which the state may not violate under any circumstances. Thomas Hobbes and Jean-Jacques Rousseau also contributed important ideas because of their emphasis on individual consent as the source of government, but each added illiberal elements, which conflicted with the existence of fundamental and inviolable rights. For Hobbes it was his embrace of authoritarian rule; for Rousseau, whose emphasis on participatory democracy was an important development of liberalism, it was a majoritarian "general will," which apparently could override any individual right. Liberalism flourished in the nineteenth-century utilitarianism of Jeremy Bentham, James Mill, and John Stuart Mill. In the works of Adam Smith and other theorists of the market, it took the form of a defense of economic liberty. In the twentieth century, liberalism has ranged from laissez-faire libertarianism to defenses of the modern welfare state.

The first systematic liberal philosophers of law were the British utilitarians Jeremy Bentham and John Austin, followed by John Stuart Mill. They were deeply committed to projects of legal reform, including penal reform and the expansion of the franchise, as crucial to the general welfare. With such reforms in mind, Bentham rejected Blackstone's *Commentaries* for their complacent view of English law as the embodiment of natural law and natural right. Austin concluded that it was pernicious to confuse law as it is and law as it ought to be. He delineated *The Province of Jurisprudence Determined* by the twin notions of command and sovereignty; the law is the command of a sovereign, an entity to which the bulk of the population is in a habit of obedience and which is, in turn, not in a habit of obedience to anything else. (In a democracy, Austin held, the people are sovereign, accustomed as it were to obeying themselves.) Moral precepts generally, including the commands of God, are not law per se.

John Stuart Mill continued the utilitarian tradition with his powerful defense of liberty of the individual against the use of coercion by the state or society. Mill's "harm principle," as it has become known, insists that the sole justification for intervening with the liberty of the individual is to prevent harm to others; his own good (legal paternalism) or the beliefs of society that what he is doing is wrong (legal moralism) cannot justify interference. Mill's contemporaneous critic, Sir James Fitzjames Stephen, in *Liberty, Equality, Fraternity,* argued that this defense of liberty was a recipe for social disintegration.

In the late nineteenth century, the realist tradition in the United States also scrutinized the links between law and morality. The realist view that law is what the judges say it is developed in opposition to the formalist picture of adjudication as the mechanical application of rules to cases. Justice Oliver Wendell Holmes' invitation to wash away assumptions about the law with cynical acid and to view the law as the bad man sees it was at least in part a pragmatist injunction not to let the law stand in the way of liberty and social progress (conceived by Holmes, as a matter of evolutionary theory). Through the writings of academics and judges such as Louis Brandeis and Benjamin Cardozo, American legal realism increasingly became identified with the liberal commitment to personal rights, such as privacy, and to the development of programs of social welfare, such as the New Deal.

The scientific positivism of the mid-twentieth century left ethical theory, including political philosophy and philosophy of law, largely in decline. A major exception to this trend, however, was Hans Kelsen's legal positivist *General Theory of Law and State*. Kelsen viewed law as a system of norms, presupposing a foundational norm. In opposition to the realists, Kelsen argued that, as such a system, law escaped the subjectivity of other normative judgments.

After World War II, Kelsen's model of law as a system of rules was taken up by H.L.A. Hart, first in his argument that the Nuremberg trials confused illegality with moral condemnation, and then in his development of a full positivist theory in *The Concept of Law*. Hart's positivism is the view that law and morality are conceptually separate—what is law is separate from what is moral. In his fundamental jurisprudential writings, Hart defended this "separation thesis" on multiple levels: the level of identifying a legal system, of identifying its rules or principles, and of the adjudication of particular cases. With regard to identifying rules or principles, for example, Hart contended that what matters is the system's accepted method of picking out rules of law—its "rule of recognition"—not the moral status of a given rule. With regard to adjudication, Hart argued that value judgments are not involved in the judge's application of "core" instances of legal rules and that, when judges step out into the "penumbra," they should be regarded as making law, with all the risks and benefits of judicial lawmaking.

Hart's insistence on this separation of law and morality stemmed importantly from his liberalism—from the view that to identify a rule as legal because of its moral status unacceptably risked the legal enforcement of morality. Mill's debate in the nineteenth century with Stephen was mirrored in the debate between Hart and Sir Patrick Devlin in the 1960s. Devlin argued that society has a right to *The Enforcement of Morals* of its own in order to prevent possibly damaging changes in its social fabric. Hart, in *Law, Liberty and Morality*, defended the *Wolfenden Report*'s recommendations for the decriminalization of "victimless" crimes such as homosexuality and prostitution, arguing as Mill had that the importance of liberty overrides concerns about social changes and disintegration, which often amount to rationalizations of the status quo. Also, recently, Mill's harm principle has received extended exploration and largely sympathetic critique in the four volumes of Joel Feinberg's examination of *The Moral Limits of the Criminal Law*.

To some extent, particularly since the legal realist movement of the 1930s, liberalism about law has been associated with skepticism about theories of the good. Many critics of liberalism have argued that it rests on the view that no theory of the good life is more justifiable than any other and that is why the state has no authority to enforce such conceptions. Critics of Mill's arguments for liberty of expression and freedom of "tastes and pursuits," for example, have accused him of assuming that all ideas of the good are equally defensible and all lives equally good. This is a misreading of Mill, who argued, instead, that we are more likely to get closer to the truth about the good in the long run if we do not presume certainty and that people are more likely to lead satisfying lives if we let them "experiment in living" and find their own good in their own way.

Since World War II, at least, liberal philosophies of law have firmly rejected the view that their position rests on skepticism about values. Hart, for example, in his classic criticism of the Nuremberg trials, argued that although the tribunal used a valid moral framework to punish those who had committed great evils, it did this inappropriately under the cover of law. Hence, it used the trappings of law to punish people for doing what was legally permissible though morally wrong. Hart took pains to explain that his criticism did not rest on moral subjectivity or relativism, but on the claim that law and morality are distinct normative systems and that threats to liberty are significant if positive morality is assumed to be part of law. Yet Hart's critics, like Mill's, have persisted in reading him as a moral skeptic. An example of this is Lon Fuller's *The Morality of Law*.

Contemporary liberalism is deeply indebted to John Rawls's *A Theory of Justice*, published in 1971. Rawls developed a theory of the right as prior to the good. Basic principles of justice—roughly, maximal equal liberty for all, and departures from equality of social "primary goods" when and only when these are to the greatest benefit of the least advantaged—should form the framework for political institutions and constitutional law. Within these structures, individuals formulate their own plans of life, sharing, Rawls assumed, the need for the same primary goods, but perhaps not much else about their visions of the good life. In the years since the publication of his book, Rawls has come to make less foundational claims for his theory. In *Political Liberalism*, published in 1993, Rawls maintains that his theory is the best reconstruction of liberalism in politics, the theory that would be constructed for their common lives by individuals with widely different conceptions of the good.

Along with Rawls, other modern writers, such as Charles Larmore, have put forth the idea that liberalism involves a special attitude on the part of the state toward individuals' conceptions of the good life. Individuals all have ideas of what makes their lives go well, of what makes life worth living, of what provides them with aspirations and motivations. The liberal state, it is said, must be neutral with respect to these conceptions of the good. There is no particular way of living that the state should favor or enforce. Nonetheless, social living requires that conceptions of the good which involve harming others be prohibited. The role of law is thus, as Mill argued, the prevention of harm, not the encouragement of particular conceptions of the good life.

This neutralist conception of liberalism has, like Mill's theory, been challenged as resting on skepticism with regard to the good. This challenge is fed by the apparent absence in liberal theories of law of communal ideals. The result has been a liberalism caught between criticism from the right and the left, defending such doctrines as respect for privacy or the rights of the disadvantaged without, it is said, any compelling theoretical basis. From the right, critics identified with communitarianism, such as Michael Sandel, argue that liberalism cannot account for conceptions of personal identity that are rooted in community and thus accept legal doctrines that do not respect community values, such as religion, and relational values, such as group and family ties. In a replay of the Mill-Stephen and Hart-Devlin debates, Sandel argues that society has a legitimate right to impose or encourage community-based identity-conferring conceptions of the good.

From the left, scholars in the critical legal studies movement in the United States argue that claims to neutrality are pretextual and conceal unacknowledged interests and relationships of power. Roberto Unger, for example, argues that liberals are committed both to liberty and the rule of law, but these fit together uneasily without commitment to a communal conception of the good. The rule of law, as embodied in legislative enactments, is the basis for order. Yet rules are subject to interpretation in adjudication and, unless one interpretation can be justified objectively and communally—as more than the judge's own values—liberty suffers, since adjudication becomes the imposition of one set of subjective values upon parties who do not share them.

Critics from the right and left thus share the charge that liberalism cannot provide a foundation for the rule of law. The right claims that liberalism ignores the value of tradition and the unchosen identity based on it; the left, that it cannot reconcile order, neutrality, and due process with liberty and justification. Perhaps the best reply to this squeeze has been developed by Ronald Dworkin, Hart's successor to the chair of jurisprudence at Oxford. Dworkin's earlier work in *Taking Rights Seriously* criticized rule-based models of adjudication, such as Kelsen's and Hart's, on the ground that they cannot account for the role of rights in adjudication. For Dworkin there is "a right answer" (or a small set of "right answers") in every legal case; this result is obtained by giving the best reconstruction of settled constitutional, statutory, and common law principles. Dworkin calls this "the soundest theory of the settled law." In the United States, Dworkin argues, the fundamental constitutional principle, underlying even liberty rights, is that each individual should be treated with equal respect and concern. On this basis

Dworkin develops a liberalism which emphasizes liberty, equality, and welfare. Dworkin argues that the right to treatment as an equal is objective because it is required by the best account of the settled law, but it is also a matter of moral principle. Dworkin answers the communitarian critique, that liberalism embodies no core social values, with the contention that it rests on the values of equality and respect for persons. He answers the critique from the left, that liberalism can realize order only by imposing subjective values, with the contention that objective values underlie existing law, in *Law's Empire*. His approach thus abandons the positivist separation between law and morality that had been a hallmark of earlier liberal theories of the law. Yet it remains clearly a liberal theory. Dworkin subsequently extended his theory in *Freedom's Law: The Moral Reading of the American Constitution* (1996).

Two other recent theorists developing objective rights-based liberal theories of the law are Carl Wellman and Rex Martin. Joseph Raz has developed a theory that emphasizes the objectivity of conceptions of the good, while insisting on the liberal right to choice regarding the good.

References

Bentham, Jeremy. *The Principles of Morals and Legislation.* New York: Hafner, 1948.

Dworkin, Ronald. *Taking Rights Seriously.* Cambridge: Harvard University Press, 1977.

Hart, H.L.A. *The Concept of Law.* Oxford: Clarendon Press, 1961.

Hobhouse, L.T. *Liberalism.* New York: H. Holt, 1911.

Larmore, Charles. *Patterns of Moral Complexity.* Cambridge: Cambridge University Press, 1987.

Martin, Rex. *A System of Rights.* Oxford: Clarendon Press, 1993.

Rawls, John. *A Theory of Justice.* Cambridge MA: Harvard University Press, 1971.

Raz, Joseph. *The Morality of Freedom.* Oxford: Clarendon Press, 1986.

Schauer, Frederick. *Playing by the Rules.* Oxford: Clarendon Press, 1991.

Wasserstrom, Richard. *The Judicial Decision: Toward a Theory of Legal Justification.* Stanford: Stanford University Press, 1961.

Wellman, Carl. *Real Rights.* Oxford: Oxford University Press, 1995.

Leslie P. Francis
Bruce Landesman

See also COMMUNITARIAN PHILOSOPHY OF LAW; CRIMINALIZATION; CRITICAL LEGAL STUDIES; PATERNALISM; POSITIVISM, LEGAL; WRONGDOING AND RIGHT ACTING

Liberality

Liberality is the virtue of generous expenditure, often associated in the aristotelian and ciceronian civic republican tradition with kings and high-born citizens, but challenged in diverse ways by later thinkers. Niccolò Machiavelli considered it politically dangerous. Michel de Montaigne ruled it the only virtue prone to tyranny. No virtue theorist since the thorough individualization of ethics in the West has considered it straightforwardly praiseworthy—despite the fact that our public buildings and spaces are very much its product still.

Aristotle's standard version of the virtue of liberality is *eleutheriotes,* sometimes translated as generosity, and it governs the proper disposition of wealth: navigating a course between stinginess and wastefulness, spending or giving in proper measure, and limiting acquisition. The related virtue of *megaloprepeia* (from the Greek roots *prepousa,* fitting; and *megalo,* large scale), usually translated "magnificence," is similar to liberality but, in contrast to it, is social in scope and concerned with great outlay. Though Aristotle is careful to say that the precise degree of outlay is relative to position and context, and therefore that liberality is possible even for the poor, the emphasis on the grand scale in magnificence has often seemed to rule out many people (though perhaps not so many *citizens*) from Aristotle's version of the life of complete virtue. For while anyone could be generous with what he possessed—"What is generous does not depend on the quantity of what is given," Aristotle says, "but on the state of the giver"—only a wealthy man could be magnificent. "A poor person could not be magnificent since he lacks the means for large and fitting expenditures; and if he attempts it, he is foolish, since he spends more than what is worthy and right for him, when in fact it is correct spending that expresses virtue." For a different interpretation, see *Sovereign Virtue* by Stephen White.

The outlay of the liberal spender must be appropriate, though, and not always large. "The liberal person will aim at what is fine in his giving and will give correctly," Aristotle tells us, "for he will give to the right people, the right amounts, at the right time, and all the other things that are implied by correct giving. He will do this, moreover, with pleasure, at any rate without pain." Aristotle's examples of liberality are familiar in type, if not in detail. The liberal man will incur "the sorts of expenses called honourable," and will limit his acquisitions likewise. When it comes to magnificent outlay, expenses will be directed to civic or religious goods—temples, sacrifices, dedications, noble competitions, feasts, warships, or choruses—and those that underwrite events which are noble and in the common interest, such as weddings or entertaining foreign visitors. Aristotle even says that "it is proper to the magnificent person to build a house befitting his riches, since this is also a suitable adornment."

While excesses of magnificence (in vulgarity) and deficiencies of it (in niggardliness) are obvious, the vices framing liberality are more complex and pose greater dangers. For example, one may be illiberal in giving to others (a deficiency) even while tending toward wastefulness in spending on oneself (an excess). One may also be too acquisitive—the "shameful love of gain" in which one receives wealth from pimps and usurers and other undesirables. This pleonectic love of wealth may then be combined, redoubling the vice, with the intemperance of lavish personal spending.

The virtue of liberality survived the transition of Aristotle's thought into the Italian civic republicanism of Cicero and his followers, translated into a Latin word derived from the root *liber,* free—as in free-spending, free with one's money. The translation does not preserve Aristotle's notion of appropriateness, but in practice the virtue did. Liberality suited the wealthy landowners who found ciceronian citizenship congenial—even if it was more honored in the breach than the observance. While not every civic republican might actually spend liberally, he could nevertheless aspire to a status in which generous public spending was frequent. At the same time, he could easily see the attraction of a public-mindedness where ego-maximization was cloaked in a mantle of noble contribution to the city. The celebration of liberality was far from being entirely hypocritical, to be sure, but there was enough hypocrisy evident in the civic republican version of liberality to provide a toehold for a stringent critic of that tradition, Machiavelli, especially when writing in his cynical moods.

Indeed, in *The Prince* Machiavelli condemns liberality as a virtue, which, like mercy and honesty, too easily turns to the ruler's disadvantage. First, it is obvious that private generosity is of no use to the prince, for it does not enhance his public reputation; so "if you wish to be widely known as a generous man," Machiavelli says, "you must seize every opportunity to make a big display of your giving." Such liberality comes with a price beyond the money spent, however, for "[a] prince of this character is bound to use up his entire revenue in works of ostentation. . . . If he wants to keep a name for generosity, he will have to load his people with exorbitant taxes and squeeze money out of them in every way he can. This is the first step in making him odious to his subjects." Far better for the prince to be known as a miser, then, for at least the people will not resent him. In fact, in characteristic inversion, Machiavelli says that there is a kind of "higher liberality" evident in the miserly ruler, for he spends only the money he truly commands, without excessive taxation. He lives within his means. The only exception to this rule is the situation in which the prince acquires wealth that belongs neither to him nor to his subjects—other people's money, in short. This, Machiavelli says, "he should spend like water."

By the close of the Renaissance, liberality was on its way to being considered a virtue exclusively of princes and kings. For even among the classes of wealthy private citizens, not many possessed both the means and the inclination for lavish public displays of spending. Discussions into the early modern period concentrate on this issue: how much should a king spend? Unusually, Montaigne agrees with Machiavelli about the pitfalls of rulers who are too liberal. The king, he says in the essay "On Vehicles," should be liberal with justice, which is dispensed according to reason, but should spend public money only where it best serves the public interest: "to ports, harbours, fortifications, and walls, to fine buildings, churches, hospitals, colleges, and the improvement of streets and roads." If he does not, and instead indulges his own whims, he risks hatred: "[T]o a monarch's subjects, who are the spectators of these triumphs, it appears that they are being given a display of their own wealth, and being feasted at their own expense."

Even when the king spends his own money, however, dangers lurk. "The subjects of a prince who is excessive in his gifts grow lavish in their demands," Montaigne says in the same essay; "they take not reason but precedent for their standard. . . . Therefore, the more a prince exhausts himself in giving, the poorer he grows in friends. How shall he satisfy desires that increase as quickly as they are fulfilled?" On this point, and on the *pleonexia* of subjects more generally, Montaigne saw more clearly than Thomas Hobbes, who opined rather hopefully in *Leviathan* that "Riches, joyned with Liberality, is Power, because it procureth friends, and servants."

Gradually, the word "liberality" acquired an additional meaning, and one that may be more familiar to contemporary ears. It came to mean generosity of mind, not money, not free-spending, then, but free-thinking—in short, tolerance. The first uses of liberality in this connection date only from the first part of the nineteenth century. In 1830, for example, Thomas Jefferson wrote of his "opponents, who had not the liberality to distinguish between political and social opposition."

Today the adjective "liberal" is not often used in connection with spending, except perhaps in slightly formal or archaic locutions, and discussion of liberality as a virtue is all but unknown. We do not depend on the largesse of kings for public outlay—though we may well find ourselves disgruntled with the targets of public spending—and the benefaction of private citizens is as often resented as praised. Yet there are some indications that liberality may be coming back into fashion as a virtue of citizens. Even now there is a vibrant culture of charity work among the wealthy. And in recent social-democratic theories of participatory citizenship the individual's contribution to the commonwealth is being to some extent rethought, as less a matter of grudgingly paid taxes and more a kind of public-spirited largesse.

The trouble here, as Machiavelli and Montaigne and our politicians all in their different ways realize, is that such liberality cannot always be counted on in times of economic trial.

References

Aristotle. *Nicomachean Ethics*. Trans. Terence Irwin. Indianapolis: Hackett, 1985.

Barber, Benjamin. *Strong Democracy: Participatory Politics for a New Age*. Berkeley: University of California Press, 1984.

The Contention Between Liberality and Prodigality. 1602. London: Malone Society and Oxford University Press, 1913.

Hobbes, Thomas. *Leviathan*. Harmondsworth: Penguin Books, 1968.

Machiavelli, Niccolò. *The Prince*. Trans. Robert M. Adams. New York: Norton, 1977.

Molho, Anthony. *Merchants, Money, and Magnificence: Florence in the Renaissance*. New York: Macmillan, 1975.

Montaigne, Michel de. *Essays*. Trans. J.M. Cohen. Harmondsworth: Penguin Books, 1958.

Murray, Gilbert. *Liberality and Civilization*. New York: AMS Press, 1979.

White, Stephen A. *Sovereign Virtue: Aristotle on the Relation Between Happiness and Prosperity*. Stanford: Stanford University Press, 1992.

Mark Kingwell

See also MONETARY POWER; TRUSTS; VIRTUE

Libertarian Philosophy of Law

With the confusion that has emerged about liberalism, so that the term is used alternatively to refer to nearly diametrically opposed sociopolitical systems, the term "libertarianism" has come to be used to refer to the sort of polity in which the right of every individual to life, liberty, and property is fully and consistently protected. Libertarianism is the political-economic theory whereby a community is just if and only if each member has his or her basic negative rights respected and protected. According to libertarians, everyone in a community must be accorded his or her sovereignty. A free market must prevail, and everyone's civil liberty is to be upheld. No one may be made subject to involuntary servitude. Even the funding of government must be secured by means of voluntary payment, not taxation.

There are different arguments in support of the libertarian legal system, and there are some differences as to how libertarians conceive of that system. However, the central tenet of libertarianism is that the highest public priority is to defend the right of everyone to life, liberty, and property.

Some libertarians conceive of law as a system of competing legal and police services. Following the writings of Friedrich von Hayek, these libertarians believe that law is itself a service to be developed spontaneously, with no agency having a monopoly on its supply. The bulk of libertarians, however, believe that the constitutional protection of individual rights must be provided by a government that is undivided, so that a court of last resort may be available to citizens who find themselves disputing over rights violations, the central source of legal trouble in a free society.

Different libertarians see the source of constitutional provisions grounded differently. Some believe that objective morality, based on human nature and the conditions facing people in communities, must underlie a bona fide legal system. Others believe that bona fide law rests on no more than the conventions identified by reference to the will of the people. Still others think that the way the common law has developed in various regions over the globe most sensibly models the nature of just law.

Furthermore, some libertarians embrace a utilitarian moral foundation in their defense of the free society, holding that the free society, especially the free market, will best promote the greatest happiness of the greatest number. Others lean toward a natural law/natural rights approach to defending the free society, holding that the moral nature of human beings, their individual responsibility to do well in life as a function of their own sovereign choices, serves to provide the basis for the libertarian polity. Yet others eschew all reference to ethics or morality and hold that libertarianism most faithfully reflects the natural, evolutionary development of human social life. There are also those who defend libertarianism because of its supposed concordance with a religious idea of human existence. Some libertarians rely on a thoroughgoing moral skepticism, following, for example, the Chinese philosophical school of taoism (mainly Lao Tzu), claiming that since nothing about right and wrong is knowable, no one could ever justify exercising any inherent authority over another.

In a libertarian polity a most basic legal protection would be accorded to the right to private property, mainly because all other rights could only be exercised fully if this right is respected and protected. Freedom of religion, artistic expression, the press, or of political participation is possible only if none is authorized to take what one owns, including one's labor and other assets. The law of property would provide the basis for identifying each individual citizen's personal sphere of authority and any violation of this sphere would not be officially tolerated. Yet the law of property would not be static, for what can be owned can change over time. Thus, for example, ownership of segments of the electromagnetic spectrum has become possible only in recent times, as has ownership of computer programs.

Moreover, the precise limits of ownership can also vary, depending on the context. Owning a huge boulder on a mountaintop, in a region plagued by earthquakes, would not imply the freedom to secure it lightly, for that would amount to a clear and present danger to people living on the mountainside. Owning a bazooka would also imply different liberties from owning a vase.

It would be the role of the courts of a libertarian polity to arrive at sensible answers to questions that arise in the course of a dynamic community life. It would be the role of legislative bodies to develop laws for new problems based on the basic principles of the libertarian constitution.

If this all appears familiar, the reason is that libertarianism is mostly the purified version of the political, legal, and economic system established in the United States of America. Libertarians would maintain that they are carrying out to its rational implications the political ideal identified by way of the Declaration of Independence or, more precisely, in the political, legal, and economic works of John Locke, Adam Smith, and other classical liberals. Accordingly, libertarians propose either a government that is required to protect, maintain, and promote the basic negative rights of all members of society or a system of competing law enforcement and adjudication that has the same objective.

One may ask what is to happen with other vital human objectives governments of most countries vigorously pursue. These include, even among western-type liberal democracies, such tasks as providing financial ("social") security for retired workers, medical care for the indigent or elderly, unemployment compensation, primary and secondary education for all, building and upkeep of roads, as well as some parks, forests, and beaches. The libertarians argue that all these and others not involving protection of rights and adjudication of serious claims of rights violation are better and more justly provided by way of the personal initiative and voluntary cooperation of members of society apart from the arm of government. Government has its hands full simply attempting to protect individual rights from criminals and foreign aggressors. Furthermore, some libertarians claim that governmental provision of these other objectives, since it must involve coercing citizens for funds and thwart the contribution of nongovernmental bodies (by means of unfair competition), is a violation of individual rights, no different from censorship or the establishment of religion.

In more general terms, libertarianism implies an unrestricted protection of individual rights as opposed to the familiar selective protection of some human activities, such as joining a religion, publishing one's ideas, and speaking one's mind.

Also, as regards some general philosophical issues, libertarianism is a minimalist theory, not explicitly addressing many topics of significance of human community life. Libertarians recognize that these topics require treatment but not by means of politics, which disintegrates from having to be spread so thin and wide when used to handle all the social problems other political theories lump under the public sector. Still, in the main, libertarians tend to embrace an individualist idea of human social existence, contending that social wholes are never concrete beings, only convenient conceptual summaries. The initiative of the individual person is, in the last analysis, the most vital feature of human community life, for better or for worse. Since the best way to secure excellence from individual effort is to hold all persons responsible for the results of their conduct and prohibit all involuntary transfer of such responsibilities—dumping, in the context of environmental affairs—the problems of community life are more likely to be solved via a libertarian than some alternative legal order.

Thus, libertarians favor privatization and the legal means of tort or product and service liability suits as blocks to malpractice in any sphere of human community life. Prior restraint, in the way of government regulation, is thought to be unjust, since it imposes burdens on individuals they have not chosen to assume, so that they are permitted to embark on some professional or commercial undertaking. Only religions leaders, members of the press, artists, writers, and most entertainers are exempt from such prior restraint (licensing, business permits, and so forth).

A couple of examples of legal measures favored or not favored by libertarians will help to further grasp the position. Libertarianism rejects the legitimacy of right to work laws, of prohibitions against racist hiring practices, of blue laws and any kind of (government) censorship, of antitrust laws (aimed at monopolies created within free markets), and of similar intrusions on free action. Libertarians may, however, approve of legal judgments against firms that fail to disclose racist hiring and related practice. (A restaurant would be free to restrict entry but would need to disclose this up front, lest it violate "reasonable man" provisions of market practices.)

Libertarians are at odds on many issues. For example, there are pro-life and pro-choice libertarians, depending on matters more fundamental than can be dealt with in politics alone. Some regard subpoenas as rights violating, others hold that consent to be governed implies consent to provide testimony where rendering justice requires it. Some embrace, others oppose, the doctrine of animal rights. Some are ardent feminists, others simply endorse universal individual human rights, whether for men, women, blacks, whites, or others. Some think children are owed parental care, others regard the relationship between parents and children akin to a voluntary contract. Some think democracy, restricted to selecting the administrators of government, is part of libertarian politics, others see this as just one possible option.

As with all seriously developed political (and indeed any) theories, the implications of libertarianism are complex and constantly emerging and being refined. What is constant is the central idea that free adult men and women, who are not under the jurisdiction of others whom they have not chosen to follow, are better suited to live a decent human life and to solve the problems they face in their communities than are people who are even just a little bit enslaved, made beholden to others against their own will. This view has been challenged by many, mostly for being naive, ahistorical, or unfeeling toward those who are unfortunate. The literature of libertarianism has by now addressed most of these challenges. The theory is thus a serious contender for the minds and hearts of the most political of animals, human beings.

References

Friedman, Milton. *Capitalism and Freedom.* Chicago: University of Chicago Press, 1962.

Hayek, F.A. *The Constitution of Liberty.* Chicago: University of Chicago Press, 1961.

Locke, John. *Second Treatise of Government.* 1690.

Machan, Tibor R. *Individuals and Their Rights.* LaSalle IL: Open Court, 1989.

Narveson, Jan. *The Libertarian Idea.* Philadelphia: Temple University Press, 1988.

Nozick, Robert. *Anarchy, State, and Utopia.* New York: Basic Books, 1974.

Rand, Ayn. *Capitalism: The Unknown Ideal.* New York: New American Library, 1967.

Rasmussen, D.B., and D.J. Den Uyl. *Liberty and Nature.* LaSalle IL: Open Court, 1991.

Rothbard, Murray N. *Power and Market.* Menlo Park CA: Institute for Humane Studies, 1970.

Smith, Adam. *The Wealth of Nations.* 1776.

von Mises, Ludwig. *Human Action: A Treatise on Economics.* 3d rev. ed. Chicago: Regnery, 1966.

Tibor R. Machan

See also Acquisition and Transfer; Liberal Philosophy of Law; Liberty; State

Liberty

Though liberty is one of the fundamental values or principles of Western society, considerable disagreement surrounds its nature, desirable extent, and relation to law. The nature of liberty or freedom (the two words mean the same thing) is most commonly identified with the lack of ("freedom from") coercion or constraint. In this view, standardly labeled "negative freedom," the people are free when others or the state do not coerce the people to abstain from what they desire, to perform what they do not desire, or to pursue alternatives other than those they might freely choose.

Negative Liberty

A crucial problem for negative freedom concerns the circumstances under which the freedom of some may be limited to enhance the liberty of others. The most widely accepted response (the harm principle) has been that individuals' liberty may only be restricted to prevent them from harming others. Such harm has typically included not only physical or mental harm, but also damage to reputation and property, as well as various social harms such as damage to the environment or public institutions.

According to the harm principle, harm is only a necessary, not a sufficient, condition for social intervention, since the extent of the harm may be too insignificant or the harm may occur in an activity in which the participants willingly accept that harm may occur to them, for instance, competitive sports. Consequently, when laws or regulations are imposed on some individuals to spare others inconsequential harm, individual liberty is unjustifiedly limited. On the other hand, harm to oneself or to others who are willing participants does not, on this principle, justify social intervention, at least when such participants are adults and are knowledgeable of their situation. When children or uninformed adults are the objects of such harm, social intervention is more obviously justified.

Nevertheless, concerns have been raised about the adequacy of the harm principle. Some object that it might justify too much coercion. If the limitation of individual behavior is dependent on legislators weighing various harms, many fear that laws or regulations may be imposed too easily on individuals to restrict their liberty. Hence, some maintain that we must also appeal to rights to liberty protected by constitutions, for example, freedom of expression, religion, or assembly. Oftentimes these rights are thought to be natural or inalienable rights that individuals possess antecedent to constitutions.

On the other hand, others claim that we must appeal to different liberty-limiting principles than the harm principle. The three most prominent include offense to others, harm to oneself (legal paternalism), and the immorality of one's actions (legal moralism).

The offense principle is invoked in cases involving pornography, obscenity, the desecration of venerable objects, as well as public instances of defecation, sexual intercourse, or nudity. The primary complaint in these cases is that people are offended, rather than harmed. The offense they experience, it is held, justifies limiting the liberty of those causing the offense.

Legal paternalism maintains that individual liberty may be limited so as to protect the individual himself or herself. A number of paternalistic restrictions appear to be readily accepted: motorcycle helmets, medical prescriptions for certain drugs, and seat belts in cars. Other protections such as proscriptions against voluntary suicide are more disputable. Once again, harm to others seems insufficient to account for many of these limitations on individual liberty.

Finally, legal moralism maintains that individual liberty may be justifiedly limited to prevent various forms of immoral behavior. Homosexuality, euthanasia, adultery, fornication, sodomy, as well as violence or exploitation of children, have been brought under this principle.

There has been considerable dispute over the nature and relations of these different liberty-limiting principles. Some have argued that the only justified restrictions on individual liberty defended by legal moralism fall under one of the other three principles. For example, only instances of immoral behavior which also harm or offend others ought to be subject to legal restriction. All other restrictions legal moralism would impose exceed the proper function of law. In this way, it is argued that legal moralism is a faulty principle. In any case, it appears that a complete account of justified limitations of individual liberty requires some combination of these principles. Which ones is a matter of considerable debate.

In all the preceding cases, the law is portrayed as limiting the liberty of some individuals. Accordingly, many individuals view the law as opposed to freedom. However, to the extent that the law justifiedly limits the behavior of some, it expands the liberty of others who might otherwise have been harmed or offended. Indeed, the role of much of constitutional law is to protect certain portions of human existence from social or political control. Thus, to think of law and liberty as simply contradictories is much too simple. They are better seen as correlatives.

Positive Liberty

Regardless of the liberty-limiting principle(s) one adopts, some maintain that negative freedom is fundamentally mistaken as an account of freedom. Instead, they maintain that liberty consists of individual self-determination or self-development, not the lack of constraint. On this second basic understanding of liberty, commonly called "positive freedom," freedom exists when individuals (have "freedom to") determine their own course of action. They are self-governing.

This view also requires substantial elaboration regarding its nature and extent, for though irrational or demented persons appear to determine their own course of action, most defenders of positive freedom would not wish to claim that such actions are free. Accordingly, those who defend positive liberty must specify the nature of the self-determination required for freedom. Not uncommonly, such further specifications involve various qualities of (for example) rationality, knowledge, emotional control, and socially good ends toward which one's self-determination must be directed. Further, since individuals live within a society, how each person's self-determination can be compatible with that of others, so that all are free, must be clearly delineated.

Laws which foster positive freedom would not aim simply to protect some people from the constraints that others impose on them. Instead, these laws would offer all individuals various powers, privileges, or rights whereby their self-determination would be protected and enhanced. For example, such measures might seek to ensure democratic resolution of important issues and to enhance the substantive participation of individuals in matters that significantly affect them.

Positive freedom also has its critics. They have charged that its defenders have been too eager to impose on everyday people the ideal conditions required for individual self-determinations to be instances of positive freedom. Thus, they argue, positive freedom leads to despotism. However, though defenders of positive freedom advisedly characterize various conditions under which people are positively free, there is no logical or historical necessity to make the further move of using governmental mechanisms despotically to impose those on ordinary people.

Other critics of positive freedom maintain that it and negative freedom are really only two different sides of the same coin. Liberty, these individuals claim, is the freedom from coercion to be or to do what one chooses. Defenders of this "unified" view of freedom claim they overcome the opposition of the two preceding views. However, they face the task of clarifying both aspects of their combined view.

Protections for Liberty

Whichever view of liberty and its relation to law one adopts, the protection of that freedom by constitutional law pertains to the relation between the state and its citizens. In some systems, for example the American, such protection does not necessarily extend to actions and relations between private individuals. Hence, constitutional guarantees of freedom of expression or religion do not themselves extend to the actions an employer may take with an employee, a church with its members, or a husband with his wife.

The protection of liberty occurs not simply through laws preventing coercion or extending various rights to individuals. It also occurs through the creation of various structures within a society. Thus, individual freedom is protected through the separation of state powers into judicial, parliamentary or legislative, and executive branches. Defenders of negative liberty will emphasize that this is simply another means to limit the coercion that powerful bodies and individuals exercise over individuals within their reach. Defenders of positive liberty will see in such structures opportunities for self-determination of individuals in that society.

Finally, several limitations regarding liberty and the law should be noted. First, constitutional and legislative law have limits beyond which their coercive powers are too crude and too slow to protect or foster liberty. Within this area popular opinion and customs have an important role to play. Second, though liberty is highly valued, the esteem in which it has been held has involved some ambivalence. Though liberty may offer people independence and self-reliance, it may also leave them isolated with little sense of power or security. In this case, freedom may seem undesirable. Thus, some people have been prepared to give up their liberty for other values. Third, liberty is one value or principle among many others, for example, justice, community, fraternity, and security. The wise legislator will recognize its high value, its complex nature, as well as its limitations.

References

Berlin, Isaiah. *Four Essays on Liberty.* Oxford: Oxford University Press, 1970.

Feinberg, Joel. *The Moral Limits of the Criminal Law.* 4 vols. Oxford: Oxford University Press, 1984–1988.

Frankel, Charles. "The Jurisprudence of Liberty." *Mississippi Law Journal* 46 (1975), 561–623.

Gray, Tim. *Freedom.* Atlantic Highlands NJ: Humanities Press International, 1991.

Hart, H.L.A. *Law, Liberty and Morality.* New York: Vintage Books, 1963.

Hayek, Friedrich A. *Law, Legislation and Liberty.* 3 vols. Chicago: University of Chicago Press, 1973.

MacCallum, Gerald. "Negative and Positive Freedom." *The Philosophical Review* 76 (1967), 312–334.

Mill, John Stuart. *On Liberty and Other Essays.* Ed. John Gray. Oxford: Oxford University Press, 1993.

Norman, Richard. *Free and Equal.* Oxford: Oxford University Press, 1987.

George G. Brenkert

See also DISTRIBUTIVE JUSTICE; PATERNALISM; RIGHTS AND LIBERTIES; WRONGDOING AND RIGHT ACTING

Life

See ABORTION AND INFANTICIDE; EUTHANASIA AND SUICIDE; WRONGFUL LIFE AND WRONGFUL DEATH

Lipsius, Justus (1547–1606)

Justus Lipsius was a Flemish philologist, political theorist, and purveyor of "neo-stoicism." A synthesis of Roman (mainly senecan) moral thought and tacitism (a style of political commentary derived from the writings of Tacitus), neo-stoicism signaled a shift away from orthodox ways of examining politics according to legal forms, and from the humanist fashion for discussing political behavior according to ideal principles. In their place, it substituted the prudential, characterized by the application of language—not just as a powerful tool of persuasion (rhetoric), but as a reliable guide to the sum of human experience. The quest for peace in a Europe being ravaged by civil and religious warfare informed Lipsius' original construction of neo-stoicism, which urged a disciplined obedience from subjects, and, on the part of governors, concentration on the means by which to achieve an internally peaceful, and simultaneously strong, state. His neo-stoic pieces were best-sellers in his day, inspiring a number of clones and adaptations in France and Spain, and, in England, finding echoes in the writings of Sir Walter Raleigh (1554–1618) and Sir Francis Bacon (1561–1626), among others. Taking their place in the growing genre of "reason of state" literature, they were also instrumental in provoking a new quest for system in political philosophy, as undertaken later by Hugo Grotius and Thomas Hobbes, at the same time influencing a generation and more of statesmen, from the Spanish Count-Duke of Olivares to the French Cardinal Richelieu. The high point of "statism" came later in the seventeenth century, personified in Louis XIV, who boasted, "*L'état, c'est moi* (The state is located in my person)," though it has been argued that Lipsian neo-stoicism underlay Prussia's march to ascendancy, achieved through militarism and the cultivation of self-discipline, ideas which indeed can be culled from Justus Lipsius' writings.

His neo-stoic synthesis was worked out in the *De constantia liber duo* (Two Books on Constancy) (1584) and *Politicorum sive civilis doctrinae liber sex* (Six Books on Politics, or Civil Learning) (1589). *Of Constancy*, written in the form of a dialogue, subtly charged contemporaries with fostering useless discussions and religious dissension. Rather than tackle divisive issues of religious dogma, Lipsius invoked stoic ideas of destiny and fate to note their affinity with the most generally held Christian tenet of providence, thus to insist upon the internalization of faith. Recourse to Tacitus helped point out the impossibility of ascertaining God's will on earth: in face of the flux of mundane experience, Lipsius urged the deployment of "constancy," which emerges from the quest for inner equilibrium ("right reason," in his terms), and which dictates that individuals have a duty to maintain their social positions and fulfill their civic responsibilities. The *Politicorum* was a compendium of classical quotations deftly held together by commentary and prudently arranged into the six books that treated, overall, various components necessary for effective governance. Excerpts from Tacitus, with his terse and often dark observations on the operations of power in early Imperial Rome, dominated the work, which epitomized Lipsius' concern to make ancient texts serve contemporary needs.

The key to successful government for Lipsius was "prudence": his authorities showed that an effective prince knew when to apply harsh measures and when leniency toward offenders would suffice. As a guide for contemporary governors, Lipsius introduced the concept of *prudentia mixta* (complex prudence), by which deceit and dissimulation were defined and set in a moral framework. He defended the teachings of Niccolò Machiavelli on the issue of deceit, and, indeed, like him, was concerned with the relationship between language and political action. However, Lipsius parted company with his Italian antecedent in adhering to an ontology of the written word, to the authority of ancient texts. Classical study, he insisted, was crucial for governors, though he considered knowledge (and power) to be beyond the ken of most people and dangerous if available to the multitude. Through his neo-stoic texts, he sought out a select audience and insisted on the use of Latin. Despite his mistrust of the "vulgar," his compositions were immediately translated into the main vernacular languages of Europe.

Lipsius was instrumental in inaugurating the fashion for Seneca and Tacitus, which persisted throughout the seventeenth century. He won acclaim for his authoritative editions of their writings, though he drew personal criticism for switching religion in an academic career that began and ended in (Catholic) Louvain, but entailed a short sojourn at (Lutheran) Jena and a longer tenure at (Calvinist) Leiden. His affiliation with the Family of Love (a clandestine sect whose members outwardly conformed to the religion of state while privately pursuing a mystical communion with God) helps explain such religious "inconstancy," which, in any case, undermined neither Lipsius' call for one public religion in a state (as he did in the *Politicorum*) nor his attachment to the classical sources of neo-stoicism. Despite his confessional acrobatics, he maintained a broad range of correspondents throughout Europe and remained a popular lecturer, striving to prepare his best students for state service through a thorough regime of classical study. His motto was "*Moribus Antiquis* (Back to the ancients' ways)," and, addressing a senecan lament, he sought to restore the value of classical literature, conceived as a repository of practical wisdom. Late in life he boasted: "*Ego e Philologia Philosophiam feci* (I turned philology into philosophy)." His boast was not an idle one, and his goal of applied philology was captured in the famous portrait by Peter Paul

Rubens, *The Four Philosophers,* showing Lipsius and three students in a study in which a bust of Seneca overlooks the teacher, who points, with Roman *gravitas,* to the wisdom to be recovered from treasured texts.

References

Morford, Mark. *Stoics and Neostoics: Rubens and the Circle of Lipsius.* Princeton: Princeton University Press, 1991.

Oestreich, Gerhard. *Neostoicism and the Early Modern State.* Trans. David McLintock. Cambridge: Cambridge University Press, 1982.

Saunders, Jason. *Justus Lipsius: The Philosopy of Renaissance Stoicism.* New York: Liberal Arts Press, 1955.

Tuck, Richard. *Philosophy and Government, 1572–1651.* Cambridge: Cambridge University Press, 1993.

Adriana McCrea

Llewellyn, Karl Nickerson (1893–1962)

Scholar, legislative draftsman, and legal theorist, the figure of Karl Nickerson Llewellyn casts a long shadow over twentieth-century legal thought.

Llewellyn was a major figure in the movement known as legal realism. In its broadest terms, the movement, which saw its heyday in the 1920s and 1930s, was a reaction to all forms of "formalism" in the law. In Llewellyn's hands, this reaction emphasized two aspects, the empirical and the philosophical.

The realists, including Llewellyn, wanted to identify the actual basis of legal decisions. Rejecting what they took to be a formalist tenet, that rules and logic decide cases, the realists set their attention on judges, for it is they who decide cases. Particularly in the first half of his career, Llewellyn believed that the tools of empirical social science could unlock the secrets of judging.

But Llewellyn, unlike Jerome Frank, located the basic unit of study more broadly than the decisions of individual judges. Llewellyn thought of law as a culture that could be illuminated by social scientific inquiry. Llewellyn located the law more broadly, focusing his attention on the intersubjective character of law; what, after Ludwig Wittgenstein, we call "practices."

In a much misunderstood line from early in the book that made his reputation, *The Bramble Bush,* Llewellyn said that what "officials do about disputes [is] the law itself." Many took Llewellyn to be saying that judges act capriciously and from individual impulse. He meant no such thing. His point was one that time has shown to be correct: that legal practice is not reducible to something which lies outside it. Law is an intersubjectively coordinated practice of argument, one that cannot be understood by positing a mechanism outside law that explains the law. Llewellyn was the first person to make this argument.

The best understanding of Llewellyn, and perhaps realism itself, comes from careful study of Llewellyn's great contribution to private law, the Sales Article (Article II) of the Uniform Commercial Code. As a realist, Llewellyn believed that judges, not rules, decide cases. From this premise, Llewellyn drafted the code to aid judges in finding the law. He believed that the source of commercial law was not statutes but business practices. His great contribution to private law was a jurisprudence of discovery: law is found in life, specifically the life of commercial actors.

Let us consider one example. Under precode common law, the agreement of the parties was a juridical concept, one composed of several elements (offer, acceptance, meeting of the minds, and consideration). Llewellyn replaced this concept with the idea that parties had a contract when those in the particular trade or business would so understand the action of the parties. Thus, if it was customary to ignore written price terms, the conduct of the parties took precedence over their written terms. What parties did was more important than any written terms, seemingly agreed to.

Llewellyn's last great work, *The Common Law Tradition,* is a sprawling, untidy masterpiece. In it, Llewellyn illustrates different styles of judging, providing a periodization for the rise and fall of different approaches. Of more immediate interest are Llewellyn's remarks on the nature of statutory interpretation. Llewellyn seems to say that for every canon there is an "anticanon," thereby giving the impression that he believed there was no rationality to the process of statutory interpretation. However, this reading repeats the error in reading *The Bramble Bush* as a relativist tract. Llewellyn railed against formalistic, unimaginative, mechanical jurisprudence. He thought law was more art than science, and the unity of his work lies in its consistent return to this theme.

References

Danzig, Richard. "A Comment on the Jurisprudence of the Uniform Commercial Code." *Stanford Law Review* 27 (1975), 621.

Llewellyn, Karl. *The Bramble Bush.* 1930. New York: Oceana, 1960.

———. *The Case Law System in America.* Ed. and intro. Paul Gewirtz. Trans. Michael Ansaldi. Chicago: University of Chicago Press, 1989.

———. *The Common Law Tradition: Deciding Appeals.* Boston: Little, Brown, 1960.

Patterson, Dennis. "Law's Practice" [review essay]. *Columbia Law Review* 90 (1990), 575.

Twining, William. *Karl Llewellyn and the Realist Movement.* London: Weidenfeld and Nicolson, 1973.

Dennis Patterson

Lobbying

Lobbying is the activity of trying to influence the opinion, behavior, or decisions of power holders, especially legislators. The existence of multiple centers of power requires lobbyists to determine where their efforts are best aimed. In the United States lobbyists are active at both the state and federal level, while in Europe there has been some transfer of lobbying effort to the decision makers of the European Union rather than those of the member states. Further, the target may be administrators rather than legislators, though the term derives from the use of the entry hall of buildings where decision makers are gathered as a place to meet constitutents or visitors. Lobby correspondents in the United Kingdom are those party to an arrangement whereby they receive information—particularly from ministers—on an unattributable basis. This system is used to place strategic leaks by politicians, but benefits journalists by providing stories. It illustrates the two-way process often involved with lobbying: those trying to influence the power holder may often have something to offer themselves, such as information, organization, or influence over voters. The two-way interaction leads to claims that decision makers have been "captured" by interest groups, on the one side, or that decision makers have "co-opted" such groups, on the other. The distinction between the lobbyist and the politician should not be overdrawn. A politician who speaks for a particular interest in a legislature, or campaigns on its behalf, is engaged in lobbying. Indeed, crucial ethical issues surround the relationship between lobbyists and politicians. For example, should politicians or legislators be allowed to accept presents, consultancy fees, retainers, and so on? If they do, should they have to declare so publicly? The Regulation of Lobbying Act (1946) in the United States requires disclosure of certain aspects of lobbying activity, primarily the self-identification of lobbyists and their financial transactions. The Nolan Committee on Standards in Public Life was set up in the United Kingdom partly as a response to the revelation that at least one member of Parliament was willing to accept a one-time payment in return for raising a particular question in the legislature. Responses to these issues depend upon views about the proper limits of privacy and confidentiality in the face of public interest arguments. Hence the Supreme Court reduced the scope of the 1946 act, while U.K. members of Parliament rejected the compulsory disclosure of their actual earnings from "outside interests." More deeply, responses depend on a conception of the democratic process and the place of lobbying, and the pursuit of interests, within it.

At one extreme of opinion, Jean-Jacques Rousseau thought that the only political system compatible with freedom was direct democracy, in which "the people" as a sovereign body made their own laws. He discountenanced intermediary associations (or interest groups) because they distorted citizens' perception of the general will (or the public interest). He did qualify this, however, by the hope that, if there were any such associations, they should be numerous. The two most radical attacks on his position allege the impossibility of self-government in a populous community, on the one side, and the conceptual incoherence of his notion of the public interest, on the other. This claim of conceptual incoherence can be extended to produce the polar opposite of Rousseau's position—the claim that in a system of representative democracy the public interest is no other than the outcome of the process of interest group interaction, which should be fostered rather than discountenanced.

There is a certain symmetry between the arguments about the desirability of lobbying and arguments about the desirability of logrolling. Both, it is said, allow for the expression of intensity of preferences, that is, an interest group can express the depth of its concern and commitment through mobilizing lobbying effort, just as logrolling allows well-placed legislators to obtain support for positions on issues of great concern by trading a vote on issues about which they have less intense preferences. The opposing arguments stress that the capacity to logroll or lobby is unequally distributed. More senior congress members, for example, are better placed to logroll, and some interest groups are better able to lobby. Work in the public choice tradition, developing arguments first systematically explored by Mancur Olson, has identified the difficulties encountered by large, dispersed, and poorly resourced interests compared to those of small, concentrated, and well-resourced groups. So we should expect, for instance, the chemical industry to be more effective lobbyists than pensioners or consumers. More generally, the concern is that both logrolling and lobbying are means of translating economic power into political influence, to the detriment of the political equality which underpins democracy or to the exclusion of a concern with general as opposed to special interests.

References

Cigler, Allan, and Burdett A. Loomis, eds. *Interest Group Politics*. 4th ed. Washington DC: CQ Press, 1995.

Dunleavy, Patrick, and Brendan O'Leary. *Theories of the State*. London: Macmillan, 1987.

Olson, Mancur. *The Logic of Collective Action: Public Goods and the Theory of Groups*. Cambridge MA: Harvard University Press, 1965.

Truman, David B. *The Govenmental Process*. New York: Knopf, 1964.

Wilson, Graham. *Interest Groups in the United States*. Oxford: Basil Blackwell, 1990.

Andrew Reeve

See also FRANCHISE AND REFERENDUM

Locke, John (1632–1704)

One of the most influential of seventeenth-century philosophers, John Locke is best known for his defenses of empiricism (in *An Essay Concerning Human Understanding*), religious toleration (in *A Letter Concerning Toleration*), natural rights, the right to resist tyranny, and (what we now call) classical political liberalism (in *Two Treatises of Government*). Locke was the foremost British spokesman for Whig political philosophy, and his writings both expressed many of the principles of the Glorious Revolution of 1688 and profoundly influenced later revolutionary authors in America and France. His most important contributions to the philosophy of law include his theory of natural law, his elaborate account of the natural rights this law defines, and his arguments for personal consent as a necessary condition of citizens' obligations to obey the law.

Locke utilized in his writings a relatively traditional, rationalist natural law theory that characterized natural law as a universally and eternally binding moral law, laid down for man by God and discernible by man through the use of reason. This law of nature requires that we preserve ourselves and, as far as possible, preserve others by refraining from harming them in their lives, liberty, or estate. Civil law (that is, the positive laws of political societies) will typically require more of us than the law of nature, but valid civil law may not require or prohibit anything contrary to natural law. Civil law which conflicts with natural law, according to Locke, is invalid and nonbinding.

Locke's chief contribution to natural law theory lay in his articulation of an extensive body of natural moral rights, which he saw as the correlates of the duties of natural law. All persons are born to equal basic rights of self-defense and self-government, which they receive fully when (if ever) they are sufficiently rational to know the law of nature and to control their actions. In addition, they may acquire special rights to property, to reparation for injuries, to the performance of promises made by others, to punish wrongdoers, to govern their families, and to make slaves of captives taken in a just war. All of these rights may be possessed even by persons in a state of nature (that is, persons living prior to the creation or otherwise without the benefit of legitimate political society).

Perhaps the most distinctively lockean of these rights are the natural rights to punish and to make property. Locke followed Hugo Grotius in holding that we may rightfully punish others who breach natural law, for they forfeit their protection under that law by the wrongful use of force. Private punishment must be proportional to the offense and intended to deter future wrongdoing. Because biased use of this natural executive right by individuals will inevitably cause social discord, Locke argued that in any legitimate political society individuals must agree to surrender this right to government, creating a governmental monopoly on retributive uses of force.

Locke also maintained that property rights can be held by persons outside of or antecedent to law-governed political societies. Persons can acquire property in unowned (or common) external things by laboring on them to some useful end. Because individuals naturally own themselves and their labor, Locke argued, mixing your labor with something makes it impossible for another to use that thing without also using what belongs to you. Thus, we can, without benefit of positive law, make property in natural objects, land, and the products of our labor. Such natural property rights are limited in extent by the requirements that we not waste what we take and that we leave for others what is necessary for them to have similar opportunities for appropriation. These rights may be transferred to others by forfeiture or by voluntary transactions (such as trades or bequests).

Locke argued that the legitimate powers of government are rights held in trust from society, and society's rights are simply those it receives from the express or tacit consent of its members and subjects. Individuals who enjoy the protection of government must be understood to have transferred to society those rights necessary for maintaining a stable polity. They thus consensually undertake an obligation to obey the society's laws and to give society jurisdiction over their land. However, society's (and hence government's) powers are limited by the rights retained by the people and by the eternal obligations of natural law. When these limits are exceeded by government, Locke maintains, the people (and in some cases individual citizens) have the right to resist and, if necessary, forcefully remove the offending government.

References

Ashcraft, Richard. *Locke's Two Treatises of Government.* London: Unwin Hyman, 1987.

Dunn, John. *The Political Thought of John Locke.* Cambridge: Cambridge University Press, 1969.

Locke, John. *Epistola de tolerantia. A Letter on Toleration.* Ed. Raymond Klibansky. Trans. J.W. Gough. Oxford: Clarendon Press, 1968.

———. *An Essay Concerning Human Understanding.* Ed. Peter H. Nidditch. Oxford: Clarendon Press, 1975.

———. *Two Treatises of Government.* Ed. Peter Laslett. London: Cambridge University Press, 1967.

Simmons, A. John. *The Lockean Theory of Rights.* Princeton: Princeton University Press, 1992.

Tully, James. *A Discourse on Property.* Cambridge: Cambridge University Press, 1980.

A. John Simmons

Logic, Deontic Legal

Deontic logic studies reasoning about norms or with norms and relations between deontic concepts. Its name originates from the Greek verb *deon,* which means "to bind." Its modern development started with a paper by G.H. von Wright, but the topic had been studied earlier by Aristotle. (A short history can be found in *La Logique des Normes* (The Logic of Norms) by G. Kalinowski.) Von Wright drew an analogy between alethic modalities (necessary, possible, impossible) and deontic modalities (obligatory, permitted, forbidden). Many theorems of deontic logic, he said, are analogous to theorems of alethic modal logic. "Forbidden" means the same as "obligatory that not," just as "impossible" means the same as "necessary that not." "Permitted" is "not obligatory that not," as "possible" is "not necessary that not." There are, however, also characteristic differences: where the necessity of p implies that p is true, the deontic counterpart of this theorem ('p is obligatory implies that p') is not acceptable.

Standard System

Von Wright laid the foundations for what is generally known today as the standard system of deontic logic. Almost every modern deontic logic is an elaboration and/or amendment of this system.

The standard system builds upon traditional propositional logic. It has the same connectives—negation ($\neg$), conjunction (.), disjunction (v), implication ($\supset$), and equivalence ($\equiv$)—and the same parameters for propositions—p, q, r, . . . It adds, however, deontic operators which range over propositions: the capitals O, P, and F, representing the deontic modalities obligatory, permitted, and forbidden, respectively. With these symbols it formulates deontic sentences: Op (p is obligatory), P(pvq) (it is permitted that p or q), p ⊃Fq (if p then q is forbidden).

The deontic operators can be defined in terms of each other. Starting with Op as a primitive (not defined) operator, we can define Pp and Fp:

Df.1 $Pp = \neg O \neg p$
Df.2 $Fp = O \neg p$

All the theorems of propositional logic are also theorems of the standard system. The specific characteristic of the standard system is, however, that it adds some deontic axioms:

Ax.1 $\neg(Op \,.\, O\neg p)$
Ax.2 $O(p \,.\, q) \equiv (Op \,.\, Oq)$
Ax.3 $O(p \vee \neg p)$

The first axiom expresses that it is inconsistent if both some proposition and its contradictory are obligatory. It is by Df.1 and propositional logic equivalent with Pp v P¬p, called by von Wright the principle of permission: any given act is either itself permitted or its negation is permitted.

The second axiom is the principle of deontic distribution: the obligation of the conjunction of two propositions is equivalent with the conjunction of the obligations of the two propositions.

The third axiom is denied by von Wright. It expresses that a tautologous proposition is necessarily obligatory (or, which is the same, that a contradiction is necessarily forbidden). It can be proven that this necessarily holds if at least one obligation or at least one prohibition exists. Therefore, if one denies the validity of ax.3, one accepts the possible existence of "empty" normative systems.

In von Wright's system, deontic operators were prefixed to act-predicates. He used capitals (A, B, . . .) to indicate act-categories (theft, murder). Connectives in the norm-content were defined (not as truth-functions, but) as performance-functions: ¬A indicates the non-performance of A. This approach has some problems. The performance of A together with the performance of B is not the same as the performance of the act A.B: A and B may be two different acts, which do not unite into one act. Therefore, the laws of propositional logic do not apply to the norm-content. To avoid this difficulty, many authors today interpret the norm-content as "proposition-like entities" or propositions, describing that some act has been performed. "Op" then says that the proposition describing that some act has been performed ought to be true. Other authors, however, believe that many of the more serious paradoxes in deontic logic arise just because of this analysis of the content of norms. They again propose deontic logics where the norm content is in some way constructed as an act.

Deontic Inference and Ideal World Semantics

Several problems have been raised concerning deontic logic generally and the standard system in particular. The first problem is a philosophical one: what, if any, is the meaning of valid deontic inference? Logical validity of an argument is traditionally defined as preservation of truth: the argument is valid if the truth of its premises guarantees the truth of its conclusion. It is an open question, however, whether normative sentences can have any truth value. If the normative sentence "one should keep one's promises" is not true or false (but perhaps valid or acceptable), because it is not a proposition stating some facts, what then does it mean to draw the conclusion that Suzy should keep this promise of hers?

The problem was already seen in the thirties by neo-positivistic philosophers and became known as Jørgen Jørgensen's dilemma: practical inferences may seem to be logically valid, but they cannot be logically valid, nor logically invalid.

Several proposals have been made to solve this problem. First, one could try to reformulate normative sentences as (true or false) propositions, for instance, propositions describing valid norms. This leads to the development of a second type of logic, a logic describing (and not expressing) norms. In positive law, however, propositions describing valid norms are dependent upon normative sentences making valid norms. We cannot say that the conclusion that Suzy should keep her promise is normatively valid on the ground that the corresponding describing proposition is true: it is the other way around. A logic describing norms is not directly relevant for reconstructing practical argument.

We may, however, interpret valid norms as descriptions of ideal worlds. Op then means that in every ideal world p is true, Pp that in at least one possible ideal world p is true. It is, using some Kripke semantics, then easy to define consistency between normative sentences: the idea is that a set of obligations is consistent if and only if there is a possible world in which all the obligatory propositions are true. A permission is consistent with a consistent set of obligations if and only if there is at least one possible world in which all the obligations can be met and the permitted proposition is true.

The validity of deontic inference is also defined with ideal world semantics. It is easy to see that O(p.q) implies Op: if in all ideal worlds p.q is true, then certainly in all ideal worlds q is true. An obligation follows from a set of deontic sentences if it is met in all ideal worlds defined by the set, a permission if the permitted proposition is true in at least one ideal world defined by the set.

A second approach is to redefine the concept of logical validity: not only preservation of truth but also, for instance, preservation of (legal) validity. The difficulty with this approach is that valid positive law is not necessarily consistent (and as a matter of fact perhaps never is). In the standard system Op.O¬p is a contradiction, necessarily not valid, but in positive law both Op and O¬p can be valid simultaneously. One should therefore redefine the concept of legal validity, to preserve its analogy with the concept of truth, but this is not unproblematic or without further problems. (See *Logic in Law* by Arend Soeteman for such a redefinition.)

Paradoxes

Standard deontic logic has been much criticized because it accepts logical theorems which seem in conflict with our intuitions. Some of these paradoxes can be solved easily, some of them cause more trouble.

In the first category is Ross's paradox, named after the Danish legal philosopher Alf Ross, who criticized some older deontic systems in 1941 because they accepted as a theorem, as the standard system also does:

(1) $Op \supset O(p \vee q)$

A possible interpretation is: if it is obligatory to post the letter, then it is obligatory to post the letter or burn it. The paradoxical flavor arises because in ordinary language the obligation to post the letter or burn it is usually taken to mean that the addressee of the norm may choose to do the one or the other. In that interpretation it is not acceptable to derive this obligation from the obligation to post the letter. If, however, we use the semantics of ideal worlds it becomes clear that no real problem exists. Op means that in every ideal world p is true. As, by propositional logic, p v q is true in every world where p is true, it follows that in every ideal world p v q is true.

Other paradoxes are more serious. This is the case with the paradoxes of commitment. In 1951 von Wright suggested that commitment "if p is the case then it is obligatory that q" could be reconstructed as "$O(p \supset q)$." This was wrong, however: in the standard system

(2) $O\neg p \supset O(p \supset q)$

is a valid theorem. Nothing is wrong with this theorem, but if one interprets the consequent as commitment, it says that if it is obligatory not to kill another, it follows that if one kills another it is obligatory to rob the victim as well. In general, if some obligation is not met, one would be committed to every other act.

A.N. Prior, who was the first to see this difficulty, suggested another reconstruction of commitment:

(3) $p \supset Oq$

This reconstruction, unfortunately, is not adequate either. It is vulnerable for the paradoxes of material implication, which are particularly damaging in deontic logic. First

(4) $\neg p \supset (p \supset Oq)$

is a theorem: every false proposition commits one to every other act. Again, nothing is wrong with this theorem, but it raises doubts about this reconstruction of commitment. Second, the negation of commitment (it is not the case that p commits to q) cannot be formulated. $\neg(p \supset Oq)$ will not do, as it entails p; $p \supset \neg Oq$ will not do either, since this would mean that if p is the case, Oq is not valid, which is much stronger than the denial of commitment.

Several attempts have been made to formulate an adequate reconstruction of commitment by defining a special deontic conditional operator. This has resulted in so-called dyadic deontic logics, in which O(p/q) means q commits to p. Von Wright was the first to present such a system (published by Hilpinen in 1971). The formal characteristics of his dyadic formulas are stipulated in three axioms:

Ax.4 $-(O(p/q) . O(\neg p/q))$
Ax.5 $O(p.q/r) \equiv (O(p/r) . O(q/r))$
Ax.6 $O(p/q \vee r) \equiv (O(p/q) . O(p/r))$

This avoids the problems of the earlier formulations. New problems, however, arise. It can easily been proven that in this system one can derive $\neg O(\neg p/r)$ from O(p/q), meaning that if in situation q one is committed to p, it necessarily is not the case that in a random different situation r one is committed to $\neg p$.

This result is clearly undesirable. Many authors have tried to solve this problem, either within the dyadic approach (von Wright, Hansson, Soeteman) or by developing other systems: incorporating notions of time (van Eck, Åqvist), making a distinction between ideal worlds and subideal worlds (Jones and Pörn), or reducing deontic logic to dynamic (action) logic (John-Jules Meyer). In general, however, solutions create new difficulties.

Contrary-to-Duty Imperatives

R.M. Chisholm developed the problem of contrary-to-duty imperatives: imperatives which arise from the fact that one does not obey another imperative. These are important for law, since the law knows of many duties of repair. Chisholm illustrated that the standard system is inadequate to reconstruct these contrary-to-duty imperatives. Consider the following sentences:

(5) It ought to be that a certain man go to the assistance of his neighbors.
(6) It ought to be that if he does go he tell them he is coming.
(7) If he does not go then he ought not to tell them he is coming.
(8) He does not go.

An obvious formal representation of these sentences in standard deontic logic is:

(9) Op
(10) $O(p \supset q)$
(11) $\neg p \supset O\neg q$
(12) $\neg p$

This, however, implies a contradiction: (9) and (10) together imply Oq, (11) and (12) imply $O\neg q$. We cannot solve this problem by reformulating (10) and (11). The sentences (5)–(8) are independent. If, however, we write (10) as

(10′) $p \supset Oq$

it follows from (12). And if we write (11) as

(11′) $O(\neg p \supset \neg q)$

it follows from (9).

One of the main questions in modern deontic logic is whether this problem can be solved within dyadic or other alternative deontic systems.

Defeasibility and Nonmonotonic Logics

A related but distinct problem with commitments is that in legal practice most commitments are defeasible. If some statute stipulates that p commits to q, then this does not exclude the possibility of exceptions in particular circumstances. If all the exceptions are known, it is possible (in theory) to formulate their absence in the condition: if p and if not these exceptions, then one is committed to q. In many cases, however, the class of exceptions is an open class.

The problem that conditional legal (and moral) norms more often than not are defeasible has recently been studied in nonmonotonic logics. Nonmonotonic logic differs in one important aspect from traditional monotonic logic: the entailment relation between premises and conclusion of an argument is much weaker. In nonmonotonic logic the addition of a new premise to the set of premises may defeat the original conclusion. If a condition of a conditional norm applies, then the norm is only presumably valid: other information concerning the particular circumstances may defeat this validity (for a recent criticism of nonmonotonic deontic logic see C.E. Alchourrón in *Deontic Logic in Computer Science*).

Nonmonotonic logic is perhaps more relevant for the reconstruction of normative systems in legal expert systems. In legal expert systems not only knowledge about legal norms is represented: the idea is that legal expert systems can find solutions for legal problems. It is much too early now to judge the usefulness of nonmonotonic logics; but it certainly marks one of the more interesting developments, which even may give such an abstract philosophical field as deontic logic practical applications.

References

Hilpinen, R., ed. *Deontic Logic: Introductory and Systematic Readings.* Dordrecht: Reidel, 1971.

———. *New Studies in Deontic Logic.* Dordrecht: Reidel, 1981.

Jørgensen, Jørgen. "Imperatives of Logic." *Erkenntnis* 7 (1937–1938), 288.

Kalinowski, G. *La Logique des Normes* (The Logic of Norms). Paris: Presses Universitaires de France, 1972.

Meyer, John-Jules Ch., and Roel J. Wieringa, eds. *Deontic Logic in Computer Science.* Chichester: Wiley, 1993.

Soeteman, A. *Logic in Law.* Dordrecht: Kluwer Academic Publishers, 1989.

von Wright, G.H. "Deontic Logic." *Mind* 60 (1951), 1–15. Reprinted in his *Logical*

Studies. London: Routledge and Kegan Paul, 1957.

———. *An Essay in Deontic Logic and the General Theory of Action.* Amsterdam: North-Holland, 1968.

———. *Norm and Action.* London: Routledge and Kegan Paul, 1963.

Arend Soeteman

See also ARTIFICIAL INTELLIGENCE AND NETWORKS; SPEECH ACTS

Love

Customs shape our modes and styles of love. If laws can influence customs, then laws can influence our modes and styles of love. Essentialists hold that love has a constant core and only its peripheral qualities may be modified; opponents of this view hold that "love" is entirely a historical construction. Both can agree that *how* we love may change without entirely changing *what* love is; *who* we love may change without changing *why* we love. If racial segregation is legal, few will have the opportunity to fall in love with persons of another race; if interracial marriages are illegal, as decided in *Loving v. Virginia,* 388 U.S. 1 (1967), then interracial love will be discouraged. If same-sex marriages are illegal, as decided in *Baker v. Nelson,* 291 Minn. 310 (1971), gay spousal love will be a legal oxymoron. If gay aliens are excludable as psychopaths, as decided in *Boutilier v. INS,* 387 U.S. 118 (1967), few will have the opportunity to love them. If homosexuals are legally stipulated to be unfit parents, as decided in *Roe v. Roe,* 324 S.E.2d 691 (Va. 1985), their children will not know their love as custodians or even as visitants, as decided in *Alison D. v. Virginia M.,* 77 N.Y.2d 651 (1991). Laws affect whom we love and how—sometimes moving ahead of social currents, sometimes lagging behind them.

Generically, love is (1) willing the good of an other (2) for the other's own sake (3) in a reciprocal relation that (4) endures. Love completes itself in (5) an ecstatic activity of self-transcendence toward an other that recenters one's affective life in the other. We increasingly find appeals to the first four points, at least, in recent decisions and proposals.

Love and law intertwine most commonly in family law, which concerns partners, siblings, and parents. Legal reasoning in this area standardly avoids mention of "love," but "the role of a loving mother" is stated *In re Nancy S.,* 228 Cal. App. 3d 836 ( ). Substitutes, however, abound: *care, affection, affinity* [notably "family of affinity" in *In re Guardianship of Sharon Kowalski,* 478 N.W.2d 790 (Minn. App. 1991)]. We find pivotal references to *emotional needs* or *emotional reasons* as sanctioned motives for adoption and marriage. For instance, section 109.119 of the Oregon Revised Statutes lets persons with "established emotional ties creating a child-parent relationship" petition for custody or visitation. A narrower Minnesota statute [Minn. Stat. sec. 257.022(2)(b)(West 1982)] offers "established emotional ties" as grounds. Appeals increasingly are turning to emotional bonding and attachment theory. Law must, in these areas at least, recognize love and law's influence on love.

Consider parental love and its legal institution. The purpose of adoption has shifted, historically, from fulfilling the need of childless couples to serving the well-being of adopted children. More than half the states have adopted this "best interest" standard. This notion of well-being, which addresses point (1), willing the good of another, is widely held to include living in a "stable, loving environment." A key debate turns on whether an "emotional bond" is likely to be facilitated most by genetic ties or actual interinvolvements; U.S. courts still typically allow adults five years to reclaim their biological offspring from adoptive parents, despite considerations of emotional continuity. Many advocates urge that a legal definition of "parent" should incorporate the imperative of serving a child's best interests, avoiding regression to a time when children were regarded as subpersons "over whom the parent has an absolute possessory interest" (*In re Alison D.,* 77 N.Y.2d 660).

Some advocates suggest that the legal definition of "parent" include reciprocity considerations as well—"mutuality," according to Bartlett, which demands that the court focus on a child's emotional need to remain connected with an adult. This is presented as a version of "best interest," but it clearly adds point (3) to points (1) and (2). Polikoff's appeal to "functional parenthood" also suggests a mutuality criterion requiring the child to expect the adult to be a parent or act as a parent. (Mutuality is problematic for the youngest children; there are also difficulties with the tacit contractualism of some of these proposals. Thomas Hobbes' 1651 argument that the moral authority of parents derives from the tacit consent of children, though dubious, has not been improved.) Bartlett also adds a custodial period of at least six months, addressing feature (4), the relation that endures, in addition to the criterion that an adult demonstrate "that his or her motive in seeking parental status is based on genuine care and concern for the child," addressing features (1) and (2).

Recognized doctrine of de facto parenthood allows parental standing so far as one regularly seeks "to fulfill both the child's physical needs and psychological need for affection and care," as is seen in *In re B.G.,* 11 Cal. 3d 679 (1974). Parenthood as a "personal and emotional relationship" is found in *In re Michael H.,* 491 U.S. 159–60 ( ). Again surrogates for "love" are pivotal, and features (1)–(3) are invoked.

Spousal love presents similar difficulties. *Griswold v. Connecticut,* 381 U.S. 476 (1965), recognized a privacy right within marriage but failed to define "marriage." Many proposed definitions reflect features (1)–(4). Divorce no longer requires "spousal fault"; that roughly half our marriages last (about the same figure for gay "lifemates") suggests an increased emphasis on love, a demand for love, a willingness to dissolve a marriage when love is no longer of the desired *kind.* Again, the law both reflects and influences our styles of loving.

Legislatures, courts, and legal theorists—against the background of a mere quarter of U.S. families consisting of a married heterosexual couple with minor children—have struggled with the notion of "family." Some advocates propose that "family" include "alternative families" who, while not related by blood, marriage, or adoption, are involved in a mutually supportive, committed relationship. However, half a dozen states have an irrebuttable "presumption of harm" standard against gay parents; many more have a rebuttable presumption standard. None has used the traditional equitable doctrines or the newer love-basic proposals in "alternative family" cases. Sodomy laws, still on the books of twenty-three states, affect family litigation, since they bar some biological parents from custody of their children and have prevented others from adopting children. Such considerations have so far trumped criteria based on features of the love definition above.

Still, in parental, custodial, and other personal relations litigation, doubtless an increasing use is made of features of the definition of love ventured in paragraph three; but none of these features can be specified once and for all. What, for instance, is to count as the "good" to be willed in a loving relationship? The National Association of Black Social Workers eschews transracial adoption. Some religious devotees demand that marriage or child rearing be limited to a particular faith, or at least to one faith to avoid spiritual confusion. Articulate pederasts argue that sexual relations between adults and children can, in certain circumstances, be "loving." Many wish to remove children from the custody of substance abusers; a few now wish to protect children from cigarette smokers. Christian Scientists have sought prayer-treatment exemptions to abuse and neglect statutes, since their vision of "care" and "good" excludes technical medicine.

It seems there is no material understanding of "love" detachable from particular visions of the good as embedded in different cultures and traditions. This raises the issue of love, not for persons, but for traditions and institutions. Love of one's community and culture, love of humankind, and love of nature are significant forms not broached here. They are, along with love of equality, love of liberty, and the like, important for the law because they form part of the motive of legal advocates, reformers, and revolutionaries.

A beautiful passage in Plato's *Symposium* finds Socrates endorsing the teaching of a seeress who claims that an essential moment in the self-transcending act of love toward ideal beauty is *love of the law.* If so, love of law is an essential moment in the development of self, since we develop self by developing practices of love. It is one with love of our communities, since customs and laws are the soul of societies. Love of law is one with love of justice, so far as justice is the point of law.

References

Cook, A.E. "The Death of God in American Pragmatism and Realism: Resurrecting the Value of Love in Contemporary Jurisprudence." *Georgetown Law Journal* 82 (1994), 1431–1517.

Cox, B.J. "Love Makes a Family—Nothing More, Nothing Less: How the Judicial

System Has Refused to Protect Nonlegal Parents in Alternative Families." *Journal of Law and Politics* 8 (1991), 5–67.
Fromm, E. *The Art of Loving.* New York: Harper & Row, 1956.
May, R. *Love and Will.* New York: Norton, 1969.
Minnow, M. "All in the Family and in All Families: Membership, Loving, and Owing." *West Virginia Law Review* 95 (1992–93), 275.
Singer, I. *The Nature of Love.* 3 vols. Chicago: University of Chicago Press, 1984.
Sorokin, P. A. *The Ways and Power of Love: Types, Factors, and Techniques of Moral Transformation.* Boston: Beacon Press, 1954.
Tillich, P. *Love, Power, and Justice.* New York: Oxford University Press, 1954.

C. Wesley DeMarco

Luhmann, Niklas (1927–)

Niklas Luhmann's outstanding achievement in the sociology of law has been to use modern systems theory to illuminate the "relative autonomy" of legal systems in advanced industrial democracies. A relatively autonomous legal system is one that is neither entirely autonomous from forces outside the legal system (politics, religion, temperament), nor entirely dependent upon them. Specifically, Luhmann uses the notion of autopoietic, or self-producing, systems drawn from the work of two biologists, Humberto Maturana and Francisco Varela.

An autopoietic system is one that constitutes the elements of which it consists out of the elements of which it consists. It is defined by contrast to allopoietic, or "other-produced," systems whose dynamic processes are entirely dependent upon, and driven by, changes in the system's environment. The core image of autopoiesis is the individual organism, ceaselessly generating elements out of elements, forming all elements into an indissoluble unity from a more complex base of energy and matter. Allopoietic systems are, by contrast, machines. Every element of an autopoietic system is produced by and produces the operations of the system. An autopoietic system is thus a network of operations that recursively generate and reproduce the network that produces them.

Elements that do not join the network of operations are outside the system, part of its environment. The environment effects operations of the system in two ways. First, the environment may "irritate" the system. It is irritation that triggers observations and correcting operations that sustain the network of operations and by which an autopoietic system opportunistically differentiates its network of operations from the environment. Second, autopoietic systems in the environment may enter into patterns of mutual irritation with the system, or structural coupling. In either case, elements from the environment play no role in reproducing the network of operations of the system. Autopoietic systems are "operatively closed." Autopoiesis thus offers a new way of understanding the autonomy of systems through "operative closure."

The core image of autopoietic law is a legal system ceaselessly generating and transforming legal materials entirely out of legal materials, hence one continuously setting and altering the conditions of its own validity. Politics, morality, and other nonlegal forces affect law in autopoietic legal systems, but do not determine the validity of legal acts and communications. Hence, law (and only law) defines what is and what is not law, and every law participates in defining what is and is not law.

Within legal theory Luhmann's notion of autopoietic law recalls Hans Kelsen's "pure theory of law" and H.L.A. Hart's "rule of recognition." The novelty of autopoietic law is that it tracks down exactly what it means for law to define law and promises to show the exact social, legal, and cultural conditions in which law defining law is possible. Hence, autopoietic law embeds Hart's "rule of recognition" and Kelsen's "basic norm" in a social practice.

Luhmann's legal theory is thus part of a general social theory. In Luhmann's social theory, social systems are autopoietic, always. The elements through which the operations of the social system work are communications. Unlike Jürgen Habermas, Luhmann does not oppose communication to system as a regulative ideal immanent within empirical social action. Instead, he opposes communication to action itself, which he regards as a choice of addressees for communication. Action, then, is a simplifying self-observation or self-description of the system by itself. The social system is comprised of the ceaseless address of communications.

Luhmann contends that the legal systems of highly differentiated societies may under certain conditions constitute autopoietic subsystems of the social system. Following Talcott Parsons, Luhmann assumes that subsystems differentiate out of the mass of communications comprising a social system by fulfilling functional needs of the larger system. The need around which functions organize is, in general, reduction of complexity and contingency in the environment of individual actors. The specific function of the legal system, Luhmann maintains, is producing and maintaining counterfactual expectations in spite of disappointments.

Luhmann constructs the function of law from simple materials. Individuals reduce complexity and the contingencies they face in their environment by cooperating with other individuals. By cooperating, individuals develop expectations of other individuals. Because other individuals also develop expectations, one develops expectations of those expectations.

The expectations of expectations pose special problems of coordination. The key problem is whether individuals are prepared to revise their expectations when another individual disappoints them—a cognitive response—or whether they are not prepared to revise their expectations—a normative response. The choice of normative versus cognitive is selectively influenced by the development of ever more successful methods of coordination driven by the persistent desire of individuals to reduce complexity and contingency.

A crucial step along the path of realizing this desire is the institutionalization of expectations, in which, according to Luhmann's definition, expectations are based on the assumed expectations of expectations on the part of third parties. Institutionalization allows the formation of generalized expectations over an entire social system, thus stabilizing expectations of expectations over many parties.

Social systems evolve more effective ways of handling the coordination problem. Luhmann's mechanisms for natural selection of methods of coordination are the familiar ones that social theory has borrowed from Charles Darwin through Emile Durkheim. The basic technique of selection is the differentiation of functionally specific subsystems of coordination. The function of the legal subsystem, according to Luhmann, is coordination of all other methods of coordination. Law, in Luhmann's terms, is congruently generalized normative expectations.

Because a fully differentiated autopoietic legal system is a subsystem performing a designated function within the social system, it cannot achieve absolute closure, unlike the social system. Luhmann thus maintains that any autopoietic legal system must be *normatively* closed and *cognitively* open. An autopoietic legal system thus maintains normative autonomy from other social subsystems, yet is at the same time constantly irritated by cognitive inputs from those subsystems and can upon occasion enter into structural coupling with them.

The structure that organizes the autopoiesis of any subsystem of the social system, that forces the differentiation of its operations from operations in the subsystem's environment, is a binary code. In a differentiated moral subsystem, the code allocates esteem and disesteem. In the legal system, however, the binary code is the necessity of deciding legal right and wrong.

References

Closed Systems and Open Justice: The Legal Sociology of Niklas Luhmann. Cardozo Law Review 13 (special issue) (1992), 1419.

Luhmann, Niklas. *Das Recht der Gesellschaft.* Frankfurt: Suhrkamp, 1995.

———. *Rechtssoziologie* (A Sociological Theory of Law). Reinbek bei Hamburg: Rowchlt Taschanbuch Verlag, 1972. London: Routledge and Kegan Paul, 1985.

Arthur J. Jacobson

M

Machiavelli, Niccolò (1469–1527)

Niccolò Machiavelli was born in Florence on May 3, 1469, into a well-known Florentine family. His father was a member of the corporation of notaries. Very little is known about Niccolò's education except that he learned some principles of law from his father and seems to have had a good knowledge of Latin, enough to be able to read the classical authors and to write his *Familiar Letters*. He was inspired by the reading of ancient historians. His youth coincided with a very difficult period in Italy's history. Italy was divided into several small states threatened from outside by the three powerful empires of Spain, France, and England. Florence with its unstable political leadership was in the center of this dispute. After the death of Lorenzo de Medici in 1492, Florence was governed by Piero de Medici, whose authority was challenged by the reform movement inspired by Girolamo Savonarola. In 1498, with the fall of Savonarola and the expulsion of the Medici from Florence, a republican regime was established. The active political career of Machiavelli began when, in 1498, he became secretary to the Florentine republic and the right-hand man of Gonfalonier Piero Soderini. As as senior civil servant, Machiavelli conducted several diplomatic missions in Italy, France, and Germany, where he met the most important political figures of his time, and acquired an exceptional knowledge of political power. His close relationship with Soderini became a serious problem for Machiavelli when the republic was overthrown by the Medici in 1513. Machiavelli was dismissed and forced to live outside Florence in San Casciano. Here began Machiavelli's career as a writer. While meditating and annotating the *Decades* of Titus Livius, he wrote *The Prince* (*De Principatibus*) in 1513. The *Discourses on the First Decade of Titus Livius* were completed by 1517. His treatise on *The Art of War* was published in Florence in 1521, and the eight books on the *History of Florence* were presented to Pope Clement VII (Giulio de Medici) in 1525. Machiavelli became well known in Florence after the performance of his two comedies, *Mandragola* and *Clizia,* in 1525. He was reinstated in a political position in 1526 but died the year after.

Machiavelli's political philosophy and philosophy of law are concentrated in *The Prince* and the *Discourses*. While *The Prince* is mainly concerned with the question of how princedoms are gained and preserved, the *Discourses* are devoted to the study of republican principles as they were achieved in the Roman republic. *The Prince* is not a treatise on philosophy of law, as such. It deals chiefly with the fruitfulness of political power and its conditions as they can be perceived through experience. As he stated in his dedication, Machiavelli wanted to communicate to the prince what he gained in his lengthy "experience with recent matters and [his] continual reading on ancient ones." The goal is a clear option for the facts as they are rather than what they ought to be. As he stated in Chapter 15, "I have decided that I must concern myself with the truth of the matter as facts show it rather than with any fanciful notion." Consequently, the analysis of political power is targeted by the end, which is success, and by the means, which are subordinated to this end. The central part of the book is devoted to the analysis of *virtù* in the prince, which is presented by

Machiavelli as the key to success. As the complement to *fortuna,* which relies only on chance and circumstances, *virtù* is within the power of the prince; it shows his talents and abilities to govern by all necessary means including ruse, hypocrisy, ferocity, and armies. Political *virtù,* for Machiavelli, is totally independent of moral virtue and has very little to do with the laws.

The first reference to laws in *The Prince* is made in relation to the attitude of new princes toward the "new institutions and customs they are forced to introduce" into principalities that were accustomed to living under their own laws. This situation requires more ability from princes, according to Machiavelli. The second reference to laws is more general and concerns the principal foundation of all states, which Machiavelli considers to be "good laws and good armies." The reasoning behind this affirmation is based on the experience that political power cannot be established on the laws only, neither on armies only, "because there cannot be good laws where armies are not good, and where there are good armies, there must be good laws."

The *Discourses* are more concerned with laws, since they bear upon republican principles, and present a fine analysis of ancient republics, Sparta and Rome in particular. In many respects, the *Discourses* could be perceived as a praise to the people, to the laws, and to the legislative sages, Lycurgus to the Spartans, Solon to the Athenians, Romulus and Numa to the Romans. The first book of the *Discourses,* in particular, insists on the primacy of good laws to preserve the republic and to maintain order and peace. Far from throwing out the idea of *virtù,* Machiavelli is trying to demonstrate how this idea is an essential element of the great legislators' success. Lycurgus is always given as an example of the legislator who succeeded in adapting the laws to the spirit of the people or the nation. His constitution lasted over eight hundred years and brought stability and peace to the city. Machiavelli is mainly concerned with fundamental laws or constitutional laws, taking for granted that "law is necessary," given the human condition. However, Machiavelli is also concerned with civil laws and the necessity for the republic to establish a judiciary system with the necessary authority "to bring before the people, or before some magistrate or council, charges against citizens."

The *Discourses,* which present the most developed thought of Machiavelli on politics, clearly reveals a man strongly opposed to tyranny and supporting the republican principle of states governed by law. However, while admiring the multitude as long as it is regulated by the laws, at the same time Machiavelli maintains his admiration also for the armed prophets or princes.

References

Barincou, Edward. *Machiavelli.* Trans. Helen R. Lane. Westport CT: Greenwood Press, 1962.

Gilbert, Allan. *Machiavelli: The Chief Works and Others.* 3 vols. Durham NC: Duke University Press, 1965.

Pocock, J.G.A. *The Machiavellian Moment.* Princeton: Princeton University Press, 1975.

Skinner, Quentin. *Machiavelli.* Oxford: Oxford University Press, 1981.

Strauss, Leo. *Thoughts on Machiavelli.* Seattle: University of Washington Press, 1958.

Guy Lafrance

Maimonides (Moses ben Maimon) (1135–1204)

Rabbi Moses ben Maimon, known to western civilization as Maimonides, is by common consensus the most important and influential Jewish scholar in the medieval era. He decisively affected the course of Jewish thought and was of some influence in western thought.

He was born in Cordoba, in Muslim Spain, and was forced by religious persecution to leave that country. After sojourning in Morocco and the Land of Israel, he ultimately settled in Egypt, where he wrote, among other major works, a *Commentary on the Mishna* [the primary document of rabbinic literature] (1168); *Mishneh Torah,* a fourteen-part summa of halakha [Judaic law] (1180); and *Guide of the Perplexed* (1190), on Judaism and philosophy. His writings, in Hebrew and Judeo-Arabic, address the major topics of concern in medieval Judaism: the definition of halakha and the relationship of the Hebrew Bible to current philosophical and scientific concepts.

With respect to issues relevant to philosophy of law, Maimonides expressed himself primarily in two works. The first was his *Mishneh Torah.* In it, he attempted to present, in complete and systematic form, a codification of halakha as developed in the vast corpus of rabbinic literature. In doing so, he aimed to be both comprehensive and systematic in a way his predecessors were not. Halakha was not looked upon as a merely legal system. It encompassed, rather, the sum of all knowledge, from the existence of God and the structure of the universe, to the maintenance of physical and mental health, as well as the ritual laws of Judaism. Moreover, uniquely, Maimonides did not let the fact that the Jews of his era did not possess political independence dissuade him from engaging in a full codification of laws pertaining to the Jewish state. In creating his *Mishneh Torah,* Maimonides also employed an entirely new system of classification of law, breaking with the previous usage of dealing with laws in the order of their appearance in the Talmud.

In his *Guide of the Perplexed,* Maimonides attempted to address the challenge that the legacy of ancient Greek philosophy, particularly that of Aristotle, presented to adherents of scripturally based religions, like Judaism. In his task, he built upon the work of both Jewish and Islamic thinkers. He asserted that the entire legal structure of Judaism was designed to facilitate the true worship of God, which he defined as the utmost development of the individual's knowledge of reality and contemplation of the divine. It was for this purpose that the Torah was given. However, Torah was designed not merely for the intellectual elite but for all people. Therefore, it included laws, ceremonies, and rituals designed on one hand to regulate society and on the other to educate people to achieve a higher level of divine service.

Part of the task of the *Guide,* therefore, is the explication of the Law of Moses in terms of its fostering the well-being of both body (moral virtues) and soul (intellectual virtues). The commandments of the Torah are divided into those, like the prohibition of murder, which the rational mind could have discovered without revelation and those, such as sabbath observance, which could be known only through divine revelation.

Maimonides' teachings received great respect as well as fundamental criticism on the part of his contemporaries and successors. While all Jewish scholars admitted his unparalleled mastery of the vast body of rabbinic halakha, there was considerable discomfort with his attempt to integrate law and philosophy and to give primacy to the study of philosophy as the ultimate divine service. There were many who felt as well that his attempts to give rational reasons for the commandments of the Torah were counterproductive in the sense that these explanations were often historical in nature and hence potentially contingent on historical circumstances, as well as often inadequate to explain both the specificities and the general principles of the commandments. For these reasons there were attempts in the thirteenth and fourteenth centuries to condemn Maimonides' works, particularly the *Guide.* Many within Orthodox Judaism to the present tend to venerate Maimonides as the architect of the *Mishneh Torah,* even as they maintain grave reservations with respect to the *Guide.*

References

Fox, Marvin. *Interpreting Maimonides: Studies in Methodology, Metaphysics and Moral Philosophy.* Chicago: University of Chicago Press, 1990.

Hartman, David. *Maimonides: Torah and Philosophic Quest.* Philadelphia: Jewish Publication Society, 1976.

Maimonides, Moses. *Guide of the Perplexed.* Trans. Shlomo Pines. Chicago: University of Chicago Press, 1963.

Strauss, Leo. *Persecution and the Art of Writing.* Glencoe IL: Free Press, 1952.

Twersky, Isadore. *Introduction to the Code of Maimonides (Mishneh Torah).* New Haven: Yale University Press, 1980.

———. *A Maimonides Reader.* New York: Behrman House, 1972.

Ira Robinson

Mair (Major), John (ca. 1467/8–1550)

John Mair (John Major, Ioannis Maioris), the Scottish philosopher-theologian in the College of Montaigu at the University of Paris and subsequently in the Scottish universities, is the first late-medieval thinker to consider explicitly the legitimacy of the Spanish conquest of the New World. In addition to his contribution to international law, Mair's ideas on the conciliarist form of government, the licitness of *cambium bursæ,* and the freedom of the seas are now recognized as original contributions to ethical, legal, political, and economic theory.

The intellectual influence of Mair on his contemporaries was widespread. Those numbered among the distinguished circle of John Mair include Scottish thinkers (Gilbert Crab, David Cranston, George Lokert, William Manderston) and Spanish intellectuals (Juan de Celaya, Antonio and Luis Coronel, Fernando de Enzinas, Gaspar Lax). Mair's influence is strongly reflected in the writings of Jacques Almain, illustrious in his day, the intellectual whose treatise called *Morals* was a standard text in the Paris Faculty of Arts. Almain's writings are referred to by Francisco de Vitoria in his discussion of right and sovereignty in the context of the legitimacy of the Spanish conquest of North America. In Spain, this influence continued well into the seventeenth century. The Dutch jurist Hugo Grotius himself cites Mair.

In the voluntarist tradition Mair defines law as the expression of the will of the lawgiver, which obliges rational creatures to perform or not perform some act insofar as the command of the lawgiver is itself in conformity with reason. This general conception of law is divided hierarchically into three broad types, divine, natural, and positive law, with natural and positive law deriving their moral legitimacy and legal authority from the divine law.

Divine law is that law which is established by the will of God either mediately through the commands of the Mosaic law, or immediately by the law of grace. Natural law, or the law of nature, is nothing other than any practical principle that is or can be known evidently through the use of reason, for example, "Nothing unbecoming and dishonest should be done." Positive, or human law, is law which is instituted for the common good and regulated by custom. Custom plays an important role in the institution and the reinforcement of positive law, but custom obliges no further than it is expressed in the written law. Custom itself is regulated insofar as it must conform to reason and thus be directed to the common good of the community. It is equally important to note that the authority of positive law does not derive its obligating force from the natural law. The precepts of positive law are not inferred from the principles of natural law, because this would imply that positive human law is reducible to the principles of natural law. This is manifestly false, because the principles of natural law are universal in nature, whereas the precepts of human law deal with particulars and are regulated by time and place. If this were not the case, then custom could have no proper role in the institution and reinforcement of positive law. Human laws are purely positive precepts which derive all of their obligating force from the will of the lawgiver.

The claim that the precepts of positive law are not directly inferred from the natural law emerges clearly in Mair's discussion of sovereignty *(dominium),* because, while Mair enumerates several different types of sovereignty, the explicit contrast developed is between natural and civil sovereignty. Natural sovereignty is based on necessity; it is that which a human being is able to seize licitly for his survival. Civil sovereignty is sovereignty acquired, retainable, and abdicable in virtue of the institution of civil law. Mair's ultimate definition of sovereignty is that it is the right of owning, having, and using something at will where no limitation of positive law is imposed by a superior power. One explicit limitation laid down in relation to sovereignty is that sovereignty is attributable exclusively to rational beings and is governed by prudential reasoning. This condition is laid down in order to exclude, among others, children, the incapacitated, and savages.

In the second book of his commentary, first published in 1510, on the *Sentences* of Peter Lombard, some of the implications of this understanding of sovereignty are developed. Mair's original discussion concerning the rights of native Indians following their conquest by the Spanish is introduced in the course of considering whether or not the rulers of Christian nations have the right to seize the lands of non-Christian nations.

Mair provides the following criteria for determining the legitimacy of conquest. In the first instance, if the ruling authority of a non-Christian nation allows the preaching of the Gospel, then the land and community under that authority are to be respected. However, if the ruling power does not allow the word of the Gospel to spread, then it is legitimate for Christian conquerors to compel the conversion of heathens in the New World. This division is defended on the grounds that deeds such as treason and heresy are legitimate reasons for denying sovereignty to rulers and their subjects. Hence, it would appear that the claim that Christian conquerors can legitimately seize the lands of the native Indians rests on the claim that the natives were something less than rational human beings, and

Mair was forced to explain why the beliefs of the inhabitants of the New World were not well founded and rational. However, it must be remarked that Mair was writing of Indian rulers without any personal experience of them and was led to envisage the equivalent of a modern-day tyrant. The response Mair gives to this question is unavoidably aristotelian, for he wished to avoid basing the rights of the conquistadors on either the emperor's temporal claims or the temporal privileges granted by Pope Alexander VI. It is a response which is both unsatisfactory and untypical of Mair, who, for the most part, was tolerant of and adaptive to change. These issues were soon taken up and justly refuted by such thinkers as Bartholomé de Las Casas and Francisco de Vitoria, who, despite accepting many of Mair's premises, rejected his conclusion.

It is reasonable to conclude that it is precisely this intolerant conclusion that can be counted as one of John Mair's most important contributions to the philosophy of law. It is a conclusion which, in its recognition of fundamental issues about rights and sovereignty, sparked heated debate in a developing Europe.

References

Broadie, Alexander. *The Circle of John Mair: Logic and Logicians in Pre-Reformation Scotland.* Oxford: Clarendon Press, 1985.

Burns, J.H. "*Politia Regalis et Optima*: The Political Ideas of John Mair." *History of Political Thought* 2 (1981), 31–61.

Durkan, John. "John Major: After 400 Years." *The Inness Review* 1 (1951), 131–157.

Grabar, Vladimir E. *Le droit politique et le droit international dans les questions de Jean Mair* (Law in Politics and International Law in the Questions of John Mair). Kiev: Académie des sciences oukraniennes, 1927 (booklet in Russian, summary in French).

Keenan, James F. "The Casuistry of John Major: Nominalist Professor of Paris (1506–1531)." *The Annual of the Society of Christian Ethics* (1993), 205–221.

Mair, John. [Commentarium in quatuor libris Sententiarum (Commentary on the Four Books of the Sentences).] *In secundum Sententiarum.* Paris, 1510, 1519, 1528. *Editio Ioannis Maioris doctoris parisiensis super Tertium Sententiarum de novo edita.* Paris, 1517, 1528. *Quartus Sententiarum.* Paris, 1509, 1512, 1516, 1519, 1521.

———. *Ethica Aristotelis Peripateticorum principis* (The Ethics of Aristotle, the First Peripatetic). Paris, 1530.

Oakley, Francis. "Almain and Major: Conciliar Theory on the Eve of the Reformation." *American Historical Review* 70 (1964–1965), 673–690.

Torrance, Thomas F. "La philosophie et la theologie de Jean Mair ou Major de Haddington" (Philosophy and Theology of John Mair (Major) of Haddington) (1469–1550). *Archives de Philosophie* 32 (1969), 531–547, 33 (1970), 261–294.

Vereecke, Louis. "La licéité du *cambium bursae* chez Jean Mair" (The Legitimacy of the lending exchange in John Mair) (1469–1550). *Revue historique de droit français et étranger* 30 (1952), 124–138.

R. Neil Wood

Mandate

See AGENCY (MANDATE)

Maritain, Jacques (1882—1973)

One of the leading thinkers in the Catholic natural law tradition of the twentieth century, Jacques Maritain was born in Paris on November 18, 1882. Following his conversion to Roman Catholicism in 1906, he undertook an intensive study of the writings of Thomas Aquinas. Maritain taught for many years at the Institut Catholique in Paris and, later, at Toronto, Columbia, Chicago, Notre Dame, and, finally, Princeton. He served as French ambassador to the Vatican (1945–1948) and was involved in drafting the United Nations Universal Declaration of Human Rights of 1948.

In his early work, Maritain sought to defend Catholic thought against the then-dominant bergsonian and secular worldviews, but, by the 1930s, he began to elaborate the principles of a liberal Christian humanism and a defense of human rights. These subjects dominated his later writings.

Maritain's legal and political philosophy lies within the aristotelian-thomistic tradition, and, following Aquinas, he distinguishes four types of law: the eternal, the natural, the "common law of civilization" (*droit des gens* or *jus gentium*), and the positive (*droit positif*). His focus is, however, on natural law.

For Maritain, natural law is not a written law; it is immanent in nature. He maintained that there was a teleological dimension to nature (though many critics have found Maritain's arguments here unconvincing), and argued that it is in terms of the specific end of a thing—the "normality of its functioning"—that one knows what it "should" do or how it "should" be used. Thus, the "natural law" is "an order or a disposition that the human reason may discover and according to which the human will must act to accord itself with the necessary ends of the human being." It "prescribes our most fundamental duties" and is "coextensive" with morality.

Moreover, Maritain emphasizes—and this is his distinctive contribution to natural law theory—that the first principles of natural law (particularly, "We must do good and avoid evil") are indemonstrable and are known connaturally or preconsciously "through that which is consonant with the essential inclinations of human nature," an activity that Maritain, following Aquinas, called "synderesis." (Critics have argued, however, that this kind of knowledge is obscure and problematic and is, therefore, inadequate as a basis for law.)

While natural law is "universal and invariable," Maritain holds that it is not founded on human nature. It is rooted in divine reason (that is, the eternal law) and is "written into" human nature by God: "[N]atural law is law only because it is participation in Eternal Law." (Some have concluded that such a theory, then, must be ultimately theological.)

Intermediate between the natural and the positive law, the *droit des gens* is concerned with human beings as social beings (for example, as citizens or as members of families), and it is inherent in all organized social life. The "positive law" is concerned with the rights and duties that exist contingently in a particular community, dependent on the stage of social or economic development and on the specific activities of individuals within it. These kinds of law are not, however, deducible from the natural law alone, are not known connaturally, and, strictly speaking, do not constitute part of the natural law, though they are rationally derivable from the first principle. It is in virtue of their relation to natural law that they "have the force of law and impose themselves on conscience."

Maritain notes that knowledge of the natural law may vary throughout humanity and according to individuals' capacities and abilities. Moreover, since one's knowledge of this law is never complete, the natural law is never exhausted in any particular articulation of it and it progressively unfolds as human life develops. This recognition of this historical element did not, however, prevent Maritain from holding that there is only one natural law for humanity.

Maritain rejects legal positivism because it provides an arbitrary standard of law, is based only on the command of the ruler (that is, it is voluntaristic), and fails to explain one's obligation to obey law. For Maritain, law is part of the moral order and, while the positive law is a product of human reason, it is not arbitrarily so and must reflect this order. Thus, when a positive law acts against the moral order, it is, strictly speaking, not a law.

Maritain's defense of natural rights reflects his analysis of natural law, and the gradual recognition of these rights has accompanied the progress in our consciousness of that law. Since each person has a duty to realize his or her nature, it is necessary to have the means to do so, that is, the rights which, since they are related to that nature, are called "natural." In large part, this respects the aristotelian principle of justice, that we should distribute to each "what is truly his or hers."

This account of natural rights also depends on Maritain's distinction between the "person" and the "individual." Human beings have a "material" side and, as part of civil society, are "individuals" who have obligations to a common, social good. However, they also have a spiritual side—they are persons. The person is a "whole," has a transcendent destiny, is an object of dignity, and "must be treated as an end."

Maritain held that natural rights are "fundamental and inalienable, [and] antecedent in nature and superior to society," but they should not be understood as "antecedent" in a temporal sense and do not form the basis of the state or of the civil law. While rights are grounded in the natural law, and while the objective of all law is the development of the human person, Maritain insists that we must not forget their relation to the common good. Nevertheless, the list of rights that Maritain recognizes extends significantly beyond that found in many liberal theories,

M

and includes the rights of workers as well as those of the human and the civic person.

Following the death of his wife, Raïssa, in 1960, Maritain went to Toulouse to live with a religious order. He remained there until his death on April 28, 1973.

While no longer as influential as it once was, Maritain's natural law theory continues to be discussed in the Americas and Europe, and there has been a revival of his ideas in Central and Eastern Europe. The American Maritain Association and the University of Notre Dame Press are currently undertaking the republication of English translations of Maritain's works.

References

Maritain, Jacques. *La loi naturelle ou loi non-écrite* (Natural Law, Unwritten Law). Fribourg, Switzerland: Éditions universitaires, 1986.

———. *Oeuvres complètes [de] Jacques et Raïssa Maritain* (Complete works [of] Jacques and Raïssa Maritain). 15 vols. Fribourg, Switzerland: Éditions universitaires, 1982–.

———. *The Social and Political Philosophy of Jacques Maritain: Selected Readings*. Ed. Joseph W. Evans and Leo R. Ward. New York: Scribner, 1955.

Maritain Studies/Études maritainiennes. 12 (1996) (thematic issue on "Maritain and the Natural Law").

Nielsen, Kai. *God and the Grounding of Morality.* Ottawa: University of Ottawa Press, 1991.

Possenti, Vittorio. "Philosophie du droit at loi naturelle selon Jacques Maritain" (Philosophy of Law and Natural Law According to Jacques Maritain). In *Jacques Maritain: Philosophe dans la cité/A Philosopher in the World,* ed. Jean-Louis Allard, 313–326. Ottawa: University of Ottawa Press, 1985.

William Sweet

Marriage Contract

A "contract" ordinarily describes a voluntary, legally enforceable agreement between two or more parties. The terms of the agreement may either come from the parties or be supplied by the law. Legally supplied terms are also of two types: "default rules" that apply only so long as the parties fail to specify otherwise, and mandatory terms imposed irrespective of the parties' wishes. The "marriage contract" is unusual among voluntary relationships in the extent to which the law restricts variation of its terms. Accordingly, the nature of marriage as a contract and its defining terms have often been controversial.

Classic proponents of marriage as contract defend the couple's freedom to specify the terms of their union. Sir Henry Sumner Maine, most famous for his insistence that "the movement of the progressive societies has hitherto been a movement *from Status to Contract,*" characterized the legal subordination of wives to their husbands as a status relationship that "deeply injured civilization." John Locke argued two centuries earlier that to the extent that the ends of marriage—procreation and the upbringing of children—did not require the husband's absolute authority, the parties should be free to accord the wife greater authority by contract. Michael Grossberg, however, concluded that such efforts often produce a change in status terms rather than contractual freedom. John Locke's call for contract, for example, serves as a midpoint between the older status of the husband as family master and the modern status of husband and wife as equals.

Immanuel Kant termed marriage a contract in a different sense. He argued that "the Contract of Marriage is not . . . a matter of arbitrary will, but is a Contract necessary in its nature by the Law of Humanity." For Kant, sexual relations involve the use of another as an object, and Kant reasoned that the only way in which such relationships could satisfy the test of fundamental respect for persons was through the couple's reciprocal acquisition of sexual rights in each other.

G.W.F. Hegel termed Kant's depiction of marriage as an exchange of contract rights "shameful." He observed that marriage involved not just "the mutual caprice" of the prospective partners, but a public celebration of entry into an institution that transcended the "individual self-subsistent units." For Hegel, marriage, if a contract at all, was "precisely a contract to transcend the standpoint of contract" in favor of "love, trust, and common sharing of their existence as individuals." Hegel's critique had two parts. The first was the insistence that marriage involves more than Kant's idea of reciprocal exchange. The second, as Jeremy Waldron explains, was part of a broader attack on "Kant's pervasive legalism"; it was an attack on the very idea of defining marriage in terms of rights. Waldron argues that, on this latter point, the difference between Kant and Hegel is more apparent than real, that "the strength and security of the marriage commitment in the modern world depends in part on there being an array of legalistic rights and duties that the partners know that they can fall back upon if their mutual affection fades."

Hegel's notion that marriage involves something more than the caprice of the spouses is, however, central to both religious and secular regulation of marriage. Modern Catholicism, for example, eschews the word "contract" for "covenant." Catholic teachings hold that the marital covenant is a sacrament that involves not only a partnership between the spouses but the presence of God. Thus, the Church distinguishes between marriages within and without the Church, and limits divorce on the basis of the biblical injunction that what God has joined together no man may put asunder.

Martin Luther, as part of his sixteenth-century break with the Catholic church, rejected the characterization of marriage as a sacrament dependent on the blessing of the Church. He reasoned that "in marriage, each of the parties owes fidelity to the other by their compact." Rooting marriage in the exchange between the spouses, he concluded that "[t]he marriages of our ancestors were no less sacred than our own, nor less real among unbelievers than believers."

Even more than Lutheran teachings, Judaism emphasizes the contractual nature of entering marriage. Louis Epstein describes Jewish tradition as dating back to a period in which neither state nor organized religion regulated marriage. Jewish law accordingly focused on marriage as a voluntary transaction, with the parties setting forth the terms of their union in a *ketubah,* or marriage contract. While both Jews and Lutherans recognize marriage as something more than a commercial contract and limit the ability of the parties to vary its terms, voluntary consent remains central. Thus, Judaism, for example, recognized mutual-consent divorce centuries before its acceptance in the United States, and Jewish law characterizes marriage and divorce as acts of the parties rather than as acts of church or state.

Civil regulation mirrors these differences. Historians attribute at least part of Anglo-American state regulation to a desire, fueled by the rise of Protestantism, to limit church influence. The U.S. Supreme Court, in the nineteenth-century cases that upheld prohibition of polygamy, treated marriage as a matter neither of religious faith nor of private agreement, but as a "basic institution of society." As such, the state regulated who could marry, prerequisites such as licenses and blood tests, the terms of the ongoing relationship, the circumstances in which the couple were allowed to part, and the consequences of marital dissolution. The couple's opportunity to vary the terms of their relationship were strictly limited. Lenore Weitzman wrote: "The marriage contract is unlike most contracts: its provisions are unwritten, its penalties are unspecified, and the terms of the contract are typically unknown to the 'contracting parties.' Prospective spouses are neither informed of the terms of the contract nor are they allowed any options about these terms."

Modern law has moved away from this pervasive regulation. The courts have relaxed restrictions on who can marry, broadened the availability of divorce, and given greater recognition to prenuptial agreements. These developments do not necessarily, however, mark an embrace of contract. Rather, Mary Ann Glendon observes, "[T]he shift that is currently taking place in American family law, far from being a shift from State regulation of status to State regulation of contracts, is a shift from regulation of the formation, effects, and dissolution of marriage to *nonregulation.* . . . [T]he State . . . now in the business of divesting itself of its marriage regulation business . . . is not likely to set up shop as an enforcer of heretofore unenforceable contracts."

The modern status of marriage as contract is thus as uncertain as it was in the time of Luther or Kant. Nonetheless, the law's mandatory terms have been remarkably stable. Marriage, according to the law in most European and American states, remains the sexually exclusive union of one man and one woman for life. While public opinion may be divided, these terms remain part of the marriage contract: (1) no western jurisdiction recognizes marriage between a man and more than one woman (polygamy) or between a woman and more than one man (polyandry); (2) marriage is legally available for homosexual couples only in Denmark, although similar legislation is pending elsewhere, and in a number of jurisdictions homosexual couples may adopt children or receive partnership benefits traditionally available only to married couples; (3) there is no legal recognition of marriages for a period other than life even in countries in which divorce is available at will; (4) the law continues to treat marriage as a sexually exclusive union whatever the agreement between the parties.

Despite the stability in the definition of marriage, other aspects of the marriage contract have changed dramatically. First, the purpose of marriage has shifted as even the Catholic church has elevated the mutual wellbeing of the spouses to equal status with procreation and provision for children in defining marital purposes.

Second, formal equality has replaced a gendered assignment of marital responsibilities. Kant, in insisting on an equal and reciprocal exchange of sexual rights between spouses, took pains to emphasize the "natural inequality" of the sexes. Anglo-American law formalized this inequality, recognizing the husband as the head of the family, charged with a duty of support in exchange for his wife's promise to love, honor, and *obey.* Modern law, in contrast, proceeds from a presumption of equality and imposes a mutual obligation of support. Despite these changes, feminists continue to criticize marriage as a patriarchal institution. Lenore Weitzman encourages women to write their own marriage contracts to safeguard their interests, and Martha Fineman advocates withdrawing state sanction from marriage as an institution, leaving only the private contract between spouses.

Third, western jurisdictions have adopted wholesale changes in the grounds for marital dissolution. Until the mid-1960s, Anglo-American law permitted divorce only upon a showing of fault. The fault requirement grew out of the marriage contract's lifetime vows, and fault initially served to release an innocent spouse from the bonds of a union that had effectively ended because of the other's misconduct. Over time, fault-based divorce also became, through the collusion of the parties, available by mutual consent. Modern reforms range from California's no-fault law, which precludes consideration of fault altogether, to reform legislation in England and New York that adds no-fault grounds to the older fault provisions. These reforms effectively remake the marriage contract from one premised on a lifelong exchange to one terminable at will.

Fourth, legal regulation of the consequences of divorce has changed. Fault-based divorce tied financial consequences to breach of the marriage contract. No fault proceeds from a concept of marriage as a shared enterprise only so long as the marriage lasts. The legal provisions for spousal support and property divisions operate as the default terms of the marriage contract, and it is with respect to such financial provisions that the courts are most willing to honor prenuptial agreements.

Fifth, the legal relationships between parent and child have shifted with the changing role of marriage. Historically, the parents' relationship determined rights and responsibilities toward children, with the law drawing a clear distinction between marital and nonmarital children and fault often influencing custody and visitation. Modern courts, in contrast, base custody and support much more directly on the interests of the children, with the result that the marriage contract, and indeed the relationship between the parents generally, plays a lesser role.

References

Epstein, Louis M. *The Jewish Marriage Contract: A Study in the Status of the Woman in Jewish Law.* New York: Arno Press, 1973.

Glendon, Mary Ann. *State, Law and Family: Family Law in Transition in the United States and Western Europe.* Amsterdam NY: North-Holland, 1977.

Grossberg, Michael. *Governing the Hearth: Law and the Family in Nineteenth Century America.* Chapel Hill: University of North Carolina Press, 1985.

Kasper, Walter. *Theology of Christian Marriage.* New York: Crossroad, 1981.

Machin, Theodore. *The Marital Sacrament.* New York: Pauline Press, 1989.

Weitzman, Lenore. *The Marriage Contract: Spouses, Lovers and the Law.* New York: Free Press, 1981.

June Carbone

See also DIVORCE AND MARRIAGE; FAMILY LAW

Marx, Karl (1818–1883)

Karl Marx never devoted sustained attention to law; hence any account of his legal philosophy must be constructed from scattered fragments. In his earliest writings Marx addressed issues within contemporary German legal philosophy; in these he engaged with G.W.F. Hegel's treatment of state and law and with the tradition of the historical school. The abiding legacy of this engagement was Marx's unreserved critique of rights. The rights of man could be nothing other than the rights of the isolated and alienated legal subject. This position Marx retained; as late as 1875 he condemned talk of "equal rights" in the draft program of the German Social-Democrats as "obsolete verbal rubbish."

Generalized, this position focuses on the abstract, formal, and universal features of law contrasted to the empirical, concrete, and particular content of actual social relations. His occasional polemical asides, for example against Jeremy Bentham, deride the abstraction and formalism of jurisprudential arguments.

Marx's treatment of law exhibits a number of other themes that coexist with his critique of rights. These may be summarized as: Law is a form of politics. Law is ideological; it gives effect to, mirrors, or is otherwise expressive of the prevailing social or economic relations. Law both exemplifies and provides legitimation to the embedded values of the dominant class. The content and procedures of law manifest, directly or indirectly, the interests of the dominant class.

Marx's imagery of base and superstructure gives rise to some philosophical problems. In *Capital: A Critique of Political Economy,* he distinguished between "the economic structure of society," which forms the base or "real foundation, . . . on which rises a legal and political superstructure and to which correspond definite forms of social consciousness." Law is assigned to the "superstructure," which "reflects" the "base" or "economic structure." Thus it is the economic structure which has causal priority in determining the character and content of the law. However, in the same passage Marx blurred this distinction: "At a certain stage of their development, the material productive forces of society come into conflict with the existing relations of production, or—what is but a legal expression for the same thing—with the property relations within which they have been at work hitherto." Here legal property relations seem to be part of the economic structure.

This is not simply a definitional matter; G.A. Cohen has attempted to resolve it by elaborating a nonlegal conception of property rights. There is a wider issue of whether legal relations (that is, the corporate form, marriage, and so forth) are actually constitutive of social and economic relations or merely reflect such relations. Karl Marx and Friedrich Engels both came to concede some "relative autonomy" to law; both used phrases such as "in the last instance" and "in the final analysis" to express this long-run sense of the determination of law and other aspects of the superstructure by the economic.

Law is ideological in a double sense; law is ideologically constructed and is itself a significant bearer of ideology. This is expressed in two theses. First, law is created within existing ideological fields in which the norms and values associated with social relations are continuously debated and struggled over. Second, the law itself is a major bearer of ideological messages, which, because of the general legitimacy accorded to law, serve to reinforce and legitimate the ideology that it carries.

Another important question for Marx's theory of law is what contribution, if any, does law make to the reproduction of class relations. This requires attention to the impact of law upon the pattern of social inequality and subordination. Two general theses are present. First, the aggregate effects of law in modern democratic societies work to the systematic disadvantage of the least advantaged social classes. Second, the content, procedures, and practice of law constitute an *arena of struggle* within which the relative positions and advantages of social classes is changed over time. The latter is most explicit in Marx's extended account in *Capital* of the struggle for factory legislation in England, legislation whose arrival he hails as a victory for the jurisprudence of the proletariat.

Marx's utopian vision of communism, epitomized by the image of the withering away of the state, implied that law had no necessary role in the classless society. This view, as much as any substantive considerations, underlines the association of law as a phenomenon of class society. Marx had no concern for the role of law as guarantor of the conditions of political and economic democracy, facilitating democratic participation, and restraining bureaucratic and state power.

References

Buchanan, Allen E. *Marx and Justice: The Radical Critique of Liberalism.* London: Methuen, 1982.

Cain, Maureen, and Alan Hunt. *Marx and Engels on Law.* London: Academic Press, 1979.
Cohen, G.A. *Karl Marx's Theory of History: A Defence.* Oxford: Clarendon Press, 1978.
Collins, Hugh. *Marxism and Law.* Oxford: Oxford University Press, 1982.
Kerruish, Valerie. *Jurisprudence as Ideology.* London: Routledge, 1991.
Marx, Karl. *Capital: A Critique of Political Economy.* Vol. 1. 1867. Moscow: Languages Publishing House, 1961.
———. "Contribution to the Critique of Hegel's Philosophy of Right." 1843. In *Karl Marx, Frederick Engels: Collected Works.* Ed. Richard Dixon et al. Vol. 3. London: Lawrence and Wishart, 1975.
———. "The Philosophical Manifesto of the Historical School of Law." 1842. In *Karl Marx, Frederick Engels: Collected Works.* Vol. 1. London: Lawrence and Wishart, 1975.
———. "Preface" to *A Contribution to the Critique of Political Economy.* 1859. Intro. Maurice Dobb. London: Lawrence and Wishart, 1971.
Sypnowich, Christine. *The Concept of Socialist Law.* Oxford: Oxford University Press, 1990.

Alan Hunt

See also MARXIST PHILOSOPHY OF LAW

Marxist Philosophy of Law

Marxist philosophy of law (MPL) has concentrated on two issues: first, how to *explain* law in the light of both class, and the marxist method for explaining how society functions, usually known as historical materialism (HM); second, the role of socialist *ethics* in law. Explanatory issues predominate in five key historical schools or tendencies: (1) Russian experimental, (2) German critical, (3) English language analytic, (4) British historical, and (5) tendencies on the cusp of MPL, which represent the development/move out of MPL to European/North American end-of-millennium radicalism. Ethical issues predominate in (6) abstract moral MPL and (7) practical political MPL. These seven schools also display a rich historical, geographical, and methodological variety. School (1) represents work done by theorists in the face of the task of implementing socialism after the Russian Revolution. School (2) comes from the famous Frankfurt school, critical of both East and West since the 1920s. School (3) has examined marxism and law under the lens of the resurgent English language political and legal philosophy of the past twenty-five years. School (4) concentrates on marxism's relevance for British legal history. School (5) both negates and preserves a distinctive marxist approach to law. School (6) has acted as a utopian current, often within other tendencies or schools, and often in opposition to the practical legal ethics of school (7), which were arrived at by those who tried to make socialism work, usually under very adverse conditions.

A fundamental task of explanatory MPL is to analyze the relation between the demands of class and HM accounts of law. Class analysis emphasizes the rootedness of law in particular class interests. HM maintains that a sufficiently elaborated philosophical analysis of the effect of economic system and class on law undermines many, if not most, analyses of the legal system as independent and autonomous. Analysis that makes class central to the development of law can proceed, as the example of D.F.B. Tucker shows, with minimal commitment to HM. In contrast, it is impossible to find HM analysis of law which does not stress class to some extent. HM analysis of law is sufficient to achieve the label MPL, but class analysis is not. However, all HM analysis of law must consider its relation to class analysis of law as a central topic and must commit itself to some class analysis. There is, admittedly, a certain paradox that emerges from these characterizations. There may be cases where legal analysis is deemed marxist because it uses HM but is less committed to class analysis than a nonmarxist account, which eschews HM. An example would be the contrast between Jürgen Habermas and Christine Sypnowich; the former uses HM analysis of law, and yet uses less class analysis than the latter, who rejects HM. In spite of this paradox, the relation of HM to class analysis constitutes a reference point against which can be analyzed all five schools of explanatory MPL.

G.A. Cohen and Evgeny Pashukanis, major exponents, respectively, of (3) and (1), are both committed to HM. Yet Tucker, also an exponent of (3), makes class more important than HM; and Sypnowich, methodologically close to Tucker because of her emphasis on rights and class, nevertheless, because of her rejection of HM finds herself cast into the ambiguous (5). Thus class analysis and HM can clash, as we also see in defining Pashukanis' place in (1). Other members of (1), such as V.I. Lenin, whose account of HM certainly lacks the subtlety and rigor of Pashukanis', were often much stronger on class.

Representatives of (5), who are for the most part interested in class analysis of law, consider that the failure of thinkers as diverse as Pashukanis and Cohen to give an adequate formulation of HM in itself, and in its relation to class, undermines MPL. Hence, as Matthew Kramer moves toward virtual abandonment of the HM component of MPL, he by no means abandons class analysis. Explanatory MPL seems to depend on HM, but nevertheless seems to thrive on class. The contrast between Tucker and Cohen suggests that a strong commitment to HM is not necessary for marxist class analysis; and the contrast between Pashukanis and Lenin suggests that HM is not even sufficient to achieve anything like a high degree of class analysis.

Schools (2) and (4) represent alternative ways of conceiving HM itself. All HM approaches must undercut, to some extent, the claims made by many, if not most, traditional philosophers of law that the legal system possesses an independent logic. For Cohen this meant that law must serve the property system, above all its nonlegal aspects. Cohen, writing in 1978, did not consider adequately the difficulties involved in giving an HM account of the form, as opposed to the content, of law, in terms of its causes in the economic system. Had he done so he might quickly have seen that the very fact that a system of laws so often takes the form of a system of rights is one of the key unsolved problems for HM, although not necessarily for class analysis of law. Of course, Pashukanis did attempt to give an account of the form of the system of law, including its rights aspect, by linking law with the market, commodity form. But (2) and (4) start from the assumption that the greatest difficulty in MPL has been the assertion of HM itself, as opposed to just emphasis on class, in the face of much confidence from other philosophers of law, that HM undermines the very enterprise of explanatory philosophy of law. To answer these critics HM would have to account for the independence and autonomy of both the content and form of legal systems. For its opponents explanatory MPL always reduced this independence and autonomy to something else that it could not be reduced to, and thus failed at its deepest task. Yet representatives of (5) even, such as Kramer, do not give up on the task of reduction, but demand it in a different or a more generalized form than HM provides.

Hence, the significance of (2) and (4), because these schools, one German and one British, have played an important role both in recent MPL, and as antecedents of (5), a movement at the cusp of MPL. Indeed, they have played the role of intermediary between traditional MPL and (5), and have played that role in North America as well as the Europe of their origin. They have been developed specifically to produce a reduction not susceptible to the charges of insensitivity to the varied cultural forms and contents of law, charges that have been raised against Cohen and Pashukanis. Schools (2) and (4) develop HM so that it can deal with law as an expression of larger cultural forces, and not just as an effect of the economy. E.P. Thompson has played an intriguing role in (4), as the defender of the autonomy and independence of the legal system within the confines of both HM and class analysis. Sypnowich, as a representative of (5), has taken up his thesis that law, paradoxically, must possess both autonomy/independence and integrity at a moral level, in order for it to serve class interests and the economic system. She sees her affirmation of class analysis and socialism, coupled with her rejection of HM, as following the lead of Thompson. Yet Thompson clearly upholds HM. Thompson's analysis of law, like Franz Neumann's and Jürgen Habermas' within (2), is precisely an attempt to work out the critique of the system of law that is necessary for HM, in terms of a morality which, first, judges the legal system, second, finds itself partially in the legal system, and third, could conceivably be reincorporated back into a system of law of the socialist future, which it would judge less harshly than the system of which it is now both part and not part.

For Thompson, if the morality and legitimacy of law are denied all reality by the ruling class that manipulates it, then law does not even serve ruling class interests. In a like vein, Neumann discovered in his historical analysis of law that the equality needed in order to rationalize the market always spilled over into a broader concept of political equality. Habermas generalized Neumann's point into the thesis that the economic system studied by HM was so incapable by itself of accounting for the development of legal society, that its explanatory force had to be balanced by the explanatory force of a posttraditional, universal morality, one which potentially had in it elements of real legitimacy.

It is clear that the conceptual history of explanatory MPL, beginning and ending with the master dispute between class analysis, HM, and the idea of the autonomy of the law, has the ultimate effect of bringing the primarily moral approach to the fore. Ernst Bloch well represents the abstract moral MPL of school (6), because he does more freely, in regard to the ethical concerns of law, what is done in a more constrained way when the moral element is subordinate to, or only part of, the master explanatory dispute over class, HM, and law's autonomy. Bloch's work also illuminates an actually existing (once) socialism, as (7), a practical political and legal application of MPL.

In regard to (6), Bloch represents a striking liberation from the whole constellation of explanatory MPL theories. For example, many of his key citations from Marx neither entail nor are entailed by class analysis or HM. By stressing Marx's advocacy of human dignity as depicting an ultimate moral ideal, stretching from the Stoics to the French Revolution and into the present, an ideal which can be incorporated, but never fully, into actual laws, Bloch's account might seem, at first glance, outside MPL—but that first glance is misleading. Bloch's abstract ethical account exemplifies (6), but also illustrates that one moral ideal wrestled with in (1)–(5) and (7) is the question of the viability of law as moral instrument. Is morality served better if law disappears (Pashukanis, Zenon Bankowski) or if law remains (Habermas, Thompson)? Once the question is posed in this way, Bloch's relation to both (6) and (7) becomes much clarified: to (6), because his work shows how part of this dispute over the necessity of law's continuing existence is purely moral and not explanatory at all; to (7), because his focus, writing first in East and then West Germany, on the morality of law within the context of the entire history of western ethics, allows an evaluation of a once actually existing socialism in terms of the question What is the ultimate moral significance of law as ideal and actuality? The issue of the morality of marxist accounts of law will certainly compete with, and may well outweigh, issues of class and HM, as marxist philosophy of law moves into the twenty-first century.

References

Bankowski, Zenon. "Anarchism, Marxism, and the Critique of Law." In *Legality, Ideology and the State,* ed. David Sugarman. New York: Academic Press, 1983.

Bloch, Ernst. *Natural Law and Human Dignity.* Cambridge: MIT Press, 1986.

Cohen, G.A. *Karl Marx's Theory of History: A Defence.* Princeton: Princeton University Press, 1978.

Collins, Hugh. *Marxism and Law.* Oxford: Oxford University Press, 1982.

Habermas, Jürgen. "Uberlegungen zum Evolutionaren Stellenwert des Modernen Rechts" (Reflections on the Place of Modern Law in Evolutionary Perspective). In *Zur Rekonstruktion des Historischen Materialismus.* Frankfurt: Suhrkamp, 1976.

Kramer, Matthew. *Legal Theory, Political Theory, and Deconstruction.* Bloomington: Indiana University Press, 1991.

Neumann, Franz. "The Change in the Function of Law in Modern Society." In *The Authoritarian and the Democratic State.* New York: Free Press, 1957.

Pashukanis, Evgeny. *Law and Marxism.* London: Ink Links, 1978.

Sypnowich, Christine. *The Concept of Socialist Law.* New York: Oxford University Press, 1990.

Thompson, E.P. *Whigs and Hunters: The Origins of the Black Act.* London: Allen Lane, 1975.

Tucker, D.F.B. *Marxism and Individualism.* New York: St. Martin's Press, 1980.

Norman Fischer

See also FRANKFURT SCHOOL (EARLY); MARX, KARL; SOCIALIST PHILOSOPHY OF LAW

Mediation, Criminal

Mediation in criminal law is founded on the premise that the law should encompass more than just the question of individual rights. Law is also viewed as relational, that is, based on the human need for interconnectedness in a community. Solving conflict has, therefore, a more expansive meaning.

Traditional and Western Societies: Personalization and Rationalization

Traditional homogeneous societies have resorted to *informal mediation* in disputes since immemorial times. The idea is simple: a figure of authority or a council of village elders, as facilitator, engage both victim and offender in a ritual of palaver and reconciliation. Victims voice their feelings of harm with a supportive community. Offenders are also invited to present their views in this ventilating process. Each becomes ready to assume his or her own share of responsibility. Everyone actively contributes to the search of a multilayered solution to overcome the conflict. A successful process is concluded by the reintegration of both parties in the circle of social cooperation, including possibly mutual apologies. The entire community endorses the solution and supports the two disputants. Most of the time, implicit social pressure to conform to this ritual and to the suggested solution are often sufficient to transform the mediation into an efficient instrument of dispute resolution.

Legal rationalization in western societies has made criminal resolution more abstract and formal, far removed from the particulars of the people in dispute. Through knowledgeable professionals, an "impersonal" society takes over the trial. It frequently leaves the victims on the side and appropriates the offender in a network of predefined rules of procedure, standardized mechanisms of qualification, and codified punishments. The case is often argued by lawyers and decided by judges, before either victim and offender have had time to be part of it. This continuing estrangement is often overwhelming and helps neither the victim to feel compensated for the pain, nor the offender to experience any desire for amendment. In this court context, the purposes of retribution and deterrence that criminal justice claim to embody do not seem to have been fulfilled. It is doubtful that the subsequent implementation of sanctions ever plays that role either, but that is another story.

Aware of the pitfalls of contemporary criminal procedure in terms of *depersonalization,* and learning from positive and negative aspects of early alternatives, political movements have militated for the development of criminal mediation, especially for small offenses where prosecution is not crucial. The hope is to help both victims and offenders claim some power in criminal resolution, and—who knows?—reduce court congestion and the crime rate. Recent reforms have been conducted to introduce criminal mediation as a procedure prior to criminal decisions. Those responsible to implement these new policies have tried to balance the needs of victims and offenders. These initiatives still need to be investigated further, in order to assess them more precisely and to refine them in the future in the interest of all concerned parties.

Mediation: Ethics of Care for Victims and Offenders

First, for *victims,* the experience of resorting to criminal mediation may have a healing effect. First steps are naturally difficult. In the legal system, people have internalized the passive role of victims; they need to be told the meaning of the whole mediation procedure. If victims agree to meet with the offender in the presence of the mediator, they can often use these meetings to express their frustration and needs, ask questions, request apology, discuss reparation, all of this helping them to come to terms with their own victimization. By itself, this has a cathartic effect, and, moreover, victims get a voice. These meetings may also open opportunities to approach in less devilish ways their offenders, especially when the latter acknowledge their guilt.

Second, for *offenders,* even if they may enter the process with second thoughts, hoping to later get a lesser sentence from the judge, they may acknowledge, like the victims, many unexpected positive effects: a better awareness of their actions, of their consequences on concrete others, of the need for reparation, and for personal improvement. They may propose to find, and agree to, symbolic or material compensation for the harm done.

From an *ethical* viewpoint, many apparent advantages stem from this two-way communication that is established between the victim and the offender. The goal is not primarily sociological or collective; it is not to re-create fictitiously some social homogeneity that does not really exist in fragmented societies, contrary to traditional ones. The goal is more psychological, intersubjective. Practically, with the mediator's help, two people are asked to reconnect to each other at a basic level, to listen to each other and to express their respective needs in a genuine dialogue, where apologies and forgiveness may lead to reconciliation. Restoring some harmony between *two* people in conflict is a heuristic prerequisite to later hope for more harmony in the community. Some people in western societies consider criminal mediation as an illusion or deception; it can nonetheless stand as a regulatory idea that moves us toward better human development, as long and difficult as this Sisyphus quest may be.

Conditions of Communication and Institutional Structure

Establishing communication is, however, never easy in a context of criminal conflict. The first obstacle has to do with the *personalities* of the participants to the mediation: some victims seek revenge; some offenders absolutely refuse to acknowledge their responsibility; some mediators are unknowingly partial. None of these features are insurmountable. Barriers can sometimes disappear by simply calling a trained mediator. In complement to interpersonal skills, mediators can use efficient methods to further *balanced communication:* they can set ground rules of confidentiality, of noninterruption of the speaker; provide each person with time to express his or her views of the offense; encourage questions about and responses to the other's views; let the disputants propose solutions to solve their conflict and possibly agree on them; and close the procedure by reminding the parties of the results of the session.

The second obstacle, *structural,* is more difficult to overcome. It refers to the status of mediation in the criminal procedure of each system. Does mediation benefit from financial support to develop beyond some isolated experiments? Since mediation is nonbinding and judges ultimately make their own independent decisions, are the mediators' actions complementary to, or undermined by, those of the judges? Is criminal mediation a token in an overall commitment to repression, or is it part of a carefully crafted policy to expand alternative dispute resolution? This involves more than a question of legal choice: it involves political philosophy.

If we agree that the law is done for the *people* and not simply for its own sake, its goals, beyond putting an end to a conflict, are to increase human autonomy and awareness of self and others, a sense of personal responsibility and harmonious belonging to the community. It is therefore congruent with a teleological spirit of the law to encourage any process, like criminal mediation, which empowers people with an active participation in the resolution of their own disputes, achieving concretely under the circumstances of a specific case high goals of personal development. By its very principles, indeed, criminal mediation aims at making victims and offenders internalize and actualize better behaviors toward others, practicing norms of respect in thoughts and deeds and not simply in words.

References

Auerbach, J. *Justice Without Law?* New York: Oxford University Press, 1983.

Bonafé-Schmitt, J.-P. *La Médiation: Une justice Douce* (Mediation: The Humane Justice). Paris: Syros-Alternatives, 1992.

Bush, R.A.B., and J. Folger. *The Promise of Mediation.* San Francisco: Jossey-Bass, 1994.

Coppens, P. "Médiation et philosophie du droit" (Mediation and Legal Philosophy). *Archives de Politique Criminelle* 13 (1992), 13–39.

Kressel, K., and D.G. Pruitt. *Mediation Research: The Process and Effectiveness of Third-Party Intervention.* San Francisco: Jossey-Bass, 1989.

Lind, E.A., and T.R. Tyler. *The Social Psychology of Procedural Justice.* New York: Plenum, 1988.

Matthews, R., ed. *Informal Justice?* London: Sage, 1988.

Six, J.-F. *Le Temps des Médiateurs* (The Time for the Mediators). Paris: Seuil, 1990.

Wright, M., and B. Galaway, eds. *Mediation and Criminal Justice. Victims, Offenders and Community.* London: Sage, 1989.

Alain Pekar Lempereur

See also ARBITRATION; DISPUTE RESOLUTION

Medieval Philosophy of Law

Medieval philosophy of law is referred to as the period from the end of Roman imperial rule in the West until the dawn of the European Renaissance, during which the philosophy of law was shaped by Christian religion as well as by the classical philosophers and jurists.

Insofar as medieval Latin thought was ultimately under the sway of Christian belief, the answer to the question What is law? was simple and straightforward. Law in the European middle ages was always the immutable divine will directed toward the plan of human salvation and damnation, accessible through revelation but fully known only to God himself. However, such an apparently uncomplicated response nevertheless produced a rich and diverse body of reflection about some of the fundamental problems in the philosophy of law, including the structure of the legal system, its moral and political foundations, and the basis for the obligation to obey it.

As with the Jews, Christians claimed to submit to a religion founded on law, albeit on the law of love rather than the Decalogue. The Christian God commanded the devout to love all humankind without reservation or distinction. In a perfect condition, many early Christians taught, human beings lived (and will again live) without a promulgated code of law. However, the fact that earthly, mortal life is imperfect, due to the taint of the sinning human will, requires law (and the enforcement thereof) in order to protect the good from the evil and to maintain a peaceful existence in which the faithful Christian may worship God. This position was perhaps articulated with greatest force in the writings of St. Augustine of Hippo (354–430), most famously in his *City of God*. For Augustine, the state and its laws were a divinely inspired creation of the human race in the wake of the expulsion from Paradise.

In view of the recognition that the law of love required supplementation in the earthly life, Christian thought during later Roman and early medieval times also integrated more mundane teachings about law, drawn especially from the stoic philosophers of pagan antiquity and from the jurists of the Roman law tradition. Classical juristic and philosophical theories of law had emphasized the guiding force of the law of nature, accessible to human beings through their faculty of reason, as the ultimate basis for all valid positive law. Medieval Christian thinkers extended the natural law principle with the simple equation, *natura, id est, Deus* (nature, that is, God), incorporating the laws of nature into God's wider plan and thus legitimizing many teachings of the pagans in the eyes of Christians. The relationship between Christian doctrine and ancient legal ideas proved to be generally congenial, particularly following the twelfth-century revival of the close study of the civil law of Rome.

Yet another set of factors shaping medieval Latin conceptions of law was generated by the operative conditions of political life. Following the collapse of Roman rule in the West, no central authority or group of authorities proved capable of establishing jurisdiction and enforcing law within Europe. Rather, the political arrangements associated with feudalism reflected the extreme fragmentation of power, rendering impossible a unified legal system. As a result, the everyday experience of law during the early middle ages was confined almost exclusively to custom of a highly localized sort. Laws were equated with those practices in which people within a village or region had engaged habitually or for such a long time that no one could recollect their origins. With a few exceptions, such as the Italian cities, justice during the early middle ages was meted out in accordance with unwritten custom whose content was determined primarily by human memory.

What changed this situation significantly was the rise over the course of the twelfth century of more centralized systems of power and jurisdiction, normally under the control of a king or similar territorial ruler. The development of these feudal monarchies was accompanied by the creation of more unified legal codes and the application of royal justice to an increasing numbers of subjects, as well as by an insistence upon the precept that valid law must be set down in writing. The model for this changed approach to law was derived from the law books of the ancient Romans, which had largely been ignored in previous centuries. Not only did Roman law provide a ready-made legislative code that the new feudal monarchs could apply, it also incorporated a hierarchical ideology that these rulers found useful, especially the claim that all binding law emanated from authorizing will of the prince. This did not necessarily lead, however, to the elimination or eradication of previous customary law. Rather, custom was often written down and integrated into the emerging legal codes of provinces and nations. The mania for legal systematization and classification that was manifest during the high middle ages even touched those locales (such as England) that resisted the imposition of the body of Roman law. The law books attributed to Glanville and Henry de Bracton, in which can be found the origins of English common law, are replete with the methods and many of the characteristic doctrines of civil law.

The medieval church found itself in a predicament not too different from that of secular rulers: mired in centuries of conflicting papal and episcopal decrees, council decisions, and patristic declarations in addition to the words of the Holy Book. Inspired by the drive for codification that stimulated civilian lawyers, the ecclesiastical jurist Gratian undertook (in his *Decretum* of 1141) the truly momentous task of reconciling the inconsistencies of church law (or canons) and establishing a coherent plan for ecclesiastical statute. Thereafter, it becomes necessary to speak of two parallel and related, but nonetheless distinct, legal methods and subject areas—those of the civilians and of the canonists. Although they shared a training based in the new phenomenon of the university, the civilians and the canonists were distinguished by their status (after 1219 priests were forbidden to practice civil law) as well as their conflicts over divergent doctrines, such as the relationship between natural and divine law. On the latter issue, the dispute concerned not whether natural law was authorized by God (all parties assumed that it was), but whether there was any means of knowing the dictates of natural law outside the revealed word. Canonists held that scripture alone yielded the terms of natural law, and hence that the law of nature was coextensive with divine law. By contrast, the civilians asserted that natural law derived from a principle of justice that, while imperfect in relation to God's justice and parasitic upon it, could nevertheless be grasped independently of direct revelation. For the canonists, in sum, we obey natural law because we know it to be the revealed will of the Lord, whereas for the civilians we obey because our natural reason, oriented toward justice, impels us to do so.

The jurists of twelfth- and thirteenth-century Europe raised a number of important issues about law and shaped the thinking of nonlawyers in this regard. Their influence can be detected in such nonlegal works as John of Salisbury's *Policraticus* (completed in 1159). Yet the work of civilians and canonists alike was primarily practical, rather than philosophical, in approach. Discourse about law moved to a more purely theoretical plane during the thirteenth century with the rise of scholasticism and the development of a full university curriculum in the arts. Associated with these events was the recovery and dissemination in the Latin world of the writings of Aristotle, especially his *Nichomachean Ethics* and his *Politics*, both translated in the mid-thirteenth century. While scholars have at times placed too great an emphasis on the intellectual transformation wrought by the reintroduction of Aristotle's philosophy into the West, it is true that Aristotle's corpus afforded an important framework for the philosophical study of law. Law played an important role in Aristotle's moral and political thought: he valued the role of the legislator and maintained that a just and well-ordered regime must be ruled according to law rather than will. Good laws, Aristotle believed, act as the best guide to ensure the virtue and happiness of citizens. Thus, he upheld the existence of an independent standard (analogous to natural law in the stoic-Christian sense) for determining the validity of law; and he specified a quality of human character, which he termed *epieikeia*, capable of amending law if its application proved inequitable in some particular instance. Aristotle also acknowledged the validity of custom, asserting that it deserved to be accorded the status of a second nature.

Such themes of Aristotle predominated in the reflections of medieval schoolmen about matters of law, in the context both of political and moral treatises and of theological tomes. Perhaps the most powerful example of medieval aristotelianism was the *Summa Theologiae* of St. Thomas Aquinas (1225–1274), which contains a separate section on law that seeks to synthesize various medieval traditions and to generate a structure within which to view the different types of law. Specifically, Aquinas proposes a quatrapartite division among eternal law, which reflects the divine governance of the cosmos; divine law, which is God's specific guidance to the human race regarding matters of salvation and beatitude; natural law, which directs all living creatures toward their survival and reproduction, as well as pointing human beings in particular toward those goods (such as social and political community) necessary for a satisfactory earthly existence; and positive law, which in aristotelian fashion educates people in those actions they must abjure or perform in order to attain virtue and avoid evil. Although law functions at different levels of generality, the dictates of each level are mutually consistent. Positive law, therefore, cannot validly require human beings to act contrary to natural, divine, or eternal law.

Aquinas insists that the obligatory nature of law, at least as regards human beings, stems from its rational character. Since people partake of reason, they obey law inasmuch as it contains a rational component. This claim has several implications. First, Aquinas rejects the view that the legitimacy of law depends solely upon will or command, thus directly challenging the Romanist position that the pleasure of the ruler has the force of law. Rather, he states in the *Summa Theologiae* that the will of any legislative power must promulgate law strictly in accordance with reason; otherwise, it sins. Hence, the legislative will is guided and constrained by reason. On the same grounds, all public powers ought voluntarily to submit themselves to law, since they recognize its inherent rationality. Moreover, Aquinas acknowledges that no person is bound in conscience to obey a positive statute that deviates from reason or justice. An unjust law does not compel, since it is not law; this doctrine, widely held during the middle ages, is given considerable justification by Aquinas. Of course, he admits that there may be prudential reasons for obeying such an irrational dictate, at least so long as religion is not violated. However, the only commands of positive law that one must obey are those consistent with reason.

While Aquinas's account of law was perhaps the most elaborate to be constructed during the middle ages, it was not immediately or widely adopted, even by his own students. Indeed, the tendency among fourteenth-century schoolmen was to stress the volitional aspect of law, to the extent that some modern scholars have detected an incipient legal positivism in thinkers of the period such as William of Ockham (1280/85–1349) and Marsiglio of Padua (1275/80–1342). While this trend has surely been exaggerated, debates about the proximate location of legislative authority in both secular and ecclesiastical spheres did intensify during the later middle ages, and so did emphasis upon the volitional aspect of law. Some authors, such as Marsiglio, sought to vest the authorization of law in the explicit and public consent of those persons to be governed by statute, thereby pointing the way toward popular sovereignty in both temporal community and church. By contrast, during the same period Augustinus Triumphus (1270–1328) argued with equal force that the pope is a law unto himself and is thus above law, his will beyond question or judgment by those over whom he rules. Similar positions were propounded on behalf of secular rulers by various later medieval schoolmen, as well as by civilian lawyers such as Bartolus of Sassoferrato (1314–1357) and Baldus de Ubaldis (1327–1400), for whom the de facto exercise of power on the part of territorial monarchs was sufficient to supplant the de jure authority of universal empire.

Yet disputes between later medieval theorists of law were less pronounced and intractable than modern scholarship sometimes suggests. None would have insisted, for example, that law was purely a matter of command without a rational ingredient, nor that reason alone was sufficient to validate any law. This reflects the fact that all legal philosophers of the time, regardless of their political and methodological orientation, still built their doctrines out of the full range of intellectual frameworks and discourses available to them: Christian theology, stoic and aristotelian philosophy, and civilian and canonist principles. A thinker such as Baldus, for instance, moved seamlessly in his writings from the technicalities of the legal practitioner to the profundities of the aristotelian philosopher. In sum, during the later middle ages, legal theorists continued to speak in a common set of languages and to be guided by a shared core of ideas.

References

Burns, J.H., ed. *The Cambridge History of Medieval Political Thought, c. 350–c. 1450.* Cambridge: Cambridge University Press, 1988.

D'Entrèves, Alexander P. *Natural Law: An Introduction to Legal Philosophy.* 1951. 3d ed. New Brunswick NJ: Transaction Books, 1994.

Fasolt, Constantin. "Visions of Order in the Canonists and Civilians." In *Handbook of European History 1400–1600: Late Middle Ages, Renaissance and Reformation.* Vol. 2, ed. Thomas A. Brady, Jr., Heiko A. Oberman, and James D. Tracy, 31–59. Leiden: Brill, 1995.

Kuttner, Stephan. "The Revival of Jurisprudence." In *Renaissance and Renewal in the Twelfth Century,* ed. Robert L. Benson

and Giles Constable, 299–323. Cambridge MA: Harvard University Press, 1982.
McGrade, Arthur Stephen. "Rights, Natural Rights, and the Philosophy of Law." In *Cambridge History of Later Medieval Philosophy*, ed. Norman Kretzmann, Anthony Kenny, and Jan Pinborg. Cambridge: Cambridge University Press, 1982.
Nederman, Cary J. *Community and Consent: The Secular Theory of Marsiglio of Padua's Defensor Pacis*. Lanham MD: Rowman and Littlefield, 1995.
Pennington, Kenneth. *The Prince and the Law 1200–1600: Sovereignty and Rights in the Western Legal Tradition*. Berkeley: University of California Press, 1993.

Cary J. Nederman

See also RENAISSANCE PHILOSOPHY OF LAW; ROMAN PHILOSOPHY OF LAW

Mens Rea

Mens rea (guilty mind) refers to the mental state which, when conjoined with an unlawful act, renders someone punishable as a criminal wrongdoer. There are several controversies concerning the meaning of mens rea and the role it plays in criminal liability. One concerns whether mens rea is a normative idea or a purely descriptive one. Another has to do with whether the mens rea requirement of criminal liability can be satisfied only by intentional wrongdoing or whether it may also be satisfied by egregious negligence measured against an objective standard of due care. A third dispute concerns whether mens rea is important only as constituting someone's moral responsibility for an unlawful outcome or whether it plays a dual role as a criterion of criminality (deciding whether the accused can be punished at all) and as a measure of responsibility for specific harms (deciding how much punishment he may legitimately suffer).

According to some, mens rea refers to whatever mental state positive law stipulates as a requirement of criminal liability. In this view, mens rea can mean intentional lawbreaking for one offense, recklessness for another, and negligence for a third, depending on what the law requires as a matter of fact. This view flows from legal positivism, for it assumes a dichotomy between a moral and a purely legal concept of a guilty mind, claiming that any normative content to the concept must be asserted from a private moral standpoint external to law as public fact.

The other view holds that mens rea refers to the very few mental states that satisfy the requirements of penal justice for punishing someone as a criminal. Proponents of this view may differ as to what the appropriate mental states are; but they agree that the legal concept of mens rea has a normative content, one that judges must read into penal statutes that are silent regarding a fault requirement, or demand from legislatures under constitutional norms of "due process" or "fundamental justice." Traditionally, the mental states thought to be requisite for criminal culpability have been variants of what is called subjective mens rea: an intention to do wrong; foresight of the high risk of doing wrong and indifference toward whether the wrong occurs; or willful blindness toward the possibility of one's committing a wrong. Recently, however, the subjectivist position has been assailed by those who argue that an egregious departure from the civil standard of care suffices for mens rea in the normative sense.

The subjectivist holds that one can legitimately be punished as a criminal only for knowingly violating someone's rights. Thus in this view the person who takes another's property believing it (however unreasonably) to be his own is not a criminal, nor is the person who sexually assaults someone in the negligently held belief that the victim consented. The subjectivist view is linked to a retributive theory of punishment. According to this theory, coercing A is legitimate only if A has willfully infringed someone's right, for only then has A given effect to a principle (the right to an unlimited liberty) whose universalization renders A's own right nonexistent. Punishment is justified only if logically implied by the denial of rights implicit in an intentional wrong, for only then is coercion authorized by the wrongdoer himself.

It would seem that, applied intransigently, subjectivism leads to the result that negligence-based liability is impermissible even for public welfare offenses (for example, pollution or selling alcohol to minors), a conclusion unflinchingly embraced by Jerome Hall, though it would render most regulatory laws ineffectual. Yet there is no logical imperative to generalize the subjectivist position in this way, for retributivism applies narrowly to transgressions against rights to spheres of personal sovereignty; it does not apply to breaches of public welfare statutes, which promote a common good rather than enforce individual rights and whose penalties are thus best understood as deterrents to harm-causing conduct.

Objectivists such as H.L.A. Hart hold that an egregious departure (by someone not unusually incapacitated) from the standard of care of the ordinary prudent person is a level of fault sufficiently serious to merit penal sanctions. In this view, the conscious choice of wrongdoing is only one way an agent might be responsible for an unlawful outcome. He is also responsible for failing to take reasonable care for another's safety, having had the capacity to do so. Hence it is not necessarily unjust to punish the unwitting wrongdoer. Because it identifies criminal liability with an agent's responsibility for a wrong, the objectivist view cannot logically stop at punishing egregious negligence. Ordinary negligence must be punished as criminal conduct as well, since the negligent lawbreaker may also be responsible for his omissions, and punishing him (albeit with less severity than the grossly negligent lawbreaker) may serve the social purposes of the law.

For the retributivist, mens rea performs a dual role in determining a person's liability to punishment. First, it establishes one's punishability as a criminal in the abstract, prescinding from the question of the appropriate measure of punishment. Thus, the willful invasion of a person's sovereignty over body or property (leaving aside any specific harm caused) renders one liable to punishment *simpliciter.* Second, mental orientation determines how much punishment the accused deserves. A fit measure of punishment depends on the type of harm the wrongdoer has caused (for instance, bodily harm or death) and on the degree to which that harm is imputable to his agency. If he intended the harm, then the harm belongs to his agency in the tightest possible sense, and so he deserves more punishment than if the harm had simply been foreseeable to someone of ordinary circumspection. In the retributivist view, accordingly, there is a distinction to be drawn between culpability for wrong (which requires subjective mens rea) and responsibility for harm (of which subjective mens rea is only the highest form). Correspondingly, there are two different ways in which a penal law might be unjust for want of the appropriate mens rea. It might (as in sexual assault with a mistaken belief in consent) impose criminal liability in the absence of intentional wrongdoing; or it might (as in constructive murder) punish the manslaughterer who did not but ought to have foreseen death with the same severity as the murderer who intended death.

The objectivist blurs the distinction between culpability for wrong and responsibility for harm. Since the only function of the mental element is to exclude from liability those not responsible for unlawful outcomes, imputability does double duty as both the criterion of punishability and as the variable to which punishment is calibrated. While this conflation of culpability and responsibility is innocuous in the sphere of regulatory offenses, it becomes problematic in the sphere of crimes. For in making agent-responsibility a sufficient condition for criminal liability, objectivism obliterates the distinction between the tortfeasor and the criminal and between moral blameworthiness and criminal guilt.

References

Duff, R.A. *Intention, Agency, and Criminal Liability.* Oxford: Blackwell, 1990.

Hall, Jerome. *General Principles of Criminal Law.* 2d ed. Indianapolis: Bobbs-Merrill, 1947.

Hart, H.L.A. *Punishment and Responsibility.* Oxford: Clarendon Press, 1968.

Hegel, G.W.F. *Philosophy of Right.* Trans. T.M. Knox. Oxford: Oxford University Press, 1967.

Stephen, Sir James. *A History of the Criminal Law of England.* Vol. 2. London: Macmillan, 1883.

Williams, Glanville. *The Mental Element in Crime.* Jerusalem: Magnes Press–Hebrew University, 1965.

Alan Brudner

See also INTENT; LIABILITY, CRIMINAL; RESPONSIBILITY

Mercy and Forgiveness

It is a matter of common knowledge that persons convicted of serious crimes sometimes ask for the court's mercy during a hearing pertaining to sentencing. What are they asking for? A lighter sentence, of course. Is a judge being asked to overlook the demands of justice in giving this lighter sentence? Does mercy have any place in institutions designed to do justice? Until fairly recently it was assumed that being merciful was one virtue among others that shape the decisions of an ideal judge. Recently this view has come under attack on grounds that a judge cannot be just and merciful at the same time. Here we will consider what we mean when we speak of mercy, what arguments have been used to deny that legal justice should be tempered with mercy, and how one might reply to these arguments. We will focus here on mercy, but the arguments can readily be translated into the language of "forgiveness."

Concept

What is mercy? (1) Is mercy in legal context one aspect of justice? No. Mercy provides a basis for treatment that is *not* demanded by justice. It involves reasons for more lenient treatment than one would otherwise receive. Mercy is related to forgiveness, though the latter (often) implies complete, as opposed to partial, removal of sanctions. (2) Would a judge who imposed a lighter sentence in order to prevent harm to persons *other* than the offender be acting with mercy? No. A judge must be motivated by sympathy or compassion *for the offender* in order to show mercy. Mercy makes its claims relative only to a judgment of guilt, a judgment that some form of hard treatment is deserved by a person. (3) Is it, as Claudia Card contends, one form of charity? Yes. Mercy is a type of charitable treatment. This third point connects with the first. If considerations of mercy are optional (relative to the rights of the offender), then they are unlike reasons of justice. An offender surely is entitled to just treatment and can *demand* it; but mercy is in some sense at the discretion of the judge, not something to which an offender has a right. We speak of the offender "pleading" for mercy, or using a related expression, putting oneself "at the mercy" of the court. Thus, it must be optional for the court to act on this plea; here is the connection with charity.

To summarize: in the legal context the claims of mercy can oppose and qualify the demands of justice as reasons for less severe (or more lenient) treatment. Compassion for the offender is the only type of reason for leniency that can qualify as mercy. Where it is truly a question of mercy, the considerations that motivate less severity do not give the offender a *right* to a lighter sentence.

Skepticism about Mercy

It has been argued that acts of mercy really involve only the *virtue* of avoiding injustice, for example, being precise in treating like cases alike, or they involve the *vice* of arbitrary treatment. In neither case is there anything that we can identify as a virtue that would temper the demands of justice. However, mercy, as it has been traditionally understood, provides a basis for just such a qualification.

Suppose A and B both committed planned and deliberate homicide. While A killed his victim in order to gain an inheritance, B acted in order to relieve great pain in a terminally ill patient who had pleaded for death. Surely it would be appropriate for the judge to accept B's plea for mercy and to give B a lighter sentence than A. However, this is not "real" mercy. These cases are sufficiently different that in doing justice a judge cannot treat them the same. B has a *right* to less severe treatment in a just system of law. From cases like these, the skeptical argument proceeds to others in which it might seem appropriate to invoke mercy in order to counter the demands of justice. Each *plausible* candidate for the category of mercy is then argued to be, not a qualification or detraction from the demands of strict justice, but precisely what justice requires.

Our account of the concept of mercy allows us to formulate the difficulty quite readily. Justice requires that like cases be treated alike. Treating like cases alike *excludes* the possibility that there are some features that are optional bases for lighter treatment. Suppose that M (some potentially mitigating factor) pertains to an individual offender and would incline a judge toward more lenient treatment. If M is relevant to the decision, then it must be considered. If the court takes M into account in any case, then it will be obliged to consider M whenever it is present. So avoiding injustice requires that there be no considerations which the judge can regard as optional—and that excludes mercy as it has traditionally been understood.

Defending Mercy

Is this skeptical attack on the virtue of mercy decisive? It has been argued that the skeptical attack oversimplifies the issues. Consider what is assumed about the point of punishing people. The above argument assumes that in asking for mercy one is asking for leniency relative to treatment that is in some sense deserved, that is, relative to some standard of justice. This seems sound enough. One does not ask for mercy, but demands justice, where one is only asking for the penalty that one actually deserves for an offense. The skeptical argument has assumed a retributivist view of criminal justice and assumed that the system cannot be justified in promoting any other values. However, legal reality may not be that simple. Legal systems also embody a standard of "public good" or utility as a part of their justificatory framework. Suppose there is good reason for thinking that under some set of circumstances the penalty deserved (because, for instance, it "fits" the offense) exceeds what can be justified on the basis of such public goods as deterrence and prevention. Suppose, for example, that a person has committed a crime for which the penalty is death, but it is discovered that the person is not dangerous and is dying of cancer. Should we rush to execute the person before this "natural" death occurs? Under such circumstances is there not room for mercy?

Utility will always provide some case (though often not a sufficient one) for the humanity which we display in releasing a person from a deserved punishment through an act of mercy or forgiveness. So, while it is true that justice itself does not provide a basis for such acts of mercy, legal systems need not be committed to the value of justice alone. Moreover, the skeptical arguments have assumed that the state has an obligation (not just a right) to exact the penalties from those who are convicted of crimes. However, as the example of the convict dying of cancer suggests, it is not obvious that we should accept this assumption.

In what sense, then, might legal forgiveness and mercy be *optional*? It is never true that the demands of justice require that a convict be released from punishment. However, unless we are prepared to accept a wholly retributive justification in which crime requires punishment, it may be within the discretion of a judge to reduce or omit the loss deserved by an offender. Within a framework that is not wholly retributivist we can accept mercy and forgiveness as among the virtues of a judge.

References

Brett, Nathan. "Mercy and Criminal Justice: A Plea for Mercy." *Canadian Journal of Law and Jurisprudence* 5 (1992), 81–94.

Card, Claudia. "On Mercy." *Philosophical Review* 43 (1972), 182–207.

Murphy, Jeffrie C. "Mercy and Legal Justice." In *Philosophy and Law,* ed. Jules Coleman and Ellen Frankel Paul, 1–14. Oxford: Blackwell, 1987.

Murphy, Jeffrie, and Jean Hampton. *Forgiveness and Mercy.* New York: Cambridge University Press, 1988.

Smart, Alwynne. "Mercy." In *The Philosophy of Punishment,* ed. H. Acton. New York: St. Martin's Press, 1969.

Twambley, P. "Mercy and Forgiveness." *Analysis* 36 (1976), 84–90.

Nathan Brett

See also Desert; Love; Retributive Rationale

Metanorms

Definition

Different terms ("empowering norms," "power-conferring norms," "norms of competence," "secondary rules," *Ermächtigungsnormen, Erzeugungsnormen, höhere Normen, normas de organización, norme sulla produzione giuridica, norme dinamico-strutturali)* are used to denote a variety of concepts of legal norms that share a common core: they are concerned with the identification of the criteria for legal [in]validity, they concern the definition for legal [in]validity of legal orders and of the norms of which a legal order consists.

A systematic analysis of the different, though related, legal phenomena depicted by these concepts of legal norms finds a fruitful point of departure in the concept of metanorms. By the term "metanorms" is here meant the set of norms which in a legal order are concerned with normative activities (for example, enactment, derogation, application, interpretation) and the set of norms which are about norms. To be more precise, the term "metanorms" is defined here as the set of norms in a legal order which concern the criteria for legal [in]validity of (1) legal acts (that is, acts whose [in]validity grounds the [in]validity of the norms they produce) and (2) legal norms which (as is the case with customary norms) are not the result of a/an [in]valid legal act.

Finding examples of the first kind of metanorms (that is, norms about normative activities) is not difficult. Legal orders have plenty of metanorms governing the ways in which norms can be given, modified, and repealed; in particular they abound in metanorms establishing what conditions are to be met for a legal act to be valid. In its turn, in spite of its apparent counterintuitive flavor, the notion of norms about norms can also be given a rich exemplification. Such, for example, are the norms defining what counts as a source of law, or establishing the hierarchy among the different sources of law; such also are the norms confining the range of validity for the norms of a legal order in temporal, spatial, and personal dimensions.

Contrary to the general attitude which assumes that all legal norms can be reduced to a unique standard type (typological monism), or at most to two main standard types, the one proper to norms and the other proper to metanorms (typological dualism), this definition implies the need to distinguish different types of metanorms. Metanorms can be distinguished according to the variety of their possible structure, function, and nature. In particular, with regard to their nature, metanorms can properly be distinguished into regulative and constitutive rules. Further, constitutive metanorms can be distinguished into different types following the typology of constitutive rules in terms of conditions.

Uneasiness of a Crucial Concept

The notion of metanorms might strike one as problematic because of its sharp departure from two long-lasting, shared legal theoretical assumptions, namely, (1) that every norm as such regulates an activity (some conduct, an instance of behavior), and (2) that every norm as such qualifies deontically the activity it regulates (the conduct, the instance of behavior) as obligatory, permitted, or forbidden.

Contrary to the first assumption, this definition of metanorms includes norms which concern norms (which are about the criteria for the legal [in]validity of norms) and thus, obviously, are about no activity at all.

Further, contrary to the second assumption, the definition of metanorms includes norms which cannot be accounted for in terms of deontic qualifications. This is obviously the case with the different types of metanorms identifying criteria of legal [in]validity of *norms*; it is also the case with most types of metanorms identifying criteria for the legal [in]validity of legal *acts*. In the former case metanorms are adeontic rules constituting [in]validity criteria for the norms of the legal order, while, in the latter, metanorms define the conditions to be met for a legal act to be [in]valid, rather than providing a deontic qualitication of its performance or forbearance.

Explanatory Scope

This concept of metanorms shows its heuristic richness by suggesting an original way to approach a variety of basic questions pertaining to different areas of legal theory, if not to solve those questions, such as (1) the theory of legal norms, (2) the theory of legal orders, (3) the theory of legal validity, and (4) the logical analysis of norms.

Moreover, and here lies its most significant merit, the concept of metanorms becomes a powerful conceptual tool for displaying the network of relations that hold among such a variety of questions peculiar to different moments of legal theory.

What does the identity criterion of a legal order amount to? When can a plurality of norms be viewed and conceived of as a legal order? What conceptual tools enable us to account for the dynamic character of legal orders? What sorts of norms are needed to account for the peculiar structure and features of legal orders? What criterion allows us to decide whether a norm is valid in a legal order? What criterion allows us to decide whether a norm is valid on its own? Such questions are but a few random examples of the basic legal issues to which the concept of metanorms provides the proper conceptual tool.

In particular, two theoretical issues in the law have already taken advantage of the concept. One has to do with the nonuniqueness of the notion of constitutive rules. Careful attention to the concept of metanorms is actually one of the main factors that promoted the elaboration of the typology of constitutive rules in terms of conditions.

The other concerns a critical review of the explanatory power of deontic calculi. Examining the pecularities in the concept of metanorms gives reasons to doubt the plausibility of interpreting formal calculi of deontic logic as calculi accounting for the logical behavior of norms that are organized into dynamic systems as legal norms are.

References

Aarnio, Aulis, and Neil MacCormick, eds. *Legal Reasoning*. 2 vols. Aldershot: Dartmouth, 1992.

Alchourrón, Carlos Eduardo, and Eugenio Bulygin. *Normative Systems*. Wien: Springer Verlag, 1971.
Gottlieb, Gidon. *The Logic of Choice*. London: Allen and Unwin, 1968.
Kelsen, Hans. "Recht und Logik" (Law and Logic). *Neues Forum* 12 (1965), 421–425, 495–500. Trans. "Law and Logic" in *Essays in Legal and Moral Philosophy,* ed. Hans Kelsen, 228–256. Dordrecht: Reidel, 1973.
Mazzarese, Tecla. "Metanorme. Rilievi su un concetto scomodo della teoria del diritto" (Metanorms. Remarks on a Difficult Concept in Legal Theory). In *Struttura e dinamico del sistemi giuridici,* ed. Paolo Comanducci and Riccardo Guastini, 125–156. Torino: Giappichelli, 1996.
Wasserstrom, Richard A. *The Judicial Decision: Toward a Theory of Legal Justification.* Stanford: Stanford University Press, 1961.
Wróblewski, Jerzy. *The Judicial Application of Law.* Ed. Zeno Bankowski and Neil MacCormick. Dordrecht: Reidel, 1992.
———. "Legal Syllogism and Rationality." *Rechtstheorie* 5 (1974), 33–46.

Tecla Mazzarese

See also HART, HERBERT LIONEL ADOLPHUS; NORMS; STANDARDS

Metaphor and Symbol

In the *Poetics* Aristotle defines metaphor as a rhetorical figure in which a name is transferred to another object. In the language of law, too, metaphor is a particular form of transposition between two semantic fields, where moving to another meaning does not imply giving up the original one, but creating a new perspective. In the legal process, metaphors are also a vehicle for symbolism, which expresses itself in rituals, and also in language through figures with symbolic character and aim.

Metaphor in Rhetoric

Aristotle's broad definition of metaphor follows four types of movements (from a genus to a species, from a species to a genus, from species to species, and for analogy). Aristotle gives pride of place to metaphor grounded on *analogy,* and it has often been limited to that. However, Aristotle also introduces *metonymy* (using one word in substitution for another according to a relation of contiguity, for example, as cause/effect, container/contained, instrument/operation, and so forth, as "bottle" for "wine," or "my word" for "my promise") and *synecdoche* (a type of metonymic transfer based on a relationship of extension, for example, part/whole, species/genus, singular/plural, as "sail" for "ship" or "mortal" for "man").

Analyzing the relation between metonymy and metaphor, Albert Henry claimed that, in metonymy, the two logically related terms on which the transfer acts are inside the same semic field while, in metaphor, the metonymic consideration occurs inside two different fields of meaning, with a final synthesis: hence metonymy is movement and metaphor is a dislocation, a continuous movement of meanings in several fields.

Metaphorical Cognition

The main characteristic of metaphor is cognitive. Aristotle notes that metaphor, like transposition of meaning and discovery of similarity, is a cognitive instrument. Through this cognition we can assimilate information and experience and adapt them to our conceptual organization of the world. M. Black, too, denies that metaphor is merely a decoration upon discourse and, developing J.A. Richard's 1936 analysis, introduces an *interaction* theory where the irreducible meaning and distinct cognitive content of metaphor is situated in a movement of transfer between two different domains of meaning, consciously selecting characteristics from them. E.G. Kittay develops this toward a *perspectival* theory: the relations governing a term's literal use are projected into a second domain that is thereby reordered with cognitive effect. Metaphor has an internal duplicity, the single expression of two distinct ideas.

D. Davidson criticizes this approach for the incoherence in its dualism: the idea of metaphorical meaning and the idea that metaphors have a special cognitive content are mistaken; metaphor is a legitimate device that denies the truth conditions in the utterance.

New Rhetoric in Philosophy of Law

For a long time academic philosophy rejected metaphor, accusing it of lacking scientific stature. However, some philosophers used metaphors and considered that abstract philosophical concepts were communicable only through metaphorical intuition. Since Friedrich Nietzsche's revaluation of the use of metaphor, its significance in philosophy has been emphasized by philosophers such as Stephan Pepper, who speaks about *root metaphors* as the original basic structure of every philosophy, Paul Ricoeur, who looks at every philosophy as the development of a *live metaphor,* and Philip Wheelright, who asserts its function of maintaining philosophy as an *open language.*

The main reappreciation of metaphor in philosophy of law came in the theory of argumentation of Chaïm Perelman and L. Olbrecht-Tyteca (1958, 1977). They restored Aristotle's rhetorical scheme and made metaphor one of the principal figures in the pragmatical persuasive aspect of argument. Discourses on topics such as law and politics permit disputes with arguments more or less plausible to achieve consensus and adhesion.

Perelman emphasizes metaphor's capacity to create presence: it can give immediate vision, moving from an abstract meaning to a concrete one. Not only is it convincing, because it is based on logical reasoning, but it also has an impact on the affective capacities.

Symbolism in Law

Departing from formal viewpoints upon law, metaphor's deep symbolic form can be observed, not explicit but perceivable in many expressions of the legal world. Metaphor's powerful effects on imagination and emotivity by its ambiguity, namely, the persuasive effect of its capacity to unify by "condensed analogy" according to Perelman, give to metaphor a distinctive symbolic aspect. By condensation, metaphor reduces the totality of aspects and becomes a symbol of some specific characteristics.

Antoine Garapon in *L'âne portant des reliques* describes legal symbolism well. Law's framework is constituted by the rituals, acts, and symbols which do not seem to have a direct utility in the legal proceedings but remain in the symbolic universe where law plays its main role. In this world the symbols are a privileged agency to confer authority on the discourses of law.

Cultural Semiotics

For losing their cognitive features and becoming the symbol for conventional characteristics, A.M. MacIver calls established metaphors *dead metaphors.* (These include catechresis: metaphor which originates in the need to name some unnamed entity, for example, the leg of a table, the foot of a mountain.)

But D.E. Cooper, instead of devaluing established metaphors, opposes only their supremacy. Metaphorical terms do not have to be evaluated according to either their true meaning or their metaphorical one, because their main function is *to cultivate intimacy* in the social sphere. Intimacy is based on an inexplicit common cultural code, which comes to efficacious understanding in the utterance. In order better to use the emotive aspects of metaphor, it is important to take account of the situation of its audience. Thus conventionality communicates a particular social image of reality. The ambiguity of metaphor, to U. Eco, is understood through an accurate semiotics of this culture.

Misunderstanding metaphor, in turn, is sometimes due to its violating social paradigms of acceptability; metaphor can challenge language norms and has to face the limits of practical acceptance. Norms for the acceptability of metaphors are pragmatically related to sociocultural taboos and limits (what we may say) and to intertextual models (what has already been said, and so can be said).

References

Black, M. *Models and Metaphor: Studies in Language and Philosophy.* Ithaca: Cornell University Press, 1962.

Cooper, D.E. *Metaphor.* Cambridge: Basil Blackwell, 1986.

Davidson, D. "What Metaphors Mean." In *Philosophical Perspectives on Metaphor,* ed. Mark Johnson. Minneapolis: Minnesota University Press, 1981.

Eco, U. *Semiotics and the Philosophy of Language.* Bloomington IN: Hackett, 1984.

Garapon, Antoine. *L'âne portant des reliques* (Mules Bearing Relics). Paris: Le Centurion, 1985.

Kittay, E.G. *Metaphor: Its Cognitive Force and Linguistic Structure.* Oxford: Clarendon Press, 1987.

Perelman, Chaïm. "Analogie et Metaphore" (Analogy and Metaphor). In *L'empire rhetorique: rhetorique et argumentation.* Paris: Librairie Philosophique J. Vrin, 1977.

Searle, J.R. "Metaphor." In *The Philosophy of Language,* ed. A.P. Martinich. London: Oxford University Press, 1979.

Shibles, W.A. *Metaphor: An Annotated Bibliography and History.* Whitewater WI: Language Press, 1971.

Monika Peruffo

Metaphysics

See ONTOLOGY, LEGAL (METAPHYSICS)

Military Philosophy of Law

From its origin in antiquity, military penal law has been more an instrument for maintaining discipline than providing justice. It has evolved independently of civil law and been shaped by the needs of military leaders and heads of state. Armed forces stand in uneasy relation to the societies that create them; they are isolated from civilian society yet remain under its influence. In the domain of military penal law, this simultaneous isolation and dependence is a source of controversy, since military law commonly reflects the liberal, monarchist, or marxist ethos of its parent societies but also accommodates the requirements of military life. The *Uniform Code of Military Justice,* adopted by Congress in 1950, is the foundation of U.S. military law. Flesh is given to its bones by the *Manual for Courts-Martial.* David A. Schlueter's *Military Criminal Justice: Practice and Procedure,* 3d edition, is the most authoritative guide to U.S. military law. Canadian military law is encapsuled in the *Queen's Regulations and Orders for the Canadian Forces.*

British-American military law has its origins in the articles of war promulgated by early British monarchs when armies were assembled and sent to battle. These articles initially remained in existence only for the duration of the conflicts that prompted them. Over the centuries, however, they were codified and became permanent. Courts-martial also evolved during this period, and specifications for their operation became part of the articles of war. Rebelling American colonists adopted contemporary British military penal law for their own armies, and the United States made no radical change in its British inheritance until it adopted the *Uniform Code of Military Justice.*

Whether in peace or at war, military endeavor requires a cohesive and tightly disciplined body capable of functioning under circumstances of extreme danger and confusion. Hence, the military is generally deemed to require instant and unquestioning obedience to command to preserve its unity and motivate ordinary human beings to face, and inflict, lethal violence.

The primacy of military discipline shapes military penal law in several ways. For relatively minor offenses military systems commonly rely on nonjudicial means whose primary purpose is reform rather than punishment. In keeping with this spirit, such methods are commonly employed in informal fashion by the commanding officers of the accused rather than trained legal officers. Sentences are often meted out in summary fashion, because strict military discipline is commonly thought to require punishment which is swift and sure.

A related facet of the requirement of discipline is a tendency to set aside concerns of justice in order to employ punishment as a deterrent to others. Hence, during World War II, the United States Army executed a single soldier who deserted during the Battle of the Bulge, Pvt. Eddie Slovak. General Dwight Eisenhower confirmed his death sentence on grounds that Slovak's execution would deter other desertions.

In the twentieth century, the independence of military law from civil law and its primary function as an instrument of discipline wielded by commanders have come under keen scrutiny. Some have urged that the system of military law should mirror its parent society's civil codes and vouchsafe the impartial trials and protection of individual rights commonly enjoyed by citizens. Others have insisted that military necessity, understood as the requirement of strict discipline and control, continues to demand that military law remain strictly independent of civilian control and remain a tool of discipline wielded by commanders.

For example, during much of its history, the military law of the United States was markedly different from civilian law. Courts-martial were often perfunctory hearings administered by officers with scant legal training. They contained little provision for appeal of decisions and few of the legal protections of the accused that are cornerstones of U.S. civilian law. The rationale most commonly offered for this system was, as usual, that military discipline demands quick, decisive judgment and punishment.

Following some thirty years of controversy, the U.S. military legal system was extensively overhauled shortly after World War II. With the enactment of the *Uniform Code of Military Justice* it came to resemble civilian law more closely and provided more of the protections citizens enjoy, though it remains independent of civilian law. Two arguments helped propel the transformation. One is that, in an era of mass, conscript armies, soldiers are also citizens and should enjoy the full range of rights and protections of other citizens, *precisely because* they endure substantial hardship on behalf of the larger society. Legal codes that functioned satisfactorily in an era of small, professional armies with few ties to civilian society, it was claimed, are no longer adequate to new conditions. A second assertion is that military discipline will be strengthened rather than weakened if soldiers are convinced that they are guaranteed the justice and fairness that their civilian peers enjoy.

However, even if soldiers remain citizens, their circumstances differ enormously from persons outside military ranks. Most important, military forces, whether in peace or at war, continue to require strict obedience and expend considerable effort to drill it into soldiers. In past years ordinary soldiers were generally not held accountable for acts performed under orders. Until World War II, U.S. soldiers could not be punished for acts performed by command. This resulted in some dismay once national leaders recognized that many of those on trial at Nuremberg claimed exculpation on grounds that *they* were obeying orders. In response the U.S. legal military code was hastily amended to stipulate that soldiers must disobey obviously illegal or immoral commands. Considerable embarrassment remains, however, for ordinary soldiers are not trained in military law and thus cannot confidently judge which orders are illegal. Moreover, military forces remain organizations that require strict obedience. Soldiers trained for instant discipline cannot seriously be expected to calmly assess their orders and disobey those which are illegal or immoral.

Nonetheless, the general trend of the twentieth century is for military law to increasingly resemble civilian law by incorporating greater procedural safeguards for those accused of misdeeds and by offering a broader array of rights for all in uniform. However, military necessity is still accommodated in as much as informal judicial procedures remain in force and the habit of strict obedience continues to be instilled.

Another feature of this century is the expanding importance of international law. International law, in its guise of the law of war, incorporates standards of conduct for all military forces and stipulates that individual soldiers be held accountable for their acts, whether under orders or otherwise. It is quite probable that individual nations will eventually adjust their military penal law to reflect international influence.

References

Canadian Department of National Defence. *Queen's Regulations and Orders for the Canadian Forces.* Rev. ed. 1968.

Generous, William T., Jr. *Swords and Scales: The Development of the Uniform Code of Military Justice.* Port Washington NY: Kennikat Press, 1973.

Keen, Maurice H. *The Laws of War in the Late Middle Ages.* London: Routledge and Kegan Paul, 1965. Reprint, Hampshire UK: Gregg Revivals, 1993.

Schlueter, David. *Military Criminal Justice: Practice and Procedure.* 3d ed. Charlottesville VA: Michie, 1992.

Shanor, Charles A., and Timothy P. Terrell. *Military Law.* St. Paul MN: West, 1980.

United States Department of Defense. *Manual for Courts-Martial.* 1984.

Gerard A. Elfstrom

See also CONSCIENTIOUS OBJECTION; REBELLION; REVOLUTION; WAR AND WAR TRIALS

Minority, Ethnic, and Group Rights

Rights have always been used to protect minorities, be they the kings and landowners of old or the members of religious and ethnic groups in the modern era. In recent decades the international community, often under the stewardship of the United Nations, has pressed for the entrenchment of human rights as the primary means to protect minorities from injustice and discrimination. These rights range from freedom of religion to freedom from hunger and the right of labor to collective bargaining. They are universal and individual rights, belonging to every human being equally.

For the more than five thousand ethnocultural minorities around the globe, however, these sorts of human rights alone are often thought to be insufficient. They demand rights not merely as human beings, but as groups and as members of groups which feel threatened within the societies in which they find themselves. This is true even in prosperous liberal-democratic states.

Group Rights and the Liberal Tradition

The postwar emphasis on human rights arose out of a liberal-democratic tradition that has systematically ignored the question of group rights. Most of the classic texts in political philosophy, from Plato to John Rawls, have presupposed an ethnically homogeneous polity. More than 90 percent of states today, however, contain significant ethnocultural minorities, and the issues which often dominate their political agendas simply do not arise in the model case. Consider the following.

Liberal theorists have produced elaborate justifications for rights to freedom of expression and universal education, but little has been written about which languages should be permitted in the public institutions of multilingual states. We are familiar with general defenses of democracy, but not with principles to determine how to fix the substate boundaries within a pluralistic political community and how to distribute powers within a federal system. How do we settle disputes about the relevant "self" in principles of self-determination and self-government? Liberals believe in freedom of movement, but what principles should guide a just immigration policy, and what demands for integration can a host society place upon its immigrants? Issues such as these seem to fall outside of the scope of a human rights approach to justice.

Kinds of Rights Demanded by Ethnocultural Communities

There is such a wide variety of rights and kinds of rights demanded by minority cultures that it would be unwise to make generalizations about their justifiability. Some are rights which would inhere in the group itself and take priority over individual rights. Others are individual rights to the conditions necessary to protect cultures. Some are demands to protect a culture from external pressures, while others are demands to allow a minority group the right to restrict the options of its own members. Some rights would have the effect of enabling a community to separate itself from the larger society, while others are intended to help the members of the group integrate themselves within that society.

When thinking about minority rights it is helpful to distinguish two general sorts of minority groups. First, there are national minorities, whose homeland had been incorporated into a larger state, usually without their consent. Second, there are immigrant minorities who have chosen to leave their homeland to settle in another state. (Some refugee communities may constitute a special category.) With this distinction in mind we can fit most demands for group rights into the following three categories.

Self-Government Rights

These are demands for political autonomy on behalf of national minorities, ranging from veto rights against central authorities to the delegation of powers to substate governments in which the minorities form a majority. At the extreme, self-government rights are used to justify secession.

Multicultural Rights

These are demands for financial support and legal protection for certain practices associated with particular ethnic or religious groups. These rights are typically demanded by immigrant groups, and in most cases they are intended to help such groups to integrate into the larger society on equal terms with members of the majority (for example, by allowing them to substitute religious holidays).

Special Representation Rights

These are demands for guaranteed representation of ethnic or national minority groups within the central institutions (parliament, supreme court, civil service, military, and so on) of the larger state. Such rights are intended to rectify systematic discrimination against, or underrepresentation of, the members of identifiable minority groups.

Cultural Membership, Autonomy, and Equality

Demands for minority rights have often been resisted by liberal-democratic theorists because they are seen as violating basic principles of freedom and equality. For example, few liberal states would be willing to offer religious minorities complete control over the education of their young. However, many philosophers now believe that a wide variety of cultural rights can be justified by extending traditional liberal arguments. In certain situations, for instance, affording special representation rights to a group may be the best way to meet the democratic requirement of political equality or the equal representation of interests. Similarly, many accommodations under the heading of multicultural rights—concerning, among other things, religious holidays, or exemptions from military dress codes for members of religious groups with conflicting dress codes—seem to be natural extensions of a liberal commitment to toleration.

Perhaps the boldest case for extending liberal principles to establish group rights of all three kinds is the cultural membership argument. It begins with liberal commitments to autonomy and self-respect and then notes that neither of these is possible for individuals without a healthy cultural context in which a wide range of choices is available. Therefore, if liberals believe in autonomy, they must be willing to give some threatened communities the means to protect their cultural context when it is under threat from the larger society. Viewed in this way, collective rights can be seen as enhancing, rather than conflicting with, individual rights and freedoms.

A similar argument for extending the role of minority languages in education and public life turns largely on liberal commitments to equality. The basic idea here is that languages in the modern world cannot survive if they are not used in public life; if minority languages die out, or if their native speakers are forced to have to communicate in the language of the majority, then these individuals will be unfairly disadvantaged in the economic and cultural marketplace. This argument, like the cultural membership argument, is presumed to be applicable primarily to national minorities, insofar as immigrants voluntarily chose to leave the more secure cultural context of their homeland.

Despite the widespread assumption that ethnocultural loyalties would fade with modernization, they have exhibited surprising resilience and remain matters of intense debate in pluralistic societies. Democratic experiments in postcolonial Africa and Asia, as well as recent developments in eastern Europe, demonstrate that resolving these issues fairly will be crucial if democratizing states are to be successful.

References

Baker, Judith, ed. *Group Rights*. Toronto: University of Toronto Press, 1994.

Kymlicka, Will. *Multicultural Citizenship: A Liberal Theory of Minority Rights*. Oxford: Clarendon Press, 1995.

Stapleton, Julia, ed. *Group Rights*. Bristol: Thoemmes, 1995.

Wayne Norman

See also Aboriginal Legal Cultures; Asylum and Refugees; Autonomy; Human Rights; Nation and Nationalism; Secession; Self-Determination, Personal

Mistake and Ignorance

One of the notoriously thorny problems in criminal law theory is determining the exculpatory or inculpatory effect, if any, of an actor not fully appreciating the circumstances or legal effect of his conduct. Ignorance implies a blank mind about the relevant aspect; mistake entails an incorrect affirmative belief. The distinction may be more formal than useful, however, since most cases of ignorance involve the mistaken belief that a state of affairs did not pertain (hereafter mistake will include ignorance as well). Mistake may also be distinguished from accident: one who shoots at a tree, but the ricocheting bullet kills a person, kills by accident; one who shoots at a person believing her to be a tree kills by mistake. Whereas inculpatory mistakes (which are outside the scope of this entry) involve the actor's beliefs being criminal but the facts innocent, exculpatory mistakes entail the facts being criminal but the actor's beliefs innocent.

The typical approach to determining whether a mistake will successfully exculpate is to classify it as to type (law or fact), what the mistake is about (for example, elements of the definition of the offense, a justification or an excuse), and whether the mistake is reasonable or unreasonable. This classificatory scheme is challenged both by philosophers who claim that the rationale for exculpating some mistakes also serves to exculpate all mistakes and by legal commentators who propound that all mistakes should be disregarded. Nearly all concede the practical difficulties of satisfactory line drawing.

Perhaps the more fundamental question is why any mistake should ever have exculpatory force. The criminal law proscribes various harms. Yet only those harms which are committed with the requisite mental state or culpability results in criminal liability—this is the standard actus reus plus mens rea formula. Even if an actor technically satisfies the definition of a criminal offense, his conduct may not be sufficiently blameworthy for punishment. A successful claim of mistake severs the inference from harmful conduct to criminal liability by denying culpability or blameworthiness. The extent to which mistakes are recognized is testament to the importance of desert as a value in criminal law. Another justification, advanced by Jeremy Bentham, is that punishing mistaken actors is pointless, since the purpose of criminal law, deterring crime, cannot be given effect because mistaken actors are, by definition, incapable of being deterred. H.L.A. Hart responded that though punishing mistaken actors does not serve specific deterrence it nonetheless enhances general deterrence—the general public will be more careful not to mistakenly engage in criminal wrongdoing. Other consequentialist arguments for disregarding mistakes include maintaining the integrity of the law. Jerome Hall claimed that allowing mistakes of law would subvert the objective nature of law required by the principle of legality—the law would become whatever one subjectively thought it to be. George Fletcher has demonstrated that recognizing mistakes fails to alter the objective nature of law. It is also claimed that allowing mistakes to exculpate will encourage sham defenses involving willful ignorance and deliberate mistakes. Moreover, the evidentiary difficulties of delving into the mind of the defendant, as William Blackstone noted in regard to mens rea, to ascertain whether a mistake is honest or dishonest is too onerous for any judge or jury. Yet, as Douglas Husak contends, this is precisely the task required in determinations of mens rea. The fate of mistakes in the criminal law is tied to the importance of mens rea and may be viewed as resting in the balance between the colliding principles of desert, justice, and fairness on one hand and consequentialist concerns on the other.

Mistake of Law

Traditionally, the hallowed adage *ignoratia juris non excusat* (ignorance of the law is no excuse) held sway. As originally applied, the principle was understandable, since the criminal law was simple and criminal offenses few—one could scarcely claim ignorance that murder or theft was wrong. With the multiplication of crimes and promulgation of offenses that prohibit conduct not intuitively criminal, a number of exceptions have been carved out of the traditional rule. A mistake has been recognized when an offense is so obscure as to fail to put the violator on "fair notice." Reliance on an official statement of law that turns out to be erroneous is widely excused, but reasonable reliance on unofficial declarations of law, even that of an expert lawyer, is not recognized. The policy consideration that criminals could opinion-shop among lawyers for advice that would immunize obviously wrongful conduct apparently outweighs arguments that reasonable reliance on statements of law, whatever the source, renders actors equally blameless. Even an unreasonable mistake of law will generate an excuse if it negates the specific intent of an offense, but a reasonable mistake involving a general intent offense will not exculpate. For example, if larceny is defined as intentionally taking the property of another and because of a mistake about property law the actor believes the property to be his, then the mistake will exculpate. Yet if larceny only has the general intent of intentionally taking property, the same mistake will not be recognized. Strict liability offenses typically do not recognize mistakes.

Mistake of Fact

Similarly to mistakes of law, a mistake of fact will exculpate if the requisite mens rea of an offense is negated. Unlike mistake of law, a mistake of fact will excuse a general intent offense but only if the mistake is reasonable, free of fault, or nonculpable. The requirement of reasonableness is also prompted by consequentialist, evidentiary concerns over disproving dishonest mistakes. Whereas some contend that a mistake must be objectively reasonable, that is, whether a hypothetical reasonable person would have made the same mistake, others claim that it need only be subjectively reasonable—judging reasonableness from the limited perspective of the actor asserting the mistake. Substantial disagreement also persists over whether factual mistakes regarding justificatory circumstances constitute justifications or excuses. One commentator has argued that a logical paradox ensues unless such mistakes are justifications.

In *D.P.P. v. Morgan,* 2 All E.R. 347 (1975), which encapsulates the profound confusion surrounding mistake, a husband lied to several men that his wife would enjoy forcible sex with them. These men then had intercourse with her, the wife resisted, and they were charged with rape. If rape requires a specific intent to rape an unconsenting person, then any mistake would exculpate; if it merely requires a general intent to forcibly have intercourse, only a reasonable mistake would excuse. If consent was instead conceived of as a justification, a reasonable mistake would either justify or excuse, depending on the theory of justification applied; an unreasonable mistake would either justify, excuse, or fail to exculpate.

References

Alexander, Larry. "Inculpatory and Exculpatory Mistakes and the Fact/Law Distinction: An Essay in Memory of Myke Bayles." *Law and Philosophy* 22 (1993), 53–66.

Christopher, Russell. "Mistake of Fact in the Objective Theory of Justification: Do Two Rights Make Two Wrongs Make Two Rights . . . ?" *Journal of Criminal Law and Criminology* 85 (1994), 295–332.

Dressler, Joshua. *Understanding Criminal Law.* New York: Matthew Bender, 1987; 2d ed., 1995.

Fletcher, George. *Rethinking Criminal Law.* Boston: Little, Brown, 1978.

Greenawalt, Kent. "The Perplexing Borders of Justification and Excuse." *Columbia Law Review* 84 (1984), 1897–1927.

Husak, Douglas. *Philosophy of Criminal Law.* Totowa NJ: Rowman and Littlefield, 1987.

Robinson, Paul. *Criminal Law Defenses.* St. Paul MN: West, 1984.

Sendor, Benjamin. "Mistakes of Fact: A Study in the Structure of Criminal Conduct." *Wake Forest Law Review* 25 (1990), 707–782.

Russell L. Christopher

See also DEFENSES; MENS REA

Mixed Rationales

Mixed theories of punishment attempt to justify it by a combination of utilitarian and retributive considerations, rather than solely in terms of one or the other.

Through most of its history, the philosophy of punishment displayed a seemingly irreconcilable opposition between the two main approaches. It appeared that punishment had to be justified either by backward-looking consideration of justice and desert, or by forward-looking considerations of social utility. Both theories, however, were found by their respective critics to have serious flaws: while retributivism ignored such a basic social aim of punishment as crime prevention, utilitarianism was committed to pursuing it in clearly unjust ways, for example, by punishing the innocent or by meting out disproportionately harsh punishments. Since the 1920s, there have been several attempts at an account that would include the partial truth of each theory, while avoiding the exaggerations and mistakes of both: an account that would accommodate the moral significance of the past *and* the requirements of the future, the demands of justice *and* those of the common good.

Each of these theories is based on a distinction claimed to be of crucial importance and to have been ignored in the preceding debates: (1) between the meaning of the word "punishment" and the justification of what it stands for, or (2) between the end and the means in punishing, or (3) between the institution and particular cases of punishment.

1. A.M. Quinton's point of departure is the first of these distinctions; his main thesis is that retributivism is an answer to the question of the meaning of "punishment," while utilitarianism provides the justification of punishment. Thus the two theories are no longer mutually exclusive, but rather complementary, as they belong to different levels of discourse. Quinton argues that the main thesis of retributivism is that a person must be guilty if he or she is to be punished, which is a logical, rather than an ethical claim, contained in the utilitarian theory of punishment by virtue of its being a theory of *punishment.* By the same token, the latter cannot be criticized for justifying punishment of the innocent, when that is expedient, since the innocent *logically* cannot be punished.

2. A.C. Ewing attempts to reconcile the two theories by arguing that the main aim of punishment is to convey society's emphatic moral condemnation of crime to that part of the public which is in need of such a lesson in morality (and in this way help prevent crimes). He claims that, unlike deterrence, this aim can only be attained if punishment is just, that is, meted out to the guilty and in proportion to

the severity of their crimes. Justice in punishment is thus a necessary means for the achievement of the end of punishment; unjust punishments are of no use for achieving Ewing's preferred aim of punishment and therefore cannot be justified.

3. Rule utilitarianism proposes to justify the institution or practice of punishment by its aim, which is crime control. However, the rules of the institution are such as a retributivist would choose (only the guilty are to be punished, and punishments should be proportionate to crimes), not on account of any intrinsic moral weight of justice and desert, but because such rules have greatest acceptance-utility. Particular punishments are justified by reference to these rules, that is, in retributive terms. The legislator goes by utilitarian, the judge by retributive considerations.

The debates have shown that none of these compromises succeed. When justice and desert are brought in as mere semantics (Quinton) or as moral, but purely instrumental considerations (Ewing, rule utilitarianism), they prove much too weak to preclude the types of injustice that compromise traditional utilitarian theories. Deliberate punishment of the innocent is indeed logically impossible, but "punishment" of the innocent is not; the public can be educated about the immorality of crime by merely apparent justice, as well as by justice that is actually carried out; a judge would have no good *utilitarian* reason to stick to the rule that only the guilty are to be punished in exceptional cases where breaking it would have best consequences. All these compromises collapse back into unqualified utilitarianism.

Like rule utilitarianism, H.L.A. Hart's widely influential mixed theory is based on the distinction between the institution and particular cases of punishment. The institution is justified by its "general justifying aim" (which is deterrence), while the distribution of punishment is determined partly by considerations of deterrence and partly by those of justice. Liability to punishment is solely a matter of justice: only the guilty may be punished. The severity of punishment is a function both of deterrent efficiency and economy, as well as the demand of justice that deterrence be not pursued by disproportionately severe punishments. However, unlike rule utilitarianism, Hart does not introduce these retributive additions to a basically utilitarian account because of their acceptance-utility, but rather as *autonomous* moral considerations that *constrain* the pursuit of utility. Therefore his theory, unlike the others, does preclude such injustice as "punishment" of the innocent and disproportionately severe punishments. It also provides a stable combination of the two main approaches to punishment, rather than collapsing back into unqualified utilitarianism under the strain of criticism.

Hart's theory has been criticized for adopting only the negative, limiting side of justice and desert (negative retributivism), while being oblivious to their positive import (positive retributivism). Justice and desert determine only the liability to punishment and the upper limit of its severity, while the decision whether those liable to be punished should indeed be punished and the establishment of the lower limit of the severity of punishments are determined solely by considerations of deterrence. The theory would therefore justify nonpunishment of the guilty in cases where considerations of deterrence do not apply and disproportionately lenient punishments when, despite their lenience, they are efficient enough as the means of deterrence. Hart is alive to the force of the former objection, at least in cases of the most serious crimes; he grants that "even the most reflective" of those who supported the punishments meted out at Nuremberg held that justice demanded that the guilty be punished, and not that those punishments were justified by their expected deterrent effects.

C.L. Ten's mixed theory is similar to Hart's and tries to accommodate this criticism by introducing considerations of comparative justice. Some of the "expressive" theories of punishment could also be seen as "mixed."

References

Ewing, A.C. *The Morality of Punishment.* London: Kegan Paul, Trench, Trubner, 1929. Reprint, Montclair NJ: Patterson-Smith, 1970.

Hart, H.L.A. *Punishment and Responsibility.* Oxford: Clarendon Press, 1968.

Primoratz, Igor. "The Middle Way." In *Justifying Legal Punishment.* Atlantic Highlands NJ: Humanities Press International, 1997.

Quinton, A.M. "On Punishment." *Analysis* 14 (1953/54), 512–517. Reprinted in *The Philosophy of Punishment,* ed. H.B. Acton. London: Macmillan, 1969.

Rawls, John. "Two Concepts of Rules." *Philosophical Review* 64 (1955), 3–32. Reprinted in *Theories of Ethics,* ed. Philippa Foot. Oxford: Oxford University Press, 1967.
Ten, C.L. *Crime, Guilt, and Punishment.* Oxford: Clarendon Press, 1987.

Igor Primoratz

See also DETERRENT RATIONALE; EXPRESSIVE RATIONALE FOR PUNISHMENT; RETRIBUTIVE RATIONALE

Mobility Rights

The rights of individuals to travel and remain may conflict with other individual rights and with the public good, and efforts to resolve these conflicts appeal to our deepest moral convictions. Some significant limitations on mobility rights may facilitate this resolution.

In the broadest sense, "mobility rights" refers both to the right to travel or remain and the right to change social status. The latter right is mainly congruent with the right to acquire property in cultures where property confers status, but other standards apply with formal castes or classes. This essay concerns the geographical or horizontal right rather than the vertical social mobility right.

This mobility right falls under the umbrella of autonomy rights, which include the rights of freedom of speech (including reading), assembly, and religion. The term "freedom" indicates this idea of autonomy, of self-management. When people invoke autonomy rights, they claim the right to choose what to say, where and when to meet, and what religion to believe. Of course, typically none of these rights is absolute, so that some speech and literature, some assemblies, and some religions are forbidden. Supporters of these moral rights hope that the law will suitably embody them. The law may also regulate these rights, but a friendly regulation seeks to preserve and enhance the entire ensemble of moral rights.

Many other rights, especially property rights, typically trump mobility rights. If we suppose a society where all land is private property, owners might post "No Trespassing" signs on their properties. If everyone did so, then an owner would have a right to move about only on his or her own land, but those without land would have to leave the territory of the society entirely. Of course, owners would likely find it useful to enter some mutual arrangements for wider travel and to grant permission to some nonowners to stay to work, or mobility rights may have enough weight to guarantee other owners, at least, access and transit. If we add publicly owned properties and government to administer them, then the weight of mobility rights would seem to be sufficient to guarantee some access and transit on this public land. Furthermore, mobility rights may require that governments provide adequate public thoroughfares through limitations on property rights or by the acquisition of land.

The 1948 United Nations Universal Declaration of Human Rights, Article 13, Section 1, claims that "everyone has the right to freedom of movement and residence within the borders of each state." However, some nation-states have denied its citizens this internal mobility right. South Africa, after mid-century until the late 1980s, required black native Africans to carry permits or passes showing what areas the holder was entitled to enter. The pass laws were intended to move labor to needed areas and to protect white-only areas from nonwhite migration. The establishment of native "homelands" gave the national government the means to assign natives to homeland areas and to restrict their movement elsewhere. Another example of the infringement of mobility rights is in the Soviet Union during the same years. Internal passports showed the permitted residence of the holder. These laws attempting to control movement were less sweeping than in South Africa and, in general, not very effective.

Governments typically impede the mobility of noncitizens by forbidding or limiting immigration. However, the U.N. Declaration, Article 13, Section 2, recognizes the right to emigrate: "Everyone has the right to leave any country, including his own, but other nations have no duty to admit emigrants." This lack of symmetry between the rights of emigration and immigration constitutes a severe restriction on mobility rights. However, given a labor surplus, transportation costs, and problems of cultural adjustment, it seems that the right of workers to live anywhere on the planet is not an optimal solution to global unemployment. On the other hand, the very wealthy thrive on worldwide mobility, since many nations welcome them as immigrants.

Given the lack of a right to immigrate, nations are free to use utilitarian arguments that limit immigration in the name of the public good. Where strong individual rights are recognized, the public good cannot easily outweigh them (the whole point of such rights is to protect the individual from majority interest or opinion). Thus, while a stronger individual right, such as a property right, outweighs a conflicting weaker individual mobility right, even this weaker individual right has priority over considerations of the public good except in extreme situations. However, if an individual is guilty of a crime, then his or her mobility rights are, in the view of John Locke, subject to a forfeiture that opens the way for both consequentialist and retributive rationales for shackles, jail, house arrest, deportation, and exile, which limit mobility rights either by confinement or by forced movement to another place, or both.

Will Kymlicka, in *Liberalism, Community and Culture,* argues that native reservations or territories in Canada may properly limit mobility and other rights of citizens of the wider nation-state to preserve the autonomy rights of the natives. If outsiders moving in destroy native culture, then many native individuals will become dysfunctional, unable to exercise autonomy. One crucial way to prevent this tragedy is to designate native territories as nonalienable: tribal property cannot be sold or divided into privately held parcels that individuals can then sell to anyone, including outsiders. The tribe may then exercise property rights to limit the residency and mobility of outsiders. What is unique to Kymlicka's argument is that these limitations of mobility rights exist not for the sake of the culture or the good of the group but for the rights of individuals. His argument can be applied elsewhere, for example to ethnic groups in the former Soviet Union.

While Kymlicka stringently limits such restrictions on mobility and other liberal rights to cases where natives meeting certain historical qualifications also have their own language, his basic argument can be extended to citizens at large who may be disabled by loss of job, home, and way of life. For example, if every citizen were assigned to a group owning a nonalienable tract of land, then no one would be homeless. Any mobility right of citizens to sleep on the sidewalks of cities could be ended, and the property rights of the collectively held land could limit the mobility right of outsiders.

Issues of immigration and emigration, as well as Kymlicka's argument for restriction of mobility rights for the sake of individual autonomy rights, indicate that mobility rights are important rights relevant to crucial moral issues.

References

Kerblay, Basile. *Modern Soviet Society.* Trans. Rupert Swyer. New York: Pantheon Books, 1983.

Kymlicka, Will. *Liberalism, Community and Culture.* Oxford: Oxford University Press, 1989.

Omond, Roger. *The Apartheid Handbook.* 2d ed. Harmondsworth: Penguin Books, 1986.

Pankhurst, Jerry G., and Michael Paul Sacks, eds. *Contemporary Soviet Society.* New York: Praeger, 1980.

Shlapentokh, Vladimir. *Public and Private Life of the Soviet People.* New York: Oxford University Press, 1989.

Edmund Abegg

See also Asylum and Refugees

Monetary Power

Under both municipal and international law, *jus cudendae monetae* (the right to coin money, that is, to create money in defined units of account and to regulate its use) is a basic attribute of sovereignty. The monetary power is conceptually complex and has a tortuous history of social development and legal interpretation.

Money

The *substantial form* can range from salt to silver coins to paper money to bank deposits in electronic form that record financial rights and obligations. Most money today is *fiat money,* created by decree or by the fractional reserve banking system. Money is best understood *functionally*: it is used (1) as a standard unit of account to express *prices* (exchange ratios), (2) as a trusted medium of exchange consisting of some standard commodity or *currency* (coins and paper money), (3) as a store of value that is a *liquid* (readily realizable and exchangeable) asset, and (4) as legal tender for purchases and payment of taxes and deferred debts. These functions are separable and produce different ideas of what money is.

The liquidity aspect of money causes disputes about how to measure the *quantity* of money and hence to controversies about policies that affect *interest rates*, the value of money. Basic money, M1, is the sum of coins and paper currency in circulation plus demand deposits in banks. Other measures (M2, M3, . . .) are used, for example, M2 consists of M1 plus savings deposits. Liquidity is a matter of degree, and the increasing sophistication and differentiation of monetary instruments make less determinate an agreed and simple measure of the money supply. There is also a question as to what extent *velocity* (the rate of circulation) should be considered in determining monetary aggregates.

Most of the contemporary money supply has been created by the modern *fractional reserve banking system*. Essentially, this involves private banks taking in deposits and, relying on the hope that not all depositors will demand their money back in the short term, lending that money to others. Some money is held in reserve to meet the immediate demands of depositors, but most is lent out at interest to (and deposited in the accounts of) borrowers. The deposits of borrowers are an additional part of M1, and therefore money has been created.

Power

The *de jure power* over money is the right of the state to decide the rights, obligations, no-rights, and freedoms of its subjects regarding money–such as the right of banks to create money, the obligation to pay taxes in legal tender, the no-right to hold gold privately, the freedom to buy foreign currencies. However, this legal power is a nullity unless backed by *de facto norms* (habits, expectations, confidence in financial institutions) at work in a civil society. The two kinds of norms, de jure and de facto, interact. They can and have diverged, especially in times of hyperinflation and other crises.

The monetary power is exercised through *central banks* (for example, Bank of England 1694, Bank of France 1800, U.S. Federal Reserve System 1913). Central banks typically are charged with two main responsibilities that uneasily coexist: to maintain price stability and to maintain conditions (such as the availability of credit) conducive to growth and prosperity. They do this by monopolizing the creation of currency (thus acquiring *seigneurage*, profits from this creation), by setting bank reserves, and by acting as a lender of last resort for banks. In modern practice they fine-tune money supply and interest rates through a system of open market operations. For example, they buy and sell financial instruments (for instance, treasury bills, foreign currencies) and set interest rates on overnight loans to commercial banks.

Philosophical Issues

Given that there are deferred debts, general *inflation* or *deflation* (rising or falling price levels) are important because they can have profound effects on the distribution of income and wealth. Inflation favors debtors, deflation creditors. On the other hand, mere price stability may leave a stagnant economy, underused resources, and high unemployment.

The exercise of the monetary power and the resultant tradeoffs in the creation and distribution of wealth may have grave social and political consequences. If there is a policy conflict between a government and its central bank, which may be a bank of some independence, which institution should prevail? Whether by direct constitutional provision, legal interpretation, or power of appointment, governments have tended to prevail. Similarly, in federal states, the central government, rather than component provinces or states, has tended to monopolize the monetary power.

There is an ongoing dispute, partly technical and partly ideological, about the creation and distribution of wealth: on one hand are those (for example, keynesians) who would use the monetary and fiscal powers of the government to influence this creation and distribution, and on the other hand are those (for example, monetarists) who would rely mainly on market forces. The exercise of both monetary and fiscal powers is severely limited by factors in international trade, investments, loans, and currency flows.

Current Problems

With the breakdown of the 1944 Bretton Woods Agreement (with its pegged rather than floating exchange rates, the International Monetary Fund for stability, and the World Bank for development) and the end of the gold standard in the 1970s, the world is in the throes of vast changes in monetary and financial powers.

Legal systems have been hard pressed to keep up with (1) the merging of formerly separately regulated institutions (banks of deposit, merchant banks, investment dealers, stockbrokers, trust companies, and insurance agencies); (2) the *securitization* of liabilities and assets (for instance, mortgages held by banks may be bundled into investment instruments and shares in them sold to others, thus transferring the risk from banks to those holders); (3) the creation of *derivatives* (financial contracts whose value derives from an underlying security such as commodities, stocks, bonds, currencies, or even index numbers) for hedging and speculative purposes; (4) the use of automatic, computerized trading programs; and (5) the electronic interlocking of global monetary, investment, and commodity exchanges and markets. The sums involved are huge—in April 1995 the world *notional* (underlying) value of derivatives was US$40.7 trillion—and can affect the ability of individual central banks to achieve their assigned goals.

With increased interdependence, complexity, and instability at the international level, there are disputes about whether the impersonal forces of the market or interventionist institutions should determine the world money supply, exchange rates, and so forth. Is there a need for a *hegemon* (a superpower or an independent world bank) to override national governments, or will multilateral agreements suffice to ensure prosperity and stability in world financial markets? De facto, world central bankers, meeting at the semi-autonomous Bank for International Settlements in Basle, have acted in concert to avert a series of potential catastrophes (for example, the OPEC oil price shock, the developing countries' debt crisis, the inflation of the U.S. dollar, the 1987 stock market crash).

Thus, instead of a regime of sovereign states using municipal law to exercise monetary power, we now have, in effect, a regime of "loose" international law—semi-independent bankers exercising on global markets ill-defined monetary powers and moral suasion. It seems likely that we face the need for new legal, economic, and philosophical ideas about the power to create and distribute money—and thus national and international legal rights and obligations regarding the real wealth it represents.

References

Gold, Joseph. *Legal and Institutional Aspects of the International Monetary System: Selected Essays.* Washington DC: International Monetary Fund, 1979.

Mann, F.A. *The Legal Aspects of Money: With Special Reference to Comparative Private and Public International Law.* Oxford: Clarendon Press, 1982.

Nussbaum, Arthur. *Money in the Law, National and International.* Brooklyn NY: Foundation Press, 1950.

Shuster, Milan Robert. *The Public International Law of Money.* Oxford: Clarendon Press, 1973.

Solomon, Steven. *The Confidence Game.* New York: Simon & Schuster, 1995.

Walter, Andrew. *World Power and World Money: The Role of Hegemony and International Monetary Order.* New York: Harvester Wheatsheaf, 1991.

Jack T. Stevenson

Montaigne, Michel de (1533–1592)

Michel de Montaigne, Gascon jurist, mayor, and advisor to kings, was one of the most influential of the legal skeptics. His legal philosophy was interwoven in his *Essays* (1580, revised 1588, further revised and posthumously published in 1595), one of the most widely read books in the French language, which was quickly translated into many foreign languages and has been reprinted frequently.

Montaigne belonged to the first generation to rediscover the writings of the ancient Greek skeptic Sextus Empiricus, after the publication of Latin translations of his work in 1562 and 1569. He pushed Sextus's critiques of knowledge and of the lawyers of his day even further, especially in "Apology for Raymond Sebond" and the last three essays of Book 3 of the *Essays.*

Montaigne's view of the legal process was quite negative. There is "nothing so grossly and widely and ordinarily faulty as the laws." He served for thirteen years as a member of the Parlement de Bordeaux, which had civil and criminal jurisdiction in southwestern France, so he knew whereof he spoke. The "lawyers and judges of our time find enough angles for all cases to arrange them any way they please." The result is not justice: "How many innocent people have we found to have been punished . . . ? How many condemnations have I seen more criminal than the crime?" Montaigne's personal attitude toward the law was to avoid the courts since "there is no remedy" for their faults.

One of Montaigne's many skeptical attacks on the law was to emphasize the variety of different laws in different times and places: "What am I to make of a virtue that I saw in credit yesterday, that will be discredited tomorrow, and that becomes a crime on the other side of the river?" Another was to point to problems with legal language: "Why is it that our common language, so easy for any other use, becomes obscure and unintelligible in contracts and wills . . . ?" That led him to the contradictions of legal interpreters: "It is more of a job to interpret the interpretations than to interpret the things." Rather than helping, "glosses increase doubts and ignorance . . . so many interpretations disperse the truth and shatter it."

The general point of departure for Montaigne's legal skepticism was our human inability to know anything for certain. He was an early opponent of witch trials, for how can we really know who is and who is not a witch? This made him a critic of capital punishment: "To kill men, we should have sharp and luminous evidence," and we do not. We cannot even trust confessions. After all, "persons have sometimes been known to accuse themselves of having killed people who were found to be alive and healthy."

In spite of all of this criticism, Montaigne opposed revolutionary change and could not even bring himself to recommend a grand reform program. How could one know that such a program would not cause more harm than good? Rather, he reminded his readers that usually the best way to live is in accord with established laws and customs, no matter how faulty, simply because they provide a bit of stability in a chaotic world. He supported the Catholic side in the Wars of Religion and served as mayor of Bordeaux and advisor to the kings of his times, chiefly recommending small reforms and opposing cruelty.

Montaigne's individualism distinguished his position from that of the absolutists of the time, such as Jean Bodin. He claimed an inner independence from politics with such phrases as "The mayor and Montaigne have always been two." His loyalty to church and state was only outward: "[P]ublic society has nothing to do with our thoughts." He lived by his own moral standard: "[S]ome things [are] illicit even against the enemy . . . not all things are permissible for an honourable man in the service of his king, or of the common cause, or of the laws."

Montaigne also opposed legal torture, the class bias of the law as practiced, and legal formalism that leads to unnecessary suffering. He was a fierce critic of theories of natural law. He opposed Niccoló Machiavelli and Giovanni Botero on "reason of state." He had no confidence in the rule of law as a panacea, but his individualism, his debunking of the grander claims of the law and of the absolute state, and his fundamental sense of fairness, probably led, through writers such as Pierre Charron and Jean-Jacques Rousseau, toward the modern liberal understanding of the law.

References

Collins, Robert. "Montaigne's Rejection of Reason of State in 'De l'utile et de l'honneste.'" *Sixteenth Century Journal* 23 (1992), 71–94.

Friedrich, Hugo. *Montaigne.* Berkeley: University of California Press, 1991.

Laursen, John Christian. *The Politics of Skepticism in the Ancients, Montaigne, Hume, and Kant.* Leiden: E.J. Brill, 1992.

Montaigne, Michel de. *The Complete Essays of Montaigne.* Trans. Donald Frame. Stanford: Stanford University Press, 1958.

Nakam, Géralde. *Les Essais de Montaigne: Miroir et procès de leur temps* (The Essays of Montaigne, Mirror and Trial of Their Times). Paris: Nizet, 1984.

John Christian Laursen

Montesquieu, Baron de, Charles de Secondat (1689–1755)

Montesquieu is known for contributing two legal concepts to legal theory in his main work, *De l'esprit des lois* (1748): the doctrine of the separation of powers in government, or *trias politica,* and the famous metaphor characterizing the role of the judiciary as one of those powers: the judge as *la bouche de la loi,* as the mouthpiece of the law. Although not considered a revolutionary thinker in his lifetime—according to W. Voisé, "trop moderne pour les Anciens, et trop conservateur pour les Modernes (too modern for the old, and too conservative for the new)"—his discussion of the types of government, with its comparison of the monarchy and the republic, paved the way for critical thought that led to the French Revolution by the turn of the century. On the eve of the American Revolution, his work was studied carefully by later authors of the constitution, such as James Madison.

Montesquieu knew the work of both legislator and judge from his own experience.

Born Charles de Secondat, later Baron de Montesquieu, he inherited the function of judge for life in the Parlement de Bordeaux and was active for several years in legislative matters and as a judge.

A striking feature of Montesquieu's approach to the concept of government is his method. The way in which rule is exercised is decisive in the characterization of a government. The complex of political and social bodies and institutions which support a government are an intrinsic part of that type of government. Montesquieu's interest in such conditions of government as climate, temperament, family structure, commerce, religion, and legal history makes him a sociologist *avant la lettre* (before the name was used). In our era, Emile Durkheim and Raymond Aron have given him credit for this sociological view of government, replacing the more traditional study of political right.

This view was based on extensive travels in several European countries. Montesquieu lived in England for two years (1729–1730), where he attended sessions of Parliament and was a member of the Royal Society. To Montesquieu, English society proved to be an additional model of government, besides the three archetypes of monarchy, despotism, and republic: a type of government that has political liberty as an end. In his perception, liberty is a result of the separation of powers, and his greatest concern was to have the three powers checked by counterpowers, with help from the spirit of the law.

The separation of powers was an idea developed by Thomas Hobbes, John Locke, and James Harrington, with whose work Montesquieu was well acquainted. His personal contributions were to add the role of the judiciary alongside the legislative and the executive powers and to secure liberty from that legal triangle by a balance among their powers, a system of checks and balances. Montesquieu's model of the separation of powers should not be seen as a dogma; its social substructure and the exceptions it requires are far more important than the structure itself.

In his sociological approach, the spirit of the laws has to do with "the various relations which the laws can have with various things," such as climate, religion, economy, size of the country, manners, and customs. This concept of law, it must be noted, cannot be taken solely as the statutory law established by the king (*loi*), but has a much wider sense (*droit*): "The law in general is human reason, so far as it governs all peoples of the earth, and the public and civil laws of each nation can be only particular instances in which this human reason applies." The spirit of the laws, as a legal concept, is a universal and unifying principle. It is linked to law in its appearance as positive law, but also to natural elements mingled with political and even divine components, in Montesquieu's observation of society in action. Guided by the spirit of the law, the judge may be seen as the mouthpiece of human reason. This is far from the traditional view of the metaphor, depicting the judge as *l'organe, en quelque façon machinal, de la loi* (the machine-like loudspeaker of the law), according to François Gény, as the *juge-automate* or, as it is phrased in English and American jurisprudence, the "mechanical view of the proper role of the judges."

Montesquieu was familiar with the mouth-of-law metaphor in English law, "which makes the King to be a speaking law, and the Law a dumbe king," as written by James I, in *The trew law of Free Monarchies* in 1598. Montesquieu implicitly approved the opinion of Lord Chief Justice Edward Coke in his conflict with King James and Archbishop Bancroft, in *Calvin's case* (1608) over the jurisdiction of common law courts and ecclesial courts, where he replaced the judge into the position of the "speaking law," thereby displacing the king.

In France the metaphor was also used in the seventeenth century in the struggle between the nobility and the king. Montesquieu places their relation into the chain of lawmakers under the dominion of time. The judge in *parlement,* as a slave of the law, is free in the name of the law. He wrote: "It is the parlement that knows all the laws made by all the kings, their outcomes, and their spirit. It would know if a new law improves or corrupts the vast whole of the others, and it says: this is how things are, this is where you must begin, this is how you will harm the whole if you don't."

This is the nonmechanical sense in which the metaphor was known on both sides of the Channel, dating back to Roman times in Cicero's statement, *magistratum legem esse loquentem* (the judge is the law actively speaking) from *De legibus* (On the Laws), the judge is the speaking law. It became a dead metaphor only after the French Revolution, with the development of legal positivism in Europe, and its kantian dichotomies.

References

Cohler, A.M., B.C. Miller, and H.S. Stone. *Montesquieu, The Spirit of the Laws.* Cambridge: Cambridge University Press, 1989.

Gardies, J.L. "La structure logique de la loi" (The Logical Structure of the Law). *Archives du philosophie du droit* (1980).

Montesquieu, Charles de Secondat Baron de. *Considerations on the Causes of the Greatness of the Romans and Their Decline.* Trans. David Lowenthal. New York: Free Press, 1965.

———. *The Spirit of the Laws.* Ed. David Wallace Carrithers from the first English edition. Trans. Thomas Nugent (1899). Berkeley: University of California Press, 1977.

Neumann, F. "Introduction." In *The Spirit of the Laws,* trans. Thomas Nugent (1947). 2d ed. New York: Hafner, 1957. Republished as "Montesquieu" in *The Democratic and Authoritarian State: Essays in Political and Legal Theory.* Glencoe NY: Free Press, 1957.

Richter, M. *The Political Theory of Montesquieu.* Cambridge: Cambridge University Press, 1977.

Schoenfeld, K.M. *Montesquieu en "la bouche de la loi."* Thesis. University of Leyden, 1979.

van Dunné, J.M. "Montesquieu Revisited. The Balance of Power Between the Legislature and the Judiciary in a National-International Context." *Rechtstheorie* 15 (1993), 451 (*Law, Justice and the State, Proceedings,* IVR World Congress, Reykjavik, 1993).

Vile, M.J.C. *Constitutionalism and the Separation of Powers.* Oxford: Clarendon Press, 1967.

Voisé, W. *La réflexion présociologique d'Erasme à Montesquieu.* Warsaw: Polska Akademia Nauk, 1977.

Jan M. van Dunné

Morality and Law

According to John Austin's version of legal positivism, laws have much in common with the orders of a gangster given at gunpoint. Just as we are obliged to comply with such orders, in a perfectly ordinary sense of the term "oblige," Austin claims that our obligation to comply with the law is of the same coercive kind. Critics of positivism—natural lawyers and others—disagree. They claim that legal obligations have their source in morality, and that, as a consequence, moral argument not only provides law with its normative force, but also plays a constitutive role in fixing the law's content. This disagreement between positivists and their critics may seem profound, but on closer inspection the disagreement seems to all but disappear.

Austin's version of positivism was very simple. He thought of law as a system of orders issued by a sovereign, backed by threats of punishment, where he thought of a sovereign, in turn, as someone whose orders are habitually obeyed but who does not habitually obey orders that are issued by anyone else. Given this conception of law it follows that the substantive morality of a legal system is fixed by whether the sovereign's orders are substantively moral in their content. Since there is no necessity that the sovereign even decides which orders to issue on moral grounds, it follows that this is an entirely contingent matter. Moral argument plays no constitutive role in determining the content of law because the law's content is fixed instead by a nonmoral fact, a fact about the content of the orders issued by the sovereign.

In the 1960s H.L.A. Hart, himself also a positivist, pointed out that Austin's version of legal positivism is vulnerable to a serious line of criticism, however. The criticism is significant not just because it leads to a revision of positivism, but also because it leads to a modification of the claim that law and morality are strictly separate. It is a datum, one which any adequate conception of law must explain, that laws are capable of persisting over time and, in particular, between the time that one sovereign stops ruling and another begins to rule. A habit of obedience to a sovereign goes out of existence with the exit of that very sovereign. A new habit takes time to develop. Austin's idea that law is a pattern of habitual obedience to a sovereign thus suggests, falsely, that there must be radical discontinuities in the law between the rule of successive sovereigns. It therefore fails to account for the continuity of law across the reign of successive sovereigns.

In order to account for such continuity Hart argued that we need to introduce a completely new element. We need to think of law not as a pattern of habitual obedience to a sovereign but rather as a set of social rules which specify, inter alia, the ways in which the power to make rules is to be transferred from one party to another. Social rules are like habits in being regularities in behavior, but they differ from mere habits in that, for a social rule to exist, enough people in the society whose behavior conforms to the pattern must suppose that there is good reason for everyone to behave in the way in question. Deviation from such a regularity is thus taken to deserve criticism, unlike departure from a mere habit. In this sense, law is essentially a normative enterprise.

Indeed, Hart thought that we could be more precise about the systems of social rules that comprise law, for he thought that all such systems comprise a union of what he called "primary" and "secondary" rules. Primary rules are rules of permission and obligation, rules which tell people how they are permitted or required to behave in various situations. Secondary rules are rules about rules. They include rules of adjudication and change that specify when, how, and by whom rules are to be administered and how and by whom rules may be changed. Most important, the secondary rules also include a rule of recognition, a master rule specifying the properties possessed by all of the other rules if they are to count as valid rules of the system. According to Hart, the master rule of recognition is constituted by a regularity in the behavior of a special subgroup of the society: the officials of the system such as lawmakers, judges, legal advocates, police, and the like. Since their behavior undergirds the existence of the regularities *as rules,* Hart claims that it is the officials, at the very least, who must suppose that there is good reason for people to behave in accordance with these regularities. It is thus the officials who must suppose that deviation merits criticism.

The idea that law is a system of social rules of the kind described allows us to account for the continuity of law across the reign of successive sovereigns. Continuity is possible because there may be regularities in the way people behave, which ground a form of criticism, even when the power to make new social rules is transferred from one party to another. These regularities, and the criticism they ground, will themselves constitute the rules which specify the ways in which such power is legitimately transferred. In other words, they will constitute rules granting *rights* of succession.

Moreover, once we see law as a system of social rules rather than a set of habits of obedience, we see that Austin's version of positivism was mistaken in a more fundamental way as well, for the existence of law does not require the existence of a lawmaker in the form of a sovereign: that is, someone who issues, but does not in turn obey, orders. Rather, those who make laws, thereby causing there to be regularities in behavior, may themselves be required to obey the very laws they make. Given that in representative democracies there do not seem to be people who are above the law in the way in which Austin supposes a sovereign to be, this is a distinct advantage of Hart's version of positivism over Austin's, for representative democracies most certainly have legal systems.

Hart thus argues for a significant revision in our understanding of legal positivism. Moreover the revision forces us to rethink the relationship between law and morality in important, and potentially radical, ways. As we have seen, Hart's theory tells us that the existence of the social rules that comprise the law requires that enough people in the society, and the officials of the system in particular, comply with the law voluntarily. For this to be so the law must be such that it is at least possible for people to act voluntarily in accordance with it. It therefore follows that laws, in order to be laws at all, must have certain very general features, at least by and large: they must be well publicized, prospective, clear, noncontradictory, relatively stable, and so on. However, as Lon Fuller points out, these features are remarkable precisely because they are themselves morally desirable. It would be unjust if people could be prosecuted for noncompliance with rules with which they were unable to comply because the rules were badly publicized, retroactive, unclear, contradictory, or changed so quickly that keeping track of them was impossible. Even according to positivism, then, the law has, and has of necessity, an "inner morality." The separation of law and morality is thus not as strict as Austin suggested.

Though Hart agreed with this conclusion, he thought that his version of positivism still had much in common with Austin's. This is because the mere existence of a set of social rules, even rules with which people can voluntarily comply if they so wish, does not guarantee all by itself the substantive *morality* of people's behavior in accordance with those rules. Such behavior, and so such rules, may still be unjust, or harmful, or in some other way immoral. Moreover, Hart argued that it remains the case, even in his version of legal positivism, that moral argument has no constitutive role to play in determining the content of law. As with Austin's theory the content of law is still fixed by nonmoral facts: facts about regularities in the behavior of a social group and the attitudes toward these regularities had by certain people within that group. Hart therefore thought that, in a relatively straightforward sense, law and morality are still separate in much the way Austin had said.

Whether Hart was right about this is, however, far from clear. The problem lies in the fact that, for Hart, the officials of the system must have certain attitudes toward the law: they must think that there is good reason both for themselves and for others to comply with the rules; they must believe that those who deviate rightly deserve criticism. What sort of criticism is deviation from the law supposed to legitimate? What is the ground of the normativity of law supposed to be?

One answer, Hart's own, is that this question has no single answer. This is because the sort of criticism involved will mirror the nature of the reasons the officials have for compliance with the rules, and, as far as Hart is concerned, there is no significant restriction on the sorts of reasons officials can have. Thus, at one extreme—and perhaps this is the typical situation in most modern democracies—the officials of the system may have moral reasons for obeying the rules of the system. They may think that acting in accordance with the rules, and so enforcing them, is morally required. At the other extreme—and perhaps this has only ever been the case in societies in which a governing elite who care for each other, but not for the rest, pass laws restricting the access of the rest of the society to opportunities and resources—the officials of the system may have purely self-interested reasons for obeying the rules of the system. They may think that the flourishing of those who they deeply care about, those in the governing elite, simply depends on everyone's acting in accordance with the rules. This may be their only reason for obeying, and so for enforcing, the rules of the system. They may give no thought to the substantive morality of their acts, or even think them immoral.

Many of Hart's critics argue that this answer is inadequate, however. As they see things, the officials of the system must have moral reasons for complying with the rules, because if officials had merely self-interested reasons for complying, then they would be unable to appeal to these reasons by way of criticism of those who deviate—the mere fact that a deviant's complying with the rules is in accordance with a judge's interests is hardly a criticism of the deviant, after all. The reasons officials have for obeying the rules, in order to be reasons that ground *criticism* of those who deviate, must therefore be reasons that those who deviate from the rules can share. The only reasons capable of playing this role are moral reasons. If the law has normative content, then that content must derive from morality, or so these critics argue.

If Hart's critics are right, then it follows that the connection between law and morality is even tighter than Hart thought. Because the existence of law is, inter alia, a matter that is fixed by the contents of the moral beliefs of the officials of the system, it follows that, even according to Hart's version of legal positivism, moral argument does indeed play a constitutive role in determining the content of law. Those who fix the content of law, the officials of the system, have no choice but to engage in moral argument. Moreover, since the officials themselves should have true moral beliefs, it follows that there is no longer such a clear line to be drawn between what the law is and what it morally ought to be.

Suppose that there are certain regularities in the behavior of a social group, regularities in behavior that are believed morally correct by the officials in that group; suppose also that we outside observers of that group believe their behavior is morally incorrect. Suppose further that we are in a position to construct an argument for this conclusion, an argument that would show that certain other behaviors in the community are morally required instead. Given that the officials of the group decide what the law is by deciding what morally ought to be the case, it follows that we must suppose not just that the officials of the system have false beliefs, but also that they have available to them an argument that they should find convincing for the alternative views that we have. We must therefore suppose that the officials of the system are mistaken in the moral reasoning that led them to formulate the law, and that this is something they could come to appreciate. Moreover, if they did, then we must suppose that they would have to change their minds and conclude that the law is really quite different from the way they currently believe it to be.

In this way of seeing things, the difference between legal positivism and natural law is thus very small indeed, perhaps vanishingly small. However, whether or not Hart's critics are right to insist that we see things in this way is a difficult matter to decide. Everything turns on whether we should call the system described earlier in which the officials act voluntarily in accordance with certain rules, though for purely self-interested reasons that nonofficials of the system cannot share, a "legal system." If so, then Austin and Hart are right that laws need not even purport to have a moral foundation. Questions like these are extremely difficult to answer, precisely because the term "legal system" becomes vague at just the point that we need precision if we are to give an unequivocal answer.

Even if we decide that they are right, however, we should immediately go on to insist that the natural lawyers are right about something as well. In the vast majority of legal systems, perhaps all those that we encounter these days, the rules are indeed thought to be morally justifiable by those who administer them. In this vast majority of cases, then, legal reasoning is inextricably bound up with moral reasoning in much the way that natural lawyers insist.

References

Austin, John. *The Province of Jurisprudence Determined.* 5th ed., 1885 ed. Robert Campbell. Intro. by H.L.A. Hart. London: Weidenfeld and Nicolson, 1954.

Dworkin, Ronald. *Law's Empire.* Cambridge MA: Harvard University Press, 1986.

Finnis, John. *Natural Law and Natural Rights.* Oxford: Clarendon Press, 1980

Fuller, Lon. *The Morality of Law.* New Haven: Yale University Press, 1969.

George, Robert P. *Natural Law Theory: Contemporary Essays.* Oxford: Clarendon Press, 1992.

Goldsworthy, Jeffrey. "The Self-Destruction of Legal Positivism." *Oxford Journal of Legal Studies* 10 (1990), 449–486.

Hart, H.L.A. *The Concept of Law.* Oxford: Clarendon Press, 1961.

Raz, Joseph. *The Concept of a Legal System.* Oxford: Oxford University Press, 1980.

Shiner, Roger. *Norm and Nature: The Movements of Legal Thought.* Oxford: Clarendon Press, 1992.

Michael Smith

See also NATURAL LAW; POSITIVISM, LEGAL

Mortgage

See SECONDARY RIGHTS

Murder

See HOMICIDE

Myth

See SAGAS, ICELANDIC

N

Nation and Nationalism

Nation, as a homeland comprising a community (one or more ethnic groups) and a territory, and nationalism, as the ideology that focuses on the nation as a major moral and political agent, are not legal concepts. These terms are not used by the law, and there is no law on the nation nor on nationalism. The normative discourse on the nation takes place on the moral and political level, but nations' claims in law are nonexistent, since "nation" is not a legal institution. The term "national" is used, especially in the context of inter- or supranational legal systems, in order to denote a "relationship to the state." In contrast with other Western languages (German: *staatlich,* French: *étatique,* Spanish: *estatal,* Italian: *statale*), English has no ordinary language adjective derived from the noun "state," and therefore "national" is used. The only legal fields where any resemblance to the term "nation" is to be found are, first, the law of "nationality," which regulates the condition for recognizing an individual as having the legal status of belonging to and falling within the jurisdiction of a state, and second, "international law," a term that originates in the classical natural law authors on the law of nations, but which is really a law between states. Where international law recognizes collective agents other than the state, for example, the right to self-determination, it refers to peoples and not to nations.

Several legal terms are connected to the concepts of nation and nationalism: the state, sovereignty, and the elements of statehood (territory, population, and administration), the parts of the state (regions, autonomous communities, provinces, states of a federation, cantons, and so on), and associations entered into by the state (international and supranational arrangements). Indirectly, several legal issues are also related to the term "nation" and to nationalist ideology: citizenship and nationality, official languages, educational and cultural policy, human rights, minority rights, popular and proportional representation, territorial autonomy, and so forth.

Legal discourse often treats "nation" as a synonym of "state," the latter being the proper legal term. This can be explained by reference to the dominant fallacy that identifies nation and state: the ideology of the nation-state or the *État-nation.* If such identification were correct, it would be inconceivable to speak of multinational or plurinational States (for example, the United Kingdom or Spain) or of stateless nations (for example, Scotland or the Basque Country) or even of nations established in two or more states (the German nation before reunification).

Nationalism has not been a fashionable topic in jurisprudence and practical philosophy, but since the late 1980s there has been growing interest most probably linked to the explosion of many forms of dormant nationalism and to the many cases of instantiation of the principle of self-determination following the dismantling of the Soviet block. The fact that prominent moral and political philosophers such as Jürgen Habermas and Alasdair MacIntyre have written about patriotism has also encouraged other philosophers to follow suit. Topics such as communitarianism, citizenship, patriotism, national identity, nation building, universalism, civil society and civic culture, self-determination, minorities' rights, and so on, are now on the practical philosopher's agenda.

Discourses on the nation can be of various types: historical, sociological, anthropological, political, philosophical. Some of these can, again, be descriptive or normative. Philosophical approaches to the nation as an institutional reality typically consider both descriptive (is) and normative (ought) issues.

The first set of questions is descriptive of sociopolitical reality. Any theory on nationalism will have to provide criteria (constitutive rules) for the definition and/or identification of the nation. The preliminary problem to tackle will be whether it is meaningful to talk of nations at all or whether nations are shams or figments of a collective imagination. On one hand, there is talk of nations at all levels and the status of nationhood is often affirmed or alternatively denied to entities that make claims to nationhood, and these claims are presumably dealt with on the assumption that criteria on the definition of the nation are available. On the other hand, the fact that it is so often impossible to find agreement on the boundaries of a nation or even on the recognition of a given entity as a nation seems to indicate that nations are not as clear-cut as, for instance, states.

Once the institutional existence of nations is recognized, the ensuing questions will inquire about the different criteria for identifying and distinguishing nations. A provisional classification would sort out objective, subjective, and reconstructive definitions of the nation. Objective definitions would try to capture a nation's essence by means of some "observable" or "evident" traits. These can be physiological, genetic, or psychological features, as well as language, dialect, history, territory, environment, location, art, music, dance, folklore, customs and traditions, laws, social organization, material conditions of existence, and ways of life. Such approaches often lead to the exclusion of minorities that do not share such features. Subjective or volitional definitions focus on the will and self-identification of the members of a nation, regardless of objective features. These theories can lead to drastic results, depending on how the will of the members is measured and how minorities are treated. Reconstructive approaches combine both criteria: the will and self-definition of the members will elaborate on certain objective features but will allow for difference and pluralism to become a characteristic feature of the nation. These theories conflate with liberalism, but at the cost of becoming rather thin. (See *Liberal Nationalism* by Yael Tamir for the best attempt.)

Once the nation is identified and constituted, nationalist theories will provide consequential rules that govern the normative relations between the nation and the nationals on one hand, and the relationships between different nations on the other.

Depending on how different nationalisms reply to questions—such as How far should the nation respect individual diversity? Should priority be given to good nationals? What are the duties of the national toward the nation? What are the duties of the nation toward the national?—one will be able to distinguish between radical or extreme nationalisms (where absolute priority is given to the nation) and liberal or minimal nationalisms (where priority is given to individual rights).

Depending on how normative theories address issues like the respect for other nations, (non)interference in other nations' affairs, protectionism, assistance, "cultural cooperation," international dispute resolution, diplomatic relations, and so on, one will be able to distinguish between imperialistic nationalisms (where priority is given to the interests of the nation) and solidary, cosmopolitan nationalisms (where the emphasis is on international cooperation and supranational arrangements).

Liberal critics question the possibility or desirability of distinguishing between nationalisms and suggest abandoning the concept altogether. Another distinction between nationalist theories derives from the relationship of nation and state. Nations that lack a state of their own claim their right to statehood through the exercise of self-determination, secession, and the constitution of a new state. This right is often denied by established states, which deploy a different form of nationalism in defense of their interests in international or supranational settings. The development of the European Union seems to offer an interesting alternative to both internal and external forms of nationalism in its quest for a truly supranational system.

References

Karlsson, M. et al., eds. *Law, Justice and the State. Rechtstheorie* 15 (1993).

Schulze, Hagen. *Staat und Nation in der europäischen Geschichte* (State and Nation

in European History). München: Springer, 1994.
Smith, Anthony. *The Ethnic Origins of Nations*. Oxford: B. Blackwell, 1992.
State and Nation. 15 *IUSEF*, Oslo. Oxford: Centre for European Law, 1995.
Tamir, Yael. *Liberal Nationalism*. Princeton: Princeton University Press, 1993.
Twining, W., ed. *Issues of Self Determination*. Aberdeen: Aberdeen University Press, 1991.

Joxerramon Bengoetxea

See also SECESSION; SELF-DETERMINATION, NATIONAL

Native Philosophy of Law

See ABORIGINAL LEGAL CULTURES

Natural Justice

Natural justice is a concept originating in English common law that embraces a number of precepts governing procedural and substantive elements of legal decision making. Natural justice (and its terminological variants—due process, procedural fairness, fundamental justice) is typically invoked by judges as a standard of censure by which the exercise of legal authority may be evaluated against moral principles thought either necessarily implied or self-evidently given by the institutional character of the legal power in issue and the scope and impact of the decision being taken.

Historically, courts held the natural justice standard to be applicable to the exercise of public authority (state action) as well as private right. They also did not distinguish between substantive and procedural usages of the concept. More recently, however, natural justice tends to be raised predominantly in contexts involving administrative agencies and other statutory decision makers, and only occasionally to review the activity of consensual and domestic tribunals. Natural justice has, moreover, acquired primarily a procedural connotation such that it is unusual to find the expression deployed as a nonprocedural standard without a qualifying adjective: hence, "substantive natural justice," and its analogous expressions "substantive due process" and "substantive procedural fairness."

As a substantive standard, natural justice was initially invoked, invariably in combination with other formulae such as "equity," "common sense," and "good conscience," as a justification for restraining the exercise of both private power (for example, the principle that a mortgagor ought not to be deprived of an equity of redemption without notice) and public power (for example, the principle of no expropriation without compensation). In these substantive usages, the concept was little more than a convenient cover for the judicial invention of principles of public policy or the judicial imposition of subjective moral choices.

The contemporary reluctance of courts to control the substance of legal decision making by invoking natural justice may be attributed in part to their development of a richer vocabulary of censure—residing both in implied common law and in constitutional standards. These standards have also enabled courts to specify the content of substantive natural justice by importing terminology with procedural overtones into their decisions invalidating decisions of public authorities. Today, doctrines such as proportionality, least intrusive intervention, equal sharing of the burden of public works, no absolute criminal liability, and so on, are among the common manifestations of substantive natural justice.

Throughout its history natural justice has most often been given a procedural content. In this usage it may be understood as comprising a particular instantiation of two complementary features of any decision-making process: the quality of the participation that should be afforded to persons affected by a decision and the kinds of reasons that properly may be offered in support of the decision that results.

As a procedural concept, natural justice originated in the early seventeenth century as a description of two maxims by which the Court of King's Bench sought by means of the writ of *certiorari* to control the procedure by which legal (typically statutory) authority was exercised. Certiorari would issue from the Court to quash decisions of "inferior tribunals" for breach of the rules of natural justice. These were said to be two: *audi alteram partem* (let the other side be heard) and *nemo iudex in causa sua debet esse* (let no person be a judge in his or her own case). Because the writ of certiorari issued only when the decision maker was performing a function broadly analogous to that of a court, these two rules soon became enshrined as elementary principles of adjudication.

The first rule, directed to the obligation of a decision maker to provide an opportunity to persons affected by a decision to make representations, has been developed over the years to comprehend a number of specific obligations. These include the right to adequate advance notice of the specific issues of fact and law to be decided; the right to a remand or adjournment; the right to counsel in the presentation of proofs and arguments; the right to call and examine witnesses and to cross-examine witnesses; the right to produce documents and to refute other documents; the right to a hearing in an open forum.

The second rule, directed to ensuring the integrity of decision making, requires that the decision maker be free from bias. Classically this has meant that the decision maker have no pecuniary interest, however small, in the outcome; that the decision maker have no relationship with any of the parties such as might give rise to a reasonable apprehension of partiality; that the decision maker approach the issue to be decided with an open mind, not foreclosed to argument by attitudes or previous off-the-record knowledge; and that the decision maker actually hear the evidence being presented personally.

In some recent judicial decisions a third rule of natural justice has been suggested: the obligation of decision makers to provide reasons for decision. This third rule can be assimilated into traditional doctrine, for it merely links the first two rules by requiring decision makers to reveal, through the obligation to craft reasons for decision that are consonant with proofs and arguments presented, that they have heard both parties and have decided a matter free of partiality or off-the-record information and assumptions.

The rules of natural justice are said to derive from an implied presumption of the common law that attaches even in the absence of explicit statutory direction. For this reason, and unlike a constitutional due process standard, their application may be excluded by the legislature. In the United States of America and in Canada, the generic concept of natural justice has also achieved recognition as a constitutional standard: "due process of law" and "principles of fundamental justice," respectively. Wherever it has occurred, the constitutionalization of the procedural due process standards has tended to displace recourse to the common law natural justice standard in public law litigation.

Constitutionalization has also led to a broadening in the scope of due process guarantees. First of all, as was historically the case with natural justice, these newer formulae are now being invoked as both procedural and substantive standards. In addition, they have been extended in application to all exercises of public authority, and not just those associated with adjudicative decisons. Hence, delegated legislative and even legislative action may be subject to constitutional control on due process grounds. Again, the allocation of public largesse by way of licenses, franchises, or welfare entitlements, although not a strictly adjudicative distributive process, is also subject to due process review.

In those parts of the common law world that have not adopted constitutional due process guarantees, the late twentieth century has seen the development of a broader implied due process standard, procedural fairness. Procedural fairness doctrines permit courts to exercise due process supervision of a panoply of public nonadjudicative decision-making procedures, otherwise not subject to review by the writ of certiorari, and therefore not subject to an implied standard of natural justice. Today the expression natural justice is itself often used in this broader sense, so that technical differences arising from the constitutionalization of standards of "due process" or "fundamental justice" aside, natural justice as an implied common law standard or judicial censure may be said to have a content and an application that is both substantive and procedural, as well as a scope that comprises both adjudicative and nonadjudicative decision-making procedures.

References

Bayles, Michael D. *Procedural Justice: Allocating to Individuals.* Dordrecht: Kluwer, 1990.

Jackson, P. *Natural Justice.* 2d ed. London: Sweet and Maxwell, 1979.

Macdonald, Roderick A. "A Theory of Procedural Fairness." *Windsor Yearbook of Access to Justice* 1 (1981), 3.

Pennock, J.R., and J. Chapman, eds. *Due Process: Nomos* XVIII. New York: New York University Press, 1977.

Schauer, P. "English Natural Justice and American Due Process: An Analytical

Comparison." *William and Mary Law Review* 18 (1976), 47.
"Symposium: Conference on Procedural Due Process: Liberty and Justice." *University of Florida Law Review* 39 (1987), 217–581.
Winston, K., ed. *The Principles of Social Order. Selected Essays of Lon L. Fuller.* Durham: Duke University Press, 1983.

Roderick A. Macdonald

See also DUE PROCESS; REGULATION; RULE OF LAW

Natural Law

The Greek philosopher Aristotle (384–322 B.C.) in his *Politics* and *Nicomachean Ethics* provided the first systematic treatment of the ethical provenance of law. What most people think of as law (statutes, codes, administrative directives, curial decisions) Aristotle located within the matrix of morality. Both morals and law, he held, require a prior ground in reason—speculative, sometimes intuitive, always practical—as itself a natural moral good. The task is to discover the underlying moral realities that define the social, ethical, and legal orders within their larger place in the cosmic order. Once discovered, moral and legal principles have to be applied with sound reasoning and prudent judgment; they have to take cognizance of unique and differing features of life's local variations, the actual conditions of social and political life in particular times and places. Thomas Aquinas, the canonical neo-aristotelian in the fourteenth century, called these derivatives "secondary rules," resulting from the application of broad principles to particular regimes, situations, and cases, so long as these "determinations" do not contravene the founding principles that give them credence and staying power in the first place. Evolution in moral development and defects in human thought and conduct account for the uneven discovery of law's morality in different societies at different times.

Natural Law

Aristotle's ethical position came to be known as the philosophy of natural law, jusnaturalism. The structure and functions of society, state, and law, he held, presuppose efficable moral ideas and reasonableness in applying them. Aristotle also noted that since some situations are not ordinary or analogous, rules of law may fail to do justice to the case at hand. As discretionary probity, equity therefore overrides legal rules when deficient or unfitting. "The equitable is thought to be just and in fact it is the just which goes beyond the written law," states Aristotle in *Rhetoric.* Justice dependent upon such discretion demands that judges be virtuous. So in Aristotle a vast literature on the virtues complements his treatment of law as a branch of ethics.

The protagonist Antigone in Sophocles' tragedy spoke of ". . . the unwritten laws of God that know not change . . . but live forever," unwittingly suggesting the standing thesis of a law-morals union: "An immoral law is not a law." The antithesis position, which denies the law-morals conceptual union, sets forth compelling rejoinders to the Antigone thesis. Thus very early was set out a natural law morality in dispute with a primary school of vigorous and trenchant opposition, positive law philosophy, that began its refutations about the same time as Aristotle's teacher Plato formulated the ethics of natural law. Its ancient credentials go back to Protagoras, Thrasymachus, Carneades, and Gorgias, moral skeptics in the dialogues of Plato.

A strong argument against natural law's claim that law is essentially a moral institution is this: given the contestability and "incompleteness" of social concepts, it does not make sense to refuse to call law that process in which all the other criteria of legality are generally present, for example, authoritative rules, right to enforce, and public recognition. Since social terms are by and large indeterminate, we cannot reasonably require that any one criterion always be represented. Even the terms of the criteria are contestable. One may reply, of course, that contestability works both ways. If it weakens the claim that a legal system *must* incorporate a moral foundation, it also weakens the claim that it cannot.

Controversies

What motivates the classical natural law school to insist on morality's informing the positive law? This motivation presages one of the dominant trends in its history and contemporary debates: the ubiquitous human fact of ulterior coercion. Because certain of our morals may be welded to just laws and to what we think justice denotes, the problem of coercion and its aggrandizement over human life has become a benchmark for natural law as it addresses law's legitimacy, authority, and requirements of obedience. Without this problematic, natural law would likely limit its scope to its original emphasis on conduct: the universal moral principles of social obligation and their natural ground, their prudent assessment when applied, and the virtues essential for aspiring to a rational and happy life.

Justice and its connection with the constituents of law and legal systems reflect Aristotle's concern with the good society. Over the years, this legal dimension gained impetus through history's narrative: political coercion and its potential for human tragedy are the rampant evil. Morality, but only if locked into law, can stand as an adversary of despots who make life miserable for mankind. Just law overrides in theory and diminishes in actuality the ulterior uses of power.

Scope

Natural law and its concomitant deliberations stretch out, as history's story moves forward, toward a comprehensive and varied sweep of claims tangential to its legal involvement. They encompass precepts of equity, for example, *nulla poena sine lege* (no punishment without a law), no unjust enrichment, no wrong without a remedy, no liability without fault, injunctions for fair distribution, relief from distress; the duty civilly to disobey the law under certain conditions; and canons of natural justice and fairness in trial proceedings (from *Torah* [*Deutero Nomy*]: "You shall not judge unfairly; you shall show no partiality; you shall not take bribes, for bribes . . . upset the plea of the just"). As well, one naturally wants legal solutions to legal problems. Giving legal postulates a moral circumference makes this possible.

"Reason is [indeed] the life of the law," is Sir Edward Coke's seventeenth-century description of the English common law, ". . . nay, the common law itself is nothing else but reason." By "reason" he meant what the constitutional historian Sir Frederick Pollock called "judicial wisdom" gained through long experience with the complexities of curial proceeding. He meant, in other words, what practical reason meant to Aristotle. Coke was drawing directly upon jusnaturalism as its classical version entered English history through canon law—and that, through the Roman tradition based on its stoic adoption.

Inalienable Rights

Well known is that the Enlightenment strongly influenced the founders of the American legal system. Natural law was in the air since its renaissance in the seventeenth century with Francisco de Vitoria and the Salamanca school, Hugo Grotius and Samuel Pufendorf, Thomas Hooker, John Locke, William Blackstone, and Edmund Burke. All saw liberty as congruent with natural law in that religious and moral life requires liberty for its meaning, justification, efficacy, and perfection. The American preoccupation with "inalienable rights" is thought by some to be the most comprehensive, best known, and authentic integration of natural law with legal institutions ever conceived. The colonists tended to believe that natural rights were *derived* from natural law. Probably the most potent concept derived from natural law theory for the American colonists was the doctrine of natural rights. We later examine the logical connection, if there is one, and note a forceful position countervailing the presumed entailment.

Semantic Problems

The Enlightenment also brought the dormancy of winter to natural law. The term was bandied about, but its interpretation radically changed, from situated precepts guided by human nature, historical experience, and prudence, to abstractions that neglected both their institutional history and their carefully crafted justifications. While enthusiasm for natural science initiated respect for discovered natural orders, it also pointed to skepticism regarding the objectivity of values. Its nonteleological structure put a rift between "facts" and "values." Language appropriate to the classical tradition gradually changed its meaning also. "Rational" came to associate with what is logical, deductive, a priori, whereas for the Greeks, "rational" defined our natural species; and because reason was elevated to a supreme moral value as a natural good, so, accordingly, our nature was akin to moral personhood, our nature was inherently normative. But in post-Enlightenment culture—heavily influenced by the success of the mechanistic and natural sciences—"nature" came to signify "arational" or "native," raw, brute, animalistic, and appetitive, or conforming to physical, mechanical, chemical, and biological laws. The valuative connotation fully disappeared. In common speech, and in the sciences, it has not returned. The burden is on philosophy to show where moral norms "come from."

Academic Renewal and Real Events

Caused in part by its intellectual recrudescence in the twentieth-century legal philosophies of the American jurist Roscoe Pound (1907–1985) and of the neo-thomist Jacques Maritain (1882–1973), but also by the academic reemergence of moral philosophy and metaethics generally, natural law regained eminence in the second half of this century. Dramatic events consolidated the rebirth. The trials at Nuremberg, Germany, after World War II, which indicted Nazi atrocities, were argued on grounds that natural law as a universally known morality precludes and supersedes military law's unquestioned, categorical obedience. Fifty years later, trials of Soviet soldiers who killed those trying to escape to the west over the Berlin Wall were also conducted by reference to the principles of natural law. Martin Luther King, Jr.'s evocative and irresistible appeal, in his "Letter from a Birmingham Jail," to moral and legal equity for persons of color, and the Supreme Court hearing in the United States in 1991 as to whether to seat the natural law jurist Clarence Thomas—each of these very different events has drawn upon natural law philosophy for its support.

Definition

Natural law's core set of criteria with respect to its juristic dimensions includes reference to (1) human nature as rational and so, (2) practical reasonableness as its method of justification when principles need to be applied to actual circumstances, and (3) a small set of substantive values ("natural goods") to be aimed at, not as means but as ends indispensable to formulating efficable precepts for right conduct, for example, the value of human life, of knowledge, of charity, truthfulness, family life, friendship, and the broad prohibition against needless harm of persons. Foremost is the *necessary truth*: do good and avoid evil, under which the others may be subsumed. (4) This aspirational posture of the natural law is cast in terms of moving from our human potential to a higher state of actuality—a kind of mandate for improvement—giving the philosophy a teleological form.

"Virtue ethics," a dimension of most natural law schools, also takes impetus from the injunction to develop habits in pursuit of these basic goods, behind which is an assumption of order. Nature is an order; therefore, human nature is an order. The moral project is to discover this human order. Natural laws are its modal fruit. They are not ideals waiting to be fulfilled in the course of time. (Only their instantiation, when not yet accomplished, stands in wait as an ideal.) Like that of the physical realm, their reality is understood "as being already everywhere established, inviolable, and finished," in a commonplace phrase. If we cannot always find them, Aquinas and others argued, it is because they are buried beneath the distortions and defects of error, falsehoods, wrong choices, and social pathologies that afflict mankind. As well, their discovery is a developing human process.

To these definitional criteria, we have to add (5) universality and universalizability, (6) the legal-moral sine qua non of intentionality and the personal freedom of the agent before moral or legal fault can be attributed, and (7) prominent especially in current writings, an echo of Immanuel Kant: "inherent dignity of the person." These last three essentials are not unique to, or original with, natural law; they are components of any moral theory.

Current Debates

The Antigone Problem

"An unjust law is not a law" would have little more than academic interest and few defenders if it were not for the perennial human problematic: politically entrenched abuses of power coupled with the obligation to obey the law. The insecurities of living under cruel regimes are exactly what some natural legalists intend to avert by their belief that a basic morality necessarily retains control over improper decrees or laws. This control seems most assured when a foundational morality resides within the law, as with the American Declaration of Independence and Constitution, *provided* its language correctly denotes real goods and duties both necessary and humane. If, however, the relevant morality is only an ideal hazily aloft in the culture, to be invoked by legislators or jurists at their will's discretion, it may not be forthcoming when needed. Opponents contend that the naturalist's fear of political power is too desperate.

The contemporary Neil MacCormick believes valid law is conceptually distinct from law's aspirations of justice and the public good. Valid law might very well be immoral;

still, it is valid, and it is law. That laws are, according to Robert George, "intelligible only by reference to the ends or values they ought to realize . . . does not entail any acceptance of substantive moral criteria as criteria of legal validity. . . ." Of course, validity, too, is a normative term. We see here the core of good sense in Hans Kelsen's (1881–1973) legal philosophy, however formal and empty of substance, in positing normativity from the start. Neil MacCormick's distinction contradicts the naturalist notion that a statute violating a fundamental law is void.

Less than Perfect Law

In addressing the Antigone problem, Aquinas spoke of corrupt, or defective, law, and a contemporary thomist, Michael Moore, suggests this same concession: a law that is "not too unjust" may morally be obeyed. This sensible qualification allows escape from the strict Antigone logic by reasonably acknowledging that some systems are legal even though they contain "not too unjust" violations of basic moral requirements. (We can readily think of circumstances where not too evil a law is often better than no law at all.) In crafting law, human beings are not God, and so the product is imperfect. There are degrees of justice and injustice. MacCormick's concession—that to speak of defects in the law does at least weaken the obligation to obey the law—goes a way toward quieting the linguistic dispute about law and morals by placing emphasis on its real functional implication: *under what conditions* may I disobey the law? The question is crucial for natural law since tradition frames the problematic for civil disobedience, viewing it as an obligation of the person of conscience. Expressions such as "perversions" or "defects" of the law diminish the absolutism of the Antigone thesis and open the way for reasonable dialogue at a crucial juncture. Still, an epistemological problem looms. If law is too fully identified with morality, then any law, regardless of its content, may be mindlessly construed as moral, and so the natural law's vigilance over arbitrary and ulterior coercion of persons is contravened; it makes no sense to raise the issue. MacCormick puts it correctly: ". . . the mere existence of a law . . . is no guarantee whatever of its moral . . . merits. . . ." Moreover, a blanket identification can equally absorb all morality into the orbit of law. This is despotism. However, if the law-morals identification is construed the other way around and all law is absorbed into the orbit of morality, this makes law voluntary and private, not publicly authoritative. Clearly this destroys the meaning of law as enforceable and, again, contravenes the legal-watchdog function of natural law. This is why the Antigone thesis formulates the more acceptable negative, "an unjust law. . . ."

Is and Ought

That facts imply certain values rests on natural law's ground in human nature. But the premise that our nature, as such and without auxiliary premises, logically entails certain moral prerogatives cannot stand. Even if logical necessity does hold between our nature and certain moral prerogatives, we still have to discriminate between those self-centered and antisocial inclinations of our nature and those disposing to empathy, generosity, reasonableness, and the virtues on which morality builds community and law stabilizes it. Hence it is essential—since no valuative conclusion can dispense with some prior valuative commitment—to posit, or discover, some modal norm, to "get the system going." Some natural legal theorists hold that human nature, even if not rational, is itself, or implicates, a modal term, much as, today, "person" holds valuative connotation. This may be circular when the hidden assumptions are brought forward, but it is promising as a direction to go, since nearly everyone would agree.

The entailment failure in the invalid, direct is-implies-ought allegation results from the fact that "nature" changed its meaning. If we could take for granted our rationality in the classical sense of practical reasoning, our preference for right reason and the moral directives that follow would scarcely require a formidable defense. Still, we have to understand this change in meaning to diagnose the problem.

A softer claim sounds reasonable: unless morality is *closely related, is relevant,* to human inclinations, it is utopian and dangerous—or inutile. This leaves open and arguable just what this close relationship is. Almost any moral school of thought, except ideological ones, would agree that some kind of fact-value alliance is essential, but it need not be strict logical inference.

A charge made by naturalists is that positivists who rest legal legitimacy on practice, or "usage" (a fact), also commit the is-to-ought error. MacCormick cleverly answers this charge by allowing that the "transformation of practice and usage into normative law" may draw upon "the mediation of some methodological or epistemological principles . . . themselves independent of moral judgment." Here, MacCormick's solution works both ways, for the naturalist too can draw upon the same types of mediating principle to transform disquieting "facts" about immoral coercion into a moral obligation to resist it.

Nevertheless, a consensus seems to be gathering that the validity of the law-morals connection is contextual. In some contexts, an obligation (value) is intended sharply to contradict and oppose an ongoing practice (fact), as when the Prophets railed against the wrongful ways into which the Hebrew tribes had fallen. Here the is/ought gap is useful. In other contexts, an ongoing practice (fact) reflects the innocent mores of a group whose identity, and perhaps survival, rests on these customs. Some norms constitute the very meaning of what it is to be a society. Some, at least, of these norms can be moral ones. Here practices evolve so gradually into the norm, that we refer to the fact as "the norm" in that society. There is no gap; the practice is the norm. (Predictions sometimes have the same modal form: "I think it will rain tomorrow" is often stated, "It ought to rain tomorrow." Nothing more is meant but that an expectable regularity appears like a norm.) Virginia Black has proposed that a semi-inductive relationship (strong induction) somewhat like that between a hypothesis and its confirming evidence may make sense of some is/ought fusions in ruling out unacceptable alternatives.

Natural Rights?

Contemporary natural law proponents like John Finnis, Henry Veatch, and Lloyd Weinreb hold that "there is . . . a genuine, strong connection between the philosophy of natural law and rights [respecting] natural law's enduring tradition and, at the same time, [reflecting] contemporary analysis of the concept of rights." The connection moves through freedom. "[T]he way in which rights constitute freedom is the way of natural law. . . . [The] connection with natural law is . . . an essential part of what we mean when we refer to human freedom and responsibility." And again, ". . . the philosophy of rights belongs to natural law." Certainly at least natural goods necessitate or presuppose a prima facie right to act to achieve them.

Leo Strauss, however, in his *Natural Right and History,* claims that a substantial difference is that natural law encompasses contractual and voluntary moral obligations (hence the right to expect, for example, that a contractual promise will be met), which include the constraints of virtue where these modify our appetites; whereas modern natural rights imply an "imperfect obligation" to leave other persons alone in their strategic interests (civil liberties). No particular values constrain individuals acting on their rights.

If not a conceptual, at least a causal relation seems to prevail between natural law and natural rights. For individuals to flourish as the natural law enjoins, the individual must enjoy the fundamental rights necessary to its expression. Nevertheless, it is true that, as Strauss emphasizes, unless the culture visibly exercises the obligations people owe to one another, or unless the people are "virtuous," natural rights cannot be effectively sustained. The causal relations are reciprocal, and both natural law and rights share a presupposition: persons are entitled to dignity and respect. We may suppose that the philosophic argument will move toward untangling the principles governing resolution of the difficult question: how to ensure both that individual rights, however justified, are not suppressed by the state, but that, whereas moral fundamentals are independent of legal systems, political sovereignties are still to be respected.

Rights discourse has by and large moved away from its problematic conceptual derivation toward understanding just which rights can be legally instrumented without inconsistency (do civil rights contradict "entitlement rights"?), and understanding the reality factors within which rights can be securely established. This is made difficult in light of our endorsing rights of national sovereignty; for it follows that, for instance, if Stockholm wishes to justify its sovereignty on positivist legal grounds, as it now does, one can only assist its citizens in taking their appeals to The Hague and persuade the Swedish government to respect the judgments of a higher, "universal" court.

Most sovereign states have no natural law, or its equivalent, structured within their highest source of legal authority. Or they have not knowingly invoked moral rules to stand as grounds of legal checks and criticism. Accordingly, questions arise: Does a transnational body have a right to supersede national law? Can a transnational law justify such a supersession?

The Future of Natural Law Studies

Current literature on the questions surveyed seems to be moving toward concessions by both naturalists and positivists, as if the seeds of truth in each were best realized through finer analyses of the points of the debate. Since theoretical ideas can often more fruitfully be persuasive when seen operative in actual situations, concrete social issues have become a favorite source for dramatizing moral philosophies.

Virtue studies have taken a central place in today's ethics curricula. Prominent are the writings of Christina Hoff Sommers, Alasdair MacIntyre, and Yves R. Simon. So, too, the character of contemporary government is coming under virtue scrutiny: the jusnaturalist principle called the rule of law is especially salient as officials wrongly harvest privileges to which ordinary citizens are not entitled. Legal education is another appropriate matrix for considerations of vice and virtue as they permeate legal cultures. In fact, legal ethics are coming to the fore in law schools.

Today's dozen or so basic book-length writings on rights theory show a marked pragmatic and international turn in which concrete cases copiously illustrate their principle and boundaries. Perhaps this focus on rights reflects the fact that actual rights have not yet circled the globe, and in fact neglect and denial of rights are more visibly widespread than ever before. Besides implementation of the legal means to eliminate violations of the human person, the alleged derivation of rights from natural law seems to pale in importance. Recognizing higher values, reciprocal obligations, and individual rights does not on the face of it depend upon their possible connections. This, however, may be superficial, since grounding rights in reality, however indirect, is always more persuasive and lasting than opportunistic agreements. One hopes that preoccupation with operable rights and their justificatory literature turns less toward conventions and conveniences than toward the alleged demands of our natural drives, leaving treaties and trade-offs to describe temporary means whereby remedies can be more immediately installed, but not fooling ourselves that contracts as such are morally ultimate.

Analyses of in situ legal cases, studied independently of theoretical grandeur, may marginally continue as problematic or novel legal phenomena continue to emerge and fascinate. Roger Shiner believes that the positivist-antipositivist debate is an eternal polarity doomed to continue in dialectical interaction. However, even if it does so, this does not imply that some basic notions may not finally take root and persist, and some resolutions of their antinomies may not occur. Daniel Skubik believes there is scarcely a debate anymore when the naturalist-positivist positions are qualified properly.

Whether a return to nature (*phusis*), to human nature as a normative idea, to universal social regularities as currently confirmed by anthropologists, or to metaphysics as a more satisfying grounding of law's meaning and purpose for the human condition—whichever of these approaches will be philosophically enshrined—it seems at least that the idea of an ontology on a deeper level of understanding does not go away. Juha-Pekka Rentto puts it mildly: "There is a nature in each human being that drives us towards something. If we accept this view, then we are natural law theorists. We believe that ontology has a normative relevance." Not only naturalists would agree.

References

Arkes, Hadley. *First Things.* Princeton: Princeton University Press, 1985.

Black, Virginia. "Turning the Corner on the Naturalistic Fallacy: An Alternative Paradigm." *Persona y Derecho* 29 (1993).

d'Entreves, A.P. *Natural Law.* London: Hutchinson, 1972.

Finnis, John. *Natural Law and Natural Rights.* Oxford: Oxford University Press, 1980.

Fuller, Lon L. *The Morality of Law.* New Haven: Yale University Press, 1964.

George, Robert. *Natural Law Theory.* Oxford: Oxford University Press, 1992.

MacCormick, Neil. *Legal Reasoning and Legal Theory.* Oxford: Oxford University Press, 1978.

Rentto, Juha-Pekka. "What Can a Discussion of Morality Learn from Aquinas?" *Vera Lex* 10 (1990), 1.

Shiner, Roger. *Norm and Nature.* Oxford: Oxford University Press, 1992.

Simon, Yves R. *The Tradition of Natural Law.* Ed. Vukan Kuic. New York: Fordham University Press, 1992.

Skubik, Daniel W. *At the Intersection of Legality and Morality.* New York: Peter Lang, 1990.
Strauss, Leo. *Natural Right and History.* Chicago: University of Chicago Press, 1953.
Veatch, Henry B. *Human Rights, Fact or Fancy?* Baton Rouge: Louisiana State University Press, 1985.
Vera Lex; Historical and Philosophical Study of Natural Law and Right (Journal of the Natural Law Society), vols. 1–14, 1979–1994.

Virginia Black

See also Conscientious Objection; Is/Ought Gap; Positivism, Legal

Natural Rights

Natural rights involve the notion that certain definable fundamental goods or opportunities are morally owed to individuals or groups. Sometimes these rights are attributed to animals and other living beings.

The concept of natural rights is more recent than natural law. Historically, the notion of a discrete right attaching to an individual or community, such as flowered with the Enlightenment, seems to have emerged sometime after the thirteenth century, before which the dominant concept of right inherited from Roman law was wedded to acts and states of affairs. Natural right in general is discussed in the concept of natural law.

Much of the relevant literature views natural rights as extant logical or decalogical entities. There is a strong, but minority, view that natural rights do not exist. The subject is complicated by lack of consensus regarding the term "natural." In this context "natural" can be viewed as either a priori, natural in the sense of inherent in nature and preexisting human society; or, given that human thought and society are part of nature, evolutionary or *emergent* only through reason and social organization. Both views would concede the real existence of natural rights, while a minority view would deny that natural rights, lacking either concreteness or clear definability, can meaningfully be said to exist at all.

The concept of a priori natural rights has been said to have its roots in the Reformation, when the appeal to reason against authority led to a new conception of the legal order as a device to secure a maximum of individual self-assertion. The conception flowered with Hugo Grotius, who wrote in 1625 in *De jure belli ac pacis* that a right is "that quality in a person which makes it just or right for him either to possess certain things or to do certain actions." This challenged the medieval notions that law existed to maintain the existing social order (drawn from Greek and Roman law) and to avoid blood feud by compensating (amercing) for wrongs (drawn from Germanic sources). Grotius proposed that law exists to express inherent moral qualities in every man, discoverable by reason, which is the measure of all obligation.

The theory of natural rights advanced in the eighteenth century with the rationale that humans possessed certain fundamental rights in a presocial state of nature, and that such rights were retained when civil society came into existence in something akin to a contractual arrangement between sovereign and subject. The British philosopher John Locke, for example, argued that the power of government was conceded only in trust, and could be taken back by the people in the event of sovereign infringement. Locke's writing influenced the American Revolution, which opened with the 1776 Declaration of Independence in which Thomas Jefferson gave preeminence to the notion of "inalienable Rights." The Virginia Declaration of Rights explained that "all men are by nature equally free and independent and have certain inherent natural rights of which when they enter a society, they cannot by any compact deprive or divest their posterity."

Since its flowering in the Enlightenment, natural rights theory has drawn from religious sources, such as the Christian natural law tradition identified with Thomas Aquinas, idealistic philosophy such as that of Immanuel Kant, and sociological theory, in which they may be identified with fundamental human drives or social norms. However, Jeremy Bentham, the founder of utilitarianism, criticized the notion of "self-evident" political rights as an "anarchical fallacy" and "pestilential nonsense," as "nothing that was ever called Government ever was or ever could be exercised but at the expense of one or other of those rights."

In the nineteenth century, a positivist and historicism reaction against idealism and rationalism made inroads against the concepts of both natural law and natural rights. Natural law was said to lack any scientific or empirical basis and to ignore the centrality of historical processes in the development of law. Hans Kelsen commented that a constitutional right "is no more 'natural' than any other right countenanced by the positive legal order."

Yet the excesses of fascism and communism, and the concerns of the individual regarding government power generally, have kept interest in natural rights alive. The Universal Declaration of Human Rights, proclaimed in 1948 by the General Assembly of the United Nations, advances "a common standard of achievement for all peoples and all nations."

American courts have treated rights enumerated in the federal and state constitutions as legally binding and as prevailing over inimical legislation. The judicial implementation of these as overruling duly enacted legislation has fueled vigorous debate over the question of "natural rights" in the United States. Political liberals and conservatives view fundamental rights as an integral and legitimate part of the legal order, while pragmatists would found them on an instrumental basis and communitarians would weigh them against the competing values of society, family, and community. Meanwhile, the British philosopher John Finnis has recently argued that natural rights are rooted in "basic practical principles which indicate the basic forms of human flourishing as goods to be pursued and realized."

References

Dworkin, Ronald. *Taking Rights Seriously.* Cambridge MA: Harvard University Press, 1977.

Finnis, John. *Natural Law and Natural Rights.* Oxford: Clarendon Press, 1980.

Grotius, Hugo. *De jure belli ac pacis libri tres* (The Rights of War and Peace, including the Law of Nature). 1625.

Kelsen, Hans. *General Theory of Law and State.* New York: Russell and Russell, 1945.

Locke, John. *Second Treatise of Government.* New York: New American Library, 1960.

Lloyd, Dennis. *The Idea of Law.* Middlesex: Penguin Books, 1964.

Pound, Roscoe. *The Spirit of the Common Law.* Boston: Beacon Press, 1921.

Rorty, Richard. *Contingency, Irony and Solidarity.* Cambridge: Cambridge University Press, 1989.

Sandel, Michael. *Liberalism and the Limits of Justice.* Cambridge: Cambridge University Press, 1982.

Frederic R. Kellogg

See also FUNDAMENTAL RIGHTS; HUMAN RIGHTS; LIBERTY; NATURAL LAW; RIGHTS AND LIBERTIES

Nazism

See FASCIST (NATIONAL SOCIALIST) PHILOSOPHY OF LAW

Necessity

A reader can gain a sense of the diversity of situations in which the defense is claimed in criminal law by noticing those in which the accused claims, "I had to do it." In addition to the usual situations considered by courts, the defense also applies in cases of provocation, coercion, or self-defense.

A variety of interpretations of the concept have been offered. One is the concept of "inevitable necessity," mentioned in *R. v. Dudley and Stephens,* 14 Q.B.D. 273 (1884). If one understands the term to mean that the accused literally had no alternative in the circumstances, the theoretical use of the concept will be minimal. In *Dudley and Stephens,* two members of a shipwrecked crew, after eighteen days adrift, killed another member who was near death, consuming him to save their lives. If one insists on the inevitability of the necessity, then the accuseds should have waited and taken no action until their victim died.

Other interpretations of the concept of necessity rely on a fundamental distinction drawn between necessity as a justification and necessity as an excuse. When framed as a justification, an accused is appealing to some value or interest superior to the legal value supporting the crime of which he is charged. When framed as an excuse, an accused acknowledges the wrongness of the action chosen but claims circumstances or character may excuse that action, or that the action is not appropriate for punishment. Both terms, "excuse" and "justification," are both general and normative; significant problems remain of considering the circumstances and the reasons appealed to when the normative claims are properly made.

Self-defense is a first situation in which necessity as a justification has been claimed as a defense. An accused could rely on self-defense when the retaliatory steps taken toward an attacker were not excessive and were a response to a life-threatening situation. Viewed in this way, self-defense would be characterized as a justification; the action would be justified because an accused was legally entitled to protect an important interest, one's person. Legal systems could require that the accused retreat when possible, but the defense as framed in Canada, as stated in the *Criminal Code of Canada,* does not require that. By contrast, an initial aggressor must clearly withdraw before relying on the defense.

Other examples outline the limits of the defense and connect it to other situations in which the defense might be claimed. Robert Nozick offers the example of an "innocent threat," an innocent person thrown down a well. Nozick wonders whether someone at the bottom of the well is entitled to use a ray gun to destroy the falling person and claim the action is justified. Another example, perhaps not involving a threat, is the case of the accused who disengaged a young man who froze on a rope ladder providing the only access to a rescue ship, *The Herald of Free Enterprise.* Those remaining in the water were denied access and were in danger of death. When efforts to persuade the young man to move failed, he was thrown off. The accused claimed necessity as a justification as a defense.

A situation where the victim was not a threat is in *Dudley and Stephens,* where the two accused killed another to save their lives. In that case the courts denied the defense because the murdered victim was not a threat. The accused were pardoned by the Crown after spending six months in prison. *Dudley and Stephens* can be usefully compared to the fictitious case of "The Speluncean Explorers" developed by Lon Fuller in his famous article in the *Harvard Law Review*; there he considers the killing of one cave explorer to save the lives of the others.

Two other cases worth grasping here are *U.S. v. Holmes,* 26 Fed. Cas. 360 (1842), and *R. v. Perka et al.,* 55 N.R. 1 (1984). In *Holmes* passengers were knocked off and thrown out of an overcrowded lifeboat to prevent its sinking. The accused first mate claimed necessity. The court denied the defense, finding that the crew should have been sacrificed before passengers. It also discussed whether lots should have been drawn. In *Perka,* international drug smugglers brought their ship ashore in Canada because they were concerned it would sink. They were charged with importing a narcotic into Canada but relied on the defense of necessity. Justice Bertha Wilson, dissenting in *Perka,* accepted that the defense could properly be understood as a justification, but insisted that the act selected by the accused must constitute the "discharge of a duty recognized by law." Since there was no conflict of duties in *Perka,* she denied the appeals. Chief Justice Dickson insisted for the court in *Perka* that the defense be characterized as an excuse precisely because "[no] system of positive law can recognize any principle which would entitle a person to violate the law because in his view the law conflicted with some higher value." In English courts this same concern was more strongly expressed in *Southwark London Borough Council v. Williams et al.,* All E.R. 175 (1971), in which squatters desperately in need of shelter trespassed to occupy empty houses owned by a local authority. The court denied the necessity defense. Lord Denning M.R. stated, "If homelessness were once admitted as a defense to trespass, no one's house could be safe. Necessity would open a door which no man could shut."

While it is understandable that the courts would properly be reluctant to enter into the determination of policy questions, it would seem that there could be cases where principled distinctions could be made allowing the defense. In Canada, Parliament has endorsed action in necessity cases by the courts as a reasonable approach to addressing the unusual situations where an appeal to the defense is made: "Every rule and principle of the common law that renders any circumstance a justification or excuse for an act or a defense to a charge continues in force and applies in respect of proceedings for an offense under this Act or any other Act of Parliament except in so far as they are altered by or are inconsistent with this Act or any other Act of Parliament."

When the defense of necessity is understood as an excuse, it is conceded that the action was wrongful but that in the circumstances the accused ought not to be punished because someone of his character would find the action chosen unavoidable. Alternatively, it would be claimed that the action chosen was not one that should be punished. In addressing the defense along the lines of excuse, jurists have resorted to the concept of "normative involuntariness," the focus being not so much on the action chosen in relation to alternatives, but rather on the nature of the person choosing. The lines of the defense would be understood in terms of Aristotle's classic example of the involuntariness of an individual's action of throwing goods overboard in a storm in order to save the ship and those on it. Chief Justice Dickson, in *Perka,* quotes from George Fletcher on "moral or normative involuntariness" and then adds: "At the heart of this defense is the perceived injustice of punishing violations of the law in circumstances in which the person had no other viable or reasonable choice available. . . ." He also sets out a number of conditions that must be satisfied for the defense to succeed. The normative involuntariness mentioned above is "measured on the basis of society's expectation of appropriate and normal resistance to pressure; . . . negligence or involvement in criminal activity do not disentitle the actor to the excuse of necessity; [and] to be involuntary the act must be inevitable, unavoidable and afford no reasonable opportunity for an alternative course of action that does not involve a breach of law."

References

Criminal Code of Canada, R.S.C. 1970, c. C-34.

Fuller, Lon. "The Speluncean Explorers." *Harvard Law Review* 62 (1949), 616.

Stuart, Don. *Canadian Criminal Law: A Treatise.* Toronto: Carswell, 1982. 2d ed. 1987.

Williams, Glanville. *Textbook of Criminal Law.* London: Stevens, 1978. 2d ed. 1983.

Jack Iwanicki

See also COERCION (DURESS); DEFENSES; NOVEL DEFENSES

Negligence, Criminal

Negligence involves inadvertent creation of a substantial, unreasonable, and unjustifiable risk of harm to others. Its role in criminal law is tied to clarification of the concept of mens rea.

In Anglo-American jurisprudence, criminal responsibility—liability to punitive sanctions—requires more than harmful conduct (construed to include inaction as well as action). The additional element is said to be a bad or guilty mind—what lawyers call "mens rea." The guilty mind must not merely obtain; it must obtain *at the time* the harmful conduct occurs (the concurrence requirement). Crimes that do not have either an explicit or an implicit mens rea requirement (known as strict- or absolute-liability crimes) are deemed exceptional and thought to require special justification. (An example of strict liability is a statute that makes it unlawful to have sexual intercourse with a person below a specified age—even if the accused reasonably believes that the other has reached the age of consent and even if the other does in fact consent to the intercourse.)

Despite its centrality to the theory and practice of criminal law, the concept of mens rea is unclear. Hyman Gross calls it a "mysterious rubric." Another complaint, according to Jean Hampton, is that "philosophers and legal theorists have found it interestingly difficult to say what *mens rea* is." Lawyers Wayne LaFave and Austin Scott, surveying the criminal law, suggest that the term "mens rea" is "too narrow to be strictly accurate," since there are and always have been crimes that require fault but no particular mental state, let alone a guilty one. The philosopher H.L.A. Hart, who has given the matter as much thought as anyone, writes that the term "mens rea" is "misleading because it [falsely] suggests moral guilt is a necessary condition of criminal responsibility."

The vagueness and ambiguity of "mens rea" are problematic. To make matters worse, there is no single mental state specified even by those crimes that *require* a guilty mind. Some crimes (for instance, common law murder) require malice aforethought, which has a special meaning in the law; others (burglary) require a specific intention to perform an act; still others (assault) require general intent. Some crimes (possession of illicit drugs) require only knowledge or belief, while others (involuntary manslaughter) require recklessness. Crimes such as negligent homicide require only negligence (albeit of a higher degree than in the law of torts). The term "mens rea," as actually used in the law, means, according to Anthony Kenny, something like "the state of mind which must accompany an act which is on the face of it criminal if the agent is to be held responsible, and therefore liable for punishment, for the action." Unfortunately, this definition is circular. Mens rea is supposed to be a necessary condition of criminal liability; but the term "mens rea" is *defined* as whatever is necessary, beyond the actus reus, for criminal responsibility.

One important philosophical task is to provide a theory or rational reconstruction of the concept of mens rea so as to facilitate communication among lawyers and between lawyers and others (philosophers, laypeople, and so on). This theory, like any theory, will abstract from particulars to get at the underlying reality or essence of mens rea. The guiding question is What, *if anything,* do the instances of mens rea have in common that distinguishes mens rea, as an element of crime, from other elements, such as the actus reus? The philosopher's objective in providing such a theory is twofold: to illuminate (the positive part) and guide (the normative part) legal practice.

A second and equally important philosophical task is to examine and criticize substantive doctrines that employ the concept of mens rea. The doctrine alluded to earlier—that except in certain carefully specified areas mens rea is required for criminal liability—has been challenged by both legal theorists and philosophers. The debate is particularly acute in the case of negligence, with some commentators maintaining that negligent behavior is an insufficient basis for criminal liability and others arguing that it is both sufficient and appropriate. The debate is philosophically interesting because one's position on the nature and necessity of mens rea in criminal law depends largely (although not entirely) on one's view of the nature and purpose(s) of criminal punishment.

The *Model Penal Code* (MPC) provides a useful point of departure. Article 2 of the MPC sets out general principles of criminal liability. Section 2 of this article states the general requirements of culpability. It is said that no person is guilty of a criminal offense unless he or she acted purposely, knowingly, recklessly, or negligently, with purposeful action being the most (and negligent action the least) culpable. Roughly speaking, one acts *purposely* when it is one's conscious object, plan, or intention to engage in conduct of a certain sort (or to produce certain results); one acts *knowingly* when one is aware of what one is doing (or of a high probability that what one is doing will produce a certain result); one acts *recklessly* when one consciously disregards a substantial and unjustifiable risk of harm to another; and one acts *negligently* when one is not aware, but should be, of a substantial and unjustifiable risk of harm to another.

To say that one *should* be aware of X is to say that a reasonable person in the actor's situation *would* be aware of X. The standard is objective in the sense that it is imposed on, rather than discovered in, the subject. Culpable negligence, according to the MPC and the common law, requires not just any deviation but a "gross" deviation from the standard of care that a reasonable person would observe in the situation, thus distinguishing it from ordinary tort negligence. A deviation is gross, ceteris paribus, when precautions against harm are very simple to take (in economic terms, comparatively costless) and the harm, should it occur, is significant.

Hyman Gross illustrates (without necessarily endorsing) the MPC culpability requirements with a case of the sleeping sailor who is asphyxiated during a fumigation of his docked ship. If the aim of the fumigators is to bring about the sailor's death, they act purposely. If their aim is to destroy rodents rather than kill the sailor, all the while knowing that the sailor will die as a result, they act knowingly. If, not knowing of the sailor's presence on the ship but knowing of the extreme risk to any sailor's life should he or she be exposed to the fumes, they proceed without inspecting the ship or otherwise issuing a warning, they act recklessly. If the fumigators broadcast several warnings but do nothing further to ensure the safety of sailors, they act negligently. In all four cases, the act of fumigation is *intentional.* Gross argues that this feature—intentionality—is the touchstone of criminal culpability. Just how culpable one is depends on one's cognitive and affective states as well as on the care with which one acts.

The normative question arising from this example is whether criminal liability is appropriate in the fourth case—the case in which the fumigators are careless with respect to the presence of sailors on the ship. Some theorists and philosophers argue that it is inappropriate, although for different reasons. Others maintain that punishment for negligence is sometimes appropriate. Nobody, of course, argues that *all* negligent actions may be punished; the debate is about whether *any* are.

One argument against criminal liability for negligence is that only acts which reflect a moral fault on the part of the agent are properly punishable, but negligent actions do not do this. The usual response is to reject the minor premise that negligently performed actions do not reflect moral fault. They can and (often) do. As Brenda Baker points out, "One of the deep-seated convictions of commonsense morality is that people are responsible for, and can properly be called to account for, their careless and negligent behaviour." The fault in such cases is said to consist in "fail[ing] to attend to or appreciate the risks or dangerousness of our conduct, . . . fail[ing] to exercise restraint over our emotions when we could have, [and] fail[ing] to bring our general knowledge or our normative standards to bear in the execution of day to day conduct." To use Gross's example, fumigation per se may be faultless, but fumigation without attention to the risks thereof is not.

Another argument against criminal liability for negligence is that it cannot possibly deter, the assumption being that the sole or primary purpose of criminalization is deterrence of what are deemed antisocial acts. One response to this argument is to deny that deterrence *is* the sole or primary purpose of criminal law; another, more localized, response is that punishment of negligent actions can deter. Common sense bears this out. If one knows that one will be responsible for harm resulting from carelessness or inattention in doing X, one has a self-interested reason to take precautions while doing X, thereby minimizing the likelihood of harm. The prospect of punishment motivates the actor to take care, to be vigilant, to pay attention—in short, to employ all of one's faculties and skills. There is no reason in principle why punishment for negligence cannot deter.

A third argument against criminal liability for negligence maintains that if liability for negligent (even grossly negligent) actions is appropriate, then so is strict liability—liability in which the actor not only did not advert to the risk of harm to others but *could not reasonably have been expected to so advert*. The argument takes the form of a logical slippery slope: (1) There are no morally relevant differences between liability for negligence and strict liability. (2) Strict liability is unjustified (except in certain special cases involving grave harm to the public, such as the sale of adulterated food). Therefore, (3) liability for negligence is unjustified.

One *could* respond to this argument by accepting the main premise concerning the logical parity of strict and negligence liability and insisting that since negligence liability is justified, so is strict liability. No commentator has adopted this strategy. Hart has taken an alternative tack. The argument fails, he says, because the main premise is false. There *is* a morally relevant difference between liability for negligence and strict liability. The difference is that the former, but not the latter, requires a subjective mental state (*not* adverting to the risk). This is morally relevant because, according to Hart, criminal law—indeed, the law generally—is a choosing system designed to guide and respect individual choice. Holding individuals responsible for inadvertence respects the choices they make and encourages them to make better choices. On the other hand, holding individuals responsible when they not only did not advert to a risk of harm but could not reasonably have been expected to so advert (as in strict liability) fails to respect them as rational, choosing beings. It treats them as manipulable objects. (For a criticism to the effect that Hart's emphasis on choice "too narrowly circumscribes the field of personal responsibility," see "Mens Rea, Negligence and Criminal Law Reform" by Brenda Baker.)

It should be pointed out that Hart's aim in rebutting this argument is not to defend liability for negligence but to show that liability for negligence is analytically (therefore possibly *normatively*) distinct from strict liability. Indeed, this is the strategy of several critics of the thesis that criminal liability for negligence is unjustified. The critics argue, in effect, that there is no *principled* reason to exclude negligence liability from the criminal law. As for whether, all things considered, gross negligence *should* be prohibited and punished, that is a matter calling for judgments of policy (including judgments concerning efficiency in the allocation of resources). It may be that the tort and regulatory systems and not the criminal justice system are the appropriate venues for addressing the problem of negligently inflicted harm.

References

Alexander, Larry. "Reconsidering the Relationship Among Voluntary Acts, Strict Liability, and Negligence in Criminal Law." *Social Philosophy and Policy* 7 (Spring 1990), 84–104.

American Law Institute. *Model Penal Code and Commentaries*. Philadelphia: American Law Institute Press, 1985.

Baker, Brenda M. "Mens Rea, Negligence and Criminal Law Reform." *Law and Philosophy* 6 (April 1987), 53–88.
Gross, Hyman. *A Theory of Criminal Justice.* New York: Oxford University Press, 1979.
Hall, Jerome. *General Principles of Criminal Law.* Indianapolis: Bobbs-Merrill, 1947. 2d ed. 1960.
Hampton, Jean. "*Mens Rea.*" *Social Philosophy and Policy* 7 (Spring 1990), 1–28.
Hart, H.L.A. *Punishment and Responsibility: Essays in the Philosophy of Law.* Oxford: Clarendon Press, 1968.
Kenny, Anthony. *Freewill and Responsibility.* London: Routledge and Kegan Paul, 1978.
LaFave, Wayne R., and Austin W. Scott, Jr. *Substantive Criminal Law.* 2 vols. St. Paul MN: West, 1986.
Wasserstrom, Richard A. "Strict Liability in the Criminal Law." *Stanford Law Review* 12 (July 1960), 731–745.
Williams, Glanville. *Criminal Law: The General Part.* London: Stevens, 1953. 2d ed. 1961.

Keith Burgess-Jackson

See also INTENT; MENS REA; STRICT LIABILITY, CRIMINAL

Negotiable Instruments

Lexicography reveals Latin roots for "negotiate" and "negotiable" in *negotium* (business, employment, occupation, affair; broadly embracing most transactions or dealings, but connoting, in mercantile contexts, trade, traffic, doing business).

Types

Certain instruments evidencing or representing proprietary rights (sometimes rights in things, sometimes obligations) are called "negotiable" as possessing (though in different combinations and in varying degrees) special attributes making them trade (with rights annexed) more easily than do other kinds of legal rights, documented or not (the vast majority). Because they are more readily sold, given as security, and transferred to agents, negotiable instruments encourage economic activity and themselves become marketable commodities.

Legal systems variously confer characteristics of "negotiability" upon (1) some classes of *orders or promises* to pay or deliver money or other things (usually "fungible," like commodities) to specified persons or to "bearer"; and (2) some *documents of title* to things, sometimes corporeal (for instance, goods), sometimes incorporeal (for instance, shares in corporations).

Characteristics

The following attributes collectively define negotiability. Not all such instruments, however, simply because they have some of these characteristics, are *called* "negotiable."

1. Negotiable instruments are *more than evidence* of the underlying obligations or property rights. In important ways, they represent them, embody them, *become property* themselves. From their inception, like corporeal moveable objects, they are in general susceptible to transfer by mere delivery. This depends upon any arrangements, express or implied, written or unwritten, arising between the transacting parties. Typical conditions are:

(a) When in *bearer* form ("in blank"), a negotiable instrument can be issued, and thereafter transferred, by delivery to anyone (for example, paper currency).

(b) When in *order* form ("in special"), the instrument can, in principle, vest through delivery only as specified. Speaking generally, if originally drawn "in special," it can, when issued, vest only in the person specified as original holder. When later transferred, if the holder specifies a transferee in his "endorsement," the instrument can vest only in the latter. (To prevent misappropriation, these specific designations, as well as other means of controlling title, for instance, "restrictive endorsements," are commonly permitted either in the original terms of the instrument or in an endorsement.) The "holder" (that is, the designated payee or endorsee in possession or, alternatively, the bearer) can then usually convert the instrument from "order" to "bearer" form, or vice versa.

Contrast *nonnegotiable* obligations or incorporeal things (and also corporeal things not simultaneously delivered). Their transfer usually involves more burdensome formalities (for example, signed agreements of sale or assignment; registrations; public notices; for obligations, almost certainly, notice to debtors of any transfer).

Moreover, *civil liability* in respect of a negotiable instrument often extends to the economic value of the underlying rights. Damages for a wrong upon it (for instance, destruction or misappropriation) may not be limited to the cost of substitute evidence even when available.

2. Within limits, acquirers of negotiable instruments, by proper negotiation, can obtain better *title* thereto than had their predecessors. An acquirer in legally defined circumstances (having largely to do with good faith and the giving of value) may be free from defects in predecessors' title, sometimes even from their complete want of title.

3. Typically, special *presumptions* inure to holders of negotiable instruments, merely from possession: notably, presumption of lawful title and of the right to enforce these instruments against all prior parties. Prior parties are normally presumed to have received value for having signed, or given over, an instrument. Holders when suing normally need not prove these facts; others must disprove them. (True, most legal systems offer some evidentiary presumption of lawful title or possession, even to possessors of ordinary charters. Negotiable instruments carry stronger presumptions, however. To enforce a contract one must normally allege and prove one's own performance. Holders of negotiable instruments generally make a prima facie case simply by exhibiting them.)

Degree and Process

Most documents of title with some measure of negotiability are, properly speaking, only semi-negotiable, having mainly characteristics in the first group. Warehouse receipts, waybills, bills of lading, and so forth, variously involve contracts to store, transport, and remit goods; rights typically (if not always) are transferable through the documents. However, acquirers are not usually protected from defects in predecessors' title to the documents or from third parties' rights in the documented property. Some scholars object altogether to applying the term "negotiable" to documents of title to things (though legislation sometimes does so). Whatever terminology is preferred, it must be understood that such instruments commonly have some special attributes characteristic of negotiability; while some documents of title (for example, corporate securities under the *Canada Business Corporations Act,* R.S.C. 1985, c. C-44, Part V) are, in substance, negotiable instruments in the fullest sense.

Negotiability, in its purest form, is usually found in certain written orders or promises to pay money, serving variously as instruments of credit and means of payment. The "promisor" on a promissory note contracts to pay the stated sum at the stated time to the payee or a subsequent holder. The "drawer" of a bill of exchange contracts that the "drawee" will pay the holder, on due presentment, with recourse against the drawer in case of "dishonor" (nonpayment). If, before paying, a drawee signs a bill, with or without adding special conditions, the drawee becomes its "acceptor," contractually bound to pay it. "Checks" are bills drawn on bankers, payable on demand. Each "endorser" can in certain ways expand or limit the endorser's liability by the terms of the endorsement. Generally, the endorser guarantees to subsequent holders the genuineness of the document, the endorser's title to it, and payment in case of dishonor. These contracts pass cumulatively with the instrument and so (by exception from normal rules of privity) can be enforced by each party directly against all prior parties. In contrast, transferors of bearer instruments without endorsement assume much narrower obligations to their immediate transferees.

The rule of *Nemo dat quod non habet* (no one can give what one does not have) imports that the acquirer of an obligation or of a thing can have no better rights than one's predecessor's. This *general rule* underlies the stability of property rights and contractual dealings. (1) Assignees of obligations normally have no better rights than assignors. (2) The law normally protects a property owner, by entitling that owner to repossession and to damages for unlawful interference (sometimes even if innocent). (3) Each innocent buyer of a stolen thing recovers, instead, damages (a) against his predecessor in the chain (as having warranted title or peaceable possession) and (b) directly against the thief for civil wrong. In principle, the loss falls ultimately upon the thief; in fact, the suable buyer nearest the thief bears the effects of the loss.

By contrast, third-party "*holders for value*" of bills and notes are commonly protected from disputes among prior parties about absence, or failure, of consideration (for example, nonperformance of the obligations for which the bill or note was given). (Even where the payee-merchant could not recover on a check given for defective goods, the merchant's endorsee usually can.)

When third-party holders can meet even stricter conditions (objective and subjective) designed to ensure their good faith, they are "*holders in due course,*" and protected even from defenses raising defects in title, like fraud, duress, even theft, though (in many jurisdictions) not usually forgery. Normal protections of debtors, and prior owners, are suppressed in favor of acquirers, who obtain good title to the paper and full right to enforce it. (Holders in due course may keep, and fully enforce, checks earlier fraudulently obtained, or previously stolen bearer notes.) A credit market in financial paper is created, and workable currency, too, which would be impossible under "nemo dat" principles.

Issues

Destroying property rights to protect them: here lie challenging issues. Should an innocent acquirer be entitled to *enforce* or retain payment of an illegal instrument, even one signed at gunpoint, or one where the owner-holder's endorsement is forged? If so, why bother posting checks rather than cash, or registering bonds in owners' names? (So-called common law jurisdictions usually protect the owner forgery victim; "civil law" jurisdictions, usually the acquirer.) Who should *bear* such losses: the immediate crime victim, the innocent acquirer, a paying institution that has disobeyed (even innocently) the payment instruction naming the genuine payee (in order to distribute economic losses optimally)?

Stephen A. Scott

References

Garland, Donald W. "A New Law of Negotiable Instruments: Revised Article 3 of the UCC." *Banking Law Journal* 109 (1992), 557.

Newell, James A., and Michael R. Gordon. "Electronic Commerce and Negotiable Instruments (Electronic Promissory Notes)." *Idaho Law Review* 31 (1995), 819.

Sommer, Hillel. "Jus Tertii Defenses in the Law of Negotiable Instruments." *Commercial Law Journal* 97 (1992), 4.

Wallenbrock, Eric. "Forged Indorsements under French Negotiable Instrument Law and the U.S. Uniform Commercial Code: A Comparative Study." *Uniform Commercial Code Law Journal* 28 (1996), 393–413.

Wickins, R.J., and C.A. Ong. "Conversion of Negotiable Instruments and Contributory Negligence." *Asia Pacific Law Review* 4 (1995), 12.

Zamphiriou, George A. "Unification and Harmonization of Law Relating to Global and Regional Trading." *Northern Illinois University Law Review* 14 (1994), 407.

C.B.G.

See also PROPERTY; SALE; THEFT AND RELATED OFFENSES

Negotiated Plea

See PLEA BARGAINING

Nietzsche, Friedrich (1844–1900)

Nietzsche was a prophet of the future. He predicted that we moderns would no longer understand law as the fabric or pattern for community, beyond our evaluation or control, but would instead understand law as the tool of a polity, an expression of human will. As Nietzsche put it: God—that is, any immutable, universal order guiding or fashioning the world from a "higher" realm—was dead.

Nietzsche's divinations have held true of many movements in jurisprudence. Positive law theories take an approach to law that seeks to separate it from cultural norms and define it "scientifically" by way of its source in human institutions. Legal realism "demystifies" law further by excavating its sources in the sociological, psychological, and political worlds of power relations and human will. Critical legal studies attacks the universalism and essentialism of "legal reasoning" and strips away law's pretensions to speak from "beyond" social and cultural contexts. All these movements seek to ground law in human will, not infinite truth.

This death of God, for Nietzsche, is itself no tragedy. The timeless universals themselves have been destructive. They taught us to despise the world in which we live, since it never measures up to the "other world" of metaphysical ideals. Nietzsche claimed in "Four Great Errors" in *The Twilight of the Idols* that these universals also taught us to despise ourselves and each other, as we used blame, shame, and punishment to bring ourselves low in a cycle expressing a *ressentiment,* rather than a celebration, of earthly power.

The tragedy Nietzsche did fear is that, once we recognized the emptiness of these absolutes, and the institutions that had been based upon them failed, we would fall victim to despair and apathy. Nietzsche feared most the spiritual weakness of the "last man," a modern who, having lost faith in a timeless, universal philosopher's god, had no measure left by which to give value to the transient human world he had been taught to devalue. The last man, Nietzsche predicted, would have no goals, no visions, nothing to honor, nothing to worship, nothing to fight for—no will to power. Nietzsche's portrait of the last man embodies the anomie, alienation, and decadence that so many writers have associated with modernity.

Much of Nietzsche's work counsels confronting the death of God head on, stripping away the universalist pretentions of moral philosophy, exposing the human genealogy of so-called absolute concepts, and recognizing law as human creativity and power. By acknowledging that all laws are human creations, Nietzsche hopes he can clear the way for an "overman" to create new values and institutions without hiding behind the emasculating "lie" of the absolute. Of "We Scholars" in *Beyond Good and Evil,* Nietzsche anticipates that these new, self-conscious, works of art will destroy the weak nihilism of anomie through a strong nihilism, a nihilism that rejects the existence of any but human valuation, human "will to power."

In executing this strong nihilism, Nietzsche sounds many themes replayed in contemporary jurisprudential writings. He excoriates the tendency to look to "universal principles" that denigrate the particular and deny relevance to the uncategorized. He exposes the philosophical mistaking of grammatical categories for ontological absolutes (for example, the subject/object distinction leads us to conclude that for every effect there must be a cause, and therefore a First Cause). He emphasizes the cultural and historical relativity of law, language, and truth itself, in *The Genealogy of Morals.*

Yet in many respects, Nietzsche's prophetic sight is more equivocal, more delphic, than that of much postmodern jurisprudence. Many passages in Nietzsche's work suggest that he questions the feasibility of his own attempt to imagine a self-conscious creation of values. How can one truly honor or respect or be obligated by one's own creations if at every moment one is also re-evaluating and re-creating them? On the other hand, he asks of "What Is Noble?" in *Beyond Good and Evil,* can one advance doctrines designed to affirm (once and for all) the fleeting and ephemeral beauty of human life without making timeless universals of them?

This tormented self-questioning suggests Nietzsche was not sanguine about western civilization's response to the death of God. Instead, Nietzsche's challenge to come to terms with modernity's equation of law with power, without alienation and without anomie, remains for us.

References

Berkowitz, Peter. "On the Laws Governing Free Spirits and Philosophers of the Future: A Response to Nonet's 'What Is Positive Law?'" *Yale Law Journal* 100 (1990), 701–722.

Constable, Marianne. "Genealogy and Jurisprudence: Nietzsche, Nihilism, and the Social Scientification of Law." *Law and Social Inquiry* 19 (1994), 551–590.

Nietzsche, Friedrich. *Beyond Good and Evil: Prelude to a Philosophy of the Future.* Trans. Walter Kaufmann. New York: Random House, 1966.

———. *The Genealogy of Morals.* Trans. R.J. Hollingdale and Walter Kaufmann. New York: Random House, 1969.

———. *Thus Spoke Zarathustra.* Trans. Walter Kaufmann. New York: Penguin Books, 1978.

———. *Twilight of the Idols.* Trans. R.J. Hollingdale. New York: Penguin Books, 1968.

Nonet, Philippe. "What Is Positive Law?" *Yale Law Journal* 100 (1990), 667–700.

Sarat, Austin. "Leading Law into the Abyss: What (If Anything) Has Sociology Done to Law." *Law and Social Inquiry* 19 (1994), 609–624.

Linda Meyer

Nihilism

The term is derived from the Latin word *nihil,* which means "nothing." The Russian author I.V. Turgenev was the first to use the term in his novel *Fathers and Sons.* Nihilism originated in the 1860s as a Russian social and reformist movement which rejected all the contemporary moral and social norms. It defended individual freedom and rational egoism and advocated the study of natural sciences for utilitarian reasons. Nihilists came to support the use of violence in order to reach their revolutionary political goals.

"Nihilism" is a word that has a clear meaning in the Russian history of ideas. Otherwise its meaning is mostly rhetorical. It can also be said that the term belongs to the vocabulary of the European continental philosophy. Anglo-American analytic philosophy has not found many uses for this term. The term is more diagnostic than analytical. In its everyday use the term has a pejorative sense, for instance, when accusing the opponent of living without any recognizable values and norms. This negative use of the word "nihilism" started soon after the term was used the first time. The term is also used in some limited contexts, for instance, in the connection with postmodern theory, but again with no clear meaning. There the term simply suggests that something is missing from the realm of values and norms. Although the term is used frequently in popular discussion, it seems to have no standard use in legal, social, and moral philosophy.

Nihilism is closely related to skepticism. A skeptic suspends his judgments concerning the truth of propositions. He may claim that he has no proof of the truth or the falsity of any given proposition. A moral skeptic extends this general argument to ethical propositions. A nihilist would say that he knows that there is no moral truth and that all moral views are worthless. Traditionally, the Russian nihilists did not extend their negative attitude to natural sciences.

If nihilism is extended to all propositions, it can be refuted by means of the following reductio ad absurdum: if you say that you know nothing, you are contradicting yourself since you say that you know that you know nothing.

Nihilism is a more radical view than moral relativism, which says that there may be moral truth, but the truth-predicate applies to several mutually contradictory propositions at the same time. If relativism denies the existence of moral truth, it claims that some moral norms are valid in their own social context. Social values are acceptable, which is exactly the position denied by a nihilist.

The view that ethical and other normative propositions are not cognitive at all but are emotive is a version of moral nihilism, although this concept is seldom applied to emotivism. The Swedish philosopher Axel Hägerström argued before World War I that such a statement as "Murder is wrong" is something like an exclamation "Murder, stay away!" Later on the Vienna Circl
and their followers adopt
no science or theory
Ethics is a purely subjec
practical matters.

Anarchism contai
cause such anarchist
Joseph Proudhon, a
manded the abolitic
necessary conditio
society. Legal nihilism clai
law is the worst possible way to orga
cial life. Law is based on coercion and violence. Anarchism is considered as a separate theory and social movement.

In the history of philosophy Friedrich Nietzsche is often mentioned as a nihilist. He denies the values of the Christian morality. He predicts a deep cultural crisis, which means the "Death of God," "decadence," and "the advent of nihilism," that is, the lack of all value. Nietzsche is not a nihilist himself because he promotes his own elitist set of values and virtues, such as those of the Superman, "who is the meaning of the earth," in his book *Zarathustra*. Nietzsche's use of the term "nihilism" is clearly diagnostic. He wants to reveal the symptoms of the dead—end of the history of the western world.

The postmodern philosophy is often referred to as a version of nihilism. It is difficult to know what this means. Jacques Derrida writes, when he discusses negative theology, as follows: "And those who would like to consider 'Deconstruction' a symptom of modern or postmodern nihilism could indeed, if they wished, recognize in it the last testimony—not to say the martyrdom—of faith in the present *fin de siècle*." Postmodernism contains some nihilist elements because it seems to deny the meaning of the concept of progress. History cannot be seen as the great testing ground of values that guide human life toward a better world. Postmodernism is influenced by Martin Heidegger's philosophy in which he expresses his concern about the nihilism of modern theory and life. Postmodern theory is interested in texts and their interpretation rather than what the text refers to. The real world seems to disappear. This may be called a nihilist result. However, the meaning of "nihilism" is so vague that no definite conclusions can be drawn.

Some uses of the term "nihilism" have their romantic overtones. Maurice Natanson, for example, has defined nihilism as follows:

…dering of reason from experience, of …phy from life, is nihilism, for what it …s is the validity of inquiry itself, or con…ousness coming into self-responsible clarity. The crisis of Western man consists in the denial of reason and the affirmation of conceptual fragmentation." Nihilism in this context is the perception and affirmation of nothingness. It is understandable that no methodological problem or school of thought can be built on this basis. Nihilism as a pure denial is the end, not a beginning.

References

Derrida. Jacques. "How to Avoid Speaking: Denials." In *The Languages of the Unknown: The Play of Negativity in Literature and Literary Theory,* ed. Sanford Budick and Wolfgang Iser, 3–70. New York: Columbia University Press, 1989.

Lowith, Karl. *Martin Heidegger and European Nihilism.* New York: Columbia University Press, 1995.

Rosen, Stanley. *Nihilism: A Philosophical Essay.* New Haven: Yale University Press, 1969.

Thielicke, Helmuth. *Nihilism: Its Origin and Nature with a Christian Answer.* New York: Schocken, 1969.

Timo Airaksinen

Nineteenth-Century Philosophy of Law

G.W.F. Hegel and Jeremy Bentham dominate the philosophy of law in the nineteenth century. They respond, not only to Immanuel Kant's synthesis of Jean-Jacques Rousseau on freedom and David Hume on habit, which closed the preceding three centuries, but also to new revolutions. French and American revolutions late in the eighteenth century inspired Latin revolutions by the 1820s and the less successful European social revolutions of 1848. Revolutionary communes and internationals were as short-lived as the reactionary alliances and ententes against Napoleon's liberties, even among monarchs who coped with them by liberalization. While in the third quarter of the nineteenth century the U.S. Civil War evinced Lincoln's liberties and constitutional populism, the Spanish-American and Boer wars at the end did so only if claims of hemispheric "burdens" by James Monroe in 1823 or Queen Victoria (r. 1837–1901) were taken at face value.

Industrial revolution, as well, climaxed throughout the century, rousing the economic theories and social concerns which preoccupied law and jurisprudence. Hegel and Karl Marx, Bentham and John Stuart Mill, all wrote the press about reform proposals. Earlier legal conflicts over religious preference subsided before rejection of any religion as oppressive. Art and literature seized upon public ills with romantic expressionism, and then social realism.

As their legal phenomena, the several revolutions evoked constitutional bills of rights, while the codifying of private law proceeded despite resistance, and statutory reforms fostered trade and suffrage. Penal procedure was used to administer associations, first those of political protesters, domestic or imperial, then of corporations and their syndical competitors.

Hegel (1770–1831) altered the entire philosophy of law by concluding his 1821 *Lectures on the Philosophy of Right, or, Natural Law and Political Science in Outline,* with *Sittlichkeit* (ethical order). "Right" culminates not in abstract though external entitlements (property, personal, and criminal law), nor in the concrete but internal duties (morality) that supersede these in the 1797 *Foundations of the Metaphysics of Morals* by Kant (1724–1804), but in public institutions and their law (ethical order). His *Phenomenology of Spirit* in 1807 presaged this, and his *Encyclopedia of Philosophical Sciences* located it in 1817. Sheer thinking in the one or sheer being in the other needs to become determinate; only thinking or being is available to make itself determinate. Recognition of this need for determination, however, already stands beyond itself; this is a negation, a determination healed by completing it. Determinacy becomes ever more concrete, as each incompleteness is healed, becoming at last in and for itself. Lord and bondsman negate each other, and so depend on each other for wholeness. So do owner and worker, offspring and citizen, constitutional legislature and executive police. "The right" (what must be as it ought to be because only it is) has worked itself clear, into legal statehood.

Law fulfills man and world, culminates in the state, and is completed in history. Law's dynamic is that "the rational is actual [what is the case]; and the actual is rational [what right demands]" (*Was vernünftig ist, das ist wirklich; und was wirklich ist, das ist vernünftig,* stated Hegel in the preface to *Philosophy of Right*). Neither clause is true separately from the other.

Separating their dialectic, however, is one traditional way to characterize their sequelae as "wings" to Hegel in nineteenth-century legal philosophy. Another is to distinguish different "schools" following the several *Critiques* of Kant: a school of pure reason, from one of practical reason and judgment. Either way uses the metaphor (drawn from seating on opposite sides of the legislative building) to contrast a "right wing" or conservative legal philosophy (historicist and nationalist, scientistic or idealist) to a "left wing" or liberal jurisprudence (from romantic "young hegelians," to the libertarian left of anarchism and the scientistic left of communism).

Right Wing

The continental *historical school* of jurisprudence agrees with Hegel on the stature he assigns history in law, but stands passive before it. Instead of law being comprehensible through its contemporary texts or immutable principles of natural law, it can only be understood in terms of its development. Initiated by Hegel's foil, Gustav Hugo (1764–1861), but made hegelian by Eduard Gans (1797–1839), the historical school found in Savigny and in Jhering its highpoint and its finale. Friedrich von Savigny (1779–1861) posited an organic connection between a people's law and its character. The customary law with which a people comes into possession of its land, *Das Recht des Besitzes* (The Law of Possession) (1803), is living law. Rudolph von Jhering (1818–1892) described law and state as the linking together of peoples' purposes (*Der Zweck im Recht* (Purpose in Law), 1877–1883), after their struggle to find autonomy (*Das Kampf ums Recht* (The Struggle in Law), 1872). Within the British historical school, Sir Henry Sumner Maine (1822–1888) in *Ancient Law* (1861) provided data to Frederick William Maitland (1850–1906) that supported a legal evolution "from status to contract." Beyond Maitland's translation of German organicism, his *Constitutional History of England* (1908) proffered evidence for this in his own jurisdiction.

History's culmination being the national state, historicism readily melds with *nationalism.* The legal system of any national state has its own rationale in terms of its own history, and needs justification from no other source. For the German nation, Wilhelm von Humboldt (1767–1835) pursued its *Bildung* (education), and Jacob Grimm its literature, while K.F. Eichhorn treated its laws. Otto von Gierke (1844–1921) wrote four volumes on medieval German law, which are the counterpart to Savigny's six (1851–1881) and Jhering's three (1852–1856) on the character of Roman law and its superiority. Gierke points how, gradually, the voluntary formation of associations became the corporate personality of the state. Early in the next century, Carl Schmitt (1888–) could drop the personification and foster the legal state's unvarnished conflict with its enemies.

Scientism linked continental thinkers in a confidence that society can be understood as a phenomenon of nature gruff toward legal forms. Charles Henri de Rouvroi St.-Simon (1760–1825), Charles Fourier (1772–1837), Pierre-Joseph Proudhon (1809–1865; *What Is Property?* 1840–1841), and Ferdinand Tönnies (*Community and Association,* 1887) do not look to Hegel for this, nor specifically to history. The importance, however, which Auguste Comte (1798–1857) gives to the dynamics of development is far different from the previous century's faith in progress. In Comte's "sociology" (the term he provided), driven by his law of the three stages that society passes through—theological, metaphysical, culminating in positive science (*System of Positive Politics,* 1851–1854)—legal activity becomes less punitive but serves to regulate scientific technology, what Mill called Comte's "frenzy for regulation."

The Origin of Species Through Natural Selection (1859) by Charles Darwin (1809–1882) gave impetus to an evolutionary jurisprudence called social darwinism. Herbert Spencer (1820–1903) chafed at the term, claiming to have named "the survival of the fittest" before Darwin in his *Social Statics* (1850), immortalized in Oliver Wendell Holmes' (himself a jural evolutionist) dissent to the *Lochner v. New York* decision, 198 U.S. 35, 75–76 (1904). From radical egalitarianism and antistatism, Spencer's jurisprudence changed throughout his *Synthetic Philosophy* (1860–1896) to support selective legislation for utilitarian purposes.

The naturalizing of legal processes continued with Weber and Durkheim, no longer in terms of historical or biological metaphors, but as phenomena and laws of social nature.

Max Weber (1864–1920) also looked to a more regulatory role for law, than its imperative and penal stature during eras of charismatic authority. Emile Durkheim (1858–1917) set this out as a movement from penal law toward restitutive law in his *Division of Labor in Society* (1893). Between them, the groundwork is laid for the sociology of law to be pursued.

British *idealists* did not resist affinity with Hegel, but dispensed with his dialectic. They shared his characterization of state law as the supreme realization of the right, but drew none of the conservative conclusions which historicists drew from that. Bernard Bosanquet (1848–1923) in *The Philosophical Theory of the State* (1899) took state as the concrete universal which is more real than the singular person. Thomas Hill Green (1836–1882) in his *Lectures on the Principles of Political Obligation* (1879–1880) presented a liberal theory of state, which left individuals free from law, but only because and until the self-differentiating social self best achieves its freedom in this way.

Left Wing

The *"young hegelians"* interested in recharacterizing religion and art affected jurisprudence despite themselves. The man known as Max Stirner (1806–1856), Bruno Bauer (1809–1882), and Auguste von Cieszkowski (1814–1894) restated religion as human phenomena: man creates religion and thereby himself as god, although finally deity steals back its attributes from man. This position of Ludwig Feuerbach (1804–1872) influenced the young Marx's views of legal alienation.

The young hegelians' liberation from alienating authority was carried further by *anarchists,* although they hardly saw Hegel as a comrade in their rejection of state law. Louis Blanqui (1805–1881) early, Michael Bakunin (1814–1876) amid, and Peter Kropotkin (1841–1921) late in the century replaced state law with relations that are consensual and not imposed. Not completely foreign to this were utopian proposals, such as Robert Owen's (1721–1858), and their perfectionist communities, which were, in fact, implanted throughout America during the century.

These utopian socialisms were completely foreign to the treatment of law by Karl Marx (1818–1883), from his early *Philosophical and Economic Manuscripts, Critique of Hegel's Philosophy of Law* (1844), and *Communist Manifesto* (1847), to his *Contribution to the Critique of Political Economy* (1859) as the first installment of his posthumous *Capital.* The *scientific socialism* Marx presented was dialectical and historical, in that its scientific laws depend upon the dynamic of negation rather than upon the positivism of scientistic jurists' causal mechanisms; but it was also materialist, in that the energy for that dialectic lies in relations of production, specifically in the ownership of means of production, rather than (upside down, as he saw Hegel) in and for the consciousness of right. Consciousness and its institutions, especially the law, are not the primary driving force of history. Law's vocation is to "wither away" as a penal prop for an incomplete stage of productive relations and to persist only as administrative regulation for the classless society replacing them.

His collaborator, Friedrich Engels (1820–1895), in *The Origin of the Family, of Private Property, and the State* (1884), was less wary than Marx either of predicting concretely the sort of legal relations which would ensue (both classless and in the intervening era of proletarian dictatorship), of extending historial materialism throughout nature, or of characterizing law not dismissively as ideology but rather as entwined with ownership in mutual causality of social relations.

Neo-kantian schools at Marburg and at Baden (setting aside one of psychological experimentation at Würzburg) ignored the hegelian track and contributed legal philosophies relating to the older master. The former school worked from the first *Critique,* with categories independent of experience, that is, immanent logical laws of pure reason; Hermann Cohen (1842–1918) and Ernst Cassirer (1874–1945) relate to this, as did Jhering and Stammler. The latter school responded to the second *Critique,* affirming a unity of cultural behaviors around the existence of independent values. While Wilhelm Dilthey (1833–1912) had more impact on cultural studies than Baden's Wilhelm Windelband or Heinrich Rickert, Georg Jellinek and Gustav Radbruch (1878–1949) are its notable neo-kantian legal philosophers. Radbruch made values autonomous, indemonstrable, and incapable of having contradictions between them resolved. The most jurisprudence can do is to make legal values coherent with some primary value, either of individuality, of collectivity, or of creativity. Rudolf Stammler

(1856–1938) set himself to counter this skepticism in law. "Right law" is recognized from the legality inherent in the positive law. It unifies individual purposes in view of the "social ideal." Radbruch and Stammler's competing influences continued out of the ninteenth century into America in the *Philosophy of Law* each wrote (1914, 1922, respectively). Out of each, Hans Kelsen (1881–1973) formalized his own powerful kantian jurisprudence.

Casting back *beyond Hegel or Kant,* Alexis de Tocqueville (1805–1859) found warm reception in England, too, for recommending how to preserve *Democracy in America* (1835, 1840) through balancing its legal powers and rousing public opinion into local self-government. More professionally, Albert Venn Dicey (1835–1922) secured this balanced rule of law with arguments for English conventional legal sovereignty in his *Introduction to the Study of the Law of the Constitution* (1885).

English Fabian socialists developed a more gradualist path toward social democracy than some continental counterparts. Also by mid-century, the *"English radicals"*—James and John Stuart Mill, Jeremy Bentham, and John Austin—formed the second stream of jurists, harkening back beyond the revolutions to the utilitarian and dispositional legal thought of Hume (perhaps of John Gay through David Hartley). Radicals advocated utilitarian legal governance of social democratic politics, that is, democratic accountability of elites through universal suffrage and majority rule. Fabians' and radicals' partners included some of the most prominent women involved in legal reform: Harriet Taylor with J.S. Mill, Beatrice and Sidney Webb, and also Harriet and George Grote. Austin's wife, Sarah Taylor, rescued his later work from oblivion, to make him the most respected jurist of the late nineteenth century. These worked similarly to Mary Wollstonecraft with William Godwin, the English property anarchist at the end of the previous century.

Jeremy Bentham (1748–1832), after dismissing his teacher William Blackstone's natural law in his *Commentary on the Commentaries,* published in part as *A Fragment on Government* (1776), plunged early into legal reform, developing plans for penal clarity, even architecturally in a "panopticon," by *An Introduction to the Principles of Morals and Legislation* (1789). After conversion to "radicalism" by James Mill, he pursued his "pannomion," a massive codification of English law, in his *Constitutional Code* (1822–1932). His resistance to revolutionary reform via natural rights did not block his advocacy for legal reforms based upon principles of utilitarian well-being through calculating maximum social benefits.

John Austin (1790–1859) provided the most thoroughly analyzed jurisprudence of the century, as well as a detailed feasibility study for his "radical" colleagues. In order to make room for reform by clarifying positive law and separating it from moral unassailability, *The Province of Jurisprudence Determined* (1832) and his *Lectures on the Philosophy of Positive Law* (1861) specified law as command by the sovereign whom a populace habitually obeys. Constitutional protections are guaranteed only by positive morality. H.L.A. Hart (1907–1992) would make critical analysis of Austin and Bentham one pole of his jurisprudence in the next century.

John Stuart Mill (1806–1873) moved in legal theory beyond his father and his godfather, by using utilitarianism of a more refined quality. Instead of denying some pleasures are higher and summing them all, J.S. Mill qualifies their value, but only while making personal creativity the highest value, which is advanced by giving no preference to any by public law. This is developed in his *Principles of Political Economy* (1848), *On Liberty* (1859), *Considerations of Representative Government,* and *On Utilitarianism* (1861). Legal force is to be employed for no other purpose than to keep persons from achieving their pleasure by harming others. Mill provides rationales for numerous exceptions, from suicide to treason. Social pressure and not legal prohibition is a sufficient sanction to achieve other beneficial social aims. Mill simultaneously recognizes, however, that tyranny by the masses would be an even greater threat to liberty than the law in the next century's liberal jurisprudence.

Catholic jurisprudence, also beyond Kant or Hegel, Rousseau or Hume, which began the century as the legal conservatism of Joseph De Maistre (1753–1821) and Louis Gabriel De Bonald (1754–1840), became by mid-century the politically reformative theory of Antonio Rosmini (1797–1855), and by its end the socially revolutionary encyclical *Rerum Novarum* (1891) of Leo XIII, reasserted at its *Quadragesimo anno* (1931) and *Centesimo anno* (1991). Another magisterial monitum from Leo closed off vital "modernist" fulfillments during the nineteenth century, but his *Aeterni Patris* (1878) summoned the neo-scholastic jurisprudence of solidarity and subsidiarity made prominent in the next by Jacques Maritain (1882–1973) and Yves Simon (1903–1961).

Kelsen, Hart, and Schmitt were to grab jural inheritances from Kant, Bentham, and Hegel. Phenomenology and the Vienna Circle would draw improved analysis of the law from the methods of Franz Brentano (1838–1917), Gottlob Frege (1848–1925), and Edmund Husserl (1859–1938). Pragmatist legal proceduralism would draw from the pragmaticism of Charles Sanders Peirce (1839–1914) or the vitalism of Henri Bergson (1859–1941). Postmodern jurisprudence would take up antihegelian romanticisms, religious in Søren Kierkegaard (1813–1855) or rhetorical in Friedrich Nietzsche (1844–1900), in the next century.

References

Bannister, Robert C. *Social Darwinism: Science and Myth in Anglo-American Social Thought.* Philadelphia: Temple University Press, 1979.

Cain, Maureen, and Alan Hunt. *Marx and Engels on Law.* New York: Academic Press, 1979.

Cornell, Drucilla, Michel Rosenfeld, and David Gray Carlson, eds. *Hegel and Legal Theory.* New York: Routledge, 1991.

Cosgrove, Richard A. *Scholars of the Law: English Jurisprudence from Blackstone to Hart.* New York: New York University Press, 1996.

Hoffheimer, Michael H. *Eduard Gans and the Hegelian Philosophy of Law.* Dordrecht: Kluwer Academic Publications, 1995.

Hosle, Vittorio, ed. *Die Rechtsphilosophie des deutschen Idealismus* (Philosophy of Law in German Idealism). Hamburg: Meiner, 1989.

King, Peter J. *Utilitarian Jurisprudence in America: The Influence of Bentham and Austin on American Legal Thought in the Nineteenth Century.* New York: Garland, 1986.

Milanovic, Dragan. *Weberian and Marxian Analysis of Law: Development and Functions of Law in a Capitalist Mode of Production.* Brookfield VT: Avebury, 1989.

Postema, Gerald J. *Bentham and the Common Law Tradition.* Oxford: Clarendon Press, 1986.

Wigmore, John H., ed. *The Progress of Continental Law in the Nineteenth Century.* Boston: Little, Brown, 1918.

Christopher B. Gray

See also EXEGETICAL SCHOOL; IDEALISTS, BRITISH; MARXIST PHILOSOPHY OF LAW; UTILITARIANISM

Norms

Normativism, namely, the opinion that law is a matter of norms, is nowadays widely shared both by legal theorists and by laypeople. This opinion is currently the majority conception of legal theory in western countries, both of common law and of statute law, and in general is implicit in modern legal thinking.

In common as well as in legal language, "norm" is often used as a synonym of "rule." Some theorists think, however, that these expressions have only partially overlapping meanings. In general, the meaning of "rule" seems to be more wide and generic than the meaning of "norm." "Rule" can be used to designate generically norms, but not vice versa. There are, in fact, rules, such as the rules of experience, that are not norms. If theorists of widely differing trends in legal philosophy agree that the law is made up of norms, they do not agree about what "legal norm" designates.

Three main conceptions or approaches to legal norms have to be taken into consideration. The first conception can be called ontological. A legal norm is here understood as a "mental entity" produced by a human act of will, but distinguished from this act, and endowed with an autonomous existence in a world of values. Hans Kelsen, the main holder of this conception, criticized imperativism and contended that legal norms, different from the orders issued by a sovereign, are prescriptive ideas, unconcerned about the events of the will that have produced them.

The legal realist theory, opposed to the duplication of reality performed by ontological normativism, set out an analysis of legal norms in terms of behaviors, in particular in terms of the behaviors of the courts. Of course, the most shrewd among the legal realists, such as Alf Ross, were fully aware that speaking about legal norms means taking into consideration not only regular, convergent behaviors in a social group—this feature is shared by legal norms and social habits—but also a particular attitude, consisting in deeming those behaviors as binding.

This attitude seems usefully connected not with feelings to be ascertained through introspective methods, but rather, with a particular use of language, that is, the use of characteristic expressions in normative terminology, such as "ought," "must," "should," "right," "wrong," indicating that a pattern of behavior is considered a general standard to be followed by the social group as a whole.

The idea that legal norms are directly dependent on language characterizes the third conception of legal norms, namely, the semantic conception. In this perspective, prevailing in analytical legal theory, a legal norm is defined as a prescriptive meaning content, obtained by interpreting a sentence that is formulated or else could be formulated. The conception of legal norms as semantic entities extends therefore also to norms which lack linguistic formulation, such as customary norms, implicit principles, norms obtained by arguing from analogy, and so on. Even if norms can be devoid of linguistic formulation, nevertheless normative meanings can be expressed in words.

Some theorists, worried about the abstractness of the notion of meaning content, have identified legal norms with prescriptive sentences or even with prescriptive utterances, that is, with speech acts which are tokens of sentences. It is nevertheless important to stress that the notions of sentence and utterance are also considerably abstract, and both presuppose the notion of meaning.

Holders of the semantic conception of legal norms cannot avoid the issue of what features distinguish legal norms from other normative phenomena, such as morals and customs. The search for special features belonging to all legal norms and only to legal norms has produced, in modern and contemporary legal thinking, many attempts to reduce all legal norms to a single norm pattern. Thus, for example, Immanuel Kant distinguished between legal imperatives, conceived as hypothetical (that is, prescribing *sub condicione)*, and moral imperatives, conceived as categorical (that is, prescribing unconditionally). In Christian Thomasius' opinion, legal norms are negative imperatives, while moral norms are positive imperatives. In Kelsen's opinion, legal norms can all be understood as hypothetical judgments expressing the specific linking of a conditional material fact (a delict) with a conditioned consequence (a punishment), and so on.

Contemporary legal theory has, however, generally abandoned the idea of special features belonging to all legal norms and only to legal norms. In fact, it is easy to become aware that the features of legal norms that are considered necessary and sufficient either are not common to all legal norms or are not exclusive to them. Indeed, in contemporary legal theory, the opinion is shared that a norm is legal when it belongs to a legal system, namely, to a normative system which has identifying characteristics, such as effectiveness and coerciveness.

The reduction of all legal norms to a single norm pattern has to be considered nowadays not a neutral, adequate description of the law, but rather a political ideal. For example, those who contend for the idea that generality and abstractness are essential characteristics of legal norms, express, in fact, the political ideal of legal equality and certainty.

The prevailing trend in contemporary legal theory is a nonreductionistic one. According to this trend, the word "norm" indicates, in law, a wide range of prescriptions which can be distinguished from different points of view. Legal norms can be distinguished, for example, with regard:

1. to the degree of binding force or prescriptive intensity: unconditioned norms, norms prescribing conditionally, directives, and so on;
2. to the universal or individual nature of the class of actions they discipline (abstract and concrete norms) and/or of the class of their addressees (general and singular norms);
3. to their function: norms which directly affect human behavior, duty-imposing or permissive norms, norms of competence, or power-conferring, constitutive norms.

Some theorists have held that permissive norms and, above all, power-conferring norms and constitutive norms, are hardly compatible with a prescriptivistic conception of the norm. This conception, however, is not weakened by the existence of permissive norms, because these norms can be reconstructed in terms of duty-imposing norms, namely, in terms of norms completely eliminating or partially limiting the scope of a duty-imposing norm.

As to the norms of competence conferring powers on private citizens or officials, it is true that these norms perform a social function different from that of duty-imposing norms. On the other hand, norms of competence can be understood as prescriptions to follow the conduct prescribed by the norms produced on the basis of a correct exercise of the competence. Moreover, it can be observed that, by reducing the law to behavior-guiding prescriptions only, a control of the compliance and the breach of legal norms becomes possible.

This is just the same for constitutive norms, that is, for the norms which immediately produce the effect they name, without requiring further human intervention (for example, abrogative norms such as "the norm x is abrogated"), as well as for the norms regulating human behaviors which cannot be fully described without making reference to the norms referring to them (for example, the norms regulating the institutional fact "marriage").

In spite of the opposite opinion held by some theorists, constitutive norms as well can be, in fact, understood as prescriptions indirectly formulated. For example, an abrogative norm can be interpreted as a prescription to the addressees of the abrogated norm, in particular to judges, not to apply it. As to constitutive norms regulating institutional fact, it can be held that such behaviors as killing or parking, too, when regulated by legal norm, cannot be fully described without making reference to legal qualifications. In this sense, all legal norms can be regarded as constitutive. Notwithstanding, they are also prescriptive.

Whatever conception of legal norms may be adopted, it is important to bear in mind that all conceptions are value-laden models and have to be evaluated not as truthful or untruthful, but as more or less suitable with regard to particular theoretical and practical ends.

References

Bobbio, N. *Teoria generale del diritto* (General Theory of Law). Torino: Giappichelli, 1993.

Conte, A.G. *Eidos. An Essay on Constitutive Rules.* In *Normative Structures of the Social World,* ed. G. Di Bernardo, 251–257. Amsterdam: Rodopi, 1988.

Hart, H.L.A. *The Concept of Law.* Oxford: Clarendon Press, 1961.

Kelsen, H. *General Theory of Law and State.* Cambridge MA: Harvard University Press, 1945.

Ross, A. *Directives and Norms.* London: Routledge and Kegan Paul, 1968.

———. *On Law and Justice.* London: Stevens & Sons, 1958.

Scarpelli, U. *Contributo alla semantica del linguaggio normativo* (Contribution to a Semantics for Normative Language). 2d ed. Milano: Giuffrè, 1985.

Von Wright, G.H. *Norm and Action.* London: Routledge and Kegan Paul, 1963.

Patrizia Borsellino

See also Logic, Deontic Legal; Metanorms; Standards; Values

Northern European Philosophy of Law

The Nordic countries share a common culture, which is manifested in the treatment and respect of law as an outstandingly important feature of social organization. Law matters as a system of substantive rules, procedures, and techniques, and this system is regarded as determinative of relevant questions. Thus the conduct of people must be subject to rules, which implies that law excludes the exercise of arbitrary power by the organs of government, that is, the legislature, the executive, and the judiciary.

The Nordic countries respect the rule of law, which stands for equality of all persons before the law and the equal subjection of both citizens and officials to the ordinary law administered by independent courts.

Within the Nordic countries there is also a common understanding of the Nordic languages, except Finnish and Icelandic. This means that there can be a fruitful exchange of views in one's mother tongue. The drawback, however, is that this debate has no impact in the international debate. One remedy is that the Nordic articles have been translated and published in the series *Scandinavian Studies in Law* by the Faculty of Law at Stockholm University since 1957. Another remedy is to publish directly in a foreign language, but at the risk that this work will have no impact within the Nordic debate.

The dominant perspective within legal philosophy has been antimetaphysical and naturalistic, as advocated by the Scandinavian realists, tending to deny any reality to "law" as traditionally understood and to make idealists and natural lawyers seem foolish. This realist approach has encountered strong opposition from the Norwegian Frede Castberg (1893–1977), professor of law at the University of Oslo, and Jacob Sundberg (1927–), professor of law at the University of Stockholm, adopting natural rights positions, and the Danes Frederik Vinding Kruse (1880–1963), professor of law at the University of Copenhagen, and Knud Illum (1906–1983), professor of law at the University of Aarhus, from a utilitarian perspective. Also the Finn Otto Brusiin (1906–1973), professor of law at the University of Turku, must be mentioned for his independent stance concerning legal thinking rooted in the nature of man, as well as for his efforts to bring international legal philosophy into contact with Nordic legal philosophy.

The Scandinavian realists stress the importance of law as the bond of the state but leave no room for a rational discussion concerning the legitimacy of law. However, if law is important, so is its legitimacy, which can and must be rationally defended. This question has led to a discussion of the adequate normative foundations of law and of the need for a critical legal science. Two approaches can be distinguished. One approach is based upon the philosophy of Ludwig Wittgenstein, transmitted in Finland by G.H. von Wright, leading to the hermeneutical-analytic perspective held by the Finn Aulis Aarnio (1937–), professor of law at the University of Helsinki, and also the Dane Stig Jørgensen (1927–), professor of law at the University of Aarhus. The other approach is based upon the philosophy of Jürgen Habermas and the Frankfurt school of critical theory, leading to the critical approach by the Finns Lars D. Eriksson (1938–) and Kaarlo Tuori (1948–), both professors of law at the University of Helsinki. This debate is still in progress. So is the debate concerning the scientific status of legal knowledge, as well as the question concerning the interpretation of law that is related to the question concerning the proper justification of legal decisions made by courts and administrative organs, where the contributions by the Swede Aleksander Pezcenik (1937–), professor of law at the University of Lund, have been influential.

Finally, there is also the strictly logical approach of rational reconstruction of legal concepts and the structure of the legal system using symbolic logic and deontic logic to present formal and precise explications of the concepts which lawyers use in their legal activities. This approach is adopted by the Swedes Lars Lindahl (1936–), professor of law at the University of Lund, and Åke Frändberg (1937–), professor of law at the University of Uppsala.

The Nordic argumentation concerning fundamental legal questions is conducted from different philosophical perspectives, taking notice of present international developments. It is to be hoped that this debate will also be noticed abroad.

References

Aarnio, Aulis. *The Rational as Reasonable.* Dordrecht: Kluwer Academic Publishers, 1987.

———. "Statutory Interpretation in Finland." In *Interpreting Statutes,* ed. D.N. MacCormick and R.S. Summers. Brookfield VT: Dartmouth, 1991.

Bjarup, Jes. "Interpretation, Reasoning and the Law." In *The Structure of Law,* ed. Åke Frändberg and Mark van Hoecke, 161–178. Uppsala: Justus Förlag, 1987.

Brusiin, Otto. *Der Mensch und sein Recht.* Ed. Urpo Kangas. Berlin: Duncker und Humblot, 1990 (English bibliography).

Castberg, Frede. *Problems of Legal Philosophy.* 2d ed. Oslo: Oslo University Press, 1957.

Jørgensen, Stig. *Pluralis Juris.* Trans. Bodil Schmidt. Aaarhus: Acta Jutlandica XLVI, Aarhus University Press, 1982.

Kangas, Urpo, ed. *Enlightenment, Rights, Revolution. A Collection of Finnish Papers.* Helsinki: Helsinki University, 1989.

Kruse, Frederik Vinding. *The Community of the Future.* Copenhagen: Einar Munksgaard, 1950.

Lindahl, Lars. *Position and Change.* Dordrecht: Reidel, 1977.

Peczenik, Aleksander. *On Law and Reason.* Dordrecht: Kluwer Academic Publishers, 1989.

Peczenik, Aleksander, and Gunnar Bergholz. "Statutory Interpretation in Sweden." In *Interpreting Statutes,* ed. D.N. MacCormick and R.S. Summers. Brookfield VT: Dartmouth, 1991.

Strömberg, Stig. *Five Essays in Historical Jurisprudence.* Uppsala: Almqvist and Wiksell, 1989.

Sundberg, Jacob. "The European Convention on Human Rights and Criminal Procedure in Sweden." In *Criminal Science in a Global Society: Essays in Honor of Gerhard O.W. Mueller*, ed. Edward M. Wise. Littleton CT: Rothman, 1994.

Jes Bjarup

See also SCANDINAVIAN LEGAL REALISM

Novel Defenses

The battered woman syndrome was first introduced to the criminal courts in the 1977 American case of *State v. Wanrow,* 88 Wash. 2d 221, 559 P.2d 548. Since then American courts have witnessed an explosion of novel defenses: premenstrual dysphoric disorder (premenstrual syndrome), posttraumatic stress disorder, kleptomania, pathological gambling, Stockholm syndrome, battered woman syndrome, rape trauma syndrome, sexual abuse syndrome, Holocaust survivor syndrome, false memory syndrome, black rage, roid (steroid) rage, urban survival syndrome, rotten social background, adopted child syndrome, and the Twinkie defense (to name just a few). In Canada, expert testimony on the battered woman syndrome was first recognized in the landmark case of *R. v. Lavallee,* 1 S.C.R. 852, 55 C.C.C. (3d) 97 (1990).

While most of these syndromes have yet to win the approval of the greater scientific community, this has not prevented defenders from appealing to them in an attempt to negate their client's responsibility for criminal behavior. In so doing, they have pressured the courts and, to a lesser extent, legislatures, to institute two types of legal change: (1) the creation of *new defenses* and (2) the *expansion* or contextualization of existing criminal defenses. Since the battered woman syndrome has captured the greatest attention from litigators, legislators, and legal theorists, it will serve as an example of *expansion.*

Attempts to create *new defenses* have captivated the public but failed to produce any substantive legal change. The scientific or clinical evidence for these defenses may be new, but critics claim that the legal arguments raised by these defenses involve standard doctrinal claims. The Twinkie defense and the abused child defense are cases in point. In his 1978 trial for the premeditated murders of Mayor George Moscone and Supervisor Harvey Milk, Dan White (a San Francisco supervisor) claimed that he was not guilty of murder due to the psychological effects of consuming too much sugary junk food. White's defense was viewed as a standard diminished capacity claim. Recently, the Menendez brothers of Beverly Hills attempted to raise an abused child defense. After two hung juries, they were finally convicted of murder in 1996. Their defense was interpreted as a traditional imperfect self-defense claim, using evidence of alleged parental abuse to support an honest, but unreasonable, belief that the parents posed an imminent threat necessitating defensive force. Even in cases where syndromes have received scientific recognition, through inclusion in the American Psychiatric Association's *Diagnostic and Statistical Manual of Mental Disorders,* 4th edition (DSM-IV), the courts have interpreted defenses which appeal to these syndromes as equivalent to existing excuses. For instance, kleptomania (listed as a diagnostically acceptable disorder in DSM-IV) and premenstrual dysphoric disorder (classified as "in need of further study") have both been treated as classic mental incapacity defenses.

Expansion, the second type of legal change, has achieved limited success. Evidence on the battered woman syndrome, for instance, has been used to expand the standards of reasonableness in self-defense law. By attending to the *context* in which battered women act—their socioeconomic circumstances, personal history, and perceptions—syndrome evidence can show how their conduct meets existing self-defense requirements of imminent danger, equal force, and necessity, even where it seems to depart from the hypothetical reasonable man standard. Syndrome evidence explains how a battered woman can legitimately perceive imminent danger where a reasonable man would not, due to her intimate knowledge of her batterer's pattern of violence. Evidence of previous injuries may justify a battered woman's seemingly excessive use of force on the grounds that she could not adequately defend herself without resorting to a weapon. The necessity of self-defense can be underscored by the lack of viable options as evidenced by inadequate police protection, ineffectual courts, and nonexistent social services. Many legal theorists and practitioners credit expert evidence on the battered woman syndrome with the elimination of gender bias in traditional self-defense standards. Originally derived from a male-biased archetype of a barroom-brawl scenario (where two men of equal strength, size, and ability confront one another), these standards have been expanded to include the experiences and perspectives of battered women.

A more radical expansionist project has been pursued by some battered woman syndrome advocates in cases that seem to lack the usual criteria of justification (for instance, when a battered woman's belief in the necessity of defensive force is found to be objectively *unreasonable* even within a broader, contextualized account of self-defense standards). In this more radical approach, syndrome advocates have attempted to endow the objective reasonable person standard in self-defense with the characteristics associated with syndrome sufferers. Instead of asking what the "reasonable person" would have believed and done under the circumstances in question, these advocates ask what the "reasonable battered woman syndrome sufferer" would have believed and done. If a "reasonable sufferer" of the syndrome would have behaved as this particular sufferer actually did, proponents hold that the defendant's conduct is reasonable and justifiable. For instance, where a battered woman's use of force seems unnecessary given available alternatives, syndrome advocates argue that the battered woman's failure to pursue these alternatives was reasonable because her affliction with the syndrome rendered her incapable of perceiving them.

Legal theorists and practitioners have questioned the wisdom of expanding reasonableness standards in this manner. Some worry about creating a stereotype of the "reasonable battered woman" to which battered women will have to conform in order to successfully plead self-defense. Others suggest that since the battered woman syndrome appears to impair cognitive abilities and perception, it should be treated as proof of a mental disorder giving rise to an excusing condition. The symptoms associated with the syndrome may well be a "normal" or "common" response to trauma, but it does not follow that persons exhibiting these symptoms are therefore reasonable. These analysts note that hallucinations and delusions are a common response to certain drugs, but syndrome advocates still want to insist that these symptoms seriously impair mental processes. Indeed, by expanding standards to include the "reasonable battered woman syndrome sufferer," analysts worry that consistency will require expansion of the standards even further to include the "reasonable mentally handicapped person" or the "reasonable psychotic." Unless we can uncover some reason why expansion should apply only to the battered woman's syndrome, some believe the expansionist's project will lead to the dilution, and ultimately, the relativization of legal standards.

Legal theorists and practitioners are currently divided on the ultimate impact of novel defenses. Some theorists believe novel defenses promote fairness and equity in law by acknowledging the fact that people legitimately differ in their ability to meet the standards of responsibility imposed by law. Others see novel defenses as a general abdication of individual responsibility that illegitimately deflects responsibility from the criminal to the abuser, a contributing condition, or circumstance. In this view, novel defenses threaten not only to dilute standards but to undermine law's universality by creating a differential system of law that holds people to different standards depending upon their particular characteristics or group membership.

References

American Psychiatric Association. *Diagnostic and Statistical Manual of Mental Disorders*. 4th ed. (DSM-IV). Washington DC: American Psychiatric Association, 1994.

Morse, Stephen. "The 'New Syndrome Excuse Syndrome.'" *Criminal Justice Ethics* 14 (1995), 3–15.

Schaffer, Martha. "*R. v. Lavallee*: A Review Essay." *Ottawa Law Review* 22 (1990), 607–624.

Schneider, Elizabeth. "Describing and Changing: Women's Self-Defense Work and the Problem of Expert Testimony on Battering." *Women's Rights Law Reporter* 9 (1986), 195–222.

Schopp, Robert et al. "Battered Woman Syndrome, Expert Testimony, and the Distinction Between Justification and Excuse." *University of Illinois Law Review* (1994), 45–113.

Patricia Kazan

See also COERCION (DURESS); DEFENSES; INSANITY DEFENSE; NECESSITY

Nozick, Robert (1938–)

Although this American philosopher's recent work covers a wide range of topics, Robert

Nozick is best known for his earlier studies in political philosophy (and, by implication, the philosophy of law) where he provides an ardent defense of libertarianism and of retributivism in punishment.

Nozick's most influential contribution to social and political philosophy is his *Anarchy, State and Utopia* (1974), in which he criticizes the accounts of distributive justice proposed by utilitarianism and by John Rawls as inconsistent with a genuine liberal individualism. The theory of justice that Nozick advances in their place and the corresponding explanations of the legitimacy of law and the state enforcement of punishment are based on a version of natural rights theory. Explicitly indebted to John Locke, Nozick's views also show the influence of Thomas Hobbes and Immanuel Kant. There are also many parallels with Herbert Spencer's rights-based political and legal theory.

Unlike Locke, however, Nozick does not claim that natural rights are derived from a natural law, and some critics charge that he provides no philosophical basis for rights beyond a doubtful intuitionism. Still, Nozick does suggest that natural rights are a consequence of the natural capacity of persons to lead integrated and meaningful lives. This notion of a capacity for a meaningful life also allows, Nozick hypothesizes, one to bridge the is/ought gap between what people are and what powers they ought to have and, hence, explains the moral weight of rights. Following Locke, Nozick identifies natural (property) rights to "life, health, liberty" and "possessions," to keep alive and to punish in proportion to any transgression of these. These rights reflect one's moral worth and dignity but are "negative"—that is, claim nothing more than "freedom from" the interference of others.

Rights, along with the entitlements they give rise to, provide a "moral space around an individual" and set "the constraints in which a social choice is to be made." They are ascribed properly only to persons and—in keeping with the independence of individuals and with the kantian principle that persons are ends, and not merely means—normally may not be encroached upon without the right-holder's consent. While all human beings possess the same natural rights, Nozick denies that all have equal "particular" rights or entitlements. To explain the moral legitimacy of an unequal distribution here, Nozick develops his entitlement theory of justice.

In Nozick's view, rights and entitlements are based on one's natural rights, not on any "end" or "common good," and can be justly acquired only in one of three ways: by initial acquisition (for instance, labor), by transfer, or by rectification (that is, compensation for past violations of rights). Nozick adds that "[w]hatever arises from a just situation by just steps is itself just." The only limit on one's holdings that he allows is a weak version of Locke's proviso in *Second Treatise of Government,* that the position of others is not worsened by an acquisition.

By defining the justice of a distribution simply in terms of how it came about, the entitlement theory is "historical." While Nozick's account of the nature of entitlements and of how they are distinct from rights is obscure, entitlement is clearly neither reducible to desert nor based on need.

Nozick's central objection to the accounts of distributive justice entailed by utilitarianism or by the principles of fairness of Rawls or H.L.A. Hart is that they are "patterned" (that is, specify that "a distribution is to vary along some natural dimension") or are "end-state" principles (that is, determine justice by looking at the outcome), rather than focus on the process by which the distribution is produced. Such accounts, Nozick objects, allow constant infringement of rights and entitlements. It is also for this reason that Nozick argues against the modern interventionist or welfare state.

Only a "minimal state" that has, as its sole function, the respect and protection of rights and entitlements is justifiable, and Nozick believes that such a state would arise inevitably—by an "invisible hand." Law, then, is based on the principles that individuals are inviolable and that only acts which violate (or risk violating) someone's rights may be restricted. While Nozick believes, like Locke, that individuals have a general right to punish, he argues that this right will ultimately default to the state and that the protection of rights through the criminal law is justified. Nevertheless, consistent with his view of justice as "unpatterned," Nozick attacks the deterrence theory of punishment—he parts company with Locke here—and advances a defense of retributivism. He develops this in a lengthy essay, "Retributive Punishment," in his 1981 volume, *Philosophical Explanations.*

In his "nonteleological" view, Nozick claims that "[r]etributive punishment is an act of communicative behavior." The purpose of punishment is to communicate to the offender that what he or she did was wrong, state how wrong it was and thereby "(re)connect the wrongdoer with correct values" by giving these values "as significant an effect in his life as the magnitude of flouting these correct values." Reformation or deterrence may be a byproduct of such an act, but neither is necessary to its justification. Nevertheless, while favoring capital punishment for "a great monster" like Adolf Hitler, Nozick is uncertain whether one ought to endorse it in general.

There have been extensive criticisms of Nozick's views. Some address fundamental issues, such as his underlying account of the nature of the person, his analysis of natural rights, his conflation of rights and entitlements, and his distinction between historical and end-state principles of justice. There have also been internal criticisms of the entitlement theory, challenges to his claim that one can justify the minimal state (and nothing more), and suggestions that his principle of rectification undermines the defense of property rights. Nozick's legal retributivism and his arguments for the state monopoly on punishment have also been contested.

While there continues to be some critical interest in Nozick's social and legal philosophy, debate has shifted to the more extended and developed libertarian views of such authors as Tibor Machan, Douglas Den Uyl, and Douglas Rasmussen.

References

Machan, Tibor. *Individuals and Their Rights.* Peru IL: Open Court, 1989.

Nozick, Robert. *Anarchy, State, and Utopia.* New York: Basic Books, 1974.

———. *The Examined Life: Philosophical Meditations.* New York: Simon & Schuster, 1989.

———. *Philosophical Explanations.* Cambridge MA: Harvard University Press, 1981.

Paul, Jeffrey, ed. *Reading Nozick.* Lanham MD: Rowman and Littlefield, 1981.

Sandel, Michael. *Liberalism and the Limits of Justice.* Cambridge: Cambridge University Press, 1982.

Sweet, William. "Les 'droits naturels' et les 'titres' selon Robert Nozick." *Lekton* 1 (1991), 81–98.

William Sweet

O

Oaths

The oath was used judicially by many of the ancestors of modern western culture, including the Hebrews, Babylonians, Egyptians, Carthaginians, Romans, Persians, and Germanic tribes. In spite of this it has inspired remarkably little philosophical discussion. Nevertheless, two major concerns have emerged: (1) the nature or analysis of the oath and (2) its role in the judicial process. Until recently, the scanty philosophical treatment of the oath concentrated on the latter, while simply assuming, without careful analysis, that the oath was a kind of ceremony colored by religion. In a passage originally attributed to Aristotle but now thought to be written by Anaximenes, the oath is defined as an affirmation without proof accompanied by an invocation of the gods. This view was clarified by Jeremy Bentham, who defined the oath as a ceremony composed of words and gesture, by means of which the Almighty is engaged to inflict on the taker of the oath punishment in the event the taker does something he or she has committed not to do or does not do something he or she has committed to do. This expresses the traditional understanding of the oath: an undertaking backed by the threat of divine punishment.

Writers often distinguish "assertory" oaths ("I swear that P is true") from "promissory" oaths ("I swear to do action A") and analyze both as akin to promises. Bentham reduces the former to the latter and argues that both are undertakings or promises which produce obligations. In his book on speech acts, John Searle includes swearing in the list of commissives (such as promising) whose propositional content is a future action of the speaker. (A commissive is a kind of speech act whose point is to commit the speaker, in varying degrees, to a future course of action.) Kent Bach and Robert Harnish likewise analyze swearing and promising together, but add that when swearing that P, the speaker both asserts the proposition P and promises to tell the truth. This reflects the dual role of swearing: committing oneself to future conduct and committing oneself to the truth of a claim about a past or present state of affairs. As yet there has been little work mapping the differences in logical grammar between promises, oaths, vows, undertakings, affirmations, pledges, and so on. It is common to treat these as philosophically and morally equivalent.

Equally important to the analysis of oaths is the nature of the obligation involved. Bentham, Searle, and Bach and Harnish, as well as most common law judges, see the oath as a means whereby someone undertakes an obligation. Searle's famous discussion of how to derive "ought" from "is" is still an excellent starting point for understanding this function. Seeing the oath as identical or closely related to promises, however, none of these authors, and very few judges, distinguish between obligations generated by promising and those generated by swearing an oath. Myron Gochnauer argues that, with the exception of vowing, only swearing involves undertaking the strongest obligation possible in the context. For him the religious aspect of the oath is conceptually accidental; the essence of the oath is the public undertaking of the strongest possible obligation, while promises are undertakings of less onerous obligations. It is not clear whether, or under what circumstances, the obligation of the oath might be considered an overriding one. It is also unclear whether they might not better be analyzed by means of Joseph Raz's notion of exclusionary reasons.

Legal scholars agree that the oath has played two major roles in western judicial process: (1) as a method of proof and (2) as a method of motivating honesty, often made a precondition of testifying ("competence"). The "decisory oath," part of the Jewish and civil law traditions, functioned to provide irrebuttable proof of an issue. Proof by oath was probably the most widespread in ancient cultures, but the motivational or testimonial use can be found as early as the Babylonian Code of Hammurabi. This second use is primary today. Legal scholars suggest the shift from one role to the other resulted from diminishing belief in a vengeful deity.

Bentham most notoriously opposed the use of the oath, but even in legal circles he has not been alone. He offers a number of arguments against using the oath. First, he argues that if failure to perform the action that the oath was intended to compel is a failure which ought to be punished, then the oath is superfluous, while if the failure is not something which ought to be punished, then the punishment is undue and mischievous. Next, if the earthly punishment for perjury is adequate, the divine punishment invoked by the oath is unnecessary, and if the earthly punishment is inadequate, then God's justice is kept in a state of dependence on human folly or improbity. Third, the oath can lead to the absurdity of the power of the Almighty being commissioned to produce incompatible effects in cases where two people swear to do mutually exclusive things. Fourth, there is the overriding absurdity of supposing that humans can make God their servant through the ceremony of the oath.

Bentham's arguments are suggestive, and if they fail, they do so in instructive ways.The first fails by not clearly recognizing that an independent obligation may arise simply because of the undertaking. Searle's speech act analysis is helpful here. The second calls for clarification of the relationship between human and divine justice, while the third raises difficult issues of incompatible undertakings and moral obligation. The latter is not a problem for Bentham, of course, with his single principle of utility, or for courts, which assume that telling the truth in a judicial proceeding is an overriding obligation for everyone. The fourth objection supposes that taking an oath can have no meaning if it does not invoke the specter of divine punishment, a view shared by the common law until the latter part of the twentieth century.

As might be expected, Bentham's major criticism of the oath is utilitarian. He argues at length that in judicial proceedings, as elsewhere, the oath is an inefficient means of providing security against deception and incompleteness, while producing a variety of mischiefs. Many legal scholars have similarly argued that the threat of punishment under the laws of perjury provides a more realistic motivation for telling the truth than the oath, and in light of the difficulties courts have had with children taking the oath, have sometimes recommended abolition of the oath for witnesses. These utilitarian-style analyses typically take a narrow view of the role and consequences of the oath.

Modern legal and philosophical scholarship has begun to look at cultural and linguistic aspects of legal practice, and a fuller understanding of the role of the oath may be emerging. In the modern world the oath has most often been thought of as having only a psychological function. The judicial process and the trial, however, are beginning to be seen as dramas or narratives of justice, expressing a long history of justice stories with mythic and moral dimensions. From such a perspective the oath has more than a psychological function. By linking the participants to powerful mythic stories it might contribute toward the social meaning and moral underpinnings of the judicial process itself.

References

Bach, Kent, and Robert Harnish. *Linguistic Communication and Speech Acts*. Cambridge: MIT Press, 1979.

Bentham, Jeremy. "Swear Not at All." 1817. In *The Works of Jeremy Bentham,* ed. John Bowring. Vol. 5, 187–237. New York: Russell and Russell, 1962.

Gochnauer, Myron. "Oaths, Witnesses and Modern Law." *Canadian Journal of Law and Jurisprudence* 4 (1991), 67–100.

Searle, John R. *Speech Acts*. London: Cambridge University Press, 1969.

White, Thomas R. "Oaths in Judicial Proceedings and Their Effect upon the Competency of Witnesses." *The American Law Register* 51 O.S., 42 N.S. (July 1903), 373–446.

Myron Gochnauer

See also EVIDENCE; RELEVANCE; SPEECH ACTS; VOICE

Obedience and Disobedience

Of the myriad philosophical issues concerning a person's relationship to political authority, the two most important would appear to be whether there is a moral obligation to obey the law and when, if ever, is what is called civil disobedience morally permissible. The first is the more basic question. It is only if one accepts that there is a moral obligation to obey the law that the question arises of when, if ever, is it morally permissible to disobey the law for the furtherance of some overall political objective.

Let us assume that a person accepts some moral obligation to the political order to which that person is subject. A person may do so for any or all of the following reasons: human beings are social animals and therefore organized social life is necessary for human existence; each individual receives the benefits of community from his fellows and therefore owes some obligation of loyalty to the political body that makes that communal life possible; it is a requirement of the natural law that an individual should obey civil law unless the civil law is grossly immoral; the individual has expressly or tacitly promised to be bound by the rules of the civil society to which that individual belongs, and so on. While, historically, the argument has been made that human beings have some moral obligation to obey the laws of any political society in which they find themselves, modern discussions of the issue confine themselves to a discussion of the moral obligation of a person to obey the law of a society which that person accepts as basically just.

For those who accept that there is such a thing as a natural law in the traditional sense, the question of a moral obligation to obey constituted authority largely answers itself. The question of a possible moral justification for disobedience only arises when positive law commands the individual to do something that is against the natural law, although, even in that situation, it might sometimes be better on balance to obey a morally questionable human law. For example, St. Thomas Aquinas noted that, "in order to avoid scandal," that is, to maintain social coherence, it may sometimes be better for the individual to acquiesce in minor breaches of the natural law than to threaten political stability by disobedience. The only example which Aquinas gives of a situation in which one should categorically never obey an immoral law is one in which human law commands one to worship an idol.

For modern writers who have found the traditional notion of natural law difficult to accept, the question of whether one has a moral obligation to obey the laws of the state seems more problematic. Some writers have accepted that the social nature of human beings and the benefits human beings receive from being members of a community create moral obligations between individuals to each other and to the political society of which they are members. Among these moral obligations is a moral obligation to obey the law. During the civil unrest occasioned by significant public hostility to the United States' involvement in the Vietnam War; however, many writers challenged this conclusion and argued that, under the conditions of modern life, there was no moral obligation to obey the laws of political society. Since membership in a political society is not really voluntary, few members of a modern society can ever truly be said to have consented to be bound by its laws. Likewise, it was argued, the benefits that one receives from membership in a political society cannot generate the obligation, because one has no choice as to whether one wishes to receive these benefits; if given a choice, one might decide not to accept some of these benefits. According to this view, therefore, any moral obligation that may arise to obey the laws of a political society arises because the laws themselves express preexisting moral obligations and/or because the effects that one's own disobedience may have on others are sufficiently socially undesirable so as to require a morally responsible person to obey the law in order to refrain from setting this unfortunate example. If, however, there is no chance that one's disobedience will set a bad example for others and if the law in question does not incorporate a preexisting moral obligation—such as a moral obligation not to physically harm other people—then the individual has no moral obligation to obey the law. The frequently given example is someone approaching a stoplight on a straight road in a flat, remote, treeless area at two o'clock in the morning. If there is no one around who might observe the transgression, and who might for this reason be encouraged to violate the law in circumstances where a violation would be morally objectionable, the driver of our hypothetical vehicle is said to have no moral obligation to obey the law. That is, if independently of the existence of the law the driver would have a moral obligation to stop the car at the stoplight, then the driver should stop, but if there is no such independent moral obligation, then whether the driver stops or not is a matter of moral indifference. Indeed it might be morally preferable that the driver not stop if, for example, by not stopping the driver could save some time and conserve fuel.

As thus stated, the argument that one has no general moral obligation to obey the law reduces to another form of act utilitarianism, that is, of the view that the moral worth of any action or failure to act is to be judged on the individual merits of the action or inaction under all the relevant circumstances rather than by whether or not the action or failure to act would comply with some general moral precept. Under this view, not only does one not have a general moral duty to obey the law but, by parity of reasoning, one has no general duty to obey any general moral norm, such as norms about promise keeping or telling the truth. For example, suppose one promises a dying friend that, after the friend dies, one will continue the friend's practice of visiting his mother's grave every week and placing flowers upon it. Over time performing that task becomes extremely onerous. Let us suppose that no living person, other than oneself, is aware that this promise has been made. The same arguments that might counsel a person not to stop at night at a stoplight in a remote area might also counsel a person not to keep this promise. No harm is caused to any human being and there is no danger of setting a bad example for others. Similar hypotheticals may be constructed with regard to any other generally accepted moral norm, such as the norm of honesty.

In short, therefore, if a person maintains—as most unsophisticated members of western societies, if not of all societies do—that there are general moral obligations and that among these is a moral obligation to obey the law, it is not possible to show that such persons are mistaken by pointing out that many legal requirements concern trivia and that some violations of the law have no harmful consequences and indeed might even provide some benefit, particularly when the violations go unnoticed. The same objections can be made to any general moral obligations. In particular instances there may be genuine benefits to be gained from breaching general moral obligations to tell the truth or to keep promises while, at the time, there is no danger of setting a bad precedent for others because no one will be aware of what one has done. It is true that much of the law concerns trivia, but that is also true of much that occurs in the realm of morals. We all have many trivial moral obligations. We all make promises about unimportant things and everyone is familiar with the notion of a "white lie."

Whether a person who accepts that there are general moral obligations also should accept a general moral obligation to obey the law therefore boils down, for most people, to the question of how important a person believes maintenance of the rule of law is to the preservation of political society. Of course, recognizing a moral obligation to obey the law does not necessarily answer the question of what a person should do in any given situation. Human beings are often confronted with competing moral obligations. Obligations of honesty may compete with obligations that arise from promises. Obligations to obey the law may compete with obligations of loyalty or with the obligation not to physically harm other human beings, and the resolution of these moral dilemmas may not be easy. These moral dilemmas are related to the sorts of questions raised by the question of civil obedience.

References

Aquinas, St. Thomas. *Summa Theologiae*. Part One of the Second Part, Questions 90 to 97. London: Eyre and Spottiswoode, 1989.

Christie, George C. "On the Moral Obligation to Obey the Law." *Duke Law Journal* 1990 (1990), 1311–1336.

Greenawalt, Kent. "The Natural Duty to Obey the Law." *Michigan Law Review* 84 (1985), 1–62.

Honoré, Anthony. "Must We Obey? Necessity as a Ground of Obligation." *Virginia Law Review* 67 (1981), 39–61.

Klosko, George. "The Moral Force of Political Obligations." *American Political Science Review* 84 (1990), 1235–1250.

Rawls, John. *A Theory of Justice*. Cambridge MA: Harvard University Press, 1971.

Raz, Joseph. *The Authority of Law: Essays on Law and Morality*. Oxford: Oxford University Press, 1979.

Simmons, John A. *Moral Principles and Political Obligations*. Princeton: Princeton University Press, 1979.
Smith, M.B.E. "Is There a Prima Facie Obligation to Obey the Law?" *Yale Law Journal* 82 (1973), 950–976.
Soper, Philip. *A Theory of Law*. Cambridge MA: Harvard University Press, 1984.

George C. Christie

See also CIVIL DISOBEDIENCE; COMPLIANCE; CONSCIENTIOUS OBJECTION; OBLIGATION AND DUTY; POLITICAL OBLIGATION; PRIMA FACIE OBLIGATION

Objectivist Philosophy of Law

A law is a rule of social conduct enforced by the government. In distinction to all other social rules and practices, laws are backed up by the government's legal monopoly on the use of physical force—by fines, imprisonment, death.

The standard for evaluating laws follows from the purpose of government. In "The Nature of Government," Ayn Rand writes: "Since the protection of individual rights is the only proper purpose of a government, it is the only proper subject of legislation: all laws must be based on individual rights and aimed at their protection." Rights can be violated only by the initiation of physical force. A proper, moral government limits its use of physical force to retaliating against those who initiate its use, in violation of rights.

By its monopoly on the use of physical force, a government is potentially the greatest rights violator in a society. The threat to rights posed by private criminals is small compared to the threat posed by governments—witness the mass slaughters perpetrated by statist dictatorships. According to Rand, it is essential, therefore, that the government's use of physical force be "rigidly defined, delimited and circumscribed; no touch of whim or caprice should be permitted in its performance; it should be an impersonal robot, with the laws as its only motive power."

This is the basis of the need for objective law. Laws must be objective in both derivation and form. "Objective" here refers to that which is based on a rational consideration of the relevant facts—as opposed to the subjective, the arbitrary, the whim-based.

An objectively derived law is one stemming not from the whim of legislators or bureaucrats but from a rational application of the principle of individual rights. Rand, in *The Virtue of Selfishness*, affirms that rights tie law to reality, because rights represent a recognition of a basic, unalterable fact, that is, of "the conditions required by man's nature for his proper survival." For instance, a law against murder is clearly derived from the individual's right to life, whereas a law compelling military service is not derived from any right, but from the alleged needs of a collective, in disdain for the individual's right to life.

Contemporary legal philosophers, politicians, judges, and bureaucrats believe that the purpose of law is to strike an ever shifting balance between the wishes and demands of various groups. In this chaos, no *principles* are invoked, only such undefined and indefinable notions as "the public interest" or, worse, "the needs of the environment." No stable, principled legal code can be derived from notions detached from reality. Such notions require a policy as "flexible" and "evolving" as the dizzying swirl of intellectual fashion that generates them. Ultimately, only the principle of individual rights, being grounded in the factual requirements of human survival, can provide the basis for law that is objectively defined and objectively applied.

As the law must be objective in its source, so it must be objective in its form: objective laws are clearly defined, consistent, unambiguous, stable, and as straightforward and simple as possible. They are also impartial and universal, in the sense of applying to all individuals as individuals rather than as members of any race, creed, class, or other collective.

In every respect, according to Rand, the law must be predictable: "Men must know clearly, and in advance of taking an action, what the law forbids them to do (and why), what constitutes a crime, and what penalty they will incur if they commit it." The ideal is to make the laws of government like the laws of nature: firm, stable, impersonal absolutes.

A crucial element in understanding objective law is provided by Rand's identification that *physical force* is the only basic means of violating rights: "It is only by means of physical force that one man can deprive another of his life, or enslave him, or rob him, or prevent him from pursuing his own goals, or compel him to act against his own rational judgment." A law defined in terms of acts of physical force, notes Leonard Peikoff, stands in stark contrast to laws forbidding crimes which are not defined in terms of specific physical acts; e.g., laws against "blasphemy," "obscenity," "immorality," "restraint of trade," or "unfair profits." In all such examples, even when the terms are philosophically definable, it is not possible to know from the statement of the law what existential acts are forbidden. Men are reduced to guessing; they have to try to enter the mind of the legislator and divine his intentions, ideas, value judgments, philosophy—which, given the nature of such legislation, are riddled with caprice. In practice, the meaning of such laws is decided arbitrarily, on a case-by-case basis, by tyrants, bureaucrats, or judges, according to methods that no one, including the interpreters, can define or predict.

A criminal who initiates physical force is attempting to make his arbitrary will, not the facts of reality, the absolute to which the victim must adjust. Similarly, nonobjective law demands that the citizen focus on and accept the unaccountable will of the law's interpreter instead of the facts of reality. Objective law reflects not anyone's will, but facts. In this sense, objective law is passive: certain defined areas are clearly marked "off limits," and, unless one crosses the line, the law respects and protects one's freedom of choice. Nonobjective law is active; it is a beast in motion. Its "flexibility" makes it the indispensable tool of dictatorships.

Ayn Rand writes in "Antitrust: The Rule of Unreason": "It is a grave error to suppose that a dictatorship rules a nation by means of strict, rigid laws which are obeyed and enforced with rigorous, military precision. Such a rule would be evil, but almost bearable; men could endure the harshest edicts, provided these edicts were known, specific and stable; it is not the known that breaks men's spirits, but the unpredictable."

Objectivity is also required in regard to every governmental activity, from the conduct of the police to election procedures. Legal objectivity, in the widest sense, includes objective methods of enacting, interpreting, constitutionally validating, and applying the law, as well as objective methods of law enforcement. Each of these is a wide and complex domain requiring multivolume treatises to specify proper procedures; but the required work has essentially been done already. The original American system of constitutionally limited government, together with eighteenth-century English common law and rules of procedure, formed a nearly perfect system from the standpoint of objectivity.

Rand's contribution to the theory of objective law is threefold. First, she provided a rational, objective basis for individual rights. Second, by identifying the fact that only *physical force* can violate rights, she made objective the basis for establishing when a right has been violated. Third, by developing a full philosophic theory of objectivity as such and then connecting this theory of objectivity with the need for government, she solidified John Locke's defense of that institution, showing in *The Virtue of Selfishness* why the law has to be objectively defined, interpreted, applied, and enforced: "*A government is the means of placing the retaliatory use of physical force under objective control*—i.e., under objectively defined laws. . . . If a society is to be free, its government has to be controlled."

References

Peikoff, Leonard. *Objectivism: The Philosophy of Ayn Rand*. New York: New American Library, 1991.

Rand, Ayn. "Antitrust: The Rule of Unreason." *Objectivist Newsletter* (February 1962).

———. *Atlas Shrugged*. New York: Random House, 1957.

———. "The Nature of Government" and "Man's Rights." In *The Virtue of Selfishness: A New Concept of Egoism*. New York: Signet, 1964.

Harry Binswanger
Thomas A. Bowden

Objectivity

The term "objectivity" as used in law is understood in three different ways: as incontestability, as impartiality, and as regulative idea.

Incontestability of Evidence

The process of the application of law tends toward obtaining an objective statement of empirical facts on the basis of which a legal adjudication is to be performed. "Objectivity" is perceived in this context in the same way as the objectivity of any empirical statement in empirical sciences. It can only be attained by the maximum elimination of any evaluative elements from such an investigation.

Hence, in law, as in the empirical sciences, the objectivity of empirical statements depends on perfecting the research methods applied, and these, in turn, are bound together with the general state of empirical knowledge. An intersubjective testability of empirical statements has been regarded since the times of Kant as the criterion of their objectivity. In empirical sciences the concept of objectivity is frequently associated with the concept of truth, especially when the postulated verifiability of the empirical statements refers to their truthfulness. Thus, objective law is law whose adjudications are based on true statements.

Impartiality

Objectivity in law can be perceived as the impartiality of the process of adjudication itself. Hence, objective law is one which sets rules and principles that obligate those who apply law (judges, juries, prosecutors, civil servants who make legal decisions, and so forth), as well as those indirectly involved in its application (legal experts, translators, stenographers, and so forth) to treat parties in the same way. They must not favor any of the parties nor have any personal or emotional involvement in the case, since this would impair the objectivity of their judgment. A number of existing legal means (such as the independence of the judiciary and of the jury, the possibility of being removed from the case, and so on) serve to ensure the principle of impartiality. A variety of such legal means at one's disposal, as well as their actual application, form the basis for evaluating whether or not a law is objective.

Regulative Idea of Interpretation: Practical Device

The objectivity of law is also identified with its objective interpretation. Although legal philosophers are reluctant about the concept of an objective interpretation of a legal text, a certain yearning for such interpretation can still be traced in literature on the subject. Lawyers and legal scholars, fully aware of the theoretical dangers ensuing from adopting the concept, frequently use terms such as "adequate," "proper," "right," instead of the term "objective." Yet, while using these terms, they very rarely believe in the real existence of an ultimate "right" or "objective" interpretation. What underlies their aspiration for finding the "right" meaning of a legal text is by no means a firm belief in the existence of a "right" meaning, but rather practical reasons. After all, a judge cannot afford to simply state that a text is equivocal, since this would render adjudication impossible. He is compelled to choose one of several possible meanings—it will often be the meaning with which a lawgiver perceived the text—and accordingly attempt a plausible justification of his choice. With the assistance of the idea of "objective" or "right" meaning, adjudication and justification become much easier.

However, in order to fully understand why lawyers, especially legal philosophers, are willing to use a concept that is theoretically both ambiguous and confusing, one should not reduce the concept of the "right" interpretation to its practical aspect. Rather, she or he should refer to the conviction, expressed occasionally in the theory of literature, that objective interpretation of a legal text is an ideal to be pursued. The concept of the "objective"/"right" interpretation of a text—in the way in which it is understood and used by theorists of legal interpretation—is an idea which is frequently perceived to be like Immanuel Kant's regulative principles (ideas): ideas which help sort out the interpreter's performance and give it some meaningful sense. While dealing with the transcendental analytic, Kant defined a number of categories which constitute, shape, and transform the empirical data perceived by the senses. However, it is not the categories that provide one with full knowledge of the phenomena encountered; it is the regulative ideas that complete the task by bringing harmony and unity into one's cognizance. Thus Kant's regulative ideas—or, as he called them, *focus imaginarius*—do not form, create, or shape anything in the way that categories do. According to W.H. Walsh, they "regulate, set guidelines for the researchers to follow in order to achieve the desired unity of science" and "constantly strive for completeness and totality" of one's cognizance. Even though such aspirations to secure the much desired completeness and totality of science may never be fulfilled, the significant role which they play is, in fact, that of constant encouraging and inspiring further research. Analysis of the works of theorists of legal interpretation clearly points to the fact that the concept of "right" or "objective" interpretation of a given legal text is mostly understood not as a belief in real existence of an ultimate, right, objective meaning of the law text, but as a kantian regulative idea.

References

Bennett, R.W. "Objectivity in Constitutional Law." *University of Pennsylvania Law Review* 132 (1984).

Fiss, O.M. "Objectivity and Interpretation." *Stanford Law Review* 34 (1984).

Hirsch, E.D. *Validity in Interpretation.* New Haven: Yale University Press, 1967.

Kant, I. *Immanuel Kant's Critique of Pure Reason.* Trans. N.K. Smith. New York: Macmillan, 1985.

Sarkowicz, R. "Über die Interpretation des Textes" (On the Interpretation of Texts). *Archiv für Rechts- und Sozialphilosophie* 82 (1996).

Walsh, W.H. "Kant, Immanuel." In *The Encyclopedia of Philosophy,* vol. 4, ed. P. Edwards. New York: Macmillan, 1972.

Ryszard Sarkowicz

See also INTERPRETATION; TRUTH; VALIDITY

Obligation and Duty

The function of normative discourse is to engender a state of mind whereby a particular state of affairs is consented to or accepted as good, right, proper, or justified. The function of ethical normative discourse is to persuade individuals to behave or refrain from behaving in a certain way, or in other words to justify the performance or nonperformance of certain actions according to criteria that could be said to constitute a morality. Thus, the function of normative discourse is to influence behavior. The normative function of legal discourse goes one step beyond that of ethical or moral discourse. Normative legal discourse functions, not only to influence behavior, but to justify the authoritative application of power to enforce the norms of the system.

The central concept of *normative* legal discourse is *legal obligation.* A legal obligation can be viewed as a *duty* from the perspective of the person having the burden to perform or refrain from performing the particular act, while the person who benefits from the duty or who can make the claim for it is often conceived as having a *right.* A person has a *liberty* or *privilege* when there is no obligation to do the act and no obligation to refrain from doing the act. Propositions about the existence of a legal obligation serve a normative function if they are used in such a way that it follows from the existence of an obligation to do or not to do a certain act that the person having the duty both ought to and is obliged to do or not do the act. Such statements can, however, serve merely a descriptive function when there is no intent to convey a normative element but merely to describe what the law provides.

The oldest approach to the normativity of legal discourse is that of *natural law* in which the normativity of the law is derived from the coherency or consistency between the content of the law and the nature of human beings and the world or universe within which they live. A law is binding if its content is consistent with the laws of nature, whether revealed by the exercise of reason or by the revelations of God. If the content of an authoritative prescription is manifestly inconsistent with the laws of nature, or reason, then it is not binding and consequently is not a true law. H.L.A. Hart has produced one of the most cogent counterarguments to this kind of explanation of normativity. Hart argues that the issue of whether or not something is a law is a separate question than whether or not it is a good law. When the two are confused we lose the clarity of validity by introducing the ambiguity of moral and ethical argument. The two issues depend upon entirely different criteria.

The coercive theories of Jeremy Bentham's and John Austin's versions of *legal positivism,* wherein law is defined as the command of a sovereign backed by a sanction, furnish an alternative explanation of the normativity of legal discourse. Such theories derive the binding nature of law from the authoritative coercive power by which the laws are enforced. Hart's critique of this perspective is generally considered to be definitive. Hart demonstrates that such theories are unable to provide a normative basis for legal obligation or the binding force of the law. Hart's now famous example of the coercive order of a gunman, demanding that another person hand over her purse, demonstrates the distinction between being obliged to do something and having an obligation to do something. It does not follow that because an individual is obliged by coercion to do an act that he or she ought to do it, which is the essence of a normative proposition about an obligation. By placing the coercive power in the hands of a sovereign authority, Hart points out that one is left with neither a plausible analysis of "being obliged" nor an adequate analysis of the normative force of an obligation.

A further explanation of the normativity of legal discourse is furnished by Hart himself. Hart argues that the source of the normativity of legal discourse is to be derived from the institutional structures of the law as they function within a social context. Hart's theory of law, known as *analytical positivism*, has much in common with J.L. Austin's theory of performative utterances, and as such constitutes a part of a general theory of social practices. Social practices such as the law or promising have two parts, the invoking features, which are constituted by a set of rules which prescribe how the practice is to be invoked, and the rules which result from the practice itself. Hart refers to the former as secondary rules and to the latter as primary rules. Hart attempts to explain the normativity of legal discourse as being derived from the union of primary and secondary rules in the context of the social practice that engenders habitual obedience and social pressures for conformity. A careful analysis of Hart's arguments, however, reveals a shift from purely descriptive uses of statements about the existence of legal obligations to prescriptive uses. Consequently, Hart's theory of law has failed to solve the very issue which he considers to be central to legal theory, the source of the normativity of legal discourse.

Theories such as *Scandinavian legal realism, American legal realism,* and even some positions within the *critical legal studies movement* take the position that the normative functions of legal and moral discourse are purely psychological in that they achieve changes in attitudes about the law, but their rationality is an illusion. If this position is correct, then the law is a fraudulent exercise whereby the power of the state is used for the benefit of special and private interests.

As with many classic debates in philosophy, such as those between free will and determinism, skepticism and objectivism, or empiricism and rationalism, both sides of the debate, while inconsistent with each other, appear to be true in certain aspects. Each side is right, but in a different way, and, since the two positions are inconsistent, we have to deny the truth in one position in order to be able to accept the truth in the other. If and when such debates are resolved (if they can ever be said to be truly settled), they are seldom terminated by one side finally predominating over the other. Resolution is achieved instead through the development of a new theoretical position transcending the argument by denying a fundamental assumption implicit in both of the traditional perspectives and by inserting in its place a different premise, which allows the relevant truths of both of the previous positions to survive without internal inconsistencies.

The traditional arguments about whether the binding force of the law is derived from its teleology or from its form, source, or validity can be analyzed in these same terms. The obvious truth of legal positivism is that the existence of an obligation depends upon the proper invoking of the practice and is not derived from the specific content of the obligation. We have a number of obligation-creating practices, such as legislating, contracting, truth-telling, and promising, whereby we can create obligations with any content, within limits. The practices themselves furnish the justification for the obligation. It is not the results of telling the truth or keeping a promising on each particular occasion which binds us to tell the truth or to keep a promise, but rather the justification of the practices themselves.

The readily recognizable truth in the nonpositivist's position is that an appeal to an obligation entails an appeal to reason. Obligations are products of practices which are justified by the teleology of the practice itself. The binding force of obligation, or its necessity, is not to be found in the causal connection between the particular content of a rule and some desirable state of affairs, but in the causal connection between the function of the practice and the ends which justify or explain its existence.

It must be kept in mind, however, that no practice is absolute. All practices function subject to a ceteris paribus clause. There are exceptions to every practice, in that no one is expected to keep a promise or tell the truth no matter what the consequences. This holds equally true for legal obligations. In situations where the existence of the legal obligation cannot function to produce the prescribed behavior, the law itself will generate an exception, such as the defense of infancy or insanity. When, for example, complying with a legal obligation will produce a worse result in terms of the teleology of the law than would not complying, then again the law will generate an exception, such as the defense of necessity or a principle that will establish a priority in terms of the teleology of the law such as the principles that persons should not profit from their wrongs, *salus populi suprema lex* (regard for the public welfare is the highest law), the nonenforceability of illegal or immoral contracts, and the abuse of right principle of the civil law. The law has certain goals which are the goals of the practice itself as a practice. These would include such objectives as certainty, decisiveness, clarity, predictability, consistency, and publicity, and so on. Then there is the matrix of goals which constitute the teleology of the content of the law itself. These would include such things as peace, safety, economic prosperity, privacy, and security, and so forth. The greater the capacity of the law to generate exceptions in a rule-governed manner where the content of the law is inconsistent with the teleology of the law, the less likely it will be that there will be an inconsistency between validity and teleology.

The concept of obligation functions as a strong kind of "ought" because it also at the same time functions to express necessity. A statement that an obligation exists is an appeal not only to reason, but to a kind of reason that is so strong or important as to leave no room for individual choice. There are many things which we ought to do, but are under no obligation to do. These would constitute a weak form of ought as contrasted with the stronger ought of obligation within which the concepts of ought and oblige merge.

Even if we can obtain an adequate theory of the normativity of legal discourse in terms of the nature and structure of obligation-creating practices, we are faced with a second problem in legal theory. The general assumption is that an adequate theory of the normativity of legal discourse will be coherent and consistent throughout the law. We have, within the legal process, however, at least two different kinds of obligation-creating practices which are central to the legal process, each having its own discourse which is inconsistent with that of the other. There is law as the rule of reason, which is founded in the discourse of moral responsibility, individual autonomy, and fundamental rights, all of which are the necessary presuppositions for action. There is also the discourse of law as fiat and, in particular, the discourse of political authority.

That is to say, we have the practice of judge-made law that assumes a theory of individual autonomy, fundamental rights, universalizability, and rationality; and we have the practice of legislation that assumes the sovereign power of the state. The fundamental presuppositions of the normativity of case-based law and that of legislation are directly contradictory. The normative foundations of rights theories and judge-made law all presuppose the moral responsibility and autonomous agency of the individual, which is inconsistent with the sovereign power of the state. This dichotomy underlies much of the dispute in political theory between libertarianism and communitarianism. No version of the social contract, as yet, has successfully reconciled the moral autonomy of the individual with the sovereign power of the state. Our actual legal practices have evolved rules which set the priorities between the different kinds of laws and the presuppositions that furnish the foundations of their normativity. Thus we have the rule of the primacy of the legislature, which permits the legislature to change any judge-made laws. Many jurisdictions provide a bill of fundamental rights, which gives a limited individual autonomy priority over the sovereign power of the state.

It would appear that normativity is relative to the discourse which constitutes the particular practice. So long as this is the case there is no foundation for a claim to an ultimate truth or justice for the law, nor for an objective foundation for normativity. Contemporary critical legal theory challenges the normativity of legal discourse on the grounds that the law is often sexist, racist, and favors economic privilege. Without a unified, objective foundation for the normativity of the law, these challenges cannot be met by merely pointing out the consistency within a legal normative discourse.

The essential logical property of normative legal discourse is the universalizability of legal judgments about obligations. *Any judgment made in regard to a particular situation, that a particular person is or is not legally obligated to do a particular act, logically entails that the judgment instances a rule of law such that anyone in a relevantly similar situation is or is not legally obligated to do the same act.* All criteria of relevancy are teleological. Universalizability functions in normative legal discourse to maintain a teleological consistency within the legal system while at the same time avoiding difficult policy, ethical, and ideological arguments. Thus case-based reasoning, of the kind manifested in the doctrine of precedent that relevantly like cases should be decided alike, is an efficient and economic form of normative rationality.

References

Coval, S.C., and J.C. Smith. *Law and Its Presuppositions.* London: Routledge and Kegan Paul, 1986.

Dworkin, R. *Taking Rights Seriously.* Cambridge: Harvard University Press, 1977.

Fuller, L. "Positivism and Fidelity to Law." *Harvard Law Review* 71 (1957–58), 630.

Hart, H.L.A. *The Concept of Law.* Oxford: Clarendon Press, 1961.

———. "Positivism and the Separation of Law and Morals." *Harvard Law Review* 71 (1957–58), 593.

Kelsen, H. *The Pure Theory of Law.* Berkeley: University of California Press, 1967.

MacKinnon, C.A. *Toward a Feminist Theory of the State.* Cambridge: Harvard University Press, 1989.

Ross, A. *Directives and Norms.* London: Routledge and Kegan Paul, 1968.

Smith, J.C. *Legal Obligation.* London: Athlone Press, 1976.

J.C. Smith

See also IS/OUGHT GAP; OBEDIENCE AND DISOBEDIENCE; POLITICAL OBLIGATION

Obligation, Political

See POLITICAL OBLIGATION

Offer and Acceptance

See CONTRACTUAL OBLIGATION

Omissions

Very broadly, the distinction of act from omission is between acting and failing to act; or between a doing or a doing-something, and a not-doing or a doing-nothing. Further refinement is clearly necessary, for not all failures to act are omissions. A nonsurgeon who fails to save a child who can only be saved through surgery would seem a case in point. Moreover, when Jack is doing something (for instance, reading a book), he is not doing a number of other things (for instance, mowing the lawn, cooking a meal), and we need some way of specifying which of the things he is not doing, if any, counts as an omission on his part.

At a minimum, three conditions seem necessary. First, Jack must have the *ability* to do whatever is in question. A nonsurgeon lacks the ability to save the child, just as a nonswimmer usually lacks the ability to save drowning people. Second, the agent must have the *opportunity* to do whatever is in question. If a swimmer never comes across a drowning person or if a firefighter never encounters people trapped in a burning building, then they do not omit to save someone. To this second condition, a restriction might be appended, namely, that the agent must have the opportunity to do whatever is in question in circumstances that are not themselves life threatening or otherwise represent catastrophic loss to the agent. A firefighter who can only save someone by going into and out of control, raging inferno would seem to fall under this restriction. Third, the agent is or will be *expected* to do whatever is in question. When we say that a surgeon or firefighter "omitted" to save a person, we in part allude to the fact that he or she is or may be expected to save individuals in certain circumstances. This helps to deal with the many things that the surgeon or firefighter do not do, at a time when he or she is doing something, and that we do not treat as omissions. At a minimum, then, ability, opportunity, and expectation are the ingredients required in order to turn a failure to act into an omission.

Not all omissions, however, are immoral/illegal ones. To have these, we need to add certain factors, for example, that the agent is under a moral and/or legal duty to do whatever is in question. (Our knowledge that the agent is under such a duty helps explain why we expect the agent to do something.) Jobs such as surgeon, firefighter, and lifeguard are in part defined in terms of the duties the job imposes upon their holders, and holders who fail to discharge these duties can be held, absent some excusing condition, to be guilty of an immoral and/or illegal omission.

This duty view of immoral/illegal omissions, in law sometimes captured by talk of feasance, nonfeasance, and malfeasance, yields a further advantage, in addition to the fact that it enables us to identify which failures to act on the agent's part are illegal omissions. It enables us to characterize omissions as the failure of the discharge of the duty to occur, where the discharge of the duty would be the completed act. In other words, once we know what the completed act would be, that is, what the discharge of the duty would be, we know what an omission or failure to achieve the completed act would be; we then construe the latter in terms of the former. If the lifeguard jumps in, she discharges her duty and saves a person from drowning; if she does not jump in, she fails to discharge her duty and so omits to save a life. We understand her omission only by first understanding what the completed act would be, if she discharges her duty.

This leads naturally into the much discussed issue of whether omissions are causes. On the analysis proffered, we need to figure out why the completed act did not occur. We want to know what the significant and distinctive factors were that explain why the completed act did not occur, why, for example, in the lifeguard case, an outcome other than life—indeed, the antithesis of life—was produced or brought about. This talk of "producing" or "bringing about" certainly looks causal but not in a billiard ball sense of causality. It represents a wider notion.

If a boulder is hurtling down the hill, and if Jill fails to push Jack out of the way, it may be tempting to regard her failure to act as sufficient in the circumstances to kill Jack. This is not true, if billiard ball causality is what is intended, for her omission does not kill Jack, the boulder does. What her failure to push him out of the way does suffice to do, however, is to allow the boulder to kill him. That is, her omission can suffice in the circumstances to allow Jack to be killed, though it is the boulder that kills him, and allowing to be killed is not the same thing as producing or bringing about. Allowing to be caused still operates with the paradigm of billiard ball causality. The rock will kill Jack, unless Jill pushes him out of the way; her failure to push him allows him to be killed by the rock. In the case of bringing about, however, the claim is that an omission is a significant and distinctive factor in bringing about a death. Jill's omission does not, or does not only, allow Jack to be killed; it actually helps to bring about Jack's death. The difference here is important: if asked what killed Jack, we cite the rock; if asked what produced or brought about Jack's death, we cite both the rock and Jill's omission. Producing or bringing about is a wider notion than causing in a strictly billiard ball sense.

Finally, we can regard what happens to Jack as both a killing and a death. As a killing, what happens to him has the rock as a necessary and/or sufficient condition of his death, and we can regard the rock as the active agent in his death in the strictest billiard ball sense. As a death, however, what happens to Jack is treated as an outcome that is produced or brought about by significant and distinctive factors in the circumstances of which Jill's failure to push him out of the way is one. Both descriptions, a killing and a death, are appropriate. A killing occurs because the rock crashes into Jack; a death occurs because the rock crashes into Jack and Jill failed to push him out of the way. Did her failure to push him out of the way kill him? Not in the same way that the rock did. However, the rock crashing into Jack is not the full story of what brought about his death. It is easy to see, therefore, why we might treat Jill's omission as a cause: death is the effect of the rock's crashing into Jack, and death is the outcome in the production or bringing about of which both the rock and Jill's failure to push Jack aside figure. Since death obtains in both cases, it might be claimed that Jill's omission, together with the rock, caused Jack's death. Though death occurs in both cases, the rock and the omission do not cause in the same sense.

References

D'Arcy, Eric. *Human Acts*. Oxford: Clarendon Press, 1963.

Feinberg, Joel. *Harm to Others*. Oxford: Clarendon Press, 1984.

Kamm, Frances. "Actions, Omissions, and the Stringency of Duties." *University of Pennsylvania Law Review* 142 (1994), 1493–1512.

Leavens, Arthur. "A Causation Approach to Criminal Omissions." *University of California Law Review* 76 (1988), 547–591.

Moore, Michael. *Act and Crime*. Oxford: Clarendon Press, 1993.

Simester, A.P. "Why Omissions Are Special." *Legal Theory* 1 (1995), 311–335.

Williams, Bernard. "Acts and Omissions, Doing and Not Doing." In *Making Sense of Humanity*, 56–64. Cambridge: Cambridge University Press, 1995.

Raymond G. Frey

See also Causation, Criminal; Causation, Tort Law; Rescue in Tort and Criminal Law; Supererogation; Virtue

O

Ontology, Legal (Metaphysics)

Legal ontology (metaphysics) is the philosophical investigation into the existence (or substance) of law. Legal ontology receives its actual meaning and significance when distinguished from the law's epistemological analysis.

In ancient and primitive societies (in which the separation, laicization, and formalization of the law had not yet occurred), the law's substance was seen as a unity between ideality and reality. Historically, in the Greco-Roman ideal of *to dikaion* (the just), law is the just thing itself, the concrete justness of the concrete case, which, as a *medium in re* (medium within the thing), is hidden in the things themselves, although its identification can only be achieved by citizens through their own communities. As survivals of this past, anthropology often uncovers ideas of law in stateless societies in which customs, contracts, and laws still form an undivided unity. Customs are normative expectations and description of the status quo, contracts record the convention actually reached, and laws reflect the decision taken by the community.

Polarization results from attempts at conceptualizing law and reducing it to the ruler's enactment. *Lex* (law) is also distinguished from the formerly undifferentiated domain of *ius* (right). As compared to *to dikaion*, this is a change in *ius*. For, in the notion of the *ius*, the behavior resulting in the *justum* (just) becomes the core element of the concept; emphasis is thereby shifted from the thing itself to its recognition and realization. Similarly, in the notions of *Recht, right, droit, diritto*, the behavior embodying the *rectum* receives emphasis. In the case of the notion of *lex* (with the meanings of λεγω such as *colligo* (gather), *dico* (tell), and *loquor* (say)), the emphasis is put on "what has been said" and "what has been collected." Thus, the earlier consideration is reasserted, according to which the standard inherent in the thing is not enough, and any genuine standard can only be found through searching for righteous human behavior.

European legal culture has been long dominated by voluntarism. First, by its expression of will, the strongest social power opposes itself to the law inherited as a tradition, then starts to control it, and finally ends up dominating it. Thereby, the quality of "legal" is eventually reduced to the arbitrary act embodied in the sovereign enactment. The understanding of law as a rule becomes separated from upright conduct. Any rule can become legal if given a posited form. Legal positivism teaches the exclusiveness of positive law: it is positive because of being posited, that is, enacted through the due procedure in the due way and form. This reduces the *ius* to the *lex*. English legal culture has always found conceptual dichotomy, or polarization, with axiomatizing pretensions. Even the statutory law is not accepted as the denial or overcoming of the idea of *ius*, but rather as a natural corollary to it. As a survival of the ancient tradition, sometimes the natural law is set against the positive law as its standard and limitation in various ways and with varied success.

Throughout the thousands of years of legal history, a number of trends in legal ontology and metaphysics were based on ideas set by the law for itself, proving by this the law's peculiar strength. The image of the law as a homogeneous and normatively closed medium, which the law suggests about itself (its existence, its self-identity, its boundaries, and its limits), has successfully subordinated philosophical reflection to the subject's ideology. Therefore, the ontology of law has to be detached from the subject's law and its ideologically formed self-image. An epistemological criticism of the law's self-definition could prove its unverifiability at most. The genuine ontological question is neither its verifiability nor the disclosure of practical interests lurking behind the ideologies, but proving why the law's ideology is an ontological component of the law's construction and functioning, its sine qua non.

Penetration of this question is mainly due to George Lukacs' posthumous ontology of social being and to some trends in deconstruction. Law is theoretically constructed, especially modern formal law, as the aggregate of teleological projections, linguistically formed. (Teleological projections are reduced to the legal transformation of social relations, or to the reflection of transcendental principles or of material determinations as norms, or to psychological effects or individual reactions, or to the stand taken by the sovereign power.) It is a commonplace that what gets realized is always more or less, but something different, from what was originally intended in teleological projections; shifts in emphasis, even if unperceivable, can end in real changes of direction in the historical process.

Such changes occur necessarily in the law, since it has its own system of procedure. Out of the heterogeneity of everyday practice, primary teleological projections must be accommodated by the law as its own secondary projections, transformed and made exclusive by its homogeneous medium.

Law is the medium of social mediation. It has no independent goal, but allows any goal to be attained through its procedures. It helps keep change orderly. It selects its contacts with other complexes. A threat of resorting to force has to stand behind it; nominally this is aimed at each and every addressee. However, it can actually be enforced only in exceptional cases. The law would certainly collapse if the need for implementing sanctions arose at a mass level. All in all, the law cannot serve as the exclusive carrier of social changes. By its symbolic reassertion it can only assist the realization of intentions in the course of their implementation. It can sanction casual deviances, if these are already isolated as the exceptions.

As social mediation, law works through the instrumentality of language, the other complex of mediation. Language can only be ambiguous and fuzzy—is completely inadequate for grasping individual phenomena—since it can resort to classifying generalizations at best. Logical subordination makes legal mediation no more than a phenomenal form. Legal professionals, through the machinery they operate, first turn actual social conflicts into conflicts within the law, then give them a formulation justifiable by logic, and strictly deducible from the positive law, and so transform them into sham conflicts.

The law must use internal technical concepts to preserve its homogeneity and to close its system normatively. It postulates its own construction by the notion of validity and its own operation by the notion of legality. These are the two pillars of its professional ideology, forming the so-called juristic worldview, a kind of normativism; this frames juristic activity within forms conventionalized within the law. It suggests the ideological presumption that expectations formed outside the law can only be satisfied by activities inside the law.

Thereby, the ontological concept of law has a wider range than positivism about rules. In addition to rules and the principles substantiating the rules' applicability, its concept includes thought patterns, conceptual distinctions, ideals, and sensibilities, as well as legal techniques and ways to proceed. Legal techniques are the kinds of representation and skill that define the genuine context of judicial reasoning in the given legal arrangement, the set of instruments which make it possible that a dynamic "law in action" will grow out of the static "law in books" in a way accepted in the legal community. Accordingly, both the legal technique and the thought-culture of the society must be recognized among the law's components.

In this way legal ontology comes close to what can be said about law by philosophy of praxis, cognitive sciences, and linguistic-philosophical analysis. Law is considered to be a historical continuum, gaplessly fed back by practice, and reconventionalized through its everyday operation. It is an artificial human construct which cannot be interpreted without attending to the community environment (that is, Ludwig Wittgenstein's *Lebensform*) and interaction.

The law's concepts are fully technicized yet, in the juristic ideology, postulate a world *as if* they truly reflected the social environment in which the law is embedded. Marxism and deconstructionism are quasi-epistemological criticisms of this reflection. They also criticize these technical concepts, as instruments of preservation which conceal the true nature of this world, falsify it, and so risk that ontological reconstruction will finally transform into an ideology.

References

Amselek, Paul, and Christophe Grzegorczyck, eds. *Controverses autour de l'ontologie du droit* (Issues in the Ontology of Law). Paris: Presses Universitaires de France, 1989.

Cojère, Alexandre. *Esquisse d'une phénoménologie du droit* (Essay in Phenomenology of Law). Paris: Gallimard, 1981.

Goodrich, Peter. *Reading the Law*. Oxford: Blackwell, 1986.

Kalinowski, Georges. "La pluralité ontique en philosophie du droit; l'application de la théorie de l'analogie à l'ontologie juridique" (Ontic Plurality in Philosophy of Law; An Application of the Theory of Analogy to Legal Ontology). *Revue philosophique de Louvain* 64 (1966), 263–280.

Kube, Vladimir. *Ontologie des Rechts* (Ontology of Law). Berlin: Duncker und Humblot, 1986.

Lang, Wieslaw. "The Ontology of Law." In *Sprache, Performanz und Ontologie des Rechts. Festgabe für Kazimierz Opalek zum 75. Geburtstag,* ed. Werner Krawietz and Jerzy Wróblewski, 221 ff. Berlin: Duncker und Humblot, 1993.

Tiscornia, Daniela. "A Methodology for the Representation of Legal Knowledge: Formal Ontology." *Sorites* (1995), 26–43.

Varga, Csaba. "Towards the Ontological Foundation of Law." *Rivista internazionale di Filosofia del Diritto* 15 (1983), 127. Also in *Law and Philosophy*. Budapest: Lorand Eötvös University Project on Comparative Legal Cultures, 1994.

Villey, Michel. "Essor et décadence du volontarisme juridique" (Rise and Fall of Legal Voluntarism). In *Leçons de la philosophie du droit,* 271. Paris: Dalloz, 1962.

Walt, Steven. "Practical Reason and the Ontology of Statutes." *Law and Philosophy* 15 (1996), 227–255.

Wróblewski, Jerzy. "Ontology and Epistemology of Law." *Rivista internazionale di filosofia del diritto* 50 (1973), 832–860.

Csaba Varga

See also JURISPRUDENCE

Oppression

See VIOLENCE AND OPPRESSION

Order

The conjunction of "law" and "order" is so familiar that it has nearly come to represent a single idea in the popular consciousness. Even philosophers of law seldom ask how these two ideas are related. A historical framework will provide the most comprehensive vehicle for discussing their relation. The emergence of human law is conditioned by a preexisting natural order; this need not imply, however, that natural order is the cause of law, or that law and order can(not) be identified with one another.

The Ancient History of Law and Order: Divine Command

Throughout the ancient world it was widely thought that through an act of divine command, cosmos (order) was separated from chaos. Since in the ancient world, divine command was generally inseparable from human and natural law, and since the gradual secularization of law in the west is predicated historically upon this religious origin, even the most ordinary assumptions about the relation between law and order refer to supernatural or metaphysical grounds.

Divine command has at least three crucial functions, and one important analogue; taken together, these clarify the complex relationship between law and order. The functions are to order place, time, and cause, and their epistemic counterparts. The analogue is human command; its order is a smaller order, or "microcosm."

Analytic/Spatial

Epistemologically, when the deity speaks, a primordial distinction is made between chaos and cosmos, permitting further distinctions, or "analysis," and derivative human knowledge. Distinctions between nature/convention, sacred/profane, and so on, are dependent upon the chaos/cosmos distinction. Metaphysically, the originary act of speaking functions to separate the chaos and the cosmos into their proper domains or regions. Until the deity localizes chaos, no concept of place is possible; hence, no space exists where further ordered beings might emerge. For example, God has to make a place for Adam before making Adam.

Synthetic/Temporal

Epistemologically, the originary act of divine command also functions synthetically. All humanly observable things are composites which appear (to the ancient mind) to have been "put together." In creating such composites, a kind of knowledge is gained. Metaphysically, the originary act of divine command functions to mark the beginning of time. If time is a form of order (as it seems to be) necessary for further orderliness, then it is hard to argue coherently that time "preceded" order. For example, the Hebrew creation account is divided into "days." Even if the divine commands are divided into separate speech acts, the implication is that these commands must be described as occurring in some sort of sequence. Hence, time is presupposed in all descriptions after the initial command ("Let there be light," and so forth).

Causal

In the ancient world, the creating word of the deity was the initial "command," and hence, the first act of speaking which could be said to have the "force of law." The deity literally lays down a law that there will be order, and it is so. Whether this positing is an act of free will or compulsion on the part of the deity varies from one tradition to another and is still a matter of serious debate among theologians.

The Human Analogue

It is not obvious that words (spoken or written) should have the power to create a limited order, binding upon human beings. The idea of human law is indebted to myths of divine command in at least a historical way. In the ancient world this analogue was sometimes an identity—the deity who spoke was considered both a legislator for the society and a member of that society. In other cases, the deity revealed the law (and therefore the proper order) for humans through a lawgiver—such as Moses, Ezra, Jesus, or Mohammed. Either way the authority the deity exercised over the natural world came to have political, social, and moral implications for human life (that is, the commander of order in the broadest sense also commanded the human order).

The prevailing precedent of having a human lawgiver or group of legislators communicate to the masses this relationship between language and order provides the basic theological, metaphysical, and epistemological warrant for the establishment of human courts and judges to preside over the human order, just as the "great judge" presides over the natural order. As the western conception of law has become increasingly secular, so the power of human language to command and create order has come to the center of concern for philosophers of law. The attempt to provide a nontheological justification of the power of human language to create and destroy order constitutes a pivotal aim in the philosophy of law.

Implications

Most contemporary philosophers of law remain fully within the analogue, rarely inquiring about the genetic or historical relation between human authority and some "ultimate authority." While this may create philosophical problems at the most basic levels of epistemology and metaphysics, it makes pragmatic sense to assume that creating laws is indeed *possible,* and that such law should be binding for human beings under certain circumstances.

Depending upon the emphasis a thinker places on the various epistemological functions of language in creating order (and regardless of whether he or she subscribes to the associated theology), that thinker will bring a correspondingly different notion of order to bear upon the idea of law itself, and hence, upon specific legal problems. For example, a philosopher who emphasizes the *analytic* function of language will be able to provide a strong account of how to interpret the black letter law, but will encounter problems in explaining how law can be justifiably originated. Order itself is threatened if new law cannot be justifiably created. Such is the problem commonly faced by nineteenth- and twentieth-century legal *positivism,* from John Austin (1790–1859) to H.L.A. Hart (1907–1992). On the other hand, a philosopher who emphasizes the *synthetic* function of language in creating order will be able to provide a rich account of the processes by which law is made, but will encounter difficulty in explaining how and when it should be applied to specific instances, since every "moment" provides another opportunity for making new law. When should prior law be binding, if ever, and why? Order is also threatened where previously made law has no authority. Such is the problem faced by nineteenth- and twentieth-century legal *realism,* from Oliver Wendell Holmes (1841–1935) to Karl Llewellyn (1893–1962), to the postmodernists. A philosopher who emphasizes the *causal* efficacy of speech will be inclined to make the performative utterance the basis of law, whether that utterance is divine as in the Catholic *natural law* tradition, or human as in J.L. Austin (1911–1960).

Also, differing versions of positivism, realism, and natural law are suggested by various ways of emphasizing the *metaphysical* function of language—as it creates order in the scope and structure of space (for example, in designating a certain property sacred or profane, public or private), time (for example, in the extent to which history is knowable and binding, in concepts such as the power of precedent and the designation of certain time periods as having a special legal significance, for example, legal holidays, tax deadlines, and so forth), and causality (for example, in the extent of free will and nature/nurture factors in influencing behavior and hence legal responsibility). Thus, the view one holds of norms and laws as such, as well as the specific norms and laws one advocates, are largely traceable to the function of order one emphasizes.

Those who hold extreme views in the philosophy of law can often be seen as reducing all the functions of language in creating order from three to just one, thereby eliminating the dialectical relationship between the root functions of law and order. For example, *anarchism* reduces all of law to individual speech acts (occupying an infinitesimal space/time region), which deny to commands all causal efficacy. The latter denial is based in the reduction of all causal order to individual free will (or corporate free will in communitarian versions, like Noam Chomsky's anarcho-syndicalism). Anarchism is on this account, therefore, an attempt to have order without law. At the other extreme, *fascism* sees order as a holistic property of the body politic, which is determinative of and concretized in the law of the state (or the will of the leader, understood as the metaphysical locus of the state). Questions of order are unnecessary where the law of the state reigns, and vice versa. This can be described as a reduction of the three order-creating functions of language to a single function (in which space, time, and causality are no longer clearly distinct).

Only two extreme views are mentioned here, and most views of the relation of law and order require more mixing and balancing of the elements and funtions of language in creating order. Nevertheless, all views are susceptible to analysis using the three functions identified.

Two Contemporary Views of Order

The two most influential contemporary views of order are those of Hans Kelsen (1881–1973) and Michel Foucault (1926–1984). Neither thinker fits cleanly into a traditional category in the philosophy of law, but Kelsen is closer to positivism while Foucault's historicist and marxist sympathies place him closer to critical legal realism.

Kelsen

Kelsen's "pure theory of law" is largely responsible for much of the current discussion of order in the philosophy of law. A simplified version follows.

For Kelsen, pure law is a normative order which can be adequately described and grasped without reference to a particular historical, political, ethical, or cultural context. Other systems of norms aside from law are possible, as are other orders, but while law does not exhaust order, it is *an* order. The principal features of legal norms are that they are descriptive, interpretive, based upon a *Grundnorm* (or "basic norm"), and created by acts of human will.

In dealing with the standard positivist dilemma over the legitimate creation of law, Kelsen suggests that newly created law derives its validity from other law, which must be ultimately traceable to the basic norm. This creates a hierarchy in both space and time to which decision makers must appeal in applying the law correctly. Specific norms are validated or invalidated through their relation to the "basic norm" (such as "the sovereign should be obeyed"), which Kelsen believes requires no justification itself (since it must be presupposed in any system of legal norms). This "basic norm" need never be fully interpreted in laws, nor even consciously realized by those who live and judge under its auspices. The "basic norm" is the source of all norms (and therefore of all valid legal norms), but Kelsen is not overly concerned with the origins and foundations of the basic norm. He identifies the social order with the natural order and relies upon science to explain the natural order.

Relative to the three functions of order indicated previously, Kelsen presents a fairly balanced account, emphasizing analysis over synthesis on foundational matters. He de-emphasizes, on one hand, the causal function of language by making law foremost a descriptive, interpretive activity, but on the other hand reintroduces the causal function at a deeper level in his voluntaristic account of the creation of legal normative meaning through acts of will. Such acts of will must occur for legal norms to be subsequently identified, interpreted, described, and systematically represented.

Foucault

Michel Foucault's complex views on order are also oversimplified in what follows. In his magnum opus *Les mots et les choses* (Words and Things), Foucault argues that general forms of order undergo ruptures in history, and that the basic structures which constitute the form of all possible knowledge in a given age (an "episteme") may quickly and completely change. These forms of order are not consciously adopted by the people living in an age, but rather, they operate as limits upon the grid of discourse in that age. All ideas which emerge in an age, whether in the human or natural sciences, art, law, philosophy, and so on, must therefore be described in terms of the prevailing form of order in that age. Due to the restrictions inherent within a given form of order, some ideas simply cannot be thought within the confines of an age.

Thus, the law of an age (like any other concrete instance of discourse) is strictly correlative to the form of that age, and the law is best described upon the basis of this relation. For example, according to Foucault in *The Order of Things,* law in the Enlightenment is justified precisely insofar as it conforms to the "genetic" and "mathetic" poles of representation, which constitute the general science of order for that age. However, for Foucault, forms of order change more quickly than human institutions, creating a historical lag in which the institutions of an age embody a notion of order no longer coherent for the people living in that age. Such a lag may occur in discourse of all sorts: historical texts (for instance, the United States Constitution) or institutions (for instance, the prisons or the courts). In time, however, historical texts and institutions can come to be reinterpreted within the context of the new form of order, in which case the institution is no longer the "same institution." It is still too early to predict the full effect of Foucault's notion of order upon the philosophy of law.

References

Foucault, Michel. *The Order of Things*. New York: Random House, 1970.

Frankfort, Henri et al. *The Intellectual Adventure of Ancient Man.* Chicago: University of Chicago Press, 1946.

Hayek, Friedrich. *Law, Legislation and Liberty*. 1978. 3 vols. Chicago: University of Chicago Press, 1981.

Kelsen, Hans. *The Pure Theory of Law.* Trans. Max Knight. Berkeley: University of California Press, 1967.

Kuntz, Marion L., and Paul G. Kuntz. *Jacob's Ladder and the Tree of Life: Concepts of Hierarchy and the Great Chain of Being.* New York: Peter Lang, 1987.

Lienesch, Michael. *New Order of the Ages: Time, the Constitution, and the Making of Modern American Political Thought.* Princeton: Princeton University Press, 1988.

Rotenstreich, Nathan. *Order and Might.* Albany: State University of New York Press, 1988.

Stumpf, Samuel E. "The Moral Order and the Legal Order." In *The Concept of Order,* ed. Paul Grimley Kuntz, 385–404. Seattle: University of Washington Press, 1968.

Voegelin, Eric. *"The Nature of Law" and Other Related Legal Writings.* Vol. 27 of *The Collected Works of Eric Voegelin,* ed. Robert A. Pascal et al. Baton Rouge: Louisiana State University Press, 1991.

———. *Order and History*. 5 vols. Baton Rouge: Louisiana State University Press, 1956–1987.

Randall E. Auxier

See also CONSTITUTIONALISM; LEGALITY; RELIGION AND THEOLOGY; RULE OF LAW

Ownership

To own something is, at least, to have some determinable range of rights over it. Ownership performs two essential legal and social functions. It determines what rights persons have over things and it determines how such rights are acquired, transferred, or alienated. Various forms of ownership, for example, private, public, corporate, communal, are distinguished from one another by means of differences in the rights they assign to owners and in the means of acquisition, transfer, and alienation of such rights. Private ownership, or liberal ownership as some have called it, is understood as being composed of the rights to possess, use, manage, the income, the capital, security, transmissibility, and the absence of term. Other forms of ownership, such as communal or public, are composed of different rights in so far as they lack the right of transmissibility. Forms of ownership also differ from one another in terms of what can be owned and the methods of acquisition and transfer. John Rawls argues that the community as a whole should be acknowledged as owning the talents and abilities of each of its members. This is a significant departure from the rights of private ownership where each person alone possesses these rights. Others have argued that rights over land and resources are not individually possessed but possessed by the community as a whole. Crimes such as theft and trespass are defined as violations of the rights owners may exercise over what they own.

A major disagreement over how ownership of things is acquired centers on how things such as land and resources are originally appropriated. One school of thought, represented by Jan Narveson and Robert Nozick and following from the arguments of John Locke, holds that unrestricted, inviolable private property rights are acquired by mixing one's labor upon what is not already owned by someone, while other schools of thought, represented by David Gauthier and Stephen Munzer, either hold that labor does not justify original appropriation of what is unowned or that the rights acquired by original appropriation are limited by restrictions, such as economic efficiency or the common social good. One contemporary illustration would be legislatively imposed environmental protection restrictions limiting rights of land subdivision or waste burial where a legislative body imposes limits on owners' rights in an effort to protect the environment from deterioration. Some would claim that this is an unjust appropriation of the rights of owners or that it is an unfair distribution of social costs in which land owners must bear a disproportionate burden. Others would argue that the legislation is a legitimate exercise of society's rights over its lands and resources.

Reductionist analyses of the concept of ownership imply that ownership can exhaustively be defined in terms of these various sets of rights, as shown by James Grunebaum, while nonreductionist analyses imply that there is something more to the conception of ownership than a set of rights. Nonreductionists believe that ownership cannot be understood solely as a collection of rights because of the way people identify and fulfill themselves in relation to what they own or because of the ways that what people own establish relations within societies, as stated by Munzer and John Christman.

Moral justifications of particular forms of ownership utilize a variety of different methods. One common method is to explain how a form of ownership is rationally compatible with a single moral principle, as do Grunebaum and Christman, several moral principles, as do Lawrence Becker and Munzer, or various conceptions of rights, as does Waldron. The moral principles can be either deontological or consequential, and there is substantial disagreement about the relevancy of economic efficiency and economic productivity to the justification. A second method, used by David Gauthier and Jan Narveson, is to derive a form of ownership from the conditions of a hypothetical state of nature. States of nature derivations differ depending upon assumptions about conditions in the state of nature that specify levels of scarcity or abundance of land and goods, the rights individuals naturally possess, and the range of rights which vest by acts of appropriation. A third method, used by Rawls, justifies the form of ownership as an implication from an original contract to establish the fundamental rules for society. The particular form of ownership chosen in the original contract or the form which would be chosen in a hypothetical contract would be considered morally justifiable. There does not appear to be any consensus about the relation of the method of justification to the form of ownership that is ultimately justified, that is, no one of the methods seems to support one of the forms over the other.

Both private ownership and communal ownership have been criticized from various moral perspectives and defended from others. Private ownership is alleged to better preserve individual freedom than other forms, especially communal ownership, because private ownership protects each owner from interference by the state insofar as inviolable private ownership rights place absolute limits on government actions. Communal ownership, it is argued, permits the state or the majority to control individual choice and to regard the individual as simply a collectively owned social asset. Private ownership, however, is criticized because in a free market economy it permits gross inequality in individuals' incomes, which leads to exploitation and to a permanent class structure in society. Defenders of communal ownership argue that greater personal equality and autonomy (in the sense of positive freedom) result from collective participation in decisions about how land and resources are to be used and developed by the community. Recently, mixed forms of ownership have been proposed in which the ownership rules for land and resources are markedly different from the rules for self and labor, as well as the rights of use and control being separated from the rights to income.

Much has also been written on the relation of private ownership to economic organization. While many have argued that private ownership with no governmental restriction on the rights of owners is essential to a free market, others have argued that a freely competitive market is possible with limits on some of the rights of owners. Among the limits on the rights of owners that are thought compatible with maintaining a competitive market are limits on the appropriation of economic rent either from one's labor or from possessions and rights to individually control resources. The role of private ownership as a necessary condition for either economic efficiency or dynamic productivity has also been questioned. The separation of management from owners' rights to income, the institutionalization of research and development, doubt about the centrality of income as a motive, and skepticism about the possibility of defining economic value independently of ownership rights are among the reasons given for doubting that only private ownership can stimulate efficiency and productivity at appropriate levels.

References

Becker, Lawrence C. *Property Rights*. London: Routledge and Kegan Paul, 1977.

Christman, John. *The Myth of Property*. Oxford: Oxford University Press, 1994.

Gauthier, David. *Morals By Agreement*. Oxford: Clarendon Press, 1986.

Grunebaum, James O. *Private Ownership*. London: Routledge and Kegan Paul, 1987.

Munzer, Stephen R. *A Theory of Property*. Cambridge: Cambridge University Press, 1990.

Narveson, Jan. *The Libertarian Idea*. Philadelphia: Temple University Press, 1988.

Nozick, Robert. *Anarchy, State, and Utopia*. New York: Basic Books, 1974.

Pollock, Lansing. *The Freedom Principle*. Buffalo: Prometheus Books, 1981.

Rawls, John. *A Theory of Justice*. Cambridge MA: Harvard University Press, 1971.

James O. Grunebaum

See also ESTATE AND PATRIMONY; FRAGMENTATION OF OWNERSHIP; GOODS; PROPERTY

P

Paine, Thomas (1737–1809)

Thomas Paine was born in Thetford, a Norfolk village about seventy-five miles from London, and died in New York City. Though Paine had great influence in his time, for example, providing some of the key intellectual underpinning of the American Revolution, he was also well ahead of his time. Jack Fruchtman states that "Paine argued for many of the policies which twentieth-century moderns have associated with the liberal welfare state: free public education, public assistance, old-age benefits, and inheritance taxes on the wealthy. The astonishing fact is that Paine argued for these policies two hundred years before the rise of the social welfare state." Fruchtman writes that, in *Rights of Man* and *Agrarian Justice,* "Paine's goal was to consider how to help the less fortunate members of society, especially the working poor." Paine frequently cites Jean-Jacques Rousseau in these works. The revolutionary Paine supported this liberalism and remains even today a hero to those on the self-described "extreme left," such as Christopher Hitchens. Many associate Paine with the leveling philosophy of some in the American Revolution.

How can we reconcile all this with Bruce Kuklick's claim that Paine "believed in laissez-faire economics"? The liberal welfare state is anathema to laissez-faire economics and libertarianism. Kuklick believes that "[t]he doctrine of a free market was coordinate with that of a powerful federal authority that would promote commercial and territorial expansion." However, a genuinely free market, by definition, cannot be propped up with government subsidies. A free market economy is a hostage to all market forces, good and bad. The Articles of Confederation failed to achieve the most desirable economic unity for the freed colonies, so the U.S. Constitution was ratified largely to achieve economic unity by centralizing power. As Kuklick observes, Paine "had always favored the centralization of government, first as a means of fighting the war, then as a precondition of a strong democratic empire. . . ."

Paine's commitment to natural rights may explain his support of a strong democratic empire. Such an empire might win governmental recognition of these natural rights shared by all around the world. Paine famously proclaimed: "My country is the world, and my religion is to do good." He was a humanist and a revolutionary "do-gooder."

Paine's greatest importance for philosophy of law is in his defense of natural law and natural rights, especially in his *Rights of Man* (1791–1792), which was Paine's response to his friend Edmund Burke's attack on the French Revolution. Paine also wrote in *Common Sense* (1776) that "[i]n this first parliament every man by natural right will have a seat." He emphasized the "happiness of the governed." Paine's philosophy greatly promotes the idea of combining natural rights with secular humanism and globalism.

Paine was rejected by the American Philosophical Society in 1781 but was finally accepted in 1785. The society gave no reason for the rejection of his nomination, but Fruchtman concludes that "Paine's argumentative style likely sparked resentment against him, especially when nomination practically meant automatic admission." Paine's success and great ability to write in an accessible and powerful style were also sources of resentment, especially since he had begun his career as a writer rather late in life (for example, "These are the times that try men's souls" and "The summer soldier and the sunshine patriot will, in this crisis, shrink from the service of their country").

The end of Paine's life held much bitterness. Symbolically, nagging frustration met his business ventures in trying literally to build bridges of his own design. Globalism appeared in Paine's hopes to build political bridges between America and England, and even between traditional enemies England and France. The ingratitude and outright hostility of many whose causes he had championed so successfully in America and France increased Paine's despair.

References

Aldridge, A. Owen. *Thomas Paine's American Ideology*. Newark: University Press of Delaware, 1984.

Ayer, A.J. *Thomas Paine*. London: Secker and Warburg, 1988.

Claeys, Gregory. *The Political Thought of Thomas Paine*. Winchester: Unwin Hyman, 1989.

Conway, Moncure Daniel. *The Life of Thomas Paine*. 2 vols. New York: Putnam, 1892.

Foner, Eric. *Tom Paine and Revolutionary America*. Oxford: Oxford University Press, 1976.

Fruchtman, Jack, Jr. *Thomas Paine: Apostle of Freedom*. New York: Four Walls Eight Windows, 1994.

Paine, Thomas. *The Complete Writings of Thomas Paine*. 2 vols. Ed. Philip S. Foner. New York: Citadel Press, 1945.

Philp, Mark. *Paine*. Oxford: Oxford University Press, 1989.

Powell, David. *Tom Paine: The Greatest Exile*. New York: St. Martin's Press, 1985.

Williamson, Audrey. *Thomas Paine: His Life, Work and Times*. London: George Allen & Unwin, 1973.

Sterling Harwood

Pardon, Parole, and Probation

See DISPUTE RESOLUTION; MEDIATION, CRIMINAL

Parenting and Childrearing

The rearing of children is an appropriate matter for legal regulation inasmuch as three distinct sets of interests are involved. *Children* are vulnerable dependents who need to be brought up within a caring, stable environment by appropriate adults with whom they can form relatively permanent, mutually affectionate relationships. *Society* has an interest in the health, well-being, education, and socialization of its future citizens. For *adult* human beings the having and rearing of children can be an extremely valuable, and perhaps centrally important, life experience. The legal regulation of childrearing should consist in an allocation of specified parental responsibilities to particular guardians. Trusting to the general generosity of strangers will not suffice. Moreover, the regulation of childrearing after birth is preferable to, though not exclusive of, the anterior control of who shall actually bear children, which is beset by considerable difficulties, both of principle and of practice.

Two broad areas of jurisprudential discussion are indicated: in *what* rights and duties does the discharge of these parental responsibilities consist? *Who* should be given these responsibilities? They are interrelated in so far as a principle of parental attribution may also specify the nature of the responsibilities. With regard to parental rights and duties, there are two further important questions concerning priority and extent: are parental rights prior to, and independent of, any parental duties, or do they derive from a prior duty to care for the child? The priority of parental rights to duties may be argued to derive simply from parental status, or from some "natural" fact, such as superior power, traditional authority, or ownership. The priority of parental duties to rights may be argued to derive from the existence of fundamental interests in the proper rearing of a child. Crucially, the proper discharge of that prior duty will limit, and determine the character of, any parental rights.

The two major factors in the determination of the extent of parental rights are a specification of what rights, if any, are possessed by children themselves, and any public interest there may be in ensuring that children are brought up a certain way. Children's rights are standardly thought of as "welfare" and "liberty." A child's right to a certain standard of health care and education straightforwardly limits what a parent may do in his rearing of a child. A parent's right to choose for his child yields to the child's liberty right to make her own choices, acquired on majority. Article 12 of the *United Nations Convention on the Rights of the Child* formalizes a now familiar, intermediary, principle that the views of a child on all matters affecting his or her interests should be given due weight in accordance with his or her age and maturity.

Society retains an interest in ensuring that all children receive a certain, basic level of care. Although the state delegates parenting duties to specified individuals, it remains *parens patriae,* parent in the last instance, caring for those children who lack a guardian, and with the right to intervene should the level of parental care fall below a specified threshold. On the whole, western law has determined that threshold by defining what shall count as significant harm to a child, rather than by stipulating a minimum level of acceptable parenting.

Two opposed models of parental rights and duties can be offered. At one extreme is *patria potestas,* whereby, under Roman law, a father rightfully exercised absolute and unlimited control over his offspring. At the other extreme is the notion of a "trust" wherein the parent and state are merely trustees, during minority, of the child's rights, a trust which must be administered solely for the child's benefit. On the whole parental rights have been "eroded" or "fragmented" over time. Two general rights retain their importance: that of autonomy—the freedom of parents to determine the best upbringing for their child—and that of privacy—the right of parents to bring up their children free from intervention by public agencies, so long as the level of parental care does not fall below the specified threshold.

In contemporary western law, parental rights are normally possessed exclusively and indivisibly; that is, they are all possessed by only one or two persons. In determining who shall have these rights biological kinship and marriage have, historically, received the most emphasis. By contrast, parental adequacy, that is, fitness to discharge the duties of care, may be important in cases of adoption or fostering, where parental rights are alienated, or in custody disputes, where opposing claims to exercise parental rights are made. However, fitness to parent does not normally determine the initial distribution of parental roles, which are assumed to follow from the existence of evident, natural ties.

The obvious context for discussion of the allocation of parental rights is the family. The generally acknowledged right to found a family comprises a right to bear children and a right to rear those one has borne. It might seem that anyone who can have children thereby acquires, at least in the first instance, parental rights over their own offspring. However, the right to bear is not an obvious correlate of a right not to bear, that is, the right to control one's fertility, nor is it an evident extension of a right to sexual autonomy or privacy. The thought that natural parents should rear their own children may owe much to the idea that the procreative act generates rights over the resultant product. This involves a proprietarian argument, due in the first instance to the labor theory of property of John Locke (1632–1704), and which, though generally discredited, continues to cast a long shadow over jurisprudential thought about parenthood.

It is also true that important social interests may be served by maintaining certain sorts of relationships and institutions, chiefly the traditional family and marriage. The family is an important intermediary association between individual citizen and state, a "haven in a heartless world," a source of diversity in lifestyles and values, and perhaps the most obvious or natural way in which parental responsibilities may be discharged. Moreover, alternatives to the family, such as communalized childrearing, can seem unattractive and are unlikely to be freely chosen by all. Yet it should be recognized that a family need not comprise two parents, of different gender, both biologically related to the dependent children.

This fact has been reinforced by the development of the new reproductive technology, which has had at least two significant consequences. The first is the pronounced separation of biological parenthood from legal and social parenthood, that is, who is causally responsible for bringing a child into being, who has the legal title of parent, and who is actually acknowledged as bearing responsibility for a child. The second consequence is the extension of the capacity to bear children to persons previously unable, such as the infertile, or unwilling in virtue of their sexual preferences. The determination of who shall rear a child, artificially conceived or gestated by a third party, will consequently involve an uncertain balancing of three types of consideration: biological kinship, parental fitness, and a social interest in privileging a certain familial structure.

In sum, the law should ensure that children are reared by someone; but the fundamental issues—who shall rear whose children and what rights to rear shall be divided among whom—remain unresolved.

References

Archard, David. *Children, Rights and Childhood.* London: Routledge, 1993.

Barton, Chris, and Gillian Douglas. *Law and Parenthood.* London: Butterworth, 1995.

Beck, Connie K. et al. "The Rights of Children: A Trust Model." *Fordham Law Review* 46 (1978), 669–780.

Blustein, Jeffrey. *Parents and Children: The Ethics of the Family*. New York: Oxford University Press, 1982.

Harris, John. "The Right to Found a Family." In *Children, Parents and Politics,* ed. Geoffrey Scarre, 133–153. Cambridge: Cambridge University Press, 1989.

LaFollette, Hugh. "Licensing Parents." *Philosophy and Public Affairs* 9 (1980), 183–197.

O'Neill, Onora, and William Ruddick, eds. *Having Children: Philosophical and Legal Reflections on Parenthood*. Oxford: Oxford University Press, 1979.

David Archard

See also DIVORCE AND MARRIAGE; FAMILY LAW; MARRIAGE CONTRACT

Parties, Contractual

According to common law, an offeror has the power to make a contractual offer to the whole world, to a specific group, or to an individual. Anyone in the position of the offeree, however, must address some specific offeror. Whenever specification is undertaken or required, an error must be relevant to the question of contract formation, and will seem to raise the issue of personal identity and how attribute differs from identity. Legal consequences diverge. A mistake merely about someone's attributes, it is said, will not avoid a contract at law, but where identity matters and when the wrong party is addressed, no contract could be formed.

Whatever judges and jurists may be heard to say about this, the issue of a contractor's identity need not raise directly any of the puzzles about personal identity discussed by philosophers. In contract formation, the problem of mistaken identity is one about reference and of what is involved specifically in *addressing* someone else. Personal identity, on the other hand, is about the problem of the criteria for the reidentification of those to whom one has already successfully referred. So a three-part distinction matters at once: (1) referring to persons (already assumed to have personal identities), (2) attributing things to them, such as creditworthiness, and (3) addressing someone, someone to whom one refers. To refer is to pick out someone so that attributions can be made. To attribute is to assign some property, feature, or characteristic, truly or falsely, to whomever one refers. To address is to single out someone (or group) as the recipient of a statement, specifically in the course of acts of referring and attributing. To make the error of attributing wealth to Mr. Poor requires referring to him, though not necessarily addressing him.

How, then, does one commit a mistake of identity but not of attribution? One suffers confusion here of a certain kind, specifically between the person with whom one deals (and so addresses) and someone else with whom one does not deal directly but also addresses. If one does not know that Dr. Jekyll was also Mr. Hyde, there is no mistake or confusion of (fictional) identities, merely a want of information about the one. Our usages about identity are not always helpful. We sometimes say, for example, that authorities in a witness protection program give someone "a wholly new identity"; this is, however, to change the individual's public attributions, such as name, appearance, address, and history. (Perhaps we speak of "new identity" because the aim is to prevent the witness's reidentification by the wrong people.) For mistaken or confused identities, A uses speech with the intention of addressing B and C in the mistaken belief that B = C. The fact that the equation fails does not prevent reference or address; it doubles it. One might bargain, for instance, directly with Ms. Thick but think, quite innocently, that she is Ms. Thin. Because singular address, we assume, was required in this case, no contract was formed—it must be void ab initio—for one party who was addressed, namely, Thin, did not accept the offer. It follows that someone duped by an alias into thinking the person one deals with is creditworthy has not suffered a confusion of identities—only an error of attribution—for address goes through to the person using the alias and no other.

The following is the problematic situation within which the law must work. Arthurs, under an apparent contract, delivers certain goods to Bold in the false belief that he is Callow. Bold then sells the goods to Dizy, who knows nothing of the mistake by Arthurs. If the dealings were face to face, without doubt A addresses B. The question then becomes whether A had addressed C as well in the belief that B = C; if so, the contract (excluding fraud for the moment) is void (as distinct from merely voidable) for identity mistake. Furthermore, D never had title to the goods she got. If the parties dealt at distance, the question simply is a more difficult one of the same order, namely, was there unrecognized dual address? However, when B is a fraud, a dilemma is forced upon the court.

How exactly should fraud count? The fraudulent act could be deemed irrelevant. When there is a confusion of identities, however induced, no contract is formed and Dizy lacks good title. In that case the court must be sure that A addressed both parties in the belief that "they" were one. This could happen if A addressed C and B interjects himself later claiming to be C. To decide that fraud is relevant to the contractual issue (the more usual course) is to decide that A was simply duped by B into a belief that B was creditworthy or otherwise desirable. This was achieved on this occasion (albeit in a way that looks as if it produced an identity confusion) by a self-introduced impersonation, rather than an alias. Once this particular deceit is seen for what it is, there is little temptation to find that A addressed the impersonated individual in his offer, even though he referred to him in the course of attribution. All that mattered to Arthurs was the creditworthiness of the party, Bold, with whom he dealt directly. The contract becomes voidable, not void, in the common law. Whether D gets good title then depends, in a sense, upon the celerity of A. Dizy will not get good title if Arthurs acts to disaffirm the contract before Bold sells to her. Indeed, it could happen in this case that Dizy will be legally required (in conversion) to pay Arthurs for the goods if they cannot be returned. This is the same result as with an innocent mistake of identity. This can be hard for innocent third-party purchasers like Dizy—a state mitigated only by the fact they often got a "deal" from Bold. The usual situation, however, is that A has not been paid, B himself had received payment from D, and A is none the wiser during this period. This situation is hard for the victims of fraud, for while A can sue B for deceit, B is likely to be judgment proof or impossible to find. Here the common law has found justice to be elusive.

References

Bronaugh, Richard. "The Place of Identity in Contract Formation." *University of Western Ontario Law Review* 18 (1980), 185.

Goodhart, A.L. "Mistake as to Identity in the Law of Contract." *Law Quarterly Review* 56 (1941), 228.

Hall, Clifford. "Some Reflections upon Contractual Mistake at Common Law." *Anglo-American Law Review* 24 (1995), 483.

Hall, J.C. "New Developments in Mistake of Identity." *Cambridge Law Journal* (1961), 86.

Samek, R.A. "Some Reflections on the Logical Basis of Mistake of Identity of Party." *Canadian Bar Review* 38 (1960), 479.

Williams, Glanville. "Mistake as to Party in the Law of Contract." *Canadian Bar Review* 23 (1945), 271.

Richard Bronaugh

See also MISTAKE AND IGNORANCE; PARTIES TO CRIMINAL CONDUCT

Parties to Criminal Conduct

The parties to criminal conduct include the principal offender and the accessory; an individual can also be held vicariously liable for the actions of another. The principal offender requires little explanation, since such persons are to be held responsible for their own criminal actions or omissions. The individual who is held to be criminally liable because he or she either is vicariously liable for another or is an accessory to a principal requires closer examination.

The basis of all criminal liability is that the accused, acting freely, possessed the mental element necessary for the commission of the crime (mens rea), that the conduct element of the crime has been fulfilled (the actus reus), and that there is a causative link between the foregoing and the harm suffered by the victim or the crime committed (causative link). These requirements are straightforward in the context of attribution of criminal liability and punishment to a principal offender. The situation becomes more complex when there are coaccused, that is, aiding and abetting, accessorial liability or art and part liability, or where the accused is held to be vicariously liable for the actions of another.

The principles of accessorial liability can be found in Roman law, and it is from this source that they were inherited, with the reception of Roman law in Europe. To establish accessorial liability there must be evidence of a common plan between the coaccused, for example, in the context of a bank robbery, where each accused had an allocated task but all are ultimately held criminally liable for the robbery, even if the role of a particular accused was only minor. Alternatively, the common plan and the shared criminal liability may arise spontaneously, for example, in the case of a spontaneous street fight or assault. The nature of the liability imposed upon the accessory is that one becomes equally liable with the principal actor for the completed or attempted crime. Liability is therefore dependent on there being a principal offender.

The actions which create such liability must not only influence but also assist the principal offender in committing the crime. It is essential that the accessory intends to assist the principal to commit a criminal act, and therefore some knowledge of the criminal activity is required. This knowledge need not be detailed for art and part liability to be created. There are three forms of activity which would result in an accessory being art and part liable with a principal offender: by counsel or instigation, by provision of material assistance for the commission of an imminent crime, and by assisting at the actual commission of the crime.

Following the principles of legal responsibility, an accessory who withdraws prior to the commission of the planned criminal offense may escape criminal liability. An accessory who withdraws at the preparation stage will not be held to be art and part liable, because there will be no evidence that this person has participated in the commission of the crime. If there is withdrawal by the accessory after the commission of the crime has commenced, then criminal liability will only be avoided if the accessory contacts the law enforcement authorities in order to prevent the crime being committed.

The attribution of accessorial liability becomes more difficult when the principal offender departs from the common or spontaneous plan. The liability of the coaccused in these circumstances is determined by the extent to which the actions of the principal were reasonably foreseeable and also if the actions of the coaccused suggest retrospective agreement, for instance, where an assault is continued on a victim after a weapon has been used. In the event that the actions of the principal are considered to not be reasonably foreseeable, or they are not retrospectively supported, each accused will be judged only on his or her own actions.

In Roman law there was a positive duty upon a slave to prevent certain offenses being committed, for example, *scelus Silanianum* was the consequence of the duty upon slaves to guard their owners at the risk of their own lives. If the slave failed to prevent the owner's murder, the slave was treated as an accessory to the principal offender. Although positive duties to prevent harm exist for certain groups, for instance, parents toward their children, failure to prevent an attack by a third party, at the risk of the parent's own life, would not attract this penalty.

Roman law punished the principal and accessory offender equally. The Christian empire placed more emphasis on subjective responsibility. The latter is still followed, and consequently there is often a gradation of penalty among offenders.

Vicarious liability is generally not part of criminal law. In Roman law it was more prominent. Ulpian in the eighteenth book on the Edicit reports: "If a slave slays with his master's knowledge, he obligates the master in full, for the master himself is considered to have slain; but if with him unaware, there is a noxal [vicarious for harms] action, since on his slave's wrongdoing he ought not to be liable for more than noxal surrender."

In modern law, vicarious liability is similar to strict liability, since both involve convicting someone who lacks any mens rea for the crime committed. Although injustice is involved in both, it is more prevalent in vicarious liability, since here no action whatsoever is required of the accused. Before vicarious liability can attach to A, it is necessary to demonstrate that the relationship of A to B is appropriate to make A responsible for B's actions. The rules of tort regarding the extent of this liability apply in criminal law. It is generally only found in the context of the relationship of employer to employee, and the employer is not to be held responsible for any offenses committed by an employee acting in pursuance of a private plan. Since the employer clearly lacks the mens rea for any offense committed by an employee, this form of liability only occurs in strict liability offenses.

Joint and several liability is unique to the law of tort. This form of liability arises automatically in the context of a partnership where all of the partners are held liable for a wrongful act, an omission, or a debt created by an individual partner in the partnership name. Joint and several liability can also be created by agreement; for example, it may be a condition of a contract that the parties assume joint and several liability for any sums owed to the supplier of goods. In these circumstances an individual is assuming in advance liability for the actions of the other parties involved.

References

Hart, H.L.A. *Punishment and Responsibility*. Oxford: Clarendon Press, 1968.

Kadish, S. "A Theory of Complicity." In *Issues in Contemporary Legal Philosophy*, ed. R. Gavison. Oxford: Clarendon Press, 1987.

Robinson, O.F. *The Criminal Law of Ancient Rome*. London: Duckworth, 1995.

Clare Connelly

See also CONSPIRACY; MENS REA; MISTAKE AND IGNORANCE; PARTIES, CONTRACTUAL; STRICT LIABILITY, CRIMINAL

Pashukanis, Evgeny Bronislavovich (1891–1937)

Evgeny Bronislavovich Pashukanis is considered to be one of the most outstanding and perspicacious of the marxist philosophers of law. He is the only marxist philosopher of law whose work continues to generate academic interest outside the circles of marxist scholarship. His theory has been labeled as "the commodity exchange theory of law."

Pashukanis made a spectacular entry into the academic and political world of bolshevik communism in 1924, in the now defunct USSR, with a little book entitled *The General Theory of Law and Marxism: An Experiment in the Criticism of Basic Juridical Concepts*. This work was a revision of a conference he delivered in 1923, which explains its dense, abstract, and clearly more suggestive than didactic character. This book projected Pashukanis from a relative anonymity—a popular judge from 1918 to 1920 and a counsellor of law from 1920 to 1924—to the summit of the newborn marxist theory of law in the Soviet Union. Thereafter, his political and academic career confirmed Pashukanis as the dean of the marxist theory of law. Pashukanis successively revised his theory from 1925 to 1937. He was executed by the political police (NKVD) in 1937 as an enemy of the people and rehabilitated in 1956.

It is a commonplace that *The General Theory of Law and Marxism*, published in 1924, assured the place of Pashukanis in the history of legal theory in the twentieth century. It is an imaginative, fascinating, and complex book. The central point for Pashukanis consists in advancing a systematic reflection on legal epistemology. In this sense, Pashukanis searched to analyze the basic juridical concepts (legal norm, legal relation, legal subject, and so forth), in the same way as Karl Marx, in his *Capital*, examined the basic concept of classical political economy. In fact, in Pashukanis's view, both legal and economic thought offer abstract descriptions of the concrete relationships that form the material base. These relationships and practices could not exist if there were not established stable patterns of expectations among the social actors. Thus, Pashukanis suggested that through the social development of a modern "commodity producing society," the basic juridical concepts acquire their status as abstract, universal, and systematic. From this epistemological position, Pashukanis rejects all the marxist tradition from Friedrich Engels, a tradition which associates the law with notions of ideology, class, and interest.

The basic epistemological reflection of Pashukanis is confirmed in his theory of juridical fetishism. Paralleling Marx's theory of commodity fetishism, Pashukanis states that the basic juridical concepts explain the hieroglyphical conditions under which people live. Pashukanis can thus identify the law as an abstract intermediary that permits social relations to function for what they are: social relations. The specific social relations which explain the morphology of law are, according to Pashukanis, the equivalent exchange of abstract rights. It should be noted that this theory of juridical fetishism is a theory of how law functions socially and has nothing to do with the concept of ideology, since it does not necessitate any relation to consciousness.

The morphology of law founded in exchange is pursued by Pashukanis in his conception of the "form of law." The legal form is affirmed as a universal equivalence between legal subjects. This universal equivalence equalizes abstractly the unequal social interests in the form of law. Thereby the law is only a modern phenomenon, a "bourgeois" concept, and the notion of feudal law is strictly a nonsense. Pashukanis is thus able to develop a highly interesting analysis about the evolution of law, the nature of postfeudal legal thought, the historical dominance of private law categories and forms of thought, the connection between legal institutions and juridical theories, the relationship between natural law theory and legal positivism, the instauration of a public authority in the law, the problematic nature of legal reasoning and legal theory in the area of public law, the relationship between law and morality, the relationship between law and punishment, and the absurdity of any conception of socialist law to which he opposed the perspective of the "withering away" of law.

Pashukanis developed a highly original sociological jurisprudential theory. However, he did not use extrajuridical concepts and never treated law as purely a mere fiction. In many respects, Pashukanis's conception of law as "social relations" rivals the individualistic and atomistic conception of law promulgated by the liberal tradition. Although the two conceptions explain the phenomenon of law by a reference to the notion of equality, this equality is purely instrumental in the liberal tradition, but in Pashukanis work it requires a closer scrutiny of the immediate role of concrete persons and concrete specific social situations. Pashukanis's theory could thus be explained as both: a humanistic project in which social and economic problems are to be treated directly as such, and a theoretical conception in which the form of law is reserved for situations of universal equivalence.

The theory of law of Pashukanis is fascinating and inspiring, but it is highly doubtful that the epistemological premises on which it was founded could be philosophically defended today.

References

Pashukanis, E.B. *The General Theory of Law and Marxism*. In *Soviet Legal Philosophy*, ed. J. Hazard, 111–225. Cambridge: Harvard University Press, 1951.

———. *Law and Marxism: A General Theory*. London: Ink Links, 1978.

———. *Pashukanis: Selected Writings on Marxism and Law*, ed. Piers Beirne and Robert Sharlet. New York: Academic Press, 1980.

Bjarne Melkevik

See also MARXIST PHILOSOPHY OF LAW; SOCIALIST PHILOSOPHY OF LAW

Paternalism

"Paternalism" comes from the Latin *pater*, meaning to act like a father, or to treat another person like a child. ("Parentalism" is a gender-neutral anagram of "paternalism.") In modern philosophy and jurisprudence, it is to act for the good of another person without that person's consent, as parents do for children. It is controversial because its end is benevolent and its means coercive. Paternalists advance people's interests (such as life, health, or safety) at the expense of their liberty. In this, paternalists suppose that they can make wiser decisions than the people for whom they act. Sometimes this is based on presumptions about their own wisdom, or the foolishness of other people, and can be dismissed as presumptuous—but sometimes it is not. It can be based on relatively good knowledge, as in the case of paternalism over young children or incompetent adults. Sometimes the role of paternalist is thrust upon the unwilling, as when we find ourselves the custodian and proxy for an unconscious or severely retarded relative. Paternalism is a temptation in every arena of life where people hold power over others: in child-rearing, education, therapy, and medicine. However, it is perhaps nowhere as divisive as in criminal law. Whenever the state acts to protect people from themselves, it seeks their good; but by doing so through criminal law, it does so coercively, often against their will.

Which acts should be criminalized and which acts are none of the state's business?

How far does one have a right to harm oneself, to be different, or to be wrong? To what extent should people be free to do what they want if others are not harmed? What is harm? When is consent free and knowing? When do we think clearly and wisely enough, and when are we sufficiently free of duress and indoctrination, to be left to follow our own judgment, and when should we be restrained by others? Who should restrain whom, and when? These are the questions raised by paternalism.

Before we examine the issues more closely, consider the very wide range of paternalistic legislation. Acts which are often prohibited by the criminal law, but which have been alleged by serious writers to be victimless or harmless, at least for consenting adults, include the following: riding a motorcycle without a helmet, gambling, homosexual sodomy, prostitution, polygamy, making and selling pornography, selling and using marijuana, practicing certain professions without a license (law, medicine, education, massage, hairstyling), purchasing blood or organs, suicide, assisting suicide, swimming at a beach without a lifeguard, refusing to participate in a mandatory insurance or pension plan, mistreating a cadaver, loaning money at usurious interest rates, paying a worker less than the minimum wage, selling a prescription drug without a prescription, aggressive panhandling, nudity at public beaches, truancy, flag burning, dueling, ticket scalping, blackmail, blasphemy, and dwarf-tossing.

Paternalism protects people from themselves, as if their safety were more important than their liberty. By contrast, the *harm principle,* famously articulated by John Stuart Mill in *On Liberty,* first published in 1859, holds that limiting liberty can only be justified to prevent harm to other people, not to prevent self-harm. More precisely, coercion can only be justified to prevent harm to unconsenting others, not to prevent harm to which the actors competently consent.

The usual legal prohibitions of murder, rape, arson, and theft are not paternalistic, since these acts harm unconsenting others; for the same reason, criminal legislation in these areas is consistent with the harm principle. Legal paternalism and the harm principle come into conflict over (1) competent self-harm and risk of self-harm, (2) harm to consenting others, and (3) harmless acts. The harm principle demands that we tolerate all three types of acts, but paternalists often wish to regulate them. If a competently consenting person is not a victim, then these three types of acts are victimless. Under the harm principle, victimless crimes must be decriminalized and virtually all paternalism over competent adults ended. The harm principle creates a "zone of privacy" for consensual or "self-regarding" acts, within which individuals may do what they wish and the state has no business interfering, even with the benevolent motive of a paternalist.

The harm principle does not bar all paternalism, however. It permits paternalism over the incompetent, such as young children, the retarded, and perhaps those whose ability to make decisions is compromised by ignorance, deception, duress, or clouded faculties. In these cases, the consent to self-harm is not competent and need not be respected. As we will see later in the discussion, the harm principle also permits what might be called self-paternalism or consensual paternalism.

Every legal system known to us seems to have some paternalistic criminal prohibitions. Conversely, the harm principle has apparently never been embraced without qualification by the laws of any country. If we wish to limit legal paternalism with a principle, the harm principle is the leading candidate. However, even informed proponents of the principle are far from agreement on (1) which acts harm only the actor, (2) which consents are valid, and (3) which acts are harmless. Finally, (4) if "harm" is defined broadly, or "valid consent" narrowly, then even the harm principle will fail to provide a meaningful zone of privacy or barrier to paternalism. Let us look more closely at these issues.

When does an act harm only the actor? Informed people disagree on whether the valid consent of recreational drug users, or truants, covers all the people likely to be harmed by drug use or truancy. If an act harms others, can we be sure that it only harms consenting others? This can be difficult to ascertain, especially if we concede with Mill that every act "affects" everyone, if only indirectly and remotely. A motorcycle rider who consents to the risks of riding without a helmet, and who suffers traumatic head injury, may harm many people who did not consent, for example, his emotional and financial dependents, fellow members of his insurance pool, and taxpayers who support highway patrols, ambulance services, and public hospitals. If increasing my taxes or insurance premiums harms me for the purposes of the harm principle, then I might be harmed by the act which the motorcycle rider thought was private and self-regarding. This special application of the harm principle is called the "public charge argument" for coercion. It is not paternalistic, since it is directed against harm to unconsenting others, not against self-harm. If we can prohibit riding a motorcycle without a helmet because of the harmful "public charge" it levies on unconsenting others, then we can prohibit eating fatty foods on the same grounds. In a welfare state which shifts costs to compensate those who harm themselves, virtually all self-harm will be other-harm too; hence virtually every corner of life could be regulated by law without violating the harm principle, and virtually all paternalism would be justified.

When is consent valid? Dueling was outlawed in large part because lawmakers believed that even those who seemed to consent to a duel were giving invalid consents procured through extreme pressure and duress. Today one hears informed people disagree on whether prostitutes, drug addicts, indigent buyers of lottery tickets, workers willing to take less than the minimum wage, and students willing to have sex with their professors are giving valid consents.

What is harm? Is public nudity harmful? Is the peddling of quack remedies for cancer harmful? Is divorce? Television violence? Well-funded commissions and independent social scientists disagree on whether pornography tends to harm women as a class. Liberals and radicals disagree on whether offended sensibilities are a kind of harm. Is harm *by omission* harm in the relevant sense? If I refuse to stop at a highway accident to render aid, or if I refuse to donate a kidney, have I caused harm? If these acts and omissions are harmless, then to prohibit them is paternalism (or legal moralism); if they are harmful, then to prohibit them is justified by the harm principle.

Sometimes a legislature will prohibit an act while conceding that the act can be harmless and the consent valid. For example, sodomy is still outlawed in many places, even for consenting adults in private. Here the issue is not consent or harm, or the effect on the unconsenting public, but the morality of the act as such. To prohibit a harmless act solely on moral grounds is a special way of acting for people's own good and making their consent irrelevant; this makes it a special form of paternalism. It is usually called "legal moralism."

Perhaps paternalism by legislators over young children and incompetent adults is as justified as paternalism over the same individuals by their parents. If so, then we must decide who is "young" and who is "incompetent" for the purposes of law. Should we use flat age cutoffs, as we do for driving automobiles and drinking alcohol? Should we use one-on-one interviews with experts, as we do for competency to stand trial and involuntary civil commitment? Age cutoffs are administratively convenient, but they are based on presumptions which we know will be false in a foreseeable number of cases; to apply them when false will be unjust. Careful interviews minimize these problems, but at such a great cost that many utilitarians find it prohibitive. Moreover, it is not at all clear that careful interviews can satisfactorily identify competency, since competency (in this context) is as much a political question as a medical one.

The harm principle holds that competent consents should take priority over benevolent legislative limits on our liberty. Paradoxically, this entails support for what might be called consensual paternalism or self-paternalism. If I make a living will when of sound mind, asking to be coerced for my own good in certain ways if I should ever become incompetent, then I am paternalizing myself, or consenting to a regimen in which others paternalize me. For this reason it is less objectionable than classical paternalism.

In a democracy, paternalism in the criminal law can to some extent be construed as self-paternalism. If "we" made the laws against usury and gambling, then "we" are restraining only ourselves. Before we justify these laws as self-paternalism, however, we must ask whether we are describing our democracy accurately or platitudinously. If laws to protect citizens from themselves were made by one nonrepresentative faction, class, or bloc, or if the electoral process is distorted so that the outcomes of elections do not represent true social consent, then we may be dealing less with consensual self-paternalism than with majoritarian (or even minoritarian) tyranny. To overlook this possibility would justify paternalism by turning a blind eye to one of its most objectionable features.

If the legislature wishes to prohibit riding a motorcycle without a helmet, it may have a paternalistic or nonpaternalistic rationale. If it believes the act is self-regarding, then it is being paternalistic; if it accepts the public charge argument, then it avoids paternalism and acts under the harm principle. There are many other ways to do what the paternalist does but without paternalism: notably, to widen the definition of harm, and to narrow that of valid consent. This fact, however, does not make arguments for and against paternalism vacuous. First, these arguments help articulate our general theory of justice, for example, by making clear that *if* an act harms only those who competently consent, then it must be tolerated. Second, we should not overestimate our freedom to rationalize here. Paternalism can be converted to nonpaternalism only when we modulate the notions of harm and consent sufficiently. While this is sometimes distressingly easy, at least as often it is an exercise in sophistry, oversimplification, or self-deception.

References

Airaksinen, Timo. *Ethics of Coercion and Authority: A Philosophical Study of Social Life*. Pittsburgh: University of Pittsburgh Press, 1988.

Buchanan, Allen, and Dan Brock. *Deciding for Others: The Ethics of Surrogate Decision-Making*. Cambridge: Cambridge University Press, 1990.

Devlin, Patrick. *The Enforcement of Morals*. Oxford: Oxford University Press, 1965.

Feinberg, Joel. *The Moral Limits of the Criminal Law*. Oxford: Oxford University Press, 1984–1988. Vol. 1: *Harm to Others* (1984); Vol. 2: *Offense to Others* (1985); Vol. 3: *Harm to Self* (1986); Vol. 4: *Harmless Wrongdoing* (1988).

Grey, Thomas C. *The Legal Enforcement of Morality*. New York: Knopf, 1983.

Hart, H.L.A. *Law, Liberty and Morality*. Stanford: Stanford University Press, 1963.

Hodson, John D. *The Ethics of Legal Coercion*. Dordrecht: Reidel, 1983.

Jordan, Shannon M. *Decision Making for Incompetent Persons: The Law and Morality of Who Shall Decide*. Springfield IL: Charles C. Thomas, 1985.

Kultgen, John. *Autonomy and Intervention: Parentalism in the Caring Life*. Oxford: Oxford University Press, 1995.

Rosenbaum, Alan S. *Coercion and Autonomy: Philosophical Foundations, Issues, and Practices*. Westport CT: Greenwood Press, 1986.

Peter Suber

See also ACTION AND AGENCY; AUTONOMY; CRIMINALIZATION; DRUGS; PROSTITUTION; WRONGDOING AND RIGHT ACTING

Patrimony

See ESTATE AND PATRIMONY

Peirce, Charles Sanders (1839–1914)

Charles Sanders Peirce is still an untapped lode for philosophy of law. Peirce's influence upon the philosophy of law is seminal, but this influence is indirect. His philosophy, even by indirection, has been catalytic upon those several approaches to legal philosophy including legal pragmatism, legal instrumentalism, critical legal theory, legal realism, and recently, legal semiotics. Conversely, legal theory and practice, especially Anglo-American common law, profoundly shaped Peirce's theory of signs and his pragmatic method. Peirce rejects absolutism and aprioristic origins of law, and insists that theory derives from the experimental, experiential ground of human relations rather than providing an abstract basis for interaction. This becomes of primary importance in philosophies of law which seek evidence for the assumption that social institutions are ideas which grow.

According to Peirce, a legal system is an open, "motion-picture" type of sign-system, in which sign-relations mediate between the encoded law and new value coming into existence. Although there is little of an explicit nature throughout the enormous volume of Peirce's work that speaks of law except in passing—implied as an exemplary, prototypical system of sign-transaction—Peirce's genius represents the profound influence of law upon him.

Max Fisch, in the introduction to *Writings of Charles S. Peirce,* called attention to significant relations between a Peircean pragmatism and the "predictive theory in law." There is not a considerable body of literature investigating the manner in which Peircean ideas become reinterpreted in Justice Oliver Wendell Holmes, and through Holmes, into the leading concepts of legal realism in the United States and possibly in Scandinavian realism, through Karl Olivecrona, Axel Hägerström, and Alf Ross. All the major writers on Peirce's influence upon jurisprudence and the development of nonpositivistic law emphasize the function of interpretation, that is, of ideas which interpret ideas in an open-ended infinite process, such that the notion of a fixed, authoritative precedent in law loses credibility. Nevertheless, the fact that Peirce did not explicitly take up jurisprudential problems as such has led many fine scholars to question his influence upon Holmes. In Roberta Kevelson's *The Law as a System of Signs* distinguished scholars from several countries, representing the distinct views from professional law and from academic philosophy, discuss aspects of Peirce's role in the law.

Even to the present day only a small portion of Peirce's work has been published, and much is accessible only in microfilm and microfiche editions. Nevertheless, with the regular and frequent colloquia on law and philosophy, which are receptive to legal semiotics and hence to the Peircean influence, the body of literature on Peirce and law has become substantial, especially in the past decade.

Despite the fact that Peirce's influence upon law is both elliptical and indirect, his theory of signs, his method of pragmatism, his link to John Locke and Boyle and thus to the notion of contract in law, present a challenge to adventurers in ideas. Peirce also provides a linkage to Montesquieu and the idea of separation of powers, as represented in the institutions of law, politics, and economics. His work has had profound impact, for example, on Friedrich von Hayek's philosophy of law and spontaneous free-market exchange in economics.

Peirce uses both the institutions of economics and of law as models for his concept of semiosis as exchange of meaning, which produces with each transaction a surplus of meaning. This concept of surplus, characteristic of open societies with free markets and open legal systems, has recently been taken up by investigators of complex systems.

Throughout Peirce's work one finds the legal concepts of contract (as noted earlier), of property as relations (in Wesley Hohfeld's sense), of mediation, judgments, legalisms, and legal fictions, and especially the strategies of rhetoric and dialectic functioning as key concepts or meta-signs.

Not only does the legal argument provide a prototypical argument for Peirce, but the very function of normativity becomes pivotal in his philosophy, linking the evidentiary aspects of fact-finding and phenomenological aspects of discovery processes with metaphysical first principles which are produced by the activities of his normative sciences. Ethics is that division of the normative sciences which connects pure rhetoric or semiotic methodology with aesthetics or the "science of values." Law as both theory and praxis is that system of signs that mediates, or connects, the actual practice of law in action with a normative ethics, which, in turn, is produced by axiological value-judgments. Such judgments are provisional, according to Peirce, and are revisable, correctable, and modifiable.

Peirce provides philosophy of law with an instrument for investigating the dynamics of law regarded as a self-corrective, cybernetic system of free interaction.

References

Braun, Christopher K. "The Systematized Universe of Legal Discourse." In *Flux, Complexity and Illusion,* ed. R. Kevelson, 33–58. New York: Peter Lang, 1993.

Brion, Denis J. "Rhetoric and the Law of Enterprise." In *Law and the Human Sciences,* ed. R. Kevelson, 61–94. New York: Peter Lang, 1992.

Cohen, Morris. *American Thought.* Glencoe NY: Free Press, 1954.

Fisch, Max H. "Introduction." In *Writings of Charles S. Peirce,* Vol. 3, ed. M. Fisch et al. Bloomington: University of Indiana Press, 1986.

———. "Justice Holmes and the Prediction Theory in Law." *Journal of Philosophy* 39.12 (1942), 85–97.

Hayek, F.A. *Law, Legislation, Liberty.* 1973. Chicago: University of Chicago Press, 1983.

Kellogg, Frederic R. "A Pragmatic Theory of Legal Classification." In *Peirce and Law,* ed. R. Kevelson, 79–98. New York: Peter Lang, 1992.

Kevelson, Roberta, ed. *The Law as a System of Signs.* New York: Plenum, 1988.

Peirce, Charles S. "Bibliography of Works, Published and in Manuscript." In *Peirce, Paradox, Praxis* and *Peirce, Science, Signs,* ed. R. Kevelson. Amsterdam: Mouton, 1990; Rodopi, 1995.

Uusitalo, Jyrki. "Abduction, Legal Reasoning and Reflexive Law." In *Peirce and Law,* ed. R. Kevelson, 163–186. New York: Peter Lang, 1992.

Roberta Kevelson

Penal Law, Philosophy of

Penal philosophy is the study of the values of justice and legality in the criminal domain. It makes use of both law and first philosophy (the study of the ground of being and its appearance).

Penal philosophy is not mere speculation about crime and the ends of punishment. It is a method and discipline for studying the facts. Starting with phenomena, it looks for the explanation of their underlying causes. It uses dialectic as the offshoot of first philosophy, but without falling into a transcendental metaphysics. It achieves rigor by relying on the vital distinctions in legal theory. Not ignoring the truth and appearances of being, it goes beyond legal formalism. It gives scope to ontological considerations, which, nonetheless, are actualized in the legal phenomena and legal formality.

Penal philosophy is not unknown in history, but it took root where the moral theory of human beings arises. Its sources derive from ancient Greece, where the public sphere received its political organization while remaining dependent upon cosmic beginnings. There, penal justice took the form of deities—Nemesis, Dike, and the Erinyes, who oversee the right order of a universe governed by retribution, the source and end of penal philosophy. Anaximander makes the idea of retribution the key to the world's development. For Heraclitus, world-making depends on punitive justice. Pythagoreans said the retributive law of *antipéponthos* rules man and the universe. Penality makes up the Greek view of nature as well as of society.

Penal philosophy's concern with law arises from its search for justice in all of its expressions. It seeks for the idea which gives law its distinctive identity. This gives it two basic concerns: (1) its *theoretical* concern for the speculative principles derived from practice and (2) its *praxeology* or *practical* concern for the dialectical relations which arise between humans and things in the course of social living.

Theoretically, it studies the usual information on penal activity in legal theory, penal science, criminology, and sociology of crime, but all from a critical perspective by determining these disciplines' interconnections. It looks for current concepts to apply the major philosophical ideas in the penal domain. It mediates the various disciplines here toward sound knowledge. It expresses the purpose of social values and individual values.

Because it is concerned with representative ideas and significant concepts, the theoretical part of penal philosophy looks also to the aesthetics of law, to explain how norms and other signs in law signify. For example, it analyzes the subjective elements in crime, to clarify the offender's culpability and its sanction. It relates the real intent and the intent as phenomenologically reconstituted by the judge according to the facts.

Penal philosophy is closely connected to jural hermeneutics. It interprets each text in need of explanation, not only its logical and rational sense, but also the onto-deontological, the historical and cultural, addressing the legally correct requirements of a case by the subtext in its legal expression.

Theoretical exercise reveals the axiological character of penal philosophy. It tries to determine the links between the wrongdoing and penal fault, and to study their repercussions upon culpability and the imposition of sanctions. Thus penal philosophy undergirds the criminal sciences.

Practical penal philosophy applies theoretical findings to the concrete actions undertaken by penal agents—judges, mediators, educators, prison officers. It puts the basic principles of penal philosophy into play there.

Practical study determines not only the purposes of punishment (penal teleology), but also the underlying relation between retribution and the utilitarian purposes of punishment. Retribution and utility are not always at odds in penal teleology. Ontological investigation of the ways of living the penal order can bring the necessary nuance to this subject. Retribution is set as a basis for punishment by appealing to distributive justice (to each one's due, the desert from one's acts). Useful ends serve present society's practical design for fostering good conduct and maintaining public order. Penal philosophy brings first philosophy into touch with the vitality of real policies concerning crime.

Beyond criminology and the contingent facts and judgments of how criminal behavior appears, it exceeds criminal treatment science by considering the offender not as having an "antisocial disease," nor a subject for experiment in the name of some misguided humanism. It steers clear of rigid criminological fashions displacing realism, invoking some utopian ethic, and dehumanizing the human being. Faced with personal dignity in all of its spiritual depth, penal philosophy looks to culpability and imputability, the gravity of crime, and the use of sanction.

By analyzing criminal activities in view of the social architectonic, the values which underlie social order, penal philosophy leads judges to seek justice without the ambiguity of legal naturalism nor the rigor of legal positivism.

References

Cotta, Sergio. *Why Violence? A Philosophical Interpretation.* Tallahassee: University of Florida Press, 1978.

Cross, Rupert, and P. Aster. *An Introduction to Criminal Law.* 7th ed. London: Butterworth, 1972.

Gionea, V. "Parallèle entre la responsabilité pénale dans le droit mésopotamien, hébreu, perse, indien et chinois" (Penal Responsibility: Parallels Between Mesopotamian, Hebrew, Persian, Indian, and Chinese Law). *Cuadernos Informativos de Derecho* 14 (1992).

Mitias, M.H. "Another Look at Hegel's Concept of Punishment." *Hegel-Studien* 13 (1978).

Tzitzis, Stamatios. "Penal Trial and the Onto-Axiological Dimension of Right." *Vera Lex* 12 (1992).

———. *La Philosophie Pénale* (Penal Philosophy). Paris: Presses Universitaires de France, 1996.

Tzitzis, S., and L.N. Dormont, eds. *Criminologie de l'acte et philosophie pénale. De l'ontologie criminelle des anciens à la victimologie appliquée moderne* (Theory of Criminal Action and Penal Philosophy: From Ancient Ontology of Crime to Modern Applied Victimology). Paris: Litec, 1994.

Walker, Nigel. *Why Punish?* Oxford: Oxford University Press, 1991.

Stamatios Tzitzis

Perelman, Chaïm (1912–1984)

Chaïm Perelman has examined what philosophers could learn from lawyers and from their actual reasoning practices. Through pragmatism, he has built an original philosophy of law but has also nurtured his general philosophy of reasonableness, the *New Rhetoric.*

Being overly dependent on contingent values and their contexts of use, legal practices are scorned by many traditions of legal philosophy. At most, they are a pale copy of an *ideal law,* stemming from a supreme legislator who imposes decrees with the force of formal necessity: be it through the laws of the universe or God (classical natural law), or the eternal prerogatives of human nature (modern natural law), or even the laws of science (legal positivism). Conversely, Perelman, a lawyer himself, does not fear the relativity of *real law* and starts from it in his philosophy.

Though still under the influence of neopositivism (Perelman wrote his dissertation on Gottlob Frege), his first major work, devoted to the idea of justice, already escapes from this "idealawism." Perelman brings out the plurality of meanings that characterizes the concept of justice and hence underlines how problems of definition may be approached differently in various contexts, circumscribing a "truth" as multidimensional.

Closer in this sense to the conventionalism of his mentor at the University of Brussels, the sociologist Eugène Dupréel (who also studied the sophists), Perelman spent all his life renewing the credit of rhetoric. Mainstream general or legal philosophy has generally preferred models that were based on absolute conclusions and did not allow discussions to continue. It has therefore looked down on rhetoric for centuries because of its reliance on incomplete syllogisms (enthymemes), opinions *(doxa),* or commonplaces *(topoi),* but also because of its incorporation of passions, emotions, and stylistic artifacts. The heritage of Aristotle's forensic rhetoric, and that of the Roman rhetoricians, like Cicero and Quintilianus, has been put aside. Perelman will revive this tradition and show that when attorneys are writing conclusions and pleading, or when judges are deliberating and writing decisions, they borrow much of their reasoning from rhetoric.

Analyzing court decisions, Perelman shows that, when facts, laws, or notions are not obvious—which happens frequently—legal reasoning stops being formal, scientific, or logical, and becomes argumentative. It is then more supple and leaves room for different opinions. Often, the premises which are used in such contexts are simply probable; they consist of arguments of variable weights, which could be maintained or replaced by another arguer. As for the transition from one argument to another, it is not absolute either; it may simply seem coherent to some extent. In consequence, the conclusion of a legal reasoning, of a series of linked arguments, is neither true nor false, but *more or less convincing and acceptable with respect to a specific audience*; it remains open to further discussion.

When do lawyers actually have the opportunity to argue? They do so about *facts,* about the multiple ways of understanding them, of qualifying them. Some facts may receive more or less emphasis, according to their easy qualification under a favorable law. Lawyers also argue about *laws*—statutes or precedents which require interpretation, or which contradict each other (antinomies), or which present gaps. Finally, they argue about *confused notions, with variable content,* like justice, equity, standards of good behavior, reasonable delivery time, and so forth.

When they expose their arguments, lawyers keep in mind whom they are trying to persuade, that is, the judge who is in front of them and who hopefully will adhere to the thesis they present to his or her assent. Similarly, when judges motivate their decisions, judges also try to convey the most convincing arguments to their own audience, which can be the court of appeal, as well as the litigants and their counsels.

In his *New Rhetoric,* Perelman has developed a very persuasive description of legal reasoning, suggesting how forensic rhetoric serves various purposes of the law: it can contribute to stability, legal decision, and problem solving, as well as to adaptability, dissenting opinions, and questioning. Promoting the first set of goals, rhetoric appears as *monist,* reducing progressively the differences between several people to a specific answer of identity. Promoting the second set, rhetoric appears in its *pluralistic* version, allowing alternative answers, that is, maintaining or reopening differences, where people may be tempted by fixed identities.

Perelman has introduced us to the double nature of language: the power of being integrative and divisive, as law itself. It is up to the speakers to choose one of these paths in relation to their audiences. If persuasion is desired, the former may well be the best; yet the other is always available. The renewal of legal rhetoric is therefore as essential for theoretical description of legal language reality as for practical prescriptions of its use.

References

Golden, J.L., and J.J. Pilotta, eds. *Practical Reasoning in Human Affairs: Studies in Honor of Chaïm Perelman*. Dordrecht: Reidel, 1986.

Lempereur, A., ed. *L'homme et la rhétorique* (Man and Rhetoric). Paris: Méridiens-Klincksieck, 1990.

Perelman, C. *Ethique et droit* (Ethics and Law). Brussels: Editions de l'Université de Bruxelles, 1990.

———. *The Idea of Justice and the Problem of Argument.* London: Routledge and Kegan Paul, 1963.

———. *Justice.* New York: Random House, 1967.

———. *Justice, Law and Argument: Essays in Moral and Legal Reasoning.* Dordrecht: Reidel, 1980.

———. *Logique juridique.* Paris: Dalloz, 1976.

———. *The New Rhetoric in the Humanities: Essays on Rhetoric and Its Applications.* Dordrecht: Reidel, 1979.

———. *The Realm of Rhetoric.* Notre Dame: University of Notre Dame Press, 1982.

Perelman, C., and L. Olbrechts-Tyteca. *The New Rhetoric: A Treatise on Argumentation.* 1958. Notre Dame: University of Notre Dame Press, 1969.

Alain Pekar Lempereur

Personal Injury

In the absence of direct proof of fault for personal injury, the doctrine of *res ipsa loquitur* permits an inference of negligence through use of circumstantial evidence, thereby aiding the jury in allocating fault and spreading loss.

A doctrine of circumstantial or indirect evidence, *res ipsa loquitur* (the thing speaks for itself) is designed to help courts deal with injuries arising from unexplained events, creating a rebuttable presumption that plaintiff's injuries from defective products were caused by negligence merely by describing the circumstances of the injury.

Measured by common experiences or expert testimony, the law reasons that certain types of events do not happen in the absence of negligence, defined by the *Restatement of the Law of Torts* as "conduct which falls below the standard established by law for the protection of others against unreasonable risk of harm." When those occurrences happen, therefore, theoretically it would be unjust if the injured party were not compensated.

Classic formulation of the doctrine comprises three elements: the event must be of the type which does not ordinarily happen in the absence of negligence; the agency or instrumentality causing the injury must have been in the defendant's exclusive control; and the plaintiff must not have voluntarily contributed to the accident. A fourth element has been suggested by some state courts: evidence as to the true explanation of the event must be more readily accessible to the defendant than to the plaintiff. The *Restatement,* however, does not require the foregoing elements, but rather requires that "other responsible causes, including the conduct of the plaintiff and third persons, are sufficiently eliminated by the evidence." Exclusive control is unnecessary.

Illustrations of situations in which *res ipsa loquitur* is used follow: an airplane crash with no apparent explanation and no detailed or specific proof despite due care in maintenance, qualified flight personnel, and normal weather conditions, leads to the conclusion that the incident would not have occurred absent negligence on the part of the defendant who controlled the instrumentality and to which the plaintiff did not contribute. Personal injury cases dealing with objects such as bricks or windowpanes falling from a defendant's premises, falling elevators, collapse of structures, escape of noxious fumes, buried water pipes that break, and exploding bottles or boilers under a defendant's control and which have been handled carefully, have also led to an inference or a presumption of negligence sufficient to permit courts to invoke the doctrine of *res ipsa loquitur.* An element of the dramatic, the unusual, and the improbable exists in many of those cases, leading courts to require that the event must be "unusual." It is obvious, however, that common experience dictates that fault is not always present when certain events occur. In those instances, therefore, *res ipsa loquitur* is inappropriate.

In close cases of vicarious liability, or cases where multiple defendants act in concert, however, application of the doctrine becomes speculative and controversial, since the question of control is often unclear. Whether defendants have exclusive control, joint control, or successive control may change liability and proof in a given fact situation. Questions of agency are ordinarily issues of fact to be determined by a jury. Questions bearing on the relationship between parties and the amount of control exercised by one over another may be prejudicial, therefore, because a jury which may hesitate finding an individual defendant liable may nonetheless find that person's employer liable. Other questions of primary and secondary or derivative liability among joint tortfeasors may also be implicated. Medical cases in which unexplained events occur also present numerous problems relating to probability and concurrent control.

Some critics of the *res ipsa loquitur* doctrine have called for its abolition entirely, on the ground that it is confused and uncertain, and some state courts have limited its application. It has been argued that the doctrine is not distinctive, and that use of the Latin phraseology adds to the general confusion surrounding it. According to some, its practical impact has encouraged a tendency toward broad assumptions favorable to liability where courts would otherwise be reluctant to adopt them absent expert testimony. There has also been greater reliance on its use in cases where a plaintiff's sufficiency of proof is problematic and his or her burden of proof difficult to sustain. Where the facts of an event are sketchy, a willingness to adopt the doctrine is apparent. In cases resulting in an injury to a plaintiff, as where a structure collapses, plaster falls, or glass or other substance is found in packaged or sealed containers of food, courts have liberally permitted introduction of the doctrine. It can be argued that such use of the doctrine amounts to the imposition on the defendant of strict or even absolute liability. Close examination of the doctrine has revealed, however, that its use approximates that used in any case of circumstantial evidence.

Critics who assail the doctrine as unsatisfactory have suggested alternative compensation plans which embrace particular categories of activities and classes of victims, essentially usurping the role of the decision maker in favor of legislative policymaking. Problematic in this scheme, however, is the consideration of whether to incorporate elements of compensation or deterrence as a legislative goal. On balance, however, because it appeals to both rationality and justice and requires a factual analysis for its application, *res ipsa loquitur* may produce a better result than other alternatives.

References

American Law Institute. *Restatement of the Law of Torts*. St. Paul MN: American Law Institute, 1939. 2d ed. 1965.

Harper, Fowler V., and Fleming James, Jr. *The Law of Torts*. Boston: Little, Brown, 1956. 2d ed. with Oscar S. Gray. 1986.

Prosser, William L. *The Law of Torts*. St. Paul MN: West, 1941. 5th ed. with W. Page Keeton. *Prosser and Keeton on the Law of Torts*. 1984.

Special Committee on the Tort Liability System of the American Bar Association. *Towards a Jurisprudence of Injury: The Continuing Creation of a System of Substantive Justice in American Tort Law*. Chicago: American Bar Association, 1984.

Speiser, Stuart M., Charles F. Krause, and Alfred W. Gans. *The American Law of Torts*. Rochester NY: Lawyers Coop, 1985.

Teshima, Joan. "Applicability of res ipsa loquitur in Case of Multiple, Nonmedical Defendants—Modern Status." *American Law Reports* 4th, 59 (1988), 201.

———. "Applicability of res ipsa loquitur in Case of Multiple Medical Defendants—Modern Status." *American Law Reports* 4th, 67 (1989), 544.

White, G. Edward. *Tort Law in America: An Intellectual History*. New York: Oxford University Press, 1985.

Marcia J. Weiss

Persons, Identity of

Problems for legal theories today (genetic technologies, terrorist threats, religious and ethnic conflicts) make personal identity a legal issue. Personal identity, unchangeable or invariable, is the essence of the human existent. Its referent is the singular which precedes and excedes the category, living past any thinking. "Singular" as a category of radical ontological otherness designates the entirety or the wholeness of a human being. The unrepeatable existentially unique act has bodily and intellectual life so inseparable that each person's existence starts with formation of its bodiliness, before any principle of consciousness, of reason, or of will appears. Personal existence comes to identity as an act, and not as the potential which various typologies make of it. It connotes an achieved dignity, which no longer has to become "realized" or "acquired" through "becoming" a person, by some lottery under the chances of a social contract. One need do no more than become the person one already is; making potency predominate over act, which every process of "acquiring human dignity" does, is to reverse this order of being.

Only thereafter is identity made explicit by *reason*, and formulated in *concepts* for the narrowed domain which the law constructs. Identity becomes "generic" and not "universal"; the human being, intelligent home of ideas, becomes conceptual and rational; the contemplative person becomes the person of action; the person in its irreducible existential singularity becomes the person as a role or "mask," recognized on the basis of abstract qualities and categories, starting with "human" and reaching, for instance, "citizen."

This does not mean the second identity leaves no room for the first. On one hand, the person takes itself as something of a kind, takes on the determinate mold which gives it the advantages of a particular status with its rights and duties under the rubric of *equality*. On the other hand, however, the person in its concrete and irreplaceable existence or its *dignity* is not lost. While identity is treated by law in terms of equality, equality then has to be set under the higher value of dignity, which is the unique core of identity for each living person, even though it is not completely "judiciable." Thus categories which express law can respect what surpasses them as a singular and vital given. The person is part of a legal and political whole and has to accommodate other persons' lives within it in "relative" and reciprocal dependence—but the person comes first, already constituted as an autonomous "whole." The person is not an outcome, capable of being leveled into uniformity, but has its own end; only as such is it open to universal treatment. There are as many personal ends, each with "dignity" and a claim to be protected, as there are human existents. Identity thus implies a twofold "relativity" inherent in the very structure of the person: relationship is turned toward other persons who are alike in substance, in view of a distributive or commutative justice; relatedness is turned, above all, toward other persons as singular, and different by analogy, in view of the demands of basic ethics.

Historical Development

Opposed views map changes in philosophy that undermine the is/ought totality or, more frequently, dismantle the biopsychical wholeness of the human being. They retain only one aspect of the object of their analysis. Particularity is substituted for singularity, "individual" is made synonymous to "particular." The individual's identity is purely descriptive, independent of any evaluation or value content; ends are given over to subjective whim. Aristotelianism (or the doctrine of the "individualization" by an "informing principle" upon a receptive "matter" with its various potentialities) had already distorted medieval thomism's interpretation. Empiricism brought this to a head, and analytical philosophy rediscovered it during the twentieth century, following criticism of the "naturalistic fallacy" by the Cambridge school, and by the normative branch of the Vienna Circle, for whom identity always finally breaks down and the person is only the role of an "agent" for discourse and the linguistic system.

Alternatively, when "is" and "ought" were kept together, only the limited conceptual and rational sense of person could be preserved. Human rationality was taken as a person's sole reality; the singular disappeared before the particularity of its kind. Within the person reduced to a thing of reason, discussion concerned only which of its parts should predominate. In the "humanist" Renaissance in Europe, "natural law" belongs to reason cut off from spirit; enlightenment comes from reason and no longer illuminates even the act of reason. Enlightenment then transcends reason, as the tradition of Plato and Augustine held.

Within human nature itself what are called the "true" and the "false" natures burst asunder: the rational part, "transcendental" in Immanuel Kant's sense, consists in the drive for recognition of moral dignity, liberty, and happiness; this asserts itself gradually over the sensible or empirical part, which is made up of instinctual drives, now devalued and judged inferior. In Cicero and ancient stoicism, in René Descartes, and then in the schools of "modern natural law," reason tries to derive a law that is generalizable, according to its own criteria, independently of the empirical facts on which it depends.

With German idealism, reason produces a law "purified" from even this content and which prevails solely by its generality over all. This is a move from one idealism to another. Personal identity first was located in reason dominating instincts, and then came to maturity in the judgment of rational "right." It flickered out with its inability to master its own logic, the prototype of the "hero" in stoic justice; it finally obliterated both lived experience and concrete trial and error, the prototype of the hero in Germanic moral life, whose "duty" and "self-respect" act against "the law of the senses." With this last movement the romantic reaction could burst forth in a nihilist flood of vital forces or, just as well, in the frenzied working of utilitarianism and the pragmatism of interests, bringing back the conception of personal identity posed by nominalism.

In a word, either the person finds its identity in the self of consciousness or reason, or else it lurks in the empirical and contingent self, which gives up discourse on the necessity of being, which has no continuity except a sequence of physically quantifiable states or the roles and social "masks" designed to provoke its various needs.

Legal Treatment

The consequences as to the person's basic protection in the law are well known. Its protection is dependent on providing factual circumstances as evidence for its claims. In *rational selfhood of consciousness,* the person claims an identity laboring under purpose. Stripped down to *empirical continuity,* in the nominalist heritage (Anglo-Saxon, Scandinavian, Italian) repeated in sociologistic functionalism, the person is reduced to its precarious material needs and shows identity only in its regularities upon a statistical curve.

Beneath *rational identity* and *empirical pseudo-identity* or *continuity,* however, the intangible given of life and a space for the existential singular can be recovered; the *identity of the living person* can be recalled, as the basis for a dignity already in place and potent enough to inspire protection or respect, at least ethically even before legally. Without it, any respect for the decisions of the law is not itself fully justified or "respectable." This way Antonio Rosmini faced empiricism and rationalism as to identity in the nineteenth century; today it is the existential personalist ("prosopological") metaphysics of personal identity as "act."

The problem for law lies in still not being able to *translate* this metaphysical and moral identity into a legal identity; for the first is absolute, while the latter, which it implies, is unavoidably relative. The metaphysical and moral "singular" has to become the "fellow citizen" of law. For example, to make a gift or to pardon (despite the legal principle of property or of responsibility) is an ethical action in complete openness. The acts show relatedness without boundary, and they express a singularity which resists legal accommodation. Law can only set up an order of exchange between "yours" and "mine" and, within the boundaries of rules addressed to everyone, cannot grasp a gift and a pardon of this kind.

Still, for enforcement to be at least "just," "justifiable," "obligatory," and worthy of respect, law must at least *not violate* personhood, namely, the unique and eminently personal ability to exist uniquely connected (and not collected) in a way that preserves all the positive value there is in the group. Law cannot make gift or pardon illusory, under the pretext that it is not verifiable by testing or statistics, not possible for a human person busily lost in society. Law cannot treat as in need of psychiatric help a person who decides "singularly" to live out a gift or a pardon, or thinks by this to remove oneself from the exchange relationships of the social contract. Personal identity in law can hold a share in the larger and fuller ethical identity, which locates itself in the higher universal ideal of the human being, held "higher" even if it is not yet always apparent or generalizable by reason. Identity is the sign of a dignity which is no more acquired than it is merited, but which is embodied in the basic fact of being a human being.

References

Bagolini, L. *Giustizia et società* (Justice and Society). Rome: Dino Ed., 1983.

de Finance, J. *De l'un et de l'autre. Essai sur l'alterité* (The One and the Other: Essay on Altereity). Rome: Gregorian University Press, 1993.

Donnelly, Samuel J.M. "Toward a Personalist Jurisprudence: Basic Insights and Concepts." *Loyola of Los Angeles Law Review* 28 (1995), 547.

Gray, Christopher B. "The Notion of Person for Medical Law." *Revue de droit de l'Université de Sherbrooke* 11 (1981), 341–415.

Hirschman, Linda R. "The Philosophy of Personal Identity and the Life and Death Cases." *Chicago-Kent Law Review* 68 (1992), 91.

Kester, M. Charles. "Is There a Person in the Body? An Argument for the Priority of Persons and the Need for a New Legal Paradigm." *Georgetown Law Journal* 82 (1994), 1643.

Massini-Correas, C.I. *Filosofia del derecho* (Philosophy of Law). Buenos Aires: Abeledo Perrot, 1994.

Noonan, John T. *Persons and Masks of the Law: Cardozo, Holmes, Jefferson, and Wythe as Makers of the Masks*. New York: Farrar, Straus and Giroux, 1976.

Ricoeur, P. *Soi-même comme un autre* (Self as Other). Paris: Seuil, 1990.

Rorty, A. *The Identity of* Persons. Berkeley: University of California Press, 1976.

Trigeaud, J.-M. *Métaphysique et éthique au fondement du droit* (Metaphysics and Ethics as the Foundation of Law). Bordeaux: Bière Ed., 1995.

Jean-Marc Trigeaud

See also Dignity; Truth

Petrazycki, Leon (1867–1931)

Leon Petrazycki, born in Kollatajewo, started medical studies, then studied law in Kiev, Berlin, Heidelberg, and Paris, received a master's degree in law in 1896 from Kiev, and a doctorate in law in 1897 from St. Petersburg. He became full professor in St. Petersburg in 1901 and a member of the Russian Duma (1906–1908) as a member of the Constitutional Democratic Party; he was imprisoned and removed from his professorial position after he signed the Vyborg Manifesto in 1906. In 1919 Petrazycki became the first professor of sociology in liberated Poland. He committed suicide May 15, 1931.

The unrecognized father of the sociology of law, Petrazycki held the original idea of creating legal policy as a science for accomplishing desired social goals and guiding society toward "rational and active love." Petrazycki successfully applied his rules of legal policy to a critique of the *Bürgerliches Gesetzbuch* (Civil Code), which made him famous in Germany. He postulated a "renaissance of natural law," an influential idea never attributed to him.

Petrazycki developed a new logic and methodology applicable to all sciences wherein "positions" (particles of the sentence) and not only whole sentences can be true or false. His methodology teaches how to build adequate theories: not "lame" theories and not "jumping" theories. Theory is lame when the explanandum is targeted toward too narrow a class (that is, something is maintained about species, when it should be asserted about genus). That cigars weighing ten grams fall down with a speed proportional to the time of their falling is contained by a more general thesis pertaining to all falling things; only those theses that relate to their objects exclusively are scientifically valid. Theory is jumping when the explanandum jumps over the explanans class (that is, something is maintained about genus, when it should be asserted about species). Marxism, for example, utilizes economic factors to explain all phenomena of social, national, and cultural character.

Petrazycki's psychology distinguishes unilateral elements (cognition, feelings, and will) and two-sided elements (emotions). He distinguished two types of emotions: appulsive (attractive, appealing) and repulsive (revolting). Emotions are the basis of morality and law and constitute the basis for legal and moral attitudes and actions.

Thus, law is made up by mutuality of "duties and claims," while morality is created by "duties." Law generates the active psyche of a citizen, convinced of one's right, while morality induces behavior generated by internal duty. Before Eugen Ehrlich coined the concept of living law, Petrazycki formulated the distinction between intuitive law (not supported by state law) and positive law (supported by the state's norms). According to Petrazycki, law plays several crucial social functions: (1) motivational (training how everyone should behave in society), (2) educative (training how to socialize behavior to societal standards), (3) distributive (training how to distribute goods and services and create economic systems, and (4) organizational (training how to construct social institutions and create the state). Also according to Petrazycki, law through history is characterized by (1) the tendency to adjudicate increased demands (tendency to attest more rights and duties), (2) the tendency to change incentives (to utilize more lenient penalties), and (3) the tendency to diminish motivational pressures to obtain the same effects.

Morality and law furnish an individual with orders which supposedly "come from above" (have a mystic character). Morality points to certain duties, "I should forgive him his ills," but does not give the right to demand those duties. Morality and intuitive law designate patterns of behavior that later could be formalized by the positive and official law. Petrazycki also developed a new sociology. Applied to law and morality, this sociology asserts that the evolution of law and morality is based on an adjustment called "puzzling purposefulness." This threefold adjustment is grounded on a modification of Charles Darwin's principle of natural selection in the struggle for existence: (1) Species adaptation inherited from ancestors corresponds to the ancestors' conditions of life but does not necessarily fit present-day conditions. (2) Individual-egocentrical adaptation tends to react aversively to pain or loss and is attracted by pleasure or gain. (3) Socio-oriented adaptation is oriented by the good of the group; this type of adaptation is "contagious." Being emotional it spreads fast, not on an intellectual but on an "infectious" emotional level, and therefore can adjust rapidly and elastically. On the basis of mutual communication and emotional contamination, social adaptation generates values, norms, and attitudes functional for the group as a whole. Thus, a social system is a system of people's coordinated behaviors guided predominantly by legal emotions.

Because Petrazycki wrote in German, Russian, and Polish, and taught in Russia before the revolution, spent some time in Finland, and eventually taught in Poland, he was not fully recognized outside of these countries. In Poland, due to his uncompromising character, he was disregarded by many. His defense of the rights of women and Jews, as well as his struggle for the autonomy of the university and the independence of science, did not gain him wide popularity.

In Poland he influenced several generations: first, followers Jerzy Lande, Jerzy Licki, Stanislaw Pietka, and critics Czeslaw Znamierowski, Jozef Zajkowski, Mieczyslaw Manelli, and Marek Fritzhand, who were one-sided and biased; second, followers Jan Gorecki, Jan Klimowski, Adam Podgorecki, and enemies and vulgarizers Maria Borucka-Arctowa, Grzegorz Seidler, and Jerzy Wroblewski, who were originally followers but later converted to marxism; third, followers Andrzej Kojder, Jerzy Kwasniewski, Waclaw Makarczyk, and Krzysztof Motyka.

Acknowledgment is given to the contribution by Andrzej Kojder and Krzysztof Motyka to this study.

References

Babb, Hugh W. "Petrazhitskii: Science of Legal Policy and Theory of Law." *Boston University Law Review* 17–18 (1937–38), 793–829.

Baum, Karl B. *Leon Petrazycki und Seine Schuler* (Leon Petrazycki and His Students). Berlin: Verlag Dunker u. Humbold, 1967.

Górecki, Jan. *Sociology and Jurisprudence of Leon Petrazycki*. Urbana: University of Illinois Press, 1975.

Petrazycki, Leon. *Aktienwessen und Spekulation* (Stocks and Speculation). Berlin: Verlag H.W. Muller, 1906.

———. *Law and Morality: Leon Petrazycki.* Trans. Hugh W. Babb. Intro. Nicolas Timasheff. Cambridge: Harvard University Press, 1955.

———. *O Nauce, Prawie i Moralnosci. Pisma Wybrane* (On Science, Law and Morality: Selected Writings). Intro. Jerzy Licki and Andrzej Kojder. Warsaw: PWN, 1985. (Multilingual bibliography.)

———. *Vvedenie v Izucenie prawa i nravstvennosti* (Theory of Law and State in Connection with Theory of Morals). 2 vols. St. Petersburg, 1907.

Podgórecki, Adam. "Unrecognized Father of Sociology of Law." *Law and Society Review* 15 (1981).

Sorokin, Pitirim. *Society, Culture and Personality. Their Structure and Dynamics. A System of General Sociology*. New York: Harper and Brothers, n.d. [1962].

Walicki, Andrzej. *Legal Philosophies of Russian Liberalism*. Oxford: Clarendon Press, 1987.

Adam Podgórecki

Phenomenology of Law

Phenomenology, as a philosophical methodology, was established by Edmund Husserl (1859–1938), a student of Franz Brentano (1838–1917) in Vienna. Husserl's philosophy, and that of his successor, Martin Heidegger (1889–1976), dominated the German philosophical scene for the first half of the century. After World War II, Husserl's work (and particularly Heidegger's) exercised tremendous influence on philosophy in France; however, it failed to make inroads in the English-speaking world.

Husserl's phenomenology is characterized by a call for a return to the things themselves as they are immediately given to consciousness. Its task is to describe the essences, the a priori structure of phenomena, by which the things themselves are given to us. Through the phenomenological reduction, the contingent elements of the world are bracketed, thus allowing the thing to appear in its eidetic purity. An ultimate reduction reveals the transcendental ego as pure intentionality, which constitutes the meaning of the world and its objects.

Although Husserl believed that his method could be applied in all the various sciences, not many legal theorists have used phenomenology and its methodological postulates in treating problems encountered in philosophy of law. Of those who have, each latched onto a particular aspect of phenomenology while leaving its other methodological concerns aside. There is neither methodological nor doctrinal similarity in the views that phenomenologists of law have espoused.

The first to use phenomenology in the law was Adolf Reinach (1883–1917), a lawyer and philosopher and a leading figure in the phenomenological movement until his untimely death. Reinach uses phenomenology to reveal the essence or the a priori structure of civil law by engaging in descriptions of certain legal concepts, such as the promise, property, representation, lending and liens, used by jurists on a daily basis. The propositions which describe these fundamental legal concepts are universal and necessary and exist independently of any human action; they are synthetic a priori and constitute the meaning of positive law.

Reinach begins his study of law by looking at the promise as one possible source of claims and obligations. After rejecting psychological explanations, he concludes that promising is a social act (like commanding, answering, warning) which must be heard before it can bind. This is a matter of a priori necessity, just as every promise presupposes that the promisor's will is directed to the action contained in the promise. Promising is an act all its own, irreducible to another, and its essence is to create claims and obligations simultaneously.

Reinach holds that his theory can neither be contradicted by legal positivism nor assimilated to a theory of natural law. On one hand, legal rules are "ought" enactments as opposed to the a priori rules, which are laws governing what is; these latter rules are grounded in the essence of social acts and cannot be refuted by historical facts. On the other hand, natural law is concerned with the norms of justice and with what ought to be; but a priori theory has as its object what necessarily is.

Reinach's theory raises several questions. First, his use of the analytic/synthetic distinction is problematic. Second, the nature of the person as the foundation for the possibility of legal-social relationships needs clarification. Third, his theory does not capture the reality of intersubjective practice. His a priori approach leaves aside the ideological and social context of law. The institution of promising as the basis of contractual obligations is not tied into nor distanced from the rise of individualism and liberalism from the fifteenth century.

Two other early German-speaking figures in phenomenology of law were Felix Kaufmann (1895–1949) and Gerhart Husserl (1893–1973), son of the founder of the movement. Kaufmann, a student of Hans Kelsen, wanted to establish the logical foundations of legal theory. While agreeing with Kelsen that laws are norms, he, unlike Kelsen, thought that it was possible to engage in a rational analysis of the ought by studying the rules which govern the use of value terms.

Husserl, over a long career as a professor of law, dealt with many issues in civil law. Husserl was a comparativist who believed that intuiting the essence of legal objects is facilitated by examining the laws in different communities.

The usefulness of the phenomenological method for understanding legal issues was picked up in France by figures such as Simone Goyard-Fabre, Paul Amselek (1937–), and Jean-Louis Gardies (1905–).

Goyard-Fabre uses phenomenological description to show the fundamental ambiguity of the law. All attempts to understand this ambiguity lead to pure thought. Without the transcendental subject, the world of law would be contingent and irrational rather than necessary and rational. Law appears as an organized form of consciousness that constitutes the meaning of legal experience according to an internal a priori necessity: human thought's need for order. Law's raison d'être resides in the transcendental function of consciousness.

Coupled to the need for order in the subjective sphere is the requirement of the respect owed to other humans in the intersubjective sphere, which constitutes the meaning of social life. The need for order and the respect of human dignity are a priori structures of human consciousness and the constitutive reason of legal phenomena. The transcendental subject is the a priori and necessary source of legal experience. In short, the transcendental ego in Goyard-Fabre's theory of law is called upon to play a role analogous to its role in explaining knowledge in general in Edmund Husserl's phenomenology.

According to Amselek, the task of phenomenology is to complete the work begun by legal positivism: to rid legal theory of metaphysical and ideological considerations by rejecting a priori interpretations and, instead, to base its explanation on the idea of normativity. However, positivism had not understood that the norm constituted the generic essence of law—its obligatory character being its specific essence—and was necessary for its philosophical analysis. This, phenomenology can do because it is a method which seeks to determine the essence of things. Sociologism and logicism thus err when they fail to capture the normative dimension of law. Such an approach is persuasive only if one accepts that Amselek has successfully bracketed our worldly attitudes and that this in turn yields normativity as the generic essence of law.

In Amselek's hands, the transcendental reduction becomes simply an epistemological tool which is used to determine the nature of the subject's attitude—which may be either technical or scientific—toward law. This use of the transcendental reduction is problematic. In the phenomenological perspective, the scientific and technical attitudes of the jurist are but two worldly psychological attitudes; there can only be one transcendental attitude, and it reveals the a priori and necessary forms of law.

Gardies draws on Reinach for his theory about the a priori foundation of legal and moral rationality. Moving beyond Reinach's intuitionism, Gardies shows that the content of norms may be logically deduced from a certain legal idea. His ultimate goal is to construct an axiomatic science of law.

Outside of France and Germany, phenomenology has found little echo, with occasional exceptions. There have been active phenomenologists in Latin America. Dutch thinkers, too, have been influenced by trends in Germany and France. There also has been a small number of American and other English-speaking authors who have worked in phenomenology.

Carlos Cossio (1902–1987) founds his egological theory of law on Husserl's transcendental ego. According to Cossio, the science of law is a science of human experience founded on culture and its object is the experience of liberty. Law is a cultural object which people create in function of certain values; law is thus not neutral toward values and the value constituted by law is a positive valuation; there is no transcendental goal, such as justice, immanent to law, which law must realize. What is immanent is the understanding of the positive evaluation. Applying his theory to judicial decision making, Cossio is led to conclude that judicial evaluation is immanent to the law, but always within the bounds prescribed by the law.

In William Luijpen's (1922–) existential phenomenology of law, rights are the correlates of justice and found the legal order. Law is indispensable for the establishment of human dignity, and its task is to guarantee as much love—the minimum requirement of human existence qua coexistence—as possible.

While the French phenomenologist Maurice Merleau-Ponty (1908–1961) never developed a systematic theory of law, William Hamrick (1944–) tries to develop a phenomenological theory of law based on Merleau-Ponty's early writings. Law is a social structure which has its origin in politics; it is one of the modes of expression of meaning and of giving life to the values in a world where there is no a priori meaning. Since the meaning of language is never completely determined, never wholly constituted, a rule may be used, by a judge for example, in a new manner. The rule now is being made to say something new, but which it was already capable of saying. This never happens arbitrarily. Law interacts with ethics and politics and yet remains distinct because each mode engages in social ordering in its own characteristic way. The task of law is to promote justice, which is conceived as a universality and is closely linked to the idea of individual freedom, and to allow the disenfranchised to be respected.

References

Amselek, Paul. "The Phenomenological Description of Law." In *Phenomenology and the Social Sciences,* vol. 2, ed. Maurice Natanson, 367–449. Evanston: Northwestern University Press, 1972.

Cossio, Carlos. "Phenomenology of the Decision." In *Latin-American Legal Philosophy.* Trans. Gordon Ireland, 343–400. Cambridge MA: Harvard University Press, 1948.

Gardies, Jean-Louis. *Essai sur les fondements a priori de la rationalité morale et juridique* (Essay on the A Priori Foundations of Rationality in Ethics and Law). Paris: Librairie Générale de Droit et Jurisprudence, 1972.

Goyard-Fabre, Simone. *Essai de critique phénoménologique du droit* (Essay on the Phenomenological Critique of Law). Paris: Klincksieck, 1972.

Hamrick, William. *An Existential Phenomenology of Law: Maurice Merleau-Ponty.* Dordrecht: Martinus Mijhoff, 1987.

Husserl, Gerhart. *Recht und Welt: Rechtsphilosophische Abhandlungen* (Law and World: Manual of Legal Philosophy). Juristische Abhandlungen, Band 1. Frankfurt: Vittorio Klostermann, 1964.

Kaufmann, Felix. *Logik und Rechtswissenschaft. Grundriss eines Systems der Reinen Rechtslehre* (Logic and Jurisprudence. Basics for a System of Pure Legal Theory). Tübingen: Mohr, 1922. Reprint, Darmstadt: Scientia Verlag Aalen, 1966.

Luijpen, William. *Phenomenology of Natural Law.* Trans. Henry J. Koren. Pittsburgh: Duquesne University Press, 1967.

Pallard, Henri. "La phénoménologie et le droit: Méthode et théorie en philosophie du droit" (Phenomenology and Law: Method and Theory in Philosophy of Law). *Revue de la recherche juridique. Droit prospectif* 13 (1988), 677–727.

Reinach, Adolf. "The Apriori Foundations of Civil Law." Trans. J. F. Crosby. *Aletheia* 3 (1983), 1–142.

Henri R. Pallard
Richard Hudson

Philosophy of Law

See JURISPRUDENCE

Plato (ca. 428–348 B.C.)

Plato's position on law is said to be a moving target. His view of law has been interpreted literally as natural, esoterically as positive, dualistically as both, and as various amalgams of the two to compose one or another kind of convention.

The most mainstream, and therefore most general, interpretations of Plato's view on law involve the natural law approach, taking seriously his discussions about moral essences, or forms or ideas, that is, objective universal truths independent of human will by which particular things existing in the world are given definition. Knowers of this natural law must seek to establish and maintain a legal order that will perfect human political associations, and thus natural law is a basis for idealism. Scholars have characterized Plato's idealism in numerous ways, however. Its essences, forms, or ideas have also been described as less objective and universal: as contrived tools for social control and even repression, as customary values of a given people and time, and as principles of social or individual utility, as noted in Huntington Cairns' *Legal Philosophy from Plato to Hegel.*

The most extreme natural law interpretation of Plato's law argues that his moral essences subsist in a realm of absolute permanence, and they subsist even if and when their particular counterparts in the world do not. Such platonic essences constitute a metaphysical foundation for the "nature" of legal and moral things and are known by reason, either by reason that simply intellects the essences without the use of logic and sense experience or, in a moderate aristotelian version, known through carefully analyzed empirical examination of the natural cosmos.

According to the aristotelian version, the essence is not metaphysical but is a *telos,* or purpose, inherent in the growth of natural things in the cosmos. In both cases, the result of discovering essence or *telos* is philosophic wisdom in absolute knowledge. For example, since the existence of all trees in the world is trees only with reference to the essence of "treeness," all just men and their just acts in the world are just only with reference to "justiceness," the natural law. Justice in this sense is the most important essence of the whole realm of forms, which constitutes the totality of the perfect essences for all existences in the world. As forms, the natural law consists of obligatory standards that naturally function in the world or that ought to be the basis for all human law. The latter claim presents a problem, however, because it suggests that natural law cannot enforce itself and, therefore, requires human agents to enforce it with voluntary will. This problem casts serious doubt on the existence of natural law and is the basis for more moderate theories and critiques of Plato's idealism.

Perhaps the fiercest critique of platonic natural law characterizes Plato as a totalitarian threat to natural human freedom. Using the *Republic* as the basis for his critique, Karl Popper argued that Plato's natural law was actually fabricated myth, a noble lie designed to subject a people to absolute philosophical rulers committed to permanence in a holistic political association. Popper rejected the possibility of natural law and perfection through the unity of philosophy and power and asserted boldly that the scientific reduction of error in knowledge and law could minimize misery among free and equal individuals and beget social and material progress. His rejection is tantamount to calling Plato a legal positivist, a malevolent noble liar who posits a myth in order to use the ignorant for the rulers' ends.

Because Popper saw future circumstances as ultimately unpredictable and therefore unknowable, he argued that platonic central planning of any kind would result in error and oppression. He applied his critique of Plato's apparent collectivism to the deterministic historicisms of G.W.F. Hegel and Karl Marx in a scathing attack on fascism and communism, respectively. Popper countered Plato's positive tyranny by proposing the "rule of law," which generally emphasizes individual liberty and legal equality by the formation of political institutions that secure traditional rights and liberties recognized through common experience and, in government, by ensuring that laws apply to rulers and subjects alike.

Some scholars see Popper's critiques of Plato's legal philosophy as destructive of platonic efforts to improve a society while maintaining its stable traditions, and thus discover in Plato a dualistic doctrine of law, both natural and human. Dualistic interpretations see Plato's laws in the *Republic* as discovered by the philosopher who ascends from the mere opinion of his culture and attains to intellection of the natural law; but the law of Plato's *Laws* remains at the level of human convention generated by a founder of a colony who must take into consideration the opinions of those to inhabit the new colony. The lawgivers must manage lawful peace among both just and unjust citizens to the end of freedom, security, friendship, and goodwill. The reason used by the philosopher here is not intellective *nous* but merely calculation of means to the end of ordered freedom, which is a basic means to living and not any virtue as an end in itself. Through music and religious education of souls, the philosopher-lawgiver elevates legal control of human passions from the baser "iron cord" of obligation, whereby citizens tearfully calculate the shame and pain of disobedience, to the nobler "golden cord" of obligation, whereby they calculate the pleasure of honor and prestige in obedience. Utility appears as virtue. Subsumed in pleasurable honor, the propensity for discord in human nature remains hidden in the harmonious consonance of the passions. Harmony of the passions is posited in the souls of the citizens through harmonic music and myth that rises to the level of divinity, and a consonant flow of tradition conserves the state through an eternity of generations. Law as human custom appears natural.

Compared to Popper's view of Plato as malevolent, this interpretation sees Plato as a benevolent noble liar who would establish laws primarily to regulate the souls of men who would in turn regulate their own bodies. Variations of this view, however, claim that Plato need not abandon his claim to philosophic knowledge of natural law to advocate instilling myth in citizens to generate an eloquent custom. The natural law of the *Republic* can certainly coexist with customary opinions necessary to govern the ignorant, even though implementation of the natural law may happen only perchance. Natural law can also coexist with purely positive human law created and enforced to maintain order, and possibly, in time, positive law might imitate the natural law.

Glenn Morrow has argued that Plato's Cretan city described in *The Laws* has many of the characteristics of modern constitutions founded on the seventeenth- and eighteenth-century constitutional theory that power corrupts, that rulers must be governed by legal institutions and procedures. Plato advocates that all citizens, including rulers, should be governed by law that is clearly and coherently formulated, publicly known, prospective, and adjudicable, and that constitutional powers should be separated in some fashion to facilitate internal checks and balances against officials. He also includes external controls, such as a citizen's right to sue officials, and legal scrutiny of officials during and at the end of their official tenure. Yet Morrow still takes somewhat seriously Plato's idealism and his hope that human law could imitate natural law.

A yet more diluted idealism can be found in interpretations of Plato as one or another kind of legal conventionalist, interpretations that further reduce his natural moral law to factual characteristics of human nature that humans value. Here, natural law is rejected, as either irrelevant or nonexistent, in favor of a morality based on universal subjective desires. They interpret Plato as holding a more hobbesian view of human nature and the necessity for law in the absence of any substantial moral essences or forms and see him as fundamentally positivistic, albeit with the possibility of absolute moral values rooted in the individual, such as the rational will never to harm oneself or anyone else. The thrust of this view sees Plato as somewhat of a social contract theorist, with legal obligation rooted in agreement to legal procedures and laws.

Although in agreement with conventional positivist interpretations to a great degree, another conventionalist interpretation sees Plato not as a positivist but as a "minimal" conventionalist, that is, as minimizing the natural law to facts about human nature that necessarily include moral values within individual human beings, but values more as an irresistible "nature" than as merely posited will. While such a nature sounds much like aristotelian *telos* in human nature, it does not involve natural ends. This conventionalism sees Plato as extolling law as the artifactual solution to discord in a world of radically individualistic human beings who each desire to live and to voluntarily pursue their own ways and ends of life, be those ends individualistic or communitarian. Law, then, is more of an instrument for coordinating pursuits of happiness and not a catalyst for cooperation to any communally virtuous or utilitarian end. Plato's portrayal of Socrates (particularly in the *Apology*) as the quintessential individualist seeking knowledge apart from the many is the symbol of the virtuous man. Individual liberty is essential to moral virtue, since coercion denies the necessity of knowledge and will in good souls or actions, both of which reside only in individuals. The virtuous life is a life of reason, and reason writ large is law among humans. The good state, then, is that which is ruled by reason as law. Such law as coordination has particular characteristics rooted in the causality found in human and physical nature. As the archetype of moral individualism, Socrates, in *Crito*, obeys the legal procedure demanding his execution because moral reason requires that his actions be rationally consistent with his nature, which includes keeping his implicit social contract with the city to obey its laws. The laws made possible the family into which he was born, his education, his own family with children, and most important his philosophic life—all of which he chose tacitly by never renouncing his citizenship and rather enjoying the benefits thereof. The moral life means living as consistently as possible as a rational man in the natural world throughout time and possibly eternity, which includes obeying oneself in one's agreement to obey law.

References

Allen, R. E. *Socrates and Legal Obligation*. Minneapolis: University of Minnesota Press, 1980.

Cairns, Huntington. *Legal Philosophy from Plato to Hegel*. Baltimore: Johns Hopkins University Press, 1967.

Kelly, J.M. *A Short History of Western Legal Theory*. New York: Oxford University Press, 1992.

Morrow, Glenn R. *Plato's Cretan City*. Princeton NJ: Princeton University Press, 1993.

Pangle, Thomas L. "Interpretive Essay." In *The Laws of Plato*. New York: Basic Books, 1980.

Popper, Sir Karl. *The Open Society and Its Enemies*. Princeton NJ: Princeton University Press, 1950.

Reynolds, Noel B. "Plato's Defense of Rule of Law." In *Philosophy of Law in the History of Human Thought, Proceedings of the Twelfth World Congress of Philosophy of Law and Social Philosophy,* Athens, 1985, *ARSP Supplementa,* vol. 2, ed. S. Panou, G. Bozonis, D. Georgas, and P. Trappe, 16–21. Stuttgart: Franz Steiner, 1988.

Wild, John. *Plato's Modern Enemies and the Theory of Natural Law*. Chicago: University of Chicago Press, 1953.

Noel B. Reynolds
Thomas J. Lowery

Plea Bargaining

Plea bargaining is a controversial procedure for prosecutorial disposition of criminal cases by exchanging charge reductions and leniency in sentencing recommendations for guilty pleas.

After a suspect is arrested and charged with a criminal offense, it must be determined whether the accused is guilty and, if so, what the punishment should be. Anglo-American judicial systems have traditionally used jury trials for the disposition of criminal cases. Prosecutor and defense attorney marshal the evidence in court, the jury pronounces the verdict, and, for those found guilty, the judge sets the sentence. Trials no longer play this dominant role. Today both verdict and sentence are typically negotiated in "plea bargains." The defendant agrees to plead guilty to an offense (often less serious than the one originally charged) and so relieves the prosecutor of the burden of proving guilt in court. In exchange, the accused is assured a sentence less severe than could be received after conviction at trial, even when discounted by the probability of acquittal. Defense attorneys can also gain, since many receive fixed fees whether there is a trial or not. Even for defendants whose only bargaining chip is the power to waive trial, counsel can still secure benefits in a fraction of the time a trial would take. Following agreement, the "trial" is usually a formal ceremony in which the judge, also enjoying a reduced workload, honors the expectation of leniency. All three—defendant, prosecutor, and judge—benefit from the agreement, while the public enjoys faster, easier, cheaper criminal convictions.

Given increasing pressures on the criminal justice system, it is not surprising that simplifying practices have evolved in the system's unregulated interstices. Our reliance upon plea bargaining has been compared with the use of judicial torture from the middle ages to the early modern period. In both cases, there was apparent difficulty obtaining desired convictions at trial. Just as the burdens of proof and adjudication are alleviated when rack and thumbscrew are used to extort an admissible confession, so too are they alleviated when a dispositive guilty plea is induced by assurances of a reduced sentence.

Although plea bargaining was once a covert feature of the criminal justice system, recent decades have witnessed robust controversy as details have come to light. While dozens of scholarly articles, books, and academic symposia have contributed to a clearer picture of the values at stake, there is no consensus on how these are to be respected. Is plea bargaining acceptable, or should it be reformed—and, if so, how?—or abolished entirely? While one cannot catalog here all the issues explored in the literature, it is possible to sketch some that have received notable attention.

Involuntariness

The comparison with judicial torture suggests involuntariness. As with torture, plea bargaining threatens a measure of suffering unless a defendant confesses. One critical strategy seeks to treat such pleas as legal nullities on the grounds of duress or coercion. Where, for example, Gunman compels Victim to hand over a wallet, Victim does not lose title to the money. Accordingly, when the accused enters a guilty plea in order to avert death or lengthy imprisonment, that agreement too should be void of legal effect. In response, defenders of plea bargaining have pointed out that, while the gunman has no right to threaten harm, prosecutors have the right—indeed are obligated—to prosecute. Plea bargaining, a prosecutorial offer of leniency in exchange for a plea, is an offer (not a threat) that improves the defendant's prospects above what they were at the pre-offer baseline, at least in those cases where defendants do not face additional undeserved punishment for requiring they state to them after trial. Critics have questioned whether one can distinguish between reduced punishments if one saves the state the expense of a trial and increased punishments if one puts the state to its proof. Which is the baseline and which is the aberration?

Unreliability

A second critical strategy fixes on the reliability of bargained-for pleas. In sidestepping trials, plea bargaining obviates scrutiny of the evidence in an adversarial setting. Conviction is based on the plea and, at best, a cursory review of its factual basis. Aside from the duress argument, it is a separate question whether we should rely on pleas that are entered to reduce vulnerability to severe punishment. Some critics complain that plea bargaining gives society poor reason to judge that those who adjudicated "guilty" are, in fact, guilty. In *North Carolina v. Alford,* 400 U.S. 25 (1970), for example, a guilty plea entered to avert the death penalty was accepted even while accompanied by the defendant's protestation of innocence. Others worry that the innocent are more likely to be punished under plea bargaining systems, due to preferring the certainty of lower punishment to the risk of nonacquittal and a greater punishment. Defenders, in reply, note the absence of data on the incidence of innocence among the convicted and observe that innocent defendants, who do not want to falsely admit guilt, are also convicted at trial only to receive more severe sentences than they would under plea bargaining.

Injustice in Sentencing

Several strands of criticism are drawn from traditional defenses of the criminal sanction. Retributivists support sentences that are proportional in severity to the seriousness of the offense. Utilitarians see the imposition of penal suffering as justifiable only if necessary to achieve such purposes as deterrence and incapacitation. However, sentence severity under plea bargaining depends largely on whether the defendant has exercised the constitutional right to trial. If the sentences imposed at trial are just, it follows that, barring happy accidents, plea bargaining will never issue in justice: either defendants will receive insufficient punishment if they are guilty or excessive punishment if innocent. Moreover, those convicted of identical offenses will receive dramatically different sentences depending on whether they waive trial. Apart from the formal injustice of treating similar cases differently, plea bargaining burdens with added punishment the exercise of the constitutional right to trial. In response, defenders of plea bargaining have called attention to an array of mitigating and aggravating circumstances that might justify mercy or leniency in sentencing. In *Brady v. U.S.,* 397 U.S. 742 (1970), for example, the U.S. Supreme Court noted that bargained-for sentence reductions are legitimate, in part, because guilty pleas are evidence of contrition.

The Contract Model

Cutting across much of this discussion is a subtle dispute about the relationship between the prosecutor and the defendant. While critics have painted plea bargains as flawed contracts, recent defenses of plea bargaining have also looked to contract theory. Consider that, for the defendant, the worst possible result is a maximum sentence following conviction on the most serious charge and, for the prosecutor, it is acquittal. Just as settlement is common in civil cases, so both parties in criminal proceedings may reasonably prefer the guaranteed half loaf to the risk of none. Because the defendant can plead not guilty and demand trial, and the prosecutor can set the charge and recommend a sentence, the two should be allowed to exchange entitlements, the defendant trading the right to plead not guilty for the prosecutor's right to seek the maximum sentence. Since each party has offered the other an expanded range of choice, the contract wrongs neither. In response, critics of plea bargaining have questioned whether prosecutors can properly enter into such agreements. Consider a "grade bargain" between a student and a harried instructor. Having glanced at the first page of a term paper, the teacher estimates that the final grade will be a D. However, if the student waives the right to a conscientious reading and critique, the instructor will award a B. Even though both parties enjoy an expanded range of choice and prefer the exchange, the contract is nonetheless illicit, but not because the student has been wronged. Like justice in grading, justice in sentencing does not require that the end result be acceptable to the parties. Critics have argued that in bargaining for guilty pleas that maximize convictions and sentences, prosecutors have misunderstood the function of their office and the constituting purposes of criminal justice proceedings.

While some jurisdictions (for example, Alaska, El Paso, and Philadelphia) have experimented with elimination and reform, the practice of plea bargaining thrives. Commentators have illuminated hidden features of the criminal justice system, stimulated reflection on the value of jury trials, and provoked inquiry into neglected questions in criminal procedure. The debate shows little sign of letting up.

References

Alschuler, Albert W. "The Changing Plea Bargaining Debate." *California Law Review* 69 (1981), 652–730.

———. "The Defense Attorney's Role in Plea Bargaining." *Yale Law Journal* 84 (1975), 1179–1314.

———. "The Prosecutor's Role in Plea Bargaining." *University of Chicago Law Review* 36 (1968), 50–112.

———. "The Trial Judge's Role in Plea Bargaining." *Columbia University Law Review* 76 (1976), 1059–1154.

Church, Thomas. "In Defense of 'Bargain Justice.'" *Law and Society Review* 13 (1979), 509–535.

Kipnis, Kenneth. "Criminal Justice and the Negotiated Plea." *Ethics* 86 (1976), 93–106.

Langbein, John H. "Torture and Plea Bargaining." *The Public Interest* 58 (1980), 43–61.

Schulhofer, Stephen J. "Criminal Justice Discretion as a Regulatory System." *Journal of Legal Studies* 17 (1988), 43–82.

———. "Is Plea Bargaining Inevitable?" *Harvard Law Review* 97 (1984), 1037–1107.

———. "Plea Bargaining as Disaster." *Yale Law Journal* 84 (1992), 1979–2009.

Scott, Robert E., and William J. Stuntz. "Plea Bargaining as Contract." *Yale Law Journal* 84 (1992), 1909–1968.

Wertheimer, Alan. *Coercion*. Princeton NJ: Princeton University Press, 1987.

Kenneth Kipnis

See also CONFESSIONS; INCLUDED OFFENSES; JUDICIAL INDEPENDENCE; JURY SYSTEM; JURY TRIALS; TORTURE

Police

See ENTRAPMENT; SUPERIOR ORDERS AND LEGITIMATE AUTHORITY

Policy, Legal

Legal policy depends on the nature of the law, and can be an active factor in influencing the content of the law, by introducing or eliminating legal values in regulation. In Hungarian legal theory on the independent role of legal policy in a democracy, the main task of legal policy is to *mediate* normative requirements into the law. However, this represents only the side which is directed at introducing the comprehensive interests of society into law.

The role of legal policy is not restricted to this, since it does not only mediate comprehensive human and democratic exigencies, but also assists in unfolding the independent role of the law. In addition, it does not mediate abstract values, but requires the practical assertion of legal needs in legislation, in the administration of law, and in compliance with these.

To this use are attached the existence of whatever legal values are available, the legal possibility for their assertion, and the suitability of the legal procedure for their assertion. For legal policy to make out adequate goals and support them, the interaction of two factors is necessary: one is the orientation of society, with its requirement for a comprehensive social policy connected to the assertion of legal norms; the other is sufficient possibilities and instruments for the law to elaborate and implement the legal values. The autonomous activity of legal policy relies on these two, which mean primarily the analysis, critique, and evaluation of the existing law, and its elaboration into an independent concept of legal policy.

It is a basic requirement of democratic legal policy that it should mediate goals, which, on one hand, do not conflict with valid legal norms (that is, preserve legal cohesion) and which, on the other, can be asserted through the instruments of law, by legal activity and legal procedure. An essential factor in this is attention to the legal profession. The lawyer can give effect in everyday legal activity to the goals as legal requirements, on the basis of professional legal knowledge. Professional knowledge is a filter in three ways. First, it indicates which value-oriented goal of legal policy is acceptable to law and, second, which activities are suitable for transformation into law (for instance, parental love as an abstract value cannot be transferred into legal rules). Third, with an eye on professional involvement, it indicates and rejects goals oriented toward disvalues.

In this way, legal policy exercises a controlling role over the goals to be transformed into law, in view of the legal profession. It also controls which goal, when transferred into law, can be realized as a legal value, because legal practice indicates, by the desuetude or nonobservance of a legal rule, that it contains prescriptions which cannot be legally implemented. In this case legal policy recommends the repeal of the given legal rule on account of its inapplicability, or the enactment of a different legal statute serving the realization of legal value.

Legal policy is a factor which builds up the concept of value and helps law build up its hierarchy of values. Out of the comprehensive system of social values, it picks out those which can be transformed into legal values and can also be asserted by legal means. Realization of the comprehensive values in humanism is an abstract requirement, and from this the comprehensive value of human rights can be made concrete and transformed into law, into constitutional provisions and individual statutes. The universal legal protection of human rights can be stressed as a value-oriented requirement of legal policy and can be institutionalized in the various branches of law, through legal guarantees of life and limb, of property and social security. These detailed rules are condensed from the comprehensive values of the law. Among these, the following can be transformed by legal policy: the rule of law, stability, and change, as well as rationality, calculability, objectivity, universality, and equity.

References

Cranor, Carl F. "A Philosophy of Risk Assessment and the Law: A Case Study of the Role of Philosophy in Public Policy." *Philosophical Studies* 85 (1997), 135.

Gottfresdon, Don, and Ronald Clarke. *Policy and Theory in Criminal Justice*. Boston: Avebury, 1990.

McNeece, C. Aaron, and Albert R. Roberts. *Policy and Practice in the Justice System*. New York: Nelson-Hall, 1966.

Stone, Deborah A. *Policy Paradox and Political Reason*. New York: Addison-Wesley, 1988.

Wonnell, Christopher. "Four Challenges Facing a Compatibilist Philosophy." *Harvard Journal of Law and Public Policy* 12 (1989), 835.

Mihaly Samu

Political Obligation

Political obligation is the moral obligation of citizens to support their states and to comply with the valid requirements of their legal authorities. Theories of political obligation generally identify the obligation to obey valid law as the most important component of political obligation, with more general obligations of support for the state or "good citizenship" as secondary elements. People's political obligations are typically taken to constitute the core of the moral relationship that exists between them and their polities, and these obligations are thus closely related to such corresponding concepts as the legitimacy or de jure authority of the state or the legal system. The classical problem of political obligation, which has been central in legal and political philosophy from the earliest recorded philosophical texts to the latest, is that of understanding when (or if) and for what reasons citizens in various kinds of states are bound by such obligations.

Theories of Political Obligation

Most theories of political obligation conservatively assume that typical citizens in reasonably just states are bound by political obligations, as most peoples' pretheoretical intuitions about the matter seem to suggest. The problem is then accordingly seen as that of defending a suitably "general" account of political obligation, one that identifies ground(s) or justification(s) of political obligation that are consistent with affirming widespread obligations. The problem can also be understood without such conservative commitments, so that an account's lack of generality is not necessarily seen as a defect. On this latter understanding, the theorist's job is simply to give as full as possible an account of political obligation, without any special concern for justifying our pretheoretical beliefs about the subject. Thus, an anarchist theory (which denied the existence of any political obligations) might on this latter understanding still constitute a successful (that is, nondefective) theory of political obligation.

Much of the modern debate about political obligation has consisted of efforts either to defend or to move beyond the alleged defects of voluntarist theories. Voluntarists maintain that only our own personal, voluntary acts—such as a contract to be bound by legal restrictions, our free consent to the authority of our government, or our free acceptance of the benefits of political life—can create obligations of obedience and support. Social contract theories, for instance, are paradigmatic defenders of voluntarist theories of political obligation. Because it is difficult to realistically portray actual political societies as very much like genuinely voluntary associations, voluntarist theories have seemed to many unable to satisfy conservative theoretical ambitions.

Theoretical responses to this difficulty have taken a variety of forms. The most basic division among these (antivoluntarist) responses is between the communitarian and the individualist positions on political obligation. Communitarians have typically maintained that our very identities are constituted in part by our roles (such as "citizen") in political society and that our political obligations are tied conceptually to, or follow trivially from, these roles. As a consequence, of course, our voluntary performances are seen by communitarians as largely irrelevant to our possession of basic legal and political obligations. Individualists have argued, by contrast, that we should not in this way think of ourselves as essentially political beings and that our political obligations rest not on our institutional roles, but on contingent relations between political societies and ourselves.

Voluntarist theories are, of course, one prominent kind of individualist view. Because of the voluntarist's apparent inability to argue persuasively for widespread political obligations, many individualists have turned instead to nonvoluntarist (but still individualist) views. Such nonvoluntarists hold that no voluntary contract, consent, or acceptance of benefits is necessary for political obligation. Simple nonvoluntary receipt of benefits may bind us to obey and support our governments, for instance, or our governments' moral qualities (such as their justice or efficiency) may ground general moral duties toward them. The individualist approach to the problem is thus affirmed, but without the apparent difficulties of voluntarism.

A third sort of response to the voluntarist's problem is to deny that it is a genuine problem. Anarchist theories, for example, have denied altogether the existence of general political obligations. As a result, of course, the voluntarist's failure to show how political obligations can be widespread is seen by the anarchist as entirely predictable. Some voluntarists have been drawn to anarchist conclusions in this way, while the inspirations for other anarchist theories have been both nonvoluntarist, individualist (for instance, utilitarian), and communitarian. In whatever form, though, anarchism rejects the conservative assumptions of most theories of political obligation.

This way of classifying theories of political obligation suggests four general categories: communitarian, voluntarist-individualist, nonvoluntarist-individualist, and anarchist. None of these four approaches to the problem of political obligation is of particularly recent vintage. Indeed, all but the anarchist theory were suggested more than two thousand years ago in various passages in Plato's dialogue, *Crito,* the first recorded discussion of the problem of political obligation. All these approaches have continued to attract adherents and continued to evolve in form even in contemporary political and legal philosophy.

Communitarian Theories

Routinely drawing their inspiration from Plato, Aristotle, G.W.F. Hegel, Edmund Burke, or Ludwig Wittgenstein, most communitarians have argued that our purposes, our values, and thus essential aspects of our personal identities are given us by our roles within linguistic, legal, social, and political communities. It is, as a result, misleading, they claim, to think (as individualists do) of our moral relation to the state as somehow optional or contingent. Citizen and state are not like unrelated contractors in economic negotiations; they are more like family members or friends. Our political obligations do not rest on externally derived moral duties, as nonvoluntarists claim. Rather, we have obligations to obey the rules of our communities because this is part of what it means to be members of those communities. To ask for further explanation of political obligation would be like asking the unintelligible question: why should our lives be regulated by what makes us who we are? Proper accounts of political obligation must appeal to justifications that are internal to our practices, not external to them.

Communitarians are thus typically committed to two general theses with clear (and conservative) implications for a theory of political obligation. The first, the "identity thesis," holds that denying one's political obligations involves unintelligibly denying the socially constituted aspects of one's own identity.

The second, the "normative independence thesis," maintains that local social practice has the power to generate moral obligations, independent of certification by some external or universally applicable moral principle.

Communitarians whose sympathies are with Aristotle or Hegel have also often argued that political community is essential to human flourishing and to the development of basic moral capacities, such as agency or autonomy. As a result, they claim, we have an obligation to belong to and facilitate those political communities that encourage this development. Once again on this line, because our political relations contribute essentially to our identities as autonomous moral agents, these relations cannot themselves be thought of as freely chosen or as dependent on moral principles that bind us independently of our legal and political roles.

Voluntarist Theories

Individualists deny that we are essentially political beings and that our political obligations are just a function of our identities as socially constituted persons. The political is seen by the individualist as a contingent, nonessential (even if perfectly typical) aspect of human life; our unchosen social and political roles cannot be assumed to justifiably define our moral responsibilities. This position is most strongly stated (or assumed) by voluntarists. The classical individualist theories of political obligation were mostly voluntarist, and nearly every voluntarist theory prior to the twentieth century was some variant of a consent or contract theory of political obligation. The terms of the modern debate about political consent were set most clearly by John Locke. According to Locke's consent theory, political obligations are grounded in the personal consent of individual members to the authority of their government or political society. This consent can be either express or tacit. However, voluntary, intentional consent of some sort is necessary for political obligation; government without popular consent is tyranny. Express consent, as given in explicit oaths of allegiance, tends not to be very widespread in modern political communities. Favorite candidates for acts of tacit consent (on which our political obligations might rest) include continuing to reside in a state one is free to leave, freely taking benefits from the state, voting in democratic elections, and accepting adult membership in a state.

Consent theory has a considerable intuitive appeal, based on the importance that persons' free choices seem to have in determining how they ought to be treated. The theory, however, has throughout its history been plagued by the complaint that it is not in fact applicable to real political life. Actual political societies are not voluntary associations, it is claimed, and real citizens seldom give even tacit consent to their governments. Indeed, all of the acts alleged to constitute tacit consent to government are typically performed without any intention to consent to government authority at all, and they are often performed unfreely, simply because of the high cost of alternatives, such as emigration. If morally binding consent must be intentional and voluntary, such facts seem to force us to the conclusion that few citizens of actual states count as even tacit consenters and that consent theory cannot adequately account for the political obligations most believe these citizens to have.

Consent theorists have often responded by specifying further conditions that must be satisfied if "government by consent" is to be achieved or by insisting that genuine, binding consent is only given by full involvement in the political life of a participatory democracy. These responses, of course, involve to a certain extent giving up conservative ambitions in thinking about political obligation. A more conservative move within the voluntarist camp has been to surrender instead the idea of consent as the paradigm ground of political obligation. Fairness theories, for instance, maintain instead that our obligations are owed as fair reciprocation for benefits freely accepted from the workings of our cooperative legal and political institutions. Consent to these institutions is not necessary for being obligated to support them and abide by their rules.

Nonvoluntarist Theories

The distance from voluntarist to nonvoluntarist (individualist) theories of political obligation can seem at first glance quite small. There are, for instance, nonvoluntarist versions of fairness theory which argue that our political obligations are grounded not in our free acceptance of the benefits of political life, but rather in our (possibly nonvoluntary) receipt of these important public goods. However, the actual theoretical distance of such accounts from voluntarism is in fact considerable. For political obligations, instead of resting on what we choose to do, are now taken to rest on what merely happens to us and on the virtues of the institutional arrangements under which we live.

The distance from voluntarism is similarly deceptive in the case of hypothetical contractarian accounts of political obligation. Our obligations, according to this approach, are determined not by our personal consent to our political authorities, but by whether we (or some suitably described, more rational version of us) would have agreed to be subject to such authorities in an initial choice situation. Hypothetical contractarianism, because it centrally utilizes the idea of contract or consent, may at first seem to be just a development of voluntarist consent theory. In fact, however, hypothetical theories do not focus on individual choice or on specific transactions between citizen and state at all, but rather on the quality of the political institutions in question. Hypothetical contractarians ask whether our laws or governments are sufficiently just or good to have been consented to in advance by rational parties, in an initial specification of their terms of social cooperation.

This emphasis on quality of government is also obvious in utilitarian theories of political obligation, despite their long-standing opposition to contractarian views. According to utilitarians, political obligations are grounded in the utility of support for and compliance with government. Because obedience to valid law generally promotes social happiness, obedience is typically obligatory. But, of course, obedience only promotes social happiness if the laws or government in question are well-framed, utility-producing devices; our political obligations are thus derived directly from determinations of governmental quality.

Anarchist Theories

Anarchism comes in many forms, from communist to libertarian. Some anarchists deny the very possibility of the legitimate state, while others deny only the legitimacy of all existing states. Some urge the destruction of existing states, others only selective disobedience to them. However, all forms of anarchism are united in rejecting the conservative assumption that most citizens have political obligations. It is illuminating to recall that much of the force of communitarian and nonvoluntarist-individualist theories of political obligation derives from the perceived failure of consent theory. As we have seen, this attack rests squarely on a conservative approach to the problem of political obligation. If the conservative assumption is abandoned, consent theory no longer appears defective. Rather, it can be taken to specify the true grounds of political obligation, grounds that are simply not satisfied in actual or possible states. Voluntarist anarchism thus reemerges as an interesting theoretical possibility.

Classical anarchism (of both communitarian and individualist varieties) recommended the abolition of the state. Late-twentieth-century philosophical anarchism merely denies the existence of (widespread) political obligation, usually on voluntarist grounds, without making any revolutionary practical recommendations. Some philosophical anarchists have argued on a priori grounds that the authority of the state is inconsistent with individual autonomy. Others have argued only that existing states fail to satisfy the voluntarist requirements for political obligation.

References

Beran, Harry. *The Consent Theory of Political Obligation.* London: Croom Helm, 1987.

Gans, Chaim. *Philosophical Anarchism and Political Disobedience.* Cambridge: Cambridge University Press, 1992.

Green, Leslie. *The Authority of the State.* Oxford: Oxford University Press, 1988.

Hirschmann, Nancy. *Rethinking Obligation.* Ithaca: Cornell University Press, 1992.

Horton, John. *Political Obligation.* Atlantic Highlands NJ: Humanities Press International, 1992.

Klosco, George. *The Principle of Fairness and Political Obligation.* Lanham MD: Rowman and Littlefield, 1992.

Pateman, Carole. *The Problem of Political Obligation.* Berkeley: University of California Press, 1979.

Rawls, John. *A Theory of Justice.* Cambridge: Harvard University Press, 1971.

Simmons, A. John. *Moral Principles and Political Obligations.* Princeton NJ: Princeton University Press, 1979.

Wolff, Robert P. *In Defense of Anarchism.* New York: Harper & Row, 1970.

A. John Simmons

See also LEGITIMACY; OBLIGATION AND DUTY

Political Philosophy

The context of the discipline has dramatically changed since 1971, when John Rawls published *A Theory of Justice*. Rawls elaborated a philosophical foundation for a liberal approach of the political sphere: the individuals are basically free and interested in pursuing their own ends, and they engage in society in order to attain these goals by putting some resources in common. This is at first glance a reelaboration of the contractualist philosophy: political authority has no intrinsic substance, it flows from the basic interests and calculations of individuals. Rawls adds an important element, however: individuals do *not* discuss the principles of justice in the framework of a classical negotiation (where everyone tries to tailor the principles to his own interests and values, so the result of the bargaining process just reflects the de facto relationship of forces, and not any intrinsic concept of justice and legitimacy). The procedure takes place once the individuals have put their basic interests behind a "veil of ignorance" so these particular elements cannot influence the negotiation process. One can say without exaggeration that virtually all the main discussions in political philosophy these last twenty-five years have turned around such a theory. Indeed, Rawls had wanted to reject the dominant utilitarian philosophy: the aggregative concept of a global utility could easily lead to a disregard of individual rights. Now individual dignity presupposes that no conception of the good is forcibly imposed on individuals: they must be innerly and freely convinced of its validity in order to be able to accept it and live according to it. So Rawls elaborated the first principle of justice, that is, the principle of equal liberty: everybody has a right to develop his or her own conception of the good, provided a same liberty is granted to the others. This principle was accepted by a wide range of "liberals," including the libertarians, who, nevertheless, strongly criticized Rawls' *second* principle (concerning the distribution of goods), and particularly the "difference principle," legitimizing only inequalities which are at the advantage of the worst-off. This could lead for them to an interventionist, at best social-democratic, at worst totalitarian, state. So the discussion with the libertarians turned around the second principle and not the first, which every "liberal" accepted as guaranteeing the eminent dignity of the individual. It seemed that Rawls could deliver the philosophical foundation for a strong defense of human rights and the constitution by judicial review.

It became apparent rapidly that this first principle was *not* that self-evident: while the debate between Rawls and the libertarians was an intraliberal dispute, an attack came, in the beginning of the eighties, from *outside* liberalism. The so-called communitarians (or at least the most progressive among them) argued that there was something fundamentally wrong in Rawls' theory of the person: the idea of self-interested individuals is basically at odds with the concept of a substantial community, that is, a set of shared ends which constitute the individual, give meaning to one's life. Liberalism was criticized as being individualist and sanctioning the modern isolation of the subject, stigmatized in particular by Hannah Arendt in *The Human Condition*. Moreover, some communitarians emphasized the dangers of liberalism for a democratic life: if individuals agree only on certain basic principles of distribution of rights and resources, there will not be any basis for a democratic life. A democratic life presupposes some shared ends, that is, a common conception of the good: without this no genuine citizenship and political commitment would be possible. Communitarians criticized Rawls' proceduralism: his principles of justice do not imply any agreement on the meaning of life, but only the acceptance of certain procedural constraints (discussing the principles under the veil of ignorance). A strong sense of community is indeed often related to authoritarian or totalitarian groups, but, communitarians argue, it is *also* necessary for the building of a democratic republic. Politics is not only the instrument of the individual ends: it must have a certain value in itself in order to allow people to struggle for *their* community. The sense of belonging is an essential problem for political philosophy, and it has no real place in Rawls' theory.

Of course, communitarianism is itself not immune to criticism: does it not represent a sort of revival of the old political romanticism? If this were true, would it not be evident that the difficulties related to the latter would unavoidably affect the former? Liberalism is too abstract and universalistic, not enough rooted into the shared ends of the historical communities. Rawls' student would retort that such an abstraction is precisely at the core of the liberal argument: the veil of ignorance *is* the movement of abstraction from particular values, which is necessary to obtain fair and universalizable principles of justice. Indeed, the liberal sense of belonging is probably too "thin" to generate a real sense of commitment and responsible citizenship, but at least Rawls' principles of justice do not impose on anybody a conception of the good he or she does not freely accept. On the contrary, the communitarian idea of a "common good" is "thicker," that is, more liable to generate a civic attachment (at best democratic); at the same time it a priori defines, so to say, the group and imposes on the newcomers values that they could not accept without a more or less "violent" (at least heteronomous) process of assimilation.

The German philosopher Jürgen Habermas, being aware of the importance and difficulties of both positions, tried to elaborate a philosophical synthesis. The solution he proposed has had so far a tremendous influence on political philosophy. Habermas wants first to preserve Rawls' separation of the right and the good, of the sphere of politics and the sphere of conscience. He thinks that this is a positive result of postkantian thought and that it should not be endangered by some trends of contemporary "postmodern" philosophy, in particular by the return to a conception of a community based on a shared sense of the good. If ethical values, which are an object of controversy, are put at the basis of political society, the situation of those who believe in another conception of the good will be unbearable: they will not be able to accept the political order as being *just,* that is, legitimate, but on the contrary they will view it as being an alien order imposed on them by force (*compelle intrare*). So legal constraint must be restricted to the sphere of justice, that is, to the implementation of principles everybody could agree on, whatever his or her own conception of the good. Habermas holds that, in order to get to such a universalistic position, the artificial character of Rawls' solution (the device of the "veil of ignorance") is finally *not* necessary. On this point, he seems to agree with the communitarian requirement that concrete individuals (and not abstract participants putting behind the veil all the elements which make sense for them and constitute their own personal history, their own "identity") take part in the debate leading to the institution of the political "republic." By doing this, however, he knows that he will not imprison again individuals in the (micro) "totalitarian" particularity of a community. Why? Because any particular set of values (what Edmund Husserl called the *Lebenswelt,* the "world of life") is, regardless of the will of the participants (who are often tempted to close it on itself in order to preserve their power), open to the "outside": as Habermas says, it possesses a "potential of universality." Such a potential is embodied in the "pragmatic" conditions of every speech act: in any society—even the closest one—people must speak, argue, solve problems, *communicate*. Now, communication precisely implies the ideal of the equality of participants, who have always already recognized, by entering the discussion, that, between them, the force of the better argument (and not the *diktat* of force) will finally prevail. Of course, such an ideal is, as Habermas has repeatedly said in order to correct misunderstandings, "contrafactual": in fact, people try to dominate others, they act in bad faith, they use rhetorical sophistry, and so on. But communication embodies by itself, nevertheless, a sort of "counterculture," that is, the repeated resort (even by paying lip service) to the ideal of an argumentation that would be free from domination. This element accounts for Habermas's rejection of Rawls' "veil of ignorance": Rawls thinks that values and interests are necessarily antagonistic and that a free agreement on the basic rules of the political game can only be attained *beyond* the particularity and conflictuality of the sphere of the good and of particular interests. Habermas seems to say to Rawls: do not be that afraid of the sphere of the good; there is a historical process of opening which necessarily affects the particular *Lebenswelte*. In one sense, Habermas thus tries to obtain the results of Immanuel Kant's (also Rawls') political philosophy (a strict separation of the right and the good, or of duty and interests) by using G.W.F. Hegel's means. Hegel criticized at the same time the abstract universalism of kantianism and the particularism of political romanticism (the theory of the *Volksgeist,* or the soul of the people). Habermas does not indeed fall back on Hegel's *Weltgeist* (the world-spirit), which leads the particular people to the final truth; he only affirms that the pragmatic conditions of communication embody a force of universalization that is present in *any* community. So he tries to present a synthesis of the two opposing major political philosophies of these years, Rawls' theory and communitarianism.

References

Habermas, Jürgen. *Faktizität und Geltung.* Frankfurt: Suhrkamp, 1993.

———. *Moral Consciousness and Communicative Action.* Cambridge: Polity Press, 1992.

Nozick, Robert. *Anarchy, State, and Utopia.* New York: Basic Books, 1974.

Rawls, John. *Political Liberalism.* New York: Columbia University Press, 1993.

———. *A Theory of Justice.* Cambridge MA: Harvard University Press, 1971.

Sandel, Michael. *Liberalism and the Limits of Justice.* Cambridge: Cambridge University Press, 1982.

Taylor, Charles. *Multiculturalism and "The Politics of Recognition."* Ed. Amy Gutman. Princeton NJ: Princeton University Press, 1992.

———. *Philosophical Papers.* New York: Basic Books, 1983.

Walzer, Michael. *Spheres of Justice.* New York: Basic Books, 1983.

Guy Haarscher

See also CONSTITUTIONALISM; POLITICAL OBLIGATION; STATE

Pornography

The criminalization of pornography gives rise to a number of thorny philosophical issues, notably how to define pornography and distinguish it (if required) from erotica; how to balance our interest in free speech and artistic expression against the harms of pornography; and what kinds of harms, if any, are constituted or caused by pornographic depictions and practices. Parallel to, and intersecting with, debates over these issues is the critical examination of the philosophical basis for the criminalization of pornography: legal moralism, paternalism, liberalism, and, most recently, feminism.

Traditionally in Anglo-American jurisdictions criminal regulation of pornography (usually termed "obscenity") aimed at maintaining "public decency" and/or protecting the vulnerable from corruption and exploitation. *R. v. Hicklin,* L.R. 3 Q.B. 360 (1868), which was widely followed, provided a test declaring material obscene if it tended to deprave or corrupt public morals. The justification for criminalizing obscenity was thus moralistic (the community may impose its morality by legal means) or paternalistic (the community may protect its members from "moral harm" by legal means). Both lines of justification were strongly criticized by liberals (most notably H.L.A. Hart in *Law, Liberty and Morality*) as violating the boundaries of the harm-to-others principle, and displacing the individual as sovereign over one's own private pursuits. Furthermore, specific moralistic justifications of criminalizing obscenity, like that of Patrick Devlin in *The Enforcement of Morals,* presupposed a (nonexistent) shared positive morality and proposed emotive tests of the community's standards, such as the notorious "intolerance, indignation and disgust." Both moralistic and paternalistic justifications failed to distinguish adequately between public displays of obscenity and their private consumption. In addition, appeals to the unique importance of free speech figured large in liberal resistance to the censorship inherent in obscenity provisions.

Uneasy about the majoritarian and irrationalist implications of appeals to community standards, and about curtailing free expression, the American Law Institute's *Model Penal Code* proposed an "oblique" approach, targeting obscenity under the regulation of business practices. This approach aimed to keep pornography "out of sight," appealing not to public decency but to the unfairness of exploiting people's desires in order to make a profit.

Notwithstanding liberal worries about the justification of obscenity laws, public concern over pornography—its proliferation, its content (the depiction [indeed, the use] of children, scenes of brutality, degradation, and sexual stereotyping), and its connection to the subordination of women and children—has grown. Feminists in particular have argued that pornography is not just offensive, but actually harmful, both in its preparation and presentation, and therefore a liberal justification for its criminalization, with the concomitant limiting of free expression, can be given. Two kinds of harm are alleged: the subordination of women (and children) through objectification and stereotyping, and increased violence toward them. Both claims are hotly contested. The first claim—that pornography subordinates women—situates pornography in a framework of discriminatory patriarchal practices which collectively deny women equality. This claim, if substantiated, is significant in justifying the limitation of speech, insofar as free speech may be seen as instrumentally valuable in promoting political goals like equality, and therefore subject to limitation when it undermines them. [Such reasoning played an important role in *R. v. Butler,* 8 C.R.R. (2d), 1 S.C.C. (1992).]

The claim that pornography contributes to violence against women and children has also been contested, with empirical research on the links between pornography and violence being cited by both the pro- and antiregulation lobby. National commissions in several countries, having examined the research, have come to different conclusions about what it proves, and therefore have also made different recommendations on appropriate legal responses. For instance, the United Kingdom's Williams Commission, unconvinced about the links between pornography and harm, recommended merely reducing pornography's offensiveness by prohibiting public displays; the written word (presumed to be avoidable) was to be fully protected regardless of content. Australian, New Zealand, and American commissions, and a series of Canadian reports, concluded that both violent and degrading pornography have harmful effects. In Canada, however, skepticism over the link persisted both in the courts, as held in *R. v. Fringe Product Inc.,* 53 C.C.C. (3d) 422 (Ont. Dist. Ct.) (1990), and in the 1985 Fraser Commission report. Some of the disagreement over the weight of the empirical research has been due to confusion over what counts as social scientific proof of a link, and how much leeway exists for courts to infer a connection. For instance, John Sopinka, writing for the majority in *R. v. Butler,* argues that although it may be impossible to prove a direct link between pornography and harm, "it is reasonable to presume that exposure to images bears a causal relationship to changes in attitudes and beliefs," which, following the Court's findings on expressions of hatred in *R. v. Keegstra,* 3 S.C.R. 697 (1990), were then taken to influence behavior.

R. v. Butler, in which Canada's Supreme Court adopted a "harms-based equality approach," is significant in accepting that pornography is harmful (in both senses identified above), in substituting risk of harm for offensiveness in the employment of community standards and in recognizing that the override of free speech entailed by upholding Canada's obscenity law (section 163) is justified. In clarifying section 163, which defines as obscene any material "a dominant characteristic of which is the undue exploitation of sex, or of sex and any one or more of . . . crime, horror, cruelty and violence," the Court included as "undue" all pornographic material involving children and material that is "degrading and dehumanizing." Sexual explicitness alone is considered erotica, not pornography; and an "internal necessities" defense is available to protect pornographic representations necessary for artistic or literary purposes. The decision in *Butler* is viewed by many as a promising step in accommodating a feminist analysis of equality within a harms-based liberal framework.

However, objections have been raised to the approach taken in *Butler*. In light of the inconclusiveness of the studies linking pornography with harm and the political nature of claims about women's subordination, is the override of free speech justified? Are the notions of "degrading and dehumanizing" and "artistic merit" clearly enough defined to protect erotica (especially erotica involving minorities) and other valuable forms of expression, and to ensure evenhanded application? Is there adequate agreement over the notion of "the risk of harm," or will the community's application of it simply reduce to moralism?

Rather than seeking legal remedies for pornography under obscenity statutes, some feminists (notably Andrea Dworkin and Catharine MacKinnon) want pornography classified as hate speech and subject to civil remedies. According to this model, pornography is viewed as a discriminatory practice, a violation of women's civil rights, against which they may seek compensation for injury. The "civil rights" approach is favored because it acknowledges the harm of inequality caused by pornography but distances itself from both censorship and the arbitrariness (or complicity) of community standards. In the United States a series of efforts have been made to put into effect the "civil rights" approach, but so far each has been blocked.

Currently in the United Kingdom antipornography groups are employing both strategies: the "civil rights" approach and the attempt to criminalize pornography by arguing for its recognition as harmful, hateful language under the *Race Relations Act*.

References

American Law Institute. *Model Penal Code and Commentaries*. Philadelphia: American Law Institute, 1985.

Busby, Karen. "LEAF and Pornography: Litigating on Equality and Sexual Representations." *Canadian Journal of Law and Society* 9 (1994), 165–192.

Chistensen, F.M. *Pornography: The Other Side*. Westport CT: Praeger, 1990.

Clark, Lorenne. "Sexual Equality and the Problem of an Adequate Moral Theory: The Problem of Liberalism." In *Contemporary Moral Issues*, 2d ed., ed. W. Cragg, 311–329. Toronto: McGraw-Hill Ryerson, 1987.

Devlin, Patrick. *The Enforcement of Morals*. Oxford: Oxford University Press, 1959.

Hart, H.L.A. *Law, Liberty and Morality*. Oxford: Oxford University Press, 1962.

Itzin, Catherine, ed. *Pornography: Women, Violence, and Civil Liberties: A Radical New View*. Oxford: Oxford University Press, 1992.

Mahoney, Kathleen. "The Canadian Constitutional Approach to Freedom of Expression in Hate Progaganda and Pornography." *Law and Contemporary Problems* 55 (1992), 77–105.

McAllister, Debra M. "*Butler*: A Triumph for Equality Rights." *National Journal of Constitutional Law* 2 (1993), 118–131.

Mill, J.S. *On Liberty*. London, 1859.

Schwartz, Louis B. "Moral Offenses and the Model Penal Code." In *Philosophy of Law*, 3d ed., ed. Joel Feinberg and Hyman Gross. Belmont CA: Wadsworth, 1986.

Elisabeth Boetzkes

See also HATE LITERATURE; PATERNALISM

Positional Philosophy of Law

See RADICAL CLASS, GENDER, AND RACE THEORIES: POSITIONALITY

Positive Duties

See OMISSIONS; RESCUE IN TORT AND CRIMINAL LAW

Positivism, Legal

The notion of legal positivism is located at the core of modern philosophical and theoretical thinking about law. From a historical point of view, it gives an adequate and unitary reconstruction of a very important part of legal thinking of the last two centuries; from a meta-theoretical point of view, it provides a clear understanding of the common conceptual presuppositions of a large portion of contemporary legal theories.

Unfortunately, in this field of research the situation is characterized by much confusion and strong conceptual differences. Some legal philosophers think that we should avoid using the notion of legal positivism, because it is too composite and heterogeneous. Others, including Norberto Bobbio and H.L.A. Hart, are of the opinion that a definition of "legal positivism" is not only possible but also fruitful, only not as a unitary definition; the notion of legal positivism should be split into distinct and logically autonomous parts (and these parts are of course differently constructed in connection with divergences at the level of legal theories adopted or presupposed). Still others, for example, Mario Jori and Neil MacCormick, rely on a unitary definition and so seem to be able to individuate a common element in positivistic legal theories, but, unfortunately, they end up by placing it at a level (methodological, theoretical, political, and so forth) that is inadequate or unsuitable. As well, there is a basic deficiency common to all these definitions that is connected with the model of definition adopted.

"Essentially Contested Concept"

Most of the scholars who deal with the definition of legal positivism presuppose that its definition is *per genus et differentiam* (by genus and difference). According to this model, the aim of the definition is to give the necessary and sufficient conditions for the correct use of the definiendum. We should be rather dubious about the existence of transitive properties, conceived as "something" which things (even cultural things) autonomously possess. The fact is that legal positivism is an "essentially contested concept," according to W. Gallie. When a concept is essentially contested, (1) most of the participants in the dispute understand each other very well, and seem to refer, to some extent, to the same "thing"; but (2) most of the participants disagree quite strongly on some basic points of the notion.

The problem with essentially contested concepts is that there is no commonly acknowledged transitive property from which to begin the definitional work. We should, therefore, abandon this traditional model and look for an alternative one. The alternative model could be called definition through paradigmatic instances and concepts.

According to this model, the definitional activity concerning general terms (above all those expressing essentially contested concepts) should be divided into two stages. In the first one, our goal should be to mention or individuate some instances of the class in question that are quite unproblematically acknowledged by the members of the community. These instances form the referential core of the notion. In the second stage our goal should be to extract from these instances a common conceptual core (the concept or the sense of the notion). The concept is the set of assumptions which isolates the common, relevant aspects of paradigmatic instances.

The Concept of Legal Positivism

We can consider as paradigmatic those instances of positivistic theories, for example, among others, John Austin's, Hans Kelsen's, and H.L.A. Hart's theories, that represent in any case some commonly acknowledged milestones of legal positivism, but that also carry out some very crucial changes in legal positivistic tradition from firmly inside its conceptual core.

All the paradigmatic instances share some basic assumptions in law, assumptions which represent the "common background of certainty" from which to begin the attempt to give a full, theoretical explanation of legal experience.

These basic assumptions can be formulated in the following way: (1) There is no difference at all, for what concerns the attribution of reference, between the expressions "law" and "positive law." (2) All positive law is, without any exception, a radically contingent human artifact from the point of view both of its production and of its evaluation and/or justification.

Explanatory comments on this kind of definition could be of some help, in order to highlight its more important implications. First, assumption (2) is expressed by an interpretative sentence that has the function of giving a precise meaning to the vague expression "positive law," contained in assumption (1). The conceptual meaning of legal positivism is in fact the outcome of positivists' commonly shared interpretation given to the expression "positive law."

Second, there is nothing really new in this definition, and it must be so, precisely because its aim is only to individuate the common core that lies in the conceptual background of all positivistic theories acknowledged as "paradigmatic" ones. It is a background that, insofar as it is taken absolutely for granted, is seldom explicitly mentioned or put under scrutiny by positivists, at least in its pure conceptual form. Of course, this interpretation of the notion of positive law is explicitly mentioned and accepted by most contemporary legal theories, but normally without the explicit aknowledgment of its conceptual role. This concept is often mistaken, on the contrary, for a methodological requisite or for a theoretical result of research; and it is clear, on the contrary, at least from the perspective here adopted, that a concept is always a presupposition and not a product of knowledge. These meta-theoretical suggestions on legal positivism do not consider the substantive content of the given definition, but rather the way in which this content is located (that is, at the conceptual level).

Third, using this conceptual definition it is quite easy to show the different ways in which the various positivistic conceptions rise from divergent interpretations of the same concept. The scope of the minimal definition, furthermore, is larger than it would seem at first sight; as a matter of fact, even Alf Ross's and Ronald Dworkin's conceptions could be legitimately labeled as "positivistic theories," just because they share with the other positivistic theories the same kind of absolute conceptual opposition to legal naturalism.

Conceptual Opposition Between Legal Positivism and Legal Naturalism

The fourth comment on this conceptual definition of legal positivism needs to be spelled out with much more care and caution, because it deals with a complex and intricate matter: the relationship between law and morals. With the help of this definition, it is possible to understand better, in fact, what kind of opposition can be postulated between legal positivism and legal naturalism. It has been said before that it is a mutually exclusive conceptual opposition. This means that each concept represents the total negation of the other; they contradict each other. We could have begun our definitional work from legal naturalism, and the result would have been the same. To obtain legal naturalism from the conceptual definition of legal positivism, it is enough to put the symbol of negation (~ or −) before both assumptions. The same would happen, of course, if we began from legal naturalism in order to obtain legal positivism.

It is useful, now, to underline some very important implications of this way of conceiving the opposition between legal positivism and legal naturalism. First of all, it is important to stress that this kind of opposition does not imply at all a supposed separation between law and morals, as might seem at first sight, adopting the traditional approach to the matter. According to this approach, the "separation thesis" is interpreted as a substantive thesis, in the sense that law and morals are conceived as two completely independent systems, and, consequently, ethical values and principles are considered as external to the law.

There are two different kinds of observations to be made in respect of this kind of approach. The first observation is that the "separation thesis," even if it is true, certainly cannot be labeled as a "conceptual thesis," and so cannot be considered as part of the conceptual definition of legal positivism. Most legal positivists, today, do not accept this thesis at all, at least in its crude substantive version. The second observation is that this thesis is, however, mistaken even for substantive reasons. It is quite easy to note here that, independently from other kinds of philosophical or theoretical arguments, there is a strong factual argument against the "separation thesis," at least if we limit our attention to the field of reference constituted by contemporary western legal systems (charter systems). In this kind of legal system ethical values are incorporated into legal principles at the level of constitutional norms. From this point of view, therefore, it might perhaps be much better to say that the law of charter systems expresses a specific moral conception (positive morality); and the consequence is, therefore, that the possible conflict between law and morals should be considered as a conflict internal to the field of ethics, a conflict between different morals. The conclusion of this line of reasoning is that a legal theorist does not need to adopt the "separation thesis" in order to remain a positivist.

There is another and more sophisticated way of conceiving the opposition between legal positivism and legal naturalism, a way which cannot be located at the commonly shared conceptual level that has been isolated with the adoption of the conceptual definition of legal positivism.

According to this second version, the separation between law and morals cannot be pursued ontologically, but only methodologically, that is, as a result of a certain kind of methodological attitude that should be adopted by jurists and legal theorists. As Bobbio notes, it is the attitude according to which they should deal with "normative materials" in a neutral way (as if they were "facts"), even when these materials are constituted by value judgments. This of course means that jurists and legal theorists should act in accordance with the "value freedom principle," the principle which is supposedly conceived as one of the basic methodological criteria for all scientists, both in natural and in social sciences.

Against this version of the opposition we could again propose the two observations made before against the "separation thesis." Before this, it is important to stress that these two observations leave out of consideration the big problem of the general fruitfulness and adequacy of the value freedom principle and of the scope of its possible applications to scientific disciplines.

The first observation against the methodological version of the "separation thesis" is again that this version, even if it is true, does not pertain to the conceptual level of the definition of legal positivism. This means that this methodological thesis does not possess at all, at least in our philosophical and juridical culture, the sort of unquestionableness and uncontestedness that a "conceptual thesis" should have. Many legal philosophers, who can be surely labeled as "positivists," have their serious doubts about the value freedom principle, at least when it is applied to the field of legal theory.

The second observation is that this more sophisticated version of the separation between legal positivism and legal naturalism is mistaken, even on its proper methodological grounds. It is enough to say here that it is highly unlikely that jurists and legal theorists could assume a neutral attitude in the context of charter systems, that is, in situations in which the object of their study is constituted (at least in part) by values. In these legal systems, in the words of Wil Waluchow,

> the interpretation of the Charter should be governed by the objects or interests it was meant to protect. If so, then it is also reasonably clear that moral arguments will often figure in Charter challenges. If one must interpret the Charter in the light of its objects, and those objects are often rights and freedoms of political morality, then it follows that one cannot determine what the Charter means, and thus the conditions upon legal validity which it imposes, without determining the nature and extent of the rights of political morality it seeks to guarantee: yet one cannot do this without engaging, to some degree at least, in substantive moral argument.

What remains at the conceptual level, we may ask now, of the opposition between legal positivism and legal naturalism? What is the correct sense of interpreting the conceptual definition of legal positivism on this matter? In answering these questions it could be said that the opposition, seen at a conceptual level, is a meta-ethical opposition in the sense that it concerns two different ways of justifying positive law from a moral point of view. Legal naturalism, in whichever way it is philosophically and/or theoretically interpreted, tries to offer an objective justification of positive law, that is, a justification which is grounded on objective values, or, at any rate, possesses, as the ultimate level (theological, ontological, anthropological, and so forth) of justification, an objective dimension. Legal positivism, in one or the other of its possible versions, offers, on the contrary, a radically relative justification. This does not mean, at least at the conceptual level, that it should not give any kind of moral justification of positive law, but, more correctly, that it can only give relative justifications, that is, justifications which are contingently valid, and are so always with reference to a set of contextually bound conditions (historical, sociological, theoretical, evaluative, and so forth) inside which justifications can be legitimately presented and possibly accepted by others.

References

Bobbio, Norberto. *Giusnaturalismo e positivismo giuridico* (Natural Law and Legal Positivism). Milano: Edizioni di Comunità, 1965.

Dworkin, Ronald. *Law's Empire*. Cambridge MA: Belknap Press, 1986.

Ferrajoli, Luigi. *Diritto e ragione. Teoria del garantismo penale* (Law and Reason: Theory of Penal Security). Bari: Laterza, 1979.

Gallie, W. "Essentially Contested Concepts." In *Proceedings of the Aristotelian Society* 56 (1955–56), 167–198.

Hart, Herbert L.A. "Positivism and the Separation of Law and Morals." *Harvard Law Review* 72 (1958), 593.
Jori, Mario. *Il giuspositivismo analitico italiano prima e dopo la crisi* (Italian Analytic Legal Positivism Before and After Its Peak). Milano: Giuffrè, 1987.
Kelsen, Hans. *Reine Rechtslehre* (Pure Theory of Law). Wien: Verlag Franz Deuticke, 1960.
MacCormick, Neil. *Legal Reasoning and Legal Theory*. Oxford: Clarendon Press, 1978.
Raz, Joseph. *The Authority of Law*. Oxford: Clarendon Press, 1979.
Ross, Alf. *Of Law and Justice*. Berkeley: University of California Press, 1958.
Waluchow, Wil. *Inclusive Legal Positivism*. Oxford: Clarendon Press, 1994.

Vittorio Villa

See also NATURAL LAW; REALISM, LEGAL

Posner, Richard Allen (1939–)

Richard Allen Posner is the central figure and the prime moving force in the law and economics movement, which has been the most influential movement in American law and legal thought of this generation. Posner has been a professor at the University of Chicago Law School since 1969 and was appointed to a position as a United States federal appellate judge in 1981. A prolific author, Posner has written over ten books and over a hundred articles, primarily on the connection between economic analysis and the law, but also on a wide range of other topics. The law and economics movement associated with Posner is the product of a combination of standard economic assumptions (all persons are always acting to maximize their preferences) and Nobel Prize winner Ronald Coase's work on the connection between legal entitlements and efficiency.

Coase's work indicated that in an ideal world without transaction costs, legal rights would end up (through voluntary transfers in the marketplace) with whichever parties valued them the most (in economic terms, this is an "efficient" distribution), regardless of which parties initially owned the rights in question. However, this effect would not occur in a world (such as ours) where there are often substantial transaction costs. What law and economics scholars added to Coase's work was the belief that the government (through legal rules and judicial decisions) should try to effect the decisions that would have been made in the market had there not been substantial transaction costs.

Posner's early writings added a number of different claims to the law and economics analysis. First, he argued that a theory of "wealth maximization" served both as an explanation of the past actions of the common law courts and as a theory of justice, justifying how judges and other officials should act. Under wealth maximization, judges are to decide cases according to the principles which will maximize society's total wealth. "Wealth" here is understood broadly, including all tangible and intangible goods and services. Additionally, since government officials can only imperfectly mimic the market in guessing how different parties value goods, judicial action will at best be only a crude approximation of the "wealth maximization" ("efficiency") that the market would create were there no transaction costs, and thus intervention to promote an "efficient" outcome is justified only where and to the extent that high transaction costs make a consensual (market) bargain between the parties impossible.

Posner's descriptive claim about wealth maximization had been that traditional common law doctrines (particularly, but not exclusively, in tort law) were economically efficient. Posner argued that this could be true, even though the judges who developed the common law rules did not speak in economic terminology, and few judges from that time had economic training. For the normative claim, Posner argued that wealth maximization retained the benefits of both utilitarianism and autonomy-based moral theories, but in a form that was more practical for determining how officials should act. Wealth maximization is better than utilitarianism, according to Posner, because willingness to pay is easier to measure than utility (happiness). It is beter than an autonomy-based approach because it allows government action even where consent to action by all affected would not be forthcoming or could not be obtained in a practical way. However, the argument goes, because the only actions allowed would be those that maximized social wealth, everyone (or almost everyone) would have consented to the actions if he or she had been asked in advance.

Posner has since pulled back from his more ambitious claims, as can be seen in *Overcoming Law,* published in 1995. His view of economics seems slightly altered, now as an "instrumental science" whose project is "to construct and test models of human behavior for the purpose of predicting and (where appropriate) controlling that behavior." According to Posner's recent writings, economic analysis need not and does not assume that all individuals try to maximize wealth or shun altruism. He now views economics as a form of thinking that can answer many questions but must sometimes leave important normative questions to others; the normative view Posner prefers is often derived from classical liberalism (as in the writing of John Stuart Mill) and sometimes from pragmatism. On the pragmatist side, Posner argues that courts have no moral duty to make present decisions fit into past precedent, though this course is often wise for prudential reasons. Where predictability is not important, coherence should carry little weight, in particular in considering how to apply the law to new questions, new technologies, and new industries. A different way of characterizing the evolution in Posner's thought is that he has moved from asserting that a certain variation of economic thought can give all the answers (both normative and descriptive), to a more general argument opposing the view that law is sufficient unto itself ("the autonomy of law"). Instead, Posner argues, legal officials should look to other disciplines, in particular economics and the other social sciences, to help create better legal rules.

References

Landes, William M., and Richard A. Posner. *The Economic Structure of Tort Law.* Cambridge MA: Harvard University Press, 1987.

Posner, Richard A. *Economic Analysis of Law.* 1972. Boston: Little, Brown, 4th ed. 1992.

———. *The Economics of Justice.* Cambridge MA: Harvard University Press, 1983.

———. *Law and Literature: A Misunderstood Relation.* Cambridge MA: Harvard University Press, 1988.

———. *Overcoming Law.* Cambridge MA: Harvard University Press, 1995.

———. *The Problems of Jurisprudence.* Cambridge MA: Harvard University Press, 1990.

Brian Bix

See also CORRECTIVE JUSTICE; ECONOMICS; ECONOMICS AND LAW; EFFICIENCY

Possession and Recovery

The word "possession" generally means the fact of control over a thing or property under a person's power. It is also used as a synonym for the thing possessed or for property. In the legal context, however, possession has been connected with certain legal effects: for instance, possession is the basis of the remedies for recovery of the thing dispossessed or of its value, the prima facie evidence of ownership, and even the substantial acquisition of ownership through prescription. It is also one of the constituent elements of crimes such as larceny. These effects have given a normative sense to the concept of possession, which has produced difficulties in understanding the meaning of possession.

In the Roman law, *possessio* consisted of *corpus* (physical control) and *animus* (an intent to possess) (*Pauli sententiae* 5.2.1; *Digesta* 41.2.3.1). But the necessity of these elements varied in each situation, such as acquisition, continuation, or loss of *possessio.* Although *possessio* was required for the usucaption, prescription, possessory interdicts, and so forth, the meaning of *possessio* was not identical in each case. For example, when a usucaptor pledged a thing, not only did the creditor possess the thing so as to be protected by the possessory interdicts, but also the usucaptor simultaneously possessed the thing for the purpose of completing usucaption (*Digesta* 41.3.16, 41.2.1.15). Or, when an owner of a land constituted servitude or usufruct, the owner was seen to have retained *possessio,* but holders of servitude and usufruct were also awarded *"possessio juris"* or *"quasi possessio"* (Gaius, *Institutiones* 2.93, 4.139; *Digesta* 8.4.2, 46.13.3.13, 17).

These features of concurrence, flexibility, technicality, and artificiality of the concept of possession remain in the modern legal systems. For instance, when a bailment is to be revocable by a bailor at will and a bailee gets possession of goods, possession lies in the bailee to maintain an action of trespass. The bailor, however, also can bring trespass, since he has "the right to immediate possession," which should be treated as possession itself, as decided in *United States of America v. Dollfus Mieg et Cie SA,* 1 All E.R. 572 (1952). Or, when a person acquires a title to land (but not yet an entry), his right to possess can be treated as possession itself by the doctrine of "trespass by relation." As well, in order to constitute adverse possession against an owner under a limitations act, the possession is more strictly construed than that of the owner, as decided in *Wallis's Cayton Bay Holiday Camp Ltd. v. Shell-Mex and BP Ltd.,* Q.B. 94 (1975); see also Articles 2229 ff. of the French civil code. In the criminal law, the *animus* element (an awareness of the situation) is relevant to determining whether the accused is in possession of an article, as noted in *Lockyer v. Gibb,* 2 Q.B. 243 (1967). Meanwhile, the significance of possession to moveable property differs from that to immoveable property. In the common law, the specific recovery of real property has been more easily allowed (as in the assize of novel disseisin, the assize of *mort d'ancestor,* the writ of right, writs of entry, the action relying on the Statutes of Forcible Entry, the action of ejectment, and so on), than that of personal property (the action of replevin). In the civil law, the maxim *En fait des meubles possession vaut titre* (for moveables, possession is as good as title), as stated in Article 2279 of the French civil code, is known.

In this manner, the meaning of possession seems to depend on the field of the law, the legal context, and the situation of particular cases. As a result, possession is said to be a vague, ambiguous, nebulous, indefinite, flexible, inconsistent, chameleon-hued, and relativistic concept. R.W.M. Dias says that "possession is no more than a device of convenience and policy," and that "the nature of possession came to be shaped by the need to give remedies." However, in order to determine the extent to which and the mode in which possession ought to be protected, it is necessary to inquire further into the nature of possession.

On one hand, possession is regarded as a subordinate means of protecting ownership or property: as possession is a prima facie evidence of ownership, it gives an adequate protection to an owner, especially who, for example, had possessed land but had been ejected from possession. There is a possibility that possessors who have no title might also enjoy this advantage; that can be seen as an unfortunate but unavoidable consequence of its purpose, to protect rightful possessors.

On the other hand, however, a possessor's possession is protected independently of ownership or proprietary rights and even against an owner who dispossessed the possessor. Several reasons why possession deserves such protection could be conceived: it may lead to the better maintenance of the peace by means of prohibiting self-help; it may be a sign of the protection for a possessor's person, which can not be disturbed without incurring guilt; further, possession as such may deserve protection, that is, the mere fact of possession may produce more right in the thing than the nonpossessor has, until someone has proved a better title.

These theoretical analyses of the nature of possession give the key to the practical questions. First, to what extent should self-help be allowed? If possession is understood as a subordinate means of protecting ownership, self-help by the true owner should be more widely allowed than under some other explanation, provided the owner has proved his right (on self-help, see Articles 859–860 of the German civil code). Second, when a possessor is dispossessed by a wrongdoer and brings an action of trespass against the dispossessor, is the latter able to defend himself by showing that some third person has a better title than the possessor (*jus tertii*)? What if the possessor brings an action of ejectment for land, or trover for goods, where the gist of the action is not an injury to possession, as in trespass, but an infringement of the right to possess? In *Armory v. Delamirie,* 1 Strange 505, 93 Eng. Rep. 664 (K.B. 1722), a chimney sweeper who had discovered a jewel was held to have acquired possession and was allowed to maintain trover against the pawnbroker to whom he had handed over the jewel for appraisal and who refused to return it. This conclusion might be justified if possession as such could be seen as a sort of substantive right. Finally, when the wrongdoer who had dispossessed the possessor sold the thing to the third party, is the possessor able to recover it from the third party? According to Articles 861 I and 858 II of the German civil code, the possessor can recover the thing when the third party was aware of the unlawful dispossession.

In any case, the judgment seems to depend ultimately on consideration of to what extent a distinction should be drawn between ownership (the right to possess) and the right of possession. The former can be characterized as a determinate appropriation of the very substance of (a part of) the thing to a person, whereas the latter has been an important element in determining the appropriation, such as the old concept of "seisin" had been.

References

The Civil Law, Including the Twelve Tables, The Institutes of Gaius, The Rules of Ulpian, the Opinions of Paulus, the Enactments of Justinian, and the Constitutions of Leo. Tr. S.P. Scott. Cincinnati: Central Trust Co., 1932. Reprinted New York: AMS Press, 1973.

Dias, R.W.M. *Jurisprudence.* 5th ed. London: Butterworth, 1985.

Donahue, Charles, Jr., Thomas E. Kauper, and Peter W. Martin. *Cases and Materials on Property.* 3d ed. St. Paul MN: West, 1974.

Justinian I. *Digest.* Tr. C.H. Munro. Cambridge: Cambridge University Press, 1904.

Rose, Carol M. "Possession as the Origin of Property." *University of Chicago Law Review* 52 (1985), 73–88.

Stoljar, Samuel. "Possession in the Civil Codes." *International and Comparative Law Quarterly* 33 (1984), 1026–1031.

Tay, Alice E.-S. "The Concept of Possession in the Common Law: Foundations for a New Approach." *Melbourne University Law Review* 4 (1964), 476–497.

Yiannopoulos, A.N. "Possession." *Louisiana Law Review* 51 (1991), 523–560.

Hiroshi Matsuo

See also ESTATE AND PATRIMONY; OWNERSHIP; PROPERTY

Postmodern Philosophy of Law

Postmodern jurisprudence is the philosophical study of law within a postmodern conceptual framework, typically poststructuralist, neopragmatist, or post-Freudian psychoanalytic. It includes work within critical legal studies, law and society theory, law and literature studies, sociological jurisprudence, semiotic legal theory, feminist jurisprudence, and critical race theory. Postmodern theories of law tend to view modernist theories of law as incoherent, descriptively inadequate, or normatively problematic, and to view modern legal institutions as incapable of securing the freedom, equality, and justice which modernist theories of law, in their confusion, promise. Postmodern theories of law aim to conceptualize and respond practically to this "crisis of modernity" without returning to premodern idea(l)s. They tend to be noncomprehensive, culturally and historically specific, robustly interdisciplinary, rhetorically ambitious, and overtly political.

Modernist Thought and Jurisprudence

Postmodernists see the diverse manifestations of modernist thought arising out of a family of related background assumptions. (1) Reality is extra-linguistic; language primarily represents reality. (2) Human reason is universal and univocal; it can understand itself, its structure and limits. By working objectively, logically, and systematically from first premises, empirical or rational, known certainly to be true, humans may acquire genuine knowledge of reality. (3) History is moving toward a *telos;* humans can purposively shape history. (4) Moral obligations arise out of neither simple power relations nor mere tradition, but rather a natural moral law available to reason, the autonomy of a rational will, natural moral sentiments, social utility, or self-interest. Human societies are best understood not as given organic unities but as systems of alterable relations among autonomous persons who are, abstractly understood, free and equal.

Modernist jurisprudence aims primarily (5) to define law, legal systems, legal concepts, and legal reasoning in an analytically rigorous and empirically sensitive way and to explain the legitimate authority of law. Modernist theories of law typically distinguish law from morality and understand the former to be a publicly promulgated and largely self-contained, self-regulating, coherent, and determinate system of generally applicable positive rules. Some theories allow that general social customs or moral norms belong indirectly to the law as a supplement necessary to ground or complete law as a system of positive rules. (6) Modernist theories of law typically explain the legitimate authority of law in terms of consensual participation in an ongoing practice of recognition and enforcement, social utility, self-interest, or some form of natural law duty. While most modernist theories of law acknowledge that in concrete cases the law (and the facts to which it is applied) must often be interpreted, they typically characterize legal interpretation and reasoning, in the ideal, as capable of determining results uniquely and objectively correct in light of unambiguous, noncontroversial, and generally applicable criteria, both logical and legal. (7) Finally, modernist theories of law typically assume that freedom, equality, and justice depend on the rule of law and other essentials of modern legal institutions. John Austin, Hans Kelsen, H.L.A. Hart, Joseph Raz, and Ronald Dworkin show modernist theory of this sort.

Postmodern Thought and Jurisprudence

Postmodern thought is born of attempts to understand and respond to a variety of perceived theoretical and practical failures of modernism. (1) Language constructs rather than mirrors reality. (2) Human reason is neither universal nor univocal, varying within and among cultures relative to distributions of social power, material conditions, and ideological commitments. Human reason seems unable to know finally its own structure and limits. (3) History transcends human agency and moves discontinuously toward no particular end. Science does not emancipate but rather enslaves persons in new ways. (4) The rationalization of politics yields irrational bureaucracies. Democracy puts in play its own disciplinary forces. The rule of law and other essentials of modern legal institutions do not always secure and often work against freedom, equality, and substantive justice. By the late twentieth century, intellectuals, artists, and activists increasingly rejected the great modernist meta-narratives (for example, varieties of liberalism, positivism, hegelianism, marxism), emphasizing the inadequacy of the modernist conception of the human being as knower and agent, the tendency of modernist projects to terminate in ironic reversal, and the violence worked on marginal groups by a totalizing modernist rationality.

Postmodern theories of law tend to draw on one or more of three main currents within postmodern thought: poststructuralism (Jacques Derrida, Michel Foucault), neo-pragmatism (Richard Rorty, Stanley Fish), post-Freudian psychoanalysis (Jacques Lacan). (5) They typically argue against the autonomy, stability, coherence, objectivity, and determinacy of legal systems, concepts, and reasoning. (6) They may argue that the normative authority of law reduces upon analysis to an ideological fiction, a form of domination, or web of contingent social practices. (7) They may characterize the law as war by other means, the reproduction of power relations through their mystification, a collective institutionalized repression of deep psychological desires, or a necessarily incoherent expression of contradictory normative commitments. They often address issues modernist theories ignore, for example, the impossibility of articulating within legal discourse certain forms of injustice, or the terrific and debilitating socialization imposed on persons as a condition of access to the power wielded within professional legal culture.

Poststructuralism and Legal Theory

Poststructuralist theories of language and culture take their name from structuralist theories. Structuralist theories analyze language or culture in terms of irreducible structural units. The sum of each unit's relations to other units determines its identity. The total system of such relations, while arbitrary, constitutes a coherent, self-regulating, self-justifying, and meaning-generating whole. Structuralist theories hold that the capacity of a particular utterance, practice, or belief to be meaningful depends not on a relationship between its basic units and a reality given independently to consciousness, but rather on its position within an arbitrary system of relationships among the structural units (linguistic, symbolic, and so forth) constituting that system. Structuralist theories aim at a synchronic description and analysis of such systems of relations.

Poststructuralists assert the impossibility of any fully adequate synchronic structuralist description and analysis of language or culture and the necessity of diachronic analysis. With respect to language, they argue that the possibility of meaningful sentences arises out of, yet never fully escapes, an unrepresentable, open-ended process within which linguistic units endlessly differentiate themselves from one another. The possibility of a word meaning anything at all in a sentence depends at every moment on the impossibility of giving its final and complete meaning in that sentence. Poststructuralists often employ a method of critical reading called deconstruction to demonstrate this impossibility and bring to consciousness the various forces which lead readers to privilege at any given moment one interpretation as final, complete, or true. It is important to note that poststructuralists do not deny the meaningfulness of language. They argue instead that the meaning of any text remains forever on its way, never fully and finally arriving, and that this feature of language must be taken seriously if humans are to take responsibility for the interpretive choices they make.

Poststructuralists tend to characterize cultural phenomena (social practices rooted in particular conceptions of self, agency, health, sexuality and gender, punishment, and so forth) as transient epiphenomena arising out of, but never fully escaping, a dynamic, diffuse, largely indeterminate, and open-ended economy of social power. Poststructuralist work in many of the social sciences consequently tends to be historically and institutionally local, politically informed, self-consciously interpretive, and often politically subversive.

Legal scholars have drawn on poststructuralist theories to argue that modern legal institutions do not, could not, and/or should not function as modernist legal theories hold. They have attempted to demonstrate the descriptive inadequacy of modernist theories of law by showing the deeply fragmented, incoherent, and unstable nature of the law as a collection of positive doctrines and rules. They have deconstructively critiqued numerous judicial opinions and legal doctrines in an attempt to reveal the ways in which the pretense of objective, logical, and stable meaning depends upon a variety of suppressed contradictions and controversial privileges and exclusions. They have argued for the incoherence, the undesirability, and the impossibility of realizing such essentials of modernist legal theories as the rule of law, the autonomy of law, the legitimate authority of law, the objectivity, neutrality, and determinacy of legal interpretation and reasoning, and the freedom and equality of the legal subject. They have also sought to illuminate historically the complex relationships between a dynamic economy of social power and the content, practice, and cultural meaning of law, paying special attention to the assimilation, disciplining, displacement, and possibility of race-, class-, and gender-based struggles for power within legal institutions and discourse.

Some legal scholars have attempted to draw on poststructuralist theories to articulate a positive postmodern jurisprudence addressing such questions as What is law? and How should legal interpretation proceed? Compared to the less difficult task of attacking modernist theories of law and modern legal institutions, this project remains underdeveloped, having proceeded not much further than the claim that the possibility of genuine justice depends on the transformation of modernist legal practices and institutions.

Neo-pragmatism and Legal Theory

Neo-pragmatism is a contemporary revival and extension of American philosophical pragmatism, the view that the meaning and/or truth of a statement is not a function of its correspondence with an extra-linguistic reality, but rather of the role the statement plays within a community or discipline. Pragmatists conceive of knowledge as a system of beliefs within which beliefs are constantly adjusted to one another in light of purposes and experience and within which no belief enjoys a fixed foundational status. Statements are true if believing them proves good or useful within a community or discipline. This means that there can be no clear distinction between fact and value, that all description and theorizing is evaluative. In the pragmatist view, theories, scientific or otherwise, do not describe reality; they are rather inference guides employed by communities of believers or inquirers.

Neo-pragmatists of the late twentieth century call such communities of believers or inquirers interpretive communities. They emphasize that every interpretive community determines what is useful or good in the way of belief from its own point of view, and they believe that there is no objective vantage point from which to evaluate the competing systems of belief of diverse interpretive communities. In this regard, they emphasize the philosophical or rational ineliminability of diverse systems of belief and interpretive communities, as well as the role rhetoric plays in moving individuals to affirm new systems of belief and join new interpretive communities. They emphasize also that individuals typically belong simultaneously to many (sometimes incompatible) interpretive communities. Membership in these communities constructs (and sometimes divides) their subjectivity. Conceptions of rationality, utility, causality, freedom, equality, history, and the like are constructed and contested within and among interpretive communities.

Legal scholars influenced by neo-pragmatism, like those influenced by poststructuralism, have attacked modernist theories of law and modern legal institutions and practices. They have argued that modernist legal theories in their description and analyses of law necessarily but covertly rely on contestable evaluative premises that ought to be made explicit. They have argued for the essentially evaluative nature of fundamental categories of legal thought assumed by modern legal institutions and practice to have some independent, neutral, objective basis (causation, consent, and so on). They have argued against the possibility of justifying methods of legal interpretation and reasoning through appeal to objective, neutral, and necessary standards of reason, emphasizing that the justification of methodological commitments, like all commitments, turns on their usefulness within a particular interpretive community. In this regard, they have emphasized the role rhetoric plays not only in the resolution of concrete legal cases, but also in academic and professional struggles between competing theories of law and legal interpretation and reasoning, and thus within the historical development of the law and legal institutions.

A great deal of neo-pragmatist legal scholarship tends to bracket and set aside larger philosophical questions and to argue against modernist theories of law and modern legal institutions, practices, and doctrines for the pragmatic consequentialist reason that they do not well serve the purposes or interests of those whom the law governs. In this regard, neo-pragmatist jurisprudence is overtly political, for it takes the instrumental evaluation of law and legal theory to be its central task, and it openly confesses the political and contestable nature of the ends the law and legal theory are to serve.

Post-Freudian Psychoanalysis and Legal Theory

One current of contemporary psychoanalytic theory, associated with Jacques Lacan, understands the subjective experience of consciousness as an effect of an unconscious economy of desire for unity with the Real within which desire is endlessly circulated and the satisfaction of desire is forever deferred. Whether it thinks itself or objects in the world, human consciousness can never satisfy its primitive desire for unmediated access to the Real. Denied direct access to the Real, consciousness seeks to satisfy its primitive desire for unity first in an Imaginary realm of fantasy. However, intersubjective communication requires more than the Imaginary can provide; it requires a shared, public, and stable Symbolic order representing the Real. The Symbolic realm, the realm of language and culture within which humans experience themselves as subjects, requires a uniform subordination or ordering of the unconscious human desire for an impossible unity with the Real; it requires positing some mythic direct access to the Real.

The law which makes possible a shared Symbolic order identifies the phallus with the desired Real. The identification of the phallus with a mythic presence given immediately and prior to representation grounds the Symbolic order, making intersubjective representation possible. Within the Symbolic order, then, the masculine assumes the privileged position of presence. Of course, human consciousness has no direct access to the Real, so the Symbolic order remains unstable, unable fully to subordinate or escape the endless play of desire in the Imaginary.

Legal scholars influenced by contemporary psychoanalytic theory have analyzed legal discourse in terms of the laws thought to govern the Symbolic order generally. They have argued that the texture and instabilities of legal discourse reflect the necessity and impossibility of overcoming the insatiable play of unconscious desire as well as the role of the phallus as mythic presence. They have also argued that as part of a masculine Symbolic order, legal discourse leaves unspeakable important hopes, desires, and possibilities of the Imaginary realm. Some feminists have argued that the identification of the phallus with a mythic presence is contingent and that it may be possible through forced contact with a distinctively feminine Imaginary to destabilize and transform the masculine Symbolic order and legal discourse.

Beyond Postmodern Jurisprudence

To date postmodern jurisprudence refers to a diverse set of attacks on modernist theories of law rather than any emerging positive jurisprudence. Perhaps it is too much and too modern, however, to expect of postmodern jurisprudence a complete theory of law. Indeed, constant critique may be the postmodern project. Postmodern jurisprudence may well remain a diverse field, within which scholars bring a variety of contemporary theoretical resources to bear on particular legal practices, doctrines, and problems (for example, adjudication and legal education; responsibility and equality; race, class, gender, and so on) without ever producing or even attempting to produce a comprehensive theory of law.

The realization of freedom, equality, and substantive justice in postindustrial, postcolonial, late-capitalist, information-oriented, pluralistic societies probably requires, however, a positive and descriptively and normatively adequate postmodern jurisprudence. Whether the postmodern theories sketched above are compatible with and provide resources sufficient to such an undertaking remains to be seen.

References

Balkin, J.M. "Deconstructive Practice and Legal Theory." *Yale Law Journal* 96 (1987), 743.

Best, S., and D. Kellner. *Postmodern Theory: Critical Interrogations*. New York: Guilford Press, 1991.

Cornell, D. *Beyond Accommodation: Ethical Feminism, Deconstruction, and the Law*. New York: Routledge, 1991.

Douzinas, C. et al. *Postmodern Jurisprudence: The Law of Text in the Texts of Law*. New York: Routledge, 1991.

Fish, S. *Doing What Comes Naturally: Change, Rhetoric, and the Practice of Theory in Literary and Legal Studies*. Oxford: Clarendon Press, 1989.

Milovanovic, D. *Postmodern Law and Disorder: Psychoanalytic Semiotics, Chaos and Juridic Exegeses*. Liverpool: Deborah Charles, 1992.

Sarat, A., and T. Kearns, eds. *The Fate of the Law*. Ann Arbor: University of Michigan Press, 1991.

Schanck, P. "Understanding Postmodern Thought and Its Implications for Statutory Interpretation." *Southern California Law Review* 65 (1992), 2505.

"Symposium: Deconstruction and the Possibility of Justice." *Cardozo Law Review* 11.6 (1990).

"Symposium: Postmodernism and Law." *University of Colorado Law Review* 62.3 (1991).

"Symposium: Transformative Discourses in Postmodern Social, Cultural, and Legal Theory." *Legal Studies Forum* 15.4 (1991).

David A. Reidy

See also AUTHORITY; CRITICAL LEGAL STUDIES; DECONSTRUCTIONIST PHILOSOPHY OF LAW; DERRIDEAN JURISPRUDENTS; PRAGMATIST PHILOSOPHY OF LAW; RADICAL CLASS, GENDER, AND RACE THEORIES: POSITIONALITY

Pound, Roscoe (1870–1964)

Scholar, philosopher of law, educator, and founder of the school of sociological jurisprudence, Roscoe Pound developed his sociological jurisprudence by drawing on the philosophy of pragmatism. Legal pragmatism was a reaction against the formalism of the jurisprudence of concepts that dominated American legal thought in the latter part of the nineteenth century. The jurisprudence of concepts used strict logic to work from first principles of law. Pound argued that it was becoming mechanical and inflexible, unable to adapt to the needs of modern society. Sociological jurisprudence called for "the adjustment of principles and doctrines to the human conditions they are to govern rather than to assumed first principles; for putting the human factor in the central place and relegating logic to its true position as an instrument."

Pound argued that it was the law in action that was truly law, not the law in the books. He saw law as a form of social engineering, an instrument for securing changing social interests.

Pound believed judges should balance competing social interests as they moved society toward an ideal. He argued that law was the queen of the social sciences and could draw on other sciences as necessary, but that judicial decision making was an art rather than a science. His theory of judicial decision making, a significant break from earlier jurisprudence, drew on Immanuel Kant's philosophy of mind.

Sociological jurisprudence was the inspiration for legal realism, which came to the fore in the 1920s. Legal realism, another form of legal pragmatism, came to overshadow sociological jurisprudence and dominate twentieth-century American jurisprudence. Pound's jurisprudence was important beyond law. It provided an intellectual basis for two new disciplines, sociology of law and administration of justice. Pound was almost single-handedly responsible for broadening the study of law in the United States. He was a prolific writer, infusing his work with ideas drawn from philosophy and European jurisprudence and linking it to other disciplines.

Pound was a central figure in two major controversies in twentieth-century jurisprudence. The first took place in 1930 and 1931 when Karl Llewellyn, one of the most influential theorists of legal realism, broke with Pound. Llewellyn began developing legal realism as a way of making Pound's sociological jurisprudence operational but began to take his work in a direction Pound could not support. In 1930 Llewellyn criticized his former teacher and mentor in an article entitled *A Realistic Ju-*

risprudence—The Next Step. He argued that Pound's writing tended to be at a high level of abstraction, too high to be practical. Pound responded with "The Call for a Realist Jurisprudence," a criticism of realism as a coherent school of legal philosophy. Llewellyn responded with *Some Realism about Realism*, defending realism from Pound's criticisms. The debate can profitably be seen as a continuation of an ancient epistemological battle in the philosophy of science between empiricism and rationalism. Llewellyn thought Pound's tendency to abstraction was the result of an unfortunate preoccupation with concepts, a holdover of nineteenth-century conceptualism. The realists urged attention to and reliance on the empirical facts. The breadth and depth of Pound's scholarship enabled him to be conscious of pitfalls that his more narrowly trained colleagues did not understand. His 1931 criticism was the classic rationalist argument against any effort to develop a too-pure empiricism: "To be made intelligible and useful, significant facts have to be selected, and what is significant will be determined by some picture or ideal of the science and of the subject of which it treats." The facts are not reliable a priori. As important as they are, the human mind just does not operate from a basis in pure fact. However, Pound did lack an adequate methodology. A methodology would not become possible until later in the century via works in the philosophy of science, such as Thomas Kuhn's.

The second controversy involved administrative law. It has grown over the course of the twentieth century to the point where some see this as the age of administrative justice. Pound was an early advocate of procedural reforms. In a 1924 article, he advocated administrative law as an important reform, a remedy for nineteenth-century conceptualism. The administrative process was a way to move beyond abstractions in the case law, a way to attend to the concrete individual and the concrete case. He saw the particularity of the decisions of administrative tribunals as a healthy antidote to the tendency to broad generalizations characteristic of the common law. Additionally, it seemed to complement his concept of social engineering. Historian Morton Horwitz notes Pound was "among the earliest thinkers to observe that the broad generalizations that characterized nineteenth century legal consciousness presupposed a homogeneous society with standardized transactions." Early-twentieth-century industrial society "undermined this traditional identification of generality with predictability." Industrial society was not homogeneous—there was enormous variation among industries. The administrative process was believed to enable the legal system to respond to heterogeneity. By 1938 Pound reversed himself and began criticizing administrative law, denouncing it as administrative absolutism. Social heterogeneity and legal predictability remained major unresolved philosophical questions until the emergence of action-based jurisprudence.

References

Horwitz, Morton. *The Transformation of American Law, 1870–1960*. New York: Oxford University Press, 1992.

Hull, N.E.H. "Some Realism About the Llewellyn-Pound Exchange over Realism: The Newly Uncovered Private Correspondence, 1927–1931." *Wisconsin Law Review* (1987), 921.

Pound, Roscoe. "The Call for a Realist Jurisprudence." *Harvard Law Review* 44 (1931), 697.

———. "The Causes of Popular Dissatisfaction with the Administration of Justice." *American Bar Association Reporter* 29 (1906), 395.

———. "The Growth of Administrative Justice." *Wisconsin Law Review* 11 (1924), 321.

———. *Jurisprudence*. St. Paul MN: West, 1959.

———. "Mechanical Jurisprudence." *Columbia Law Review* 8 (1908), 605.

———. "The Scope and Purpose of Sociological Jurisprudence." *Harvard Law Review* 24 (1911), 591 (Pt. 1); *Harvard Law Review* 25 (1912), 140 (Pt. 2) and 489 (Pt. 3).

Sayre, Paul. *The Life of Roscoe Pound*. Iowa City: College of Law Committee, 1948.

———, ed. *Interpretations of Modern Legal Philosophies: Essays in Honor of Roscoe Pound*. New York: Oxford University Press, 1947.

Wigdor, David. *Roscoe Pound: Philosopher of Law*. Westport CT: Greenwood Press, 1974.

Nancy Rourke

See also ACTION-BASED PHILOSOPHY OF LAW; LLEWELLYN, KARL NICKERSON; REALISM, LEGAL; SOCIOLOGICAL JURISPRUDENCE

Powers and Rights

Rights and liberties to act form one set of fundamental legal conceptions, while powers and immunities to make changes in these form another, as two distinct but interacting sets of jural relations, in Wesley Newcombe Hohfeld's analysis. These four legal advantages have corresponding legal disadvantages: duties and no-rights to act, with liabilities and disabilities to undergo changes in those. (Hohfeld innovated the terms "no-right" and "disability.")

Jural Relations

These eight fundamental legal conceptions Hohfeld arranged schematically as (I) correlatives and (II) opposites, within (i) the set of rights and (ii) the set of powers. Others added (III) jural contradictories. These legal advantages (starred below) and disadvantages are not to be confused with various material advantages and disadvantages, to which the legal ones are merely empirically and contingently associated.

(I)Jural Correlatives	*(i) Rights Set*	*(ii) Powers Set*
	right*	power*
	& duty	& liability
	liberty*	immunity*
	& no-right	& disability

Applying this to the rights set, first: suppose claimant A has a right to a claimable object x in relation to B, any other person who would have judicial standing to deny A's claim. B, as to an x, would have a duty not to interfere with A. Hohfeld called this correlative of a right and a duty a primary jural relation, the relation that, as conventionally agreed, authorizes A coercively to enforce, as to an x, the duty B owes A, that is, to make B's performance of the duty nonoptional.

Unlike jural correlatives, jural opposites do not describe the relation between two parties, but rather focus on each party. Once the correlatives are assumed, then the opposites must follow with analytic necessity.

(II) Jural Opposites	*(i) Rights Set*	*(ii) Powers Set*
	right*	power*
	& no-right	& disability
	liberty*	immunity*
	& duty	& liability

Thus, if as a primary jural relation, as to an x, A has a right, then A cannot have a no-right; nor if A has a no-right can A have a right. Similarly, as to an x, if B has a duty, then B cannot have a liberty; nor if B has a liberty can B have a duty.

The scheme would make no sense if it permitted that, in a dispute between A and B as to an x, A has both a right and a no-right and B has both a duty and a liberty. Some call this focus on one party jural contradiction, but others have discerned jural contradictions, which they call the true opposites, as relations between parties. As to an x, if A has a right, then B cannot have a liberty (B must have a duty).

(III) Jural Contradictions	*(i) Rights Set*	*(ii) Powers Set*
	right*	power*
	& liberty*	& immunity*
	no-right*	disability
	& duty	& liability

The secondary jural relation is the controversial one. In the correlatives, A may have a no-right and not a right. That is, in relation to A, B is free to do as B chooses in regard to an x and A has no right to interfere. Hohfeld's point is that without the conception of a no-right, jural relations would make no sense for bridging the gap between theory and practice. The place of a no-right would be either empty space, which indicates conceptual incoherence, or a space falsely filled with a duty, a duty on A as the opposite of A's right. This covertly turns B's liberty into a right and imposes a duty on A not to interfere with B's liberty. This obscures the independent significance of the conception of a liberty and a no-right and permits a duty on A without public justification.

Powers

As with no-right in the rights set, so in the powers set the missing concept Hohfeld innovates, for unifying the scheme as to powers, is disabilities. These missing pieces establish an immunity and a disability as correlatives in secondary relation, as a power and a liability in primary relation. The powers, like the rights, also have the support of jural opposites and contradictories to give their jural correlatives coherence in thought and action.

Unlike the rights set, however, the problem with the powers set, as Hohfeld recognizes, is more fundamental. The intrinsic nature of a power as such is a metaphysical mystery, and too close an analysis of it will not be useful. It suffices to observe as part of the scheme how a power operates as a real legal relation. The first thing noticed is that all changes in a given, existing legal relation between A and B come from a voluntary fact or group of facts superadded to it; involuntary facts are negligible. Frequently the volitional control over superaddable facts by one person is paramount, and therefore that person is in the A position. A superadds the facts of expressed intention and thus alters both "rights" clusters as to an x to accord with the material purposes A desires to realize.

Applications

The shrimp salad has perhaps become Hohfeld's classic example to show that, among the fundamental legal conceptions, the liberty and no-right relation is a real legal relation. Suppose (1) A has the right to the salad, that is, no one has the better right or title to it. Suppose further A says to B: "Eat the salad if you can, but I do not agree not to interfere with you." B is now "at liberty" to eat the salad, and, if B does eat it, A has a no-right against B eating it. However, says Hohfeld, A also has no duty not to eat it, but rather, like B, a liberty to eat it.

Moreover, (2) even if B does not get to eat the salad (A eats it first), having merely a liberty still makes B better off legally (but not necessarily materially: B may not like shrimp, it may make her sick) than C, a third person who never had the legal advantage or opportunity to eat the salad.

On the other hand (3), since A's expressed intention in exercising his powers puts A under no duty to B not to revoke B's liberty to eat the salad, then if A creates its full ownership in C, before B eats it, C has a right to it, and A and B alike have a duty to C not to interfere with C exclusively dealing with it. (If, on the other hand, as legal formalists argue, A has not a no-right, but a duty not to interfere with B's liberty, A could not revoke B's liberty without violating A's duty.)

By having (4) the background cluster of "rights" that gives A paramount volitional control over the salad, besides exercising a power to create a revocable license, A also has powers to make a gift of the salad, sell it, trade it, deal with it by contract, put it in trust, simply waste it, and so on. It all depends on what facts as to the salad within A's volitional control A, by expressed intention, superadds in relation to another person.

A more typical test of the legal reality of a liberty and a no-right relation is the business of competing for customers. (Customers are the x in the jural relation, like the salad, but as persons, unlike the salad, they individually have their own powers to create jural relations.) In business, neither A nor B as competitors has a duty not to interfere with the other in attracting the same customers. Rather, they are both "at liberty" to get all or most of the customers, even if it "unfairly" causes great material disadvantage (financial and emotional harm) by putting the other party out of business.

At least, the material loser has initially the legal advantage and equal opportunity to get some or all of the customers, something not possible if on the superadded legal facts one of the competitors has a right, for instance, by contract with the customers or by statutory monopoly, to deal exclusively with all of them. According to the legal facts as superadded by contract or statute, one competitor (for example, B) would no longer have the liberty to deal with the customers, nor merely a no-right to interfere with a liberty of the other competitor (A), but instead B would have a duty not to interfere with A's right exclusively to deal with them.

Criticisms

Perhaps the most misguided criticism of Hohfeld's rights scheme sees its conception of a liberty as atomistic. To be sure, this is a plausible view if liberty is taken in the conventional sense, as the absence of all duty between all persons as to all things claimable by any two persons. Obviously, Thomas Hobbes' conception of a liberty as license or anarchy is not the conception of a liberty in Hohfeld's rights scheme. This scheme, it should not be forgotten, is applied in judicial reasoning; the law is its background. Just because A and B, for example, are both at liberty to eat all the salad or to get all the customers does not mean they have as their background right Hobbes' right to interfere as they please with the equal liberty of the other to compete for the larger share. In fact, as the scheme makes explicit, they have the no-right to interfere, and if they interfere they have infringed the fundamental immunities of every person not to be liable to change by deprivation of rights to life, liberty, and property except by due process of law.

Controversy still continues over Hohfeld's seemingly amoral use of the word "liability," as of right, duty, and liberty. The conventional terms merely mark the schematic positions of the eight fundamental legal conceptions. They acquire their meaning from the functions they serve in the scheme, as determined by the rules of the game, so to speak, a game that is well played when judges squarely and openly face issues of justice and policy.

Another frequent but misguided criticism of Hohfeld's rights scheme has it necessarily favoring the so-called conservative ideology of private property rights. This criticism mistakenly assumes that only private parties can be in the A position. As far as the rights scheme is concerned, the opposite can be true. A statute as the expressed intention of a legislature can always be in the A position of superadding facts to change legal relations for the simple reason that the legislature's volitional control over claimable things, unless disabled by constitutional law, is supposedly always paramount over private parties.

The chief controversy over Hohfeld's rights scheme is his conception of a no-right and also his innovation of a disability. What point does a liberty have if the no-right to interfere with it is not itself a duty with the coercive enforcement it alone authorizes? These concepts, however, have value beyond analytic clarity, the value of making issues so precise that, so to speak, they answer themselves. Justifying the injustice of depriving A of his right to x would be difficult. There is much less to justify, simply by narrowing the issue to the destruction not of A's total right to sue as to an x, but to the destruction only of that part of A's power to enforce B's duty by a lawsuit rather than in some other way.

References

Friedman, W. *Legal Theory*. 5th ed. New York: Columbia University Press, 1967.

Fuller, Lon L. *The Morality of Law*. Rev. ed. New Haven: Yale University Press, 1969.

Hohfeld, Wesley Newcombe. *Fundamental Legal Conceptions as Applied in Judicial Reasoning*. Ed. Walter Wheeler Cook. New Haven: Yale University Press, 1919. Rev. ed. 1923. Reprint, 1946 with a new foreword by Arthur L. Corbin.

Kocourek, Albert. *Jural Relations*. 2d ed. Indianapolis: Bobbs, Merrill, 1928.

Llewellyn, Karl. "Powers." In *Encyclopedia of the Social Sciences,* vol. 7, 400. New York: Macmillan, 1932.

Paton, George Whitecross. *Jurisprudence*. 3d ed. Ed. David P. Derham. Oxford: Clarendon Press, 1964.

Pound, Roscoe. *Jurisprudence*. Vol. 4. St. Paul MN: West, 1959.

Radin, Max. *Law as Logic and Experience*. New Haven: Yale University Press, 1940. Reprint, Hamden CT: Archon Books, 1971.

Stone, Julius. *Legal System and Lawyers' Reasoning*. Stanford: Stanford University Press, 1964.

Williams, Glanville. "The Concept of Legal Liberty." In *Essays in Legal Philosophy,* ed. Robert S. Summers, 121. Oxford: Basil Blackwell, 1968.

Eugene E. Dais

Powers of Government

The term refers to government's normative powers, not its de facto ability to achieve its ends. In modern society the organs of the state, which form government in the broadest sense, claim supreme normative authority. Normative authority implies the power to change the normative positions (that is, rights, duties, powers, and so forth) of the persons and groups living in society. As the highest normative authorities, the organs of the state claim (1) the supreme power to enact norms, (2) the supreme power to interpret these norms, (3) the supreme power to enforce norms, (4) the supreme power to take specific measures (for instance, to use and organize force) to maintain their authority, and (5) the reflexive power to regulate their own exercise of power by enacting, interpreting, and enforcing constitutional norms concerning the first four powers.

Powers (1) and (2), the power to lay down norms and the power to interpret preexisting norms, are often seen as two distinguishable types of action. According to this view, legislation involves the creation of general norms, while legal interpretation consists of applying general, preexisting norms to particular cases. This theoretical separation makes it possible to separate these activities physically and institutionally, so that the power to enact norms and the power to interpret them are vested in separate organs.

This view of the powers of government is based on the development of a particular conception of law. First, law needs to be conceived as a product of human activity. The theories of natural law, from the medieval times down to John Locke, saw the legislative function as a primarily judicial one: the task of the legislator was merely to interpret the already existing laws of nature. According to this view, the fundamental distinction was between legislative and administrative (or "political") functions. According to the separation doctrine, by contrast, the content of laws was determined by the organs of the state only, even if their legitimacy was ultimately derived from natural law. Second, laws have certain formal characteristics: it is their generality, rather than their substantial correctness, that distinguishes them from other authoritatively made decisions. Thus, the legitimacy of the law, even when nominally derived from prepositive natural rights, can rest on the legitimacy of the processes of legislation, adjudication, and enforcement. The separation of these processes was conceived as a precondition for their legitimacy. The separation doctrine was thus a step from substantial to procedural legitimation of the law.

Third, the separation presupposes that positive norms have relatively stable and independent meanings that can be grasped by the interpreter. Here the question is whether the difference between the creation and the interpretation of norms can be defined in a systematic way. Thus, the strict requirement of separation between legislation and adjudication was often connected with a view that regarded the application of existing laws as an unproblematic, even quasi-mechanical process. While the legislator had no right to apply norms, the judiciary had no need to complete the existing law with judicial lawmaking.

The separation of interpretative and legislative powers was seen as conducive to human liberty in two ways. First, because legislators could make only general norms, they had fewer opportunities to use the powers of government to their own ends. The separation guaranteed that law was applied in a consistent and impartial way. Second, it made possible the limitation of legislative power by positive laws. Although these limitations were enacted by legislators themselves, there was a separate agency, the independent courts, which could control legislators and make sure that they acted within the prescribed limits. The independence of courts introduced a "loop" into the hierarchical idea of sovereignty formulated by Jean Bodin and Thomas Hobbes, a conception adopted by radical democrats and conservatives alike. The separation doctrine was, in a sense, an attempt to circumvent the problem of sovereignty. By means of the separation of powers, every power holder in the state was brought under the normative control of some other power.

Historically, the most influential normative theory of the powers of government is the classical tripartite doctrine of the separation of powers originating with Montesquieu. According to this theory, (1) the powers of government are divided into the legislative power of enacting laws, the judicial power of interpreting laws, and the executive power of enforcing laws, making administrative decisions, nominating officials, and conducting foreign policy. (2) These powers are conferred by the constitution on different bodies and persons. (3) The three branches of government are coordinated and autonomous, and none is subordinate to the others. (4) No branch of government can exercise the powers allocated to the other branches. (5) The different branches exercise control over each other.

There have been different interpretations of this classical doctrine. All the interpretations, however, have had a common starting point: they have shared the first four postulates above and justified them by the liberty argument. In the version of the separation doctrine promulgated by Thomas Jefferson and the theorists of the French Revolution, the legislative, judicial, and executive branches of government were all responsible to the sovereign people, not to each other. In the less radical views of the Federalists and of Benjamin Constant, the separation of powers constituted the basis of the relations of mutual control among the different branches. The working of the system as a whole was assumed to be the guarantee of individual liberty: if one branch of government tried to usurp more power than was allotted to it in the constitutional scheme, the other branches would counteract it. Within this tradition, one could more easily justify such practices as judicial review of legislation.

The separation doctrine has been criticized from several viewpoints. Some have pointed out that it has never been fully realized in any actual legal system: in addition to their stated functions, courts also create norms, and legislatures also interpret laws. Furthermore, it is not clear why the number of separate powers should be precisely three. In fact, the executive function has always had a residual character in the tripartite classification. Some theorists have made a further separation within the executive branch, distinguishing between its normal powers of executing laws and special prerogative powers, the latter being related especially to the conduct of foreign affairs and the handling of emergencies.

It has also been argued that certain twentieth-century developments—the increasingly dominant role of executive power in parliaments, the ever increasing body of norms created outside legislatures, and the growth of state bureaucracies—have made the doctrine of separation descriptively irrelevant. Finally, there seems to be an inevitable tension between the separation doctrine and all notions of sovereignty. Accordingly, legal and political theorists who reserve the central governing role to the sovereign (the people or the state, for example) are inclined to reject the idea of separation.

References

Constant, Benjamin. "Principles of Politics." 1815. In *Political Writings*, trans. and ed. Biancaria Fontana, 171–305. Cambridge: Cambridge University Press, 1988.

Hamilton, Alexander, James Madison, and John Jay. *The Federalist*. 1787–88. London: Dent, 1978.

Marshall, Geoffry. *Constitutional Theory*. Oxford: Oxford University Press, 1971.

Montesquieu, Charles-Louis de Secondat. *The Spirit of Laws*. 1748. Trans. Thomas Nugent. New York: Haefner Press, 1949.

Vile, M.C.J. *Constitutionalism and the Separation of Powers*. Oxford: Clarendon Press, 1967.

Eerik Lagerspetz

See also JUDICIAL REVIEW; LEGISLATION AND CODIFICATION; MONTESQUIEU

Pragmatist Philosophy of Law

Pragmatism is the most significant philosophy native to the United States. Begun by Charles Sanders Peirce in the 1870s, pragmatism developed into a distinct philosophical movement some thirty years later, largely due to the work of William James. Its other principal architects include John Dewey, Clarence Irving Lewis, and, in Britain, F.C.S. Schiller. Pragmatism enjoyed its period of greatest influence during the first third of the twentieth century, though a significant revival in neo-pragmatic thought began to take hold in the century's final decades.

For Peirce and James, the principal thrust of pragmatism was methodological. Less a new philosophical theory than, as James put it, "a slow shifting in the philosophic perspective," pragmatism emerged in large part as a critical response to traditional academic philosophy. Peirce derided idle philosophical debate where conceptions of truth bear no practical importance to actual problems of human knowledge or belief. James opposed the tendency of philosophical rationalism to postulate absolute, immutable a priori truths said to be prior and superordinate to knowledge derived from observation and experience.

As to its positive aims, pragmatism is not a philosophy describable in terms of a single hypothesis or doctrine. The term "pragmatism," taken in its most precise sense, refers generally to the philosophical movement characterized by the set of overlapping, though somewhat inconsistent, theoretical ideas and attitudes of its founders. Several of these ideas bear particular relevance to law, and during the heyday of pragmatism they exerted significant influence over the direction American legal philosophy was to take. Four interrelated themes of pragmatism stand out.

Fallibilism and the Evolutionary Growth of Knowledge

Peirce stressed that no conceptual ordering of experience can be known to be true with absolute certainty. Every conceptual scheme contains at least the possibility of error and stands subject to disproof by further experience. Yet James emphasized the salubriousness of pragmatic fallibilism, for the rejection of one previously held truth, and its replacement by another, reveals the evolutionary nature of knowledge and signals positive growth toward a greater understanding of reality.

Contextualism

The pragmatists considered the world, what James called the "perceptual flux" of existent particulars, to be chaotic and discontinuous. They thus regarded the process of conceptual translation of object into idea, while secondary to the existent particulars, as essential to human life, for it results in a deeper understanding and adds value to the otherwise valueless concrete percepts. Yet how we perceive the outside world, take it in, classify, and order it, depends upon the problems, interests, and purposes we have in mind. Hence, to pragmatism, context is critical to what we experience, how we think, and which beliefs we hold to be true. Truth claims can only be understood relative to context.

Instrumentalism

Peirce had stressed that inquiry, to be meaningful, must be directed toward the attainment of knowledge that will settle actual philosophical or scientific doubts. He insisted that a clear concept must have practical consequences. James and Schiller agreed, while turning the focus of pragmatism away from strictly intellectual inquiry to the problems of human life. James described the pragmatic method as requiring that concepts and theories be tested according to what concrete difference the truth of one side rather than the other will make in anyone's actual life. As Schiller put it, the truth of a proposition depends, according to pragmatism, on its "consequences to someone engaged on a real problem for some purpose."

This instrumentalist aspect of pragmatism became the defining feature of Dewey's philosophy. He characterized instrumentalism as "an attempt to constitute a precise logical theory of concepts, of judgments and inferences in their various forms, by considering primarily how thought functions in the experimental determinations of future consequences." Instrumentalism thus became for Dewey a theory linking logic and ethical analysis.

Workability

A final theme of pragmatism that bears especial importance to law is captured in James's pithy phrase that truth is "the expedient in the way of our thinking." James meant by this that the truth of an idea or concept depends upon whether believing it to be true "works satisfactorily." The satisfaction here is not material or proprietary, but intellectual. According to James, we accept propositions as true when they serve our basic intellectual interest in possessing a conception of reality which consists of a set of beliefs that fit together harmoniously and consistently.

From the outset, pragmatism was a philosophy linked to law. During the years he was formulating the pragmatic method, Peirce associated with an informal group of intellectuals in Cambridge, Massachusetts, known as the "Metaphysical Club." Several members of the club were trained in law, most notably Oliver Wendell Holmes and Nicholas St. John Green.

Some years later Green wrote a series of essays on the law of torts. An ardent follower of Jeremy Bentham, Green found that the instrumentalist orientation of pragmatism, where concepts are held up for comparison according to their practical consequences, meshed well with Bentham's principle of utility. Arguing in a decidedly pragmatic way, Green became a vocal critic of judicial decisions. He took strong issue with the doctrine of stare decisis, set out to expose the fictitious character of certain established common law rules, and derided judges for treating certain legal principles, such as the distinction between "proximate" and "remote" causation in tort liability, as if they were scientific axioms, rather than evaluative distinctions articulating merely degrees of certitude.

Holmes's pragmatism is far less clear and straightforward. While he is generally seen as a pragmatist and sometimes credited as one of the movement's founders, he never endorsed it directly, and in his private correspondence he distanced himself from it emphatically. Few of his judicial opinions proceed according to pragmatic reasoning; many redound with an absolutism unfitting to the pragmatic temperament, and the influence of Bentham appears in his opinions far more pronounced than does that of Peirce or James. Nevertheless, many of his jurisprudential writings reflect pragmatic principles, at least in a general way. His strident criticism of legal formalism, for example, parallels the pragmatists' rejection of philosophical absolutism. The substantial contributions he made over the years to classify and order the common law likewise harks back to the pragmatic notion that conceptions of reality reflect the conceptual ordering that we ourselves impose on the flux of sensible experience. The predictive theory of law he set forth in the essay "The Path of the Law" bears some resemblance to the instrumentalist emphasis in pragmatism on testing hypotheses according to their anticipated consequences.

In a short essay entitled "Anthropology and Law," published in 1893, Dewey cited Holmes as providing an accurate account of the development of law and legal principles.

Apart from the reference to Holmes, Dewey's essay provides an important insight into how he saw law as a pragmatic enterprise. According to Dewey, legal principles do not exist antecedently in an abstract realm waiting to be discovered; rather, they come into existence as practical responses to concrete problems. Over time, the original problems and contexts fall away, and the responses come to be treated as fixed principles of right. Whether and for how long a single principle or even an entire area of law remains part of a legal system depends upon "the practical value, the working utility, of the rules themselves." Dewey stressed that continuity in law is critical. Yet laws are modified, continuity altered, according to the "practical usefulness" of the legal rules in question.

It was others not associated in any way with the founding of pragmatism who contributed furthest to imparting its principles into American legal thought. As early as 1909, a popular jurisprudence text written by Munroe Smith explained the development of legal principle to a generation of law students and young lawyers in seemingly pragmatic fashion. The most important and influential voices of pragmatism in law, however, were those of Roscoe Pound and Benjamin Cardozo. While Pound seldom acknowledged explicitly being influenced by pragmatism, it stands forth clearly as an ever present undercurrent in his work. His most singular contribution to American legal theory, the method of sociological jurisprudence, aimed to focus attention on the social effects of legal doctrines and institutions. He included in his program of sociological jurisprudence an examination of judicial decision making. He looked at the factors courts reference in reaching their decisions, as well as the ideals and psychological impulses that influence them. He also recommended various institutional changes in law and lawmaking, such as the creation of a Ministry of Justice to draft laws rectifying anachronisms in the common law. From its analyses to its recommendations, his program of sociological jurisprudence reflected a pragmatic orientation. It avoided doctrinaire theorizing, taking the form of a concrete jurisprudence fashioned to bring about practical results.

Like Dewey, but in a far more complete way, Pound also articulated an evolutionary view of legal history. He identified five stages of legal development, each characterized by the practical purposes or ends that the rules and doctrines at that stage are formulated to satisfy. The five stages are (1) "primitive law," where the end is basic legal order; (2) "strict law," aimed at making the legal order certain and uniform; (3) "equity and natural law," marked by the relaxing of strict law according to basic ethical considerations; (4) "maturity of law," where once again certainty becomes the predominant interest, now expanded to include security of expectations and equality before law; and (5) "socialization of law," where normative sociological ends take ascendancy. Understanding law at any of these stages, according to Pound, requires looking at it pragmatically, as a concrete process directed toward harmonizing potentially conflicting wills so as to maintain social order. Legal rules should not be thought of as universal, abstract principles of right, but as "represent[ing] experience, scientific formulations of experience, and logical development of the formulations."

Similar to Pound, Benjamin Cardozo set out to construct a concrete jurisprudence. His principal contribution to legal thought came in the four methods of judicial decision making he set forth in *The Nature of the Judicial Process*. He explained that

> [t]he directive force of a principle may be exerted along the line of logical progression; this I will call the rule of analogy or the method of philosophy; along the line of historical development; this I will call the method of evolution; along the line of the customs of the community; this I will call the method of tradition; along the lines of justice, morals and social welfare, the mores of the day; and this I will call the method of sociology.

Cardozo claimed that these methods set the parameters of judicial inquiry once a judge has identified the applicable legal rule and precedent cases. While judges possess the important power of performing this essentially pragmatic task of analysis, Cardozo stressed that their discretion is very limited. Judicial inquiry does not grant them freedom to impose their ideas of justice, morality, or social welfare on the law. Just as Dewey thought that his instrumentalist method of inquiry bridged logic and ethical analysis, Cardozo saw his methods of judicial inquiry performing a similar function. For most often, he maintained, adhering to the logic of established law and legal history will advance the underlying interests of justice and social welfare more than would the shaping of a new legal doctrine born of a judge's sense of justice.

Cardozo did not, however, spurn outright the overruling of precedent. Like Pound, he recommended that a governmental Ministry of Justice be created with the power to legislatively rid the law of archaic rules that no longer serve a worthwhile purpose. His recommendation led, some years later, to the creation of the New York Law Review Commission, a body entrusted with precisely the power he outlined. He also approved of the unusual judicial practice of prospective overruling, where a court applies an existing but problematic legal rule to the case before it, with the declaration that henceforth it will follow a different rule. In his judicial capacity, Cardozo overruled precedent when he found such action called for by the pragmatic logic of judicial inquiry. His opinions in *MacPherson v. Buick Motor Co.*, 217 N.Y. 382, 111 N.E. 1050 (1916), and *Pokora v. Wabash Railway Co.*, 292 U.S. 98 (1934), illustrate this.

The pragmatic jurisprudences of Pound and Cardozo proved highly influential throughout the 1920s and 1930s. Their work, together with the philosophy of pragmatism in general, provided a significant philosophical stimulus for what became the American legal realist movement. By the time of World War II, however, pragmatism fell into disfavor among American philosophers, and its influence over legal thought waned. Toward the end of the twentieth century, a spirited neo-pragmatic renaissance began to gain currency among philosophers. A nascent neo-pragmatism in legal thought followed. Most early work in this vein has taken one of two forms. Some take a historical approach. Thomas C. Grey, among others, has conducted a painstaking review of Holmes's writings and correspondence to settle the question of his relationship to pragmatism. Others seek to infuse pragmatic principles into contemporary legal thought. They borrow themes from pragmatism, for example, contextualism, the possibility of a plurality of viewpoints, and the rejection of absolutism, which they then use in creating their own legal theories. Often these theorists link pragmatism to another theoretical perspective such as feminism, postmodernism, or the economic analysis of law. The prospects for this line of neo-pragmatism are vast, but the verdict on what these theorists accomplish will be a long time coming.

References

Brint, Michael, and William Weaver. *Pragmatism in Law and Society*. Boulder CO: Westview, 1991.

Cardozo, Benjamin. *The Growth of the Law*. New Haven CT: Yale University Press, 1924.

———. *The Nature of the Judicial Process*. New Haven CT: Yale University Press, 1921.

Dewey, John. "Anthropology and Law." Vol. 4 of *The Early Works, 1882–1898*. Carbondale: Southern Illinois University Press, 1971.

Grey, Thomas C. "Holmes and Legal Pragmatism." *Stanford Law Review* 41 (1989), 787.

Holmes, Oliver Wendell, Jr. *Collected Legal Papers*. New York: Harcourt, Brace, and Howe, 1920.

Patterson, Edwin W. "John Dewey and the Law." *American Bar Association Journal* 36 (1950), 619.

Pound, Roscoe. *Interpretations of Legal History*. 1923.

———. "The Scope and Purpose of Sociological Jurisprudence." *Harvard Law Review* 24 (1911), 591; 25 (1911), 140; 25 (1912), 489.

"Symposium on the Renaissance of Pragmatism in American Legal Thought." *Southern California Law Review* 63 (1990).

Douglas Lind

See also POSTMODERN PHILOSOPHY OF LAW; REALISM, LEGAL

Precedent

Law is a mechanism the proper function of which is to promote justice. Precedent lubricates this mechanism. A legal system which does not respect precedent is inherently unjust; the machine grinds to a halt. These metaphors are alluring and seem to convey a compelling, commonsense picture. It is therefore surprising that the notion of precedent is fraught with philosophical difficulties. The doctrine of binding precedent states that a legal judgment is bound by previous judgments in similar cases; a judge must stand by the earlier decisions. Hence another name for the docrine is *stare decisis*. It is necessary to distinguish two versions of this doctrine. In a hierarchical system where some courts are superior in authority to others, a doctrine of vertical stare decisis requires courts to follow the decisions of courts in a higher tier. Horizontal stare decisis enjoins courts to follow their own decisions and those of courts of the same rank. The Supreme Court of the United States has ruled that the obligation to follow the law made by a superior court is stronger than the obligation to observe horizontal stare decisis. It may be questioned, however, whether this ruling is correct either as a matter of policy or as a matter of law.

The rationale behind the doctrine of binding precedent is that justice demands that similar cases be treated similarly, but two problems immediately arise. First, there is a fundamental moral question: why is justice best served by treating similar cases in similar fashion? Second, is it possible to say what counts as "similar" in a way precise enough to make the doctrine usable?

An impatient response to the first of these questions might be that it is true by definition that to treat similar cases differently would be unjust. Yet in many societies it is not considered unjust for the rich to buy privileged education for their children, or to pay for faster, better treatment than a person in equal need of medical care can afford. Typically, the view is not that it is right that everyone have equal access to these goods, and that some people buy an unfair advantage, thereby cheating the system. Rather, the capitalist view is that there is nothing inequitable about people having differential access to these goods. In many jurisdictions it is possible to buy a favorable legal verdict or to receive unequal treatment under the law in virtue of the position one holds in the society; this is the practice, if not always the official theory. What, if anything, is wrong with treating dissimilarly persons who have perpetrated similar wrongs? The justness of a policy of stare decisis may be defensible, but it needs to be defended, not assumed.

The second question invites us to provide a criterion for similarity. Anything is similar to anything else in one way or another. It is an amusing exercise to pick two items that, at first sight, have nothing in common and then to search out a respect in which they are similar. This may require some ingenuity, but there is a simpler, algorithmic method: nominate a property F possessed by the first item, and a property G possessed by the second. Then the two items are similar in that they share the disjunctive property of being F-or-G. Although this exercise may seem a mere recreation, the underlying problem is central to the theory of precedent in law. Thus (to take a familiar example), consider Judge Benjamin Cardozo's decision in *MacPherson v. Buick Motor Co.*, 217 N.Y. 382, 11 N.E. 1050 (1916). Cardozo ruled that Buick, if negligent, was liable to the purchaser MacPherson if MacPherson was a member of the class of persons foreseeably harmed by that negligence. What general rule of law can be extracted from this ruling? One might posit a general rule applying to all car manufacturers, but perhaps that is not general enough. To all vehicle manufacturers? To all providers of goods and services? The rule must be general if it is to determine decisions in subsequent cases, but it must not be so wide as to embrace relationships not sufficiently similar to the one between Mr. MacPherson and Buick. So the problem lies in finding a principle for formulating a law which is *appropriately* general. In most instances this may not be difficult, but there will be occasions when subtle distinction reveals dissimilarities between two cases, and a choice about whether or not to frame a rule subsuming both may be controversial.

One benefit of adopting a strict doctrine of binding precedent is that such a policy helps promote certainty and consistency. When precedents bind, those who contemplate committing an offense transparently similar to one that has recently received judicial punishment can discover the exact tariff in terms of judicial penalty, and will, if they are thinking straight, factor this knowledge into a decision about whether to perform the act or to desist. Those who wish to sue can receive from their lawyers accurate estimates of the likelihood of succeeding. There is also the thought that the interest of fairness is best served by strictly following previous decisions. However, these benefits must be weighed against the costs of rigid adherence to precedents.

The most obvious cost is that morally wrong decisions do not get righted; legal development is inhibited. For example, in an Australian case, *Dugan v. Mirror Newspapers Ltd.*, 22 A.L.R. 439 (1979), the plaintiff, who was a convict serving a life term for a capital felony, was held not to have the right to sue the newspaper for defamation, because he was "attained," that is, his blood was corrupt, he was notionally dead, and had thus forfeited his legal rights! Six of the seven judges at the High Court of Australia succumbed to the precedential power of this archaic doctrine.

In recent times, moral thinking on issues such as euthanasia, homosexuality, and abortion has become more liberal, but common law judges have been reluctant to depart from precedent and to make judgments which reflect changes in the ambient moral norms. One reason for this conservatism is that many judges feel that, as officials who were not democratically elected, they are not entitled to overturn established law.

In many common law systems there is now provision for departing from precedent, but the exercise of this creativity is normally reserved for the highest court in the land. Thus, in the United Kingdom, the Lord Chancellor announced, in the so-called Practice Statement of 1966, that the House of Lords uniquely would be at liberty to "depart from a previous decision when it appears right to do so." This marked a radical change in the practice of being strictly bound by its own decisions that the House had laid down for itself in *London Tramways Ltd. v. L.C.C.,* A.C. 375 (1898).

A puzzle attaches to such announcements on precedent. Are they themselves rules of law? If not, then what is their status? If they are, then whence do they derive their authority? Consider Lord Halsbury's statement, in the *London Tramways* case, that the House of Lords is bound by its decisions. One may wonder whether that very statement is a decision binding on the House. Its status as such could not have been established by any previous decision, for previously decisions were not binding, yet the alternative would be that the statement is the source of its own authority; it pulls itself up by its own bootstraps.

References

Cross, Rupert, and J.W. Harris. *Precedent in English Law*. Oxford: Clarendon Press, 1991.

Goldstein, Laurence. *Precedent in Law*. Oxford: Clarendon Press, 1987.

———. "Some Problems about Precedent." *Cambridge Law Journal* 43 (1984), 88–110.

Goodhart, A.L. "Precedent in English and Continental Law." *Law Quarterly Review* 50 (1934), 40–62.

Kempin, Frederick. "Precedent and Stare Decisis: The Critical Years 1800 to 1850." *American Journal of Legal History* 3 (1959), 28–54.

Postema, Gerald. "On the Moral Presence of Our Past." *McGill Law Journal* 36 (1991), 1153–1180.

Practice Statement (Judicial Precedent), 3 All E.R. 77 (1966).

Rogers, John. "Lower Court Application of the 'Overruling Law' of Higher Courts." *Legal Theory* 15 (1995), 179–204.

Schauer, Frederick. *Playing by the Rules: A Philosophical Examination of Rule-based Decision-Making in Law and Life*. Oxford: Clarendon Press, 1991.

Williams, Glanville. *Salmond on Jurisprudence*. London: Sweet and Maxwell, 1930. 11th ed. 1957.

Laurence Goldstein

See also DISCRETION; JUDICIAL REVIEW; STANDARDS

Prediction Theory

See HOLMES, OLIVER WENDELL, JR.

Preventive Detention

Preventive detention is detention by the state of persons thought to be dangerous to the safety of the community. It differs from detention imposed as punishment in that it is aimed neither at retribution nor at deterrence, but only at incapacitation of the dangerous person. It may, in practice, be limited to persons who have been convicted of crimes, but it need not be. It also differs from involuntary commitment of the mentally ill in that persons preventively detained may be legally sane; and it differs from quarantine in that the danger to be prevented, in the case of preventive detention, is the likelihood that the dangerous person would intentionally cause harm, while in the case of quarantine it is the likelihood that a contagiously ill person would unwittingly communicate a disease to others.

While it is sometimes said that no one may be confined who has not been convicted of a crime, the truth is that most jurisdictions have one form or another of detention based not upon conviction for a past crime, but rather upon predictions of dangerousness. There is, for example, denial of pretrial bail on grounds of dangerousness; more disquieting are statutes that permit the indefinite detention on grounds of dangerousness of various sorts of offenders after they have completed their prison sentences. The question is whether such practices can be morally justified. They require such justification, of course, because they constitute an enormous intrusion into the personal freedom of the person detained. While preventive detention is not in fact intended as punishment, and may not be intended to carry any stigma, the truth is that detention as a potential criminal does carry with it much of the stigma of incarceration for past crimes. While the legislature's intention may be to make life more comfortable for the detainee than for the convicted criminal, there are limits to what can be done to make confinement bearable.

Predictions

Some commentators have thought that preventive detention could not be justified. It is of course notoriously difficult to predict who will commit a violent crime in the future, and Alan Dershowitz has argued that while preventive detention might be acceptable if predictions were accurate, it is morally unacceptable while predictions are unreliable. This stands as an objection to preventive detention only for those who believe that the rate of "false positives" in predicting future dangerousness is unacceptably high. There are courts and legislatures that appear to believe that something close to certainty is now possible; whether or not they are right, what concerned Dershowitz is obviously not a concern for them.

The Value of Freedom

Andrew von Hirsch, on the other hand, argues that even if complete certainty were possible in predicting dangerousness, it would be wrong to detain people on the basis of future crimes. The argument he fashions is not entirely persuasive, however; it depends upon the high value we place upon freedom, and that premise might as easily support the contrary conclusion. Where von Hirsch argues that since we value freedom so highly we cannot countenance the deprivation of freedom involved in preventive detention, someone might equally well argue that since we value freedom so highly we cannot permit behavior that we know will limit the freedom of potential victims.

Preventive Detention and Punishment

Other commentators have argued that preventive detention can be justified. Michael Davis has argued that preventive detention can be justified as punishment for past crime, and a similar argument can be made for treating it as self-defense: if the person who is predicted to commit very serious crimes in the future is made aware of this prediction, then (assuming that present detention is the only way to prevent those crimes) either the person will offer to have oneself committed voluntarily or will be guilty of reckless endangerment. If the person is guilty of reckless endangerment, then he or she may be detained as punishment (or in self-defense). The sentence for reckless endangerment is of course limited; but if the sentence runs out and the person is still unwilling to commit himself, he may be sentenced again, and so on indefinitely. Either way the person cannot complain about indefinite detention; either the person has consented to it or is guilty of a crime. Thus the state does one no wrong if it simply chooses to lock that person up involuntarily. Since the conclusion of the argument is that we do not wrong those we preventively detain, it would seem to follow that we do not owe them compensation either.

Compensation

In some jurisdictions compensation is provided to those who are quarantined because of a dangerous disease. The thinking, apparently, is that people so quarantined, through no fault of their own, are being confined for the common good; therefore, by analogy with the taking of property for the common good, they ought to be compensated. Why should those who are preventively detained for the common good not be compensated as well? Ferdinand Schoeman, for one, has argued that preventive detention is comparable to quarantine and has suggested (without argument) the possibility of compensation. (See also Lionel Frankel.) The argument that might be made here is that, as with the defense of necessity, it is reasonable to permit the state to take away from an individual something to which all people are entitled—freedom—for the general good, but only so long as the harm to be prevented is great enough and compensation is made.

However, if the dangerous person is guilty of the crime of reckless endangerment, as Davis believes, we have taken away nothing to which that person has a right if we lock him up. Certainly Davis is right insofar as someone who presently intends to commit a crime, and who has begun to act accordingly, is concerned. In such a case the state would be justified in acting either in self-defense or as punishment. The difficult case, and the case generally involved in preventive detention, is the case of someone who is predicted to be highly likely to commit a crime in the future, but who does not presently intend to commit any crime. The question, therefore, comes down to this: does the future offender, who at this time has no intention of breaking the law, have a present obligation to lock himself up, as Davis believes, and, if he does not, is he guilty of present wrongdoing in neglecting a responsibility to prevent his future violations? If that is so, then in locking that person up the state is merely interfering with an activity that one has no right to be engaged in, namely, causing an endangerment of the public. However, if that person has no responsibility to prevent crimes that he has not yet decided to commit, then although the harm to be prevented may justify detaining the person, we make the community secure at his expense. In the latter case, it is reasonable to suppose compensation is due; in the former, not.

References

Davis, Michael. "Arresting the White Death: Involuntary Patients, Public Health, and Medical Ethics." (photocopy)

Dershowitz, Alan. "The Law of Dangerousness: Some Fictions about Predictions." *Journal of Legal Education* 22 (1970), 24–47.

Floud, Jean, and Warren Young. *Dangerousness and Criminal Justice*. Totowa NJ: Barnes & Noble, 1981.

Frankel, Lionel. "Preventive Restraints and Just Compensation: Toward a Sanction Law of the Future." *Yale Law Journal* 78 (1968), 229–267.

Schoeman, Ferdinand. "On Incapacitating the Dangerous." *American Philosophical Quarterly* 16 (1979), 27–35.

von Hirsch, Andrew. "Prediction of Criminal Conduct and Preventive Confinement of Convicted Persons." *Buffalo Law Review* 21 (1972), 717–758.

Michael L. Corrado

See also Mobility Rights

Prima Facie Obligation

W.D. Ross introduced the notion of a prima facie duty as part of his response to moral theories according to which all right actions have some common feature that makes them right. In particular, Ross rejected G.E. Moore's version of utilitarianism: if α is a right action (performed by a moral agent M at time t), this is because no other action (by M at t) would produce more good than α. For Ross, maximizing goodness is one among many right-making features of actions. An action may also be right because it is a case of keeping a promise, not injuring someone else, making amends for a previous wrong, distributing benefits justly, and so forth. If having feature F can make an action right, then any action with feature F is said to be a prima facie duty for the relevant agent. So agents always have a prima facie duty to keep promises, not injure others, and so on. But an agent can do his or her prima facie duty, yet not act rightly, because agents can have conflicting duties. (By analogy, pushing a ball north can make it move north, though not every ball pushed north moves north; and ceteris paribus, a ball pushed north moves north. Not every ball pushed north moves north, however, since a ball can be pushed in different directions at the same time.)

Suppose Molly promised to meet a friend for lunch. On her way there, Molly comes across an accident where she can render needed aid to the victims. Molly has a prima facie duty to meet her friend, and a prima facie duty to render aid. In this case, Ross would say that Molly's "duty proper" is to render aid; that is, helping the victims is what Molly ought to do. However, benificence does not always outweigh promise keeping. (By analogy, gravitation does not always outweigh electromagnetism, or vice versa.) Suppose Molly promised to give an old car to a nephew, but by giving the car to a local charity Molly would produce just slightly more good, taking into account all the consequences of her action—including any social consequences of breaking her promise. Ross would claim that, here, Molly ought to keep her promise. Crucially, he thinks that reflective moral agents will agree; but utilitarians might well dissent.

Ross emphasizes the personal character of duty. He argues that utilitarians distort morality, by reducing all morally significant relations between persons to just one: being the beneficiary of another's actions. However, if breaking a promise is *sometimes* right when an agent has conflicting prima facie duties, one wants to know what makes an action right in such morally complex cases. (Some philosophers contend that agents facing moral dilemmas cannot act rightly, but this is not Ross's view.) Ross is skeptical that any *theory* can answer our question. Perhaps all we can say is the following: if α is a right action (performed by M at time t), this is because no other action (by M at t) would have a complex of right-making features that is *more* important than the complex of right-making features had by α. Absent some independent account of moral importance, this can seem unsatisfying.

The goal is not to provide a decision procedure that determines, for those who do not already know, an agent's duty proper in any given case of moral conflict. On the contrary, Ross assumes that normal humans have an intuitive capacity for judging what they ought to do in particular cases. Such judgments are revisable. One might learn only later that an action had some right-making feature, or one's views about how to balance various prima facie duties might change over time, though Ross expects substantial stability here, at least in mature agents. At any given time, considered moral judgments are our best guide to right action. We should not follow the dictates of a moral theory that conflicts with these judgments. (Utilitarians might retort that theorizing is part of considering and that it is reasonable to reject intuitions which conflict with otherwise plausible theories.) An agent may not, however, judge as she pleases on Ross's view. If Molly judges an action right because it is a case of promise keeping, she must give weight to promise keeping in future deliberations. If Molly has judged it right to keep a promise, even though breaking the promise would produce slightly more good, Molly should judge that giving the car to her nephew is the right thing to do.

References

Brink, D. "Moral Conflict and Its Structure." *Philosophical Review* 103 (1994), 215–247.

Dancy, J. "An Ethic of Prima Facie Duties." In *A Companion to Ethics,* ed. P. Singer. Oxford: Blackwell, 1991.

Gowans, C. *Moral Dilemmas*. Oxford: Oxford University Press, 1987.

Moore, G.E. *Ethics*. Oxford: Oxford University Press, 1912.

Pietroski, P. "Prima Facie Obligations, Ceteris Paribus Laws in Moral Theory." *Ethics* 103 (1993), 489–515.

Ross, W.D. *Foundations of Ethics*. Oxford: Oxford University Press, 1939.

———. *The Right and the Good*. Oxford: Oxford University Press, 1930.

Searle, J. "Prima Facie Reasons." In *Philosophical Subjects,* ed. Z. van Straaten. Oxford: Oxford University Press, 1980.

Paul M. Pietroski

See also Civil Disobedience; Conscientious Objection; Imperfect Obligation; Obedience and Disobedience; Obligation and Duty; Political Obligation

Privacy

"Privacy" is a recalcitrant concept whose meaning, function, and value are disputed among philosophers and legal scholars. Proponents of privacy rights disagree over the interpretation of privacy and the range of application entailed by the two laws governing its use: tort and constitutional law.

Tort law defends against intrusion upon identities, disclosure of information, and photographs that would inevitably lead to a transgression of a subject's "inviolate personality." There are four separate torts, according to William Prosser, that contribute to the common criticism that tort law on privacy is not uniform and its moral implications are vague: (1) intrusion upon solitude, (2) disclosure of personal facts, (3) placing a person in "false light," and (4) misappropriating a person's image. In general, these attempt to "keep separate" the interests and values of one party from public scrutiny. They do not, however, entail a coherent content of "privacy." Theorists claim that the contexts are so varied that attempts to provide a moral ground of privacy become splintered into arguments against informational and noninformational access. Those who adopt informational restriction as a criterion of privacy draw too narrow an account. For example, there are people exposed to observation, not under informational surveillance such as prisoners and the homeless, but who nonetheless are without privacy.

The majority of theorists support the restriction against noninformational access, since it infringes the agent's personal autonomy. Decisions regarding lifestyle, professional pursuits, marital relations, and choices of endearment express a kind of character that emanate from their private and intrinsic interests. Human flourishing follows only if dignity of personhood is separated from threats of a kind that manipulate instead of enhance one's self-respect. Variations of this position are supported by Jeffrey Reiman, S. I. Benn, and Anita Allen. The core of meaning and value of privacy is control over their own lives; that is, preventing conditions that would neutralize their autonomy and jeopardize their identity. Noninformational access claims consider unwanted observation as a form of "theft" of personhood.

Constitutional law of privacy parallels these values insofar as it protects the domain of control in our lives with respect to intimate choices. For example, in *Griswold v. Connecticut* (1965) and *Stanley v. Georgia*, U.S. Ga., 89 S.Ct. 1243 (1969), constitutional law supports the right of privacy when the state infringes upon the autonomy and intimacy of marital relations including the right of intimate expression in one's home that may involve obscene materials.

Critics of privacy rights argue that this lack of coherence among the interests demonstrate the implausibility of "privacy." According to Judith Jarvis Thomson, rights to privacy claims are masked claims to property or personhood. Protection of a valued domain can be accomplished without appealing to privacy. For example, a pornographic picture being secured in a safe may be accessed by means of an X-ray device. The issue is stealing, not privacy. There are other claims, she cites, that violate a bond of personal relation and their liberty to express terms of love or anger in one another's company. She does not consider these instances of privacy per se, but circumstances from which privacy derives. Julie Inness disagrees with Thomson's reduction of privacy, maintaining that the value of ownership is beyond material possession. Two faculty members conversing in the faculty lounge may curtail the topic and tone of the conversation upon the entrance of another person (colleague or not). Instead, it is the "zone of ownership" intruded upon that alters one's way of choosing to express an opinion.

Neither ownership nor personhood exhausts the meaning of privacy. Reductionist arguments fail to support "underivability" as a necessary and sufficient condition of privacy. Cases involving privileged information, sexual intimacy, and control over the plans of life express derived, yet valued, separation from the public domain. Privacy lies at the core of one's intimate decisions about information and intimate access to ourselves.

Inness's account of intimacy provides a foundation and conceptual focus for privacy values. It entails respect for another's autonomy that embody one's love, liking, and care. Were privacy conceived as respect for personhood alone, it would imply more than the intimacy account warrants. The concept of intimacy shapes one's self-image and respect for others and advances a common ground between tort and constitutional privacy law.

References

Bronaugh, Richard E. *Philosophical Law: Authority, Equality, Adjudication and Privacy*. Westport CT: Greenwood Press, 1978.

Inness, Julie. *Privacy, Intimacy and Isolation.* New York: Oxford University Press, 1992.

Thomson, Judith Jarvis. "The Right to Privacy." *Philosophy and Public Affairs* 4 (1975), 295–314.

John M. Abbarno

See also HOMELESSNESS AND RESIDENCY; INTIMACY

Private Law

The distinction between *jus privatum* (private law) and *jus publicum* (public law) is attributed to the Roman jurist Ulpian, who drew a distinction between laws which govern relations between citizens and the government and the principles which govern the relations of citizens with one another. In common law countries the term tends to embrace the principles of both the common law and equity, while, in the civil law jurisdictions, the realm of private law is based principally on Roman law and its divisions into the law of persons, of things, and of actions. Blackstone, in his *Commentaries on the Laws of England,* also used this threefold Roman division. These areas have over time been influenced by three major philosophical streams deriving from the classical authors, from Christianity, and, since the Enlightenment, from liberalism. The liberal stream is at present itself being criticized by the critical legal studies movement, and from neoclassical natural law and communitarian perspectives.

The classical contributions came largely from Plato, Aristotle, and Cicero. St. Augustine at the end of the classical period placed many of Plato's ideas into a Christian context, as St. Thomas Aquinas later developed certain principles of Aristotle in a Christian framework. All of these authors shared a notion of justice as something objective, something which exists in fact and is not merely a matter of social convention or agreement. In particular, Aristotle, Cicero, Augustine, and Aquinas argued that there exists a natural law which transcends historical differences, the principles of which are the essence of justice. Laws which violate these principles are inherently unjust. Aristotle also contributed the notion of commutative justice, which refers to principles governing the exchange of goods between persons. This notion of there being certain immutable principles which should lay the foundations for just relations governing the exchange of goods between citizens had a marked influence on the development of contract and commercial law. The basic principle of commutative justice is that we should give due return for what we have received. This was developed by the philosophers of the middle ages, especially Aquinas, but was later undermined by the notion, which arose in the work of Francisco de Vitoria (ca. l483–1546), professor at Salamanca, that the only ground for an obligation was an act of will of a superior directed to moving the will of an inferior. This position was taken on by Thomas Hobbes in his work *De Cive*. According to Hobbes, a contract is a declaration of will by the parties and involves either the transfer of right by one party to another or the giving up of rights by one party in favor of another. This required that the will of a party to a contract must be expressed in such a way as to be known to the other party and that the transfer of rights must be accepted by the beneficiary in order to complete the contract. From Hobbes' position the most important element is the issue of consent or agreement, not the inherent justness of the terms to which consent was given.

The law, however, seems to be turning full circle back to an emphasis on principles of commutative justice. As P.S. Atiyah observes in his seminal 1979 work, *The Rise and Fall of Freedom of Contract*, there has been a decline in promise-based liabilities and a growth in benefit-based and reliance-based liabilities. This involves a circumscribing of the freedom-to-choose doctrines by the judicial application of equitable principles to contract cases and by legislation prescribing the terms of employment contracts, loan contracts, and standard term leases. The tendency is for the law of civil obligations to move away from a theoretical framework based on the *assumed* obligations of individuals, to a framework of judicially *imposed* obligations. This growth in benefit-based and reliance-based liabilities is dissolving the traditional division between tort and contract. It is also raising issues about the nature of the relationship between contract law and the restitutionary doctrine of unjust enrichment, especially the issue of whether the doctrine should give rise to a general cause of action.

The law of civil wrongs is also in a state of fluidity, with the major issue being whether to retain the element of fault as an essential aspect of a tort or whether to move toward policies of strict liability. There is also the related concern of whether to analyze the action from the perspective of its social and economic consequences or to continue to focus on the negligent quality of an action. Richard Posner argues that the utilitarian principle of wealth maximization underpins the private law of obligations and, accordingly, that the law should focus on the social and economic consequences of actions. On the contrary, Ernest Weinrib argues that the central principles of the law of tort are the proximity of relationship between defendant and plaintiff and the doctrine of causation. If such a position is accepted, then personal fault retains its centrality and strict liability principles should be reserved for exceptional cases. Richard Epstein has summarized the problem as one of trying to develop a framework which can relate conceptions of right and wrong on the one hand, with considerations of costs and benefits on the other.

In the realm of property law there are two distinct and apparently competing doctrinal traditions: the continental Romanist conception of property as *dominium* over things, and the common law conception of ownership, according to which many possible kinds of property entitlement are held by different people in relation to a single source of wealth.

The two principal forms of property in the modern world are land and company securities. However, the expansion of biotechnology has given rise to such issues as the possibility of property rights in body parts or in potential life, while the rise of environmental problems has opened a new area of proprietary rights in natural resources. There has also been an expansion of property law into the realm of the ownership and preservation of "cultural capital," such as artifacts, rituals, and sacred tribal information. As the realm of property law becomes more expansive and complex, it is argued by some that the Roman concept of *dominium* is not sufficiently adaptable to deal with the new forms of proprietary interests.

Within the area of company law there is also a growing tension: between nineteenth-century principles of corporation law, which were formulated in a period when mercantilist ideas were dominant, and the contemporary trend of the judiciary to hold that company directors should consider not only the good of the shareholders, but also the common good, when making investment decisions. This trend corresponds to the return to an interest in principles of distributive justice, which parallels the return to considerations of principles of commutative justice, in contract law. Both trends reflect the concern that liberalism, especially in its economic rationalist form, has not been able to protect the common good.

References

Atiyah, P.S. *The Rise and Fall of Freedom of Contract*. Oxford: Clarendon Press, 1979.

Caenegem, R.C. van. *An Historical Introduction to Private Law*. Cambridge: Cambridge University Press, 1992.

England, I. *The Philosophy of Tort Law*. Brookfield VT: Dartmouth, 1993.

Posner, R. *Economic Analysis of Law*. Boston: Little, Brown, 1992.

Weinrib, E. *Tort Law*. Brookfield VT: Dartmouth, 1991.

Tracey Rowland

See also Commutative Justice; Contractual Obligation; Distributive Justice; Public and Private Jurisdictions; Unjust Enrichment and Restitution

Products Liability

Products liability law concerns the question of who, usually as between the manufacturer of a product and the victim of a product accident, should bear legal responsibility for the losses resulting from the accident. The paradigmatic case involves the user of a product who is injured while using the product. For example, power circular saws are equipped with a spring-operated guard that is supposed to close automatically over the blade when the saw is removed from the wood being cut. If the saw is dropped, damaging the guard, or if sawdust clogs up the guard mechanism, the guard may fail to close. In such a case, if the user lowers the saw to his leg after sawing a board, the now unguarded blade may cut his leg. The problem for products liability law is who should bear the losses resulting from such an accident—the injured user or the manufacturer of the saw.

This is also a problem of moral philosophy: which party involved in a product accident has moral responsibility for the consequences? According to law, the resolution of this problem is dependent upon particular factual matters concerning the manner in which the product was designed, marketed, manufactured, and used. It is also dependent upon the interrelationship of numerous legal issues, which involve at bottom (1) the expectations of both the manufacturer and the user, (2) the fault of the manufacturer and the user, and (3) the causal connection between such expectations, fault, and the accident.

Strict Liability

Modern products liability law is widely thought to be based on no-fault principles of "strict liability," so that the maker's and user's fault would seem to be irrelevant in determining responsibility. Moral philosophy does support the application of strict-liability principles in two contexts where no-fault principles are strongly rooted in the expectations of both parties—accidents principally attributable to (1) a manufacturer's misrepresentations of fact about a product's safety, such as a representation that sawdust will not cause a saw's blade guard to jam, and (2) manufacturing flaws.

Powerful reasons within the ideals of freedom and truth support a rule of strict liability for accidental harm resulting from innocent but false assertions of product quality. When a manufacturer makes safety "promises" in an effort to sell its products, its very purpose is to convince potential buyers that the promises concern matters that are both important and true. Safety information is important and, hence, valuable to users because it provides a frame of reference that permits users to shift their limited cognitive and other resources away from self-protection, responsibility for which is thereby placed upon the manufacturer, toward the pursuit of other goals. In this manner, true safety information adds value to the product by enhancing the autonomy of the user, for which value the consumer fairly pays a price. So, if the information is not true but false, the purchaser loses both significant autonomy and the benefit of his bargain. Since an important purpose of the law is to promote autonomy, and the equality of the buyer to the seller as reflected in their deal, the law should demand that the seller rectify the underlying falsity and resulting inequality in the exchange transaction if harm results—whether or not the seller should have realized that the price unfairly reflected value that was false. More general, communal interests are also promoted by the enforcement of such promises, for the confidence of all members of the community in the trustworthiness of others is fundamental to positive interpersonal relations, in general, and to commercial efficiency, in particular.

Moral theory also supports strict principles of liability in manufacturing flaw cases. It is the very essence of an ordinary exchange transaction that the buyer pays appropriate value for a certain *type* of "good" comprised of various utility and safety characteristics common to each unit of that type produced by the maker according to a single design. Both the maker and the buyer contemplate an exchange of a standard, uniform monetary value for a standard, uniform package of utility and safety. At some level of abstract awareness, most consumers know that manufacturers sometimes make mistakes, and that the cost of perfect, error-free production for many types of products would be exorbitant. However, while consumers may abstractly comprehend this practical reality, their actual expectation when purchasing a new product is that its important attributes will match those of other units that are sold as, appear to be, and cost the same. When a purchaser pays full value for a product that appears to be the same as every other, only to receive a product with a dangerous hidden flaw, the product's price and appearance both generate in the buyer false expectations of safety which deny the right to truth. Moreover, a hidden flaw that injures a consumer violates the right to treatment equal to that afforded other consumers. Thus, both equality and the expectations of the parties, rooted in truth and freedom, support the maker's responsibility for harm from latent manufacturing flaws.

Fault-based Liability

Notwithstanding the appropriateness in moral theory of strict liability principles in misrepresentation and manufacturing flaw cases, the more interesting products liability problem of accountability concerns the maker's responsibility for (1) failing to warn of known and unknown hazards and (2) failing to design its product so as to provide the maximum of protection to all persons against all dangers. In both of these important contexts, involving problems of warnings and design "defectiveness," the law has applied principles that it calls "strict" but which are based on principles of optimality and feasibility and, hence, are really predicated on fault.

One of the most perplexing doctrinal problem in products liability law today is the question of who should bear responsibility for risks that neither party fairly could expect. If a product's dangers are both unknown and unknowable at the time of manufacture, the manufacturer's comprehension of and ability to prevent them may be said to be beyond the "state of the art." In such cases, where neither party has the means to possess the truth concerning the product's dangers, the law fairly may revert to a naked freedom model, since the parties are exchanging a product that they both (mistakenly) believe to be reasonably safe. As both parties know that the possession of absolute truth by either one is unattainable, they both rationally should choose *ex ante* (before the fact) to make and price the deal efficiently, according to their (fair) expectations concerning risks of injury known and knowable at the time, rather than including in the product's price an excessive "premium" for insurance against such unknown risks as might eventuate in harm *ex post* (after the fact).

When a consumer's prior expectations concerning product safety are fractured by an accident, and the manufacturer did not affirmatively *create* the unmet expectations, principles of utility and efficiency should help define a moral basis for deciding liability. Unlike values such as freedom and truth that are immensely difficult to value and compare, notions of utility and efficiency reflect the equal worth of all affected parties and hence provide a principled basis for comparative analysis that informs the "defectiveness" issue in design and warnings cases. The principle of utility dictates that actors seek to maximize communal welfare and, commensurately, that they seek to minimize waste. If a consumer suffers injury from an inefficient product risk—one that was excessive for the benefits achieved—the manufacturer may be faulted on moral grounds for causing waste (assuming that it was feasible to reduce the risk). However, if the maker carefully and fairly determines that the benefits of a particular design exceed its inherent dangers, then consumers who suffer injury unavoidably from those dangers may not fairly challenge the manufacturer's "legislative" design decision, a decision which was proper by hypothesis.

Consumer Responsibility

Principles of freedom and equality suggest that careless consumers should bear responsibility for their accidents. When the user of a product has the dominant control of risk, responsibility for resulting harm lies at least partially with him. If the consumer causes an accident by using the product inefficiently, in a manner or for a purpose that he knows to be improper, then he is morally responsible for the waste under principles of utility. The user has no moral claim to force others to bear the harmful consequences of his careless choices made and actions taken in derogation of others' rights or of his own dignity as an autonomous human being, for the freedom right possessed by consumers contains within itself the responsibility to act rationally and with due respect for the equal freedom right of other persons.

Products liability law is firmly rooted in moral theory. Principles of freedom and equality, as well as notions of truth, expectation protection, and utility, all have played a major role in fashioning the rules of liability and defense in this area of the law.

References

Attanasio, John B. "The Principle of Aggregate Autonomy and the Calabresian Approach to Products Liability." *Virginia Law Review* 74 (1988), 677.

Ausness, Richard C. "Compensation for Smoking-related Injuries: An Alternative to Strict Liability in Tort." *Wayne Law Review* 36 (1990), 1085.

Hubbard, F. Patrick. "Reasonable Human Expectations: A Normative Model for Imposing Strict Liability for Defective Products." *Mercer Law Review* 29 (1978), 465.

Kotler, Martin A. "Utility, Autonomy and Motive: A Descriptive Model of the Development of Tort Doctrine." *University of Cinncinnati Law Review* 58 (1990), 1231.

Owen, David G. "The Moral Foundations of Products Liability Law: Toward First Principles." *Notre Dame Law Review* 68 (1993), 427.

———. "Products Liability: Principles of Justice." *Anglo-American Law Review* 20 (1991), 238.

———, ed. *Philosophical Foundations of Tort Law*. Oxford University Press, 1995.

Schroeder, Christopher H. "Rights Against Risks." *Columbia Law Review* 86 (1985), 495.

Schwartz, Alan. "Proposals for Products Liability Reform: A Theoretical Synthesis." *Yale Law Journal* 70 (1988), 353.

Sowle, Kathryn D. "Toward a Synthesis of Product Liability Principles: Schwartz's Model and the Cost-Minimization Alternative." *University of Miami Law Review* 46 (1991), 1.

David G. Owen

See also FAULT; STRICT LIABILITY, CRIMINAL; TORTS

Professional Ethics

Professionals can be identified by their special expertise, their formal education, and their providing an important service to their clientele. Linked to these features and relevant to problems that arise in professional ethics is the professional's commitment to a value that defines both their expertise and service. For lawyers, that value is justice; for physicians, health; for scientists, truth; and so on. Professionals are likely to perceive such values as dominant and overriding, while nonprofessionals are not. Problems in professional ethics, therefore, arise when the values dominant within a profession come into conflict with others.

Often, the defining values of a profession are reflected in a profession's code of ethics conceived by self-regulating members of the profession itself. Such codes appear to license behavior that would be immoral outside of the profession. The American Bar Association, for example, requires lawyers to zealously defend clients believed to be guilty, and the Hippocratic oath urges physicians to promote health without regard for the patient's own priorities. Scientists, who do not operate with a code of ethics, are committed to expanding knowledge even when such knowledge has deleterious effects. If, then, a pervasive feature of professionalism is principles permitting conduct that would be immoral outside the profession, the question to be asked is, how is this possible? What makes being a professional a reason for engaging in conduct that is apparently wrong?

Two powerful traditions in ethics, kantian and utilitarian, suggest that the very concept of a professional ethics is incoherent. For the first, the distinguishing feature of ethical principles is their universalizability. For them, actions have moral worth when they conform to principles that are binding on all rational beings as such. This means that any principle binding only upon a special interest group cannot be a moral principle at all. In this view, it would be absurd to claim that there is a moral code for, as an example, scientists but not for stenographers. If the code is a code of ethics, it is binding on both.

Similiarly, in putting forward the "greatest happiness principle," utilitarians argue that we must, before acting, consider how our action will have an impact on all those affected, with each person's interests counting as one. However, scientists, for instance, in their unfettered pursuit of truth, do not particularly care how the results of their research are put to use, nor do lawyers particularly care whether the defense of their clients contributes to the general good. We thus have an apparent paradox: either our understanding of ordinary ethics is not as Immanuel Kant or the utilitarians conceived of it, or professionals are wrong to think there is a code of ethics specifically for them. Given the powerful appeal of these two moral traditions, the burden of proof is squarely upon those who would defend a professional ethics.

Supporters of professional ethics typically argue that the paradox is more apparent than real, that a professional ethics is reconcilable with ordinary morality. Some writers on professional ethics look to justify professional conduct by appealing to the institutional structure and the place of the professional within that structure. This is especially the case in the legal profession where lawyers operate in an adversary system. The theory behind the system is that each side of a controversy is entitled to an advocate who would defend his or her cause before an impartial judge and jury whose job is to decide the merits of the case. It is not the lawyer's job to decide guilt or innocence; that is the job of the judge and jury. The lawyer is playing a part in a system that will work if the others play their parts as well. In this view, lawyers are permitted to engage in morally questionable conduct (provided it is legal) on the grounds that they are players in a system out of which justice emerges. In a similar vein, it might be argued that society is better off as a whole if scientists are left to the unfettered pursuit of truth. Thus, it is not as if the code of ethics governing lawyers (or scientists) is inconsistent with a kantian or utilitarian ethics; rather, the professional's code of ethics addresses itself to the special circumstances of the professional's life. In other words, the claim is that a code of ethics, with its precepts specifically tailored for the professional, informs and gives content to the largely formal principles of morality.

Another way of reconciliating professional with ordinary ethics is by arguing that professionals, with their special responsibilities, have "privileges" that correlate with these responsibilities. The claim here is that privileges function as special rights that are carved out of the rights of others. Thus, the ambulance driver exercises a privilege when he exceeds the speed limit during a medical emergency even though exceeding the speed limit is ordinarily forbidden to non–ambulance drivers.

However one reconciles professional with ordinary ethics, what must be shown is that being a professional is somehow relevant to engaging in questionable conduct, for, clearly, simply being a professional will not carry the burden of proof. Compare, in this light, the professional assassin working for the mob with the government-employed secret service agent. While both are professionals for whom killing is part of the job, it is the latter but not the former whose conduct is allowed. The reason for this is presumably because being a secret service agent is reconcilable with ordinary morality in a way that being an assassin for the mob is not.

References

Baumrin, Bernard, and Benjamin Freedman, eds. *Moral Responsibility and the Professions*. New York: Haven Publications, 1983.

Bayles, Michael. *Professional Ethics*. Belmont CA: Wadsworth, 1981.

Callahan, Joan C. *Ethical Issues in Professional Life*. Oxford: Oxford University Press, 1988.

Davis, Michael, and Frederick Elliston. *Ethics and the Legal Profession*. Buffalo NY: Prometheus Books, 1986.

Goldman, Alan. *The Moral Foundations of Professional Ethics*. Totowa NJ: Rowman and Littlefield, 1990.

Kipnis, Kenneth. *Legal Ethics*. Englewood Cliffs NJ: Prentice-Hall, 1986.

Luban, David, ed. *The Good Lawyer*. Totowa NJ: Rowman and Littlefield, 1983.

Joram Graf Haber

See also ETHICS, LEGAL; ROLE

Prohibited Substances

See DRUGS

Promulgation

According to *Black's Law Dictionary*, to promulgate means "[t]o publish; to announce officially; to make public as important or obligatory." *Promulgating* a rule is not the same as *pronouncing* the rule: while a statute, decree, decision, or regulation may be pronounced in secret, it would be contradictory to suppose that it had been promulgated in secret. The practical issue for the criminal law is whether a law may be enforced that has not been promulgated, or whether the state may punish someone for violating a law that was not, at the time of the crime, promulgated. In this context, the state has promulgated a rule with respect to a certain individual if that individual was aware of, or should (morally) have been aware of, the existence of the law, and understood, or should (morally) have understood, its meaning.

The Common Law

It may come as a surprise to learn that, as a matter of principle, some courts have enforced rules against defendants who could not even have known of the existence of those rules. The traditional common law position appears to have been that citizens are presumed to know what the law is, whether or not it has yet been promulgated. Recently courts have been of two minds about this issue. In the United States the Supreme Court has held, in *Lambert v. California,* 355 U.S. 225 (1957), that where circumstances do not call one's attention to the possibility that behavior might be prohibited (that is, where there is not sufficient notice of the existence of the prohibition), the law may not be enforced unless the defendant had actual knowledge of its existence. It is not clear, however, whether this ruling requires the general promulgation of criminal laws; the law at issue in the case was a regulation requiring the registration of felons, and the problem was that there was no reason for a felon to know of the requirement. Since we all should know that murder is wrong, however, it may be consistent with the ruling to suppose that laws against murder and other clearly harmful acts need not be promulgated. *Lambert* has not given rise to any progeny, and it has not prevented lower courts from enforcing laws that had not been published at the time of the crime.

In *United States v. Casson,* 434 F.2d 415 (D.C. Cir. 1970), for example, a conviction was upheld for a federal crime committed after the bill that created the crime was signed by the President but before it was published. The court cited Lord Edward Coke for the proposition that the public was presumed to know what the Parliament had enacted. The summary of the common law given in that case appears still to be an accurate portrayal of the state of the law, at least in a number of jurisdictions. Indeed, there are still jurisdictions that permit courts to create common law crimes. It would be difficult to imagine a power more inconsistent with a requirement of promulgation.

Nature of Law

By and large, philosophical discussion of promulgation has revolved around two questions. The first is whether anything can be law that has not been promulgated. According to Thomas Aquinas (1225–1274), "Promulgation . . . is required in order for a measure to possess the force of law." In recent times Lon Fuller (1902–1978) has argued that promulgation is an essential feature of law, so that we cannot be said to have a system of law at all unless there is promulgation. Indeed it seems odd to say that a certain law exists in a community when the community is unaware of that law. Still, most people in most jurisdictions are in fact ignorant of much of the criminal law, and yet we find little difficulty in calling it the law and holding them to it. It is true that the law is available, had they the time and resources to explore it. However, it is also true that, in practical terms and for most people, large parts of the criminal law may as well have been passed in secret, for all they know of it. It does not seem to offend any logical or metaphysical principle to suppose that even those parts of the criminal law are law, and that the community is bound by them.

The Moral Issue

The second question is whether any standard that has not been promulgated can have a moral claim to be law; or, to put it another way, whether a law that has not been promulgated *ought* to be enforced. Clearly, given the existing inadequacy of promulgation, this question is of the greatest interest; yet it has been given the most cursory treatment by philosophers. It appears to be generally assumed that promulgation should be a condition of enforcement, but that conclusion is not a straightforward consequence of either utilitarian or retributivist approaches to the criminal law. Jeremy Bentham (1748–1832), for example, listed cases in which the law had not been promulgated as being among those in which punishment would be inappropriate as having no effect. Efficacy alone would not, in spite of what Bentham thought, support a failure-of-promulgation excuse: although utility may dictate that a law must eventually be promulgated, the most efficacious way to promulgate it may be to punish the first person to violate it, even though that person had no notice of the law. If punishment is in fact the most effective (least costly) way to announce the law, then the person punished cannot raise the objection that the law was not promulgated; his punishment is itself justified as a means of promulgation and of deterring others.

Particular versions of retributivism may also encounter difficulty supporting a requirement of promulgation. Retributivists who see punishment as something called for by the offender's violation of the moral law, for example, may not find promulgation a moral condition of enforcement. For although the law may be one way to teach morality, it is not the only way morality can be known. Each of us knows the difference between right and wrong, especially when issues of serious harm to others are concerned; at the very least we know what our community thinks of these matters.

Thus one who has violated a moral rule can be deserving of punishment regardless of whether the particular rule has been announced; since he should have known what he did was wrong, it would not be unfair to punish him. Thomas Hobbes (1588–1679) suggests such a view in connection with the principles of "natural law": "The Lawes of Nature [unlike other laws] therefore need not any publishing, nor Proclamation; as being contained in this one Sentence, approved by all the world, Do not that to another, which thou thinkest unreasonable to be done by another to thy selfe." Hobbes did not believe the same to be true of the purely positive law. Nevertheless, the consequences of taking such a view seriously can be alarming and may be seen in those systems of criminal law that give the judge the right, in the form of a *principle of analogy*, to punish those who, without violating any written law, are thought to have contradicted some unwritten code such as the will of the state or of the community. The criminal codes of both Nazi Germany and the Soviet Union in the early years contained such a provision.

The view that makes the clearest case for an excuse based on the failure of promulgation is the view that the justification of the criminal law lies in principles of self-defense. As that theory has been developed by Warren Quinn and others, it justifies the *threat* of punishment, not punishment itself, in terms of crimes prevented; punishment itself is justified derivatively. If what justifies the criminal law is its role as a threat, then punishment can be justified only if notice has been given. Where a law was not promulgated, no threat was made to prevent the offensive behavior, and punishment cannot be justified as a consequence of a justified threat.

References

Aquinas, Thomas. *On Law, Morality, and Politics*. Ed. W.P. Baumgarth and R.J. Re-

gan. Indianapolis: Hackett, 1988 (*Summa Theologiae* I–II, Q. 90, art. 4).
Beccaria, Cesare. *On Crimes and Punishments*. Trans. Henry Paolucci. Indianapolis: Bobbs-Merrill, 1963.
Bentham, Jeremy. *Introduction to the Principles of Law and Morals*. Ed. J.H. Burns and H.L.A. Hart. London: Methuen, 1970.
Fuller, Lon. *The Morality of Law*. New Haven: Yale University Press, 1969.
Hobbes, Thomas. *Leviathan*. 1651. London: Oxford University Press, 1909.
Murphy, Joseph, "The Duty of the Government to Make the Law Known." *Fordham Law Review* 51 (1982), 255–292.
Robinson, Paul, "Are Criminal Codes Irrelevant?" *Southern California Law Review* 68 (1994), 159–202.

Michael L. Corrado

See also EX POST FACTO LEGISLATION; MISTAKE AND IGNORANCE

Proof

See EVIDENCE

Property

Every society has domains of valuable resources which are subject to interpersonal and intergroup regulation by cultural norms or by a regime of law. Because "property" is defined by these social domains and norms, theories that explain, justify, or critique property practices are socially and historically conditioned to a high degree.

In Greek antiquity, Pythagoras and Plato advocated communistic property rights because private property was seen to be socially divisive and contrary to individuals' transcendental development. Plato further argued that communal property leads to the best social order. In opposition, Aristotle argued that private property arises naturally from innate self-interest and encouragess economic activity, social harmony, and moral development. In the Roman empire, with a mature legal system and a wide knowledge of the property practices of different societies, philosophers such as Cicero and Seneca argued that private property was based on conventions of civil law, and that prior to civilization and its legal fabrications, there must have been a "Golden Age" in which property was common and disputes were few. This romantic image fused with the Christian "Garden of Eden" account of an aboriginal "natural" human condition prior to humankind's "fall" to conventional civilization. With this history of Greek and Roman beliefs, the questions for property theory were fixed for almost two millennia: does communist or private property best fit human nature, and how can we explain transitions between these two?

For example, St. Augustine argued that God gave the material world to all humankind as common property, and that private ownership arises as stewardship authorized by God through civil government in accordance with the principle of best use. After the restoration of Aristotle by Aquinas, scholastic philosophers began to argue that private ownership was natural and arose prior to civil law. John of Paris and John Fortescue developed the labor theory of property, explaining that private ownership results from individual labor applied to the common store of nature. For Marsillius of Padua, the innate human sense of free will transmutes mere use into personal control and that into a natural sense of ownership.

As theories of human nature became more psychological, so too did property theory. René Descartes' mechanistic psychology based on animal spirits and passions included an innate desire to acquire those things that are useful. Thomas Hobbes argued that humans motivated by selfish passions and set in the common store of nature must have been in constant warfare until reason caused them to give up common property rights to all things and to accept private property protected by civil power. For Baruch de Spinoza, reason was as much a part of natural psychology as passions, and private property was legitimized by reasonableness, not by power. John Locke's revival of the labor theory of property was integral to his psychology of perception and agency: just as a perceptual property belongs to the object whose activity caused the perception in the perceiver, so too does an economic property belong to the person whose activity caused the property to be appropriated from the common store of nature. In the eighteenth century, Francis Hutcheson and others in the British empiricist tradition began developing the idea of a possessive instinct. However, for David Hume, property arises because people want to maintain the cognitive comfort and utility of their established associations of ideas. For Jeremy Bentham, property is a legally secured expectation of future utility. G.W.F. Hegel's psychological theory was that property is necessary for the self-actualization of the personality.

The quest for the natural origins of property led not only to psychology but also to ethnography. Starting in the seventeenth century, property theorists were increasingly citing ethnographic evidence. For example, Hugo Grotius had argued that the original, natural human condition in the Garden of Eden was akin to the simple communal societies of North American native people. Locke took this archetype of "the wild Indian, who knows no enclosure and is still a tenant in common" as the starting point to explain how private property rights arise from invested labor. Montesquieu's and Jean-Jacques Rousseau's accounts of property relied heavily on accounts of ancient societies and primitive peoples, and in the nineteenth century, it became the norm to expect property theory to fit ethnographic evidence. Lewis Morgan's account of a progressive development of property rights from primitive tribes to contemporary European civilization strongly influenced Karl Marx's and Friedrich Engels' accounts of the coevolution of the social organization of production and the ownership of the means of production. Sociologists Herbert Spencer and Thorstein Veblen, also using ethnographic evidence, argued that private property developed to serve social stratification generally. George Mead argued that private property arose when the aboriginal organic community was disrupted by the intrusion of outsiders, such as traders, spouses, and captives.

However, for a number of reasons, including the growth of secularism, the perceived threat of marxism, the political struggles inherent in social policy debates about property rights, and the endlessly complex elaborations of private ownership schemes (for example, time-share real estate, derivative securities, ownership of genes), mid-twentieth-century property theory moved away from the classical questions to seemingly descriptive accounts of private ownership. For example, F. Snare's semantic analysis formalized property as three rules: (1) owner may use object X without interference, (2) others may not use X without owner's permission, and (3) owner may recursively transfer the first two property rights to another person. Economic descriptions of property have included Hardin's logic of the "tragedy of the commons" and Richard Posner's reduction of property to mechanisms of productive efficiency. Another example is Reich's descriptive analysis of the functions of investment property, leading him to define "new property" as a right to an income, including income from social benefits programs.

Future developments in property theory will probably be found in scholarship arising from critical legal theory, from feminist jurisprudence, and from the interdisciplinary mix of law with the social and behavioral sciences. Theories of property, especially descriptive theories, can be challenged for hidden ideological biases and for lack of empirical confirmation. Critical legal theorists such as Duncan Kennedy have been actively debating with law and economics theorists on topics of property. Feminist scholars such as C.M. Rose have been developing new forms of critical argument to show that property theory is commonly presented in a male voice and structured to exclude women's perspectives. In support, interdisciplinary social scientists such as Floyd Rudmin have shown that men conceive ownership more as absolute and exclusive control and that women conceive ownership more as responsibility and self-reference. Replicated cross-cultural studies have further challenged traditional property theory, for example, by showing Locke to be factually wrong: where people do get their food by hunting and gathering, their labor does not lead to private property rights. In conclusion, because property is a social phenomenon, the philosophy of property law will necessarily be constrained by historical context and by empirical claims.

References

Avila, C. *Ownership: Early Christian Teachings*. London: Sheed and Ward, 1983.

MacPherson, C.B. *Property: Mainstream and Critical Positions*. Toronto: University of Toronto Press, 1978.

Marcel, G. *Being and Having: An Existential Diary*. Trans. K. Farrer. Glasgow: University Press, 1949.

Munzer, S.R. *A Theory of Property:* Cambridge: Cambridge University Press, 1990.

Parel, A., and T. Flanagan. *Theories of Property: Aristotle to the Present*. Waterloo ON: Wilfred Laurier Press, 1979.

Rose, C.M. "Property as Storytelling: Perspectives from Game Theory, Narrative Theory, Feminist Theory." *Yale Journal of Law and Humanities* 2 (1990), 37–57.

Rudmin, F.W. "Cross-Cultural Correlates of the Ownership of Private Property: Two Samples of Murdock's Data." *Journal of Socio-Economics* 24 (1995), 345–373.

———. "Milder Differences in the Semantics of Ownership: A Quantitative Phenomenological Survey Study." *Journal of Economic Psychology* 15 (1994), 345–373.

Schlatter, R. *Private Property: The History of an Idea*. New Brunswick NJ: Rutgers University Press, 1951.

Snare, F. "The Concept of Property." *American Philosophical Quarterly* 9 (1972), 200–206.

Floyd W. Rudmin

See also ACQUISITION AND TRANSFER; GOODS; OWNERSHIP

Prosecution, Private

A private prosecution, in its purest form, is a criminal prosecution instituted and conducted by a private individual rather than an agent of the state. However, private prosecutions are not restricted to purely criminal proceedings. They may also be concerned with the prosecution of such quasi-criminal matters as regulatory or public welfare offenses (including, to take one notable example, the enforcement of pollution control legislation).

The private prosecution process is to be contrasted with the system for the public prosecution of common law crimes, which sees criminal conduct prosecuted at the instance of the state. In common law countries crime is ordinarily regarded as an offense not simply against the individual but against the state. This conception of the importance of the criminal act is tied to the belief that crimes should be prosecuted in the name of the state by state officials. This belief in turn has led to the establishment of public prosecution systems in both common law and civilian jurisdictions throughout the western world. With the rise of public prosecution has come the diminution of the role and importance of private prosecutions.

The antecedents of private prosecution are considerably more ancient than those of public prosecution. At the time of the Norman conquest, all prosecutions were conducted by private citizens. By contrast, the public prosecutor did not become a feature of English law until the late nineteenth century. It is only a comparatively recent addition to common law legal traditions that has allowed state officials (such as the attorney general) to assert paramount claims to the carriage of a prosecution. Indeed, in the eighteenth century, state officials had no formal ability to take over the conduct of a private criminal prosecution without the private prosecutor's consent. Today, the attorney general in Canada is able to intervene in a private prosecution as a matter of unfettered official discretion pursuant to a grant of statutory authority. This power of intervention is not restricted to the intervention and carriage of an action but extends so far as to validate an official intercession whose sole purpose is the entry of a stay of proceedings. The statutory roots of this power to stay proceedings are traceable to the first Criminal Code of Canada (1892) and derive ultimately from the somewhat different common law nolle prosequi power. Historically, all prosecutions were private and, in England, the theory evolved that the prosecuting police officer was simply a citizen in uniform. The right of private prosecution has come to be regarded as a fundamental English constitutional right. This has not precluded discussion of the wisdom of narrowing the right to institute prosecutions privately. Despite reputable calls for such reform, or even abolition (as was the case with the recommendations of 1981 British Royal Commission on Criminal Procedure), the impetus for change has been resisted. The Law Refom Commission of Canada even went so far in 1986 as to recommend modestly enhancing the scope and power of private prosecutors. Nevertheless, the significant limitations on the long cherished right to launch and conduct criminal prosecutions must be recognized. In terms of frequency of use in the criminal process, the right of private prosecution must be regarded as substantially eroded, even if it has not been completely eliminated. However, the frequency of the use of the private prosecution power is not viewed as an accurate measure of its value.

In Canada and throughout the common law world the vast majority of prosecutions is initiated by the police. (Some jurisdictions do not allow charges to be laid, even by the police, unless they are first screened or approved by a public prosecutor.) Whether the charge is laid by the police or a public prosecutor, the usual practice is for the charge to be prosecuted by a public official, usually a Crown attorney. This fact has been said to strengthen the social justification for the retention or expansion of private prosecutions since, in a public prosecution system, only where the prosecutor has failed to exercise his or her discretion to prosecute will the private individual feel the need to undertake the prosecution of an offender personally. A noteworthy contrast is to be found in the United States where the private prosecutor has virtually no role to play in the criminal justice process. Private prosecutions based on the English model were rejected by colonial settlers, and this development was entrenched with the American War of Independence. The dominant system in that country today is the district attorney–led public prosecution system. The citizen's role in this criminal justice process is confined to that of complainant.

The value of private prosecutions aside, there are, at least in Canada, significant fetters, both practical and procedural, on the wholesale resort to the use of the power. As the seriousness of the charge in question increases, the restrictions on the ability of an individual to prosecute a case privately become more severe. Thus, while there are few, if any, restrictions on the right to prosecute a summary conviction case (that is, the most minor form of criminal charge) privately through to the conclusion of trial, matters become procedurally more complex when the charge in question is more serious and consequently must be prosecuted by indictment. Indeed, in Canada the active involvement of the attorney general becomes imperative if the charge is privately laid and the offense is indictable. In such instances the consent of the attorney general must be formally obtained by the private prosecutor before the case may be carried forward. Moreover, assuming a consent is granted, the question is open as to whether the consent to the preferring of an indictment necessarily means that the private prosecutor can personally conduct the prosecution. Canadian courts have been left to struggle with this uncertain dynamic. Realistically, it would seem likely that any attorney general prepared to consent to the preferring of an indictment at the behest of a private citizen would perforce be prepared to undertake the prosecution of such a matter at trial.

There is a debate of considerable proportions surrounding the question of the value or utility of preserving or enhancing the ability of citizens to prosecute crimes privately. Proponents of private prosecutions, such as the Law Reform Commission of Canada, argue that private prosecutions are valuable to the general enforcement effort. The private prosecution operates in effect as an informal review of discretionary powers. This view gains force when it is the state itself, or some arm of it, that is regarded as a potential malefactor as, for example, environmental activists contend that the state can be on those occasions when ecological concerns are at issue. Private prosecution introduces a method of inducing accountability into a process or system that might be viewed with suspicion by those who otherwise have little, or no, access.

The private prosecution process has been extolled by its proponents as a salutory form of citizen/victim participation in the legal system. This form of participation is thought to promote and enhance democratic values by fostering an image of effective citizen involvement in the administration of justice within the state.

Critics of private prosecutions, such as the Royal Commission on Criminal Procedure, contend that they are costly, result in inconsistency in practice, inspire malicious persons to commence prosecutions that are not carried to appropriate conclusion, lack necessary professionalism, objectivity, and expertise, and may be motivated by thoughts of private gain through the extortionate use of legal proceedings.

As regards the issue of malice and abuse, defenders of private prosecutions reply that the form of retribution that is exacted by a citizen's resort to legal processes is preferable to other unregulated forms of citizen self-help. Nevertheless, the potential for abuse inheres in the notion of private prosecution. It is for this reason that such systems, including Canada's, provide for a measure of supervision and oversight by a responsible public official possessing the power to intervene and stay proceedings in genuine cases of abuse of process. As the chief justice of Canada noted in the case of *Dowson,* 62 C.C.C. (2d), 286 S.C.C. 288 (1982): "The right of a private citizen to lay an information, and the right and duty of the Attorney General to supervise criminal prosecutions, are both fundamental parts of our criminal justice system."

References

Burns, P. "Private Prosecutions in Canada: The Law and a Proposal for Change." *McGill Law Journal* (1975), 269.

Davis, P.L. "The Crime Victim's 'Right' to a Criminal Prosecution: A Proposed Model Statute for the Governance of Private Criminal Prosecutions." *DePaul Law Review* 38 (1989), 329.

Law Reform Commission of Canada. *Private Prosecutions*. Working Paper 52. Ottawa, 1986.

Royal Commission on Criminal Procedure. *Prosecutions by Private Individuals and Non-Police Agencies*. Policy Study No. 10. London, 1980.

Samuels, A. "(4) Non-Crown Prosecutions: Prosecutions by Non-Police Agencies and Private Individuals." *Criminal Law Review* (1986), 33.

Webb, K. "Taking Matters into Their Own Hands: The Role of Citizens in Canadian Pollution Control Enforcement." *McGill Law Journal* 36 (1991), 771.

Stanley A. Cohen

Prostitution

Although definitions of prostitution vary in scope, and these differences affect the scope and direction of substantive discussion, for the purposes of this article it is best defined simply as commercial or mercenary sex. Prostitution gives rise to two questions in legal and social philosophy: Should it be legally proscribed? Is it morally wrong?

Prostitution and the Law

The legal status of prostitution today differs from society to society. In most western countries prostitution as such is not illegal, but it is often restricted or regulated to some extent; in some countries legal prohibition of associated activities (for example, soliciting) is almost crippling. In the United States, prostitution is illegal in all states except Nevada. Whether it should be prohibited or restricted is a question that brings up the philosophical problem of the limits of legal curtailment of individual liberty. The answer will depend on the liberty-limiting principle or principles one subscribes to.

If one accepts only the *harm to others* principle, one should be opposed to the legal prohibition of prostitution, provided it involves only consenting adults. Even a widely interpreted conception of public harms seems to call only for certain restrictions relating to marketing and a measure of regulation in order to protect public health. The *offense to feelings* principle leads to the same practical conclusions: the feelings of the public can be sufficiently protected by restricting prostitution and related activities in appropriate ways, so that persons whose feelings are liable to be offended need not be exposed to them.

Paternalistic arguments for legal suppression of prostitution point out its occupational hazards: venereal diseases, violent behavior of clients, exploitation by madams and pimps, extremely low social status and social ostracism of prostitutes. These arguments are flawed, as such hazards are for the most part brought about or greatly increased by the very legal prohibition of prostitution they are meant to justify (and the concomitant condemnation of prostitution by conventional morality). Not all paternalistic arguments are circular in this way, however: hazards to the personal sex life of the prostitute are real, considerable, and not a consequence of the illegality of prostitution, but rather inherent to it. Still, if paternalistic laws are only to protect the individuals from their decisions and actions that are not (fully) voluntary (*weak* paternalism), these hazards can only justify legal prohibition of prostitution by minors or incompetent adults, and provisions that make sure that the choice of prostitution as an occupation is reasonably free and informed (which, as a matter of fact, it very often is not). If paternalistic legislation is to go beyond this, and to prevent competent adults from making a free and informed decision to engage in commercial sex, it will have to be based on a moral conception of what is good or proper for human beings admittedly alien to the individuals whose liberty is infringed. However, this (*strong*) version of paternalism is much less attractive as a liberty-limiting principle; it is not an independent principle at all, but merely a version of legal moralism.

Legal moralism is an appropriate ground for making prostitution illegal in societies where moral condemnation of prostitution is widespread and strong enough. This liberty-limiting principle is so controversial, however, that arguments proceeding from it are unlikely to gain general acceptance.

Today, the most lively and theoretically interesting opposition to prostitution comes from feminists. Although a critical attitude to prostitution is adopted by most currents of contemporary feminism, the view that mercenary sex should be legally prohibited is not. The balance of argument on the legal status of prostitution is clearly in favor of decriminalization.

The Morality of Prostitution

Some hold that commercial sex is morally wrong, to be avoided, and, if possible, eradicated as a social practice (although not necessarily suppressed by law). This view is shared by many moral and social conservatives and by many feminists. Others adopt the liberal or contractarian view of prostitution, claiming that it is not morally wrong as such, and that as long as there is no violation of basic moral rules prohibiting coercion, deception, and exploitation (which apply to sex just as to anything else), commercial sex should be seen on a par with any other commercial activity.

Perhaps the most popular argument for the immorality of prostitution is that some things simply are not for sale and that sex is one of them. While the first part of this claim is surely compelling, the second is less so. It is usually based either on the traditional view of sex as bound up with marriage and procreation, or on the understanding of sex as part of important personal relationships characterized by mutual feelings of closeness, concern, love, and the like. However, adherents of the marriage-and-reproduction view of sex should not judge prostitution too harshly. They should rather tolerate it, since it does not endanger, but complements and strengthens the institution of marriage. Research carried out in the United States and the United Kingdom has shown that approximately three quarters of prostitutes' clients are men who are and intend to stay married, and who resort to prostitutes in order to obtain sexual gratification they do not receive from their spouses. The other, "sentimentalist" view of sex can be plausibly advanced only as a moral ideal, and not as a norm that should, or indeed could, be imposed and backed up by the threat of moral sanctions for noncompliance. Therefore it cannot be the ground for moral condemnation of casual sex in general and prostitution in particular. Such sex falls short of the ideal, but that does not even show that it has no value at all, let alone that it is positively morally wrong.

Another line of argument is that prostitution is immoral because it is degrading. It may be considered degrading either because mercenary sex is impersonal or merely instrumental, or on account of the intimate character of sex, or because the prostitute sells her body, herself. The first two arguments are incomplete. Much of social intercourse is impersonal and instrumental, and it should be shown, rather than assumed, that *only* individuals interested in each other as persons, or brought together by mutual sexual love, may engage in sex acts. The argument from intimacy seems to commit one to the implausible conclusion that a nurse attending to the intimate hygiene of a disabled patient is doing something degrading and morally wrong. Finally, what the prostitute sells is, strictly speaking, neither her body nor herself, but rather a specific sexual service.

Feminist critics of prostitution insist that we should try to understand and evaluate it within its social and cultural context, rather than in the abstract. When approached in this way, it can be seen to be implicated in the inequality and oppression of women. Now this does not apply to many noncapitalist societies, nor indeed to all types of prostitution that exist in capitalist societies. However, it may well be true of many, if not most, varieties of mercenary sex characteristic of contemporary capitalist society. Thus feminist critics do have an important point, not about prostitution as such, but about a considerable part of the practice as it exists in our society: when we attend to the actually existing mercenary sex in our own society, we find that much of it does express and reinforce the inequality and oppression of women. In so far as it does, it is indeed morally unacceptable.

References

Ericsson, Lars O. "Charges against Prostitution: An Attempt at Philosophical Assessment." *Ethics* 90 (1979/1980), 335–366.

Jaggar, Alison M. "Prostitution." In *The Philosophy of Sex: Contemporary Readings,* 2d ed., ed. Alan Soble, 259–280. Savage MD: Rowman and Littlefield, 1991.

Pateman, Carole. *The Sexual Contract.* Cambridge: Polity Press, 1988.

Primoratz, Igor. "What's Wrong with Prostitution?" *Philosophy* 68 (1993), 159–182. Reprinted in *Human Sexuality,* ed. Igor Primoratz. Aldershot: Ashgate, 1997.

Richards, David A.J. *Sex, Drugs, Death, and the Law.* Totowa NJ: Rowman and Littlefield, 1982.

Schwarzenbach, Sybil. "Contractarians and Feminists Debate Prostitution." *New York University Review of Law and Social Change* 18 (1990/1991), 103–130. Reprinted in *Human Sexuality,* ed. Igor Primoratz. Aldershot: Ashgate, 1997.

Shrage, Laurie. *Moral Dilemmas of Feminism: Prostitution, Adultery, and Abortion.* New York: Routledge, 1994.

Igor Primoratz

See also CRIMINALIZATION; DRUGS; DUELING; PATERNALISM; WRONGDOING AND RIGHT ACTING

Psychiatry

The interaction between law and psychiatry has not always been a happy or productive one. The value systems of each are different and often sharply conflicting. Lawyers stress civil liberties and individual rights; psychiatrists emphasize their role in helping people without expressing particular concern for their rights. Any account, therefore, of the relationship between law and psychiatry must inevitably address the conflict between the disciplines. One sees this conflict particularly in the debate over civil commitment where the battle lines are drawn around the conceptual issue of whether mental illness is a disease and the normative issue of when it is appropriate to limit a person's liberty.

In the 1970s, when the antipsychiatry movement enlisted lawyers in an effort to eliminate civil commitment, a group of lawyers led by Bruce Ennis championed Thomas Szasz's controversial claim that most alleged cases of mental illness are not illnesses at all but instances of social deviancy; as such, they are beyond the realm of the health professional's expertise and represent a coercive attempt to keep "undesirables" at bay. Against this view, mainstream psychiatrists argued that mental illness was a disease that necessitated treatment when the patients were dangerous to themselves or others.

Whether or not mental illness is a disease ultimately depends upon a satisfactory analysis of the concept of "disease." Construed narrowly, "disease" means disease *of the body.* From the libertarian's perspective, any broader interpretation invariably contains a value judgment suggesting that psychiatry is a form of social control. The history of medical views on masturbation is a case in point. In the eighteenth and nineteenth centuries, when sexual activity was thought to be bad for the soul, masturbation was believed to be a dangerous disease.

While not denying that "disease" means disease of the body, mainstream psychiatrists see mental illness as a disease which, affecting the brain, manifests itself in aberrant behavior. Not unlike a diseased pancreas, which manifests itself in diabetes, since it is the pancreas's job to secrete insulin, a diseased brain manifests itself by aberrant behavior, since it is the brain's job to regulate conduct. To psychiatrists, their work is no more value-laden than the work of endocrinologists.

One's position on the status of mental illness will often determine one's position on involuntary civil commitment. If mental illness is not a disease in any respectable sense of the term, then civil commitment represents a violation of due process. Conversely, if mental illness is a disease, then psychiatry may be justified in treating noncompliant patients when these patients are dangerous to themselves or others. Citing the right to self-determination, antipsychiatry lawyers argue that we have more to fear from psychiatrists depriving patients of their civil liberties than we have from patients presenting a danger to society. Psychiatrists, on the other hand, cite the relative unimportance of such a right in dysfunctional or dangerous psychotic individuals as well as the reversibility of psychosis through medical treatment. No mainstream psychiatrist will deny the right of a person to be psychotic so long as the person presents no danger to himself or herself, although there is considerable debate over what this entails. Mainstream psychiatrists argue that a person's inability to take care of himself or herself on account of mental illness presents a danger to that person. Antipsychiatry lawyers maintain that such an analysis of "danger" is too broad to be of service and carries with it the potential for abuse.

Because today there is a general consensus that "patients" who are acutely ill and dangerous may be committed and treated without their consent, the real issue concerns patients who while not presently dangerous to themselves or others are *potentially* dangerous. The typical scenario involves the patient who is involuntarily treated while acutely ill, responds to therapy, and promises to again become dangerous upon being released. The hard question is what to do with these patients when, judging by their past history, they are noncompliant outside the hospital setting. On one hand, the Fifth Amendment protects them from being committed against their will if they are in no imminent danger to themselves or others. On the other hand, in the absence of policing, such patients typically become dangerous and a threat to society. In this regard, psychiatry has become a victim of its own success.

To be sure, there are other issues in which law and psychiatry intersect and which are philosophically interesting. Perhaps the most interesting of these is the insanity defense, which has come under recent attack and has been eliminated in certain jurisdictions. If it is true that moral responsibility is binding only upon people who are accountable for their actions, then those whose criminal conduct stems from schizophrenia and manic-depressive illness should not be responsible for their crimes any more than a person who strikes another during an epileptic seizure. Whether this philosophical truism extends to criminal misconduct owing to PMS, "black rage," or "parental abuse" is a question that has recently been debated and is likely to receive further attention.

References

Bloch, Sidney, and Paul Chodoff. *Psychiatric Ethics*. Oxford: Oxford University Press, 1981.

Brooks, Alexander C. *Law, Psychiatry and the Mental Health System*. Boston: Little, Brown, 1974.

Isaac, Rael Jean, and Virginia C. Armat. *Madness in the Streets: How Psychiatry and the Law Abandoned the Mentally Ill*. Glencoe IL: Free Press, 1990.

Haber, Joram Graf. "The Freedom to Be Psychotic?" *Journal of Law and Health* (1987–1988), 157–71. Reprinted in *The International Library of Essays in Law and Legal Theory: Medicine and the Law*. Ed. Bernard M. Dickens. Brookfield VT: Dartmouth, 1993.

Jacob, Joseph. "The Right of the Mental Patient to His Psychosis." *The Modern Law Review* 39 (1976), 17–42. Reprinted in *The International Library of Essays in Law and Legal Theory: Medicine and the Law*. Ed. Bernard M. Dickens. Brookfield VT: Dartmouth, 1993.

Joram Graf Haber
Lina Levit Haber

See also Insanity Defense; Preventive Detention

Public and Private Jurisdictions

In legal, as well as in political, philosophy there is a constant need to distinguish the public from the private realms of human existence. In western culture the separation of the public domain from that of the private is traceable to Aristotle, who thought that the polis offered greater opportunities for a full life than could be realized within the more restricted domestic realm. While law has been less concerned than political theory with the maintenance of such elementary distinctions, they do have jurisprudential significance. Problems of jurisdiction and the scope of legal authority often engage the division between public and private life that originated within the classical tradition of political philosophy.

Western legal systems have always regulated important aspects of family life. With the decline of ecclesiastical jurisdiction, secular law has assumed an even greater authority over vital domestic matters such as marriage, divorce, and inheritance. The attack of modern feminism upon the classical public-private dualism has put increased pressure upon the law to extend its jurisdiction more deeply into family life. To the ancients, the life of the household was not of intrinsic importance, but modern feminism has demonstrated the fallacy of this conception. Its critiques have led to some important reforms, such as increased attention by the criminal law to the problem of domestic violence. However, there are some deeper reasons why law has traditionally maintained some distance from the intimacies of domestic life.

The limits to the coercive power of law are often not fully appreciated. Some of these limits can be understood within the framework of the public-private distinction. Intimacy generates emotion. When passion rules a relationship, the writ of law is powerless. Domestic conflicts engage intense feelings; although law must prevent, as well as punish, overt wrongdoing, it cannot change how one person in such an intimate relationship feels about another. Moreover, in order to administer justice, law must treat the parties to any conflict as mutually distinct from one another. This externality is, as Immanuel Kant noted, an aspect of the public quality of law.

Externality also limits the jural regulation of evil actions. In his *Treatise on Law* St. Thomas Aquinas taught that human law could not repress all vices but only the most serious wrongs, whose prohibition is indispensable to civilized life. Such wrongs, in addition to being overt, also must be amenable to proof by objective criteria. These aspects of the public-private distinction can be seen in the developing law of sexual harassment in the workplace. The Supreme Court held in *Harris v. Forklift Systems*, 114 S.Ct. 367 (1993), that one has a cause of action for harassment only if, in addition to the perception of harm in the mind of the complainant, the circumstances are such that a reasonable person would have considered the environment to be hostile or abusive.

Abortion is another area which places great strains upon the public-private distinction within the law. On the one hand, the decision of a pregnant woman as to the future of the pregnancy is an intensely private matter. Since the choice deeply engages her emotional and moral life, it is resistant to external coercive authority. However, the practice of widespread abortion profoundly affects the community at large. Every civilized society has some responsibility to protect innocent life. In trying to delineate the jurisdiction of law in the field of abortion, courts and legislatures have tried to strike some balance between the public and private dimensions of this controversial issue. An example of this can be found in *Planned Parenthood of Southeastern Pennsylvania v. Casey*, 112 S.Ct. 2791 (1992).

The tension between the public and private aspects of human conflict can be seen in other areas where law has struggled to establish its legitimate jurisdiction. Historically, law came into existence as a substitute for private vengeance, and this development laid the foundations for the criminal law, as well as the law of tort, which compels restitution for private injuries. As for crimes, the essential advance was the recognition that an act of violence was a public wrong punishable by the state. In modern life, the private aspects of violence—its effects upon the victims and their families—has gained renewed attention. This is, in part, the result of the influence of the mass media, which tends to make every aspect of social existence a matter of personal concern.

Those who suffer, directly or indirectly, because of the actions of criminals, are now more able to express their grievances before the courts. In some jurisdictions they can gain public compensation for their losses and also have some influence upon both the severity and the longevity of the punishment. How far these practices can be extended without compromising the paramount jurisdiction of public law is an interesting and important question. The impartiality of the legal process, as well the ability of governing authority to show mercy, can be jeopardized if the requirements of justice become indistinguishable from demands for revenge.

To Aristotle, the domestic realm was inferior to the public world because the home was the locus of economy as well as of reproductive labor. In the modern world, domestic cottage industries and crafts have been replaced by large corporations, which, far from home, produce goods and services on a massive scale. As the modern economy becomes the dominant social reality, it assumes a public importance. This shift away from domesticity has implications for law as well as for politics.

Economic analyses of law abound, and the preeminence of economics has led to a reformulation of the ideals of justice. Classical law was inspired by a tripartite vision of justice. It governed relations between individuals (commutative justice), the claims which the individual could make upon the state (distributive justice), and the claims which the state could make upon the individual (legal justice). The "law and economics" school of contemporary jurisprudence virtually eliminates the last two categories and restricts the jurisdiction of the law primarily to the first. Commutative justice, which regulates the domain of private transactions, is of central importance.

Economists see most problems of justice as arising out of individual initiatives and personal relations which have acquistion and exchange as their objective. The law of property, contract, and commercial transactions are considered to be the essential legal subjects in a market-oriented democracy. Developments in areas such as product liability are limited by the desire to give license to free enterprise.

This reduction of the public to the private is inspired by a liberal ideology. Classical distributive justice addressed the relation between the individual and the larger society, thus enlarging the scope of personal responsibility. Products liability, for example, would be more complicated once the distributive, as well as the commutative, dimensions are taken into account. This perspective is being replaced by a paradigm of isolated individuals whose only relations are those of mutual advantage. For economists, arithmetic equality takes precedence over geometric proportion. Neither the relative position of the individual within society nor his or her particular circumstances have any relevance to the distribution of societal burdens and benefits.

To close the gap between public and private life one must assume that the political and the personal are indistinguishable, but legal reason and method are largely impersonal. Through dialogue and persuasion the process of law attempts to create a shared conception of right and justice. This requires public collaboration with others who are different from ourselves. The appeal of legal discourse is to aspects of reasonableness which are matters of common understanding.

The collective realization of the ends of law requires inclusive participation and the widest possible range of meaning. This calls forth a *philia*, or civic friendship, which transcends self-absorption. Law must be compassionate, but it must also draw upon a general range of values which can be dispassionately applied. To do complete justice there must be the enforcement of public values—such as due process of law—which are of critical importance to human freedom.

References

Anderson, David C. "Expressive Justice Is All the Rage." *New York Times Magazine* (Jan. 15 1995), 36.

Aquinas, Thomas. *Treatise on Law*. Chicago: Henry Regnery, 1963.

Arendt, Hannah. *The Human Condition*. Chicago: University of Chicago Press, 1962.

Dabin, Jean. "General Theory of Law." In *Legal Philosophies of Lask, Radbruch and Dabin,* vol. 4 of *Twentieth Century Legal Philosophers Series,* trans. K. Wilk. Cambridge MA: Harvard University Press, 1950.

Finnis, John. *Natural Law and Natural Rights*. Oxford: Clarendon Press, 1980.

Fletcher, George. *Rethinking Criminal Law*. Boston: Little, Brown, 1978.

Kant, Immanuel. *The Metaphysical Elements of Justice*. 1797. Indianapolis: Liberal Arts Press, 1965.

Nozick, Robert. *Anarchy, State, and Utopia*. 1974. Boston: Little, Brown, 1986.

Posner, Richard. *Economic Analysis of Law*. 3d ed. Boston: Little, Brown, 1986.

Taylor, Charles. *The Ethics of Authenticity*. Cambridge MA: Harvard University Press, 1992.

Cornelius Murphy

See also FAMILY LAW; MARRIAGE CONTRACT; PRIVATE LAW; STATE ACTION

Pufendorf, Samuel (1632–1694)

Samuel Pufendorf was born in a Saxon village near Chemnitz, Germany, in the same year as John Locke and Baruch Spinoza. They were the dark times of the Thirty Years' War. He studied theology, then jurisprudence, at the University of Leipzig, and he was taught philosophy at Jena by the cartesian thinker Erhard Weigel, who was also to become a friend. He entered the diplomatic service, and in 1660, in very difficult political circumstances, wrote and published his first work, the *Elementa jurisprudentiae universalis* (Elements of Universal Jurisprudence), which applies Weigel's method, *more geometrico* (geometric method). Carl-Ludwig, Elector of the Palatine, to whom the book is dedicated, offered him a chair of natural law at the University of Heidelberg. After the publication of *De statu Imperii Germanici* (The State of the German Empire) in 1667, he was severely criticized and chose to accept the post offered him by the King of Sweden, Charles XI, at the University of Lund. Here he composed his greatest work, the *De jure naturae et gentium* (Natural Law and the Law of Nature), published in 1672, followed, in 1673, by the *De officio hominis et civis juxta legem naturalem* (The Obligation of Man and Citizen According to Natural Law).

Charles XI invited Pufendorf to Stockholm, where he fully satisfied the monarch's expectations by writing a Swedish history, *Eris Scandina,* in 1673. Later, Pufendorf set out for Berlin, where he wrote and dedicated his *De habitu religionis christianae ad vitam civilem* (The Christian Religion in Civil Life) to Frederic-Guillaume—a book of ethics more than of jurisprudence, but in which the sensitive problems of the times (individual liberty, tolerance, authority of the Church) are broached. In his last book, *Jus feciale divinum* (Special Divine Law), Pufendorf expressed his point of view on civil and religious peace. True to his doctrine, he continued to develop his ideas in terms of the strong principle of natural law. In 1694, King Charles XI accorded him the dignity of Swedish Free Baron. Pufendorf died in the same year. He was an extraordinary scholar. While his work evoked both jealousies and eulogies, his great reputation has not diminished. Gottfried Leibniz's word, *Parum jurisconsultus et minime philosophus* (hardly a jurist and less a philosopher), is unfair. Pufendorf remains, along with Hugo Grotius, of whom he is a fearsome critic, the strongest exponent of natural law theory.

The originality of Pufendorf's work lies in his rational and systematic architectonic (it is, says Pufendorf, a "systematic science of natural law"), as well as in its ontological foundation in the fundamental law decreed by divine will.

From 1660 on, and particularly in the *Elementa jurisprudentiae universalis*, Pufendorf expresses the idea of rationality that sustains his juridical and ethical reflection. His working method is clear: he starts from definitions and axioms in order to deduce, *more geometrico*, their logical consequences. "Jurisprudential science" must be built on undoubted principles by a *concatenatio,* or series, of rules which, as he says in a letter to Johann Christian Boineburg, is made possible by a deductivist method. In the *De jure naturae et gentium*, Pufendorf emphasizes, however, the difference in approach necessary for considering *corpora naturalia* and *corpora moralia*. Indeed, there is an irreducible ontological gap between *entia physica* and *entia moralia* (physical entities, moral entities). Hugo Grotius and Thomas Hobbes are simply wrong in believing that there can be the same certainty in moral as in physical or mathematical sciences. Consequently, says Pufendorf, the experimental observation of the human condition must satisfy the a priori dictates of reason. He also explains meticulously to his Swedish objectors that the *lex fundamentalis* (fundamental law) of his system is not a rational postulate but a principle derived from human nature and known from observation.

The philosophical foundation of the system is more important, however, than its methodological aspects. Pufendorf explains that everywhere in the universe human nature, created by God according to his supreme and transcendent will, is governed by the *lex naturalis*. This natural law is not a law of nature, but the rule or the supreme norm by which God introduces meaning, order, and value in the human world, the world where the *entia moralia* are able to add a work of culture to their primitive nature. It is the rule uniting liberty and nature. In their specific area, humans must obey natural law because it is the order of a superior: it takes, for them, the prescriptive form of command and obligation to obey.

Natural law is, therefore, principally an ethical rule. If it is true, as Hobbes and Spinoza contend, that its first expression is a *jus naturae,* which means an original will of life, it cannot be understood as a scheme of individualistic naturalism. Humans are not insular beings. In so far as natural law governs nature as a whole, it is fundamentally a rule of *sociability*. This means that it is not only an inclination to live in society, but an *obligation* to work for the general good of the largest human community. Consequently, natural law as *norma agendi* (norm for acting) carries its regulative power, its intrinsic normativity, in all forms of society, in private as well as public affairs. It governs the *jus rerum* (the law of things, for instance property or usufruit) and the *jus personarum* (the law of persons, for example, parental or domestic power). In the analysis of these notions, Pufendorf always accords priority to human dignity. This is why he condemns unreservedly theft, fraud, and slavery. In civil societies (whose emergence he explains by the three moments of a social contract: *pactum unionis, pactum ordinationis, pactum subjectionis*; the agreements to unite, to achieve order, and to accept authority), the political law, with respect to the sovereign as well as the citizens, is never independent of the ethical components of natural law. It would never have occurred to Pufendorf to pose jurisprudence in terms of autonomy and to justify it in terms of natural law alone. The legal order and moral orders are founded in the metaphysical teleology of divine natural law. When Pufendorf discusses the law of nations (*jus gentium*), he shows that it proceeds in its various manifestations from the rational capacities by which humans understand and actualize natural law inscribed in the world by divine will. In such a thesis, he widens Francisco Suaréz's theory of law, according to which divine power and human power cooperate to build a legislative apparatus. Pufendorf extends this idea beyond the state's frontiers to the community of the whole human species.

Many interpreters have found in this universalistic view the roots of our modern international law, but Pufendorf's merit is elsewhere. Thinker of justice, order, and peace, he holds that everyone has the *duty* to assume obligations dictated by natural law, that national frontiers cannot alter the imperative character of natural law, that even warring states are bound by this law. The law of nations must define the norms governing relations between states before war, during hostilities, and after war. When conventions dictate the behavior of belligerent parties, their pacts, agreements, and alliances can be drawn according to natural law alone. Thus, their ultimate and transcendent basis ties them to a holy and inviolable oath.

In all his work, philosophical, historical, or theological, Pufendorf develops the same strong idea of natural law. However, it would be a singular error to read this work as if it adopts the individualistic and rationalist premises of occidental modern philosophy. For Pufendorf, natural law is the principle of unity put into the world by the transcendent will of God. With this thesis, he remains tributory to the largest body of classical and medieval philosophy. The influence of stoic morals, and especially the idea of harmony between humans and nature, is present in his manner of thinking about the probity of human action. This is why he says morality and law in the areas of private and public law are always inseparable. In proposing his directives for the law of nations, he makes the classical notion of bona fides a fundamental principle requiring that positive conventions between states be bound by it. Although Pufendorf refers to concepts such as moral person, individual consciousness, goodwill, responsibility, tolerance, and so on, his theory of law of nations is marked by the imperative duty inscribed in natural law: the *ethical obligation to obey the principle of sociability*. Refusing the individualistic perspectives of rationalist humanism in which he foresees a danger for the cultural and spiritual destiny of humanity, and consequently not yet near the enlightened ideas of the eighteenth century, he remains tied to a very classical conception of morals and jurisprudence in his theory of natural law.

References

Carr, Craig L. "Pufendorf, Sociality and the Modern State." *History of Political Thought* 17 (1996), 354–378.

Diesselhorst, M. *Zum Vermögenrechtssystem Samuel Pufendorf* (Samuel Pufendorf's System of Legal Power). Göttingen: Schwartz, 1976.

Fiorillo, V. *Tra egoismo e socialità: Il giusnaturalismo di Samuel Pufendorf* (Between Egoism and Socialism: The Natural Law of Samuel Pufendorf). Naples: Joveni Editore, 1992.

Goyard-Fabre, S. *Pufendorf et le droit naturel* (Pufendorf and Natural Law). Paris: Presses universitaires de France, 1994.

Krieger, Leonard. "History and Law in the Seventeenth Century: Pufendorf." *Journal of the History of Ideas* 21 (1960), 198–210.

Pufendorf, Samuel. *On the Duty of Man and Citizen According to Natural Law*. Ed. James Tully. Trans. Michael Silverthorne. Cambridge: Cambridge University Press, 1991.

———. *On the Law of Nature and Nations. Eight Books*. Trans. Basil Kennet. London: R. Sare, 1717.

———. *The Political Writings of S. Pufendorf*. Ed. Craig Carr. Trans. Michael Silverthorne. Oxford: Oxford University Press, 1994.

———. *Samuel Pufendorf's On the Natural State of Men*. Trans. Michael Seidler. Lewiston NY: Edwin Mellen Press, 1990.

Seidler, Michael. "Religion, Populism, and Patriarchy: Political Authority from Luther to Pufendorf." *Ethics* 103 (1993), 373.

Skinner, Andrew S. "Pufendorf, Hutcheson and Adam Smith: Some Principles of Political Economy." *Scottish Journal of Political Economy* 42 (1995), 165.

Simone Goyard-Fabre

Punishment

History, literature, religion, and practical observation all suggest that punishment has always played a central role in organizing human relationships. For many reasons, this is neither surprising nor troubling. For other reasons, it is both. To understand the phenomenon and the moral challenges it poses, both perspectives need careful exploration.

Human relationships are characteristically rule governed. There are many reasons for this. At various stages of life, human beings are incapable of meeting even their most basic needs without the help of others. Each of us needs the support and protection of adults if we are to survive. At every stage of our lives, each of us is vulnerable to physical assault, theft, and the destruction of property. Rules provide the framework for mutual assistance and cooperation. They help to define what is permitted and what is prohibited. If they are not enforced they cannot do their job, and cooperation becomes more difficult or perhaps even impossible.

Punishment has a natural place in this picture. It responds to the anger, resentment, and sense of injustice that those who break basic rules generate. It acts as a disincentive. It is one way of ensuring that those who respect the rules do not end up worse off than those who do not.

On the other hand, punishment is morally problematic. One of the most basic rules of civilized society is that deliberately inflicting pain and suffering on others always requires careful justification. Punishment has in the past almost always been accompanied by pain and suffering sometimes of a brutal and barbaric nature. Even today, capital punishment is widely practiced. Even where it has been abolished, offenders can be and frequently are sentenced to very long prison terms in institutions where living conditions are difficult, monotonous, and frequently dangerous. Yet punishment, particularly harsh punishment, has not been shown to be an efficient or an effective tool of enforcement. In additional, typically, the weight of punishment falls most heavily on the poor and the marginalized members of society.

For all of these reasons punishment needs to be justified both in principle and in practice. Providing this justification requires answers to four questions: Is the practice of punishment *ever* justifiable and if so under what conditions? What *kinds* of punishment are justified and must they involve suffering? *Whom* are we entitled to punish? *Who* is morally entitled to inflict punishment?

Traditionally, the responses to these questions have been either backward looking or forward looking. Backward-looking justifications see punishment as a response to moral wrongdoing. An offense by its very nature creates an injustice by inflicting an unmerited harm on a victim or by conferring an undeserved and unfair benefit on the offender. The purpose of punishment is to remove the undeserved benefit and correct the harm done by imposing a penalty or hardship on the offender that matches the seriousness of the offense committed. According to this account of the matter, punishment constitutes just retribution for voluntary or intentional wrongdoing.

Retributivist justifications of punishment are found in Greek, medieval, and modern western philosophy and are deeply embedded in Jewish, Christian, and Muslim theology, though in none of these faith-traditions are they the only account of punishment offered. They have been articulated and defended by some of the most influential philosophers in the history of modern thought, for example, Immanuel Kant and G.W.F. Hegel. Finally, retributivist justifications have had a profound impact on the development of western legal institutions. The law of evidence, the requirement that guilt be established beyond a reasonable doubt, and the principle of mens rea all testify to this fact.

The most common and pressing concern with retributivism is its association in the minds of many with the idea of vengeance. Conflating the two, however, is unjustified. The pursuit of vengeance or revenge is almost always undisciplined and intemperate. Those seeking revenge frequently misjudge the harm or wrong to which they are responding and react in an excessively harsh manner, perpetrating in their turn further injustice. The result is frequently a revenge cycle with escalating responses from which there seems no escape. Consequently, though vengeance is frequently exacted in the name of just retribution, it rarely has that quality. In contrast, just retribution is assumed to require impartial judges, guided by laws that ensure a fair trial, who are directed to ensure that punishment fits the crimes committed and is imposed only on those persons found guilty in a court of law for the offense for which they are to be punished.

Retributive justifications of punishment face other tests that are not so easily parried, however. Justifying an appropriate system of tariffs or penalties is one. Here popular appeal is frequently made to the *lex talionis*, "An eye for an eye and a tooth for a tooth." Yet such formulas quickly break down in the face of the ingenuity with which human beings inflict unjustified harm on each other. What, for example, does the *lex talionis* recommend as an appropriate penalty for brutal sexual assault, defamation of character, dishonesty, kidnapping, or terrorism? On the other hand, if the *lex talionis* is abandoned, retributivists are left with a principle of proportionality that recommends simply that the punishment inflicted vary with the moral seriousness of the offense committed. While this advice is clearly of some value, it provides no guidance in determining the kinds of punishments that are morally justifiable, capital punishment, for example, or corporal punishment, or solitary confinement, or heavy fines, and so on.

Retributivist accounts have been criticized on other grounds as well. Their critics argue that they conflate legal and moral wrongdoing in ways that seem particularly inappropriate in modern western pluralistic societies. They appear to leave little room for important values, like compassion, forgiveness, and mercy, when responding to offenders. Perhaps the most telling criticism, however, is that retributivism requires that the guilty be punished even when it is clear that neither the offender being punished nor the community will benefit directly as a result.

In contrast to retributivism, forward-looking justifications require that punishment be administered only where it confers benefits that outweigh the suffering it imposes. Traditionally those benefits have been of two sorts, benefits accruing to the individual being punished and benefits accruing to victims and society. For many people, the idea that punishment might be imposed with a view to the welfare of the person being punished has a paradoxical character. Nevertheless, it is deeply entrenched historically in discussions of the subject, for example, the Old Testament book of Job and Plato's *Protagoras*. Theories of punishment in this category are typically welfare oriented and focus on punishment as a tool of rehabilitation, treatment, correction, reform, or moral education.

Deterrence-oriented theories have also been advanced to justify punishment. One of the benefits of this approach is that it seems to provide clear guidance as well as clear limits in sentencing offenders. In this view no punishment should be inflicted that imposes more harm or suffering on the offender than it prevents by deterring the offender from repeating the crime or by reducing the likelihood that others will follow in the offender's footsteps.

Although both welfare-oriented and deterrence-oriented theories have found varied and sophisticated defenders and have exerted considerable influence on the development of punishment and sentencing theory in this century, it is generally conceded that both are subject to the same telling criticism. If the goal is purely forward looking, why punish only those who break the law intentionally or voluntarily? Why wait for people who pose a threat to society to commit offenses before requiring that they undergo treatment or rehabilitation? Indeed, why not replace the moralistic language of guilt and innocence, punishment and retribution with the vocabulary of treatment, rehabilitation, and behavior modification, for example? In short, it is not at all clear that there is room in purely forward-looking theories of punishment for the idea of justice.

These telling criticisms of the two traditional justifications of punishment have stimulated a wide range of responses. Some theorists (for example Jeffrie Murphy and Jean Hampton, Wesley Cragg) turned their attention to a re-examination of retributivism and its relation to justice, mercy, forgiveness, hate, and resentment. Others (for example, R.A. Duff, Jacob Adler) have attempted to connect secular notions of punishment with the idea of penance. Attempts have been made to construct hybrid accounts of punishment combining the best features of retributivist and utilitarian justifications (for example, H.L.A. Hart, R.A. Duff) and have been extensively criticized (for example, Nicola Lacey, Wesley Cragg). The relationship between punishment and suffering or hard treatment has been extensively explored. Finally, the function and role of punishment in law enforcement, sentencing, and corrections has been analyzed.

Two conclusions emerge from the contemporary debates over the nature and role of punishment in a modern democratic society. First, the concept of punishment is complex and contested. Second, in spite of the failure of modern punishment theory to provide a convincing, persuasive justification, formal instruments of punishment continue to be regarded by theorists and the public alike as essential components of contemporary society.

References

Adler, Jacob. *The Urgings of Conscience: A Theory of Punishment.* Philadelphia: Temple University Press, 1991.

Bentham, Jeremy. "Principles of Penal Law." In *The Works of Jeremy Bentham,* vol. 1, ed. J. Bowing. Edinburgh: W. Tait, 1838.

Cragg, Wesley. *The Practice of Punishment: Toward a Theory of Restorative Justice.* London: Routledge, 1992.

Duff, R.A. *Trials and Punishments.* Cambridge: Cambridge University Press, 1986.

Hart, H.L.A. *Punishment and Responsibility.* Oxford: Clarendon Press, 1968.

Hegel, G.W.F. *Philosophy of Right*. Trans. T.M. Knox. Oxford: Oxford University Press, 1942.

Honderich, Ted. *Punishment: The Supposed Justifications*. Harmondsworth: Penguin Books, 1969.

Kant, Immanuel. *Philosophy of Law*. Trans. E. Hastie. Edinburgh, 1887.

Lacey, Nicola. *State Punishment*. London: Routledge, 1988.

Martin, Rex. *A System of Rights*. Oxford: Clarendon Press, 1993.

Murphy, Jeffrie G., and Jean Hampton. *Forgiveness and Mercy*. Cambridge: Cambridge University Press, 1988.

Plato. *Protagoras*. In *The Great Dialogues of Plato,* trans. W.H.D. Rouse. New York: Mentor Books, 1956.

A. Wesley Cragg

See also DESERT; DETERRENT RATIONALE; EXPRESSIVE RATIONALE FOR PUNISHMENT; INCAPACITATIVE RATIONALE; MIXED RATIONALES; REHABILITATION AND HABILITATION RATIONALE; RETRIBUTIVE RATIONALE; SENTENCING; VENGEANCE

Punitive Damages

The common law routinely allows the award of damages in civil suits to *compensate the plaintiff*. "Punitive damages" refers to the award of damages in civil suits to *punish the defendant*. The common law traditionally allowed punitive damages only in a narrow class of torts such as slander, in which the injurer harms the victim's dignity. American state courts and legislatures have expanded the class of cases that permit punitive damages to include many civil wrongs in which the defendant's moral culpability goes beyond negligence. A recent study disclosed that eight of America's fifty states allow the award of punitive damages for gross negligence, while thirty-seven require intentional wrongdoing or something similar, such as "malice," "wanton and reckless" behavior, "callous disregard" for safety of others, or "deliberate exposure to undue risk."

The award of punitive damages outside the narrow class of dignitary torts is unusual in America and unknown in many other countries. Even so, punitive damages represent a significant risk to some American defendants. Juries set punitive damages with minimum guidance from judges, so awards are unpredictable. To illustrate, the ratio of punitive damages to compensatory damages awarded recently by juries varied from as low as 1/10 to as high as 410,000/1, and jury in one recent case awarded $5 billion in punitive damages. Furthermore, many private insurance contracts do not cover liability for punitive damages, and some states outlaw insurance against liability for punitive damages. There is little wonder that defendants continue to argue (without success so far) that punitive damages fall under the prohibition of excessive fines by the Eighth Amendment to the United States Constitution.

When sued for punitive damages, the defendant risks criminal punishment without receiving the protections of a criminal proceeding. For example, the plaintiff must prove his case by the "preponderance of the evidence," as opposed to "beyond a reasonable doubt." This fact has prompted debate about the purpose and justification of punitive damages. Three rationales are offered.

First, punitive damages may be awarded as a surrogate for compensatory damages in cases where punishment is easier to quantify than injured dignity. This rationale should receive little weight today, regardless of its historical importance, because compensation now extends to all manner of ephemeral harms.

Second, scale economies in adjudication imply that deciding the two issues of compensation and punishment in a single trial, rather than having two separate trials, saves transaction costs. Thus the private plaintiff may assert that he should be "rewarded" with punitive damages for doing the state prosecutor's work.

Third, punitive damages reduce the frequency with which wrongdoing goes unpunished. The frequency may be reduced in two ways. First, the private plaintiff may provide the resources and motivation that the public prosecutor lacks to punish some defendants. Second, the private plaintiff enjoys the advantages of a civil procedure, whereas the public prosecutor suffers the disadvantage of criminal procedures. Reducing the frequency with which wrongdoing goes unpunished serves the goals of retribution and deterrence.

When should punitive damages be awarded? How large should they be? American court practice is currently lawless in the sense that predicting punitive damages is impossible in particular cases from knowledge of the law and a description of the facts. Juries are not receiving sufficiently definite instructions about punitive damages to keep their findings within reasonable bounds. A definite rule for punitive damages can be derived if the damages are used to correct errors, which cause wrongdoing to go undeterred, in assigning liability. For example, if a person who steals $100 faces the probability of getting caught with probability ½, then the enforcement error of ½ can be offset by setting liability equal to $200.

The implicit rule in this example can be stated precisely with the help of some notation. Let L represent the full cost of an accident to its victim. Let D denote damages. Compensation is "perfect" when the victim is indifferent between having the injury and damages, or having no injury and no damages.

$$D = L <=> \text{perfect compensation}$$

Let B denote the (marginal) burden of care. Let p denote the amount by which the probability of an accident increases when the injurer fails to take care B. Thus, spending B reduces expected accident costs by pL. Social efficiency requires taking care when it costs less than the expected savings in accident costs:

$$pL > B <=> \text{take care } B$$
$$pL < B <=> \text{do not take care } B.$$

To provide incentives for social efficiency, courts should declare the defendant "negligent" and impose liability when $pL > B$, whereas courts should declare the defendant "nonnegligent" when $pL < B$. This liability standard, known as the "Hand Rule," was promulgated in *U.S. v. Carroll Towing*, 159 F. 2d 169 (1947), and enshrined in the Second Restatement of Tort as the definition of negligence.

The Hand Rule implicitly assumes that courts apply the formula without error. Specifically, the Hand Rule assumes that negligent injurers are held liable with probability 1. In the absence of error, punitive damages are not needed for deterrence. In the presence of error, however, punitive damages can perform the role of correcting enforcement error. To see why, assume that negligent injurers are held liable with probability q, where $q < 1$. Thus q denotes the probability that the injurer who does not take care B will be held liable for the resulting accident. Instead of weighing the social loss pL against the burden B, a rationally self-interested decision maker will weigh the expected liability qpL against the burden B:

$$qpL > B <=> \text{take care } B$$
$$qpL < B <=> \text{do not take care } B.$$

This behavior results in too little care relative to the efficient level of care prescribed by the Hand Rule.

To see how punitive damages can correct enforcement error, let r represent the ratio by which punishment increases damages above the perfectly compensatory level. Thus the injurer who faces punitive liability must pay total damages equal to rL. A rationally self-interested decision maker will follow the rule:

$$rqpL \geq B <=> \text{take care } B$$
$$rqpL < B <=> \text{do not take care } B.$$

The preceding decision rule reduces to the Hand Rule when $r = 1/q$. In other words, social efficiency is restored when the *punitive multiple r equals the reciprocal of the enforcement probability 1/q*. Setting punitive damages according to this rule minimizes the sum of the cost of wrongdoing and its prevention, as required for optimal deterrence.

Enforcement error has another important behavioral consequence. If the legal standard is clear and precise, the injurer can avoid liability by satisfying it exactly. If, however, the legal standard is vague and uncertain, the injurer may want to exceed the putative standard in order to provide a margin for enforcement error. The injurer will want a margin of error in the event that liability jumps from zero to a large number at the point where precaution falls below the legal standard. Thus uncertainty about the legal standard causes most injurers to *minimize their costs by exceeding* it.

Conversely, the injurer who deliberately falls short of the putative standard risks large liability. Given the large risk, he might just as well save a lot by taking very little care. (In technical terms, there is a discontinuity in liability costs at the legal standard caused by a nonconvexity in the injurer's cost function.) Thus uncertainty about the legal standard causes some injurers to *minimize their costs by deliberately falling far short* of it. This fact provides a behavioral test for intentional harm. If the failure to take care is deliberate, care will usually fall far short of the legal standard. Thus "gross negligence" is a good indicator of deliberate wrongdoing. If the failure is accidental, care will usually be close to the legal standard.

Juries could be instructed to award punitive damages for harm caused by gross negligence and to set punitive damages at the level required to overcome enforcement error as specified by the rule of the reciprocal. However, the practical politics of the bar do not augur well for legal reform along these lines. A more ad hoc approach to reform is to impose statutory ceilings on punitive damages, or to transfer decisions about punitive damages from jury to judge. The unsatisfactory state of punitive damages and the politics of the bar guarantee that this controversy will not go away.

References

Chapman, Bruce et al. "Symposium: Punitive Damages." *Alabama Law Review* 40 (1989), 687–1261.

Cooter, Robert. "Punitive Damages, Social Norms, and Economic Analysis." *Law and Contemporary Problems* (1998).

Ellis, Dorsey. "Fairness and Efficiency in the Law of Punitive Damages." *Southern California Law Review* 56 (1982), 1.

Ghiardi, James D., and John Kircher. *Punitive Damages, Law and Practice*. Wilmette, IL: Callaghan, 1981–85.

Landes, William, and Richard Posner. "An Economic Theory of Intentional Torts." *International Review of Law and Economics* 1 (1981), 1271.

Landes, William, and Richard Posner. *The Economic Structure of Tort Law*. Cambridge MA: Harvard University Press, 1987.

Polinsky, A. Mitchell, and Steven Shovell. "Punitive Damages." *Harvard Law Review* 111 (1998), 869.

Redden, Kenneth, and Linda L. Schlueter. *Punitive Damages*. Charlottesville VA: Michie, 1989.

Shavell, Steve. *The Economic Analysis of Accident Law*. Cambridge MA: Harvard University Press, 1987.

Robert Cooter

See also DETERRENT RATIONALE; FAULT; LIABILITY, PROTECTIONS FROM CIVIL; RATIONAL BARGAINING; TORTS

Pure Theory of Law

See KELSEN, HANS

Purpose, Legislative

The purpose of law is a key concept in any theory of legal interpretation. It may, broadly, be understood to denote those aims, functions, or values whose implementation is the task of legal rules in general. Legislative purpose in the strict sense refers to the explicit or implicit aims of a statute or of the legal provisions contained therein.

Doctrine

The earliest theories of legal interpretation were designed to meet the needs of jurisprudence to systematize the law; they thus incline toward a doctrinal interpretation. From the mid-nineteenth century in Europe, two theories were developed concerning the goal of the interpretation of law: the subjective theory of the historical and psychological will of the lawmaker (*voluntas legislatoris*) and the objective theory of the immanent sense of the law (*voluntas legis*). The second theory holds that each law has its own aim or purpose, which may well differ from the lawmaker's original intention.

According to H.L.A. Hart, the problem of interpretation lies in the fact that the rules of law are general standards of conduct expressed or transmitted by terms that, in both legislation and precedent, are equally general. The use of such general terms, or what Hart refers to as the "open texture" of language, introduces an indeterminacy in the rules and an uncertainty in their application. When the cases examined obey the core of settled meaning of the words of the rule, interpretation is problem-free. However, when those cases lie in an area of verbal penumbra, interpretation encounters difficulties that can only be resolved by turning to the aim or general purpose of the rule in question. Thus Hart applies the linguistic criterion in plain cases and the complementary criterion of the purpose of the rules in problem cases. For the rest, he retains the positivist thesis of a separation of law and morals.

In opposition to legal positivism, which, according to Lon Fuller, is beset by the fear of a purposive interpretation of law, Fuller holds that (1) the interpretation of a rule of law requires us first and foremost to determine its purpose, and that (2) "it is in the light of this 'ought' that we must decide what the rule 'is.'"

Ronald Dworkin attacks the analytic conception, which, in his view, separates legal theory and practice, jurisprudence and adjudication. Dworkin conceives of law in its entirety as an interpretive concept. Legal interpretation is constructive or "creative," and purpose has a fundamental place therein. Yet the purpose to be established is not that of the lawmakers, but that of the interpreter of the rule. Accordingly, the interpreter should take account of various factors, but especially the ideas, convictions, beliefs, and assumptions of the community that shares that (legal) social practice. Nevertheless, Dworkin fails to shed much light on the way in which the purpose of law is actually construed.

Operation

In the field of operative interpretation Jerzy Wróblewski constructs a theoretical model for the interpretation and judicial application of law in statutory law systems.

The model holds that interpretation should only begin when doubts arise concerning the direct meaning of a legal rule. In such cases the determination of the meaning of the rules is conducted through three distinct contexts that correspond to three groups of interpretive directives and to three kinds of legal interpretation. These directives, which are used to clarify the meaning of the rules, take the following order: (1) linguistic directives, which appeal to common natural language, legal language, legal definitions, and so forth; (2) systemic directives, whereby the rule to be interpreted is held to be consistent with the remaining rules in the system; and (3) functional directives, involving a wide range of sensitive issues, the most prominent of which is the purpose of legal rules.

The functional directive for purpose is described as follows: the aim of any legal regulation is the implementation of certain values and that aim is what is termed the purpose of the law. The problem lies in determining what purpose each particular rule or statute has. To determine what the purpose is, one can appeal either to the purpose attributed to the rule by the historical lawmaker or to the purpose attributed by the contemporary lawmaker. Static theories, which claim judicial decision making is bound to legal rules, prefer the first option. Dynamic theories, which defend free judicial decision, favor the second.

Robert Summers and Neil McCormick hold that legislative purpose is a teleological/evaluative argument and that the mode of its determination may be either to reference the deliberations of those involved in the production of the statute at the preliminary stage (*travaux préparatoires*), or to reflect on the rational aims an ideal lawmaker attributes to the statute and which the latter seeks to implement. In principle, however, a close reading and careful study of the full text of the statute may be sufficient to determine the general purpose of the statute or of some of its legal provisions.

Closely connected to the concept of purpose are other functional interpretive directives, such as the task of social control specifically allotted to each statute, and the extralegal values and rules to which the statutes are frequently related. A matter that is also close to the question of purpose is the substantive reasons argument, which makes direct reference to values of an economic, political, or moral kind, whose implementation is the task of rules belonging to the legal system.

The legislative purpose argument is in any case a strictly legal means of interpretation, which is to be based on the very statutes and on the rules and principles formulated in the system and which should be confined to those limits. It should not be confused with arguments of policy, morals, or other kinds, which allude to the social aims and functions attributed to statutes but do so from positions outside the legal system.

References

Dworkin, Ronald. *Law's Empire*. Cambridge MA: Harvard University Press, 1986.

Fuller, Lon L. "Positivism and Fidelity to Law: A Reply to Professor Hart." *Harvard Law Review* 71 (1958), 630–672.

Hart, H.L.A. *The Concept of Law*. Oxford: Clarendon Press, 1961.

———. *Essays in Jurisprudence and Philosophy*. Oxford: Clarendon Press, 1983.

MacCormick, D. Neil, and Robert S. Summers. "Interpretation and Justification." In *Interpreting Statutes. A Comparative Study*, ed. MacCormick and Summers, 511–544. Aldershot: Dartmouth, 1991.

Marmor, Andrei. *Interpretation and Legal Theory*. Oxford: Clarendon Press, 1992.

Wróblewski, Jerzy. *The Judicial Application of Law*. Dordrecht: Kluwer, 1992.

José López Hernández

See also INTENT, LEGISLATIVE; INTERPRETATION; JUDICIAL REVIEW

R

Radbruch, Gustav (1878–1949)

Born in 1878 in Lübeck, Germany, Gustav Radbruch was professor of criminal law and philosophy of law at the universities of Königsberg, Kiel, and Heidelberg. Radbruch became active in the Social Democratic party and served as Minister of Justice of the Weimar Republic. In 1933 he was dismissed from his chair in Heidelberg by the Nazi regime. After World War II he was recalled and became dean of the faculty of law, contributing to the reorientation and reorganization of legal education in Germany. He died in 1949.

His main works are *Einführung in die Rechtswissenschaft* (Introduction to Jurisprudence, 1910), *Grundzüge der Rechtsphilosophie* (Philosophy of Law, 1914), *Kulturlehre des Sozialismus* (Cultural Theory of Socialism, 1922), *Entwurf eines Allgemeinen Deutschen Strafgesetzbuchs* (Draft of a New General German Criminal Code, 1922), *P.J. Anselm Feuerbach. Ein Juristenleben* (P.J. Anselm Feuerbach: A Jurist's Life, 1934), *Der Geist des englischen Rechts* (The Spirit of English Law, 1946), and *Vorschule der Rechtsphilosophie* (Elementary Course in the Philosophy of Law, 1947).

In Berlin, Gustav Radbruch studied criminal law with the reform criminologist Franz von Liszt and philosophy of law with the neokantian Rudolf Stammler. Influenced by the "Southwestgerman Neo-kantian School" (especially by Heinrich Rickert and Emil Lask, but also by Ernst Troeltsch and Max Weber), he conceived law as an empirical and normative cultural science: "Jurisprudentia est divinarum et humanarum rerum notitia, iusti et iniusti scientia" (Jurisprudence is knowledge of things human and divine, the science of the just and the unjust). Radbruch was a methodological dualist, distinguishing strictly between values and facts, the "ought" (*Sollen*) and the "is" (*Sein*), and consequently between the normative sciences concerned with ideas, principles, and ideal states (*Wertgesetzmäßigkeiten*) and the empirical sciences concerned with the present, past, and future realities (*Naturgesetzmäßigkeiten*). The science of law was for him an empirical ("systematically constructing") science, concerned with the problems of human coexistence, and at the same time a normative ("interpreting") science, concerned with the values of law (security, functionality or utility, and justice) and with the "right" and "just" law that allows the best possible implementation of those values.

The philosophy of law is for Radbruch especially important because it has the function of reflecting upon the normative dimension implied in the legal systems, a dimension which he conceives as specific "cultural forms" and manifestations. This normative dimension, subject of the philosophy of law, comprehends the values and goals of the law, the idea of law, and the notion of ideal law. The philosophy of law leads naturally, in Radbruch's conception, to legal policy, which as an "art of the possible" examines the possibilities of realization of the "ideal" and "just" law. While the philosophy of law relates the empirical legal reality to the basic, normative ideas it implies and is based upon, legal policy tries to mediate practically between the normative and the empirical dimensions of law, transforming the concrete legal reality according to the basic ideas it presupposes.

Radbruch elaborates in his philosophy of law a theory of justice as the highest criterion of positive law and the goal of the legislature. In his theory of justice Radbruch conceives justice as a formal normative idea, based on equality, and aiming at universality, without neglecting psychological and sociological factors.

After World War II Radbruch tentatively turned to a moderate natural law position, holding that in certain extreme cases the "unjust" positive law ("unlawful law") must cede to the higher demands of justice ("übergesetzliches Recht").

References

Engisch, K. "Gustav Radbruch als Rechtsphilosoph" (Gustav Radbruch as Philosopher of Law). *Archiv für Rechts- und Sozialphilosophie* 38 (1949/1950), 305–316.

Kaufmann, A. *Gustav Radbruch. Rechtsdenker, Philosoph, Sozialdemokrat* (Gustav Radbruch. Legal Theorist, Philosophy, Social Democrat). Munich: Piper, 1987.

Patterson, E.W. "Introduction." In *The Legal Philosophies of E. Lask, G. Radbruch, and J. Dabin.* Trans. Kurt Wilk. Cambridge MA: Harvard University Press, 1950.

Wolf, E. "Gustav Radbruchs Leben und Werk" (Gustav Radbruch's Life and Work). In G. Radbruch, *Rechtsphilosophie,* 17–79, Stuttgart: K.F. Koehler, 1950.

Thomas Gil

Radical Class, Gender, and Race Theories: Positionality

Theorists have developed "positional" critiques of the law that assess law from the point of view of a particular economic or social "position" such as class, gender, or race. Positional theories constitute slices of theories of inequality. Accordingly, no matter how neutral laws may appear on the surface, a deeper analysis reveals that law serves the interests of some groups at the expense of others. For example, while the idea of citizenship may seem neutral and inclusive, the original Constitution of the United States excluded slaves and women from the ranks of citizens. Perhaps less conspicuously, current laws reflect class, gender, and race biases, deeply and diffusely embedded throughout the legal system.

Positional critiques stand between liberalism and communitarianism. Liberals place a premium on individual preferences, while communitarians emphasize the critical role played by community in shaping the self. Positional theories find that liberal individualism fails to confront the problems of group injustice and that the communities celebrated by communitarians often exclude groups. Positionalists differ as to which excluded group—class, gender, or race—warrants the closest attention.

Class

Classical marxists characterize class in terms of the ownership of the means of production. The ruling class owns the means of production, while the working class sells their labor to the ruling class. The law promotes cleavages between ruling class and working class by forcing issues into a mold that favors the ruling over the working class. Collective bargaining, for example, serves more as a co-opting tool for the ruling class than as a means of empowerment for the working class. Labor law promotes the structural inequality between ruling and working classes and recasts the disputes into contractual ones, shorn of any reference to class conflict. Similarly, the criminal law favors the rich and the powerful. So, for classical marxists, class conflict determines legal formulations and developments. While neo-marxists reject the thesis that class determines law, they see law as reflecting the dominance of some economic interests over others.

Recent developments in radical legal theory—critical legal studies (CLS), feminist jurisprudence, and critical race theory (CRT)—incorporate marxist insights, but these positional analyses reject the claim that law is a tool of class domination. CLS criticizes marxists for having privileged the problems of class. CLS concerns itself more with the particular effects of ideology on consciousness and everyday social relations than with the overall effect of modes of production on class power.

Positional Indeterminacy

The categories underlying legal principles and doctrines (or, in another version, flexibility of legal narratives) can yield competing or contradictory results, which serve to benefit some groups at the expense of others. CLS proponents claim that law is politics. If we deconstruct law, we will find that it serves the interests of an identifiable political group. Influenced by poststructuralists like Michel Foucault and postmodernists such as Jacques Derrida and Jean-François Lyotard, CLS rejects liberal appeals to universal justice and instead promotes a politics of resistance that is situated and local.

Gender

Feminists agree with many of the critiques offered within CLS, but they also find them limiting. Feminists transform the CLS claim that "law is politics" into "law is sexual politics." Some feminists claim that CLS and legal scholarship have undervalued or ignored how law subordinates women. CLS theorists talk about but have not fully experienced domination and oppression. Gender positionality begins with listening to the experience of women, which other perspectives undervalue. Yet women and feminists do not speak with a single voice. Therefore, feminists have expanded the idea of "women's experience" to include the experiences of lesbians and bisexuals.

Feminists criticize law as a patriarchal institution. The law plays an important role in perpetuating a hierarchical structure that subordinates women to men. Gender is socially constructed within a hierarchy of male domination.

Do women, being basically similar to men, require equal treatment or do women, being significantly different, require special treatment? Many feminists attempt to escape from the sameness/difference duality. For them, equality is not simply a matter of determining the appropriateness of same and different treatment but rather of questioning the grounds for sameness and difference. An alternative is to return to more fundamental notions like disadvantage, domination, and oppression—ones that initially defined patriarchy.

Race

CRT agrees with positional critiques of liberalism. By focusing on intent in equal protection analysis, liberals privilege the viewpoint of perpetrators over that of victims. They see the appeal some liberals make to a color-blind constitution as disguised racism.

CRT adherents reject the appeal made by some feminists to a unitary essentialist feminist experience. They agree with feminists that CLS privileges white male experience, but they accuse feminist jurisprudence for doing the same for white female experience. Thus, CRT argues for the inclusion of a distinct voice of color in legal scholarship. Others have found the call for a collective subject known as a "person of color" guilty of the same essentialism found in early feminist jurisprudence. As a remedy, they propose expanding a race-conscious perspective to include Chicano, Asian American, Native American, and other perspectives.

For many positionality theorists, narratives and stories fully reveal the complexities of positionality. Stories, with multiple and shifting subject positions, best capture the extent to which what you see depends upon where you stand. The myth-making aspect of storytelling creates a new collective subject with a history from which individuals can draw to shape their identities.

Positionality

While the positional analyses have been largely confined to legal scholarship, they have had an impact on the practice of law. Feminist legal theory has affected issues such as rape, sexual harassment, reproductive freedoms, and pregnancy rights in the workplace. CRT has had considerable influence in discrimination law and on issues such as hate speech.

Each positional perspective has served as a corrective to the others. As a result, none of these perspectives can ignore class, gender, or race. Class, race, and gender—deeply embedded in one another—constitute distinct forms of inequality. Theorists are now developing analyses of how these positions intersect and effect one another in concrete legal settings. The grouping "black female" is not simply a combination of being black and being female. Rather, it forms a distinct form of oppression. Discrimination claims brought under Title VII of the United States Civil Rights Act do not recognize "black female." So, a claimant must choose to bring evidence under sex or race discrimination but not both.

The next step will be the development of a theory that exposes the power dynamics underlying the positions. Theories of positionality have come under postmodernist influences that reject universalistic appeals to justice in favor of fragmented and heterogeneous conceptions and discourses about justice. While postmodernism has opened up the law to the authenticity of other voices, it has mired positional critiques in relativism by shutting off those voices from universal sources of power. The challenge lies in mediating the tension between modernist universal visions and postmodern critiques to find a general sense of social justice that embodies the multiple voices and particular contexts of disadvantaged groups.

References

Bartlett, Katherine T., and Rosanne Kennedy, eds. *Feminist Legal Theory: Readings in Law and Gender*. Boulder CO: Westview Press, 1991.

Boyle, James, ed. *Critical Legal Studies*. New York: New York University Press, 1994.

Caudill, David S., and Steven Jay Gold, eds. *Radical Philosophy of Law: Contemporary Challenges to Mainstream Legal Theory and Practice*. Atlantic Highlands NJ: Humanities Press International, 1995.

Crenshaw, Kimberlé, Neil Gotanda, and Kendall Thomas, eds. *Critical Race Theory: A Reader*. New York: New Press, 1993.

Delgado, Richard, and Jean Stefancic. "Critical Race Theory: An Annotated Bibliography." *Virginia Law Review* 79 (1993), 461.

Hunt, Alan. *Explorations in Law and Society: Toward a Constitutive Theory of Law*. New York: Routledge, 1993.

Kairys, David, ed. *The Politics of Law: A Progressive Critique*. 2d ed. New York: Pantheon Books, 1990.

MacKinnon, Catharine. *Toward a Feminist Theory of the State*. Cambridge: Harvard University Press, 1989.

Smith, Patricia, ed. *Feminist Jurisprudence*. Oxford: Oxford University Press, 1993.

Thomas W. Simon

See also Derridean Jurisprudents; Difference Theory; Feminist Philosophy of Law; Postmodern Philosophy of Law

Rational Bargaining

Rational bargaining is the procedure whereby two or more rational agents, who stand to gain by coordinating their behavior but whose claims to the benefits of such cooperation are incompatible, reach unanimous agreement on a mode of cooperation that determines the distribution of the benefits; the availability of the benefits is conditional upon such an agreement being reached.

Traditional conceptions of the social contract can be naturally construed as bargaining situations, so it seems likely that a clearer under-

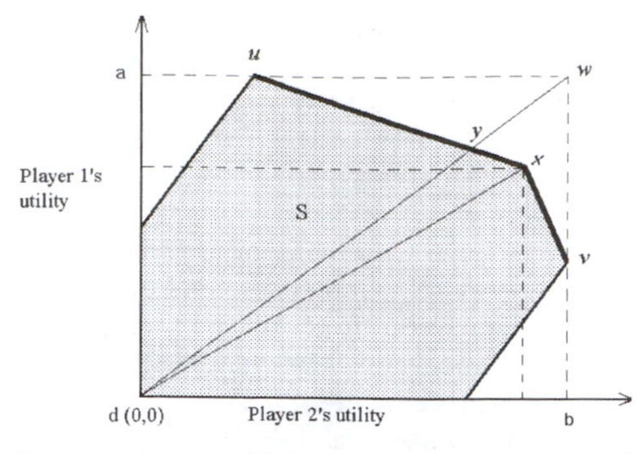

Outcome Space and Disagreement Point in Typical Bargaining Problem in Which n = 2.

standing of the dynamics of bargaining will illuminate philosophical issues which theorists of the social contract have sought to resolve: the nature and limits of state legitimacy and of the correlative obligation to obey the law, how citizenship might be compatible with autonomy, the nature of distributive justice, and so on. Mathematical treatments of bargaining form a part of game theory; they are of philosophical interest first and foremost as a resource for theorists of rational strategic choice. Recently, however, these formal treatments have also been appealed to at crucial points in the arguments of moral and political philosophers, most notably in the work of David Gauthier.

As a part of the theory of games, the theory of bargaining presupposes utility theory, as developed by John von Neumann and Oskar Morgenstern, Frank P. Ramsey, Leonard J. Savage, and others. According to utility theory, given sufficient information about preferences, we can define, for each agent, a *utility function* which assigns a numerical value (a utility) to each possible outcome of a situation. The significance of the value can be expressed in the following way: it is a necessary condition on the rationality of an agent that the agent act as if to maximize the expected value of the outcome as determined by the agent's utility function. Although some philosophers have supposed that utility theory involves substantive assumptions about philosophical psychology, it can plausibly be construed as an attempt to make more precise a very ordinary notion of consistency of choice and preference.

A game is defined by identifying, for each possible combination of strategies selected by the players, the expected utility for each player of the outcome resulting from that combination. A typical bargaining problem is given by identifying the *outcome space*—the utility payoffs to each player for the outcome of every possible mode of cooperation or identifying an agreed-upon combination of strategies—and the *disagreement point*—the payoffs accruing to each player in the event that no agreement is reached on a mode of cooperation. As the term implies, an outcome space, where the problem involves n players, is standardly represented as a set of points in n-dimensional space, where the players' utility scales are given by the axes, as in figure 1. (For the sake of simplicity, we shall here restrict our attention to the case in which $n = 2$.) Here S is the outcome space: the set of all points whose coordinates represent the utilities for each player of the outcomes of all possible modes of cooperation. The availability of randomized strategies ensures that the outcome space will always be convex and compact. The origin can always be stipulated to coincide with the disagreement point d, because choice of a utility scale, like choice of a temperature scale, is a matter of stipulation.

Once S and d have been defined, then, the bargaining problem can be stated thus: what point or set of points in S is it rational for the players to agree upon as representing the best (that is, most preferred) outcome each player can expect, given that each player is, and knows every other player to be, a utility maximizer? Notice that, although the outcome of bargaining is an agreed-upon mode of cooperation, the bargaining process itself is envisioned as noncooperative—each player makes offers and concessions solely with a view to maximizing his or her own utility. Since the problem was first formulated by John Nash in 1950, the usual approach has been to set out axioms stating conditions it seems reasonable to expect any solution to fulfill and, ideally, to show that only one solution fulfills all such conditions. This was the approach of Nash himself, who proposed the following four axioms: (i) Pareto optimality: there must be no outcome which affords every player a greater utility than the solution outcome. (In our example this axiom restricts solutions to the more heavily drawn northeast boundary of S between u and v.) (ii) Symmetry: if the bargaining situation is symmetrical, that is, the same for all the players, then the solutions should afford all the players the same utility. (iii) Independence of equivalent utility representations: if one bargaining problem is derived from another by positive linear transformations of the players' utility functions, the solution of the new problem can be derived from the solution to the old by means of the same transformations. (iv) Independence of irrelevant alternatives: if one bargaining problem is derived from another solely by enlarging or reducing the space of feasible outcomes, then the solution to the new game will be the same as the solution to the old, unless the new solution is outside the boundaries of the old space or the old solution is outside the boundaries of the new space.

Nash proved that, for any bargaining problem, there is one and only one solution that conforms to all four of his axioms. This solution is the outcome which maximizes the geometric average (that is, maximizes the product) of the utility gains to each player beyond their payoffs at the disagreement point. In our two-person example, this outcome is represented by the point x on the boundary of S which maximizes the area of a rectangle, two of whose sides lie along the axes and which has line dx as its diagonal.

Opponents of Nash's solution have frequently pointed out that it yields very implausible results in certain cases. (It is not clear that any single solution will be immune to such criticism.) However, if Nash's solution is rejected, at least one of his axioms must be rejected too, since they uniquely define it. The axiom most often denounced is that of the independence of irrelevant alternatives, and this does indeed seem the least self-evident of Nash's four. The main alternative solution to have been given philosophical application is that favored by Gauthier, which is based on the work of Howard Raiffa, Ehud Kalai and Meir Smorodinsky, and Alvin Roth. In the two-person case, the solution ("solution G") has been proven to be uniquely determined by Nash's axioms (i)–(iii), with a monotonicity axiom replacing Nash's axiom (iv). The basic idea is this. The *ideal point* w is defined as (a, b), where a and b are the utility payoffs of the feasible outcomes most favorable to player 1 and player 2, respectively. In any nontrivial bargaining problem, the ideal point will be outside the space of feasible outcomes. Solution G is represented by the point y at which a straight line between d and w intersects the Pareto-optimal boundary of S. At this point, each player receives as high a payoff as is compatible with their both receiving the same proportion of their maximum payoff. Roth proved in 1979 that, unfortunately, there is no such solution for bargaining problems with more than two players. Gauthier has proposed instead his (unaxiomatized) solution G′. G′ is determined by the *principle of minimax relative concession*, according to which the largest concession made by any player should be as small as possible, where a player's concession is measured as a proportion of the utility gain beyond the disagreement point represented by the maximum possible payoff.

The most immediate philosophical application of these theoretical considerations is to problems of distributive justice, where what is to be apportioned is not utility but social values (John Rawls' "primary goods," for example, or Amartya K. Sen's "capabilities"). If this kind of distribution is treated as a bargaining problem, its solution presents itself as a candidate for the most just outcome. This is roughly Gauthier's strategy. However, many remain unconvinced that justice can be essentially the by-product of a noncooperative game—including Rawls himself, who has made it clear that his discussion of bargaining is an unessential part of his theory. Furthermore, the definition of d—in this application, the state of nature—is a matter of great philosophical contention.

References

Binmore, Ken, and Partha Dasgupta, eds. *The Economics of Bargaining*. Oxford: Blackwell, 1987.

Gauthier, David. *Morals by Agreement*. Oxford: Oxford University Press, 1986.

Harsanyi, John. *Rational Behavior and Bargaining Equilibrium in Games and Social Situations*. Cambridge: Cambridge University Press, 1977.

Kalai, Ehud, and Meir Smorodinsky. "Other Solutions to Nash's Bargaining Problem." *Econometrica* 43 (1975), 513–518.

Luce, R. Duncan, and Howard Raiffa. *Games and Decisions*. New York: Wiley, 1957.

Nash, John. "The Bargaining Problem." *Econometrica* 18 (1950), 155–162.

Roth, Alvin. *Axiomatic Models of Bargaining*. Berlin: Springer Verlag, 1979.

Von Neumann, John, and Oskar Morgenstern. *Theory of Games and Economic Behavior*. Princeton NJ: Princeton University Press, 1944. 2d ed. 1947.

James Doyle

See also GAME THEORY; PUNITIVE DAMAGES; SOCIAL CONTRACT

Rawls, John (1921–)

The American political philosopher John Rawls is best known for *A Theory of Justice*, which provides a philosophical justification of the liberal and democratic institutions of a constitutional democracy. Rawls argues that the most appropriate conception of justice for a democratic society is "Justice as Fairness." It guarantees equality of certain basic liberties, provides fair access to equal opportunities for all citizens, and mandates that inequalities of wealth and position are to be designed so as to maximally benefit the least advantaged members of society. Drawing on the social contract tradition of John Locke, Jean-Jacques Rousseau, and Immanuel Kant, Rawls contends that free persons who are fairly situated and ignorant of their social positions and individual interests would all choose and agree to these principles. To protect their interests, they would prefer Justice as Fairness to utilitarianism, the principle of efficiency, and other alternatives.

Rawls' first principle of justice is "Each person has an equal right to a fully adequate scheme of equal basic liberties which is compatible with a similar scheme of liberties for all." The principle protects—not liberty, as such, or the freedom to do as one pleases—but certain specified liberties: liberty of conscience and freedom of thought, equal political rights and freedom of association, the freedoms specified by the liberty and integrity of the person (including the right to hold personal property, but not to its unlimited accumulation), and the rights and liberties covered by the rule of law. Rawls sees these rights and liberties (as opposed to some other list) as basic, because they are essential to exercising the capacities (or "moral powers") that enable us to pursue a conception of our good and engage in social cooperation.

These liberties are basic in two ways. First, they have priority over all other social values; equal liberty cannot then be infringed for the sake of greater social utility, economic efficiency, or even greater economic equality. In this sense they are fundamental liberties. Second, they are inalienable—persons cannot give up or bargain away their basic liberties for the sake of greater individual utility. Rawls' account then implements a specific ideal of persons as equal citizens deserving of equal respect. Equal respect, on his account, requires equality of certain rights and liberties, even if a person may not appreciate their significance.

The abstract liberties of Rawls' first principle can be applied to specify more particular constitutional rights and liberties. For example, freedom of thought gives rise to such rights as freedom of speech, press, and expression; political rights of participation underwrite equal rights to vote, hold office, assemble, and join and form political parties. Rawls sees the rule of law as essential (but by no means sufficient) to the freedom of democratic citizens, since laws establish a basis for settled and legitimate expectations, thereby enabling people to plan their activities. In his view, the rule of law requires rights and procedures guaranteeing that similar cases be treated similarly, the public promulgation of well-defined laws, no ex post facto laws or laws imposing duties impossible to perform, due process, and the right to an impartial and open trial, and so on.

Notably absent from Rawls' list of basic liberties are freedom of economic contract and the right to control and accumulate productive property. Rights of property and contract are defined and regulated according to the second principle of justice. This "difference principle" regulates permissible inequalities, or differences in rights. It says that social and economic inequalities (1) must attach to offices and positions open to all under conditions of fair equality of opportunity and (2) must be to the greatest benefit of the least advantaged members of society. Imagine the spectrum of feasible economic and property systems. The difference principle says that system is just where those who are least advantaged (in terms of income and wealth) do better than the least advantaged in any other system. This standard is to be applied by legislators in regulating the complicated system of laws and conventions that constitute an economic system. Rawls argues that a market system best satisfies the difference principle, since markets allocate productive resources efficiently, but it will be a market system in which distributions of the social product, or rights to income and wealth, are decided, not by markets alone, but by nonmarket transfers guaranteeing each citizen a social minimum. (A "property owning democracy" and liberal socialism satisfy this requirement, but not laissez-faire capitalism, or even the welfare state as traditionally conceived.) A social minimum guarantees the fair value of the basic liberties: it is a prerequisite for their effective exercise and so is essential to effective freedom.

The account of democracy that emerges from Rawls' view is not simple majoritarianism. It is a constitutional democracy where the rights and liberties defining the status of free and equal citizens are protected against majority infringement within ordinary lawmaking procedures. Rawls sees judicial review as a legitimate democratic institution, but only when it is exercised for these purposes and ordinary democratic legislative procedures are incapable of self-regulation.

References

Rawls, John. *Political Liberalism*. New York: Columbia University Press, 1993.

———. *A Theory of Justice*. Cambridge MA: Harvard University Press, 1971.

Samuel Freeman

Raz, Joseph (1939—)

Joseph Raz was a doctoral student of H.L.A. Hart at Oxford University and has taught at Oxford since 1972; he is currently its professor of the philosophy of law. His work has been influential in legal theory, political theory, and moral philosophy (including important work on the role of different kinds of reasons within moral thought). Raz's work in both political theory and moral theory emphasizes "well-being" (autonomy is also important in Raz's analysis, but its importance derives from its instrumental value in promoting well-being).

The present summary focuses on Raz's contributions to legal theory. While Raz's work on legal theory can be seen as carrying on and defending H.L.A. Hart's legal positivism (the view that there is no necessary connection between law and morality), Raz's approach departs from Hart's at a number of points.

Two concepts central to Raz's analysis are the "sources thesis" and the centrality of authority, both of which are discussed in *The Authority of Law.* Raz claims that the "social thesis" is at the core of legal positivism: that "what is law and what is not is a matter of social fact." Raz asserts a "strong" version of the "social thesis," which he calls the "sources thesis": "A jurisprudential theory is acceptable only if its tests for identifying the content of the law and determining its existence depend exclusively on facts of human behavior capable of being described in value-neutral terms, and applied without resort to moral argument."

This restatement of the legal positivist's separation between law and morality is tied to, and supported by, a distinction between deliberating as part of the process of coming to a decision, as well as the execution of the decision once made. As Raz noted in *The Concept of a Legal System*, "Executive considerations are . . . substantive positivist considerations." When judges are merely applying decisions already reached (by the legislature or by prior court decisions), they are executing decisions already made (determining what the law *is*); when judges consider moral factors in creating a new rule, or in considering possible changes to an existing rule, they are deliberating about what the law *should be*. Raz suggests that law can best be seen as consisting of "the authoritative positivist considerations binding on the courts" and that it "belongs essentially to the executive stage of the political institution . . . of which it is a part." Under this analysis, courts generally apply both legal and nonlegal considerations.

Second, it is in the nature of law (of a legal system) that it claims legitimate authority. Raz's analysis ties together law, authority, and practical reasoning. For Raz, the connection between authority and practical reasoning is a general one: authorities and authoritative reasons affect our moral deliberations; where there is an authority (which we recognize as such), our decision is based at least in part on what the authority (whether that authority is the law, a sacred text, a religious leader, an army commander, and so forth) states we should do; we incorporate the authority's weighing of the relevant factors rather than simply weighing all the relevant considerations for ourselves. In Raz's terms, stated in *Political Reason and Norms*: "The authority's directives become our reasons. While the acceptance of the authority is based on belief that its directives are well-founded in reason, they are understood to yield the benefits they are meant to bring only if we do rely on them rather than on our own independent judgment of the merits of each case to which they apply." The phrase "the benefits they are meant to bring" refers to the argument that one treats a source as authoritative if, as noted in "Facing Up," "conforming with its directives is more likely to lead one to conform better with reason than acting independently of it would."

There is a connection between the first and second theme. As law purports to be authoritative, it would defeat that purpose if citizens would have to figure out for themselves (by moral reasoning) what various legal rules meant.

It is important to note that while Raz believes it distinctive of legal systems that they claim to be authoritative, Raz does not believe that there is a prima facie moral obligation to obey the law. In other terms, Raz asserts that there is no (additional) moral obligation to follow a prescription or prohibition simply because it was promulgated by a legal system (even if it is a generally just legal system).

References

Raz, Joseph. *The Authority of Law.* Oxford: Clarendon Press, 1979.

———. *The Concept of a Legal System.* 1st ed. Oxford: Clarendon Press, 1970. 2d ed. 1980.

———. *Ethics in the Public Domain.* Oxford: Clarendon Press, 1994.

———. "Facing Up." *Southern California Law Review* 62 (1989), 1153–1235.

———. *The Morality of Freedom.* Oxford: Clarendon Press, 1986.

———. *Practical Reason and Norms.* 1st ed. London: Hutchinson, 1975. 2d ed. Princeton: Princeton University Press, 1990.

The Works of Joseph Raz (Symposium). *Southern California Law Review* 62 (1989), 731–1235.

Brian Bix

Realism, Legal

Legal realism is an intellectual movement in American law schools that became influential during the 1920s and 1930s and whose influence continues to be felt to the present. The "realists"—figures like Karl Llewellyn, Jerome Frank, Joseph Hutcheson, Felix Cohen, Herman Oliphant, Walter Wheeler Cook, Leon Green, Underhill Moore, Hessel Yntema, and Max Radin, as well as intellectual forebears like Oliver Wendell Holmes—argued against the dominant "mechanical jurisprudence" or "formalism" of the day, which held that judges decide cases on the basis of distinctively *legal* rules and reasons that justify a unique result in every case. The realists argued, instead, that a careful look at how judges *really* decide cases reveals that they decide not primarily because of law, but based on their sense of what would be "fair" according to the facts of the case. Legal rules and reasons figure simply as post hoc rationalizations for decisions reached on the basis of nonlegal considerations.

Context and Background

American legal realism was largely a movement of academics at two prominent law schools in the northeastern part of the United States: Yale and Columbia. There were exceptions on both counts. Frank, for example, was a lawyer with considerable trial experience, who (like many realists) later worked in President Franklin D. Roosevelt's "New Deal" during the 1930s and eventually served as a federal judge; he never held an academic appointment. Figures like Green and Yntema, though associated at times with Yale or Columbia, spent large parts of their career at other elite American law schools (Texas and Michigan, respectively). Among legal theorists, the realists are notable for the sizable number who also enjoyed distinguished careers in the practice of law, including, for example, William Douglas (appointed to the U.S. Supreme Court by Roosevelt) and Thurman Arnold, founder of a prominent Washington, D.C., law firm that still bears his name. Most of the key figures in realism, however, held academic appointments at Columbia and/or Yale during the 1920s and 1930s.

Realism arose in an intellectual culture that was deeply "positivistic," in the sense that this culture viewed natural science as the paradigm of all genuine knowledge and thought all other disciplines (from the social sciences to legal study) should emulate the methods of natural science. Chief among the latter was the method of *empirical testing*: hypotheses had to be tested against observations of the world. Thus, the realists frequently claimed that existing articulations of the "law" were not, in fact, "confirmed" by actual observation of what the courts were really doing. Also influential on some realists was behaviorism in psychology, itself in the grips of a "positivistic" conception of knowledge and method. The behaviorist dispensed with talk about a person's beliefs and desires—phenomena that were unobservable and hence could not serve as empirical checks on theories—in favor of trying to explain human behavior strictly in terms of stimuli and the responses they generate. The goal was to discover laws describing which stimuli cause which responses. Many realists thought that a genuine science of law should do the same thing: it should discover which "stimuli" (for instance, which factual scenarios) produce which "responses" (that is, what judicial decisions). This understanding of legal "science" is most vivid in the work of Moore. Other realists invoked scientific "metaphors" more loosely, for example, when they talked about the necessity of "testing" legal rules against experience to see whether they produced the results they were supposed to produce.

Legal Indeterminacy

The realists famously argued that the law was "indeterminate." By this, they meant two things: first, that the law was *rationally* indeterminate, in the sense that the available class of legal reasons did not *justify* a unique decision (at least in those cases that reached the stage of appellate review); and, second, that the law was also *causally* or *explanatorily* indeterminate, in the sense that legal reasons did not suffice to explain why judges decided as they did.

Realist arguments for the rational indeterminacy of law generally focused on the existence of conflicting, but equally legitimate, canons of interpretation for precedents and statutes. In 1950 Llewellyn demonstrated, for example, that courts had endorsed *both* the principle of statutory construction, that "[a] statute cannot go beyond its text," and the principle that "[t]o effect its purpose a statute must be implemented beyond its text." However, if a court could properly appeal to either canon when faced with a question of statutory interpretation, then the "methods" of legal reasoning (including principles of statutory construction) would justify at least two different interpretations of the meaning of the statute. In that case, the question for the realists was: why did the judge reach that result, given that law and legal reasons did not require him to do so? In *The Bramble Bush* Llewellyn made a similar argument about the conflicting, but equally legitimate, ways of interpreting precedent (which he called the "strict" and "loose" views of precedent).

Notice that the realist argument for the indeterminacy of law—really the indeterminacy of law and legal reasoning—is based on an implicit view about the scope of the class of legal reasons: that is, the class of reasons that judges may properly invoke in justifying a decision. The realists appear to assume that the legitimate sources of law are exhausted by statutes and precedents and that a method for interpreting a statute or precedent is legitimate insofar as it has been endorsed or accepted by some court. Unfortunately, the realists themselves never gave arguments for these assumptions. Later writers, like Ronald Dworkin, have argued that much indeterminacy in law disappears once we expand our definition of the legitimate sources of law to include not only statutes and precedents, but also broader moral and political principles that underlie the latter.

The Core Claim

All the realists agreed that the law and legal reasons are rationally indeterminate (at least in the sorts of cases that reach the stage of appellate review), so that the best explanation for why judges decide as they do must look beyond the law itself. In particular, all the realists endorsed the following claim: in deciding cases, judges respond primarily to the stimulus of the facts of the case, rather than to legal rules and reasons (hereafter "the core claim"). Several points bear noting about the core claim.

First, it is not simply the trivial thesis that judges must take account of the facts of the case in deciding the outcome. Rather, it is the much stronger claim that in deciding cases, judges are reacting to the underlying facts of the case, *whether or not those facts are legally significant*. Second, the core claim is not the thesis that legal rules and reasons *never* affect the course of decision; rather, it is the weaker claim that they generally have no (or little) effect, especially in the sorts of cases with which the realists were especially concerned, namely, that class of more difficult cases that reached the stage of appellate review. Third, many of the realists advanced the core claim in the hope that legal rules might be reformulated in more fact-specific ways. Thus, for example, Oliphant spoke of a "return to *stare decisis*," the doctrine that rules laid down in prior cases should control in subsequent cases that are relevantly similar. Oliphant's critique was that the "legal rules," as articulated by courts and scholars, had become too general and abstract, ignoring the particular factual contexts in which the original disputes arose. The result was that these rules no longer had any value for judges in later cases, who simply "respond to the stimulus of the facts in the concrete case before them rather than to the stimulus of overly general and outworn abstractions in [prior] opinions and treatises." Oliphant argued that a meaningful doctrine of stare decisis could be restored by making legal rules more fact-specific. So, for example, instead of pretending that there is a single, general rule about the enforceability of contractual promises not to compete, Oliphant suggested that we attend to what the courts are really doing in that area, namely, enforcing those promises when made by the seller of a business to the buyer, but not enforcing those promises when made by a (soon-to-be former) employee to his employer. In the former scenario, Oliphant claimed, the courts were simply doing the economically sensible thing (no one would buy a business, if the seller could simply open up shop again and compete); while in the latter scenario, courts were taking account of the prevailing informal norms governing labor relations at the time, which disfavored such promises. Green took the same approach to torts, organizing his groundbreaking 1931 textbook on torts not by the traditional *doctrinal* categories (for example, negligence, intentional torts, strict liability), but rather by the factual scenarios in which harms occur: for example, "surgical operations," "traffic and transportation," and the like. Realists like Llewellyn and Moore tried to systematize the point for commercial law: in adjudicating commercial disputes, they claimed, judges generally try to enforce the norms of the prevailing commercial practice in which the dispute arose. Llewellyn, who later drafted Article 2 of the *Uniform Commercial Code*, incorporated this understanding of adjudication into the code: the code, in effect, tells judges that what they "ought" to do in most commercial disputes is simply enforce the customary practices and norms in the trade.

Two Branches of Realism

In fact, there was a division among realists over the question of how to explain why judges respond to the underlying facts of the case as they do. The "sociological" wing of realism—represented by writers like Oliphant, Moore, Llewellyn, and Cohen—thought that judicial decisions fell into *predictable* patterns (though *not*, of course, the patterns one would predict just by looking at the existing rules of law). From this fact, these realists inferred that various "social" forces must operate upon judges to force them to respond to facts in similar, and predictable, ways. These "social" forces included the economic background of the judges and their professional socialization experiences. It was these factors, rather than rules of law, that account for decisions and determine the response judges have to the underlying facts of a case.

The "idiosyncracy wing" of realism, by contrast—exemplified most prominently by Frank and Hutcheson—claimed that what determines the judge's response to the facts of a particular case are idiosyncratic facts about the psychology or personality of that individual. Thus, Frank notoriously asserted in *Law and the Modern Mind* that "the personality of the judge is the pivotal factor in law administration." (Note, however, that no realist ever claimed, as popular legend has it, that "what the judge ate for breakfast" determines her decision!) Frank, under the influence of Sigmund Freud's psychology, felt that it would be impossible for observers to discover the crucial facts about personality that would determine a judge's response to the facts of a particular case. As a result, Frank concluded that prediction of judicial decision would be largely impossible; the desire of lawyers and citizens to think otherwise, Frank suggested, reflected merely an infantile wish for certainty and security.

Frank's skepticism about our ability to predict how judges will decide cases flies in the face of the experience of most lawyers: while the outcome of some cases is hard to fathom, most of the time lawyers are able to advise clients as to the likely outcome of disputes brought before courts. Yet, despite the fact that Frank's skepticism sits poorly with practical experience, a striking feature of the long-term reception of realism (about which more follows) is that Frank's view is often taken as the essence of realism. This "Frankification" of realism does justice neither to the majority of realists who felt that judicial decision was predictable—because its determining factors were identifiable social forces, not opaque facts about personality—nor to those realists, like Oliphant, who envisioned a refashioned regime of legal rules that really would describe and predict judicial decisions, precisely because they would take account of the particular factual contexts to which courts are actually sensitive.

Legacy of Legal Realism

Within American law and legal education, the impact of legal realism has been profound. By emphasizing the indeterminacy of law and legal reasoning, and the importance of nonlegal considerations in judicial decisions, the realists cleared the way for judges and lawyers to talk openly about the political and economic considerations that in fact affect many decisions. This is manifest in the frequent discussion—by courts, by lawyers, and by law teachers—of the "policy" implications of deciding one way rather than another. The modern legal textbook is largely an invention of the realists as well. The "science" of law envisioned by Christopher Langdell, dean of Harvard Law School in the late nineteenth century, was to be based exclusively on a study of the opinions issued by courts: from these, the scholar (or student) could formulate the rules and principles of law that governed decisions. The realists, who very much shared the ambition of making the study of law "scientific," disagreed profoundly with Langdell over what that entailed. For if the realists were correct that judges' published opinions at best hint at and at worst conceal the real nonlegal grounds for decision, then the study only of cases could not possibly equip a lawyer to advise clients as to what courts will do. To really teach law, the realists thought, it was necessary to understand the economic, political, and social dimensions of the problems courts confront, for all these considerations figure in the decisions of judges. Thus, the modern legal teaching materials are typically titled "Cases *and Materials* on the Law of . . . ," where the materials are drawn from nonlegal sources that illuminate the various nonlegal factors relevant to understanding what the courts have done.

Although the realists profoundly affected legal education and lawyering in America, they have had less influence within recent Anglo-American jurisprudence. The history of realism in this respect is complex. With the advent of World War II, many scholars (especially at Catholic universities) criticized the realists on the grounds that their attacks on the idea of a "rule of law" simply gave support to fascists and other enemies of democracy. At the same time, scholars at Yale (notably Harold Lasswell and Myres McDougal) propounded a watered-down version of realism under the slogan of "policy science." These writers emphasized the realist idea of using social scientific expertise as a way of enabling legal officials to produce effective and desired results.

In the 1950s, American legal education was swept by the "legal process" school, which largely suppressed the lessons of realism. The legal process school identified the distinctive institutional competence of judges as providing "reasoned elaboration" for their decisions; this could be done well or poorly, and it was the business of legal scholars to monitor the performance of judges in this regard and thus to help ensure that judicial opinions would provide a reliable guide to the future course of decision. Absent in all this was any principled response to the realist argument that the law and legal reasoning were essentially indeterminate. (Within Anglo-American jurisprudence, the work of Ronald Dworkin is usefully understood as a philosophical defense of the legal process conception of adjudication.)

The decisive blow for realism as a jurisprudential movement, however, was dealt by the English legal philosopher H.L.A. Hart. In his seminal 1961 work, *The Concept of Law*, Hart devoted a chapter to attacking "rule-skeptics," by whom he meant the realists. Hart characterized the realists as offering an analysis of the "concept" of law according to which by "law" we simply mean a prediction of what the courts will do. Hart effectively demolished this "predictive theory of law." For example, according to the predictive theory, a judge who sets out to discover the "law" on some issue upon which she must render a decision is really just trying to discover what she will do, since the "law" is equivalent to a prediction of what she will do! These, and other manifestly silly implications of the predictive theory convinced most Anglo-American legal philosophers that realism was best forgotten.

The difficulty, of course, was that the realists were not offering a predictive theory of law: they did not seek an understanding of the "concept" of law, as did Hart. They were concerned with prediction because of its practical significance for lawyers advising clients, not because they were advancing semantic claims about how we use words. In most respects, Hart's analysis of the *concept* of law, in fact, fits comfortably with the rest of realist jurisprudence. Moreover, it is striking that on the one real issue where Hart and the realists have a genuine disagreement—namely, over the empirical question of how often legal rules actually affect the course of judicial decision—Hart does no better than simply to assert what the realists deny.

Meritorious or not, Hart's critique had the effect of turning the attention of professional philosophers away from legal realism. In the 1970s, and continuing into the 1980s, nonphilosophers associated with the critical legal studies (CLS) movement brought the realists back to prominence within American legal thought. CLS, however, invented its own version of realism, one more congenial to its distinctive theoretical ambitions. For example, while claiming to embrace the realist claim that the law is indeterminate, CLS writers went beyond realism in two important respects. First, unlike the realists, many CLS writers claimed that the law was "globally" indeterminate, that is indeterminate in all cases (not just those that reached the stage of appellate review). Second, unlike the realists, CLS writers generally grounded the claim of legal indeterminacy not in the indeterminacy of methods of interpreting legal sources, but rather in the indeterminacy of all language itself. Here they took their inspiration—albeit very loosely (and often wrongly)—from the later Ludwig Wittgenstein and deconstructionism in literary theory.

CLS writers also made much out of an argument against the "public-private" distinction, an argument due to the Columbia economist Robert Hale and the philosopher Morris Cohen. Although Hale has become the favorite legal realist of CLS, it bears noting that Hale was not a lawyer and was regarded as only a marginal figure by the other realists. Cohen, though sometimes lumped with the realists, was better known at the time as a critic of realism.

The argument attributed to Hale and Cohen runs basically as follows: since it is governmental decisions that create and structure the so-called private sphere (that is, by creating and enforcing a regime of property and contractual rights), there should be no presumption of "nonintervention" in this "private" realm (that is, the marketplace) because it is, in essence, a public creature. There is, in short, no natural baseline against which government cannot pass without becoming "interventionist" and nonneutral, because the baseline itself is an artifact of government regulation. Despite the blatant non sequitur involved (it does not follow that it is normatively permissible for government to regulate the "private" sphere from the mere fact that government created the "private" sphere through establishing a structure of rights), this argument proved very popular with legal academics into the 1990s, and became central to the CLS version of realism (a version well represented in the introductory materials and selections in *American Legal Realism* by W.W. Fisher et al.).

While realism changed the way lawyers, judges, and law professors thought about law, and while realism continues to be a reference point for many writers in legal theory, developing a sympathetic philosophical understanding of the realists themselves remains a task for the future.

References

Fisher, W.W. et al., eds. *American Legal Realism*. New York: Oxford University Press, 1993.

Frank, Jerome. "Are Judges Human? Parts I & II." *University of Pennsylvania Law Review* 80 (1931), 17–53, 233–267.

———. *Law and the Modern Mind*. New York: Brentano's, 1930.

Holmes, Oliver Wendell, Jr. "The Path of the Law." *Harvard Law Review* 10 (1897), 457–478.

Leiter, Brian. "Legal Realism." In *A Companion to the Philosophy of Law and Legal Theory*, ed. Dennis Patterson. Oxford: Blackwell, 1996.

Llewellyn, Karl. *The Bramble Bush*. New York: Oceana, 1930.

———. *The Common Law Tradition: Deciding Appeals*. Boston: Little, Brown, 1960.

———. "Remarks on the Theory of Appellate Decision and the Rules and Canons about How Statutes Are to Be Construed." *Vanderbilt Law Review* 3 (1950), 395–406.

Moore, Underhill, and Theodore Hope. "An Institutional Approach to the Law of Commercial Banking." *Yale Law Journal* 38 (1929), 703–719.

Schlegel, John Henry. *American Legal Realism and Empirical Social Science*. Chapel Hill: University of North Carolina Press, 1995.

Twining, William. *Karl Llewellyn and the Realist Movement*. Norman: University of Oklahoma Press, 1973.

Brian Leiter

See also DECONSTRUCTIONIST PHILOSOPHY OF LAW; INDETERMINACY; NATURAL LAW; POSITIVISM, LEGAL

Rebellion

Rebellion is thoroughly interwoven with a variety of other concepts including civil war, revolution, insurrection, and insurgency. Distinguishing and refining the concepts requires attention to nuance. Rebellion is almost, by definition, unlawful within the purview of any positive metropolitan law. Treason, in one form or another, is always prohibited, so rebellion must be illegal under the municipal law of the state in question. On the contrary, the rebels see the established government and the countermeasures it takes against them as illegal.

International law has generally been in accord with municipal treatment of rebellion. While international law generally permits civil war, it distinguishes three stages: (1) rebellion, (2) insurgency, and (3) belligerency. In the first of these stages all the force of international law is on the side of the government suppressing the rebellion. Help from outside states to the "rebels" constitutes illegal intervention. In general, while rebellion itself is not illegal under international law, it gives no protection to participants in a rebellion (save international human rights, extended to all). Once a full-scale revolution is under way, international law describes it as an "insurgency" and the legal position of the rebels changes significantly. In an insurgency, rebels begin to achieve the status of a protected international party including the protection of the laws of war.

This would include protection for noncombatants, prisoners of war, and the sanctity of truces and guarantees of safe conduct. Although positive international law is, by no means, congruent with just war theory, the latter, like the former, better fits fully developed revolution and revolutionary war than rebellion at an early stage.

There are two exceptions to this categorizing of the concepts and principles of just war theory. Two principles of just war theory frame the moral question of rebellion at this early stage with precision. The crux of the moral issue of rebellion can be expressed under the just war notion of legitimate authority. First, how can a group rebelling against a presumptively legitimate government ever be justified? What could possibly constitute proper authority on the part of the rebels? A second, and more important, just war requirement that seems applicable is that the violent resistance be launched in a just cause. Why do you rebel? What is your moral justification? This leads to one of the often discussed and most contentious issues in political philosophy: the right of rebellion. That is, do a people have a right to rebel against a presumptively "legitimate" government and, if so, under what conditions?

Thomas Aquinas is perhaps the first to explicitly address the right of rebellion at length. Sedition is a mortal sin, for it makes war upon "the unity and peace of a people." It is opposed to "the unity of law and common good," as well as to justice. However, that is not the end of the tale, for a tyrannical government not only fails the standard of justice, but has as its purpose the private good of the tyrant. Thus, if the tyrant's rule can be overturned without greater harm than the tyrant presently visits on the people (an application of the *rule of proportionality*), it is just. This, Aquinas points out, is not sedition, it is defense against sedition. For the tyrant, who harms the people for his own advantage, is the one guilty of sedition.

The right of rebellion continued throughout the late medieval and early modern period to be inarticulately formulated and neither defended nor refuted with special cogency. Then came John Locke's *Second Treatise of Civil Government*, containing what is surely the most famous defense of rebellion in western thought. (Locke also writes briefly on a right of rebellion in "A Letter on Toleration.")

Locke's theory of political obligation is based on tacit consent. One consents to be governed so long as one's property, that is, life, liberty, and estate, is adequately protected. If it is not, and especially if the rulers themselves become a threat to said property, then the citizen has a right to resist. Again, like Aquinas, Locke believes it is the corrupt or tyrannical ruler who actually initiates war upon the citizens. Should he "take away and destroy" their property or "reduce them to slavery under arbitrary power," then a tyrant attacks the citizens. Here, the citizens' right to self-defense takes over and justifies resistance.

However, Locke introduces another moral consideration. The government must *actually* be behaving in a tyrannical manner, *genuinely* threatening their life, liberty, or estate. The mere opinion of the citizen is not sufficient. Citizens are responsible to God to be correct. By mounting rebellion, they appeal to God, and the moral propriety of their action will be told in the success or failure of a revolution.

Locke's theory had enormous influence. The French *philosophes* combined an evolutionary, historical theory of revolution like that of Aristotle or Polybius with Locke's approval, of revolution, which made revolution natural and, therefore, acceptable. Such a view in one form or another was expressed by Jean Le Rond D'Alembert, Montesquieu, Denis Diderot, Voltaire, and Jean-Jacques Rousseau.

In what was soon to be the United States, Thomas Paine and Thomas Jefferson, most explicitly, adopted a lockean justification of rebellion. The *Federalist Papers* clearly presuppose the right of rebellion; however, the authors believe that its necessity in a constitutional republic is obviated, which means they hedge the right rather significantly. Subsequent to the American founding, Henry David Thoreau and even Abraham Lincoln, among many others, clearly asserted a right of rebellion when the government ignores the rights of citizens. Likewise in Britain, John Stuart Mill and Acton occasionally enunciated, and more often took for granted, a right of rebellion. It would seem that this right has become an integral part of virtually any form of western liberalism.

Probably the most powerful and well known voice against a right of rebellion is Immanuel Kant's. Although liberal in much of his political philosophy, there is no right of rebellion against a formally legitimate head of state (as opposed to a usurper or rebel).

Of course, liberalism is not alone in defending rebellion as an appropriate response to certain political or social abuses. Indeed, marxism can be seen as a far more ambitious project of justification of revolution than liberalism ever was. One is entitled to rebel, but not only against particular tyrannical governments or particular tyrannical measures of government. Now, the very nature of all of society, as determined by economic processes and arrangements, exploits and oppresses a large class of people. The warrant, then, for rebellion is not merely to overthrow a government or even a type of government, but an entire society with its whole social, economic, political, legal, and religious structure. Its purpose is not merely to correct political ills but to advance history and create a new, entirely different kind of social life.

There are special cases of a right to rebellion, and they pose different and difficult problems for moral theory and international law. Rebellion against a conqueror or colonial power is one case where the right of rebellion is more strongly presumed than in general. The issue in this case is, most centrally, one of legitimate authority. A foreign power has prima facie no legitimate power to govern an alien people. The case of succession or irredentism is much more difficult and goes beyond this short survey.

Whether it be broadly aristotelian as in Thomas Aquinas or liberal as in John Locke or radical as in Karl Marx, a justification for rebellion can be seen as fitting into just war theory. A justified rebellion carried out under a right to rebel satisfies the first maxim of just war theory, that is, the *jus ad bellum* requirement that the cause be just. The second relevant just war requirement is that it be carried out by proper authority. In this case, those with proper authority could only be morally justified rebels. For the application of the other principles and categories of just war theory, it will better serve to consider a rebellion which has advanced to organized civil war, or at least to the stage at which international law describes as "insurgency."

References

Akehurst, Michael. *A Modern Introduction to International Law*. 5th ed. London: Allen and Urwin, 1984.

Aquinas, Thomas. *Summa Theologica*, II–II, Qu. 40, "Of Sedition."

Arendt, Hannah. *On Revolution*. New York: Viking Press, 1963.

Berger, Peter L., and Richard John Neuhaus. *Movement and Revolution*. Garden City NY: Doubleday, 1970.

Friedrich, Carl J., ed. *Revolution*. In *Nomos*, vol. 8. New York: Atherton, 1966.

Tucker, Robert C. *The Marxian Revolutionary Idea*. New York: Norton, 1969.

James W. Child

See also POLITICAL OBLIGATION; REVOLUTION; SUPERIOR ORDERS AND LEGITIMATE AUTHORITY

Reception

Reception refers to the transfer of legal concepts across time and space. It thus forms part of a large and ancient debate (*translatio studii*) concerning the nature of social identity and change. In concentrating on the nature and techniques of legal transfers, it forms part of diffusionist social theory, which teaches the primacy of social borrowing. Many forms of reception are also compatible, however, with local and particular forms of social development and hence with some features of evolutionist social theory.

Thinking in terms of reception of law appears, however, to be a relatively recent phenomenon. It became current with the process of reception of Roman law in medieval Europe and is thus closely related to the emergence of nation-states and legal positivism. Reception in this modern sense assumes that identifiable and indigenous legal institutions or rules can be the object of a process of transfer from one particular legal jurisdiction to another. It may thus be the object of formal, legal control and can be seen as superfluous if domestic sources of law are entirely adequate. This formal, positive concept of reception requires further explanation, but it cannot be taken as representing the only form of reception.

Prior to the emergence of nation-states there was movement and circulation of legal ideas. Greek law and philosophy influenced Roman law; the *ius gentium* (the law of nations) of the Romans influenced their *ius civile* (municipal law); religiously inspired law influenced secular law. If the sources and boundaries of law are not formally and exclusively established, law is a matter of influence and persuasion. Distant ideas may play an important role in the process and may even be preferred, since they are not the product of local, dominant forces. A precursor to the notion of reception may thus be seen in the relatively free circulation of legal ideas that preceded the emergence of national legal positivism. The existence and use of legal maxims (for example, *pacta sunt servanda*, agreements are to be kept) typified this process.

The reception of Roman law in medieval Europe was facilitated by the historical mobility of legal ideas. The most evident sign of this was the importance of transnational legal writing or doctrine in the creation of the European *jus commune* (shared law). At the same time, however, national forces led to the domestication of Roman law and to the idea of reception itself. This was facilitated by the use of national legislation or through formal pronouncement by courts, as when the German Imperial Supreme Court explicitly adopted Roman law in 1495 as a residual source of law.

The dominance of formal legal positivism over the last two centuries has turned the attention of legal theorists mainly to the creation and consistency of national law. Reception thus became a largely neglected study and, where discussed, was seen as an element in the formal process of national lawmaking. Comparative law was the main vehicle in this process, seen as a useful aid in the process of refinement and articulation of national rules. Today, however, reception has re-emerged as a major process in the world, and it is necessary to consider a number of different types of reception.

Reception may be seen as formal or informal in character. Formal reception is usually effected by means of legislation, as when a receiving jurisdiction states that the law of another jurisdiction is received as of a precise date. This practice was current in the colonial era, and its effects continue to be felt today in many jurisdictions. It is compatible with the contemporary concept of a legal system, which may formally incorporate an element originally external to itself. Formal legislative reception may also be more particular and more disguised, as when a receiving jurisdiction reenacts a particular law or text of another jurisdiction without acknowledgment of its source. Tracing the process of reception becomes more difficult in such cases, in spite of the formal process of the reception. Formal reception may also be accomplished by national courts, whose decisions may call for reception of the law or laws of a foreign jurisdiction, usually as they existed at a given date.

As a formal process, reception may also usually be characterized as functional in character, dependent on the will of the agency effecting the reception. A number of functions may thus be assigned to reception, including cultural assimilation, economic dominance, efficiency, political authority, political alliance, or legal need (usually expressed in terms of the inadequacy of local sources). Frequently a number of these functions may be evident and relied upon by the agent of reception.

Reception may also be more informal in character. This was the case for the freer movement of legal ideas prior to the nation state. Informality also typified the transnational doctrinal writing of medieval Europe, relying frequently on common Roman sources. Informal reception has also, however, been a continuing, ongoing process which has paralleled formal reception and has even occurred in its absence.

Informal reception occurs when legal officials (lawyers, judges) take cognizance of law identifiable as foreign and make active use of it in their legal reasoning. If the decisions of these officials are recognized as lawmaking (*stare decisis*), this form of reception may exhibit formal characteristics. Usually, however, the number of such officials and the incremental nature of the process are incompatible with a formal lawmaking process. It is also the case that regular use of foreign authority, usually referred to as "persuasive," precludes development of a strong concept of national *stare decisis*.

Informal receptions may be functional in character. The reception of civilian learning in the United States in the nineteenth century was an essential element in the construction of local sovereignty and local law. More often, however, informal reception is nonfunctional in character, or limited to the function of dispute resolution. This is the case for circulation of case law in the Commonwealth and for much of the contemporary influence of U.S. law abroad. Informal, nonfunctional reception presents no threat to local particularity and to the evolution of local societies. Foreign law is simply used as a suppletive source of law, as needs require. Informal, nonfunctional reception poses, however, a major challenge to contemporary systemic legal theory, since it is not controlled by any formal legislative or judicial rules. The emergence of legal "epistemic communities," linked by modern technology over state boundaries, will reinforce contemporary tendencies to informal, nonfunctional reception.

References

Chiba, Masaji, ed. *Asian Indigenous Law in Interaction with Received Law*. London: KPI, 1986.

Glenn, H. Patrick. "Persuasive Authority." *McGill Law Journal* 32 (1987), 261–298.

Hoeflich, Michael. "Transatlantic Friendships and the German Influence on American Law in the First Half of the Nineteenth Century." *American Journal of Comparative Law* 35 (1987) 599–611.

Lee, Hyeong-Kyu. "Die Rezeption des europäischen Zivilrechts in Ostasien" (The Reception of European Civil Law in East Asia). *Zeitschrift für vergleichende Rechtswissenschaft* 86 (1987), 158–170.

Pappachristos, A.C. *La réception des droits privés étrangers comme phénomène de sociologie juridique* (The Reception of Foreign Private Law: A Phenomenon of Legal Sociology). Paris: Librairie générale de droit et de jurisprudence, 1975.

Reimann, Mathias, ed. *The Reception of Continental Ideas in the Common Law World, 1820–1920*. Berlin: Duncker und Humblot, 1993.

Vinogradoff, Paul. *Roman Law in Medieval Europe*. Cambridge: Speculum Historiale, 1968.

Watson, Alan. *Legal Transplants: An Approach to Comparative Law*. 2d ed. Athens: University of Georgia Press, 1993.

Wiegand, Wolfgang. "The Reception of American Law in Europe." *American Journal of Comparative Law* 39 (1991), 229–248.

Wise, Edward. "The Transplant of Legal Patterns." *American Journal of Comparative Law* 38 (Suppl.) (1990), 1–22.

H. Patrick Glenn

See also AFRICAN PHILOSOPHY OF LAW; COMPARATIVE LAW; CONFLICT OF LAWS; CUSTOMARY LAW

Recovery

See POSSESSION AND RECOVERY

Rectificatory Justice

See CORRECTIVE JUSTICE

Referendum

See FRANCHISE AND REFERENDUM

Refugees

See ASYLUM AND REFUGEES

Regulation

Defining the term "regulation" presents a conceptual problem parallel to the problem of defining law. Indeed, some of the most relied-upon definitions by nonjurists bear a striking resemblance to positivist definitions of the term "law." Thus, according to Barry Mitnick, regulation is "a process consisting of the intentional restriction of a subject's choice of activity by an entity not party to, or involved in, that activity" or, according to Alan Stone, "a state-imposed limitation on the discretion that may be exercised by individuals or organizations, which is supported by the threat of sanction."

If "regulation" thus appears to invade the province of law, what is its own province? All contemporary accounts of regulation juxtapose and contrast the functioning of markets with what is typically referred to as "regulatory intervention." That is, but for regulation, the sphere of human endeavor in issue would be governed by private choices and economic incentives. Most frequently, generic forms of market failure—natural monopoly, imperfect information, externalized costs, and public goods—are invoked as rationales for regulations. Thus, regulation of entry into and pricing in public utility markets was in the past justified on the grounds that these industries were natural monopolies; that is, given economies of scale, the lowest cost provider was a single firm. Regulation of disclosure in securities markets was justified by information deficiencies in the unregulated market. Environmental regulation controlling emissions and factory tecnology was justified on the basis that pollution imposed external costs not reflected in the price of goods produced. The expropriation and protection of park land was needed to create and maintain a public good that would not be provided by the market.

Implicit in this form of reasoning is that regulation is only justified when markets do not function properly. "Deregulation" is therefore justified when conditions change so as to allow competitive markets to exist or, indeed, when the original claim that the market failed is challenged. This justification has proved particularly compelling when applied to the natural monopoly rationale for regulation, which has been generally disputed on the grounds that technology will permit more than one low-cost provider (for instance, in the telecommunications sector). When the existence of a natural monopoly is challenged, deregulation has meant principally the removal of pricing and entry restrictions so as to allow competition. In other spheres, deregulation has meant that the market is being used as a substitute for regulation. Thus, for example, self-regulation is relied upon to a greater degree to produce adequate disclosure. Market incentives are relied upon in building tradable pollution emissions credit regimes. What was formerly understood to be public goods, such as government-supplied statistics, are sold as a service on a cost-recovery basis.

In addition to the definition of regulation as state intervention into the market, there is a formal legal definition of the term "regulation," which refers to the concept of delegated legislation. Whereas a statute is an instrument adopted by the constitutionally competent legislative body, a regulation is an instrument adopted pursuant to a statute by a duly delegated authority, such as a member of a cabinet or an administrative agency.

There is a conjuncture, according to Roderick MacDonald, between the narrow legal definition of "regulation" as delegated legislation and the notion of regulation as state intervention into the function of the markets. Typically, regulatory policy is achieved through the formal mechanism of delegated legislation promulgated by independent regulatory agencies given broad public-interest authority. A large part of the attack upon the legitimacy of administrative agencies, the "headless fourth branch of government," is directed at their capacity to legislate without having a direct democratic mandate. It is inherent to the effort to control market pricing and entry that broad discretion must be granted to some steering agency. This discretion can nevertheless be subject to public hearings and standards of accountability, which are then absent as responsibility is shifted to the market in the wake of deregulation.

The question that is begged by distinguishing regulation from markets is: what *are* the institutional and legal underpinnings of the market? In other words, is there a form of regulation that assures the existence of markets? Much financial regulation fits uneasily into the cast of "market failure regulation." Capital adequacy rules and liquidity requirements designed to maintain confidence in financial institutions are as coercive as entry and pricing controls. However, they are understood as part and parcel of the functioning of capital markets rather than as limits on competition within them. Indeed, competitition (antitrust) law, which aims to restrict monopolistic practices and to foster the conditions of economic rivalry, is not traditionally understood to be a form of regulation but can dramatically restrict market choices, for example, through blocking mergers and acquisitions. Indeed, "deregulation" has in many contexts endowed competition law with greater importance, thus shifting from one form of market oversight (the command-and-control regulatory agency) to another (the competition watchdog).

References

Macdonald, Roderick. "Understanding Regulation by Regulations." In *Regulations, Crown Corporations and Administrative Tribunals*, ed. I. Bernier and A. Lajoie. Toronto: University of Toronto Press, 1985.

Mitnick, Barry. *The Political Economy of Regulation*. New York: Columbia University Press, 1980.

Stone, Alan. *Regulation and Its Alternatives*. Washington DC: Congressional Quarterly Press, 1982.

Richard Janda

See also ECONOMICS AND LAW; LEGISLATION AND CODIFICATION

Rehabilitation and Habilitation Rationale

Reform as a concomitant of punishment has formed the basis of twentieth-century rehabilitative theory. While the latter half of the nineteenth century was almost wholly informed by the principle of deterrence, the criminological positivism of the twentieth century led to the introduction of the ideology of reform and treatment of the criminal offender. The Gladstone Report (England) in 1895 ushered in a new era which sought to balance the combined objectives of deterrence and rehabilitation. Focus on individual characteristics led to a more elastic system of punishment, which assumed that differences between offenders should be measured on an ongoing basis to assist in assessment of the reform of the offender. Indeterminate sentences, parole, treatment, and training models for prison and probation systems were introduced as part of the new era of rehabilitative theory. This rehabilitative theory has informed and continues to have impact on sentencing practice and the corrections system.

Rehabilitative theory has come under considerable attack from legal theorists. The theory has been criticized by utilitarian and retributive theorists. It is argued that rehabilitative theory does not provide appropriate punishment for an offense, either in terms of reduced recidivism or in terms of justice. It has also been argued that rehabilitation does not provide adequate denunciation of an offense. Indeterminate sentencing has been referred to as too lenient, allowing release of an offender before the completion of the sentence actually imposed by the court, or too harsh, allowing the incarceration of an individual for a period of uncertain duration under the guise of treatment or training. Criticism is also focused on the fact that rehabilitative sentences often lack the voluntary participation of the offender and, consequently, lack the willing involvement of that offender. It can be argued that where an offender has no choice in relation to the type of sentence imposed or the way in which that sentence will be carried out, a significant hurdle is placed in the way of achieving positive results for the offender.

When assessed from a feminist perspective, rehabilitation does not provide a solid foundation on which to base sentencing. Rehabilitation seeks to instill in the offender the will to lead a good and useful life as defined by the social rules and conventions of the time. Rehabilitation, by definition, means to restore another to privileges, reputation, or proper condition; it means to restore to effectiveness or normal life by training. For the female offender, normal life has traditionally meant a condition of subordination to the interests of men and subservience in relationships with men. The reality of female offenders coupled with women's historical and present position in society leads to the conclusion that rehabilitation does not provide an acceptable foundation for sentencing theory for the female offender.

Unemployment, poverty, and physical and sexual abuse characterize the lives of women who find themselves in contact with the criminal justice systems. While it can be said that this picture is true for offenders generally, it can be argued that the female offender's reality of physical and sexual abuse economic disadvantage, and often racial discrimination demands gender-specific attention. The importance of such review is further illustrated by the fact that the criminal justice system continues to be defined and peopled largely by men.

Female offenders are marginalized within society. Their crimes often, either directly or indirectly, are the result of single parenthood and a past life experience of physical and emotional abuse. The concept of punishment, whether aimed at retributive justice or the objective of crime prevention and protection of society, has focused on adherence to social rules. In relation to female offenders, these rules incorporate gender-based objectives which not only deny women equal status in society but enforce oppression and punish behavior that does not conform to recognized gender and reproductive roles.

Habilitation identifies a new conceptual approach in sentencing the female offender. The objective of habilitation can be defined as enabling or endowing the offender with the ability to participate in and to make a meaningful contribution to a society accountable to women on the basis of gender equality.

The concept of habilitation requires a shift from classical response-oriented theories of punishment to a sentencing model which recognizes that the offender is responsible and accountable for actions, but also goes further to provide options which would break the cycle that has brought the offender into the criminal justice system. This model requires the involvement of the community and demands protection of the community by focusing on the concept of accountability of the offender.

In constructing a sentencing theory which seeks to provide the offender with options to address past life experience and future objectives, the offender must play an active and leading role. Options must allow the offender to address the problems of past experiences in terms with which the offender is capable of dealing and must provide realistic and constructive avenues to assist in future development. Habilitation must not restrict its scope to a sentence period which reflects a measure of punishment. Ongoing support and assistance to the offender is necessary to effect lasting enablement and, as a result, must be built into social services which are available outside the criminal justice arena.

The sentencing of female offenders provides the criminal justice system a significant challenge in the development of criminal legal theory. It requires the development of a sentencing theory which seeks to enable offenders to participate equally in society without gender inequality. It requires moving beyond mere recitation of principles of equality and fairness to construct a sentencing system which recognizes the offender's life experience, demands that the offender take responsibility for actions, and provides useful avenues to allow the offender to participate as a responsible citizen in the community. Habilitation changes the focus from punishment to participation, to enable the female offender to work toward a positive future and to make responsible choices.

References

Adelberg, Ellen, and Claudia Currie, eds. *Too Few to Count: Canadian Women in Conflict with the Law.* Vancouver: Press Gang Publishers, 1987.

Cragg, Wesley. *The Practice of Punishment: Toward a Theory of Restorative Justice.* London: Routledge, 1992.

Cross, Rupert, and A. Ashworth, eds. *The English Sentencing System.* London: Butterworth, 1981.

Lombroso, C., and E. Ferrero. *The Female Offender.* New York: D. Appleton, 1900.

Mukherjee, S.K., and J.A. Scutt, eds. *Women and Crime.* Sydney: George Allen and Unwin, 1981.

Report of the Standing Committee on Justice and Solicitor General on Its Review of Sentencing, Conditional Release and Related Aspects of Corrections: Taking Responsibility. Chair, David Daubney. Ottawa: Queen's Printer, 1988.

Ruby, C. *Sentencing.* Toronto: Butterworth, 1987.

Sechrest, L., S. White, and E.D. Brown. "The Prospects for Rehabilitation." In *Corrections: An Issues Approach*, ed. L.F. Travis, M.D. Schwartz, and T.R. Clear. Cincinnati: Anderson, 1983.

von Hirsch, A., and K.J. Hanrahan. *The Question of Parole: Retention, Reform, or Abolition?* Cambridge MA: Ballinger 1979.

Wilkins, Leslie. *Consumerist Criminology.* London: Heinemann, 1984.

Charalee F. Graydon

See also Feminist Philosophy of Law; Punishment; Radical Class, Gender, and Race Theories: Positionality; Sentencing

Reinach, Adolph (1883–1917)

Adolf Reinach, the founder of phenomenological philosophy of law, trained in both philosophy and law. In 1904 he completed his doctoral thesis on the concept of cause in criminal law under Theodor Lipps (1851–1914) in Munich; subsequently, he completed his legal studies in Tübingen. In 1909 he submitted his *Habilitation* under Edmund Husserl (1859–1938) in Göttingen and was appointed to a position in philosophy. He quickly became a central figure in the phenomenological movement; some students considered him more important than Husserl. Reinach was one of the original coeditors of the *Jahrbuch für Philosophie und phänomenologische Forschung*, and his most important work, "The Apriori Foundations of Civil Law," appeared in the first volume of that journal. As Husserl notes, he was one of the most promising young philosophers in Germany, but unfortunately that promise was cut short by World War I: Reinach was killed in Flanders in 1917.

In "The Apriori Foundations of Civil Law," Reinach examines basic concepts in various areas of private law: personal rights and obligations and their origin in the promise; real rights, especially property; and powers found in representation, mortgages, and liens. His theory of "social acts," which forms the basis of his analysis of many legal concepts, anticipates J.L. Austin's (1918–1960) and John Searle's (1932–) work on speech acts and may even surpass it in many regards.

Reinach's a priori has ontological priority and not merely logical or cognitive precedence. In his realist ontology, there are legal structures (*Sachverhalte,* or states of affairs) that are a priori, universal, timeless, and intelligible. They have the same ontological status as mathematical concepts—such as the various figures of Euclidean geometry or simple arithmetic truths, for example, $2 \times 2 = 4$—which humankind discovered but did not invent.

The phenomenological method makes possible the discovery of the a priori foundations of law. According to Reinach, there is too much variation in the positive laws adopted by different societies over time for the jurist to come upon the foundation of law through induction. Instead, he claims these foundations are intelligible and that people can even intuit them directly.

Reinach shows, for example, how the study of the a priori content of the promise reveals its essence. He rejects any notion of reducing the promise to a declaration of intention because the latter creates neither rights nor obligations. Instead, he adopts a very intuitionist stance, claiming that the pure intuition of the essence of a promise reveals the promise as a social act that addresses the future conduct of the promisor toward the promisee. This, when combined with what is revealed by the pure intuition of the a priori content of renunciation, yields the following propositions: the promise is irrevocable; the rejection of the promise extinguishes the personal right and obligation that it created; performance terminates the obligation; the obligation may be assigned, but the personal right may not.

Reinach claims that his phenomenological method of analysis of the a priori should be generalized and applied to other areas, such as criminal, constitutional, and administrative law.

The statements which express the a priori foundation of law are neither tautologies nor statements based on experience, but are precisely like Immanuel Kant's synthetic a priori statements in pure mathematics. Reinach criticizes Immanuel Kant for limiting unnecessarily the sphere of the synthetic a priori, which he expands to cover also the a priori states of affairs that provide the condition of possibility of positive law.

Although Reinach criticizes legal positivists for being incapable of explaining the foundations of law, he denies that his work is a new version of natural law. Unlike natural law, his a priori is not rooted in human nature. Just as the truth $2 \times 2 = 4$ exists independently of human nature, so do the a priori foundations of law.

Reinach's a priori legal concepts provide the possibility of positive law, but they need not be realized in actual laws. As he notes, it is possible for governments to adopt laws which do not accord with the a priori. Although positive law cannot do what is impossible—such as place the promisee under an obligation to the promisor—which would lead to nonsense, nor can it require the necessary; it can differ from what its a priori foundation requires.

In his brief career, Reinach started a program of research which went beyond the philosophy of law. His complete works (published only in 1989) include articles on William James, Immanuel Kant, David Hume, Paul Natorp, an introduction to philosophy, a paper on phenomenology, and works on the concept of number, the essence of movement, and a phenomenology of religion. Although many authors have noted that, despite the excellence of his work and the clarity of his writing, Reinach has not been much read, his main influence—until the recent reawakening of interest in his more general philosophical concerns and his theory of "social acts"—has been in philosophy of law.

References

Brettler, Lucinda Ann Vandervort. *The Phenomenology of Adolf Reinach: Chapters in the History of Knowledge and Legal Philosophy* (thesis). Montreal: McGill University, 1973.

Burkhardt, Armin. *Soziale Akte, Sprechakte und Textillokutionen. A. Reinachs Rechtsphilosophie und die moderne Linguistik* (Social Acts, Speech Acts, and Textual Illocutions. A. Reinach's Legal Philosophy and Modern Linguistics). Tübingen: Max Niemeyer Verlag, 1986.

Gardies, J.-L. "La philosophie de droit d'Adolf Reinach" (The Philosophy of Law of Adolf Reinach). *Archives de Philosophie du Droit* 10 (1965), 17–32.

Husserl, Edmund. "Adolf Reinach." Trans. Lucinda Vandervort Brettler. *Philosophy and Phenomenological Research* 35 (1974/1975), 571–574.

Mulligan, Kevin, ed. *Speech Act and Sachverhalt. Reinach and the Foundations of Realist Phenomenology*. Dordrecht: Martinus Nijhoff, 1987.

Reinach, Adolf. "The Apriori Foundations of the Civil Law." Trans. J.F. Crosby. *Aletheia* 3 (1983), 1–142.

———. *Sämtliche Werke* (Complete Works). Critical text edition. 2 vols. Ed. Karl Schuhmann and Barry Smith. München: Philosophia Verlag, 1989.

Zelaniec, W. "Fathers, Kings, and Promises: Husserl and Reinach on the A Priori." *Husserl Studies* 9 (1992), 147.

Richard Hudson
Henri R. Pallard

See also PHENOMENOLOGY OF LAW

Relevance

The law of evidence, which is part of a larger body of procedural law, contains a cluster of interrelated concepts that are both practically important and theoretically interesting. These concepts, which include admissibility, relevance, materiality, and sufficiency, are employed by practicing lawyers and judges. Teaching them to prospective lawyers is one of the tasks of legal education. The task of the philosopher is twofold: first, to analyze the concepts, showing how they are related (the conceptual part), and second, to rationalize or criticize the value judgments that underlie certain evidentiary doctrines that employ these concepts (the normative part).

The basic rule of Anglo-American jurisprudence, as reflected in Federal Rule of Evidence (FRE) 402 for United States courts, is that only relevant evidence is admissible. This, by itself, does no more than preclude the introduction of irrelevant evidence. There is also a presumption (expressed in FRE 402) that relevant evidence is admissible. The presumption, however, is rebuttable. Otherwise relevant evidence may be excluded by the judge where, according to FRE 403, "its probative value is substantially outweighed by the danger of unfair prejudice, confusion of the issues, or misleading the jury, or by considerations of undue delay, waste of time, or needless presentation of cumulative evidence." Thus, subject to certain explicit exceptions known as exclusionary rules, all and only relevant evidence is admissible in court.

Relevance has been called "[t]he cornerstone of modern evidence law," according to Dale Nance. As noted by John Strong, to say that a proposition, p, is relevant to some other proposition, q, is to say that the probability of q being true given the truth of p is greater (or less) than the probability of q being true not given p. Relevance is the relation between propositions in which the truth of one proposition increases or decreases the likelihood that the other proposition is true. Less formally, according to *Black's Law Dictionary*, a fact is relevant when it relates to, bears upon, or is connected with the matter in hand or some point or fact in issue. As such, relevance is an either/or concept, not a matter of degree. Proposition p is either relevant to q or it is not; it makes no sense to say that p is quite relevant to q or that p is more relevant than r to q. To say that p is *irrelevant* to q, conversely, is to say that p has no bearing on the truth of q—that they are logically unrelated.

Relevance must not be confused with materiality. Every legal case, civil or criminal, rests on or presupposes a set of facts, some of which, typically, are in dispute. The disputed facts are said to be "in issue." To say that a fact is material is just to say that it is in issue or otherwise of consequence to the outcome of the case. So while person X's being in a tavern at a certain time and place may be relevant to whether X was intoxicated shortly thereafter, that fact (assuming it is a fact) is immaterial if X's intoxication is not in issue in the case and does not otherwise affect its outcome. FRE 401 conflates the concepts of relevance and materiality in its definition of "relevant evidence" as "evidence having any tendency to make the existence of any fact that is of consequence to the determination of the action more probable or less probable than it would be without the evidence."

Sufficiency differs from both relevance and materiality. To say that evidence is sufficient is to say that it is enough, given a certain standard, to establish the point in issue. The aim of an advocate is therefore to introduce relevant, material evidence that, taken together, suffices to establish the essential facts of the case so that a verdict or judgment will be rendered favorably to his or her cause. Standards can and do differ depending on the type of case. In criminal law, at least in Anglo-American jurisdictions, the standard is proof beyond a reasonable doubt. In most civil law cases, the standard is proof by a preponderance of the evidence. In some civil law cases, the standard is intermediate: proof by clear and convincing evidence. To say that an *item* of evidence is *admissible* is to say it belongs on the scale; to say that a set of evidence is *sufficient* is to say that its side of the scale is heaviest.

Besides analyzing these and other concepts, the philosopher of law takes an interest in the normative and epistemic foundations (if any) of certain rules that exclude relevant and material evidence. These so-called exclusionary rules are often explicitly grounded in public policy. Examples include character and other-crimes evidence as proof of behavior on a particular occasion (FRE 404), evidence of subsequent remedial measures as proof of negligence (FRE 407), evidence of offers of compromise or settlement as proof of liability (FRE 408), evidence of insurance as proof of liability (FRE 411), and evidence of promiscuity or past sexual behavior as proof of consent to intercourse on a particular occasion (FRE 412). It is argued, for instance, that to admit evidence of subsequent remedial measures as proof of negligence would be to discourage such measures, which is against public policy.

Among other things, the philosopher of law wonders whether the traditional exclusionary rules have a common rationale—fairness, for example. If not, how are the different values (truth, fairness, and perhaps others) being weighed and compared? A more fundamental question concerns the rationale for restricting evidence to that which is relevant. The usual answer is that the primary value of the trial system is truth, and that only relevant evidence conduces to truth. It has been argued that some or all of the extant exclusionary rules can be understood as instruments to the efficient production of truth or true belief.

To illustrate, take the exclusion of explicit, gory photographs in a murder trial. A judge may exclude such photographs on grounds that their probative value is substantially outweighed by the danger of unfair prejudice or confusion of the issues (FRE 403). This *appears* to be a case in which truth is sacrificed for some other value, for example, fairness to the defendant, but it can also be viewed as a means of *promoti*ng truth (true belief). If the photographs so shock and discombobulate the jury that they cause the jurors' emotions to overwhelm their reason, and if reason is essential to arriving at truth (as seems plausible), then excluding the photographs promotes truth and not just fairness. It may be that other exclusionary rules can be rationalized in a similar manner.

What is needed, and what the philosopher by training is equipped to provide, is a theory of relevance that both (1) explains why all and only relevant evidence is (presumptively) admissible and (2) makes sense of the various exclusionary rules that have developed. It may be that some portions of existing law will be seen as anomalies in the light of this theory, in which case the theory will treat them as mistakes to be ignored or excised. Jeremy Bentham and John Henry Wigmore are among those philosophers or philosophically minded lawyers who set out grand theories of evidence, theories that continue to be studied by the likes of William Twining.

References

Bentham, Jeremy. *The Rationale of Judicial Evidence*. Ed. John Stuart Mill. 5 vols. London, 1827.

Burgess-Jackson, Keith. "An Epistemic Approach to Legal Relevance." *St. Mary's Law Journal* 18 (1986), 463–480.

Goldman, Alvin I. "Epistemic Paternalism: Communication Control in Law and Society." *Journal of Philosophy* 88 (March 1991), 113–131.

Henze, Donald F. "The Concept of Relevance." *Methodos* 13 (1961), 11–23.

Lempert, Richard O. "Modeling Relevance." *Michigan Law Review* 75 (1977), 1021–1057.

Nance, Dale A. "Conditional Relevance Reinterpreted." *Boston University Law Review* 70 (May 1990), 447–507.

Slough, M.C. "Relevancy Unraveled." *Kansas Law Review* 5 (1956), 1–15.

Strong, John W., ed. *McCormick's Handbook of the Law of Evidence*. 4th ed. St. Paul MN: West, 1992.

Twining, William L. *Theories of Evidence: Bentham and Wigmore*. London: Weidenfeld and Nicolson, 1985.

Wigmore, John Henry. *Evidence in Trials at Common Law*. 10 vols. Boston: Little, Brown, 1983.

Keith Burgess-Jackson

See also EVIDENCE; TESTIMONY AND EXPERT EVIDENCE

Religion and Theology

All phenomena pertaining to the belief in and worship of deities, both natural and supernatural, fall under the heading "religion." Such deities are believed in and are worshiped whether they truly exist or not. "Theology" is the systematic articulation and critique of these same subjects.

Precedental Development

Religion and law are equally ancient and were originally indistinguishable. At their origin we should refer to them both using a single word, and "custom" seems the best term. When in tribal cultures matters of custom come into question, and the questions exceed human wisdom, the priests or elders traditionally turn to their deities for assistance in reaching a decision. Once a decision has been made, it can become a binding precedent to be applied subsequently in similar cases. Customs, in the present sense, are not precedents until they are self-consciously adopted and affirmed by the group or its leaders, being thereby more or less formalized.

Precedent gradually becomes the functional engine for the secularization of law, since as a culture ages, and if it grows and becomes increasingly complex, precedent increasingly lessens the need for direct appeals to the deity. With the emergence of a "functioning precedence," custom begins to develop and differentiate. Without its emergence, there is no evidence that a culture will become more complex or differentiated.

Why precedent begins to take hold of a culture and fuel its differentiation (secularization, specialization, and fragmentation) is difficult to explain. Some authors suggest that the advent of writing is a crucial moment in moving a culture, via the power of a functioning precedence, toward substantive precedent—from custom to religion and law. Writing preserves a detailed account for many generations of the decisions of kings, priests, and presumably the deities themselves, their meanings and their interpretation.

Once such a precedental historical consciousness has begun to emerge in a culture, the gap between theory and practice widens, and theological as well as legal-philosophical issues also emerge. In the early stages, this nascent division between theory and practice gives rise to such ancient notions as "divine command," the view that a divine being speaks and a moral and/or natural order is thereby created. A culture would not beget a doctrine such as divine command unless there were already some awareness of a split in function between law and religion.

Between 2200 and 1750 B.C., among the Babylonians the power of precedent had developed to a stage of articulation recognizable as legal philosophy on one hand, and theology on the other. The Code of Hammurabi can be seen as an attempt to repair the split, since its authority is both secular (from the king) and sacred (from the sun-god Shamash), and since it is a set of precedents—282 decisions of Hammurabi dealing with most of the current categories of criminal and civil law.

Procedural Influence

The practices associated with the legal adjudication of guilt or innocence in custom-based cultures were also ritualistic religious ceremonies. This is the source of procedural influence of religion upon law. As the power of precedent has grown, the level of ritual associated with the administration of concrete law has gradually diminished, but it has not disappeared. For example, the widely found practice of having jurors and witnesses take an oath to a deity before hearing evidence, reaching a verdict, or speaking into the record is a vestige of this ancient association. Many other procedures in modern courts are traceable to practices found in custom-based cultures and to ancient attempts to seal the split between religion and law. The general atmosphere of ritual found in modern courts (along with our intuitive sense that this atmosphere is appropriate) is also attributable to this connection.

Regarding procedural influences, not only has religion influenced law, but law has influenced religion. One may see this in the widely accepted metaphor of the deity as a judge with final authority and omniscient understanding, as well as later in the procedures adapted from more secular legal traditions. For example, procedures of the Roman courts were appropriated by the medieval Christian church. This was partly a consequence of the adoption of Latin as the sacred language, since the most refined interpretation of this language resided in its written law and legal philosophy. The Christian church was obliged to draw upon this body of language in order to translate and interpret its own scriptures. There is also a general tendency for more developed religions to become increasingly legalistic as their notions of orthodoxy become refined over time via this point of contact between theological reflection and legal precedent.

Methodological Influence

A much later development in the interplay between religion and law is that, as the body of laws and religious doctrines has accumulated, and the amount of preserved written reflective criticism upon each area has built up, an increasing need to develop a theoretical apparatus for sorting, classifying, and interpreting all the precedents and their interpretations has also appeared. Above and beyond a mutual influence of procedures, therefore, a reflective, abstract analogue to procedural influence has emerged, here designated as an influence of "method." Method (for instance, of interpretation) allows legal philosophers and theologians reflectively to formulate abstract principles for interpreting and classifying the texts peculiar to their respective disciplines. Since both disciplines deal with historical texts and are founded upon the power of precedent, it is not surprising that any method of interpretation which proves illuminating in one discipline is often borrowed by the other. A contemporary example is the way in which legal philosophers have drawn upon the method of biblical hermeneutics developed by the theologian Friedrich Schleiermacher (1768–1834). The wider influence of the nineteenth-century German high criticism, for example, form criticism, historical criticism, and scientific philological analysis, has also been profound.

Legal philosophy and theology today often look to developments in secular philosophy and linguistics (language analysis, semiotics, deconstruction, and so on) for their methodological ideas. Understanding the influence of theology upon legal philosophy is complicated by the same questions which accompany any effort to understand the relation between two distinct bodies of theory.

Jurisdictional Issues

Since law and religion are so closely related in ancient history, since both are precedental in function and structure, and since both lay claim to an authority to decide pressing normative matters which exceed human wisdom, they have often fallen into conflict over jurisdiction. The contemporary issues regarding the relation between church and state are only one example of this conflict. What is clear about common law, for example, is its close connection to the folkways and mores of the Anglo-Saxons on one side and the procedures of the Normans on the other. Both the Anglo-Saxon norms and the Norman procedures are the offspring of an earlier association with religion. In the case of the Normans, this was primarily a negative influence, in that they had already developed a de facto separation of ecclesiastical and secular law, and even a small body of legal philosophy (in which are developed early versions of the idea of a crime against the public good and the idea of a separation between church and state). Yet this development among the Normans could only have arisen from a situation in which the closeness of religion and law in Norman culture had become problematic, as the history of the Normans confirms. Even though the body of precedent subsequently produced by the common law tradition was very secular and progressive in its day, its precise connection to religion has remained an ill-defined and problematic area in England.

This problem has been inherited by a large number of modern nations which took their essential directions in law from the rule established by the British Empire. In Great Britain, a functional separation of jurisdiction has emerged in spite of a substantive identity between church and state, and the issue can hardly be said to have been resolved. Many other nations have addressed their jurisdictional viewpoint to weaknesses in the British tradition, but in different ways. Some nations, such as the United States and Canada, have insisted upon a substantive as well as functional separation between church and state, while others, such as a number of nations formerly under British control in the Middle East, have chosen a substantive as well as functional identity of church and state. Other groups have sought political solutions to these jurisdictional problems, such as the separation of Hindu India from Muslim Pakistan.

The question theologians and legal philosophers must ask is: can the principle of the separation of church and state, religion and law, be cogently defended? What would the basis of such a defense be? The identity of religion and law has both historical precedent and logical advantages. It is more easily defended in the abstract than separation. The idea that two variant bodies of practice and belief (religion and law) can simultaneously claim ultimate authority over individual people seems contradictory. Unless one body yields to the authority of the other, the individual's position is impossible. A system which creates such contradictions appears irrational on the surface.

How is the separation defended? Many have argued that reason is a suitable substitute for divine authority, while others have said that consensus among the people, or democratic processes through which the people make their collective will manifest, are adequate substitutes. Still others appeal simply to utility or raw power. Yet these arguments are made at the expense of another legal principle, religious freedom, and not only contradict themselves, but also ultimately yield to the authority of law over that of religion in saying that the free exercise of religion is guaranteed because of the law. If the free exercise of religion is at bottom a legal issue, then religion has no authority of its own. The question accompanying the suggestion that utility, raw power, consensus, the will of the majority, and reason are adequate substitutes for divine authority is: what is the justification for declaring that these substitutes are adequate replacements for divine authority? Does not religion, and perhaps even the legal principle of religious freedom, demand that some extralegal authority be reserved for religion? It is here that religion and its theology confront law and legal philosophy in the contemporary arena.

The confrontation is bewildering in its complexity. For example, even if one's religion is based upon a traditional belief in God's omnipotence, one might still give a dozen different theological justifications for the use of power in enforcing the secular law. If one's theology states that God is love, one might still give many religious justifications of the employment of force in enforcing the secular law (for example, the criminal is evil, or it is God's will that our nation prosper, and so forth). In short, so long as one's theology and one's religion can conflict in both form and content, a gap will exist in which law and legal philosophy may enter and exercise influence. The Quaker who sees a contradiction between the pacifist theology and the day-to-day behavior of Quakers might be tempted to invest a fuller confidence in the rule of law and its articulation in legal philosophy. Similarly, an attorney who daily witnesses the contradiction between the high ideals of a given legal philosophy and the corrupt practice of law in the courts might be more inclined to allow a religion and its theology to fill the gap in authority thus created. Therefore, clear thinking about the jurisdictional conflict between law and religion is not as simple as analyzing either the law and legal philosophy of a given nation, or the religion and theology of a given faith.

The philosophical defense of a separation of church and state is obliged to confront these contradictions if it aims to defend a separation of church and state. Otherwise, the more obviously rational solution of an entirely legal or entirely religious authority, that is, a totalitarian society, prevails in argumentation. The totalitarian stance is more parsimonious and unitary, and in most every way logically superior to the separation stance, unless one can defend philosophically the greater value of diversity and complexity in the forms of human association. Such a defense is fraught with difficulties, both theoretical and practical, and this accounts for the enormous difficulty of this issue.

References

Cassirer, Ernst. *The Myth of the State*. New Haven CT: Yale University Press, 1946.

Curry, Thomas J. *The First Freedoms: Church and State in America to the Passage of the First Amendment*. New York: Oxford University Press, 1986.

Frankfort, Henri et al. *The Intellectual Adventure of Ancient Man*. Chicago: University of Chicago Press, 1946.

Greenawalt, Kent. *Religious Convictions and Political Choice*. New York: Oxford University Press, 1988.

Hayek, Friedrich. *Law, Legislation and Liberty*. 3 vols. Chicago: University of Chicago Press, 1973–1979.

Levy, Leonard. *The Establishment Clause: Religion and the First Amendment*. 2d ed. Chapel Hill: University of North Carolina Press, 1994.

Reichley, James. *Religion in American Public Life*. Washington DC: Brookings Institution, 1985.

Stokes, Anson Phelps. *Church and State in the United States*. 3 vols. New York: Harper and Bros., 1950.

Voegelin, Eric. *"The Nature of Law" and Other Related Legal Writings*. In *The Collected Works of Eric Voegelin*, vol. 27, ed. Robert A. Pascal et al. Baton Rouge: Louisiana State University Press, 1991.

———. *Order and History*. 5 vols. Baton Rouge: Louisiana State University Press, 1956–1987.

Randall E. Auxier

See also ABORIGINAL LEGAL CULTURES; CUSTOMARY LAW; ECCLESIASTICAL JURISDICTION; INDIAN PHILOSOPHY OF LAW; ISLAMIC PHILOSOPHY OF LAW; JEWISH LAW; OATHS; ONTOLOGY, LEGAL (METAPHYSICS); ORDER; PRECEDENT

Renaissance Philosophy of Law

Like the Renaissance in all its manifold aspects, Renaissance legal philosophy has deep roots in earlier thought. As students of the period are aware, scholarly and artistic developments in the late middle ages had already begun to evince the humanistic, individualistic, and naturalistic orientation that was later to flower in the Italian Renaissance and still later to engulf Europe generally. Crucially, these developments never involved, or even presaged, an actual turning away from the Christian theological preoccupations that had so thoroughly characterized the medieval period. Rather, their dominant feature was the adaptation of traditional, theologically oriented forms and ideas to newer and more secular concerns, as the latter were generated by the sweeping social, economic, and political changes then taking place in western Europe. It was this trend, with its attendant intermingling of the worldly and the otherworldly, the practical and the spiritual, the human and the divine, that quickly developed into that supercharged explosion of multidimensional human creativity known as "the Renaissance."

The case was not appreciably different in the philosophy of law. The late medieval period is rife with forerunners of the theorizing that characterizes legal philosophy in the Renaissance; these forerunners serve as theology-based foundations for the mixture of ecclesiastical and secular jurisprudential reasoning that was to follow. They include, for example, the precisely specified divisions among "eternal," "divine," "natural," and "human" law developed by Thomas Aquinas (1224–1274) and others of the late scholastic tradition. They likewise include the manner in which these thinkers carefully allotted to each legal species its appropriate role in relation to the affairs of God and humankind. Indeed, they embrace the whole of Aquinas's legal philosophy, and a rich array of related ideological innovations. So fundamental were these developments to the legal thought of the Renaissance period itself, that the present entry must presuppose some familiarity with at least the central elements of medieval philosophy of law.

Marsilius of Padua (ca. 1275–1342) is the first legal theorist of importance in the early Renaissance. Remarkably for his time, he not only drew a sharp distinction—as Aquinas had done—between the moral and religious sphere on one hand, and the political on the other, but he held that the people actually affected were the only legitimate source of authority within the latter sphere. He thus regarded the law governing the body politic as the legislative prerogative exclusively of those to whose conduct it pertained. He saw the law in question as predominantly coercive, addressed to regulating the conflicts that inevitably arise among individuals so that the disagreements do not become disruptive to the society at large. He maintained that even the political power of the Church and its popes must thus be subordinated to that of the people. Evidently the legal categories with which he worked came straight out of medieval thought, although he dramatically reversed some of the traditional relations among them.

William of Ockham (1285–1349), an English scholastic philosopher of the Franciscan order, represented at least two strains of thought running counter to the doctrines of Marsilius. He regarded the highest law in all matters to be the law of God, and he saw as its aim not the constraint of the people, but rather their liberation. Thus, Ockham considered the pope, in his role as supreme head of the Church and representative of God on earth, as the final authority on all societal affairs whatsoever. Nevertheless, he took the pontiff to be subject to such legal checks as might prove necessary to prevent tyrannical abuse of his papal authority, for, contrary to the law of God, such abuse threatened to curtail the freedom of the people if allowed free reign. Evidently, like Marsilius, Ockham worked with traditional categories. Moreover, he was fully as much an innovator: if in respect of where the ultimate legal *authority* lies he was less humanistically inclined than Marsilius was, in respect of the ultimate *aims* of the law, he was evidently the more humanistic of the two thinkers.

Whereas both Marsilius and Ockham took everyone to be bound alike by political law, certain governmental administrators of the fourteenth and fifteenth centuries were inclined to exempt rulers from the constraints of such law. Bartolus of Sassoferrato (1314–1357) was one of these administrators, although he thought it would be best if rulers abided by the law anyway, on a voluntary basis. A much more renowned thinker of the period to grant special, supra-legal authority to heads of state was Niccolò Machiavelli (1469–1527). The famed Florentine political theorist regarded the preservation of the ruler's own authority as primary and was therefore willing to see the sovereign bend, break, or even totally suspend the established laws, if pragmatic concerns so argued in what might otherwise prove to be difficult circumstances for him. Yet another supporter of such exemptions from the law was Jean Bodin (1530–1596) in France, who went so far as to *identify* law simply with whatever the sovereign decrees, echoing in this view certain medieval notions of the relation of God to the moral law.

In sharp dissent from these autocratically inclined theorists, and following instead Aquinas's thesis that positive law should always be subject to evaluation in terms of a higher natural law, thomists of the Renaissance identified unjust political laws as an important variety of instances in which the law is nonbinding upon anyone. The English jurist John Fortescue (ca. 1394–1476), his compatriot Christopher St. Germaine (1460–1549), the Italian cardinal Robert Bellarmine (1542–1621), and later the Puritan clergyman Thomas Hooker (ca. 1586–1647) were among thomistic legal theorists of the period promoting such a natural law–dependent view. They followed Aquinas likewise in the opinion that while natural law is not man-made, no higher authority is required to propound it or to evaluate positive law in terms of it, because its nature is openly accessible to human reason.

The theorists so far discussed attended to law exclusively as it applied to individuals residing in a given state or subject to its governance. However, as the rise of nation-states brought international relations into prominence, such thomists as the Spanish monks Francisco de Vitoria (ca. 1492–1546) and Francisco Suárez (1548–1617) sought to extend the concept of natural law to the area of international affairs. In an extensive body of writings, these thomists urged that we should see rights, obligations, and the other conceptual constructs of natural law theory as belonging not just to individual persons in their dealings with one another and the state, but also to nations in their dealings with other nations. Thus, even if no international legislative body had ever codified a positive law to cover international affairs, the same rational faculties that enable our apprehension of the natural law in the civil sphere provide us access to it in the international arena as well. If this is correct, then relations among states do not obtain in the legal vacuum that otherwise threatens. The Dutch Protestant legal theorist Hugo Grotius (1583–1645) was noteworthy for making extensive further contributions to natural law theory in its international applications.

References

Allen, Carleton K. *Law in the Making*. Oxford: Clarendon Press, 1964.

Cairns, H. *Legal Philosophy from Plato to Hegel*. Baltimore: Johns Hopkins University Press, 1949.

Carlyle, Robert W. *A History of Medieval Political Theory in the West*. New York: Barnes & Noble, 1953.

Frederich, C.J. *The Philosophy of Law in Historical Perspective*. Chicago: University of Chicago Press, 1963.

Gewirth, Alan. *Marsilius of Padua and Medieval Political Philosophy*. New York: Columbia University Press, 1951.

Kelley, J.M. *A Short History of Western Legal Theory*. Oxford: Clarendon Press, 1962.

Luscombe, D.E. "Natural Morality and Natural Law." In *The Cambridge History of Later Medieval Philosophy*, ed. Norman Kretzmann et al. Cambridge: Cambridge University Press, 1982.

McGrade, A.S. "Rights, Natural Rights, and the Philosophy of Law." In *The Cambridge History of Later Medieval Philosophy*, ed. Norman Kretzmann et al. Cambridge: Cambridge University Press, 1982.

Rowan, Steven W. *Law and Jurisprudence in the Sixteenth Century: An Introductory Bibliography*. St. Louis: Center for Reformation Research, 1986.

Vinogradoff, Paul. *Outlines of Historical Jusisprudence*. London: Oxford University Press, 1910–1921.

Robert B. Barrett

See also MEDIEVAL PHILOSOPHY OF LAW; SIXTEENTH- TO EIGHTEENTH-CENTURY PHILOSOPHY OF LAW

Republican Philosophy of Law

The legal theory of the Roman republic, as revived and elaborated in Renaissance Italy, commonwealth England, and the legal traditions of the French and American revolutions, is here called republican legal theory.

Republican legal theory developed out of the jurisprudential and constitutional legacy of the Roman *res publica* (public concerns), as interpreted by subsequent admirers in Italy, England, France, and the United States. Leading republican authors include Marcus Tullius Cicero (106–43 B.C.), Niccolò Machiavelli (1469–1527), James Harrington (1611–1677), Algernon Sidney (1622?–1683), John Adams (1735–1826), and (more controversially) subsequent self-styled "republican" legislators such as Abraham Lincoln (1809–1865) and Charles Renouvier (1815–1903). Many important writers outside the republican tradition also reflect its strong influence, including Montesquieu (1689–1755), Jean-Jacques Rousseau (1712–1778), and Immanuel Kant (1724–1804). These three also illustrate the close connection between republican ideas and the European Enlightenment leading up to the French and American revolutions.

The central concepts of republican legal theory include pursuit of the common good, popular sovereignty, liberty, virtue, mixed government, and the rule of law, linked by a Roman conception of *libertas* that defined justice between free people as subjection to no one's will or interest, but only to general laws approved by the people for the common or "public" good of the community.

Republican theorists have usually followed Cicero's conception of Rome's republican laws and institutions, as set out comprehensively in his treatises *De officiis* (on duties), *De legibus* (on the laws), and *De republica* (on public concerns). Other fundamental texts include the first ten books of Titus Livius (59 B.C.–A.D. 17) in his history of Rome, the sixth book of the *Histories* of Polybius (ca. 205–123 B.C.), and much less importantly, the works of Aristotle (384–322 B.C.), insofar as they anticipate and justify Roman practices. Of these authors only Cicero primarily concerned himself with legal institutions, not just in his monographs, but also in letters and orations, including the widely read *Philippicae* and speeches against Catiline. Cicero and Livy took the proper province of legislation to be the public interest or *res publica*, protected by laws established in advance, to avert the influence of private considerations. Private interests (*res privata*) also deserved protection, within their own sphere, defined by public deliberation. The republican tradition justified popular sovereignty as a necessary check on self-interested factions, but only under the guidance of an infrequently elected legislative council or "senate." Necessary components of a "republican" constitution on the Roman model include a bicameral legislature, standing laws, and elected magistrates.

Constitutional law has always been the central concern of republican legal theory, but several other components of the republican tradition have provided judges, legislators, and lawyers with standards of virtue and a vocabulary for legal discourse. Republican public virtue (*virtus*) is a disposition to serve the common good. The *Lives* of L. Mestrius Plutarchus (ca. 50–120) supply a rich source of republican narratives and models of civic virtue. Cornelius Tacitus (ca. 55–120) and Gaius Sallustius Crispus (86–34 B.C.) contain salacious accounts of the vices that emerge when republican principles decline. All three authors had considerable influence on the aims and invective of subsequent republican theorists.

The central project for republicans since Cicero consists in reviving the liberty, principles, and virtue of the Roman republic, while avoiding the vices and constitutional flaws that led eventually to the tyranny of emperors and tragedy of civil war. Cicero had proposed frequent rotation in office for executive officials and a strengthened senate, to control both the magistrates and popular assembly. Machiavelli suggested in his *Discorsi sopra la prima Deca di Tito Livio* (1517–1518) that republics thrive best in poverty and war, which unite citizens in pursuit of the common good. He concluded that wealth and leisure made Rome too corrupt to be free. Harrington agreed in his *Commonwealth of Oceana* (1656) and advocated limits on landholding and rotation in office, to maintain the civic equality necessary for true republican virtue. Sidney's *Discourses Concerning Government* (1698) argued that wealth would actually strengthen the republic, and he endorsed representation in the popular assembly to check the excesses of direct democracy. Adams' *Thoughts on Government* (1776) and *Defence of the Constitutions of Government of the United States of America* (1787–1788) also embraced representation, with the added check of a veto in the chief executive. James Madison (1751–1836), writing *The Federalist* (1787) under the republican pseudonym of "Publius," praised the American republics' central constitutional reform, which totally excluded direct democracy from any active role in legislation.

Despite their different proposals for protecting republican liberty and virtue, all the main authors in the republican tradition shared a basic conception of the constitution and legal order that they sought to revive. This embraced pursuit of the common good through standing laws, ratified by controlled popular sovereignty, in a bicameral legislature of senate and democratic assembly, to be executed by elected magistrates. Republicans agreed that unelected kings or any other uncontrolled power in the constitution would lead to self-interest and corruption. Liberty and the common good depended on "mixed government" and a "balanced constitution." During the age of European revolution many theorists reluctant to define themselves as "republican" accepted aspects of this ideology. Montesquieu supported monarchy, which made it impossible to endorse or even accurately to describe republican government. However, he did embrace the common good and rule of law in *De l'esprit des lois* (1748), as well as balanced government, the senate, and a (representative) popular assembly. Rousseau viewed a sovereign popular assembly as the essential attribute of legitimate government. His essay *Du contrat social* (1762) insisted on ratification of all laws by a general vote of the people, as was done in Rome. Rousseau would have restricted the senate to a purely executive function. Kant proposed in *Zum ewigen Frieden* (1795) the creation of an international federation of republican states, to provide the basis for perpetual peace.

Rousseau's identification of liberty with law, and law with the common good, repeated the republican formula of Cicero, Machiavelli, Harrington, Sidney, and even Montesquieu, who put it into a monarchical context. Rousseau differed only in his program for realizing republican virtue. Republicans since Harrington had endorsed representation as a technique for purifying the popular will. Republicans since Cicero and Polybius had praised mixed government as the best control of private passions. Rousseau, however, preferred the democratic formula that only plebiscites make law. He attributed this idea of a unitary state to the Spartan king Lycurgus, which reflected his general preference for Spartan equality to republican balance—even to the extent of accepting slavery for some to maintain the liberty and virtue of the rest. Montesquieu had also admired Spartan poverty and virtue. Both authors insisted that republican purity could only survive in small states or cantons, like Sparta and Geneva. French unicameralism and the Reign of Terror under Maximilien Robespierre (1758–1794) both derived in large part from Rousseau's fascination with the homogeneity, poverty, and asceticism of Sparta. Rousseau's direction has colored the tone of French republicanism ever since and marks the beginning of separate republican traditions in France and the United States.

The republican revolution of the American Civil War represented a rejection of "Greek" republicanism, with its frank reliance on slavery, and a return to the Roman rhetoric of liberty and Cicero's condemnation of servitude as a violation of natural law. American republicans never feared commerce or wealth, and the new "Republican" party sought to maximize both and reinvigorate the common good through a widened electorate and universal rule of law. The Fourteenth Amendment to the United States Constitution protected the original Constitution's guarantee of a "republican form of government" by forbidding the states to deny any person the equal protection of the laws or to deny citizenship and its privileges to any persons born in the United States.

The strongly republican nature of early American constitutionalism produced a senate, a bicameral legislature, elected executives, balanced government, popular sovereignty, and broad commitments to the "general welfare," "liberty" and "due process" of the law. Yet twentieth-century American constitutionalism developed after the World War II toward a dry "legal process" theory that endorsed the frank pursuit of self-interest by an atomized and unreflective electorate. The recent American republican constitutional revival emerged in response to moral dissatisfaction with postwar liberal interest-group pluralism as a suitable basis for any just legal order.

The republican revival began among intellectual historians such as Gordon Wood (1933–) and J.G.A. Pocock (1924–) in the 1960s and 1970s, followed in the late 1980s by legal academics such as Cass Sunstein (1954–) and Frank Michelman (1936–), who argued that the United States Constitution reflects an ideology of shared citizenship and common purpose that might justify judicial intervention against self-interested legislation. Their primary arguments concerned republican deliberation and the common good, rather than republican institutions. This self-styled "liberal" republicanism echoes Rousseau, Montesquieu, and the American antifederalists in questioning the value of popular sovereignty in a very large and pluralistic republic and in preferring the local democracy of smaller cantons and communities.

Liberal critics of republicanism question whether this heightened civic federalism can solve the problem of pluralism without an intolerable threat to personal autonomy. For many, the very idea of a shared common good appears a veil for intolerance and oppression. Republicanism implies the possibility of collective objectivity and seems alarmingly antidemocratic in its reliance on the senate and judiciary. Roman checks and balances intentionally frustrate the immediate will of the people to serve their common good. If private desires and personal interests are everything, the self-denial of republican virtue must be pointless.

Liberal fears of republicanism reflect liberal fears of government that go back at least as far as the English Revolution of 1688. When they are not virtuous the people may be dangerous, and even Cicero feared the tyranny of the mob more than the tyranny of kings. Sometimes in the wake of civil war monarchs promise safe and stable government. Rome settled for Augustus (63 B.C–A.D. 14), England for Charles II (1630–1685), and France for Napoléon Bonaparte (1769–1821). In each case subjects received from their sovereign guarantees that protected the private sphere while ceding public power to the state. Benjamin Constant (1767–1830) frankly distinguished the (republican) "liberty of the ancients," in *De la liberté des anciens comparée à celle des modernes* (1819), "for which we are no longer fit," from the (liberal) "liberty of the moderns"—liberty to pursue one's own private pleasures in peace. Modern liberalism emerged from the older republican tradition, when full republicanism no longer seemed attainable.

Republican legal theory remains America's central contribution to modern legal discourse, through the United States Constitution's practical demonstration that popular sovereignty may seek liberty and justice in pursuit of the common good, through the rule of law, checks and balances, a deliberative senate, and a stable judiciary, without collapsing into tyranny and civil war. The Roman republic provided a model and inspiration for republican theorists in America, as it had in Italy, England, and France. The United States, however, became the first nation since Rome to make this system work, through the innovation of representation in the popular assembly. Republican theory triumphed so completely in America that its origins are largely forgotten. Most modern legal discourse is in some sense "republican," because republican theory is so deeply entrenched in the universal institutions of contemporary constitutional government. Almost every generation experiences some return to republican first principles, as well as new attempts to build civic community and a revived legal order from the ruins of the west's oldest and most persistent legal and political philosophy.

References

Fabre, M.H. *La République. Sa perception constitutionnelle par les Français* (Republic. Its Constitution as the French Perceive It). Aix-en-Provence: Edisud, 1987.

Michelman, Frank. "The Supreme Court 1985 Term—Foreword: Traces of Self-Government." *Harvard Law Review* 100 (1986), 4–77.

Nicolet, Claude. *L'idée républicaine en France: Essai d'histoire critique* (The Republican Idea in France: An Essay in Critical History). Paris: Gallimard, 1982.

Pocock, John G.A. *The Machiavellian Moment: Florentine Political Thought and the Atlantic Republican Tradition*. Princeton NJ: Princeton University Press, 1975.

Sellers, Mortimer. *American Republicanism: Roman Ideology in the United States Constitution*. Basingstoke UK: Macmillan, 1994; New York: New York University Press, 1994.

———. "Republican Impartiality." *Oxford Journal of Legal Studies* 11 (1991), 273–282.

———. "Republican Liberty." In *The Jurisprudence of Liberty*, ed. Gabriël Moens and Suri Ratnapala. London: Butterworth, 1995.

"Symposium: The Republican Civic Tradition." *Yale Law Journal* 97 (1988), 1493–1723.

White, G. Edward. "Reflections on the 'Republican Revival': Interdisciplinary Scholarship in the Legal Academy." *Yale Journal of Law and the Humanities* 6 (1994), 1–35.

Wood, Gordon S. *The Creation of the American Republic, 1776–1787*. Chapel Hill: University of North Carolina Press, 1969.

Mortimer N.S. Sellers

See also DEMOCRATIC PROCESS

Rescue in Tort and Criminal Law

The common law traditionally has recognized no general duty to aid another person in danger.

This position was expressed most forcefully in *Bush v. Amory Manufacturing* (1897), where the court declared that there was "a broad gulf" between wrongfully causing injury ("misfeasance" or wrongdoing) and merely failing to protect another against harm ("nonfeasance" or not-doing). The negative duty to refrain from wrong was a legal obligation, while the affirmative duty to prevent injury was generally "a moral obligation only, not recognized or enforced by law." In other words, the law did not require a person to be a Good Samaritan.

The traditional rule has been defended by Richard Epstein and other libertarians on the ground that individuals generally should be free to act as they like, so long as they cause no harm to others. Assistance should be a matter of charity or contract, not coercion. For the state to compel one person to act solely for the benefit of another would constitute an infringement of individual liberty.

In response, some theorists, such as Joel Feinberg, contend that one who fails to prevent harm may under some circumstances be said to have caused the harm. They acknowledge, however, that this holds true only where there is an antecedent duty to act. The crucial question, therefore, is whether the law ought to recognize such a duty.

Several arguments have been advanced for a duty to rescue. First, many writers, including James Barr Ames (in Ratcliffe's *The Good Samaritan and the Law*) and Ernest Weinrib, advocate such a duty on moral grounds. In opposition to the legal positivism of *Bush*, they contend that the law should be brought into greater harmony with moral principles. (In his work, however, Weinrib reconsiders this position, and instead develops a theory of legal formalism following Immanuel Kant, according to which law is based on a conception of right that is prior to a conception of ethics—a view that leads him to reject affirmative duties in tort law.)

Ames Weinrib, in "A Duty to Rescue," and others have also elaborated a utilitarian rationale for requiring rescue. This position may be traced back to Jeremy Bentham, who suggested that it should be the "duty of every man to save another from mischief, when it can be done without prejudicing himself." Similarly, while some law-and-economics scholars, including William Landes and Richard Posner, have questioned the efficiency of a duty to rescue, others, such as Richard Hasen, have made a persuasive case for the duty on economic grounds.

The common law rule has also been criticized from a cultural feminist perspective. Thus, Leslie Bender argues that the doctrine reflects a traditional or masculine view that emphasizes abstract rules based on individual liberty and autonomy. Drawing on the work of Carol Gilligan, Bender contrasts this view with a feminist ethic that focuses on caring, relationship, and responsibility. This perspective supports a duty to rescue rooted in the interconnectedness of human beings. Similarly, some communitarians seek to ground that duty in an individual's responsibility to the community.

These arguments constitute a powerful critique of the traditional Good Samaritan doctrine. At the same time, they all confront a common difficulty: that of reconciling the duties that they would impose with individual rights. Morality, utility, efficiency, interconnectedness, and community might support the imposition of affirmative duties beyond those that would be acceptable in a liberal society. Just as the libertarian position on rescue may sacrifice these values for the sake of individual liberty, the countervailing views may pose the opposite problem.

One effort to resolve this dilemma would view rescue in terms of the rights and duties of liberal citizenship. Drawing on the social contract tradition, this approach would hold that the ends of a liberal community include the protection of its members from criminal violence and other forms of serious harm. Individuals have a fundamental right to such protection by the community. In return, they have an obligation to assist the community in providing this protection, by notifying the authorities or otherwise aiding a fellow citizen in peril. Failure to rescue violates a duty both to the community itself and to the particular victim, and thus may give rise to both criminal and civil liability. In this way, it may be possible to develop a justification for rescue that combines the liberal emphasis on individual rights with the countervailing themes of community, responsibility, and the common good.

In recent decades, some jurisdictions in the United States have moved toward establishing such a duty. Several states, responding to the Kitty Genovese case and other notorious incidents, have enacted laws requiring individuals who witness a violent crime to notify the police. Vermont, Minnesota, and Rhode

Island have gone further, establishing a general duty to provide reasonable assistance to any person exposed to grave physical harm. It is not yet clear whether these laws, which provide for criminal penalities, will also provide a basis for liability in tort.

Most jurisdictions continue to adhere to the traditional rule that there is no duty to rescue. Over the past century, however, courts have steadily narrowed this rule by recognizing a wide range of "special relationships" and other circumstances that will give rise to affirmative duties. In addition, most jurisdictions seek to encourage rescue through so-called Good Samaritan laws, which make rescuers immune from tort liability for any injuries caused by their efforts, unless they are grossly negligent.

References

Bender, Leslie. "A Lawyer's Primer on Feminist Theory and Tort." *Journal of Legal Education* 38 (1988), 3–37.

Epstein, Richard A. "A Theory of Strict Liability." *Journal of Legal Studies* 2 (1973), 151–204.

Feinberg, Joel. *The Moral Limits of the Criminal Law*. Vol. 1. New York: Oxford University Press, 1984.

Hasen, Richard L. "The Efficient Duty to Rescue." *International Review of Law and Economics* 15 (1995), 141–150.

Heyman, Steven J. "Foundations of the Duty to Rescue." *Vanderbilt Law Review* 47 (1994), 673–755.

Ratcliffe, James M., ed. *The Good Samaritan and the Law*. Garden City NY: Anchor, 1966.

Weinrib, Ernest J. "The Case for a Duty to Rescue." *Yale Law Journal* 90 (1980), 247–293.

———. *The Idea of Private Law.* Cambridge MA: Harvard University Press, 1995.

Steven J. Heyman

See also Imperfect Obligation; Omissions; Supererogation

Residency

See Homelessness and Residency

Res Ipsa Loquitur

See Personal Injury

Responsibility

Responsibility may be understood in a number of ways, some related and some utterly independent of each other. Talk of responsibility for events, typically ones that are untoward, unwelcome, unhappy, illegal, and so forth, may sometimes amount to nothing more than the identification of the event, object, person, or whatever, that was the cause, or one of the causes, of the event in question. For example, it might be said that the electric storm was responsible for the power outage that damaged the hard drive in a computer. Such causal responsibility ascriptions are almost always made in the past tense. Not all entities that are causally responsible for something, however, can or should be held responsible for its occurrence in the other senses of "responsibility": moral and legal. For example, it may be the case that a very young child was causally responsible for breaking the vase, though it may be inappropriate to hold that child responsible, morally or legally, for breaking it. To hold an entity responsible in both the moral and legal sense is to hold it accountable, answerable, for the event in question. Some things, such as the storm, cannot answer or be held to account for what they cause. It makes no sense to seek restitution from them or to require that they compensate injured parties for their harm-causing or that they suffer for that harm-causing.

To be held to account an entity must have, or be believed to have, certain capacities and abilities: those generally believed to be necessary to be an appropriate subject of punishment, blame, praise, and so forth. What those capacities are has been the subject of considerable argument in the philosophical and legal literature. Two types of capacities are typically defended. One type addresses the state of the entity at or before the time of the event. Generally, especially in law, these include having a certain mental condition with respect to the performance of the act that led to the harm-causing. The standard requirement in criminal law is that the accused must be shown to have had the intent to do the offending deed knowing it to be wrong or improper. The accused must have the mens rea, the guilty mental state, with respect to the act. Liability to punishment is excluded if the act can be shown to have been unintentional or done under certain forms of duress. Aristotle, when discussing conditions for holding people responsible, focuses on excusing conditions and basically refines those to two types, actions performed under compulsion and those performed because of ignorance. We should not be held responsible, on his account, for what we do, if the action's true source lies outside ourselves, as when, to use one of Aristotle's examples, a captain loses control of his ship to an overpowering wind that blows it well off course. Further, we should not be held responsible (or at least not fully responsible) if we were ignorant of crucial particular aspects of events we are causing by our actions, as when we reasonably mistake one person for another.

The second type of criterion focuses on the assessment of the efficacy of punishing the offending entity with respect to the commission of the offense. The efficacy of punishment, of course, may be tied to the mens rea issue, but it might be understood as a totally different matter. One might decide not to hold another responsible for what he or she did because we judge that nothing is to be gained, either for society or for the offender, from doing so or because we believe there may be social disvalues that outweigh the value of punishing, even though there is no disagreement over whether the individual committed the offense with the appropriate mens rea. In such cases we are likely to say that the offender is causally and morally responsible for the offense but is not to be held legally responsible. The person did it and did it with the intent of doing it and knowing full well it was a bad thing to do, but no social penalty is affixed to the commission of the specific act or to the type of act for some reason that is deemed to be overriding from the social, political, or legal point of view, for example, the immunity of unions' job actions from prosecution as crimes against property.

H.L.A. Hart noted that law does not explain why the mens rea conditions are deemed necessary for criminal responsibility. We should suspect that the law's inclusion of those conditions reflects its adoption of the moral doctrine that a person should only be held to account for an offense that person did intentionally and that people should not be held responsible for doing things if they could not have done otherwise than they did. Such an idea is found in Aristotle and has been defended by moral philosophers for centuries. Of course, in the determination of legal responsibility the doctrine requires that we somehow get into the head of the accused, not at the time of trial, but at or before the commission of the offense. That is typically a very difficult thing to do. More important, however, the doctrine, sometimes called the principle of alternate possibilities, has been the subject of a great deal of debate among philosophers, especially in recent years. Harry Frankfurt persuasively argues that this doctrine is false and not a central element of responsibility. His work on the subject has given rise to a large and growing body of literature debating the principle.

The law itself does not always insist on the tight link between responsibility and the mens rea condition. There is a category of offenses for which one can be held responsible and punished regardless of one's state of mind at the time of the act. They are strict liability offenses and include bigamy and statutory rape. In those cases only causal responsibility is required for legal responsibility. In still other cases legal and moral responsibility may be assessed, even though there is no showing of causal responsibility. For example, parents may be held vicariously responsible for the destructive behavior of their minor children. Moral responsibility is also sometimes assessed for failures to act in which there is no causal responsibility for the untoward event. In some jurisdictions laws have been passed to outlaw certain kinds of failures to act, even though the harm-causing was originally not brought about by the person who is failing to act. Such "Bad Samaritan" laws have been widely debated because they appear to impose a legal responsibility for an injury on someone who may only be a bystander or a passerby. The basis of these laws, however, may lie in a moral responsibility, again widely debated, to provide positive aid to those in obvious need.

Kurt Baier distinguishes causal responsibility from agent responsibility, which is, for him, assignable, assumable, or acquirable responsibility and can only be held by persons. It is by virtue of agent responsibility that persons can be held responsible for untoward events and so be responsible to others for things that happen. Baier further identifies dimensions of agent responsibility in terms of task responsibility, answerable responsibility, and culpable responsibility. These distinctions relate to Baier's basic assumption that agent responsibility must involve at least two persons: one who is responsible for something and another to whom the first is responsible. Hart distinguishes senses of the word "responsibility" under four classifications: role responsibility, causal responsibility, liability responsibility, and capacity responsibility. Role responsibility involves a collection of duties, a "sphere of responsibility," associated with a particular station or job in society to which one must pay heed for a protracted period of time. Parents qua parents have role responsibilities, as do doctors, lawyers, and others in their professional capacities. That is, in virtue of the specific positions they occupy in society, individuals have obligations and duties with which persons not in those positions are not saddled. Hart's account of role responsibility is similar to Baier's notion of task responsibility, though task responsibility extends to short-term as well as long-term duties. Individuals become role or task responsible either by assuming, being saddled with, or being assigned jobs or social stations.

People are not uncommonly referred to as responsible in another way. We believe that such people are disposed to take seriously and diligently perform their role and task responsibilities regardless of whether they assumed, were assigned, or were saddled by them.

References

Fingarette, Herbert. *On Responsibility*. New York: Basic Books, 1967.

Fischer, John Martin. *Moral Responsibility*. Ithaca: Cornell University Press, 1986.

Frankfurt, Harry. *The Importance of What We Care About*. Cambridge: Cambridge University Press, 1988.

French, Peter. *Responsibility Matters*. Lawrence: University Press of Kansas, 1992.

———. *The Spectrum of Responsibility*. New York: St. Martin's Press, 1991.

Glover, Jonathan. *Responsibility*. London: Routledge and Kegan Paul, 1970.

Hart, H.L.A. *Punishment and Responsibility*. Oxford: Oxford University Press, 1968.

Watson, Gary. *Free Will*. Oxford: Oxford University Press, 1982.

Peter A. French

See also DEFENSES; LIABILITY, CRIMINAL; MENS REA

Restitution

See UNJUST ENRICHMENT AND RESTITUTION

Restitutionary Rationale

In civil law cases, courts routinely require people to make restitution to those they have accidentally, carelessly, or negligently damaged. In the criminal law, the practice of requiring offenders to make restitution—to restore their victims to the condition they enjoyed before the offense—is both less common and more controversial. Victims of crime typically have a right to file civil suits against those who have harmed them, but the state, acting through the criminal law, usually aims to punish criminals, not to exact restitution from them. Whether restitution ought to be part of the criminal remedy, however, or even to replace punishment altogether, is now the subject of a lively debate among legal philosophers.

The idea of requiring restitution of criminals is an old one, but its modern revival owes much to the claim that the victims of crime are too often overlooked and ignored. Many people seek to protect the rights of the accused and many others to ensure swift and severe punishment for those convicted of crimes, according to this claim, but few seem interested in the rights of the victims. One remedy for this neglect, Stephen Schafer and others have suggested, is to ensure that the wrongdoer's punishment includes an effort to make restitution to his or her victim. "Correctional restitution holds a threefold promise," Schafer has argued, "in that it compensates the victim, relieves the state of some burden of responsibility, and permits the offender to pay his debt to society and to his victim."

Promising as they may be, restitutionary schemes present a number of practical problems. One is that criminals cannot be required to make restitution to their victims unless they are apprehended and convicted—a fate that many criminals apparently escape. Another problem is the difficulty of determining the proper amount and form of restitution. Exactly what does the criminal owe to the person he burgled or blinded, robbed or raped? What if money simply cannot repair the damage to the victim? However, these problems plague all forms of punishment, as the advocates of criminal restitution point out. Criminals cannot be fined or incarcerated until they are caught and convicted, and the number of days, months, or years that an offender should serve in prison for committing a particular offense is by no means obvious, nor is it clear that their imprisonment always benefits their victims. A third problem—that of exacting restitution from offenders once they have been convicted—seems to fall peculiarly on restitutionary schemes. No matter how poor or inept they may be, criminals are still capable of serving time in prison, yet they may be so poor and inept that they have no real chance of making complete restitution to their victims. The advocates' response to this problem is that some restitution is better than none. Moreover, restitution is more likely than imprisonment to contribute to the reform of criminals, because it is more likely to lead them to recognize and take responsibility for the wrong they have done.

Interest in criminal restitution has also raised important issues in the philosophy of law. These issues involve the distinction between crimes and torts and, more generally, the nature of punishment. To some, restitutionary schemes threaten to collapse the distinction between crimes and torts—and therefore between criminals and tortfeasors. If we require the thug who maliciously assaults someone to make restitution to his or her victim, for example, we are placing the thug on a par with the hapless person who accidentally injures another person. Criminals, however, are not mere tortfeasors who must make amends for their misdeeds; they are dangerous culprits who deserve to be punished—that is, made to suffer—for the wrong they have done to others.

Proponents of restitution respond to this complaint in two quite different ways. Most seem to take the position that restitution ought to be regarded as a form of or supplement to punishment—as punitive restitution—and therefore as no threat to the distinction between crimes and torts. Restitution can always be combined with imprisonment and other forms of punishment, they note, and even when it is not, the demands of restitution may well strike the offender as unpleasant. Such is likely to be the case when criminals must pay the full costs of their victims' suffering, including the costs of lost opportunities and of mental or emotional anguish, and the cost to society of capturing and convicting them as well.

Other advocates of restitution respond by arguing for a system of pure restitution. According to this view, the distinction between crimes and torts obscures the fundamental requirement of justice: those who harm or violate the rights of others must repair the damage they have done. The aim of a criminal justice system, therefore, should be to secure the restitution of victims, not to punish criminals who have supposedly offended against the laws of society or the state. According to Randy Barnett, then crime may be defined, without any reference to mens rea, as "an offense by one individual against the rights of another. The victim has suffered a loss. Justice consists of the culpable offender making good the loss he has caused."

These different responses to the problem of distinguishing crimes from torts indicate the main lines of an intramural debate between proponents of pure and punitive restitution. Pure restitutionists argue from a libertarian or neoclassical liberal position that takes society to be an aggregation of individuals who need a system of laws and law enforcement to protect their rights and interests against the accidents, mistakes, and depredations of other individuals. Punitive restitutionists insist that this point of view fails to account for important categories of criminal offense, especially crimes of endangerment, such as drunken driving and attempted but unsuccessful crimes. In addition, pure restitution cannot adequately provide for those who are not direct victims, but nevertheless suffer the "secondary harm," as noted by Margaret Holmgren, of crime when they must take extra precautions, pay higher insurance costs, or simply endure the suspicions and anxiety that accompany criminal activity.

This concern for "secondary harm" may explain why restitutionary programs so often include a community service element, for if criminals owe a debt to society as well as to their particular victims, as punitive restitutionists believe, then the best way to discharge this debt is to make restitution to the community in the form of community service.

References

Barnett, Randy. "Restitution—A New Paradigm of Criminal Justice." *Ethics* 87 (1977), 279–301.

Dagger, Richard. "Restitution—Pure or Punitive?" *Criminal Justice Ethics* 10 (1991), 29–39.

Hajdin, Mane. "Criminals as Gamblers: A Modified Theory of Pure Restitution." *Dialogue* 26 (1987), 77–86.

Henderson, Lynne N. "The Wrongs of Victim's Rights." *Stanford Law Review* 37 (1994), 937–1021.

Holmgren, Margaret R. "Punishment as Restitution: The Rights of the Community." *Criminal Justice Ethics* 2 (1983), 36–49.

Schafer, Stephen. *Compensation and Restitution to Victims of Crime.* Montclair NJ: Patterson Smith, 1970.

Richard Dagger

See also PENAL LAW, PHILOSOPHY OF; PUNISHMENT; UNJUST ENRICHMENT AND RESTITUTION

Retributive Rationale

The two main theories of punishment are the utilitarian, which is forward looking and asks, "What good will punishment do?" and the retributive, which is backward looking and asks, "What punishment do criminals deserve?" For the utilitarian the punishment's total effects—the benefits of prevention and deterrence less the harm to the criminal—must be better than the effects of every feasible, alternative way of dealing with crime. Utilitarians reject retribution because it aims to harm the criminal without producing a compensatory benefit for anyone. They argue that if retribution does no good it is just revenge, and if it is justified *because* it does good, it is not *retributive* punishment. Retributivists accept deterrence as a socially desirable by-product of punishment, but the punishment itself must be deserved, else it is not really punishment but merely using a person to change criminals' motives.

There are at least four ways to characterize retribution. According to the first view, retributive justice is independent of both vengeance and utility, and it is simply perceived to be right that wrongdoers suffer. A difficulty with this stark version of retribution is that disagreements about "moral perception" seem to be intractable.

The second (and most popular) version says that retributive punishment is what fits and suits the crime, as a counterpoise to the crime that undoes it in the realm of justice. Thus Immanuel Kant speaks of the right of requital, the *jus talionis,* and G.W.F. Hegel says punishment is an annulment of the wrong. The view leads easily to "an eye for an eye," death for a murder. There is reason to think this was the voice of the soft-hearted in biblical times: one can take only one eye for an eye, only one life for a life (and not the criminal's family). How does it apply to modern crimes? Should rapists be raped, swindlers swindled, and what should we do with propertyless vandals? The eye-for-an-eye doctrine gains some persuasiveness from the equivalence impled in the Golden Rule question, "How would you like it if that were done to you?"—that is, perhaps it is fitting that it be done to you if you do it to them.

The third version construes desert contractually, so that the winning team deserves the prize, workers their paychecks, and criminals their punishments, because these are tacitly promised by virtue of rules and practices. The state might be said to "sell" crimes: if you steal, the price is this, if you murder, that, and criminals who deny they should pay for their crimes are like any consumers who deny they should pay. The problem is the move from "if you do X, you will get Y" to the criminal's deserving Y; at the least, this is not what most people mean when they say a cruel murderer deserves punishment.

The fourth view says that retributive justice originates in revenge, but becomes a moral idea when institutionalized in certain ways. Revenge turns into retributive justice when (among other conditions) it (1) is done by the state, not by the victims or their relatives, (2) is in accord with promulgated rules that are applied consistently, and (3) is done in a cool hour by officials without personal interest in the criminal or victim. The view is not that some new thing called "retributive justice" appears and replaces revenge, but that retributive justice is the same thing as sanitized revenge. How, however, does one establish this identity, and why should not the result be that retributive justice is lowered to the moral level of revenge?

In any version of retribution there are calibration problems: it is easy to compare two crimes and judge one worse than the other, but this says nothing about what punishment warrants. When we slide a scale of punishments past a scale of crimes, how do we know where to stop, that is, how do we know how much punishment fits a given degree of harm and responsibility?

Nonetheless, the idea of just desert is not eliminated as easily as is sometimes thought. Shunning, shaming, holding in disgrace, are all varieties of retribution, for we shame or shun people for what they did, not because it is utile. Victims of crime, worldwide, insist on judicial retribution. Moreover, an asymmetry of positive and negative desert seems difficult to justify: most people who reject retribution would be loathe to claim that saints, Good Samaritans, and heroes should receive their praise, rewards, and medals only because these are positive reinforcements, and not because they deserve them.

"Organic" and communitarian defenders of retribution claim that if a society's courts did not punish heinous crimes, the society would not be felt to take its own values seriously; it would dishonor itself, appear poor spirited, and citizens' sense of social identity would be diminished. Think, for example, how women were made to feel when rapists were punished lightly or not convicted. Think how most Israelis would feel, and be viewed by others, if Israel declined to punish Adolph Eichmann because his punishment would not deter his kind of crimes and, given this, Israel did not think it should sacrifice the positive utility of Eichmann's contented retirement. We should note, however, that in claiming that failure to punish has these undesirable consequences, the question arises concerning whether we have a defense of retribution or just another example of retribution decomposing into utilitarianism as soon as justification is sought.

The problem is that most people accept, with seeming inconsistency, both retributive and utilitarian grounds for punishment. One possible reconciliation of the two, within a rule utilitarian framework, is that while the general practice of judicial punishment has utility, which justifies it, particular acts of punishment are based largely on retributive considerations. To what, however, does a judge appeal when deciding on a sentence? If it is utility, we do not have a case of retributive punishment, and if the judge's reasons are retributive they are, to the judge, in no need of being part of a practice with utility. Another problem is that rule utilitarianism implies that the public's false beliefs, for example, that so-and-so should suffer because he deserves it, can in the aggregate do much good. If the public knew this, however, they would not believe anyone should suffer because they deserved it, and then the aggregate good would not occur. The question then arises whether, in the tradition of Plato's paternalism, philosophers should hide the fact that no one should suffer solely because he or she deserves it, much as some philosophers think that religion, while false, nonetheless is good for most ordinary people; in which case the philosophers' job is to seek the truth, and keep it to themselves.

Can retributivists hold that some criminal punishment is justified because it is deserved and other punishment is justified only because it protects society, so long as they do not call the latter punishment retributive? However, retributivists not only think some people deserve to be punished, they also believe people should be punished only if they deserve it. Some philosophers, such as Anthony Quinton, and S.I. Benn and R.S. Peters, argued in the 1950s that retribution and utility are compatible because retribution is no more than the claim that only the guilty may be punished, that this is a "logical point" about the meaning of "punishment," and hence utility is left with the field regarding how much one should punish. Yet many people claim to have a sense that in terms of retribution alone some punishments are too severe or too lenient.

There still may be room for both. A retributivist can let utility set the degree of punishment in cases where our retributive feelings have nothing precise to say. This accommodation accepts the general idea that evildoers and lawbreakers, and only these, may be punished. The accommodation also allows the degree of punishment, between the extremes of too severe and too lenient, to be set by legislators who are reacting to how much they and the public hate and fear the crime and to how difficult the crime is to deter.

References

Benn, S.I., and R.S. Peters. "Punishment." In *Social Principles and the Democratic State*. Ed. Benn and Peters, 173–195. London: Allen and Unwin, 1959.

Hart, H.L.A. *Law, Liberty, and Morality*. Stanford CA: Stanford University Press, 1963.

Hegel, G.W.F. *The Philosophy of Right*. Trans. T.M. Knox. Oxford: Oxford University Press, 1942.

Mabbott, J.D. "Punishment." *Mind* 48 (1939).

Oldenquist, Andrew. "An Explanation of Retribution." *Journal of Philosophy* 95 (1988).

Quinton, Anthony M. "On Punishment." *Analysis* 21 (1954).

Andrew Oldenquist

See also DESERT; DETERRENT RATIONALE; EXPRESSIVE RATIONALE FOR PUNISHMENT; INCAPACITATIVE RATIONALE; MIXED RATIONALES; PUNISHMENT; REHABILITATION AND HABILITATION RATIONALE; RESTITUTIONARY RATIONALE; VENGEANCE

Retroactive Laws

See EX POST FACTO LEGISLATION

Revenge

See DESERT; VENGEANCE

Revolution

International law does not take cognizance of revolution until it has reached a level where rebels command significant organized forces and control substantial amounts of territory. The first of these stages is usually designated insurgency. The second, where a civil war has given birth to what is virtually a new national state, is called belligerency. The Confederate States of America constitutes a perfect example of an entity created out of a civil war that reached the state of belligerency. When such a fully developed nation-state emerges with organized armies in uniform, a front and rear area emerge. Here, the application of the laws of war and of just war theory which underlies it are little different than for conventional war. Of course, as in any conventional war, the opposing sides under *jus ad bellum* might or might not be fighting for a just cause and with proper authority. It is the moral and political notion of a right to rebellion to which the rebel side must appeal for both just cause and proper authority. The rules of war (of how it is to be waged) and *jus in bello*, the moral foundations of those rules, all treat civil war in the belligerency stage as they would the powers involved in any conventional war.

The interesting case is the interim stage between rebellion and belligerency, namely, insurgency. For insurgencies create unique and serious problems for both the laws of war and just war theory. If we assume that the insurgents are rebelling with just cause and, therefore, have proper authority, the problem remains of how such an insurgency can legally and morally be fought. Moreover, reciprocal problems face the regime resisting revolution. How can armed resistance efforts at suppression be both legal and moral?

The special problems posed by revolutionary, especially insurgency and counterinsurgency warfare, break down into two main areas, those of guerrilla war and terrorism. Terrorism is very much a topic unto itself, since it occurs outside the context of revolution as often as it occurs in it. Thus, we will not address terrorism further here.

The most definitive feature of revolutionary war at the insurgency stage is the guerrilla war. Guerrilla war is a means of waging war, so it would follow that the problems it poses, both in its prosecution and to governments that would resist it, would be those ordered under *jus in bello*.

There are several indicia of guerrilla versus conventional war. (1) The strategy of the guerrilla is not to take and hold territory. (2) Consequently, there is no clearly defined front or rear area. Any part of the territory over a large area is equally likely to see an outbreak of fighting, for (3) the guerrillas, with great freedom, choose, as much as possible, the times and places of attack. Also, since neither the guerrillas' locations nor identities (among noncombatants) are known to the enemy on defense, uncertainty is maximized. (4) The uncertainty of identity is accomplished by the guerrillas' ability to blend into the civilian population. (5) This, in turn, assumes at least the grudging and tacit support of the civilian populace, if not their enthusiastic participation. (6) This support is used by the guerrillas, as we have said, to hide themselves but also to prompt the government forces to attack the whole civilian population. (7) Such attacks further alienate the people from the government and cement relations between the guerrillas and the people. There is one other key feature of guerrilla warfare. (8) The guerrillas tend to live off the land and the civilian populace. Thus, (9) their communication and supply lines are intermittently nonexistent and never well established. (10) This makes the handling of prisoners of war very difficult for them. That, along with the intense hatred such internecine bloodletting often causes, invites atrocities against prisoners of war at worst and mistreatment and severe deprivation at best.

These features of guerrilla war pose a number of legal and moral problems for the guerrilla leadership. Features 3 and 4, noted previously, create a problem under both the

Hague and Geneva conventions, both of which require that all combatants, including guerrillas, must "wear a fixed distinctive sign visible at a distance," and they cannot secrete weapons but must carry them openly. The reason for this is twofold and is clear. First, it gives "fair notice," as it were, to opposing forces, differentiating guerrillas from terrorists and assassins. Second, it allows the opposing government to direct fire at combatants while discriminating them from noncombatants.

The lack of a uniform gives rise to another moral and legal problem posed by features 4 through 7. The guerrilla, by fading into the civilian population, draws government fire on the whole people. He does this knowingly. Is he then responsible for the government's violation of noncombatant immunity? Indeed, is he violating noncombatant immunity? Authorities divide upon this. Michael Walzer believes that the guerrillas are not responsible, while Paul Ramsey believes that they are. Clearly, there are intricate issues of legal cause and double effect here, but they are beyond the scope of this short entry.

The one further moral problem is posed by features 8 through 10. Does anything about guerrilla war justify neglect, mistreatment, or even execution of prisoners of war, perhaps on the grounds of necessity? Walzer, to cite one authority, no doubt correctly concludes that the answer is no. The Geneva Convention requires that prisoners be treated as well as one's own troops. Of course, this constitutes great cost and inconvenience to guerrilla fighters, but not obviously more than the same standard that is applied to the established government that opposes them or to either side in a conventional war. Morally and legally proper care of POWs is always an expensive and troublesome business in any war.

What of the established government? What legal and moral problems does it face in waging a counterinsurgency war? The primary problem is that of honoring the principle of noncombatant immunity. This difficult problem is, as we have seen, due to the very nature of guerrilla war and guerrilla tactics, as well as a result, perhaps, of conscious efforts of the guerrillas to get government forces to violate noncombatant immunity.

For many years, rebels of any sort were considered traitors and outlaws within metropolitan law. Moreover, they had no status whatsoever in international law. Not only were enemy combatants routinely tortured and executed, but parlays, truces, and guarantees of safe passage were not respected. Most outrageous is that noncombatant immunity was intentionally and massively violated. The suppression of such rebellions was viewed as a war against a people or a class. Sometimes the existence of racial, ethnic, or religious differences contributed to a feeling that rebels had no moral standing, but, just as often, no such distinctions were necessary.

Whatever conceptions of insurrectionists might once have been, it is clear today that they have standing before both international law and just war moral theory, not merely as possessors of human rights but as combatants or noncombatants, respectively. Thus, the principle of discrimination (or the doctrine of noncombatant immunity) is very much in force. However, what can the forces of the established government do when guerrillas continually hide among the people, often not wearing uniforms (or other insignia or clear marking) and not openly bearing arms? One thing seems clear to all authorities: a wholesale abrogation of noncombatant immunity is never justified.

Guerrilla war, the standard modus operandi of rebels during the problematic insurrection stage of a revolution, is perhaps the most difficult form of warfare from a moral and legal point of view. This is true because it is conceptually difficult, with many gray areas and a few genuine moral conundrums. However, it is true even more because it sets armies of radically different types, usually with radically different scales of armaments, against each other in intimate and continuing contact with noncombatants. Of course, this does not justify the commission of war crimes and violations of human rights.

References

Debray, Regis. *Che's Guerrilla War*. Trans. Rosemary Sheed. Harmondsworth: Penguin, 1975.

Haycock, Ronald, ed. *Regular Armies and Insurgency*. London: Croom Helm; Totowa NJ: Rowman and Littlefield, 1979.

Johnson, James Turner. *Can Modern War Be Just?* New Haven CT: Yale University Press, 1984.

———. *Just War Tradition and the Restraint of War: A Moral and Historical Inquiry*. Princeton NJ: Princeton University Press, 1981.

O'Brien, William V. *The Conduct of Just and Limited War*. New York: Praeger, 1981.
O'Neill, Robert J. *General Giap: Politician and Strategist*. Melbourne: Cassell Australia, 1969.
Walzer, Michael. *Just and Unjust War*. New York: Basic Books, 1977.

James W. Child

See also HUMAN RIGHTS; REBELLION; TERRORISM; TORTURE

Rhetoric

See ANALOGY; METAPHOR AND SYMBOL; VOICE

Rights and Liberties

Contemporary discussions of the nature of rights usually begin with the distinctions first explicitly drawn in Wesley Hohfeld's work. Hohfeld restricted his investigations to legal rights, but most philosophers working on rights theory have thought his findings readily applicable to discussions of moral rights as well.

Kinds of Rights

Hohfeld considered the term "rights" to be ambiguous, and so he identified four distinct kinds of "jural advantages" that this term could signify. Each of these advantages is related by necessary and sufficient conditions to its peculiar "jural correlative," held by another, "disadvantaged," party. The first of Hohfeld's rights is a *claim right*. According to Hohfeld, a person P has a claim right against Q to some treatment if and only if Q has a duty to P to provide that treatment. The relevant treatment can cover an enormous range of cases, from the provision of goods and services to refraining from interfering with certain of P's activities.

Hohfeld called a second kind of right a *privilege*; today this kind of legal or moral protection is usually referred to as a *liberty right*. A person P has a privilege (or liberty right) against Q to perform some action A if and only if P has no duty to refrain from performing A. These are the rights familiar from Thomas Hobbes' state of nature. With such rights, Q, the disadvantaged party, is said to have a *no-right* vis-à-vis P's actions. This simply means that Q has no claim right against P that would obligate P to perform any particular action. Note that a person's being privileged or at liberty to perform (or refrain from) an action does not entail that others must refrain from interfering with the right-holder's undertakings. A person may have a liberty right to sit on the park bench of his or her choice, but this is compatible with another's hurrying to occupy the seat first. Liberty rights free one from duties but do not constrain the actions of others toward the right-holder.

Claim-rights and privileges specify the existence of duties and permissions. The remaining two sorts of rights determine the conditions under which duties and claims can properly be assigned. Consider a *power*, the third kind of Hohfeldian right. A person P has a legal (or moral) power over Q with respect to some legal (or moral) relation if and only if P has the capacity to alter that relation. Those who stand to have their legal or moral relations so altered are said to have a *liability*. Being under a legal (or moral) liability is not necessarily disadvantageous. All citizens are under a legal liability of being beneficiaries of a generous testator. Those drafting wills have the power to alter the legal relations of others by executing a legal document in the proper way. On the assumption that the laws governing such transactions are morally justified, the legal powers of testators are also moral powers, since a duly executed will also alters the moral claims and duties of third parties.

The fourth kind of Hohfeldian jural advantage is an *immunity*. According to Hohfeld, a person P has a legal immunity from Q with respect to legal relation R if and only if Q is unable to alter R. The person disadvantaged in such a relation is said to have a *disability* with respect to that relation. A frequently cited example of an immunity right is that of free speech. This right disables the government from interfering with most forms of communication among citizens. A disability is not a duty; it is not that the government should not interfere with speech, because the interference is somehow legally (or morally) wrong for it to do so. Rather, the government *cannot* interfere. Laws licensing such interference are invalid, rather than merely unjustified.

If we allow that powers, liberties, and immunities are proper rights, then the familiar claim that rights always generate correlative duties must be false. The converse is also false. There are duties—most prominently, imperfect duties—that fail to generate correlative rights.

Rights and Duties

There is the further question, with regard to claim rights: are they identical to their correlative duties, or are they distinct from, but related by necessary and sufficient conditions with, their correlative duties? Jeremy Bentham, John Austin, and Hohfeld all thought of the relation as one of identity; a claim right was thought to be nothing but the duty of another to treat the right-holder in a particular way. Contemporary skeptics about rights are inclined to see matters this way, but others, most notably Joel Feinberg, argue for the thesis that claim rights are distinct from, and ground, their correlative duties, in the sense that such duties are generated only because it is appropriate to confer a particular claim right.

Because the identity thesis is more economical, the onus is on its opponents to show what greater advantage is gotten by having a claim right, as opposed simply to another's being duty-bound in particular ways. These advantages mostly concern the benefits of self-respect that come when one can "stand on one's rights" and demand certain treatment as one's due. The right-holder alone can demand the performance of a duty, or release another from his other-regarding duty. This greater control over the duties of others translates into greater control over one's own affairs, creat a sphere of dominion that is said to be obtainable only through rights relations.

Interest and Choice

When rights ground duties, the source of such duties is the right-holder's interests or autonomy, rather than some extraneous concerns possibly bearing little connection to the right-holder. This casual description actually masks a deep division among rights theorists, namely, whether the protection of interests, or the respect for an agent's choices, is the appropriate basis for rights ascription. Bentham and Austin, as well as Salmond, and contemporary philosophers David Lyons, Neil MacCormick, and Joseph Raz, all hold that the duties imposed by claim rights are grounded in concern for protecting certain of the right-holder's interests. An agent has a (claim) right so long as one of his interests is strong enough to generate a duty in another. H.L.A. Hart and Carl Wellman, on the other hand, hold that rights are essentially devices for protecting the choices of the right-holder. This "will" or "autonomy" view, clearly inspired by Immanuel Kant, shares with his ethics the implication that animals and nonrational beings generally are outside the scope of the community of rights. Hart took this as a benefit of his theory; others are less sanguine.

Principles for delineating the scope of the rights community are derived only mediately by opting for an interest or choice-based theory. Ultimately, the choice between an interest and will-based account depends on the justificatory basis for rights theory. Standardly, there are three major candidates: natural rights theory, contractarianism, and consequentialism. It is possible to distribute these justifications across different domains; a lockean theory, for instance, would see human rights as natural rights and would accord civil rights on a contractarian basis, while justifying much of the positive law consequentially. When we narrow our focus to the domain of fundamental moral rights, however, this spirit of pluralism is very little in evidence.

Fundamental and Consequential Rights

Consequentialists traditionally have been skeptical about such rights. Act utilitarians in particular have been highly suspicious of moral rights that prohibit the performance of maximally beneficial actions. However, this skepticism derives from a monistic value theory that sees only pleasure or desire-satisfaction as intrinsically good. Some recent consequentialist theories have endorsed pluralistic value theories that incorporate rights-respect as an intrinsically valuable goal to be maximized. These accounts retain the act consequentialist implication that no right is absolute. In circumstances where more rights can be vindicated only by sacrificing those of a few, these latter must be overridden. Other consequentialists (for example, Wayne Sumner) see a set of rights-conferring rules, justified by the overall social good that results from respecting such rules, as the only plausible way to ground moral rights.

Contractarians share the consequentialist suspicion regarding the possibility of underived natural moral rights, but take a pessimistic view of the project of reconciling consequentialist theories with fundamental moral rights. Contractarians see morality as a fundamentally social, cooperative enterprise whose roots are mirrored in a hypothetical social contract that generates basic moral rights.

This process of justification is also thought by many, most notably John Rawls, to yield a set of moral rights and duties that can best generate allegiance among the citizenry and so best ensure social stability. The particular schedule of rights that emerges from such a justificatory scheme depends crucially on the characterization of the hypothetical contractors, the options they are choosing from, and the circumstances of their deliberations.

Opponents of contractarianism often pose the following dilemma. Either there are moral constraints imposed on the contracting parties or there are not. If there are, then these are the fundamental bases for moral theory; rights are derivative at best, and the contract device is expendable in favor of direct argumentation employing these more fundamental moral considerations. If, on the other hand, moral constraints are absent, or largely absent (as in rights theories following Hobbes), then the moral force of the emerging principles is vitiated.

For natural rights theorists, the reason that persons have (for example) a right to life is not because recognizing this brings about increased social welfare or because hypothetical contractors would have agreed to accord such a right. Rather, there are certain features of persons (particular needs or capacities) that are by themselves sufficient to generate fundamental moral rights. Such rights in turn ground the whole, or a large part, of ethical theory generally. Ronald Dworkin, for instance, sees the dictates of morality as derivable from a fundamental right of each person to equal respect and concern.

Critics of natural rights theories charge that such theories are founded on the supposed fallacy of deriving moral prescriptions from solely nonmoral premises. They claim that no description of natural facts is sufficient, without the addition of moral bridge premises, to generate moral conclusions. Yet the addition of such premises would undermine the claim of natural rights theorists to have identified underived, fundamental moral rights. Bentham most famously (in "Anarchical Fallacies") expressed skepticism of such a position by denouncing such rights as "nonsense upon stilts."

Among Bentham's many objections to natural rights is his complaint that such rights (to life, liberty, happiness, property) were far too general to confer determinate moral protections in particular instances. Further, their very breadth ensured that they would conflict with one another, thus defeating the absolutist claims of the natural rights theorists. Bentham was right to see the issues of scope and stringency so closely connected, but there is nothing about a natural rights theory that requires seeing rights as absolute or as having contents so broadly described.

Scope and Stringency

Tensions between scope and stringency are at the heart of analyses of rights conflict. When rights appear to conflict, one may narrow the content of one or both of the competing rights. Alternatively, one might reduce a right's stringency, demoting it from an absolute protection—one that overrides all possibly competing moral considerations—to a prima facie protection. The broader the content of a right, the greater chance it has of conflict, and so the greater the pressure for reducing it to a prima facie, overridable protection.

Since many different distinctions are often gathered under considerations of scope, it is best to do some sorting. *Inalienable* rights, the focus of the worst of Bentham's wrath, may be either prima facie or absolute and may be quite broadly or narrowly drawn. Inalienability in fact refers neither to scope nor stringency, but rather to the right-holder's disability in waiving or transferring the relevant right. *Negative* rights require that others refrain from acting in certain ways, while *positive* rights require another's provision of goods, services, or treatment. *General* rights are those whose content is more or less broadly drawn, as opposed to more *specific* rights. There are no determinate criteria of application for this distinction; rather, the terms merely represent varying degrees along a spectrum of descriptive breadth.

The distinction between general and specific rights is very different from that between *universal* and *special* rights, which refers not to the content of rights, but to the scope of the domain of rights-holders. Universal rights are those had by all persons, while *special* rights are those that arise only in virtue of the right-holder's distinctive characteristics or special relationship to another. *Human rights* are examples of universal rights; rights to use a certain TV, or to the exercise of particular authoritative powers, are special rights had only by a particular subset of persons. The distinction between special and universal rights is again different from that between *rights in rem* and *rights in personam*. The former are rights holding against all other agents; the latter hold only against certain others.

Each of these distinctions is logically independent from one another, and a right's falling on one side of a distinction is compatible with its falling on either side of the remaining ones. For instance, an in personam right may be universal, negative, and fairly general (for example, a right not to be killed by one's parents). It might also be special, positive, and rather specific (for example, the right of employees to one week of annual sick pay from their employers). It might be universal, positive, and somewhat specific (for example, the right to a friend's assistance if such assistance is rendered at minimal cost and is necessary to avert very serious injury), and so on.

Rights and Progress

Though the notion of rights has never been without its detractors, rights theory has recently been the object of especially sustained attack from feminist, communitarian, and marxist critics. These critics claim that rights are individualistic, patriarchal, and/or bourgeois devices that cripple progressive social causes. Defenders of rights typically claim that even the most progressive social arrangements require persons to be regulated by some rights, both for coordination purposes and to ensure the very self-respect needed by citizens participating in egalitarian practices and institutions. Addressing these challenges has yielded a contemporary body of literature on rights that has yet to be surpassed in its subtlety and argumentative rigor.

References

Austin, John. *The Province of Jurisprudence Determined*. London, 1832.

Bentham, Jeremy. *Introduction to the Principles of Morals and Legislation*. Ed. Burns and H.L.A. Hart. London: Athlone Press, 1970.

Dworkin, Ronald. *Taking Rights Seriously*. Cambridge MA: Harvard University Press, 1978.

Feinberg, Joel. "The Nature and Value of Rights." *Journal of Value Inquiry* 4 (1970), 243–257.

———. *Social Philosophy*. Englewood Cliffs NJ: Prentice-Hall, 1973.

Hart, H.L.A. "Are There Any Natural Rights?" *Philosophical Review* 64 (1955), 175–191.

Hohfeld, Wesley. *Fundamental Legal Conceptions*. New Haven CT: Yale University Press, 1919.

Rawls, John. *A Theory of Justice*. Cambridge MA: Harvard University Press, 1971.

Sumner, L. Wayne. *The Moral Foundations of Rights*. Oxford: Clarendon Press, 1987.

Wellman, Carl. *A Theory of Rights*. Totowa NJ: Rowman and Allanheld, 1985.

Russell Shafer-Landau

See also ENTRENCHMENT; FUNDAMENTAL RIGHTS; HUMAN RIGHTS; IMPERFECT OBLIGATION; POWERS AND RIGHTS

Risk Assessment

The use of science in the assessment and management of risks has assumed increasing importance in the regulatory processes of modern government. Governments are under pressure to protect their publics from the risks to health and welfare posed by hazardous substances introduced into the environment by the activities of modern technological society. However, those who benefit from risk-imposing activities fear that "overregulation" of risks stifles economic and technological development and prevents the realization of many compensating social benefits. The expansion of international trade and trade agreements creates additional pressures for the regularization of risk assessment methodologies and safety standards among trade partners to prevent safety issues from being used as nontariff trade barriers.

In response to these pressures, public regulatory agencies look to the various "risk sciences" to provide rationales for regulatory decisions that are reliable, objective, and "neutral" with respect to the competing values brought to safety debates by the various stakeholder groups. Otherwise, risk regulation decisions can be challenged as violating the fundamental principle of administrative law that it not be applied arbitrarily and capriciously. Legal developments in western countries, most notably in the United States, have granted stakeholders the right not only to demand regulatory action, but also to challenge risk regulatory decisions in the courts or other administrative bodies and to require them to be defensible by accepted criteria of scientific evidence and safety standards.

However, regulatory science can rarely provide the kind of reliable and objective conclusions assumed by these demands. Regulatory science is often distinguished from "research science" in this respect. Regulatory science is mandated to answer practical policy questions that cannot await the time and data collection needed to obtain a result that meets the high confidence levels of research science. Further, the questions posed to this "mandated" science are often not purely empirical or scientific. They are what have been termed "trans-scientific," in the sense that they involve issues of political or moral judgment. Nowhere is this more evident than in risk assessment "science," where the very concept of "risk" (defined as probability times magnitude of harm) is itself a mix of empirical and normative elements. (How, for example, is "harm" to be defined and measured?) Thus, Liora Salter comments that mandated science must combine the "truth-seeking" features of science with the "justice-seeking" features of the legal process.

The uncertainties endemic to regulatory science render its findings open to a wide range of interpretations and thus divergent assessments of risk. These uncertainties, together with the "trans-scientific" aspects of risk issues, make risk assessment and management activities inherently political exercises. No matter how strongly risk regulators rely upon the best science, they must in the end make interpretive judgments requiring the invocation of political values around which there is rarely a social consensus and which, consequently, will be subjected to intense criticism by stakeholders with competing interests in risk decisions. Those whose political values "lose" in the risk regulatory debate inevitably see the administrative decision as unscientific, and thus as arbitrary and capricious.

The problem of how to handle the "politicization" of risk regulatory science has been a matter of intense debate among risk analysts and regulators. Some have suggested that risk regulation be divided into two very distinct phases. The first, the phase of risk assessment, is seen as a primarily empirical, scientific task of measuring the magnitude of the risks to health or well-being, which should be kept as free of "political" influence as possible. The second, the phase of risk management, is explicitly recognized as "political," insofar as it is required to make explicit value judgments, such as the setting of safety standards (what risk magnitudes are acceptable, and for whom?), the allocation of management costs, and fair compensation for imposed risks.

In some jurisdictions (for instance, the United States) the two-stage view of risk regulation has led to the setting of very explicit and rigorous standards of scientific review of risk assessments and to the insulating of these scientific judgments from political influence. Only the risk management decisions in these jurisdictions are then subjected to a broad range of political judgments and procedures. These procedures include the explicit setting of safety standards by statute (for example, the infamous "Delaney clause" in the U.S. Food, Drug, and Cosmetics Act, prohibiting the use of any food additives known to cause cancer in humans or animals), as well as guarantees of stakeholder consultation and consent to risk management strategies.

In other legal jurisdictions the recognition that the risk assessment science is itself infused with political value judgments has led to skepticism of the two-stage view and thus to less clearly defined scientific standards in the risk assessments underlying regulatory decisions. In these jurisdictions, the procedures tend to be less formalized and greater room for regulatory discretion tolerated. In recognition of the value-laden nature of the regulatory science itself there is greater openness to case-by-case consultation with stakeholders at the risk assessment level itself.

Among the value choices commonly recognized to bear upon the assessment of risk are the following:

1. The question of who should bear the burden of scientific proof. Should the burden of proof lie with the parties who allege that a product is "safe" or those who allege it to be "unsafe"? Risk producers naturally prefer the adoption of the criminal law principle of "innocent until proven guilty." Others, especially those who represent the potential risk bearers, argue that in the realm of administrative law governing the assessment of risks the principle should be reversed—"hazardous until proven safe." If high standards of scientific proof are also demanded, the placing of the burden of proof can lead either to the systematic overestimation or underestimation of risks by regula-

tors. Some commentators argue for a mediating principle between the two extremes, such as the adoption of a neutral stance, with "weight of evidence" as a standard of proof.

2. There is also the closely related question of the standard of proof appropriate to risk assessment. In criminal law the usual requirement is that the finding of guilt be "beyond all reasonable doubt." The analogous requirement in administrative law would be a 95 percent confidence level (the standard of research science) for the conclusion of safety or of risk. In regulatory science, such confidence levels are rarely obtainable. Most regulatory regimes adopt less demanding standards of proof, which are closer to the common law standard of "more likely than not" (for instance, "weight of evidence").

There is a more basic value underlying the selection of these methodological norms in risk assessment. It is the choice each regulatory system must make: should uncertainties in the regulatory science be handled by erring on the side of safety or on the side of risk? This, in turn, reflects a social choice between benefits and risks. Different jurisdictions weigh these values differently, and this weighting will be reflected in the kind of scientific and procedural requirements demanded of these administrative decisions.

References

Douglas, Mary, and Aaron Wildavsky. *Risk and Culture*. Berkeley: University of California Press, 1982.

Harrison, Kathryn, and George Hoberg. *Risk, Science, and Politics: Regulating Toxic Substances in Canada and the United States*. Montreal: McGill-Queen's University Press, 1994.

Lowrance, William. *Of Acceptable Risk: Science and the Determination of Safety.* Los Altos CA: William Kaufman, 1976.

National Research Council. *Risk Assessment in the Federal Government: Managing the Process*. Washington DC: National Academy Press, 1983.

Salter, Liora. *Mandated Science: Science and Scientists in the Making of Standards.* Boston: Kluwer Academic Publishers, 1988.

Shrader-Frechette, Kristen. *Risk and Rationality.* Berkeley: University of California Press, 1991.

Conrad G. Brunk

See also ECOLOGY AND ENVIRONMENTAL SCIENCES; EMPIRICAL EVIDENCE; PUNITIVE DAMAGES; RATIONAL BARGAINING; REGULATION; TESTIMONY AND EXPERT EVIDENCE

Robbery

See THEFT AND RELATED OFFENSES

Role

Role is the set of behaviors, determined by society, for any individual's standing, in virtue of which each individual knows just what to expect from anyone in a particular situation.

With the notion of one's "role" the individual becomes an object of study for the social sciences. According to Paul Ricoeur:

> If we assume . . . that an individual's activity is dictated by the structure of the role one inhabits, we can take that both as a proposition which can be confirmed within a social science, and as the assumption which is built into taking up the sociological point of view; in the second case, to say that an individual is socially determined, is simply to say that one must be understood in this way when studied sociologically; the first case, on the other hand, is to hold that sociology shows that the outward behavior of an individual is reducible either to taking on a socially prescribed role, or to following the rules which allow one to play these roles."

Friedrich Nietzsche firmly placed the classical Greek conception of a theatrical role into sociological perspective. Sociology and social psychology are where the numerous questions concerning the notion of role are developed, dealing especially with authority, community, social conflict, conformity and deviance, institution, game, and personality. The notion of role is fundamental for all writers who relate the functioning of society to individual conduct.

C.H. Cooley and G.H. Mead set these perspectives into a systematic theory. Mead saw in role an indispensable tool for explaining the origin of the person. *Role taking* is the interior act by which the subject adopts and takes on another's attitude, the mental process which lets the individual adapt to contemporaries' activity and makes possible one's participation in social activity. Due to this "internalization" and "interdramatization," the individual can see himself or herself from the other's point of view and gains awareness of his or her own personality. Two aspects of the person must be distinguished: the *me*, a complex of others' attitudes which the organism takes on itself, corresponds to "the generalized other" (the whole set of roles of otherness, that is, the presence of society in the individual); whereas the *I*, the organism's response to others' attitudes, is constituted from the reactions of the individual to the social situation that individual has interiorized. This is the dimension of spontaneity and of creativity.

Ralph Linton linked role to status. Each individual in society occupies a particular position or "status," which imposes duties to be carried out and functions to exercise, but also confers rights. This ensemble of functions, duties, and rights is called one's "social role." The "role" stands for the conduct expected from an individual in a specific social situation, given that individual's social standing. Playing the role implies a "group" perspective and corresponds to one's "overt activity."

Walter Coutu stressed the distinction between *role playing* (manifest and external conduct, one's behavior, overt activity) and *role taking* (taking on or assuming a role from the symbolic point of view, an internal fact, implicit in action). This is the source for the distinction between the meanings of "role" used by sociologists (*role playing*) and by psychologists (*role taking*, a mental activity, with many senses—simulation, unreality, play). This puts opposition between their terms of art, such that the sociological "role" is kept from the slightest whiff of psychology: the police officer who sets out to arrest a gangster or the soldier who has to fire on an enemy cannot experience the slightest feeling toward them. Only in special cases, such as the play activity of the child, do the two meanings reunite, to form a third type of role, *playing-at a role*: at play the child expresses in external movements the activity of an *other* whose presentation he or she has internalized and whose role he or she plays.

For T. Parsons, four *pattern variables* enter in, which let roles be classified into opposed pairs: "universal/particular," "specified/diffuse," "affectively neutral/nonneutral," "achievement oriented/ascribed."

F.L. Bates locates each person within several statuses; so we must investigate not only the set of attitudes expected from a person because of their status, but above all the possible conflicts to which the interlinked complexity created by the several statuses gives rise. Robert Merton identifies the *status-set* (the set of roles associated with the same individual and making up his or her status), which goes hand in hand with the increasing complexity of the *role-set* (all those who share a role). Since the individual has to oversee more numerous and complex roles all at the same time, more refined choices are required in ever more demanding role conflicts.

In organizational sociology, every organization has an ensemble of roles distinguished from one another to a greater or lesser extent (systems of normative *constraints* to which *agents* adapt themselves) and of *rights* correlative to these. These rights, since they are known to all the actors in an organization, create *role expectations* that reduce uncertainty in transactions, even though individuals still keep some room to maneuver. Various factors enter in to modify one's accountability, such as the "distance" individuals always put between themselves and the roles they play; or the "variability" among the normative constraints attached to roles; or the "ambivalence" of these limitations. This room for autonomy leads to *systematic effects* of great social importance.

In social psychology, the learning of roles in the genesis of the person is stressed. Jean Piaget came to conclusions similar to George Herbert Mead's on interiorizing the roles of associates. The concept of role also becomes useful in grasping such problems as group discussion, familial structure, the process of acculturation, deviant behavior, professional groups, and means of persuasion: playing a role helps one to adopt new views. The importance of this for a mass communications society is obvious. Roles are put into three categories: (1) *institutional roles* within the total society, which approximate the fundamental personality, such roles as the biosocial ones of age or sex, or ones of social class, professional grouping, and associations; (2) *roles in particular groupings*, such as leader or as member of a group; and (3) *personal roles*, such as the mass media present them.

Juridical roles are employed by some authors to describe legal agents' share in autonomy. They also are used to reintroduce the notion of status and to integrate it into a global theory of legal interaction: role conflicts can lead to recognition of legal rationalities that are opposed and that explain the changes over time in legal systems observed by sociologists. In a legal context, roles are less open than in sociology or social psychology: in law, roles are arranged into statuses that are definite and detailed. Fulfilling social roles outside the law or in violation of rights-holders, however, leads to conflicts which go beyond mere deviance and lead to extensive changes in the law.

References

Arnaud, André-Jean. *Critique de la raison juridique*, I, *Où va la sociologie du droit* (Critique of Legal Reason, I, Whither Sociology of Law). Paris: Librairie générale du droit et de jurisprudence, 1981.

Crozier, Michel, and Erhard Friedberg. *L'acteur et le système. Les contraines de l'action collective* (Agent and System. Constraints on Collective Action). Paris: Le Seuil, 1977.

Dame-Castelli, Mireille. "Rôle." In *Dictionnaire Encyclopédique de Théorie et de Sociologie du droit*. 2d ed. Paris: Librairie générale du droit et de jurisprudence–EJA, 1993.

Deutsche, K.W. "On Political Theory and Political Action."*American Political Science Review* 55 (1971), 11–27.

Linton, Ralph. *The Cultural Background of Personality*. 1945.

Mead, George Herbert. *Mind, Self and Society*. Chicago: University of Chicago Press, 1934.

Merton, Robert K. *Sociological Ambivalence and Other Essays*. New York: Free Press of Glencoe, 1976.

Ricoeur, Paul. "La pensée et les ordres de realité" (Thinking and the Levels of Reality). In *Tendances principales de la recherche dans les sciences humaines et sociales*, vol. 2, ed. Jacques Havet. Paris: Mouton/UNESCO: La Haye, New York, 1978.

Rongère, P. "Rôles et conflits de rôles en droit du travail" (Roles and Role Conflict in Labor Law). In *Études en droit du travail offertes à André Brun*, 451–476. Paris: Librairie sociale et économique, 1974.

Seidman R. "The Judicial Process Reconsidered in Light of Role Theory." *Modern Law Review* 32 (1969), 516–531.

André-Jean Arnaud

See also Sociology of Law; Standing

Roman Philosophy of Law

Roman philosophy of law can be considered as *the* philosophy of law, because the Romans invented law as an art or science (*ius redigere in artem*). The eclectic way Roman philosophy adopted Greek philosophy was reinforced by the nature of legal work: always open to different arguments and adverse to a unique reason or system.

Origins

Prejudice against classicism wrongly presents Roman law as being static and monolithic, a kind of image of *recta ratio* (right reason) itself. This was not true by any means. In the beginning Roman priests specializing in the new art, law, acted like sociologists—they tried to see what was going on in society and stylized good procedures as rules (the axiological work). Once the principal rules had been laid down, however, they argued over the correct answers to problems, they formed legal fictions or used equity to solve difficult cases (their truly dialectical work). The written texts were interpreted as mere descriptions of correct ways of doing things in society, not the sacrosanct positivity of justice. The practical genius of Rome can be seen in this trial and error procedure, and the greatness of a period like the classical Roman one can be evaluated by its capacity to deal with controversy and a plurality of conceptions.

Decadence

At the end of the third century, neo-platonic ideas corrupted the original aristotelian positions. The influence of Plotinus, Porphirius, Proclus, and even St. Augustine on juridical thought dissolved the isolation of juridical reason into a syncretic moralism and invaded law with political matters. The first tendency can be seen in new and vague conceptions of natural law. The second tendency appears in two legal principles: voluntarism in the creation of laws (*quod principi placuit, legis habet vigorem*, whatever suits the ruler has the force of law) and the claim that the prince is not bound by his own laws (*princeps legibus solutus est,* the ruler is loosed from laws). Both tend toward an authoritarian and utopian political conception, deriving in the last instance from the *Republic* and the *Laws* of Plato.

The stoic influence was not so heretical and slid into the original *corpus* with the same ease as the Christian legacy. From this derive ideals of dignity in every person, even the slave. Some consider that this was also a source for the extension of natural law to animals. Cicero was a great transmitter of stoic ideas. His description of natural law manifests that source: *Est quidem vera lex, recta ratio, naturae congruens, sempiterna* (This is true law, right reason, concordant with nature, and everlasting).

Roman eclecticism permitted the traditional vision of Roman legalism (associated with empire by some, with the civic strong virtues of the republic by others), but also allowed a dialectical and pluralistic perspective that is closer to the origins and the prosperity of that civilization.

Codification

Writings of Ovid and Horace, with the jurisprudential writings of Cicero and others, can be mined for Roman legal philosophy. The great treasure from which Roman philosophy of law is extracted, however, is the compilation by the Byzantine emperor Justinian in the sixth century A.D., the *Corpus Iuris Civilis*. The compilation treats several matters and is composed of different parts: a legal code (*Codex*); the collection of new laws (*Novellae*); the official and unique manual for law learning and teaching, the Institutes (*Institutiones*); and, the most famous of all parts, the Pandects (*Pandectae*) or Digest (*Digesta*). This is a kind of encyclopedia made up of a structured system of nine thousand quotations on all subjects of legal knowledge from the most important Roman authors, such as Gaius, Papinianus, Paulus, Ulpianus, and Modestinus. Tribonian, minister of the emperor, coordinated this cathedral of juristic thought, helped by only four professors and eleven lawyers, in only three years.

Despite having suffered all the conflicting influences, the Digest still contains the principal points of a complete philosophy of law. From the first entry, rules (*regulae*) come from law (*ius*), and law (*ius*) comes from justice (*iustitia*) and never the opposite: *Est autem ius a iustitia, sicut a matre sua, ergo prius fuit iustitia quam ius* (Law is from justice, as from its mother, so there was justice before there was law), because rules (even the apparent holy written texts of laws) are nothing but the narrative or the linguistic signs of law. Nature presides and prevails over law: what nature forbids cannot be allowed by any law.

Law is not defined, but presented in short but eloquent sentences. The most important, by the fact it contains a whole *topica* of the different elements at play in justice, is from Ulpian, at the very beginning of the Institutes: *Iustitia est constans et perpetua voluntas ius suum cuique tribuens* (Justice is the reliable, lasting will to render each his due). Law regards three topics: justice (the perpetual will of the just), person (each one who has rights—and everybody has rights), and one's own (*suum*, the right thing, the due or the just—what is owned by someone). This constitutes an exquisite theory of the ontology of law.

The professional interest that supports this knowledge and the respective practices, the priests, pay homage to the goddess Justice. No mere metaphor, their science of law (*Iuris prudentia*) is the knowledge and perception of some divine things and some human (nature in general, the nature of things, *natura rerum*, and the nature of humankind), prior to knowledge of the just and unjust, which is specific to law.

The Romans, finally, left a general theory of norms (obligations and contracts, and so forth) which underlined the internal side of each law, the attributes it has to have to exist according to justice. In short, juridical acts, to exist, must respect the three juridical commandments: do not abuse your right (*honeste vivere*), see the limits of your own right, by another man's right (*alterum non laedere*), and the most specific and well-known: render to each one's due (*suum cuique tribuere*).

Revival

The revival of Roman law in the late medieval centuries, beginning with the universities and the first glossators, underlined the power (*potestas*) of the emperor in order to benefit the rising power of royal centralization in Europe. Since then, especially in the reconstruction of history at the hands of Enlightenment philosophers such as Montesquieu and Jean-Jacques Rousseau, a myth of Roman law and its philosophy was created. In that myth the decadent *dura lex sed lex* (Law may be inhumane, but still law) had as prominent a role as civic virtues and republican mores in public law. Neglect of the creative power (*auctoritas*) of the praetor, the Roman judge, especially in what concerned such flexible techniques as legal fictions, identified the spirit of Roman law with a legalism that helped institutionalize legal positivism during the late eighteenth and nineteenth centuries in continental Europe.

Prospect

With the ontology and epistemology of the new knowledge, with a program for its practitioners, a legitimation for its power (rooted in nature, and then in society and values), and a theory of its acts, the Romans not only had a philosophy of law but were the true philosophers, those who put into practice the love of *sophia* (wisdom) and not a mere verbal simulacrum. With Roman law, we knew for the first time law itself—free from other normative social orders—and philosophy in action.

References

Berman, Harold J. "Roman Law in Europe and the Jus Commune: A Historical Overview with Emphasis on the New Legal Science of the 16th Century." *Syracuse Journal of International Law* 20 (1994), 1.

Ducos, M. *Les romains et la loi: Recherches sur les rapports de la philosophie grecque et de la tradition romaine à la fin de la république*. Paris, 1984.

Gorecki, Danuta M. *Roman Law: A Selected Bibliography of Books Written in English*. Chicago: American Association of Law Libraries, 1978.

Hoeflich, Michael H. "Bibliographic Perspectives on Roman and Civil Law." *Law Library Journal* 89 (1997), 41.

Norr, Knut Wolfgang. "Technique and Substance: Remarks on the Role of Roman Law at the End of the 20th Century." *Syracuse Journal of International Law* 20 (1994), 33.

Reiman, Mathias, ed. *The Reception of Continental Ideas in the Common Law World, 1820–1892*. Berlin: Duncker und Humboldt, 1993.

Riga, Peter. "The Influence of Roman Law on State Theory in the Eleventh and Twelfth Centuries: A Study of the Roman Glossators and Their Influence on Modern State Theory." *American Journal of Jurisprudence* 35 (1990), 171.

Roman Law. (Symposium) *Tulane Law Review* 66 (1992), 1591.

Samuel, Geoffrey. "Epistemology, Propaganda and Roman Law: Some Reflections on the History of Subjective Right." *Journal of Legal History* 10 (1989), 161.

Villey, Michel. *Le Droit Romain. Son actualité* (Roman Law Today). 1945. 8th ed. Paris: Presses universitaires de France, 1987.

Watson, Alan. *The Spirit of Roman Law.* Athens: University of Georgia Press, 1994.

Zimmerman, Reinhard. *The Law of Obligation. Roman Foundation of the Civilian Tradition.* Cape Town: Beck, 1992.

Zuchert, Michael P. "'Bringing Philosophy Down from the Heavens': Natural Right in the Roman Law." *Review of Politics* 51 (1989), 70.

Paulo Ferreira da Cunha

See also HELLENIC PHILOSOPHY OF LAW: PRIMARY SOURCES; HELLENISTIC PHILOSOPHY OF LAW; MEDIEVAL PHILOSOPHY OF LAW

Rosmini, Antonio (1797–1855)

Antonio Rosmini(-Serbati)'s spiritual quality (as priest, doctor of theology, and founder of the Institute of Charity and later the Congregation of Providence) was no obstacle to his diplomatic and political activity as ambassador of the Piedmontese Government to Rome in 1848. His negotiations failed, war with Austria began instead of an Italian confederation under the pope, two of his works were put on the Index, and both he and the pope went into exile. Pope Pius IX considered making him a cardinal and forbade all attacks against him when Rosmini resumed charity work in Domodossola alongside active intellectual work and fervent mysticism. However, Pope Leo XIII condemned forty of his propositions in 1888, resulting in a cloud of silence, today being lifted to reveal his orthodoxy.

Rosmini created the Society of Friends (*Società degli Amici*) to seed a Catholic Encyclopaedia, its principles the reverse of the Enlightened French one. His philosophy had its sources in Plato and Augustine, although his eclecticism was able to achieve some synthesis with modern views, particularly Immanuel Kant's. His philosophical ideas on law occur in *Filosofia della Politica* (1837), *Progetti di costituzione* (edited in 1952), including *Costituzione secondo la giustizia sociale* (1827), and *Filosofia del Diritto* (1841–1845). They began earlier in his manuscript on *Property* (*Frammento sulla proprietà*, ca. 1825), and particularly in the three *Frammenti della Filosofia del diritto e della politica* (published in 1886–1888). Other works include *Principi della scienza morale* (1831), *Trattato della coscienza morale* (1839), and other ethical writings within his global system.

Philosophy of law has a central place in Rosmini's thought. For him, society and politics are not absolute realities, but are always a function of the person (conceived as being responsible for his own acts); society is a society of persons. Person is the major value and category of all his work; he achieves the vital connection of law and morals by means of a constant reference to truth and person. The function of law, one form of truth, is to provide for human needs, beginning with that essential need for a person's safety. So, this conception of person, related to law, rejects both the empirical individualism of the Enlightenment, with its subsequent utilitarianism, and the individual's dissolution into idealistic universalism as occurs in G.W.F. Hegel. Consequently, even the theory of society becomes part of a theory of justice. This leads to a conception of law determined by justice; such a conception of justice implies a moral root.

Concern for the restoration of the Church liberties and criticism of the Enlightenment's revolutionary legacy led him in *Frammento sulla proprietà* (Short Essay on Property) to at first rigorously conceive of social and political ties as relations between proprietors, with the ruler above all, and the state as nothing but the general corporation of owners. Property was the condition for any possible equality, and right was identified with property as the real absolute right of the person.

Rosmini moved on from this position, however, to propose a social contract of monarchy mixed with republicanism, although with no illusions about its codification, except on the technical level, and no enthusiasm for its separation of powers. Despotism is seen not as the monopoly of only some forms of government, but as always arising whenever the decisions of any sovereign cannot be judged, even if that sovereign be "the people."

The idea of a political (or constitutional) tribunal occurred to him, in order to moderate the influence of the property owners upon legislative power. In the political field, the last synthesis is the common subordination of state and individuals to justice. Rosmini remained a defender of natural law, considered as the capacity of "feeling the just and unjust in relation to truth, as which it presents itself," truth related to different situations or beings. This is a corollary from his theory of "the shape of truth" at a moral level. So, natural law is not conventional but, as part of the moral order, it is the supreme guarantor of personal dignity and right, that is to say, the principal vector of justice. Law itself, coming from the moral duty of respecting other persons, is considered in a subjective way, as the ability of persons to act when protected from others by moral law. Formal law is "a notion of the mind used for making a judgment about the morality of human actions, which must be guided by it." Therefore, right is derived from duty (the juridically specific duty to allot one's due to each—*suum cuique tribuere*), and not the opposite; all individual subjective rights persist in that moral relation, because they have a "utilitarian" or "eudemonological" rationale. In the chain composed by reality/truth/morals/natural law right, this last element must be in harmony with its ethical basis.

While law and right must be moral, according to natural justice, there is for him a most perfect and higher justice (*giustizia soprannaturale*), that is inspired or even formed by grace, and that is God's justice, which Rosmini identifies with charity, a spiritual love that unites human and God. This mystical face of Rosmini's thought is not always disguised in his superficial eclecticism of a religious rationalist: it is significant that he chose to begin the section on "The Essence of Right" in his *Philosophy of Right* with this passage from Cicero's *De legibus*: "These things arise because we are naturally inclined to love our fellows, which is the foundation of right."

References

Adam, Michel. "Actualité de Rosmini" (Rosmini Today). *Revue de Philosophie Française* 2 (1994), 195–202.

Bataglia, Felice. *La Filosofia del Diritto in Rosmini* (Philosophy of Law in Rosmini). Intro. Giovanni Ambrosetti. (Quaderni di Iustitia, 31.) Rome, 1980.

Cotta, Sergio. "Filosofia pratica e filosofia politica: conoscitive o normative? La posizione di Rosmini" (Practical Philosophy or Political Philosophy: Cognitive or Normative? Rosmini's View). *Rivista Internazionale di Filosofia del Diritto* 3 (1990), 392–411.

Darós, William R. "Ética y derecho según Rosmini" (Ethics and Law in Rosmini). *Revista Rosminiane di Filosofia e di Cultura* 86 (1992), 15–26.

Feibleman, James K. "Ethical Variations on a Theme by Rosmini-Serbati." *Tulane Studies in Philosophy* 6 (1957), 53–66.

Mathieu, Vittorio. "Etica e politica in Rosmini: la mediazione del diritto" (Ethics and Politics in Rosmini: The Mediation of Law). *Rivista Internazionale di Filosofia del Diritto*, 3 (1990), 432–440.

Rosmini, Antonio. *Opere*. Ed. E. Castelli. Padua, 1936– . Trans. D. Cleary and T. Watson as *Works*. Durham, UK: Rosmini House (*Rights of the Individual*, 1993; *Rights in the Family*, *Rights in God's Church*, *Unified Social Right*, *The Essence of Right*, 1995).

Siacca, M. F. *Il pensiero giuridico e politico di Antonio Rosmini* (Antonio Rosmini's Legal and Political Thought). Florence: Sansoni, 1962.

Trigeaud, Jean-Marc. "De la persone à la propriété dans la philosophie juridique et politique d'Antonio Rosmini" and "Activité personnelle, bien juridique et bien esthétique chez Rosmini" (Person and Property in the Legal and Political Philosophy of Antonio Rosmini; Personal Acts, Legal Goods, and Aesthetic Good in Rosmini). In *Essais de Philosophie du Droit*. Genoa: Studio Editoriale de Cultura, 1977.

———. "Rosmini: l'Europe et le droit. Sur le dépassement du politique" and "L'unité de l'expérience des valeurs morales et juridiques d'après la philosophie rosminienne" (Rosmini on Europe and the Law: Beyond Politics; The Unity of the Experience of Moral and Legal Value in Rosmini's Philosophy). In *Persona ou la Justice au double visage*. Genoa: Studio Editoriale de Cultura, 1990.

Paulo Ferreira da Cunha

Rousseau, Jean-Jacques (1712–1778)

Jean-Jacques Rousseau's philosophy of law derives entirely from the general will as presented finally in the *Social Contract.* Here Rousseau addresses these questions: Who is the legitimate sovereign? How do government and state stand to law? What is law?—valid law?—just law? What is the relationship of personal equality and liberty to law? What relations obtain among the general will, equality, the common good, self-interest and law?—natural rights, natural law, and divine law?—law to democracy? How does property differ from possession? What is just punishment?—justifiable censorship?

What is the general will? The simplest answer is "all citizens willing the good of all citizens." Each citizen has a particular will, which may be expressed in willing one's own perceived good only or in willing the good of a particular group, as sports fans do for teams. Each citizen also has a general will, which is expressed by voting for laws that secure the good of all on matters of common concern. All particular wills are possible rivals of the general will in weakening desire for the common good. The general will, then, is only all willing the good of all on a universal matter.

Next are Rousseau's answers to the questions, in order. The people as legislators of law constitute the only legitimate sovereign. Elected government executes the law. The state is all citizens as subject to general-will law. State and citizen are autonomous; each obeys rules it gives to itself. Law is the command of the general will. A law exists "when the entire people enacts something concerning [the good of] the entire people." A law is valid only if every citizen participates. A law is just if all citizens will the good of all subjects. Every law is valid and just.

Equality exists before and under the law, since the law comes from all equally and applies to all equally. Law gives equality and freedom if each is treated by right as an equal legislator and as one ruled autonomously. General-will law creates three distinctions of freedom: political liberty, each citizen is entitled to membership in the sovereign; civil, each is protected by law; and moral, each autonomously "obeys laws one gives to oneself" as a citizen, and thereby is not subject to the wills of others or one's passions. Autonomous liberty identifies human nature and direct democracy.

Law jointly satisfies equality, self-interest, the common good, and justice. Since each citizen is equal as legislator, and acts from self-interest, each must seek a self-interest in the common interest and legislate for the common good. With the common good, fairness and justice are satisfied.

Rousseau vacillates on natural rights, constitutional rights, natural law, and divine law. He realizes their value against tyranny, since they posit moral standards superior to the authority of the sovereign state. For the same reason, however, they compete with general-will law. His consistent position is that because of what it provides, its nature and limits, general-will law outranks external moral standards if a choice is necessary.

Because the general will overrides, Rousseau's direct democracy opposes liberal democracy. Consider property. For John Locke's liberal democrat, property is an independent natural right, support of which justifies government. Rousseau holds that mere possession is legitimated as property when held by legal right. Some personal possessions are of no interest to the common interest. However, should push come to shove and your land becomes necessary, the general-will requirement overrides even your legal right. Again, consider just punishment: the death penalty is just if one assents to it. "It is in order not to be the victim of a murderer that a person consents to die if he becomes one." As a citizen legislator, one may decide with others that the common good requires the death penalty for murder, and then prescribe that law to oneself. If one becomes through murder an instance of that universal law, one accepts the justice of the punishment. One may consider censorship justifiable if it fosters self-rule.

Rival interpretations of Rousseau read differently his philosophy of law. The totalitarian or collectivist interpretation claims that Rousseau is illiberal, denies personal freedom, sacrifices the individual to the superpersonality of the state and its mystical will, and prepares the individual for willing sacrifice by inflamed patriotism and hidden machinations. The liberal interpretation replies that Rousseau's highest values are freedom, equality, and democracy, that Rousseau decries a state that sacrifices even one citizen, that by contract citizens relinquish natural rights but receive their equivalents strengthened as law, and that the general will parallels and secures natural law, leaving all power and authority to citizens. Both interpretations find favorable texts. The totalitarian cites the state as a moral person, with its own will where citizens are "forced to be free," reliance on *la main cachée* (the hidden hand) of the legislator and patriotism. However, the state as a moral person is a legal concept and is not totalitarian. The liberal interpretation fails to appreciate the primacy of equality; freedom as self-rule; rejection of representatives, representative parties, and parliament; and the priority of the general will. Both interpretations seem anachronistic.

References

Cell, H., and J. MacAdam. *Rousseau's Response to Hobbes*. New York: Peter Lang, 1988.

Chapman, John. *Rousseau—Totalitarian or Liberal?* New York: AMS Press, 1968.

Dent, N.J.H. *A Rousseau Dictionary*. Oxford: Basil Blackwell, 1992.

Derathe, Robert. *Jean-Jacques Rousseau et la science politique de son temps* (Jean-Jacques Rousseau and the Political Science of His Time). Paris: Librairie Philosophique J. Vrin, 1970.

Goldschmidt, Victor. "Rousseau et le droit" (Rousseau and the Law). In *Victor Goldschmidt, Ecrits*, vol. 2, 129–159. Paris: Librairie Philosophique J. Vrin, 1984.

Neumann, F. *The Rule of Law*. Leamington Spa UK: Berg Publishers, 1986.

Roosevelt, Grace G. *Reading Rousseau in the Nuclear Age*. Philadelphia: Temple University Press, 1990.

Rousseau, Jean-Jacques. *Jean-Jacques Rousseau on the Social Contract with Geneva Manuscript and Political Economy*. Ed. and trans. Judith Masters. New York: St. Martin's Press, 1978.

———. *Jean-Jacques Rousseau, Oeuvres Completes*. Vol. 3. *Du Contrat Social Ecrits Politiques* (Jean-Jacques Rousseau, Complete Works, vol. 3. The Social Contract and Political Writings). Ed. B. Gagnebin and M. Raymond. Dijon: Bibliotheque de la Pleiade, Editions Gallimard, 1966.

———. *The Political Writings of Jean Jacques Rousseau*. 2 vols. Ed. C.E. Vaughan. Oxford: Basil Blackwell, 1962.

Jim MacAdam

Rule of Law

Rule of law is the supremacy of law, a normative standard requiring that the state's coercive power be confined within known and settled boundaries declared in legal rules and principles. All persons, including the chief executive and other government officials, are equally under the law and held accountable. All within the regime have a fair opportunity to plan their conduct with knowledge of the predictable response of the state and avoid sanctions if they choose; this requires the certainty and clarity of law. Some sphere of individual liberty is thus guaranteed, even if the laws are to some degree oppressive, and the reluctance of the powerful to subject themselves equally to invasive procedural and substantive laws will limit actual domination.

In Plato's *Laws*, Aristotle's *Politics*, Thomas Aquinas's "Treatise on Law" in *Summa Theologica*, and John Locke's *Second Treatise of Government*, the rule of law develops as a regulative ideal opposed to unconstrained political power. English constitutional history and common law, in the struggle against prerogative power, contributed to the institutional and theoretical elaboration of the ideal. It is central to all forms of modern liberalism, including the German tradition of the *Rechtsstaat* stemming from Immanuel Kant. Since no one is above the law, there are implications for every role in the regime. In lawmaking, the rule of law implies some sort of constitutionalism to regulate and legitimize the process: rules and principles must exist to determine whether a law has been duly enacted or passes some other test of validity. Arguably, no substantive constitutional constraints are implied by the rule of law by itself, except that law must aim for the characteristics that allow subjects to guide their conduct by it. Lon Fuller's account of these is fundamental: generality, promulgation and publicity, nonretroactivity, clarity and determinacy of application, consistency, capability of being obeyed, stability, and the actual administration of law in accordance with declared rule.

In the application of law to cases, the rule of law requires impartial and publicly established tribunals following established procedures that reasonably ensure fairness, the right to a hearing before such tribunals (thus the great historical importance of habeas corpus to the rule of law in common law nations), the independence of the judiciary, and minimal reliance upon subjective interpretation and discretion. Although Albert Venn Dicey argued that all sanctions must originate in ordinary courts applying ordinary law, arguably the use of state power by administrative and regulatory agencies need not by itself violate the rule of law if appropriate quasi-legislative and quasi-judicial standards are observed, and sufficient legislative and judicial control is exercised, ensuring that these agencies are under law.

In the enforcement of law by prosecutors and police, the rule of law requires conformity to publicly established procedures and policies to ensure that law is not perverted through arbitrary or biased enforcement, and that crimes are not perpetrated under color of law. The rule of law requires that law enforcement officers ultimately be answerable for their conduct in ordinary courts, although when misconduct falls short of crime internal disciplinary tribunals may also promote the rule of law. Since it often seems unguided by principles and is usually hidden from public scrutiny, prosecutorial discretion is a standing danger to the rule of law.

Because personal liberty is most at stake, in the criminal law, the normative force of the rule of law is especially strong and undergirds the maxim "No crime, no punishment without law." Especially strict requirements of promulgation, notice, clarity, and certainty of law, as well as scrupulous procedural regularity, must be observed. The rule of law is one ground for the asymmetrical position of defendant and prosecution—the prosecution seeks a direct imposition of state coercion to punish the defendant, and this kind of full power over a person must be treated with great suspicion and precisely confined. Although state coercion enforces both process and judgment, the state is not directly seeking to enforce its own commands in tort and contract. The parties to the dispute stand in symmetrical relationship: here rulings in groundbreaking cases seem inevitably somewhat ex post facto, and the rule of law is served by the judicial creation of reliable rules and principles for the future. By providing a stable framework for avoiding and resolving disputes, the increasing scope of the rule of law promotes free exchange of goods and services and enables individuals to pursue their own ends more effectively.

In full takings of property through eminent domain, the exigency of the rule of law seems intermediate between tort and crime, since the state takes the initiative, yet does not assert the power to deprive property owners of full personal liberty: even in the absence of a constitutional guarantee such as in the United States, a rule-of-law government at least normally owes compensation. When arguably there is a partial taking through the imposition of burdensome state regulation, the rule of law still triggers at least judicial scrutiny to determine impartially whether compensation is due.

Underlying the aspiration for the rule of law is the rejection of domination and power as a basis for the polity: all are subjected to the sovereign law, and neither individuals nor factions (even a majority faction) govern by imposing their arbitrary will. The maxim "A government of laws and not of men" captures the crucial distinction between impersonal, impartial law and personal, arbitrary power.

Critics claim that this distinction is always illusory. Though intermingled, various perspectives are discernible. Marxists see law as largely a mask for class interests and thus a form of domination by faction. Michel Foucault and followers see power as all-pervasive, even though not personal or factional in origin. Deconstructionists (following Jacques Derrida) assert that contradictions and incoherence riddle the law, and they attack the very possibility of determinacy of meaning. Legal realism and critical legal studies deny the cogency of legal reasoning and undermine the distinction between law and politics: social and political commitments hide behind always available legal arguments on opposing sides of any interesting legal controversy.

The more abstract a legal principle, the more uncertainty there is in its application. Broad norms, such as the due process and equal protection clauses of the U.S. Constitution, generate such perplexity that a watertight distinction between law and politics seems unrealistic. However, that does not mean that no rule-of-law considerations operate in applying such norms, for increased clarity and at least moderate stability are achievable.

References

Altman, Andrew. *Critical Legal Studies: A Liberal Critique*. Princeton NJ: Princeton University Press, 1990.

Dicey, Albert Venn. *Introduction to the Study of the Law of the Constitution.* London: Macmillan, 1885. Reprint of 8th ed. Indianapolis: Liberty Classics, 1982.

Dworkin, Ronald. "Political Judges and the Rule of Law." In *A Matter of Principle*, ed. Ronald Dworkin, 9–32. Cambridge MA: Harvard University Press, 1985.

Fuller, Lon L. *The Morality of Law*. New Haven CT: Yale University Press, 1964.

Hayek, Friedrich A. *The Constitution of Liberty*. Chicago: University of Chicago Press, 1960.

Henley, Kenneth. "Abstract Principles, Mid-Level Principles, and the Rule of Law." *Law and Philosophy* 12 (1993), 121–132.

Neumann, Franz. *The Rule of Law: Political Theory and the Legal System in Modern Society*. Leamington Spa UK: Berg Publishers, 1986.

Raz, Joseph. "The Rule of Law and Its Virtue." In *The Authority of Law: Essays on Law and Morality*, ed. Joseph Raz, 210–229. Oxford: Clarendon Press, 1979.

Schauer, Frederick. *Playing by the Rules: A Philosophical Examination of Rule-based Decision-Making in Law and in Life*. Oxford: Clarendon Press, 1991.

Shapiro, Ian, ed. *The Rule of Law: Nomos XXXVI*. New York: New York University Press, 1994.

Kenneth Henley

See also CONSTITUTIONALISM; DUE PROCESS; EMINENT DOMAIN AND TAKINGS; JUDICIAL REVIEW; NATURAL JUSTICE; STANDARDS

Rules

See NORMS

S

Sagas, Icelandic

These literary masterpieces inquired into the viability of self-governing societies of free people. Between Iceland's founding ca. 870 and its submission in 1262 to the Norwegian monarchy its inhabitants had originally fled, Iceland was a republic. Its government consisted of four Quarter Courts, or "Things," to which was later added a fifth court of appeals and the Althing (founded ca. 930), a combination supreme court and legislature. Freemen, on behalf of themselves or their households and kin, could bring cases before the courts. In theory these were adjudicated in accordance with a body of laws recited over a three-year period at the Althing by the Law-Speaker, the republic's only paid official. In practice, support from chiefs and their followers was needed to obtain a verdict in the absence of any law enforcement machinery. Most disputes arose over women, inheritances, and the increasingly scarce resources (land, timber, fish, livestock), which compelled the poor island of under a hundred thousand people to seek Norwegian protection after the republic degenerated into a violent, feuding aristocracy.

In the years of Iceland's decline and shortly thereafter (ca. 1215–1350), the great sagas were written. They deal with the strengths and weaknesses of the republic and the reasons for the persistence and then collapse of its legal system. The sagas present profound yet ultimately indecisive meditations on the legal and moral issues raised by the existence of republican Iceland in a world of monarchical and feudal states. Was the Althing an adequate forum that regulated the conduct of free people until it declined, or was the republic marred by violence and injustice from the start? Were monarchy and submission to the Christian church better solutions for keeping order among hot-tempered Vikings than the consensual Things, or were they the pathetic, last-resort aftermaths of a republic that had squandered its precious freedom?

The sagas raise fundamental questions of legal philosophy through the medium of Iceland. They invoke a panoply of interpretations to such questions as Should an innocent yet contentious person be outlawed for the sake of civic peace? Should the form and technical points of law be preserved to ensure social stability, even if injustice is done to individuals? Should people take the law into their own hands to undo unjust verdicts? Should compromise solutions which placate powerful interests override the claims of aggrieved individuals to absolute justice? Such issues are repeatedly dealt with in two of the greatest sagas—*Njal's* and *Eyrbyggja*.

Njal's Saga most explicitly makes the law its theme, for Njal is Iceland's greatest legal sage. His birth in 930 was the year the Althing was founded. The burning of his house, himself, and most of his kin is the saga's central incident, representing the symbolic destruction of the republic and its law. Njal has previously tried heroically to contain feuds brought about by his hot-tempered friends and family. His murder is not punished at the Althing because the law has degenerated into corrupt lawyers pleading technicalities. Njal's followers do not accept the acquittal, and the Althing then turns into a battlefield, symbolizing the deterioration of the republic into rampant feuding and vengeance-taking among leading families. Anarchy finally gives way to Christian forgiveness, the hoped-for outcome of this parable of Iceland's republican greatness and decline.

Eyrbyggja Saga—the story of the people of the Eyr Peninsula in western Iceland—presents virtually every legal problem which caused feuds during the republic. Runaway slaves, unfaithful wives, beached whales, and tensions between Christians and pagans cannot even be contained within Iceland or among the living. The quarrels spill over into Greenland and the New World, and ghosts return to haunt the living. The Althing is powerless to stop an escalating series of feuds, which leads to the destruction of the virtuous pagan priest Arnkel at the hands of the unscrupulous Snorri. The saga's heroes are the community of free people who strive in vain to end the terrible violence which brought down the republic shortly before this saga was written.

No body of literature rivals the sagas in taking as its theme the nature of law and the ability of republican institutions to do justice. Iceland was the only republic to survive in the western world from the decline of Rome to the rise of Switzerland and was well aware of its unique status. While it lost its independence in 1262 and did not regain it until 1944, Iceland secured its place in history and legal philosophy through its sagas—of which there are hundreds, many still untranslated or unpublished—which dramatically probe the virtues and defects of self-governing communities of free people.

References

Andersson, Theodore M. *The Icelandic Family Sagas: An AnalyticalReading*. Cambridge MA: Harvard University Press, 1967.

Byock, Jesse. *Medieval Iceland: Society, Sagas, and Power*. Berkeley: University of California Press, 1988.

Magnusson, Magnus, Hermann Palsson, and Paul Edwards, eds. *Njal's Saga* (1960); *Eyrbyggja Saga* (1989). London: Penguin Books.

Miller, William Ian. *Bloodtaking and Peacemaking: Feud, Law, and Society in Medieval Iceland*. Chicago: University of Chicago Press, 1990.

Pencak, William. *The Conflict of Law and Justice in the Icelandic Sagas*. Amsterdam: Rodopi, 1995.

William Pencak

Sale

In the common law tradition, a sharp division separates the sale of goods from the sale of land, the former historically the preserve of the courts of common law and the latter of the courts of equity. Time has not been considered of the essence in a sale-of-land agreement, largely because the market in land is not as volatile as that in goods and because the sale of land has been marked by the difficulty of making title and the need to comply with demanding formal requirements. The law of sale of goods, on the other hand, was formed on the basis of mercantile dealings in commodities, and even today that law has a markedly commercial flavor. Given the absence of a common law division between civil and commercial law, the fault line has separated, instead, sale of land and sale of goods contracts. In the civil law tradition, there is no sharp division between sale of goods and sale of land, but there is (though some national legal systems have departed from this) a division between civil and commercial law.

The contract of sale of goods has some claim to being the most important of the nominate contracts in the development of a general law of contract. It was one of the Roman consensual contracts and is the transaction that underpins the market economy. The seller, in return for a money consideration called the price, delivers goods to the buyer and tranfers title (or ownership) to the buyer. A sale contract may be concluded in widely diverging circumstances, from the instantaneous "one shot" transaction of buyer and seller who will never see each other again to the repeat transaction of buyer and seller engaged in continuous dealings, sometimes concluded under an exclusive distributorship or requirements contract. The goods may be bought for personal consumption or for resale, perhaps after undergoing a manufacturing process.

Despite the expression *caveat emptor,* the common and civil law of sale have long imposed duties on the seller concerning the quality of goods supplied. Drawing from Roman law, the civil law systems have favored the protection of the buyer against latent defects in the goods. The favored remedies in the event of seller breach are price reduction or a setting aside (or redhibition) of the contract with damages if the seller is at fault (which professional sellers are presumed to be). The common law, somewhat differently, imposes on business sellers implied obligations of reasonable fitness of the goods for the buyer's purpose and of merchantable quality. These obligations allow a wide range of goods to be suppied, sometimes even defective ones, depending upon the context of the sale, the price paid, and the words that pass between the parties. Liability is strict and damages are commonly awarded. The commitment of the common law to privity of contract has meant that buyers have traditionally been unable to pursue remote sellers further up the distribution chain, and nonbuyers injured by faulty goods have had no recourse against the retail, or indeed any other, seller. These difficulties have been overcome in numerous countries by case law and legislative means. Mention can be made of the Product Liability Directive in the European Community, designed to establish level competitive conditions among manufacturers in the Community by the approximation of national laws.

The common law of sale was developed mainly through a series of nineteenth-century cases that were then subjected to monumental treatises by Lord C. Blackburn and Judah Benjamin. The hallmark of Blackburn's work was the scientific organization of sale around the transfer of ownership, which proprietary event had a profound and general effect upon the contractual rights and duties of the party. This preoccupation of the law with title was in the present century strongly criticized by Karl Llewellyn, the principal architect of the *American Uniform Commercial Code* who, favoring "narrow issue thinking," preferred solutions to individual problems that were sensitive to commercial usage and responsive to practical problems. Lord Blackburn's views, however, found their way into the Sale of Goods Act 1893, enacted by the Westminster Parliament and adopted throughout the British Empire (except for civil law jurisdictions such as Quebec). Ontario was the last common law province in Canada to adopt the Imperial Act, which it did in 1920. In the United States, the act was also the model for Williston's Uniform Sales Act 1906, which was adopted by a substantial number of states before it was superseded in the 1950s and after by Llewellyn's *Uniform Commercial Code*. S. Williston's monumental treatise on the law of sale was thus rendered in practical terms obsolete and went the same way as other great American treatises in modern times.

The other great English treatise on sale was by Benjamin, a former Confederate Minister of War who arrived in England as a refugee from Louisiana in the 1860s after the defeat of the South. As a civilian, it is not surprising that his work, which has endured to this day, was larded with references to the civil law. From being largely a comparative text, it flourishes to this day in a very different form as a detailed practitioners' work largely orientated on the treatment of international sales decisions. The marked feature of these cases is that they concern large-scale commodities dealings concluded between multinational companies who refer their disputes to London arbitration, even though they, and their dealings, usually have no material connection with England. Commodities dealings on forward delivery terms frequently take the form of string contracts involving many parties in the buying and selling of just one cargo. The reality is that forward delivery contracts are tantamount to unregulated futures dealings. The parties to such contracts display a keen concern for technical contractual rights and a lack of patience for the failings of their contractual partners. Litigation is keenly contested between disputants, who appear to find no difficulty in carrying on business as usual with each other during the course of such litigation.

In domestic terms, sale is usually one of the first contracts to attract legislation and codification. The same is true in the field of international unification where, in response to the perceived shortcomings of the unification of conflict of laws rules, attention has been turned to the unification of the substantive law itself. The German jurist Rabel firmly placed the unification of sale on the international agenda before World War II. Two conventions, concerned with the unification of sale and with rules on the formation of contracts, were concluded at The Hague in 1964. They attracted very few adherents, one reason being the lack of third world involvement in the process. That was corrected when the establishment of the United Nations Commission on International Trade led to a renewal of the work of unification involving a wide range of countries of all types. Adopted at a diplomatic conference in Vienna in 1980, the Convention on the International Sale of Goods has been implemented by a large number of countries, including the United States, Canada, China, Argentina, much of the former socialist world, and most of the countries of western Europe (but not the United Kingdom). It has also served as the model for domestic law reform in Scandinavia. This convention favors flexible solutions and keeping the contract alive in the event of disputes. It has some similarities with the Uniform Commercial Code (Article 2) but stands in marked contrast with the rules of English law, which favor certainty at the expense of flexibility and are therefore more palatable to the world of commodities dealers.

References

Benjamin, J.P. *Treatise on the Law of Personal Property with References to the American Decisions and to the French Code and Civil Law*. London: Sweet and Sons, 1868.

Blackburn, C. *A Treatise on the Effect of the Contract of Sale on the Legal Rights of Property and Possession in Goods, Wares and Merchandise*. London: Stevens and Sons, 1845.

Bridge, M.G. *The Sale of Goods*. Oxford: Clarendon Press, 1997.

Guest, A.G. et al. *Benjamin's Sale of Goods*. 5th ed. London: Sweet and Maxwell, 1997.

Honnold, J. *Uniform Law for International Sales under the 1980 United Nations Convention*. 2d ed. Deventer: Kluwer, 1991.

Llewellyn, K. "Of Warranty of Quality in Law and Society I, II." *Columbia Law Review* 36 (1936), 699; 37 (1937), 341.

———. "Through Title to Contract and a Bit Beyond." *New York University Law Review* 15 (1936), 159.

Ontario Law Reform Commission. *Report on the Sale of Goods*. 3 vols. Ottawa: Ministry of the Attorney General, 1979.

Williston, S. *The Law Governing the Sales of Goods at Common Law and under the Uniform Sales Act*. Rev. ed. New York: Baker, Voorhis, 1948.

Zulueta, F. de. *The Roman Law of Sale*. Oxford: Clarendon Press, 1945.

Michael G. Bridge

See also ACQUISITION AND TRANSFER; CONTRACTUAL OBLIGATION; JUSTICE IN CONTRACT, CIVILIAN; NEGOTIABLE INSTRUMENTS; OWNERSHIP; POSSESSION AND RECOVERY

Savigny, Friedrich Carl von (1779–1861)

Friedrich Carl von Savigny, the German jurist, was leader of the historical school of law and one of the most influential legal thinkers of the nineteenth century. Savigny was not a legal philosopher in the traditional sense of someone inquiring into what is right and just, nor did he want to be. One of his most fundamental postulates was that legal philosophy, concerned with ideas of justice, must be separated from jurisprudence, concerned with the nature and meaning of positive law. Savigny concentrated his efforts entirely on the latter. He was therefore primarily a theorist of positive law.

His ideas are best understood in their historical context. Savigny lived during the shift from the eighteenth-century age of reason to nineteenth-century historicism. He was the most influential advocate and outright symbol of this shift with regard to law. Thus, most of his views were reactions against the law of reason and were manifestations of the new historical spirit. This is particularly true for his theory about the nature of law, which became the credo of the historical school. The eighteenth century had distinguished between timeless natural law, originating in reason, and positive law, made by the legislator. Savigny disregarded the former as speculative and reformulated the origin of the latter. For him, positive law emanated from silent, internal powers working within the people. Law, like language, expressed the spirit of the people, the *Volksgeist*. *Volk* was not an ethnic or sociological concept but a cultural idea; *Volksgeist* meant the characteristics of a culture. Law was expressed, then, mainly through custom, but at later stages of civilization also through the ideas of jurists. With the culture, law grew organically over time. It thus emerged, as Savigny wrote, from the innermost character and the history of a people. In short, law was neither a metaphysical nor a legislative phenomenon, but rather a cultural and historical one.

As such, even positive law was not truly a product of the legislator, but of history. It was not something the present could make at will, but a heritage of the past. It was positive not in the sense of made, but of being given. Savigny viewed attempts actively to shape law according to current needs with skepticism. He opposed codification and legislative change because they interfered with the organic growth of the law. Law should be left largely unto itself, explored and refined by scientific experts, the jurists. Thus, Savigny's fundamental attitude is perhaps best characterized as jurisprudential laissez-faire.

This view of law determined his concept of jurisprudence. Jurisprudence was essentially historical, tracing the law's development in order to reveal its true principles. Yet the ultimate goal of the discipline was to arrange these principles in a system. In contrast to natural law, however, jurisprudence was not to *construct* such a system. Instead, as a true science, it was to bring an already inherent organic order to light. Jurisprudence was therefore both historical and scientific as expressed in Savigny's term "historical science of law" *(geschichtliche Rechtswissenschaft)*.

Savigny's conviction that the elements of a logical system were latent in the actual sources was a manifestation of his "objective idealism," according to Joachim Rückert, that is, of his belief that in historical reality there was sense and order. The "is" and the "ought," the real and the ideal, were united in his view of history as a genesis of true principles. Savigny saw every element of life as part of a higher, organic whole *(Glied eines höheren Ganzen)*.

Regarding its political function, Savigny defined law as the boundary between the various individual spheres of liberty in society. Its function was not to enforce moral principles but to guarantee a free space in which they could flourish. Here, he sounded like a nineteenth-century liberal, although politically he was a moderate conservative.

There has been much debate about who most influenced him. One finds traces of Immanuel Kant, Johann Fichte, F.W.J. Schelling, and Johann von Herder, and many of his ideas are reminiscent of Montesquieu and Edward Gibbon. Today, the romantic element is considered less dominant than the classicist features of his thought. Savigny has often been compared with Goethe, in part because of his olympian attitude and his brilliant literary style.

Savigny was also one of the greatest Roman law scholars of all times and the leading legal historian of his age. Many of his works were translated into English, among them his 1814 manifesto *Vom Beruf unserer Zeit für Gesetzgebung und Rechtswissenschaft* (On the Vocation of Our Age for Legislation and Jurisprudence), which concisely presents his fundamental beliefs.

References

Gale, Susan. "A Very German Legal Science: Savigny and the Historical School of Law." *Stanford Journal of International Law* 18 (1982), 123–146.

Kantorowicz, Hermann. "Savigny and the Historical School of Law." *Law Quarterly Review* 53 (1937), 326–341.

Reimann, Mathias. "Nineteenth Century German Legal Science." *Boston College Law Review* 31 (1990), 837–897.

Rückert, Joachim. *Idealismus, Jurisprudenz und Politik bei Friedrich Carl von Savigny.* Ebelsbach: R. Gremer, 1984.

Wolf, Erik. *Grosse Rechtsdenker der deutschen Geistesgeschichte.* 4th ed. Tübingen: J.C.B. Mohr, 1963.

Mathias Reimann

Scandinavian Legal Realism

This term is applied to theories of a group of jurists from Denmark, Norway, and Sweden. The starting point is the philosophical perspective put forward by the Swedish philosopher Axel Hägerström (1868–1939), holding the chair of Practical Philosophy at the University of Uppsala from 1911 until his retirement in 1933. Hence also the label "the Uppsala School of Legal Thinking." The most prominent members are the Swedes A.V. Lundstedt (1882–1955), professor of law at the University of Uppsala, Karl Olivecrona (1897–1980), professor of law at the University of Lund, Per Olof Ekelöf (1906–1990), professor of law at the University of Uppsala, the Dane Alf Ross (1899–1979), professor of law at the University of Copenhagen, and the Norwegian Torstein Eckhoff (1916–1993), professor of law at the University of Oslo. Tore Strömberg (1912–1993), professor of law at the University of Lund (1961–1977), also upheld the view. Some of their writings have been translated into English and have aroused an interest in their perspective on law and legal knowledge in the Anglo-American world. Their basic perspective is antimetaphysical, subscribing to Hägerström's stated aim "to destroy metaphysics, if we ever wish to pierce through the mist of words which has arisen out of feelings and associations and to proceed 'from sounds to things.'" This can be seen as a version of realism in the sense of the doctrine that there are real entities within the scientific area of thought. This doctrine can also be described as a version of materialism or naturalism. The Scandinavian realists hold that whatever exists can only be satisfactorily explained in natural terms of facts. This is a proclamation of the omnicompetence of science and its claim that scientific descriptions must be presented in terms of empirical observations and that scientific explanations are causal explanations. Materialism or naturalism must be taken seriously within the area of law and morality. This is the fundamental message using the term "realism," as Ross points out, as the slogan of the school in their battle against the prevailing jurisprudential perspective of idealism. The term "idealism" denotes the way of thinking in terms of ideals of justice and human rights to be used as standards of evaluation of the existing—positive—legal system, its rules and their application on the one hand and the idea of positive law as an inherently normative system of valid rules with binding force grounded in the will of the sovereign on the other.

Scandinavian legal realism is then to be seen as a revolt against the established perspective on justice and law, originating in the 1920s and mounted upon the epistemological foundation provided by Hägerström's theory of knowledge of reality. The Swedes follow Hägerström, who also has influenced Ross, although Ross later took his inspiration from the Vienna school of logical positivism. The writings of Ross have in turn had a great impact on Norwegian and Finnish jurisprudents who generally ignore Hägerström's philosophy. Hägerström and his followers by contrast claim that logical positivism is an untenable approach to scientific thinking of and about law. Despite this difference, they all share a common platform in their naturalistic perspective that science is the only form of knowledge, that there is nothing in the world beyond what can in principle be scientifically known, that metaphysics is nonsense which must be eliminated, and finally that philosophy provides the foundation for law and legal knowledge by supplying a conceptual analysis of legal concepts and the concepts used in legal science. For Hägerström this conceptual analysis is based upon a historical and psychological investigation into the nature of ideas, whereas for Ross it is based upon a logical inquiry into the meaning of propositions.

For Ross, propositions are rejected as metaphysical propositions by reference to the principle of verification put forward by the logical positivists. Hägerström's rejection of ideas as metaphysical ideas is based upon the materialist view that only what can be seen or touched is to be admitted as real.

What is common to the realists is the doctrine that a proposition which does not admit to being reduced to enunciations of facts can have no real and intelligible meaning. From this antimetaphysical doctrine of meaning the realists claim that law and legal thinking abound with metaphysical concepts, for example, the concepts of right, duty, the validity or binding force of legal rules, and the will of the state. People in general and lawyers in particular suppose they are talking sense when they use such concepts, but this is an illusion. As a matter of fact, they do not use concepts but only words without any meaning. This may have a profound effect on the behavior of people who suffer from this illusion. This can be illustrated in the magical or supernatural elements of primitive superstition, which are also found in Roman law and natural law and which still dominate modern thinking.

The aim of the realists is to cure people, including lawyers, of their nonsensical ideas, thus liberating them from the religious and metaphysical stages of believing that law is to be seen as commands of a sovereign will or that there are ideals of human rights or justice to be implemented by law. The aim of the realists is to bring about the scientific stage of thinking in terms of natural facts and their causal relations. In this battle the realists appeal to a causal theory of meaning according to which the meaning of a sentence or a word is the response, or range of responses, produced by the sentence or word as a sign of ideas in one's mind.

The causal theory of meaning is then combined with the naturalistic perspective that ideas must refer to observable facts. Hence it follows that, cognitively speaking, there can be no such thing as legal rules as commands based upon the will of the sovereign, nor legal rules as norms based upon practical reason. Thus the prevailing legal theories of positivism and natural rights are untenable from the scientific perspective. From this perspective law can only be understood as fact. Legal concepts, for instance, the concepts of rights and duties, do not refer to any observable facts; hence they are, cognitively speaking, meaningless, although room is found for using these concepts solely as technical tools of representing empirical data. Whether this is a satisfactory analysis is a matter of dispute among the realists.

From the realist perspective the only proper view is that legal rules and concepts are metaphysical sentences and words devoid of any cognitive meaning. However, they have a function of expressing feeling addressed to and regulating the behavior of officials, especially judges, by calling forth the appropriate response in terms of feeling to follow the rules on pain of sanctions. The crucial fact is that the cause as well as the effect of issuing legal rules can be discovered empirically. Hence legal rules can be defined in terms of "independent imperatives" (Olivecrona) or "directives" (Ross), having the function of regulating the behavior of people. Thus the realists take an instrumental perspective on law as an impersonal social machinery subject to natural causation.

In the end the machinery of law is controlled by the officials, who also are constituted by the system. The system is operated according to the interest of society or the interests of specific classes. It follows that there is room for a scientific discipline dealing with law as a natural fact. Thus there is legal knowledge as sociological knowledge put forward in scientific propositions based upon the observation of facts. For Ross this legal knowledge is the scientific knowledge of predicting what the courts or officials will do. Legal science is a branch of natural science. For the Swedes legal knowledge is scientific knowledge to be used as guidance for courts and officials deciding disputes. Legal science is a branch of social science, and the task is to offer guidance concerning the interpretation and application of legal rules by the courts. What is common is the thesis that reason must be seen as instrumental rationality concerned with the efficient means to given ends. There is no such thing as substantive rationality concerned with the rationality or morality of the ends to be pursued. The reason why this is the case is the distinction between fact and value, endorsed by all realists. As a matter of fact, values are not part of the fabric of the world, and moral thinking is just as infected with metaphysics as legal thinking. There are no moral propositions, hence no such thing as ethics or moral knowledge. This is Hägerström's famous doctrine that moral sentences do not express any cognitive moral propositions but are rather expressions of feeling or interests. Thus Hägerström was among the first in the twentieth century to present what is called an emotive theory of ethics, which is dubbed "value-nihilism" by his opponents. According to Hägerström's moral skepticism, there can be no knowledge of values; hence values are feelings or illusions.

All realists subscribe to this moral skepticism, which depends upon a contrast between the sciences dealing with facts and ethics dealing with values. There is knowledge of facts, including the fact that people express their moral feelings. In this sense there is a scientific study of moral feelings, that is, moral sociology or moral psychology, which deals with facts. However, there can be no scientific discipline concerned with whether the moral feelings have any truth value, since they are expressed in sentences which, cognitively speaking, are meaningless utterances. It follows that criticism of the legal system in moral terms can be dismissed as nonsense or metaphysics. Despite the claim that nothing is objectively right or wrong on the theoretical level, the realists claim that they are entitled to hold fast to their own basic feelings of what is valuable in life. People may thus have a private morality, but there can be no such thing as public or ideal morality independent of law. Hence the need for laws to pursue and secure social harmony and to influence people's moral opinions. This is Olivecrona's thesis that it is the law which is the cause of morality, not the other way around.

For the realists the basic social values are to establish and maintain peace and social welfare within the state and among states based upon respect for law as the cement of society. No state can function satisfactorily if it does not have a peaceful order, and some other public goods as well, provided by the state through law. Law in turn can be upheld primarily by suggestion and conditioning, secondarily by the use of force monopolized by the state. The need for law can then be explained on a scientific basis because the alternative of breaking the law is anarchy or chaos. Hence the rejection of natural or moral rights as mischievous but dangerous nonsense. Hence also the rejection of the communist ideal of abolishing law altogether. Law is essential in the state as a method of rational social control, and it is an illusion to think that the use of force can be eliminated. If the state is a necessity for social order and the well-being of the citizens, it is easy to infer that its representative institutions should govern for the good life and that all citizens should have their well-being underwritten by law.

This is the position held by A.V. Lundstedt advancing the method of social welfare based upon the need of people rather than the method of justice based upon freedom and human rights. Lundstedt's approach is, despite his vigorous protests, a version of utilitarianism, which is rejected by Olivecrona and Ross as metaphysics. So is the method of justice. Law is a fact, an important social fact for the maintenance of order in society. Whether this order is legitimate and just cannot be rationally discussed. It must be noticed that Torstein Eckhoff offers a contribution concerning the distribution and allocation of private and public goods.

Although the Scandinavian realists did not found a lasting school, they left a lasting spirit in the Nordic countries, especially their moral skepticism combined with the claim to turn legal science into scientific and instrumental knowledge describing the causal relations among legal facts. The political thought of the school is made manifest in the Nordic welfare states' stressing of equality and utility rather than liberty and human rights, based upon the respect for science and its application as a contribution to welfare and as a weapon against legal dogma and popular superstition.

The Scandinavian realists, by way of conclusion, have also met opposition, partly by attacking the epistemological foundation as a version of idealism rather than realism. The Scandinavians hold that what there is, is what we can think about, and this is necessarily true, because the idea of something that we could not think about makes no sense. The rejoinder, however, is the realist position, which holds that what there is extends beyond the reach of our minds. Further, the Scandinavians confuse or neglect the difference between law as prescriptive rules and law as descriptions, which is related to equating reasons and causes. Their moral and legal epistemology may also be questioned, since this reduces legal and moral discourse to something which is essentially nonrational, a matter not of argument but of psychological pressure and efficacious manipulation. This is founded upon the causal theory of meaning, which is untenable.

The views of the Scandinavian realists is still a lively issue, as can be seen from the Swedish debate between Jacob Sundberg, a former professor of jurisprudence at the University of Stockholm who was charged, by his colleages, with corrupting the students by preaching that the Swedish legal system—and its prominent lawyers—ignores basic human rights. Jacob Sundberg had to resign from his chair in 1993.

References

Bjarup, Jes. "Epistemology and Law According to Axel Hägerström." *Scandinavian Studies in Law* 29 (1985), 13–47.

———. *Skandinavischer Realismus* (Scandinavian Realism)*: Hägerström-Lundstedt-Olivecrona-Ross*. Freiburg: Verlag Karl Alber, 1978.

Eckhoff, Torstein. *Justice: Its Determinants in Social Interaction*. Rotterdam: Rotterdam University Press, 1974.

Geiger, Theodor. *Vorstudien zu einer Soziologie des Rechts* (Prolegomenon to a Sociology of Law). 4th ed. Berlin: Duncker und Humblot, 1987.

Hägerström, Axel. *Inquiries into the Nature of Laws and Morals*. Trans. C.D. Broad. Intro. Karl Olivecrona. Uppsala: Almqvist and Wiksell/Otto Harrasowitz, 1953.

———. *Philosophy and Religion*. Trans. R.T. Sandin. London: Allen and Unwin, 1964.

Lundstedt, A.V. *Legal Thinking Revised*. Stockholm: Almqvist and Wiksell, 1966.

Olivecrona, Karl. *Law as Fact*. 1939. 2d ed. London: Stevens, 1971.

Ross, Alf. *Directives and Norms*. London: Routledge and Kegan Paul, 1968.

———. *On Law and Justice*. London: Stevens, 1958.

Ross, Alf. *Towards a Realistic Jurisprudence*. Trans. A.I. Fausböll. Copenhagen: Einar Munksgaard, 1946.

Shils, Edward. "Academic Freedom at the University of Stockholm." *Minerva* 29 (1991), 321–385.

"Soziologische Jurisprudenz und realistische Theorien des Rechts" (Sociological Jurisprudence and Realist Theories of Law). *Rechtstheorie* 9 (1986). Ed. Eugene Kamenka, Robert I. Summers, and William L. Twining. Preface by Aleksander Peczenik. (Articles on Scandinavian realism by Jes Bjarup, Enrico Pattaro, Silvana Castignone, Carla Faralli, Stig Jørgensen, Jacob W.F. Sundberg, and Annika Lagerqvist Almé.)

Strömholm, Stig, and H.H. Vogel. *Le "réalisme scandinave" dans la philosophie du droit* ("Scandinavian Realism" in the

Philosophy of Law). Preface by Michel Villey. Paris: Librairie générale de droit et de jurisprudence, 1975.
Sundberg, Jacob W.F. *Haegerstrom and Finland's Struggle for Law*. Littleton CT: Rothman, 1983.

Jes Bjarup

See also NORTHERN EUROPEAN PHILOSOPHY OF LAW

Science
See EMPIRICAL EVIDENCE

Scottish Enlightenment

This period of extraordinary intellectual activity, centered on the cities of Edinburgh and Glasgow, ran from perhaps 1760 to 1790, though some scholars would expand the life span a decade or more in both directions. The period is typified by a famous observation, attributed to a certain Mr. Amyat, King's Chemist—"a most sensible and agreeable English gentleman," according to printer and antiquarian William Smellie—who remarked: "Here I stand at what is called the Cross of Edinburgh, and can, in a few minutes, take fifty men of genius and learning by the hand."

The conflux of talent was indeed remarkable, for living and working in Scotland at this time were, among others, David Hume, arguably Britain's greatest philosopher; Adam Smith, founder of modern economics; Thomas Reid, expositor of "common sense" philosophy; Adam Ferguson, one of the founders of sociology; William Robertson, groundbreaking developmental historian; William Cullen, teacher of clinical medicine; and James Watt, of steam-engine fame. Nor were able minds lacking in the field of law and jurisprudence. In addition to Smith, professor of jurisprudence at Glasgow University, were Henry Home (Lord Kames) and James Bumett (Lord Monboddo), who plotted the connections between law and philosophy through practical investigations, while John Millar and Francis Hutcheson anticipated later developments in legal philosophy by examining the relations among law, social structure, and history.

The 1707 Act of Union that joined England to Scotland (refashioned "North Britain" by southern politicians) brought many changes to Scotland, including the obvious and decisive loss of sovereignty. However, many important institutions were left intact by the Union, including Scotland's legal, educational, and religious systems. To this day, though attempts at regaining sovereignty have repeatedly failed, Scottish civil law retains important differences from English common law, notably the middle-course jury verdict of "not proven" in cases where there is insufficient evidence to convict. This independent legal tradition was crucial to national self-regard in the years following the Act of Union, when patriotism was necessary protection against English condescension, and was made central by the celebrated "moderate literati of Edinburgh," Enlightenment Scotland's leading lights, many of whom had trained as lawyers in the civil law tradition favored in the Dutch universities they habitually attended.

These literati drew on the previous work of the seventeenth-century Scottish jurists to articulate the principles of Scottish law and, moreover, to adapt those principles to the new demands of vibrant commercial society. According to David Daiches, one student of the period, Viscount Stair's *Institutions of the Law of Scotland,* first published in 1681, broke the ground by placing "the study of the legal system of Scotland in a context of philosophical inquiry into the fundamental principles of law and their relation to morality, social structure and customs, politics, and economics." Later efforts by Sir George Mackenzie (1684), Lord Bankton (1751–1753), John Erskine (1754), Lord Kames (1760), and Baron David Hume (the philosopher's nephew) continued the "legal contextualist" tradition of Stair.

Perhaps of equal importance in this tradition was Gershom Carmichael, first professor of moral philosophy at Glasgow University, a chair held later by Francis Hutcheson and Adam Smith. Carmichael was largely responsible for establishing the tradition of natural jurisprudence in the Scottish universities of the day, and his annotated edition of Samuel Pufendorf's *De officio hominis et civis* was made a set text in moral philosophy at Glasgow and thus influenced several generations of students. Sir John Plingle, professor at Edinburgh University, also adopted Carmichael's Pufendorf at around this time. Together they set the terms of legal debate as Scotland became more prosperous and, hence, struggled with questions of justice in a commercial society no longer obviously susceptible to Ciceronian virtues of the civic republican sort.

Hutcheson, Smith, and Kames were the leading lights in this debate. Hutcheson, drawing on Carmichael's rather idiosyncratic interpretation of John Locke's *Second Treatise,* argued that land ownership was the best foundation of civil government and civic virtue. He posited an original contract of landowners who together created and maintained society, their duties to the poor spelled out not by that contract but by natural law. This contractarian aristocracy was criticized by both Hume and Smith, who were more cognizant of the commercial nature of Scottish society in the 1760s. Smith suggested that the civic republican virtues were no longer to the point, and indeed tended to serve the interests of a rich elite rather than justice for the poor. In *The Wealth of Nations* he argued, famously, that free markets would guide a society not to more equality, or more virtue, but more justice.

This was novel use of the natural law tradition that had been endorsed in Scottish jurisprudence since at least Stair's *Institutions.* That tradition—from Thomas Aquinas to Samuel Pufendorf and Hugo Grotius to John Locke and Beyberac—had embraced a right to private property but had likewise enshrined the right to a fair price and the obligation of the rich to help the poor. Under Smith's reading, the fair price was set by what the free market would bear, the obligation to the poor by the increased prosperity of active investment. There was therefore, in his view, no in-principle conflict between the rights of the rich and the needs of the poor.

Kames, too, employed the natural law tradition to illuminate the social situation in Enlightenment Scotland. He also shared the sociological approach to law that Smith exhibited in his *Lectures on Jurisprudence.* A judge in the Court of Session, Kames was even more keenly aware than Smith of how the philosophical issues played out in courtroom practice. His *Historical Law Tracts* and *Principles of Equity* are extended attempts to spell out law as a "rational science" for "every person who has an appetite for knowledge." Therefore, he attempted to show how the law's "principles unfolded," and how it possessed crucial "connections with manners and politics." According to his contemporary, John Millar, Kames's writings refashioned the natural law tradition as "a natural history of legal establishments," crowning the work of Scotland's other "speculative lawyers." The law, said Kames, became "only a rational study when it is traced historically, from its first rudiments among the savages, through successive changes, to its highest improvements in civilized society."

Like his countrymen, Kames was particularly concerned with the emerging needs of a newly commercial society, one where progress was a central goal. He was critical of "antiquated" common law and advocated extensive statutory improvements under the broad heading of "equity." This principle of natural law, which draws, among other sources, on Aristotle's discussion of justice in Book V of the *Nicomachean Ethics,* calls for sensitive application and case-by-case flexibility in principles of justice. Advocating it, especially in his *Principles of Equity,* Kames came close to writing a general social theory to match the general jurisprudential history offered in the *Tracts.*

The irony is that, as a means to realize equity, more statutory law approaches self-defeat. Further rules do not necessarily help existing rules find better application. For his part, Smith was skeptical of Kames's entire project, and commented in a letter to Hume (12 April, 1759) that it was no more than an attempt to make "an agreeable Composition by joining Metaphysics and Scotch law." Certainly Smith's work has proved more influential than Kames's, who is today known less for his detailed legal theory than for his startling, but rather poorly worked out, proto-Darwinian ideas on natural selection (popular drawings of the day invariably show him with a monkey's tail). If nothing else, Smith was more prescient. His keen sense of emerging commercial society's needs, in Scotland and elsewhere, contributed to the economic theory that underwrites the limited-government branch of classical liberalism, whose hero he remains.

References

Campbell, R. H., and A. S. Skinner, eds. *The Origins and Nature of the Scottish Enlightenment.* Edinburgh: J. Donald, 1982.

Chitnis, Anand C. *The Scottish Enlightenment: A Social History.* London: Croom Helm, 1976.

Daiches, David. *The Scottish Enlightenment.* Edinburgh: Saltire Society, 1986.

Daiches, David, and Peter Jones, eds. *A Hotbed of Genius: The Scottish Enlightenment.* Edinburgh: Edinburgh University Press, 1986.

Davie, George. *The Scottish Enlightenment and Other Essays*. Edinburgh: Polygon, 1991.
Hont, Istvan, and Michael Ignatieff, eds. *Wealth and Virtue: The Shaping of Political Economy in the Scottish Enlightenment*. Cambridge: Cambridge University Press, 1983.
Phillipson, Nicholas T., and Ronald Mitchison, eds. *Scotland in the Age of Improvement*. Edinburgh: Edinburgh University Press, 1970.
Rendall, Jane. *The Origins of the Scottish Enlightenment*. London: Macmillan, 1978.
Sher, Richard B. *Church and University in the Scottish Enlightenment: The Moderate Literati of Edinburgh*. Princeton NJ: Princeton University Press, 1985.

Mark Kingwell

See also HUME, DAVID; PUFENDORF, SAMUEL

Secession

Until the early 1990s the question of secession was almost entirely ignored by philosophers, and it remains complicated by a confluence of legal, moral, and political issues.

Secession is the withdrawal of a population and its territory from the authority of the state of which it had been part. It differs from mass emigrations and from the annexation of territory by a foreign state. A successful secessionist movement typically sets up its own state, although irredentist secessionists wish to separate from one state in order to join another. Secessionist movements can also operate at the substate level, where a region desires to separate from one subunit (for example, a province or city) to join another or to attain the same status itself.

The Legality of Secession

Secessionist movements fall within the scope of both domestic and international law. Very few constitutions recognize a right of secession. In theory, secessions could be facilitated in domestic law through the normal process of amending the constitution. Since such procedures typically give veto powers to the nonseceding regions, they can hardly be said to confer a *right* of secession.

There are aspects of both formal and customary international law that bear on the legitimacy of secession. Formally, the *United Nations Charter*, Article 1(2), states that a central purpose of the organization is to "develop friendly relations among nations based on respect for the principle of equal rights and self-determination of peoples. . . ." Articles 55, 73, and 76(1) confirm this principle, as do a number of subsequent U.N. resolutions. While this principle was invoked during the period of decolonization, most experts agree that it does not imply a legal right of secession. The 1970 *Declaration on Friendly Relations* makes clear that the principle shall not "be construed as authorizing or encouraging any action which would dismember or impair, totally or in part, the territorial integrity or political unity of sovereign and independent States. . . ." The reason for this formal distinction between decolonization and secession is clear: most member states in the United Nations contain significant ethnic minorities, and their governments would not endorse resolutions which would legitimize or encourage secessionist movements within their borders. Many philosophers are inclined to view this distinction as morally arbitrary.

Most experts also doubt that there is a right of secession implicit in customary international law. It is not the practice of states to recognize the existence of new states simply because the populations in secessionist territories desire independence. Even in the case of the breakup of the Soviet Union, the international community did not confer recognition on the new states until the Russian government did. There was some early recognition of Slovenia and Croatia during the breakup of the Yugoslav Federation, but this was treated as a case of a state dissolving rather than as a matter of secession. In general, anomalies and inconsistencies in recognition of seceding territories can be explained by the strategic interests of the states conferring recognition.

The Morality of Secession

Many believe there is a *moral* right of peoples to self-determination. "Peoples" here is usually interpreted to refer to groups with an ethnocultural identity. Good arguments can be given for why such groups may require a degree of political autonomy. For example, this may reduce discrimination against them, or it may be the best way to enable them to preserve their languages and cultures. However, most philosophers do not think that such a principle can ground a right of peoples to secede, since there are more than five thousand ethnic groups in the world, and it seems inconceivable that more than a small fraction could have their own states.

In order to determine whether some particular group, S, may have a right of secession, most theorists assume that moral considerations in addition to the principle of self-determination must come into play. Some concentrate on substantive considerations such as whether S has been discriminated against, whether S has representation in the central government, whether the culture of S is threatened, whether S had been illegally incorporated into the larger state within recent memory, or whether the economic resources of S are unfairly exploited by the larger state. While such factors do seem relevant, it is also difficult to see how, in many cases, they could be judged impartially by a national or international body attempting to evaluate the legitimacy of a secessionist claim.

Another approach focuses on procedural criteria. In the most straightforward case, a secession is legitimate if and only if the majority within S desires (and votes) to secede. Such a principle is typically derived from either a principle of free association, a consent principle of legitimacy, or a basic principle of majoritarian democracy. The simplest versions of these principles would have to be modified to account for the widely held view that if an act is wrong it is not made right by the mere fact that a majority votes for it. An injustice caused by a particular secession (for instance, because a wealthy region attempts to leave a state in order not to have to share its resources) is not necessarily made right by a majority vote within the seceding region.

Others have questioned the deduction of a principle of secession from a principle of democracy. In declaring that the people should rule, democracy takes for granted that we know the relevant boundaries of the people; yet this is precisely what secession calls into question. The idea of democracy itself cannot explain who is entitled to vote in a plebiscite to determine who should be entitled to vote in the future, and any appeal to ethnocultural criteria for defining "the people" is foreign to the idea of democracy per se.

The Politics of Secession

In the absence of clear legal procedures and widely accepted moral principles, secessionist movements press their claims in the political and military arenas. In democratic states, nationalist movements with a territorial base within one or more subunits will sometimes escalate their demands to the point of secession. If so, it is natural that at some stage they will hold a plebiscite, and it is likely that a simple majority vote will be taken as sufficient to justify secession. (Those objecting to the simple-majority criterion would be made to look undemocratic or unfair.)

One way of thinking about the legitimacy of secession, which combines the realities of law, morality, and politics, is to consider which constitutional secession procedure would be appropriate for a given state. For example, we might imagine the procedure that would be agreed to if the regional and cultural groups in a particular country were founding a democratic union in a fair bargaining situation. We might expect such parties to agree on a requirement that a plebiscite be held in the seceding region, that the vote necessary to secede be set at 60 percent or higher, and that there be a formula for valuing and dividing assets and budget surpluses or debts. In effect, such a conclusion would constitute a fair procedure for secession within a given state. The super-majority requirement would be justified for reasons similar to those which recommend super-majorities for other constitutional amendments. Of course, it would be very difficult to entrench and legitimize such a procedure once a secessionist movement in a state has already gathered steam.

References

Buchanan, Allen. *Secession: The Morality of Political Divorce from Fort Sumter to Lithuania and Quebec*. Boulder CO: Westview, 1991.

Eastwood, Lawrence S. "Secession: State Practice and International Law After the Dissolution of the Soviet Union and Yugoslavia." *Duke Journal of Comparative and International Law* 3 (1993), 299–349.

Young, Robert A. "How Do Peaceful Secessions Happen?" *Canadian Journal of Political Science* 27 (1994), 773–792.

Wayne Norman

See also MINORITY, ETHNIC, AND GROUP RIGHTS; NATION AND NATIONALISM; SELF-DETERMINATION, NATIONAL; SELF-DETERMINATION, PERSONAL

S

Secondary Rights

Secondary or accessory rights of property are the rights one person has upon the property of another. The common law recognizes a number of interests individuals may have in the property of others. Such interests may have a narrow purpose, such as ensuring the payment of debts. This is the case with mortgages and artisan's liens. A mortgage allows a creditor to foreclose on and sell the property of a delinquent debtor. An artisan's lien allows one who has worked on the property of another to retain possession of the property until compensated for his or her services. Such interests may also involve the broader use of another's property, as is true of easements, profits, and licenses. An easement grants one a right of way in the land of another. A profit is the right to obtain something from another's land, such as timber or crops. A license is similar to an easement, except that, unlike an easement, a license is revocable at will. Such interests may even control what another can do on his or her own property, such as covenants that compel or restrict an owner's activities.

The existence of these secondary rights within the common law exposes the philosophic complexity of the common law's concept of property. Within common law jurisprudence, one can detect three conceptually distinct senses of property: (1) property as thing, (2) property as relation between person and thing, and (3) property as relation between persons. The ordinary understanding of property most closely resembles the notion of property as thing. However, secondary rights within the common law reveal the inadequacy of this ordinary understanding of property because of the way these rights involve different persons having different relations to the same thing. For example, a typical homeowner with a mortgage retains control of his or her residence so long as the homeowner makes timely payments to the bank holding the mortgage. Should the homeowner fall behind in these payments, the bank may assume control of the residence. Understanding mortgages thus requires the second conception of property—property as relation between person and thing—in order to explain the different property rights of the homeowner and bank. These different rights stem from the different relations each has to the same thing. Because mortgages involve at least two legal actors, they also implicate the third sense of property—property as relation between persons. While the property rights of the homeowner and bank involve their different relations to a thing, such rights also involve their relation to each other.

In exposing the philosophic complexity of the common law's concept of property, secondary rights bring to the fore a number of important issues. In implicating the notion of property as a relation between person and thing, for example, secondary rights raise the issue of the nature of ownership. If secondary rights contemplate differing relations to the same thing, are all such relations those of ownership, or is the relation of ownership distinctive in some way? The common law's ambiguity in this connection underlies a modern doctrinal conflict regarding mortgages. Some jurisdictions adopt a title theory of mortgages; others prefer a lien theory. In title theory jurisdictions, the creation of a mortgage conveys title to the party holding the mortgage. Thus, such party is deemed to be the legal owner of the mortgaged property. In lien theory jurisdictions, ownership remains with the party taking out the mortgage. The holder of the mortgage is merely granted a lien against the mortgaged property.

From a theoretical perspective, there are a number of possible strategies for resolving the common law's ambiguity regarding the nature of ownership. Each strategy in turn provokes additional issues. One strategy understands ownership as involving the most extensive relations with a thing, but the meaning of "extensive" is problematic here. What makes one set of relations more extensive than another? Another strategy sees ownership as involving a particular distinctive relation with a thing, but the difficulty here lies in identifying the specific relation denoting ownership. What grants this relation its preeminent status? A third strategy denies the need for a rigorously analytic general definition of ownership. Taking its cue from legal practice, this approach seeks instead to analyze and clarify the particular relations between persons and things recognized under the common law. However, this approach fails to account for the persistence and power of the concept of ownership within so much of contemporary discourse.

Along with revealing general issues regarding the nature of ownership, secondary rights under the common law raise the question of the particular status of such rights. The question of the particular status of secondary rights arises out of the tension between the notion of property as relation between person and thing and the notion of property as relation between persons. Because secondary rights implicate both senses of property, their status in this connection is ambiguous. Put in terms of a traditional legal classification, the ambiguity is this: Are they rights *in personam* or *in rem*? Rights in personam arise primarily out of a relation to a person; rights in rem arise primarily out of a relation to a thing.

Doctrinally, the common law dealt with this ambiguity by introducing significant distinctions. Consider the common law's distinction between an easement appurtenant and an easement in gross. An easement appurtenant is one which enhances its holder's use of another parcel of land—referred to as the dominant tenement. An easement in gross exists independent of its holder's ownership of an additional parcel of land. Under the common law, a holder of an easement appurtenant transferred it with the sale of the dominant tenement, but the common law regarded an easement in gross as purely personal and therefore inalienable. Modern rulings have created exceptions to this doctrine.

Thus, an easement appurtenant has the character of a right in rem. It is a right that arises primarily out of its holder's relation to a thing—the dominant tenement. When the holder changes his or her relation to the thing by selling the dominant tenement, the holder loses the easement appurtenant. An easement in gross, however, has an in personam character. It arises primarily out of its holder's relation to a person—the owner of the land in which it exists. Thus, the common law's restriction against its alienability made sense: sale of an easement in gross was impossible because it would sever the very relation which gives rise to the right.

From a theoretical perspective, however, this common law distinction is subject to challenge. An easement in gross may be easily reconceptualized as a right in rem. This is because by its very character it also involves its holder's relation to a thing—the land in which it resides. Given this ambiguity in its status as a right, the willingness of modern courts to create exceptions allowing the sale of easements in gross is unsurprising. Such ambiguities in legal theory allow for the practical development of the law.

References

Becker, Lawrence. *Property Rights: Philosophic Foundations*. London: Routledge and Kegan Paul, 1977.

Reeve, Andrew. *Property*. Atlantic Highlands NJ: Humanities Press International, 1986.

Waldron, Jeremy. *The Right to Private Property*. Oxford: Oxford University Press, 1988.

Jeffrey Nesteruk

See also ESTATE AND PATRIMONY; FRAGMENTATION OF OWNERSHIP; SECURITY

Secondary Rules

See METANORMS

Security

Security is used in three related senses in the law: mutual protection, secured transactions, and documentary securities. The concept that is central to all three senses is that of safety or, more precisely, prior protection against loss, particularly the loss of life or property.

The philosophically most significant sense, the focus of the political and legal philosophy of Thomas Hobbes, John Locke, and Jean-Jacques Rousseau, is that people band together for *mutual protection* against others. The driving force behind the hypothetical *social contract* employed in all three theories is the actual well-founded fear that people have for each other. No one can be secure in holding a possession when others can wrest it away. So the idea of being secure in one's person and property suggests a collective agreement where each is protected from each other by the creation of a protective association or government with a monopoly of power (or at least so much power as, in Hobbes's colorful and perceptive phrase, "to hold men in awe").

The quest for security formed the primary impetus for the development of civilization—the concentration of things valued into *defensible places* where they could be collected, preserved, and developed. At some point prehistorically, people gathered together in protected communities—whether behind palisades (for example, as seen both in pre-Columbian excavations in the New World and ancient Celtic and Germanic ones in the Old) or stone walls (for example, in the civilizations of the Euphrates valley)—and created city life. The walls of Nineveh made possible Assyrian civilization. Isolation by water (as in Crete) or wasteland (as with Egypt) could have the same effect, as could proximity to the sea (for instance, Lorient in Brittany). Athens, Rhodes, and Troy had substantial walls in addition to their seaside locations.

The rise of kings, tyrants, and *ruling classes,* so far as our knowledge goes, is largely attributable to the protective role played by such individuals. The prima facie justification for focused leadership and the special rights acquired by warrior classes rested on their ability to provide for secure living. As walls became inadequate and warrior classes too sparse to do the job (with the advent of advanced weaponry), the justification for such special status began to evaporate and was slowly replaced by the nation-state, conscription, and democracy.

The great revolutions of the seventeenth to twentieth centuries constituted the transitional mechanism for moving from hired protection to *collective protection,* and the movement from government by acquisition and heredity to government by social compact. Nevertheless, the fundamental rational justification of government is security for people, places, and things. A government that cannot provide for local security forfeits the legitimacy required to actually govern.

Aggressive war endangers security, and the twentieth century saw two attempts to move the concept of collective security to *international status* with the formation of the League of Nations in 1919 and the establishment (beginning in 1945) of the United Nations. The League attempted to replace the system of alliances that had developed in the preceding century. The purpose of those alliances was to present a too fearful prospect for any potential transgressor. However, potential transgressors also built similar alliances and the result was larger and wider wars. The League itself failed because some major powers (for example, the United States) were not members, and the League lacked war-making power. The United Nations, despite many impediments to the successful provision of collective security (1) now has all major nations as members and (2) now has war-making power. What it lacks is a monopoly of power or even enough power to hold major nations in awe. What seems to be developing (beginning with the Korean War, 1948–1953) is a method of co-opting major nations for U.N. peacekeeping purposes. When this can be done, the protective security of the United Nations is effective.

The second sense in which security appears centrally in any legal system is in the concept of the *secured transaction.* In its simplest expression it is this: in a contract or covenant in which one (or more) of the parties has not yet performed, the party (or parties) that has performed (in whole or part) obtains at the outset a security interest in the property of the nonperforming party (or parties), the actual possession of which guarantees the future performance of the as yet nonperforming party.

There are many secured transactions of the sort defined. The most ubiquitous and transparent is the *mortgage.* For example, Able sells Baker Whiteacre, transferring all of his rights in Whiteacre to Baker. Baker gives Able a million dollars, three quarters of which Baker has borrowed from Citicorp (in this example, a bank). Baker gives Citicorp a mortgage to Whiteacre so that if Baker does not pay Citicorp $750,000 when due, Citicorp is entitled to get Whiteacre as if Able had sold it to Citicorp at the outset. So the mortgage secures Citicorp's interest in Whiteacre regardless of what Baker does.

Suppose the value of Whiteacre itself might decline to less than Citicorp's interest in it ($750,000). Citicorp can protect its investment by securing from Baker (at the outset) a *note* for $750,000, which says that regardless of the mortgage to Whiteacre held by Citicorp Baker personally owes Citicorp $750,000. This note, as it stands, is unsecured because when Citicorp goes to Baker for the $750,000 Baker may be worth less than $750,000 (perhaps nothing). So Citicorp may require that Baker put up other material of value at the outset worth $750,000 to secure the note, that is, to make sure that Baker pays off the note as or when due. This material is called *collateral* and may be held in *escrow* either by Citicorp or by Dave, a stakeholder, who will give it to Citicorp on proof that Baker has defaulted on his note to Citicorp.

These are two familiar instances of secured transactions; two others equally familiar are the lien and the title (as in automobile title). The *lien* is instituted (or attached) by a creditor to secure payment of a debt. Usually this is done by a filing with some central authority (like a title registry) or a court. The lien runs with the property to which it is attached and constitutes a defect in the free alienability of that property. Any purchaser takes subject to the lien, unless or until it has been discharged, much as a purchaser of a mortgaged property takes it subject to the mortgage. This sort of interest cannot be eliminated unless the lien or mortgage is satisfied. In all cases of secured transactions courts will routinely enforce mortgages, notes, and liens in the absence of significant and compelling defenses (for example, infancy, fraud, duress, insanity). *Titles,* for example, to real property, when registered require a conveyance signed by the titleholder that empowers the taker to register the property, thereby cutting off other unregistered claims. The action of registering a title (with a title office) perfects title in the purchaser. Title, where provided for by statute, can be issued for automobiles, airplanes, and ships. Ownership cannot be perfected without a conveyance (in the proper form) by the title owner followed by registration. Perfection secures the transaction in as much as courts (along with their attendant police power) will routinely protect the validity of registered claims in the absence of significant and compelling defenses.

These are the elementary forms of secured transactions. Secured interests can be expressed in many ways and in nearly every kind of property, tangible and intangible.

The third sense in which security is typically used is nominative. Here the object called a *security* is a thing itself; usually, but not always, a certificate representing an equitable position in a company (stocks) or evidence of a debt (bonds). They are called securities because, in virtue of their issuance, the holder already has a secured interest in the issuer's wherewithal as represented by the stock or bond. *Stocks* represent proportionate shares in the company as stated on the certificate. Stocks may be with or without voting power; with or without the right to buy further shares, get dividends, or share in a winding up of the enterprise. A *bond,* however, evidences a debt the enterprise has to the holder, and the bond includes rights to compensation, preference in repayment, and other matters attached to it. Both kinds of securities may be sold, unless otherwise encumbered, to anyone for whatever price the parties agree upon. In mature settled markets both stocks and bonds may be registered, and their exchange is usually regulated by some enforceable national legislation. The more mature and settled the market, the more secure the holder's interest is, but that security does not include price stability, which is the function of the market.

Futures contracts, puts, calls, and other *market devices* are not themselves securities but contracts to buy and sell securities. The more mature and stable the market is, within which they are traded, the more like the securities they are derived from they appear.

References

Atiyah, P.S. *Promises, Morals and Law.* Oxford: Clarendon Press, 1981.

Fried, Charles. *Contract as Promise.* Cambridge: Harvard University Press, 1981.

Hobbes, Thomas. *Leviathan.* 1651.

Locke, John. *Second Treatise of Government.* 1690.

Nozick, Robert. *Anarchy, State, and Utopia.* New York: Basic Books, 1974.

Bernard H. Baumrin

See also DETERRENCE, STRATEGIC; NEGOTIABLE INSTRUMENTS; SECONDARY RIGHTS

Self-Defense

Moral and legal philosophers have focused on the circumstances and conditions under which the use of force is rendered permissible, despite its nominal violation of a norm, in the context of self-defense. Self-defense force is virtually universally deemed permissible when (1) a culpable (2) aggressor (3) wrongfully attacks (4) an innocent victim (5) who uses necessary (6) proportional force (7) against the aggressor's present or imminent attack (8) from which there is no retreat (9) with the intention or motive of defending himself. The debate about which of the above elements are necessary and sufficient involves the delicate balancing of interests between the aggressor and the defender. Even when all these elements are satisfied, however, there is disagreement as to whether defensive force is right, proper, and good or whether it is merely permissible, tolerable, and not wrongful. Although self-defense is normally discussed as a justification (despite the technical violation of a norm, the act is not wrongful), self-defense may also be excused (wrongful violation of a norm that would be unfair to punish) when one or more of the requisite elements are not met.

Various theories have been advanced, none of which are entirely satisfactory, to account for the permissibility of force in self-defense. Disagreement regarding the theories reflects and parallels the disagreement over which of the elements must be present. Under the moral forfeiture theory, by attempting to violate another's right to life, the aggressor forfeits his own right to life. Thus the defender may use lethal self-defense without violating the aggressor's right to life because the attacker has forfeited it. The theory has been extensively criticized because it justifies unnecessary, disproportional, and retaliative force. The theory of personal autonomy stresses not the devaluation of the aggressor but the enhancement of the defender's rights. It postulates that wrongful aggression breaches a sphere of autonomy enjoyed by all, as well as breaching right itself. Since right must never yield to wrong, the defender not only has the right but the duty to exercise defensive force. Critics note that this theory too fails to incorporate the principle of proportionality: lethal force, if necessary, is permissible, for instance, to prevent the theft of an apple. The right to resist aggression theory holds that everyone has a right against the state to be protected from aggression. Since the state cannot always prevent aggression, it grants the right of self-defense. Because the right is derived against the state, the right can be limited (unlike under the former theories) by the principles of necessity and proportionality. Yet self-defense is seen as not merely a civic right but also a moral right independent of the state.

Subjective or Objective

The subjective, or agent-relative, theory of self-defense judges the permissibility of force on the circumstances as the agent (reasonably) believes them to be; the objective, or agent-neutral, theory looks to the actual circumstances. The two theories collide when (1) an agent uses defensive force against what he or she reasonably, but mistakenly, believes is a wrongful attack (mistaken self-defense) and (2) an agent believes he or she is wrongfully using force unaware of circumstances which would render that force permissible as self-defense (unknowing self-defense). The subjective view would justify (1) but not (2), whereas the objective theory would justify (2) but not (1). Supporters of the subjective view argue that as long as the mistake is reasonable in (1), the agent is free of fault and should not be judged to have acted wrongfully. Objective theorists reply that the apparent attacker in (1) is equally free of fault and was wrongfully harmed—the agent should only be excused. In (2), objective theorists argue that since the actual circumstances require the use of self-defense force, the agent's ignorance of those circumstances should not bar a justification. Subjective theorists reply that one cannot permissibly use defensive force without having good reasons. It has recently been argued that the objective approach, as applied to both (1) and (2), sustains internal contradictions.

Imminence

Critics of the traditional imminence standard argue that its purpose is merely to ensure that defensive force be absolutely necessary. Thus, if self-defense is necessary now to prevent a certain but distant (in time) attack because when the attack finally becomes imminent defensive force is ineffective, the standard should be broadened to one of necessity. A requirement of imminence, supporters contend, insures that the defender uses force against a certain attack and not a speculative one. Yet suppose that a three hundred-pound prison inmate has been raping his hundred-pound cellmate every day for a month. Further suppose that prison guards have turned a deaf ear to the smaller inmate's complaints, escape is impossible, physical resistance is ineffective, and the larger inmate tells the smaller that he will rape him when he awakes from his nap. While the larger inmate is asleep, the smaller inmate breaks his aggressor's arm to prevent the threatened rape. Many would argue that such a case illustrates the unfairness of a strict imminence requirement.

Innocents

In between the general permissibility of self-defense against villainous aggressors and the impermissibility of defensive force that harms innocent bystanders is a gray area involving self-defense against those who are dangerous but no less morally innocent than the defenders. In a range of situations falling under the rubric of innocent aggressors, philosophers have questioned why self-defense is justified against attacks by, for example, toddlers shooting guns, psychotic aggressors, or people who have been slipped violence-inducing drugs. In cases known as innocent threats, the permissibility of self-defense is even harder to explain. Suppose a very fat man is pushed off a cliff and will land on an innocent agent below, saving the fat man but killing the agent. The agent does not have time to move out of the way but conveniently has a ray gun that can vaporize the fat man. The fat man is morally innocent and is not even "aggressing," so how could the use of self-defense be permissible? The innocent shield situations are perhaps the most difficult to analyze, especially for those justifying force in the former situations but not against innocent bystanders. Suppose an evildoer is driving a tank, with a baby strapped to the front, at an innocent agent with the intent of murdering her. Her only defense is to fire an antitank gun, which can kill the evildoer inside, but it also kills the baby. The difficulty lies in whether the baby is to be classified as an innocent bystander or as an innocent threat/aggressor. For those who find the baby to be an innocent bystander, what if the baby is instead strapped to the fat man pushed off the cliff?

References

Alexander, Lawrence A. "Self-Defense, Justification, and Excuse." *Philosophy and Public Affairs* 22 (1993), 53–66.

Christopher, Russell L. "Unknowing Justification and the Logical Necessity of the Dadson Principle in Self-Defence." *Oxford Journal of Legal Studies* 15 (1995), 229–251.

Dressler, Joshua. *Understanding Criminal Law*. New York: Matthew Bender, 1987.

Fletcher, George P. "The Psychotic Aggressor—A Generation Later." *Israel Law Review* 27 (1993).

———. *Rethinking Criminal Law*. Boston: Little, Brown, 1978.

Greenawalt, Kent. "The Perplexing Borders of Justification and Excuse." *Columbia Law Review* 84 (1984), 1897–1927.

Kadish, Sanford H. "Respect for Life and Regard for Rights in the Criminal Law." *California Law Review* 64 (1976), 871–901.

Robinson, Paul H. *Criminal Law Defenses*. St. Paul MN: West, 1984.

Schopp, Robert, Barbara Sturgis, and Megan Sullivan. "Battered Woman Syndrome, Expert Testimony, and the Distinction between Justification and Excuse." *University of Illinois Law Review* [1994], 45–113.

Thomson, Judith Jarvis. "Self-Defense." *Philosophy and Public Affairs* 20 (1991), 283–310.

Uniacke, Suzanne. *Permissible Killing: The Self-Defense Justification of Homicide*. Cambridge: Cambridge University Press, 1994.

Russell L. Christopher

See also DEFENSES

Self-Determination, National

It is often said that, when a nation determines itself, then it is free. The view that national freedom means self-determination is very different from another view, according to which the more a nation is able to do, the freer it is. A nation which determines itself cannot necessarily do many different things, for example, because of economic reasons, and a nation which can do many things does not necessarily determine what it does. The view that national freedom is self-determination should also be distinguished from a view according to which a nation is free when it has no unsatisfied interests or needs. On one hand, a nation may have unsatisfied interests even if it determines itself. On the other hand, the interests of the nation may be satisfied even if it does not determine itself.

Right of Nations to Self-Determination

Historically, among the philosophy classics, the right of nations to self-determination has often been vigorously defended. Perhaps G.W.F. Hegel (1770–1831) is the most renowned representative of the idea that nations and nation-states should seek their freedom by developing their autonomy. However, the right of national self-determination was defended as early as 1670 by Baruch de Spinoza (1632–1677) in his *Tractatus Theologico-Politicus*. From a very different point of view from those of Hegel or Spinoza, the right of nations was sympathetically treated also by the utilitarian philosopher John Stuart Mill (1806–1873) in his brief essays called "A Few Words on Non-Intervention" (1859) and "Of Nationality" (1867). Niccolò Machiavelli (1469–1527) and later, for example, David Hume (1711–1776), argued for so-called *real* or power politics in international relations, and the ideas of *real* politics have unexceptionally been related to the notion of the right of national self-determination.

It is important to note that a holder of the right for national self-determination may be either a nation or a nation-state. Within the borders of a given nation-state there may be several "nations" or "peoples." On the other hand, one nation or people may inhabit territories of several nation-states. Broadly speaking, a nation-state is a "country," a territory with citizens and a state. Granting a right to self-determination to nations will yield entirely different results from granting the same right to nation-states. Whereas in the former case the results would be radical, in the latter they would be conservative. An unspecified claim for national self-determination only tells us that either nations or nation-states are entitled to self-determination.

In referring to the right of national self-determination, it is crucial, first of all, to define those acts which are thereby justified and, secondly, those acts that are thereby forbidden. If the right of national self-determination protects nations or nation-states only from military intervention, the scope of the right is quite narrow. It is obvious that a nation-state may be unable to determine its own affairs, even if it has not been a target of military intervention. This is why it is sometimes said that the right of national self-determination also protects nations or nation-states from diplomatic and economic aggression. According to this definition, the scope of the right is of course wide, and one may wonder if it is too wide. Can we, for instance, reasonably say that the right of national self-determination has been violated, if a nation is in economic difficulties due to the economic policies of another nation? James Rosenau and Jeff McMahan discuss various aspects of this question.

When one defines the scope of the right of national self-determination, it is not necessary to presume that all interventions constitute violations of the right. A nation performs an intervention when it influences the internal affairs of another nation; the right of national self-determination prohibits acts of this kind. However, a claim that not all interventions violate the right of national self-determination may still be reasonable: If we by "intervention" mean, for example, intentional cultural influence and if we think that the right of national self-determination protects a nation only from military aggression, then intervention obviously does not violate the right of national self-determination. This is one reason why it has often been thought that there can be so-called justified interventions. Intervention is justified, it is claimed, when it does not violate the right of national self-determination. Another reason for the idea that there can be justified interventions is the viewpoint that intervention may be justified even if it does violate the right of national self-determination. It may be, the argument goes, that there are *superior moral reasons* for intervening, even if intervention violates the nation's right to determine its own affairs. So it seems that the relationship between the notion of "the violation of the right of self-determination," the notion of "intervention," and the notion of "morally unjustified intervention" is this: all violations of the right of self-determination are interventions, but not all interventions are violations of the right of self-determination, and not all violations of the right of self-determination are morally unjustified.

The right of self-determination and noninterventionism imply different kinds of obligations to nations and states. Let us suppose that nation A intervenes in nation B, and nations C and D display utter indifference with regard to the event. According to both the right of self-determination and noninterventionism, the action of nation A is (probably) morally wrong. However, it may be argued that according to the right of self-determination, the actions of nations C and D are also morally wrong. Perhaps the conceptual nature of rights is such that actors are obligated to *protect* the general respect for rights. If this is so, then the right of self-determination provides better protection against foreign interventions than does noninterventionism, since noninterventionism does not obligate nations to look after those nations that, against their duties, still intervene.

Problems of the Right of Nations to Self-Determination

The right of nations to self-determination is not an unproblematic idea. Some people think that this right does not have morally acceptable grounds. In the literature, especially Charles Beitz and Henry Shue have criticized the idea of the right of nations to self-determination.

In many countries individual rights are systematically violated by the state power or by other more or less organized forces. People are tortured in prisons. People are "disappeared." There are no fair trials. Primary goods are distributed extremely unequally. Ethnic and linguistic minorities are discriminated against. People who accept the unexceptional reading of the right of national self-determination seem to accept also the view that nothing tangible should be done in order to improve the living conditions in these societies. According to critics, the talk about the right of national self-determination is often ironic and cynical, since in many societies a *nation* or a *people* does not determine anything: only tyrants and the armed forces do. This criticism raises several questions. Should we, in some cases, allow humanitarian intervention, an intervention on behalf of human rights? If so, should we allow humanitarian intervention implemented by the military forces as well? If so, whose army is the proper one to implement that intervention? In general, is it possible to force a nation to respect political rights? On the other hand, is it, as has been argued by Michael Walzer, that a nation's internal freedom can only be won by the nation itself? What is the significance of cultural differences to the notion of "political freedom" in this context? Is it true that the right of nations to self-determination condemns all humanitarian interventions? At least according to the liberal interpretation of international law, this is not necessarily the case.

The problems related to humanitarian intervention are not the only problems with the idea of the right to national self-determination. One difficult further question concerns who are eligible for national self-determination, a problem analyzed by Avishai Margalit and Joseph Raz in "National Self-Determination." Suppose that the right of self-determination belongs not to nations but to nation-states: only those entities that are at the moment called nation-states are eligible for self-determination. The result is that no nation which lives in the territory of a nation-state is justified to secede, and claims like "We have a right to our own state" can never be justified. This is certainly not a satisfactory implication, for, among other things, this makes it impossible to compensate past wrongs done by conquering states.

So perhaps we should think that the right of self-determination belongs not to nation-states but rather to nations only. This idea, however, is not intuitively compelling either. First, if all nations were nation-states, there would be serious difficulties in preserving any kind of international order and security. Second, if all nations were entitled to establish their own state, there would be no agreement to exactly which groups were nations. Many ethnic, linguistic, and territorial minorities along with other groups claim that they are nations, but many majorities do not agree with them. In usual cases, it is hard to judge who is right. Perhaps majorities do not recognize the nationhood of minorities just because of economic reasons; perhaps minorities claim that they are nations just because of economic reasons. If all nations are entitled to establish nation-states, it is extremely important to define which entities are nations: in a sense, nation-states own the territory their citizens inhabit and hence all the resources of the territory.

However, it is unclear why a nation should be entitled to establish its own nation-state. Even if we knew which social groups were nations, there would not necessarily be any point in concluding that these groups have a right to establish a state. If nation-states discriminate between their citizens and foreigners, as they in fact do, then there must be some morally relevant difference between insiders and outsiders. Even if we could say that all groups with property F are nations, we could not conclude that all groups with property F are entitled to their own state. This conclusion would follow only if the property F were a morally relevant one, and it is hard to see what could be that property in practice. Perhaps there is nothing in nationhood which would justify nations to establish their own nation-state.

References

Beitz, Charles. "Nonintervention and Communal Integrity." *Philosophy and Public Affairs* 9 (1980), 385–391.

Elfstrom, Gerard. "On Dilemmas of Intervention." *Ethics* 93 (1983), 709–725.

Emerson, Rupert. "Self-Determination." *American Journal of International Law* 65 (1971), 459–475.

French, Stanley, and Andreas Gutman. "The Principle of National Self-Determination." In *Philosophy, Morality, and International Relations,* ed. Virginia Held et al., 138–153. New York: Oxford University Press, 1974.

Margalit, Avishai, and Joseph Raz. "National Self-Determination." *Journal of Philosophy* 87 (1990), 439–461.

McMahan, Jeff. "The Ethics of International Intervention." In *Ethics and International Relations,* ed. Anthony Ellis, 24–51. London: Manchester University Press, 1986.

Mill, John Stuart. "A Few Words on Non-Intervention." In *Essays on Equality, Law, and Education,* ed. J.S. Mill, 111–124. Toronto: University of Toronto Press, 1984.

Rosenau, James. "Intervention as a Scientific Concept." *Journal of Conflict Resolution* 13 (1969), 149–171.

Shue, Henry. *Basic Rights: Subsistence, Affluence, and American Foreign Policy.* Princeton NJ: Princeton University Press, 1980.

Twining, William, ed. *Issues of Self-Determination.* Aberdeen: Aberdeen University Press, 1991.

Walzer, Michael. *Just and Unjust Wars: A Moral Argument with Historical Illustrations.* New York: Basic Books, 1977.

Juha Raikka

See also HUMAN RIGHTS; NATION AND NATIONALISM; SECESSION; STATE

Self-Determination, Personal

Self-determination has a moral and a legal meaning. As a moral concept, it can be used in the articulation of the freedom to choose; as a legal concept in the philosophy of law, it defends individuals as the bearers of rights, it treats persons as legal personalities. The two dimensions constitute a whole. They can be separated only for analytical purposes; otherwise they should not be separated.

Self-determination is characterized by self-mastery, self-reliance, and creativity—the construction of values via action; willingness to weigh reasons, learn from mistakes, and beware one-sided belief, not thinking for oneself; and imposing self-generated principles for choosing to be or not, for thinking for others, and for caring for them profoundly—instead of unduly for only one's own. Here, the genesis of this philosophical conception of self-determination is traced in three prominent philosophers: Plato, Immanuel Kant, and G.W.F. Hegel.

In Plato's *Republic,* self-determination is presented as the moral property of a person whose life is guided by quest for self-mastery. Indeed, a person attains wholeness, calm, and harmony only when he or she finally controls the meandering desires, by the self-generated power of self-mastery. The self-determining being is the one who successfully triumphs over the burdensome and rude pressures of the desires of the soul.

For Plato, the soul is constituted of reason, desire, and spirit. The well-ordered soul attains order only when desire and spirit are guided by reason. The disordered soul, by contrast, is dominated either by excessive desire or by excessive spiritedness, neither of which excesses is helpful to a being who is seeking to determine the course of his or her life, particularly in regard to the distribution of food, sex, and shelter, the cardinal stuff of everyday life.

Strictly speaking, then, a soul structure that is not founded on the infrastructure of reason leads to disaster, produces a disposition of slavishness to the moods of desire, whereas a soul that is consciously motivated by self-mastery, or the possibility of attaining it, is on its way of understanding the meaning of self-determination. Self-mastery is the property of a self that is determining its choices. Plato allows at all times a moderate satisfaction of desire. He is vociferously opposed only to the excessive surrender to the temptations invoked by desire. In fact, a moderate use of desire is part of the absolute proof of a triumphant self which has subdued desire by the power of reason.

Kant in the seventeenth century essentially revisits Plato's conception of self-determination as self-mastery. He merely radicalizes this conception by adding a strong disdain of the desires, considerably stronger than Plato's. Plato was interested in curbing the influences of desires in their interaction with reason and spirit, by allowing a moderate surrender to desire. In direct contrast to Plato, Kant is almost fanatically opposed to the mere presence of desire in any human action.

A self which is determining the movement of its actions ought to be particularly aware of the dangerous presences of desire in the form of feelings. Surely, humans are beings who feel. This is a biological fact that Kant knew as well as everybody else, but this brute fact need not incline us to surrender to the effects of feelings. Rather, it is a fact that ought to humble us to pay a profound attention to the fragility of human nature, its disposition toward succumbing to evil, precisely because of the nature of our feelings.

It is because we are beings who feel that we occasionally encounter difficulty in controlling these feelings, which are the sources of heteronomy (reason blended with feelings) by autonomy (pure reason freed from the contamination of feelings). A self-determining being is the one who listens to the moral law and, through it, will obey the right law, knowing that moral law is the law of pure practical reason. Such a person is autonomous, fully capable of legislating for himself in the realm of action. One of the most articulate defenders of Kant's perspective is the contemporary American philosopher John Rawls. His celebrated books, *A Theory of Justice* and *Political Liberalism,* seek to apply that perspective to the examination of justice in the modern philosophy of law.

By the time that self-determination occupies a place in Hegel's mind, it is inventively made a part of the philosophy of law. Self-determination as (1) self-mastery, Plato's move, and (2) as autonomy, Kant's formulation, is now looked at not merely as an isolated product of individuals' action but significantly as part of the historical web, most specifically as a facet of positive law, the law of institutions, as passed by a rational and ethical state. According to Hegel, it is not enough for individuals to be self-determining, which at any rate cannot be realized by solitary selves. Individuals must live and be trained by laws that would help them to be self-determining. Freedom for Hegel is not merely a natural fact that could be owned by individuals. It is rather an outcome of growth, evolution. Individuals can become self-determining and that self-determination itself is a product of struggle, wars, and contestations. Self-determination is not given to individuals. They have to earn it, sometimes by resorting to violence, so that they can be freed from dominators, masters, tyrants, and so forth. It is Hegel who adds an active dimension to self-determination by arguing that freedom, or the right to determine one's destiny, is not a brute fact, as Plato and Kant seem to think, but rather a possibility, a historical becoming. It is ultimately the ethical duty of the rational state to defend constitutionally the rights of self-determining individuals, as the bearers of intrinsic rights.

References

Hegel, G.W.F. *Hegel's Philosophy of Right.* Trans. T.M. Knox. London: Oxford University Press, 1981.

Kant, Immanuel. *The Foundations of Morals.* Indianapolis: Bobbs-Merrill, 1975.

Kiros, Teodros. "Self-Determination." *Journal of Social Philosophy* 22 (1991), 92–101.

Plato. *The Republic.* New York: Basic Books, 1968.

Rawls, John. *Political Liberalism.* New York: Columbia University Press, 1991.

———. *A Theory of Justice.* Cambridge: Cambridge University Press, 1971.

Taylor, Charles. *Sources of the Self.* Cambridge: Harvard University Press, 1989.

Teodros Kiros

See also AUTONOMY; LIBERTY; SELF-DETERMINATION, NATIONAL

Self-Reference

We know from more than two millennia of experience that self-referential statements, such as the liar's ("This very statement is false"), can be debated by philosophers and logicians endlessly without producing consensus on their solutions. We should not be surprised, then, if self-referential laws produce paradoxes that puzzle lawyers. What is surprising, though, is that some of these paradoxes bother only the logicians and philosophers who study law from outside—and do not bother lawyers at all. This fact should interest philosophers of law even more than the paradoxes themselves.

Alf Ross argued that a constitutional amending clause could not be used to amend itself; the act could be reduced to a formal self-contradiction. He did not know, or did not acknowledge in his essay, that self-amendment is commonplace in legal history. If it is contradictory, that fact had never been noticed before and had never bothered either legal officials or citizens. What if Ross is right that self-amendment is contradictory? We may want to conclude that the legal practice of self-amendment is invalid, even if it has been accepted by citizens and courts wherever it has occurred, just as inconsistent theories are false even if widely accepted. Conversely, we may want to conclude that in some circumstances law can harbor contradiction, just as essays and novels may harbor contradiction. Ignoring some qualifications, these are the positions of Alf Ross and Peter Suber. There may be other explanations better than these, but these are enough to show that self-reference in law is not a minor curiosity; in this case it raises profound questions about the boundaries of legal change and the nature of legal rationality.

While self-amendment has occurred in almost every state that has an amending clause, the act is rarely as important for practice as it is for theory. It can be seen as a variation on the theme of the paradox of omnipotence: can a deity create a stone so heavy she cannot lift it? If she can, there is a stone she cannot lift; and if she cannot, then there is a stone she cannot create. Either way, she seems to lack classical omnipotence. An amending clause seems to be legally omnipotent, because it can modify any law in its system, perhaps including itself. However, we can ask of it what we asked of the deity: can it limit itself irrevocably? If it can, then there is a limit it cannot overcome; and if it cannot, then there is a limit it cannot enact. However, if the amending power is not legally omnipotent, then no lawmaking power is legally omnipotent. Are we to conclude, then, that in a democracy the people cannot make any law at any time? Here is where the theoretical question can become quite practical.

In the contract tradition, can the founding generation give consent to a constitution which binds its successors forever—or must we seek consent from each generation? If the omnipotence of one generation allows it to bind its successors irrevocably, then its consent can establish a constitution over the dissent of its descendants. If the equal omnipotence of the succeeding generations means that they can overrule any decision made by their ancestors, then the consent of each generation will be needed. If legitimate government derives from the consent of the governed, then we must wade into the paradox of legal omnipotence in order to decide whose consent matters or to decide legitimacy. Suber argues that a self-applicable amending clause can repeal any previous law, which makes all limits on the people's power revocable. It follows that the only irrevocable limit on the people's power is that they cannot enact other irrevocable limits on their power. This is consonant with the rule in England and the United States that one legislature cannot bind its successors irrevocably.

It also follows that John Austin's theory of sovereignty is false in holding that every sovereign is both unlimited and illimitable. If the supreme legal power (usually the amending power) is unlimited, then it can limit itself irrevocably; and if it is illimitable, then it can-

[illegible] then [illegible] could only be a[illegible] by another court, and a determined advocate could push back the regress indefinitely.

Some legal circles are problems, not solutions. If A and B make a contract in Illinois, and B violates it in Indiana, A will consult the contract to see whether Illinois or Indiana law applies to the breach. Suppose the contract specifies Illinois law. Illinois law may in turn require the parties to use the law of the state where the breach occurred. However, Indiana law may require them to use the law of the state where the contract was made. Such a circle is called *renvoi*. Similarly, the accidental side effect of many rules made over many years may be that an estate must be divided among claimants when A has priority over B, B over C, and C over A. If laws were simply rules, like software rules, then these situations would precipitate the legal equivalent of infinite loops. Because *renvoi* and circular lien problems are solved in finite time, in principled ways, lawfully, by human decisions which face the need to escape absurd literalism, they provide important clues to the sense in which laws are not simply rules and law itself is more a human enterprise than a formal system.

There are other cases in which legal powers or institutions act on themselves in a way which raises the specter of paradox. Can Article VII of the U.S Constitution establish the conditions of its own establishment? Can the English House of Lords abolish itself? Can a judicial decision (*London Street Tramways,*

force of
to be fol-
be overturned
an a court consti-
a postrevolutionary
ity of the revolution, the
Can a court declare a consti-
ment unconstitutional (*U.S. v.*
0)? Can a will forbid anyone to
its validity, on pain of being excluded
he estate (*in terrorem* clauses)? Can a
itten contract declare that the parties have
no oral amendments or qualifications to the written terms (integration clauses)? Can a treaty bind a nation to ratify it (Article III of the Kellogg-Briand Pact of 1928)? Can a "sunset clause" in a statute trigger the invalidation of the statute at a certain time, including the sunset clause? Can the effective date provision of a statute authoritatively declare, before the effective date, that the statute is not yet authoritative? Can a doctrine of desuetude (invalidation through nonuse or obsolescence) become invalid over time through desuetude?

References

Fletcher, George. "Paradoxes of Legal Thought." *Columbia Law Review* 85 (1985), 1263–1292.

Gilmore, Grant. "Circular Priority Systems." *Yale Law Journal* 71 (1961), 53–74.

Goldstein, Laurence. "Four Alleged Paradoxes in Legal Reasoning." *Cambridge Law Journal* 38 (1979), 373–391.

Hart, H.L.A. "Self-Referring Laws." In *Essays in Jurisprudence and Philosophy,* ed. H.L.A. Hart, 145–158. Oxford: Oxford University Press, 1983.

Hicks, J.C. "The Liar Paradox in Legal Reasoning." *Cambridge Law Journal* 29 (1971), 275–291.

Rinaldi, Fiori. "Dilemmas and Circles in the Law." *Archiv für Rechts- und Sozialphilosophie* 51 (1965), 319–335.

Ross, Alf. "On Self-Reference and a Puzzle in Constitutional Law." *Mind* 78 (1969), 1–24.

Suber, Peter. *The Paradox of Self-Amendment: A Study of Logic, Law, Omnipotence, and Change*. New York: Peter Lang, 1990. (Contains a bibliography on self-reference in law.)

Tammelo, Ilmar. "The Antinomy of Parliamentary Sovereignty." *Archiv für Rechts- und Sozialphilosophie* 44 (1958), 495–513.

Teubner, Gunther. *Reflexive Law: Autonomy and Regulation*. Berlin: Walter de Gruyter, 1986.

Peter Suber

See also AMENDMENT; CODIFICATION; LEGISLATION AND CODIFICATION

Semiotic Philosophy of Law

Semiotics was introduced as a distinctive method of analysis of and inquiry into law in the 1970s, although the term appears in passing as early as the 1960s. Semiotics of law is today a covering term for two main approaches which seem to have originated independently from one another. One main approach derives from the theory of signs, or "semiotic," of Charles Sanders Peirce; the other grows out of continental approaches to semiology, which derives from structuralist/functionalist linguistic paradigms. The dialogue between investigators of these two major discourses on law and semiotics has evolved over more than two decades. This exchange has produced and sustained symposia and publications of the highest intellectual quality. Participants in these legal semiotics communities cross over today from peircean to greimasian paradigms on selected issues and on problems of mutual overlap concerning, in particular, comparative legal cultures, international law, and contrastive studies on civil law and common law principles. Especially in the comparative study of legal semiotics as a general idea and its relationship to several other approaches to the law, such as pragmatism, critical legal theory, instrumentalist, postmodernist, including its opposition to legal positivism as a whole, semiotics of law makes important contributions.

Notable in both major approaches to semiotics of law is an ability to effect interdisciplinary perspectives on key issues, and to also bring about unifying points of view from cross-national, cross-cultural concerns. In keeping with the peircean notion that semiotics is a process of interpreting and evolving meaning in all systems of signs and sign-relationships, both approaches to law and semiotics represent open doors and intellectual receptivity to experimentation in the linking together of discrete discourses into more comprehensive relations; in fact, there are as many connections as are represented by the academic divisions of modern universities. Examples of work in these emergent cross-disciplinary relations are those of Robin Malloy in law and economics, Denis Brion in chaos theory, William Pencak in history, Pertti Ahonen in political science, Willem Witteveen in literature, and David Caudill in psychoanalysis.

The first explicit colloquium on law and semiotics took place in the context of the summer institute on semiotics studies that was held at the University of Toronto in 1977. This workshop followed closely upon the first publications on the topic of law and semiotics. The first international colloquium on law and semiotics was held at Indiana University in Bloomington, as part of the annual meeting of the Semiotics Society of America in 1983; proceedings of this meeting were published by Indiana University Press in 1986.

In 1984 the Center for Semiotic Research in Law, Government, and Economics was established at Penn State under the direction of Roberta Kevelson. During the following year this center, in collaboration with four similar research centers at Venezuela, France, England, and Italy, under the respective directions of Roque Carrion-Wam, Eric Landowski, Bernard Jackson, and Domenico Carzo, established the International Association for Law and Semiotics, with its official organ, the *International Journal for the Semiotics of Law/Revue Internationale de Semiotique Juridique*.

Studies and development of the concept of semiotics of law are largely tied to the activities of both the International Association for Semiotics and Law and the Center for Semiotic Research in Law, Government, and Economics. The former conducts annual symposia, on topics that range from rights of human beings to images of justice, and has included such topics as proof in law, didactic approaches for instruction in legal semiotics, and citizenship and the global state. The latter organizes conferences on such topics as action and agency, comparative legal cultures, consensus, and semiotics and the human sciences. Three series of volumes have been published under the auspices of the center, which serve as research tools in the development of the idea of semiotics of law. In addition to these two primary colloquia on semiotics and law, several smaller special sessions are included on the regular programs of international congresses, for example, the International Association for Semiotics and Structuralism and the International Society for Philosophy of Law and Social Philosophy.

Resistance to binding definition of semiotics of law is shared by those who follow the American pragmatic method of Peirce as well as by those who espouse the saussurean/greimasean linguistic model, despite the fact that different sets of presuppositions and principal ideas are operative in each case. Yet each approach also regards a taxonomy of semiotics of law as a common language, which makes possible communication among scholars whose matrix disciplines, national idioms, and ideological preferences are vastly different.

In summation, there is general agreement from the perspective of semiotics of law that (1) the law represents a prototype of social institutions that relates normative values to actual, lived human affairs, since the law is a mediating system of signs; (2) legal systems are open systems which grow and evolve dynamically by means of interpretations, rhetorical strategies, and dialogic construction of legal discourse; and (3) law in theory and practice is not a mirror of aprioristic, eternal values, but is an ongoing experiment of human beings creating provisional balance between expanding freedoms and assent to self-controls.

References

Ahonen, Pertti, ed. *Tracing the Semiotic Boundaries of Politics*. Bloomington: Indiana University Press, 1993.

Brion, Denis. "Modern Witchcraft: The Semiotic Power of Community Cosmology." In *Action and Agency*, ed. Roberta Kevelson, 95–116. New York: Peter Lang, 1991.

Caudill, David. "Jacques Lacan and Our State of Affairs." In *Law and the Human Sciences*, ed. Roberta Kevelson, 95–114. New York: Peter Lang, 1992.

Goodrich, Peter. *Reading the Law*. Oxford: Basil Blackwell, 1986.

Jackson, Bernard S. *Semiotics and Legal Theory*. London: Routledge and Kegan Paul, 1986.

Kevelson, Roberta. *Inlaws/Outlaws*. Lisse and Bloomington: Peter de Ridder and R.C.L.S.S., 1977.

———. *The Law as a System of Signs*. New York: Plenum, 1988.

———, ed. *Codes and Customs*. New York: Peter Lang, 1993.

———, ed. *Spaces and Significations*. Amsterdam: Rodopi Editions, 1995.

Landowski, Eric, with A.J. Greimas. *Semiotique et sciences sociales* (Semiotics and the Social Sciences). Paris: Editions de Seuil, 1976.
Malloy, Robin Paul. "Planning for Serfdom—An Introduction to a New Theory of Law and Economics." *Indiana Law Review,* 25 (1992), 621–632.
Pencak, William. *Signing In.* New York: Peter Lang, 1993.
Sabota, Katerina. *Sachlichkeit, Rhetorische, Kunst der Juristen* (Objectivity, Rhetoric, and Legal Practice). Frankfurt: Peter Lang, 1990.
Witteveen, Willem. "The Rhetorical Labours of Hercules." *IASL* 3, 9 (1990).

Roberta Kevelson

See also HERMENEUTICAL PHILOSOPHY OF LAW; SPEECH ACTS; VOICE

Sentencing

A sentence is an imposition, requirement, or prohibition directed against someone who has been identified as having committed an offense by a sentencing authority in response to the alleged offense. Sentences have traditionally been linked in the public mind with hard treatment or punishment, though both linkages have been challenged by sentencing and punishment theorists. In modern legal systems, sentencing is a task normally undertaken by a court presided over by a judge in accordance with law set down by a legislative authority. The discussion that follows will look at the purposes that sentencing has been thought, historically, to serve, the evolution of sentencing theory and practice particularly in this century, and finally the types of sentences and their rationale that are typically imposed in modern legal systems.

One of the oldest and most persistent purposes of sentencing is to secure justice by ensuring that those found guilty of breaking criminal laws receive their just deserts. This approach to sentencing is avoidably backward looking and punishment oriented. It requires sentences that impose penalties that fit the crime committed. That is to say, the severity of the penalty imposed must both reflect and be in proportion to the moral gravity of the offense. It also requires that like cases be treated alike. This view of justice is traditionally captured by the image of the goddess of justice blindfolded as a symbol of objectivity and impartiality, holding scales in one hand to symbolize the careful balancing of penalty with offense committed, and a sword in the other, symbolizing the coercive and punitive character of the sanctions imposed. This approach to punishment connects directly to retributive theories of punishment.

A second approach with equally ancient roots rejects the view that the purpose of sentencing is to correct past wrongs. It proposes as an alternative that a sentence should be imposed with a view to reducing the likelihood that similar events will recur in the future. In this view, a sentence should aim at deterrence, reform, education, or rehabilitation. Where deterrence is the goal, the purpose of a sentence can be either to reduce the likelihood that the person being sentenced will repeat the offense in question or discourage others who might otherwise engage in similar behavior from doing so.

Historically, sentencing practice has varied enormously from society to society and from period to period. Arguably, however, it has been dominated either by the pursuit of retribution or deterrence or both. This is perhaps at least partly explained by the fact that both purposes are relatively easily communicated to the public and in practice closely related. Deterrence-oriented sentencing typically varies with the perceived gravity of the offense, and retribution-oriented sentencing is typically punitive in nature and hence likely to serve also as a general as well as a specific deterrent.

Although modern sentencing practices have been deeply influenced by these historical patterns, they have also departed from them in significant ways. Perhaps the earliest sign of change was the emergence of the penitentiary in the eighteenth and nineteenth centuries. Prior to that time, prisons were used to confine people until they could be punished or until they corrected the wrong they had committed (failure to repay a debt, for example). Penitentiaries, on the other hand, were introduced as instruments of reform, a place where an offender could contemplate the wrongness of his ways (in the first instance the inhabitants of penitentiaries were virtually exclusively men) and repent.

While the introduction of penitentiaries marked a significant shift in thinking about the purpose of punishment, it was still firmly within the scope of a classical approach to sentencing whose focus was at root a response to moral culpability. By the end of the nineteenth century, this idea was under seige. Its demise as the dominant sentencing paradigm was marked by the emergence of criminology, a discipline committed to building scientifically grounded responses to what would increasingly be described using the morally neutral nomenclature of deviance and mental illness. Under the influence of the emerging behavioral sciences, sentencing theory shifted to devising sentencing prescriptions designed to return deviants to socially acceptable patterns of behavior. By the mid-twentieth century, this trend was firmly entrenched in virtually all western democracies.

The resulting shift in sentencing manifested itself in three ways. First, sentencing and correctional practices focused increasingly on offenders as individuals and not on their crimes. With this came a shift in the language of sentencing toward treatment, rehabilitation, and risk assessment. Second, the moral character of criminal behavior was deemphasized as the goal of sentencing shifted from assessing the moral gravity of an offense to preventing recidivism. Finally, the range of discretion granted to sentencing authorities in determining appropriate sentences was progressively broadened. One distinctive manifestation of this trend was the emergence of the indeterminate sentence, which required that an offender be held until cured, rehabilitated, or reformed.

The last two decades, however, have once again seen a striking reversal of outlook as the concept of coercive rehabilitation has come under increasingly hostile moral and empirical scrutiny. Imposed programs of treatment and rehabilitation have been widely criticized as manipulative, incompatible with moral principles requiring that human beings be treated as ends and never as means only, and largely ineffective in preventing recidivism. The result has been a dramatic return in many parts of the western world to sentencing based on just deserts and deterrence.

Changes in sentencing theory and practice have been accompanied in this century with significant changes in the kind and range of sentences available to modern sentencing authorities in sentencing offenders. These changes have been marked by two trends: first, a moderation in the brutality of punishment, the second an increasing range of options. That the institution of punishment has over human history provided the occasion and the excuse for the expression of the most brutal cruelty is hardly a matter of controversy. The Roman practice of crucifixion, the Inquisition with its use of grotesque forms of torture, and drawing and quartering and similar punishments imposed by modern European sentencing authorities prior to the nineteenth century are abundant witness to that fact. Indeed, the elimination of brutality and cruelty in sentencing has been one of the persistent and central demands of legal reformers throughout human history. It would be a mistake to think that the humanization of punishment has been entirely successful. The continuing need for organizations like Amnesty International bears ample witness to this truth. At the same time, it would be churlish to ignore the substantial progress that has occurred.

Although the institution of penitentiaries, including the notions of penance that lay behind them, became itself an instrument of incredible suffering, its appearance marked a major step toward a rethinking of punishment. More important were the major penal reforms that followed in the late nineteenth century and then progressively through to today. An important symbol of change is the recognition in charters and bills of rights and freedoms that cruel and unusual punishment is an infringement of an important and universal human right. A second major accomplishment has been the gradual elimination of capital punishment, which today continues to be practiced among western liberal democracies only in the United States. A third major achievement has been the gradual recognition that people are sent to prison as punishment, not for punishment. As a consequence, subhuman living conditions are much less common and the subject of vociferous public and international criticism when uncovered. Equally welcome is access on the part of inmates of prisons to medical care, adequate diets, educational and occupational training, and recreational opportunities, as well as the separation of juvenile and adult offenders, which characterizes most modern penal systems. The introduction of community sanctions (for example, community service orders), probation, parole, and victim/offender mediation has also widened the range of sentencing options in important and innovative ways.

Whether these reforms in sentencing practice will continue into the twenty-first century remains to be seen. The dramatic shift back to retributive- and deterrence-oriented sentencing—accompanied as it has been with a loss of confidence in such practices as parole, rehabilitation, mediation, and judicial discretion—is being accompanied in the last two decades of the twentieth century by increased prison populations in many countries, longer sentences (particularly in the United States), reduced emphasis on training, education, and similar programs, and increasing imposition of sentencing laws that are mechanical or algorithmic in their application.

In conclusion, sentencing and its reform continues today, as it has throughout human history, to pose urgent challenges. Some will see grounds for optimism that progressive responses to those challenges are still possible in the fact that the theory and practice of sentencing and punishment continue to be as vigorously debated by scholars, journalists, and politicians alike today as at any time in recent history.

References

Beccaria, Cesare. *On Crimes and Punishments.* Indianapolis: Bobbs-Merrill Educational Publishing, 1963.

Christi, Nils. *Limits to Pain.* Oxford: Martin Robertson, 1981.

Cragg, Wesley. *The Practice of Punishment: Toward a Theory of Restorative Justice.* London: Routledge, 1992.

Fogel, David, and Joe Hudson. *Justice as Fairness: Perspectives on the Justice Model.* New York: Anderson, 1981.

Foucault, Michael. *Discipline and Punish: The Birth of the Prison.* New York: Vintage Books, 1979.

Garland, David. *Punishment and Welfare: A History of Penal Strategies.* Aldershot: Gower, 1985.

Roberts, J. *Empirical Research on Sentencing.* Ottawa: Department of Justice (Canada).

von Hirsch, A. *Doing Justice: The Choice of Punishments.* New York: Hill and Wang, 1976.

Walker, N., and M. Hough. *Public Attitudes to Sentencing: Surveys from Five Countries.* Aldershot: Gower, 1988.

Wootton, B. *Crime and the Criminal Law.* London: Sage, 1963.

Wright, M., and B. Gallaway, eds. *Mediation and Criminal Justice: Victims, Offenders and Community.* London: Sage, 1989.

Zimring, Franklin E., and Gordon J. Hawkins. *Deterrence: The Legal Threat in Crime Control.* Chicago: University of Chicago Press, 1973.

A. Wesley Cragg

See also CRIMINOLOGY; DETERRENT RATIONALE; EXPRESSIVE RATIONALE; MERCY AND FORGIVENESS; MIXED RATIONALES; PUNISHMENT; RETRIBUTIVE RATIONALE

Separation of Powers

See POWERS OF GOVERNMENT

Sex, Commercial

See PROSTITUTION

Sexual Abuse

Three main kinds of sexual abuse are sexual harassment, rape, and spousal battering. Statistics show that victims of these behaviors are predominantly women, the perpetrators, men. The main philosophical issues are what constitutes these behaviors and how this is decided. Traditional views reflected in both the construction and implementation of the law and in society at large display a bias against the victim and support and perpetuate myths about men and women. Recent feminist views recognize both the sexist assumptions upon which traditional answers are based and group harm done to all women from any instance of these behaviors, and aim to take the burden off the victim.

Rape

According to *Black's Law Dictionary,* English common law defines rape as the "illicit carnal knowledge of a female by force and against her will." This definition of the law interprets rape to be done by a man to a woman, but not a husband to a wife; it must involve penetration of the vagina by a penis; it must be forcible.

The issue of consent (whether intercourse is against a person's will) is the most controversial: traditional law requires that the rape be nonconsensual and that the rapist know his act does not have the consent of his victim. Rape of wives is still not recognized in many states, because a woman's consent to marriage is taken to be an implicit consent to have sex with her husband at his will; she is property he owns, to which he has a right. For other women, the courts have looked for physical evidence of resistance by the victim, so that if a woman were unable to resist physically because the rapist was too strong, or because she had a submissive personality (which is encouraged and rewarded in a patriarchal society), or because she was too drunk to protest, the act would not be considered rape because the woman is believed to have consented. It has been very easy for a rapist to escape conviction by arguing that he believed that a woman consented: by dressing provocatively, by voluntarily choosing to go to a place where rape is a possibility (such as a bar), by kissing a man, by having intercourse with the rapist or with other men, and so on. Moreover, women are seen as primarily emotional beings so that their protests and cries of rape are often interpreted to be blown out of proportion. Often, men believe that women mean "yes" even when they say "no"; they think that women enjoy being raped, thereby allowing the rapist to claim innocence of intention. The law has favored the rapist especially in the case of date rape for these reasons, together with the assumption that the male sex drive is very strong and uncontrollable such that if a woman "comes on" to him the man cannot be expected to stop short of intercourse.

Feminists challenge sexist assumptions underlying the assessment of whether rape has occurred. Why should not a woman act provocatively, and why does that give a man a right to rape her? Why does consenting to be kissed mean that the woman implicitly consents to having intercourse, since this is not a logical step in the formation of other agreements? Feminists have argued that the burden of proof as to whether sex was consensual should be on the rapist to show that he got consent, not on the victim to show that she did not consent. Questions of consent—whether the man asked the woman throughout the sex act if she wanted to go further and if what they were doing was acceptable to her—are more relevant in determining whether she consented than whether he believed she had consented (because of what she wore or where she socializes or whether she was unable to fight off her attacker).

The main drawback of the feminist position is the case of the woman who is fearful of speaking her view because she has been indoctrinated by a patriarchal society to believe that women are supposed to be demure and submissive to men's wills. Her consent is probably false. Perhaps an argument about what she would have consented to were she not a victim of patriarchy would solve the problem.

Sexual Harassment

According to Anita Superson, sexual harassment has been defined by EEOC *Guidelines on Discrimination Because of Sex* as unwelcome or unwanted sexual advances by one person who has power over another, either with the threat of reprisal (quid pro quo harassment) or by "unreasonably interfering with an individual's work performance or [creating] an intimidating, hostile, or offensive environment" (hostile environment harassment). Sexual harassment was established to be a form of sex discrimination prohibited under Title VII, in the landmark case *Meritor Savings Bank, FSB v. Vinson,* 477 U.S. 57 (1986).

Traditionally, the law construes sexual harassment subjectively, as determined by what the victim feels and what the perpetrator intends. Victims must have serious cases of repeated incidents of harassment showing extreme emotional distress or tangible economic detriment. The law does not protect victims who are harassed by a number of different people, who have institutional power over their harassers, who do not complain out of fear, and who do not suffer grievous harm.

The traditional view puts the burden on the victim to complain and to establish that the behavior is unwelcome or annoying, or that it creates an intimidating and hostile environment. Many victims hesitate to complain for fear of repercussions. Victims often doubt themselves, partly because of the way women are raised and treated under patriarchy, partly because harassers often send ambivalent messages, and partly because of the way women are treated when they do complain. Many do not seek punishment of the harasser, but merely want the behavior to stop. Many have no other career and educational choices and must continue to interact with their harasser. Many women believe sexist myths and stereotypes and as a result do not recognize harassment for what it is.

Even when women do complain, as in the case of rape, it is all too easy for the perpetrator to claim innocence and win his case by showing that the victim welcomed or was not annoyed by the behavior. In *Lipsett v. Rive-Mora,* 669 F. Supp. 1188 (1987), the plaintiff was discharged from a medical residency program because she did not react favorably to her professor's requests to go out for drinks, his compliments about her body, and questions about her personal life, on the grounds that she initially smiled when she was shown lewd drawings of herself and was called sexual nicknames, evidence that she did not find the comments unwelcome. In *Swentek v. US Air,* 830 F.2d 552 (4th Cir. 1987), a harasser was excused after he made obscene gestures to a flight attendant on the grounds that she previously used vulgar language and discussed her sexual encounters: it was judged that she would not be offended by and would welcome the comments. Harassing professors try to justify their behavior on the grounds that they are bombarded daily with the temptation of provocatively dressed young women, as if the students' apparel indicated that they welcomed the treatment. As with the case of rape, the perpetrator's behavior is often excused because it is natural, uncontrollable, and flattering, and the victim is judged as being too sensitive and too easily annoyed or offended. Judges have ruled that women working in a "man's world" must come to develop a thick skin and put up with this "normal" behavior, instead of requiring or even expecting men to change.

Feminists have offered an objective definition of harassment designed to cover even the most seemingly minor cases of harassment. They take sexual harassment to be any instance of behavior by a member of the dominant class that expresses and perpetuates the attitudes that a member of the subjugated class is inferior because of her sex. This definition has the advantage that it recognizes the harm done to all women by a single instance of harassment: the behavior reflects and reinforces sexist attitudes that women are inferior to men and ought to occupy certain sex roles (for example, sex objects, motherers, nurturers). It also has the advantages that it prevents the harasser from claiming innocence because he did not believe the woman was bothered by his behavior, and it allows for a case of harassment to be made even when women are reticent to complain. The definition must, however, be made consistent with freedom of speech.

Woman-Battering

Traditionally, woman-battering has been excused or even accepted by society, partly because wives have been seen as property of their husbands, partly because family issues were and still are considered private matters with which the state ought not to interfere.

The courts and the police have treated victims of woman-battering in the same way they have treated victims of rape and sexual harassment. Women are said to deserve their abuse because they did something to provoke the man, by saying or not saying certain things or by indicating in any way that they were not properly upholding their expected role as wives. Police historically have not gotten involved in domestic disputes and have not arrested abusers unless the victim's injuries were severe enough to require hospitalization. Police officers and judges do not try to remove the perpetrator from the victim's home, or at least provide the victim with some protection, but aim instead to preserve the family unit. Yet judges are quick to use the fact that women stay with their abusers as evidence that the situation was really not that bad. The truth is that many women are economically dependent on their abusers, or fear they will have their children taken away from them, or, as statistics bear out, fear death at the hands of their abuser.

The debate is not as much over whether battering has occurred as it is over how much women can be expected to endure. Feminists want to eradicate the view that women deserve abuse because they are to blame for inciting their abusers and for being unable to control them. Feminists want to eliminate sexism in society so that women truly have options other than remaining with abusers and men are not taught that abusing women is a sign of masculinity. Better police protection and legal remedies are required.

References

Griffin, Susan. "Rape: The All-American Crime." In *Women and Values: Readings in Recent Feminist Philosophy,* ed. Marilyn Pearsall, 176–188. Belmont CA: Wadsworth, 1986.

MacKinnon, Catharine A. *Sexual Harassment of Working Women: A Case of Sex Discrimination.* New Haven: Yale University Press, 1979.

Paul, Ellen Frankel. "Sexual Harassment as Sex Discrimination: A Defective Paradigm." *Yale Law and Policy Review* 8 (1990), 333–365.

Pineau, Lois. "Date Rape: A Feminist Analysis." *Law and Philosophy* 8 (1989), 217–243.

Superson, Anita M. "A Feminist Definition of Sexual Harassment." *Journal of Social Philosophy* 24 (1993), 46–64.

Tong, Rosemarie. *Women, Sex, and the Law.* Savage MD: Rowman and Littlefield, 1984.

Wright Dziech, Billie, and Linda Weiner. *The Lecherous Professor: Sexual Harassment on Campus.* Boston: Beacon Press, 1984.

Anita M. Superson

See also COERCION (DURESS); FEMINIST PHILOSOPHY OF LAW; RADICAL CLASS, GENDER, AND RACE THEORIES: POSITIONALITY; STRICT LIABILITY, CRIMINAL

Sixteenth- to Eighteenth-Century Philosophy of Law

European jurisprudence at the dawn of the period spanning the sixteenth to eighteenth centuries operated within three main traditions: those of civil law, canon law, and customary law. Deriving from the texts of classical Roman law (*Corpus iuris Iustiniani,* compiled in the sixth century), civil and canon law were "modern" academic disciplines with a pedigree going back to the foundation of universities in the twelfth century, when jurists became engaged in the political controversies between Italian provinces and the Holy Roman Empire over superior jurisdictional authority, a legacy that was given further impetus at the end of the fifteenth century when Roman law was officially "received" at imperial courts throughout Germany, displacing local and municipal practices of customary law. With canon law pertaining mainly to ecclesiastical courts and church issues, customary law can be described as a vernacular tradition based on custom, prescription, and the authority of the past. Its "unwritten" character distinguished it from the tradition of Roman law; in France, Spain, and particularly England, commentators praised and idealized their "common law" as (first) a *lex non scripta* and (above all) in harmony with the character of the nation. One of the main themes in the three centuries under consideration here was the emergence of "national jurisprudence" and the accompanying transformation of customary into national law.

In fact, three main issues dominated European legal thinking in this period. The first was an inherited concern to articulate (or rationalize) the principles of law in a given state, which involved a debate over "method" in both teaching and interpreting law, and which grew into the concern to codify national bodies of law. The second was the assertion of a particular tradition of jurisprudence as the source of all authority in a nation, which developed into the question of the fundamental nature of the concept of the sovereign nation-state and also expanded into comprehending theories of imperial (or federal) relationships. The third emerged from theories of territorial sovereignty and gave birth to the modern notion of international law. These issues intersect in relation to both the contemporary political controversies which spawned them and the role of civil law in providing a vocabulary and a set of concepts and procedures in which they were worked out. Legal practice itself was transformed by the growing secularism of the period, as well as by a distinctively new scientific approach to questions of justice, authority, and liberty, the sanctity of property, and the nature and punishment of crime. The profession of law expanded dramatically during these three centuries, in tandem with an increasingly litigious spirit at large but due perhaps above all to the growing importance of "written" law in settling disputes and informing national consciousness (as well as due to the quasi-universal adoption, or adaptation, of "civil" procedures in different national contexts).

The process which ultimately developed, in the eighteenth century, into the concern to codify national bodies of law can be traced to the early Italian Renaissance when, postulating that Roman law was universal, "civilians" conferred on it something of an ontological status and set about recovering the fundamental principles inhering in the original Justinian texts. From their glosses and commentaries the discipline of "civil science" was born: the scholastic approach came to be called the "Italian method" (*mos italicus*) and its followers Bartolists (after its most renowned exponent, Bartolus, who undertook a quest to recover the "reason" or spirit of the law). Sixteenth-century jurists from Claude de Seyssel (d. 1520) to Alberico Gentili (d. 1608) adhered to this tradition, although its method was increasingly criticized by humanists, beginning with Lorenzo Valla and his scrutiny of the Donation of Constantine. Inaugurating a tradition of "legal humanism" (not to suggest there also came into being a trend for "illegal" humanism), Andreas Alciato, Ulrich Zasius, and Gillaume Budé sought to extract the original reasoning of the Justinian texts by recourse to textual exegesis and juridical lexicography. At the University of Brouges the so-called French school of jurisprudence (*mos gallicus*) developed strong anthropological and historical perspectives, thus introducing the field of comparative law. In his "bipartite commentaries" on the Justinian texts Eguinaire Baron noted French equivalents for Roman legal and political terms in 1550, but Etienne Pasquier's *Interpretation de Institutes de Justinian* (unpublished until the nineteenth century) ended up as a critical review, and comparisons could become even more invidious, as in François Hotman's *Antitribonian* (1567). In England, John Selden's *History of Tithes* (1618) exemplified the power of the historical and comparative method in contesting English clerical claims to levy tithes (which they based on "divine" sanction), and this method developed substantially during the eighteenth century with Giambattista Vico (*Scienza nuova* (New Science) [1725]) and Voltaire (*Dictionnaire philosophique* (Philosophical Dictionary) [1764]); it culminated in two very distinct applications: Montesquieu's *De l'esprit des lois* (1748) and Edmund Burke's *Reflections on the Revolution in France* (1790).

Burke was far from discussing principles of law as conceived earlier (or even contemporaneously on the continent); in between, the movement for juridical nationalism had triumphed, aided and abetted by the contest between civilians and vernacular jurists. Through the medieval compilation, *Consuetudines feodorum* (Feudal Customs), civil law itself had recognized native traditions, and in an attempt to "civilize" the vast number—and sometimes contradictory nature—national (or feudal) customs, jurists in France, Spain, Germany, and England had attempted to reconcile Roman and native laws. So, for example, Louis le Caron produced the *Pandectes, ou Digestes du droit françois* (1587) and William Fulbeke (in England) his *Parallel or Conference of the Civil Law, the Canon Law, and the Common Law of this Realm* (1618). John Cowell compiled his *Institutes of the Lawes of England,* published in 1651 as a counter to Sir Edward Coke's *Institutes of the Common Lawes of England,* published in 1628–1644, which Coke had conceived to serve as a great legal textbook to complement his eleven-part compilation of cases, the *Reports* (1600–1615). Cowell and Coke are usually noted as instances of the contest between rival systems of jurisprudence and their political counterparts—absolutism versus constitutionalism. However, their legal writings also pertained to the growing concern to organize unwieldy bodies of national law. In England, despite appeals for rationalization [from radicals during and after the Civil War (1642–1660)] and the intermittent interest in creating commissions to reform the law (the most famous being perhaps the Hale Commission of the early 1650s), the systemization of law was eschewed.

On the continent, however, the quest for system prevailed, involving, from René Descartes to Gottfried Leibniz to Immanuel Kant, philosophers as well as jurists. While Montesquieu would seek to uncover the "spirit" of the laws, a number of his antecedents and contemporaries sought rather to extract their reason (*ratio legum*), thus to define law, both in general and in its various component parts, and also ascertain principles of equity and justice, custom and sovereignty, and (more and more, as the eighteenth century wore on) "public utility." The British Isles produced a number of participants in this discussion, including Francis Bacon, who, civilian-like, sought to extract the "maxims" of law, and involving, much later, Jeremy Bentham, who invented the word "codification." But continentals showed a much greater affinity with the idea of "written reason," the *ratio scripta* fundamentally associated with original Roman law. This rationalism was at one with the principles of the eighteenth-century Enlightenment, pervading the movement for unified legal codes within heterogeneous states. Prussia finally produced a systematized code in Frederick the Great's *Allgemeines Landrecht* (1794), but the crystallization of Jean-Baptiste Colbert's (seventeenth-century) goal of a standard legal system for France had to await the Napoleonic phase of the revolution, while in Austria the *Principles of Compilations* (1753) yielded only a draft *Codex Theresianus* by century's end.

If the movement for codification symbolized the triumph of the concept of reason in articulations of national jurisprudence, that same concept pertained to two other important questions preoccupying legal and political thinkers of the era, questions involving the nature of political authority and the idea of law as the basis of all political relationships. The

Hapsburg-Valois contests of the early sixteenth century had divided civilians into camps of "Citramontanes," who upheld the formula that the emperor was literally "lord of the world" (as glosses on the title *Cunctos populus* [all peoples] affirmed), and "Ultramontanes," who maintained that the civil law was authoritative "not by reason of empire," as a modern formula has it, "but by the empire of reason." As a consequence of the outbreak of religious warfare and ongoing confessional disputes (roughly, 1560 to 1690), assertions of the sovereignty of the law developed into a prolonged debate over the nature of sovereignty itself. In France, Jean Bodin produced his influential *Six Livres de la République* (1576) in which he set out a systematic defense of absolutism in terms of the lawmaking role of the sovereign, while in England, James I (1603–1625) maintained that a king exercised authority by divine right and was, indeed, *lex loquens* (speaking law). Yet the "just king," James declared, bound himself as well as his people to the "fundamental laws of his kingdom." Seeking, against James, to claim the common law as the repository of the fundamental laws of England and as anterior to kings, Sir Edward Coke pronounced upon its "immemorial" character, insisting that Magna Carta and other such laws guaranteeing English liberties were no mere specimens of positive law, even though promulgated in time by particular kings and parliaments, and in response to particular grievances; rather, they were confirmations of long custom, reaffirmations of an ancient constitution that existed, according to Coke, since "time out of mind." The Spanish Jesuit Francisco Suárez also disputed Jacobean claims of divine right, in this case by asserting a notion of popular sovereignty based on natural law, which, for Suárez, derived from "divine law" and was accessible through the human faculty of reason. In both England and France theories of popular sovereignty became the basis for resistance to (heretic or erring) monarchs, as argued in England by Catholic polemicists against Elizabeth I (1558–1603) and supporters of Parliament in the Civil War against Charles I (for example, by Henry Parker in 1642). The concept of popular sovereignty was also harnessed in polemics arguing the deposition of such monarchs (as in the *Vindiciae contra tyrannos* [Claims Against Tyrants] [1579]). At the end of the seventeenth century, John Locke's *Two Treatises of Government* echoed the same theme in justifying revolution against what he considered a no longer legitimate king.

Between John Locke and Francisco Suárez, however, an intellectual revolution had occurred, leaving Suárez as the culmination of scholastic natural law theorizing. His *De legibus* (1612), though replete with Cicero's notion of political society originating from a civil compact between rational individuals, also drew its assumptions from Thomas Aquinas and Aristotle, setting civil society within a teleological framework, issuing from divine accordance. While natural law and contract theory would continue to permeate western political thinking, culminating, perhaps, in the writings of Jean-Jacques Rousseau and the ideologies that galvanized the American independence movement and the French Revolution, these owed less to Suárez than to the "modern" school of natural law, worked out in the first half of the seventeenth century mainly by Hugo Grotius and Thomas Hobbes. Both stood aloof from (and repudiated) earlier arguments centering on legal sovereignty, which was already suffering from blows of moral relativism, issued first by Niccolò Machiavelli then, later in the sixteenth century, by Michel de Montaigne in France and Justus Lipsius in the Netherlands. Taking into account the "prudential" (rather than legal) prescriptions of these skeptical observers of human nature and society, Grotius and Hobbes derived the fundamental principles of civil society from a philosophy of minimalist ethics: the principle of self-preservation and the ban on wanton injury of another. For Hobbes, this meant that the right of self-preservation was yielded to the sovereign in exchange for laws by which individuals (subjects) were guaranteed survival and the security to pursue their business, and the ban on wanton injury was upheld by the sovereign, Hobbes' Leviathan. The idea of the state as an autonomous moral sphere came to gain currency, influencing all subsequent political and moral theories. In his *Dialogue Between a Philosopher and a Student of the Common Laws of England* (1661), Hobbes took on Coke's idea of the "artificial wisdom" preserved in the common law and countered with the abstract reasoning of the philosopher (*mathematici*) to further present his concept of the state as philosophically rather than authoritatively sanctioned. Yet it was the latter that prevailed in England, especially after the Glorious Revolution (1688–1689) affirmed Parliamentary sovereignty and the rule of English (common) law as the safeguard from the tyranny of absolutism and the guarantee of individual rights. Such a conception of the English constitution, together with Locke's view of limited sovereignty and inalienable natural rights, permeated "American" concepts of federated empire—until, that is, 1776, when American "patriots" charged the English Parliament with tyranny and acting against nature. In *Common Sense* (1776), the English radical Tom Paine supported American independence with arguments based on the law of nature, invoking in one instance the parallel of a maturing colony and a child coming of age and ready to make its own way in the world.

While Hobbes played a key role in the emergence of the concept of the state and in identifying the fundamental principles of political behavior, Grotius applied the philosophy of minimalist ethics to the problem of relationships between states. His *De juri belli et pacis* (1625) established the model for the modern notion of international law, a model taken up and developed by Samuel Pufendorf in *De iure naturae et gentium* (On the Law of Nature and Nations, 1672). For Grotius, the problem of the "laws of nations" had become acute and in need of address since Holland, in his day, was staking expansionist claims against the Iberian states in territories in the Atlantic, Pacific, and Indian oceans. In *De iure praedea* (1609), he had already declared the principle of acquisition by occupation as a right based on "nature." His theory of open and unpossessed seas gave way, in his later work, to the greater concern for regulations among states: the principles of keeping treaties, restoring unjust gains, and reparation of injuries, all of which he derived from the moral force of the precepts of natural law, conceived as a species of self-interest (the need for self-preservation). This focus, as well as his systematic approach in setting down the laws to be recognized and upheld by all nations, distinguished Grotius from earlier Spanish theorists discussing the laws of nations: legalists like Francisco de Vitoria and Juan Ginés de Sepúlveda, in the early sixteenth century, and, later, Suárez, all of whom wrote in the tradition of Roman law, in which laws regulating nations derived from usage and custom and were thus part of human, positive, not natural law. Grotius nevertheless maintained the idea of the "just war," an idea later rejected as barbarous by Voltaire and Immanuel Kant. In his *Metaphysics of Morals* (1796), Kant went so far as to call for a congress of states whose purpose would be to monitor international affairs and settle disputes in a civilized fashion.

Two aspects of legal practice that changed dramatically in the period surveyed here remain to be noted. The first is the displacement, by formal legal proceedings (particularly in the burgeoning urban centers of Europe), of "informal" means of dealing with social miscreants, when neighbors, through *charivari* or rough music, exerted their own moral force to create conformity in a locality. The second is the disappearance of witchcraft as a crime punishable by courts, which reflects the secularization (and greater skeptical spirit) of not only law but all facets of cultural and intellectual life. Both these issues pertain, too, to the growing proliferation of lawyers in the period.

References

Brewer, John, and John Styles, eds. *An Ungovernable People: The English and Their Law in the Seventeenth and Eighteenth Centuries*. New Brunswick: Rutgers University Press, 1980.

Burns, J.H., and Mark Goldie, eds. *The Cambridge History of Political Thought, 1450–1700*. Cambridge: Cambridge University Press, 1991.

Davis, Natalie Zemon. *Society and Culture in Early Modern France*. Stanford: Stanford University Press, 1975.

Kelly, J.M. *A Short History of Western Legal Theory*. Oxford: Clarendon Press, 1992.

Keohane, N.O. *Philosophy and the State in France: The Renaissance to the Enlightenment*. Princeton: Princeton University Press, 1980.

Pagden, Anthony, ed. *The Languages of Political Theory in Early-Modern Europe*. Pt. I. Cambridge: Cambridge University Press, 1987.

Pocock, J.G.A. *The Ancient Constitution and the Feudal Law: A Study of English Historical Thought in the Seventeenth Century. A Reissue with a Retrospect*. 1957. Cambridge: Cambridge University Press, 1987.

Shapiro, Barbara J. *Probability and Certainty in Seventeenth-Century England: A Study of the Relationships Between Natural Sci-*

ence, Religion, History, Law, and Literature. Princeton: Princeton University Press, 1983.
Tiernay, Brian. *Religion, Law, and the Growth of Constitutional Thought, 1150–1650*. Cambridge: Cambridge University Press, 1982.
Wootton, David, ed. *Divine Right and Democracy: An Anthology of Political Writing in Stuart England*. Harmondsworth: Penguin Books, 1986.

Adriana McCrea

Skepticism

Skepticism, the doubt or suspension of judgment about truth and justice in the law, is both an overarching theoretical disposition and a ubiquitous tool in legal interpretation and argumentation. Best understood in contrast to its dialectical opponents, its many forms are used by practitioners, judges, teachers, and philosophers to undermine the claims of those who assert knowledge of the truth about any matter. Skepticism undermines dogmatic or doctrinaire interpretation and argumentation based on any theory with claims to truth, objectivity, or right answers from natural law to legal positivism, from intentionalism to formalism, from kantianism to marxism, from Hans Kelsen to Ronald Dworkin to Jürgen Habermas.

In practice, skepticism is most likely to be used against those who are trying to establish some fact or doctrine and have to carry a burden of proof. It has undeniably affected legal vocabulary in many ways. For example, doctrines of "reasonable doubt" and "probable cause" are responses to, and ways of living with, skepticism.

The many forms of skepticism can be distinguished in several ways. Starting with the question, skepticism about *what*?, we might begin with category distinctions. Doubts about the reality of things in the universe are usually labeled "ontological skepticism," and doubts about our ability to know them are usually labeled "epistemological skepticism." One might be skeptical about the existence of justice in the universe (ontological skepticism), but not at all skeptical about a court's judgment concerning the conventionally defined innocence or guilt of a particular defendant (epistemological dogmatism). Alternatively, one might have no doubts about the general possibility of achieving justice (ontological dogmatism), but doubt the ability of a particular system to recognize it (epistemological skepticism).

Another dimension for distinguishing skepticisms can be imagined as a quantitative axis between total, universal doubt and very specific partial doubt. At one extreme, global skepticism doubts the truth of 100 percent of all claims whatsoever. An intermediate skepticism might recognize our ability to know some truths, but not others, such that we can know 40 percent or 50 percent or 60 percent of the relevant truths. The most limited local skepticism would cast doubt on, for example, a particular kind of evidence or even a particular witness, which we might think of as skepticism about less than 1 percent of the universe of knowledge claims.

A third dimension categorizes skepticisms in terms of historical traditions. Some skepticisms draw self-consciously on the history of philosophical skepticism, going back to Pyrrho, Arcesilaus, and Carneades. Cicero's *Academica* and his report on Carneades in *De re publica*, Diogenes Laertius's *Lives of the Eminent Philosophers*, and Sextus Empiricus's *Outlines of Pyrrhonism* and *Against the Rhetoricians* (the law teachers of the day) are our chief sources on the ancient tradition. In early modern Europe, Michel de Montaigne's criticism of law and legal interpretation drew on the rediscovery of the works of Sextus Empiricus. Hugo Grotius cast his modern natural law as an answer to Carneades. Thomas Hobbes, David Hume, Immanuel Kant, and G.W.F. Hegel developed their philosophies of law in self-conscious debate with, and often acceptance of, the skeptical tradition. Many contemporary anglophone skeptics, however, are nonhistorical, apparently unaware of the rich treasure of skeptical arguments and tools available in these works.

A fourth dimension for the distinction of skepticisms is functions. For some, skepticism is a way of life and results in a sort of philosophical closure. The ancient skeptics claimed that they started out disturbed by opposing positions on many issues; became convinced that there are equipollent arguments on both sides of them; suspended judgment on such issues; found themselves in *ataraxia*, or mental tranquility; and lived in accordance with customs. For others, skepticism is entirely a matter of utility: it is used to win in court.

A fifth dimension is psychological and sociological sources. The ancient skeptics reported that skepticism gave them tranquility, but would have no answer for others who said that skepticism made them nervous; from their accounts we might conclude that attitudes toward skepticism are a matter of personal temperament. It has also been observed that many philosophical skeptics began their careers as lawyers. Adversary systems seem most likely to stimulate skepticism. Trained to argue either side of any issue according to which side is paying them, lawyers may become disposed to doubt that either side represents the truth in any larger sense. Rather, we agree to act as if the truth is what the judge or jury declare it to be.

In American jurisprudence, legal realism has sometimes been called skeptical because it argues that what passes for justice is merely power and that legislators and judges can do whatever they want. Oliver Wendell Holmes earned the sobriquet "the Great Skeptic," in part for such assertions as that the common law is not a "brooding omnipresence in the sky." His alternative was a legal realism that held that rights extend only as far as the ability of political movements to demand and enforce them. The school of legal realism of the 1930s generally followed his analysis but added reformist proposals, and the notion was further developed by critical legal studies in the 1970s and 1980s. It is important to recognize that although realists are usually skeptical of establishment claims of justice and truth, they are not at all skeptical about their own analysis of what really happens and what should happen in the law.

Similar things can be said about yet another variation on legal realism, economic analysis of the law. A theory of skepticism in jurisprudence has been advanced by Richard Posner, one of the originators of that movement. He argues that there is nothing special about legal reasoning that cannot also be found in other types of reasoning, and that it often does not yield determinate outcomes. While he is skeptical of other dogmatisms, he is not skeptical of his own dogma of the economic analysis of law.

In recent years, skepticism in legal intepretation and argumentation has received a measure of cross-fertilization from skeptical theories of hermeneutics from other disciplines ranging from natural science to biblical studies to postmodern literary studies. A well-publicized representative of this movement is Stanley Fish, who delights in declaring that accepted dogmas, such as "freedom of speech," are conceptually impossible. His skepticism, however, is only partial because he declares that his diagnosis is "the truth."

Criticism of skepticism often centers on the self-referential implications of skepticism. If you doubt everything, would you also have to doubt your skepticism? Another criticism insists that people could not live according to skepticism, because they would walk off cliffs if they were not sure that they were there. In theory, these are well-known conundrums, answered in the literature of the historical tradition described above. In practice, these are not usually serious objections to skeptical legal arguments, because skepticism is usually the tool of the party that does not have the burden of going forward. A lawyer may doubt that his or her client is innocent and still go forward with raising doubts about the client's guilt.

A final charge is that skepticism leads to legal and political nihilism, conservative quietism, or paralysis, since skeptics doubt all reasons for doing anything. However, the skeptics of the skeptical tradition always reported that they lived in accordance with appearances, customs, beliefs, and opinions in the absence of truth and certainty. If appearances, customs, beliefs, or opinions justified it, they would engage in vigorous action. Thus, skepticism in legal interpretation and argumentation can be used on behalf of almost any legal or political position, except those that can only be justified by doctrinaire dogmatism.

References

Fish, Stanley. *There's No Such Thing as Free Speech, and It's a Good Thing, Too.* Oxford: Oxford University Press, 1994.

"Interpretation Symposium." *Southern California Law Review* 58 (1985), 1–725.

Laursen, John Christian. *The Politics of Skepticism in the Ancients, Montaigne, Hume, and Kant.* Leiden: E.J. Brill, 1992.

Levinson, Sanford, and Steven Mailloux. *Interpreting Law and Literature: A Hermeneutic Reader.* Evanston: Northwestern University Press, 1988.

Nathan, Daniel O. "Skepticism and Legal Interpretation." *Erkenntnis* 33 (1990), 165–189.

Posner, Richard A. "The Jurisprudence of Skepticism." *Michigan Law Review* 86 (1988), 827–891.

John Christian Laursen

See also DECONSTRUCTIONIST PHILOSOPHY OF LAW; ERROR, DECEIT, AND ILLUSION; INDETERMINACY; TRUTH

Slavery

The idea that one human being can own another stretches as far back as recorded history. From ancient China and Egypt through Greece and Rome, slavery has been a widely accepted practice, and sophisticated legal rules have grown up around the institution of slavery. Only since the American Revolution released a new ideology of individual freedom have western cultures resoundingly rejected slavery.

Despite the fact that slavery disappeared in parts of western Europe, such as England, as early as the tenth century A.D., western Europeans, particularly the Spanish, Dutch, and English, drew upon the legacy of slavery in the ancient Mediterranean and its survival in some forms in Spain in establishing slavery and the legal rules to govern it in North and South America. Following quickly on Spanish explorations in the Caribbean, Spanish settlers enslaved the native people. When the efforts to use native slaves failed, Spanish merchants introduced African slaves into Central and South America and the Caribbean in the early sixteenth century. The English settlers in the Caribbean modeled their practices on the Spanish slavery. From the British colonies in the Caribbean, slavery spread to mainland British North America. By 1680, Virginia and Maryland had both well-developed laws regulating slavery. South Carolina, which borrowed its slave laws from Barbados, had a slave majority from shortly after its founding in the 1680s until about 1740.

There was some opposition to slavery, which took hold in British North America in the middle of the seventeenth century, from the time of initial settlement. Based largely on the Golden Rule, Quakers argued that slaveholding violated God's law. Nevertheless, the calls for abolition of slavery remained relatively ineffectual until the era of the American Revolution. In the wake of the Enlightenment, English law rejected slavery even while English merchants profited from the slave trade to America. Blackstone wrote in his *Commentaries on the Law of England* that the "spirit of liberty is so deeply implanted in our constitution . . . that a slave . . . the moment he lands in England . . . becomes a freeman." Likewise, in *Somerset v. Stewart,* 98 Eng. Rep. 499, 510 (1779), Lord Mansfield wrote that slavery "is so odious that nothing can be suffered to support it, but positive law." American courts interpreted Mansfield to mean "the air of England will not support slavery."

In America, a growing ideology of freedom seemed destined to lead to the termination of slavery. Thomas Jefferson's optimistic rhetoric in the *Declaration of Independence* that all men are created equal is probably the strongest evidence of the humanist impulses of the revolutionary generation. In 1779, Pennsylvania, for instance, passed a gradual abolition statute, followed by Massachusetts in 1782. In Virginia, William and Mary professor St. George Tucker proposed a scheme for gradual emancipation in his 1803 edition of Blackstone's *Commentaries.* However, some historians have argued that it was the very existence of slavery that led Americans—particularly Virginians—to understand the value of freedom and to fight the revolution.

Americans struggled with the dilemma of slavery in the wake of the revolution. It was in the early nineteenth century, when the humanism of the American Revolution gave way to economic and social reality, that Americans, particularly southerners in the areas growing tobacco, rice, and cotton, began to oppose the gradual abolition of slavery. Southern thinkers, such as John C. Calhoun of South Carolina, articulated a theory why slaves should be kept in bondage. Calhoun voiced his belief that slaves formed the basis of southern society—its wealth and its culture—and that any attempt to end slavery would result in catastrophe. Southerners often pointed to San Domingo, where slaves led by François-Dominique Toussaint had violently claimed their freedom in the 1790s, as an example of the South's likely fate. Academic writers, such as William and Mary professor Thomas Roderick Dew and University of Virginia professor Albert Bledsoe painted Hobbes-like visions of southern society. They argued that an individual's freedom was greatest in societies in which (white) individuals were protected from harm to their persons and property. Thus, to maximize freedom, southern society had to carefully protect property in slaves and protect against slave revolt, which was best accomplished in their minds by supporting slavery against all challenges and by placing strict controls on the discussion of slavery and on the activities of free blacks.

Such ideas expressed themselves in the judicial opinions of southerners. In opinions like *State v. Mann,* 13 N.C. 263 (1827), the courts allowed masters a free hand in disciplining slaves, right up to killing them. Southern courts also protected against free blacks by sharply limiting manumission of slaves as well as by not allowing free blacks to enter the state, and against potentially rebellious slaves by harsh punishment and even outright banishment of deviant slaves. Similarly, the state legislatures and courts prohibited the distribution of abolitionist literature.

Southern judicial thinking on slavery and on the benefits of slavery—as well as the dehumanization of slaves—culminated in the *Dred Scott v. Sanford* opinion, 60 U.S. (15 How.) 393 (1857), delivered in May 1857 by Chief Justice Roger B. Taney. Taney denied that blacks had any rights that the judicial system was required to respect. He also recognized the rights of individual states to have the property of their citizens protected from taking by the federal government (and also, by extrapolation by taking from the northern states), thus adopting much of the southerners' political philosophy and their interpretation of the Constitution.

Abolitionists and others who opposed slavery had long recognized that the law provided a significant barrier to humanizing the institution of slavery. "Over and above" the institution of slavery, Harriet Beecher Stowe wrote in her antislavery novel *Uncle Tom's Cabin,* "there broods a portentous shadow—the shadow of the law." The law both prevented manumission and provided for the collection of debts, which often required slaveholders to sell slaves away from the families in order to pay debts. Reform of the law, abolitionists thought, was necessary to cleanse slavery of its immorality.

The law of slavery posed a particularly significant moral dilemma for northern judges who opposed slavery. The judges' obligation to uphold the Constitution required them to return fugitive slaves to their owners or to punish those who had helped slaves escape. The judges adopted several avenues, ranging from resignation from the bench, to evasion of the pro-slavery law whenever possible, through enforcement of the law. Justice Story's opinion in *Prigg v. Pennsylvania,* 41 U.S. (16 Pet.) 539 (1842), is believed to be an example of a moderate approach of an antislavery judge. In *Prigg,* Story held that northern states may do nothing that interferes with the return of fugitive slaves, thus invalidating Pennsylvania's requirement that suspected fugitives must be brought before local magistrates before they were returned South. The *Prigg* decision, however, had the effect of absolving northern states from cooperating in the return of slaves, thus also hindering the recapture of fugitives.

The best informed opinion of scholars is that dispute over slavery—and in particular the concern of southerners that Abraham Lincoln would take away their property rights in slaves—precipitated the American Civil War in April 1861. The rise of the Republican party occurred largely because of opposition to slavery and the moral dilemma posed by southern slave law. The termination of slavery, promised by Lincoln's 1862 Emancipation Proclamation, achieved constitutional status in the Thirteenth Amendment, adopted in 1867, thus completing the revolutionary dream.

References

Calhoun, John C. *The Works of John C. Calhoun.* Charleston SC, 1851–1855.

Cobb, Thomas Reed Root. *The Law of Slavery.* Philadelphia: Lippincott, 1858.

Cover, Robert. *Justice Accused: Antislavery and the Judicial Process.* New Haven: Yale University Press, 1977.

Davis, David Brion. *The Problem of Slavery in the Age of Revolution: 1770–1823.* Ithaca: Cornell University Press, 1978.

Faust, Drew Gilpin. *A Sacred Circle: The Dilemma of the Intellectual in the Antebellum South.* Baltimore: Johns Hopkins University Press, 1977.

Fehrenbacher, Don E. *The Dred Scott Case: Its Significance in Law and Politics.* New York: Oxford University Press, 1978.

Watson, Alan. *Slave Law in the Americas.* Athens: University of Georgia Press, 1990.

Wood, Gordon. *The Radicalism of the American Revolution.* New York: Vintage, 1992.

Alfred L. Brophy

See also EQUALITY; LIBERTY; MOBILITY RIGHTS

Smith, Adam (1723–1790)

Owing to his *Inquiry into the Nature and Causes of the Wealth of Nations* (1776), Adam Smith became one of the most famous authors in the history of printing; yet he was also an outstanding scholar in law and the philosophy of law. His lectures in moral philosophy at the University of Glasgow (1752–1764) included a section on justice, which,

> being susceptible of precise and accurate rules is, for that reason, capable of a full and particular explanation. Upon this subject he followed the plan that seems to be suggested by Montesquieu; endeavoring to trace the gradual progress of jurisprudence, both public and private, from the rudest to the most refined ages, and to point out the effects of those arts which contribute to subsistence, and to the accumulation of property, in producing correspondent improvements in law and government.

So wrote John Millar, Smith's most prominent student, himself a professor of (civil) law at Glasgow in 1761. Significantly, Smith was awarded an honorary doctoral degree in law when he resigned his chair to become a tutor to the later Duke of Buccleuch. Although his will demanded that nearly all of his manuscripts be burned, two student transcripts of his *Lectures on Jurisprudence* have been preserved. They reveal an excellent knowledge of Roman as well as contemporary law. These must be used instead of his intended book on natural law; the evidence suggests that it would have been a well-developed treatise, analytical as well as normative, historical as well systematic in its approach.

Smith's treatment of law is basically outlined in his first published book, *The Theory of Moral Sentiments* (TMS) (first edition in 1759). In all the subsequent editions (which he carefully prepared himself until the last year of his life), he asserted his intention to give himself "an account of the general principles of law and government, and of the different revolutions they have undergone in the different ages and periods of society." He certainly would have established "a theory" or "a system of what might properly be called natural jurisprudence"; by that he meant "the natural rules of justice" or "the general principles which ought to run through and be the foundation of the laws of all nations." In this context, Smith chides other lawyers for not having written such a treatise yet; in his opinion, "it was very late before the *philosophy of law* [as one of the first authors explicitly to use that term] was treated of by itself." In his view, Hugo Grotius was the only author who had taken on such a task. Systems of positive laws are always but a more or less imperfect attempt toward such a system of natural jurisprudence. Judges are appointed for that purpose, but often the constitution of a state is merely an instrument of power in the hands of the prominent orders or the constitution of the judicature is defective. In Smith's original concept at least, the other parts and purposes of jurisprudence and law were police, revenue, and arms (to which was added the law of nations), besides justice; these were ruled not by the principle of justice, but of "expediency," according to Millar, and they were elaborated in part in *The Wealth of Nations*.

Two other elements in TMS seem particularly noteworthy. Smith develops a theory of a threefold human vulnerability. Injuries may be physical (affecting the person) or psychical (affecting the reputation), or they may affect one's property. If an injury is inflicted by other people, and perhaps even intentionally, then justice or individual rights are violated and, through the moral working of sympathy, a resentment arises within the (impartial) spectator. Thus the origins of law in general and penal law in particular are to be found in real emotional features and phenomena, rather than in abstract and exclusive principles of retribution or (utilitarian) calculation. Of course, this original impetus is further refined in the philosophico-legal process, by criteria such as impartiality, consistency, and coherence that ensue from the concept of the really impartial spectator.

The other legacy of TMS is the definition of justice (the predominant aim of public and private law, including penal law) as a "negative virtue," a virtue which tells us to abstain from doing something, namely, hurting our neighbor. Thus the law cannot, in general, demand positive actions, but only an attitude of sitting still and doing nothing. Furthermore, the "rules of justice" must be precise and enforceable, they must relate only to external actions, in contrast to moral rules, which generally demand positive actions and are rules within human beings. Smith compares the latter with aesthetic and stylistic considerations, the former with rules of grammar. It remains an interesting and open question whether Smith considered lawmaking as a voluntaristic, sovereign command or as an intricate consensual process inspired by concepts of natural law and even cautiously recognizing a right to resistance. Adherents of either interpretation will find explicit passages in TMS that support their respective views.

The lecture notes from Smith's students, *Lectures on Jurisprudence*—LJ(A) from 1762–1763 and LJ(B) from 1763–1764—differ in regard to two important features: (1) The treatment of *individual topics* is generally more comprehensive in LJ(A), while the *range of subjects* is wider in LJ(B); LJ(A) stops after two thirds of the section on "Police." (2) The *sequence* in "Justice" is radically different. LJ(A) is very historical, beginning with Francis Hutcheson with private law, that is, property and other rights, goes on to domestic law, and ends with "Public Jurisprudence." LJ(B) adopts "the method of the civilians," starting with government, then to family and household, ending with private law (including "Deliquency," that is, penal law). Smith demonstrates a knowledge of legal topics, including Roman law, that is substantially more profound than the knowledge displayed in comparable treatises on moral philosophy.

The *Lectures'* historical, sociological, and descriptive analysis uses a four-stage theory of humankind's development, as hunters and fishers, shepherds, in agriculture, and in commerce, making the analysis multifactorial. This is artfully intertwined with the evolution of property and thereafter with forms of government. In this historical perspective, government is established to protect the rich from the encroachment of the poor. Following Samuel Pufendorf and Hutcheson, Smith distinguishes between natural rights and adventitious rights that include property and contract and are conceivable only after the institution of government. At the last two stages, legal disputes are multiplied, and thus law and juridical institutions become more and more complex.

References

Brühlmeier, Daniel. *Die Rechts- und Staatslehre von Adam Smith und die Interessentheorie der Verfassung* (Theory of State and Law in Adam Smith, and the Interest Theory of the Constitution). Berlin: Duncker und Humblot, 1988. (English summary in *Law & Social Inquiry* 16 (1991), 615–634.)

Cairns, John W. "Adam Smith's Lectures on Jurisprudence: Their Influence on Legal Education." In *Adam Smith: International Perspectives,* ed. Hiroshi Mizuta and Chuhei Sugiyama, 63–83. New York: St. Martin's Press, 1993.

Haakonssen, Knud. *The Science of a Legislator: The Natural Jurisprudence of David Hume and Adam Smith.* Cambridge: Cambridge University Press, 1981.

MacCormick, Neil. "Law and Economics: Adam Smith's Analysis." In *Legal Right and Social Democracy,* 103–125. Oxford: Clarendon Press, 1982.

Smith, Adam. *Essays on Philosophical Subjects,* ed. W.P.D. Wightman, J.C. Bryce, and I.S. Ross. Oxford: Clarendon Press, 1980.

———. *Lectures on Jurisprudence,* ed. R. Meek, D.D. Raphael, and P. Stein. Oxford: Clarendon Press, 1978.

———. *Lectures on Rhetoric and Belles Lettres,* ed. J.C. Bryce. Oxford: Clarendon Press, 1983.

———. *The Theory of Moral Sentiments,* ed. D.D. Raphael and A.F. Macfie. *The Glasgow Edition of the Works and Correspondence of Adam Smith,* vol. 1. Oxford: Clarendon Press, 1976.

Stein, Peter. "Adam Smith's Jurisprudence—Between Morality and Economics." In *Jubilee Lectures Celebrating the Foundation of the Faculty of Law of the University of Birmingham,* 137–151. London: Wildy, 1981.

Stewart, Dugald. *An Account of the Life and Writings of Adam Smith, LL.D.* In *Essays on Philosophical Subjects,* ed. W.P.D. Wrightman, J.C. Bryce, and I.S. Ross. Oxford: Clarendon, 1980.

Winch, Donald. *Adam Smith's Politics. An Essay in Historiographic Revision.* Cambridge: Cambridge University Press, 1978.

Daniel Brühlmeier

Social Contract

Contractarian or contractual theories are modern political theories that explain the origin of civil or political society in terms of an express or tacit agreement (contract, compact, covenant) among a group of free individuals in an actual or hypothetical state of nature. These individuals agree to establish a commonly recognized political authority to safeguard *natural rights,* such as their right to life. The term "social contract" connotes either a contract among individuals, or a contract between individuals and their sovereign. The leading exponents of this modern tradition—Thomas Hobbes (1588–1679), John Locke (1632–1704), Jean-Jacques Rousseau (1712–1778), and Immanuel Kant (1724–1804)—focused only on the contract among individuals.

Historical Background

The ancient Greeks discussed different versions of a social contract. For example, as noted by Plato in *Republic,* Book II, Glaucon claims that it is in the interest of all to covenant with one another to avoid committing injustice. Moreover, Socrates contends, according to Plato in *Crito,* that Athenians ought to obey laws because they have tacitly agreed to do so. The Greeks also discussed a secular version of natural law. For example, Aristotle in *Nicomachean Ethics* divides political justice into transculturally valid justice (natural justice) and contextually valid justice (legal justice). The stoics adopted and developed the idea of a universally valid natural law. Cicero is a good example of their influence in Roman jurisprudence. In *De re publica* he defines true law as right reason according to nature, universally and eternally valid for all. Roman jurisprudence influenced medieval Christian natural law, especially St. Thomas Aquinas's legal philosophy. In *Summa theologiae* Aquinas defines natural law as the will of God apprehended by human reason, and, therefore, universally valid for all. For Aquinas, a community confers political authority on a sovereign contingent upon the promotion of the *common good,* and if a violation of this good occurs, the community acts rightly by revoking its allegiance and consequently deposing the tyrant.

Consent

Contractarians ground legitimate political authority on a hypothetical *voluntary* agreement among individuals rather than on nature, tradition, or might. The roots of political voluntarism can be traced back to St. Augustine's conception of free will as necessary for ascribing moral responsibility to people. Political voluntarism is also implicit in Aquinas's and explicit in Francisco Suárez's political writings. Moreover, it appears in Hobbes when he argues for an unconditional covenant among people to institute and obey a sovereign provided their lives are protected. Unlike Hobbes, however, Locke rejects the notion of an unconditional duty of obedience. For him the legitimacy of political authority depends upon the end for which it was instituted, namely, the preservation of the natural rights to life, liberty, and estate. If these rights are infringed, the *trust* between the community and the magistrate (government) is canceled, and the people have a right to appeal to heaven (revolution) to establish a new legislative body. Unlike Locke's idea of conditional sovereignty (conditioned upon the preservation of natural rights), Rousseau argues for absolute popular sovereignty. The *general will* of the citizens, Rousseau contends, can never be represented in its legislative capacity, but it should be represented by the government in its executive capacity. Although the general will is always what it ought to be, the vote of the majority conditions it. Rousseau's ideal citizens are obliged to obey the will of the majority only if each citizen is allowed to vote on what the general will is and on what the content of the law should be. However, unlike Locke, he stipulates no right to revolution. Therefore, he provides no safeguard against the tyranny of the majority. Similarly, Kant provides no protection against tyranny. Like Hobbes, he argues that sovereignty is inalienable. Once people covenant with one another to confer it upon someone, it can never return to them. If it could, the authority of a sovereign would be limited; however, this is conceptually incoherent. Thus Kant, unlike Locke and Rousseau, rejects the notion of popular sovereignty as self-contradictory. For him the citizens of a commonwealth should act not only *as if* they have consented to abide by a hypothetical social contract, but also *as if* they have consented to obey the law. Like Hobbes, he insists that citizens have an actual unconditional duty of obedience.

Contemporary Debate

By reformulating traditional contractarianism into an ideal conception of political justice, John Rawls offers a penetrating critique not only of utilitarian political theories, but also of communitarian theories. Unlike traditional contractarians, Rawls presupposes an *original position* rather than a state of nature to justify the adoption of egalitarian and reasonable principles of justice. These principles are chosen from behind a *veil of ignorance* by equally situated rational egoists. By omitting personal information that may taint the impartiality of the alleged principles (for example, social status, natural talents, or different conceptions of a good life), the veil should guarantee that these principles are not only reasonable but also fair. Consequently, Rawls calls his theory *justice as fairness*.

Objections

While contractarians supply heuristic tools for evaluating political institutions, they cannot adequately explain why contractees should keep their promises. Hypothetical contracts generate only hypothetical obligations. Yet hypothetical obligations oblige no one. Moreover, since the notion of a nonbinding contract is incoherent, it follows that a hypothetical contract is no contract at all. According to G.W.F. Hegel, since the validity of private rights (contractual and property rights) depends upon public rights as defined by the laws and institutions of the state, the private cannot legitimize the public (the law). On the contrary, Norberto Bobbio held that the legitimacy of the private depends upon its being sanctioned by the law. If the main goal of contractarians is to justify political authority, they fail to accomplish it. Nonetheless, if political authority can indeed be justified, it must be justified on consequentialist grounds or on concrete considerations of justice rather than on hypothetical considerations. If this is so, then the hegelian objection remains a formidable challenge to contractarianism.

References

Barker, Ernest, ed. *Social Contract: Essays by Locke, Hume, and Rousseau*. Intro. Ernest Barker. New York: Oxford University Press, 1947.

Bobbio, Norberto. "Contract and Contractarianism in the Current Debate." In *The Future of Democracy*. Trans. Roger Griffin. Ed. and intro. Richard Bellamy. Minneapolis: University of Minnesota Press, 1987.

Hampton, Jean. "Contract and Consent." In *A Companion to Contemporary Political Philosophy,* ed. Robert E. Goodin and Philip Pettit. Cambridge MA: Blackwell, 1993.

Hobbes, Thomas. *Leviathan*. Ed. Richard Tuck. New York: Cambridge University Press, 1991.

Kant, Immanuel. *The Metaphysical Elements of Justice*. Trans. and intro. John Ladd. Indianapolis: Bobbs-Merrill, 1965.

Locke, John. *Two Treatises of Government,* ed. Peter Laslett. New York: Cambridge University Press, 1970.

Medina, Vincente. *Social Contract Theories: Political Obligation or Anarchy?* Savage MD: Rowman and Littlefield, 1990.

Rawls, John. *A Theory of Justice*. Cambridge MA: Harvard University Press, 1971.

Riley, Patrick. *Will and Political Legitimacy: A Critical Exposition of Social Contract Theory in Hobbes, Locke, Rousseau, Kant, and Hegel*. Cambridge MA: Harvard University Press, 1982.

Ritter, Alan, and Julia Conaway Bondella, eds. *Rousseau's Political Writings*. Trans. Julia Conaway Bondella. New York: Norton, 1988.

Vincente Medina

See also CONTRACTUALIST PHILOSOPHY OF LAW

Social Philosophy

The international organization in which lawyers, philosophers, and others cooperate on questions in the philosophy of law is called the International Association of Philosophy of Law and Social Philosophy (in the original German: *Internationale Vereinigung für Rechts- und Sozialphilosophie*). This name expresses the conviction that the understanding of the nature of law and the treatment of related philosophical problems presupposes a grasp of the social context in which law is embedded.

While legal philosophy as well as political philosophy are well-defined and institutionalized branches of study, the term "social philosophy" has a much vaguer and contested sense. Neither the *International Encyclopedia of Social Science* nor the *Encyclopedia of Philosophy* has entries for "social philosophy," and not all who use the term would agree with the author of the entry in *Handwörterbuch der Sozialwissenschaften* (Manual of Social Studies), Jürgen von Kempski, that it denotes theories of predominantly reformatory-utopian character. Although the term, or derivatives like "social philosophers," is used in the titles of a number of books, the contents of these vary considerably and are often difficult to distinguish from that of books on political philosophy or sociological (or social) theory.

If one wants to give the term a more definite sense, and to delineate a problem area that deserves to be studied under the name "social philosophy," one has to presuppose a conception of philosophy in its relation to the various branches of science, like the German *Wissenschaft* taken in a broad sense to include the humanities and the social sciences. One such conception combines the idea of philosophy as "the mother of all sciences" with the idea that, after these have developed into separate branches of study, two roles are left for the philosophers in relation to them. Georg Simmel has suggested these roles by the use of spatial metaphors: each science borders on philosophy, on two levels. "Below" it we have philosophical analysis of its presuppositions and its methods; "above" it we have speculative attempts to build a total picture of the part of reality with which it is concerned, a picture which the science in question cannot deliver, since it never finishes its task and only reaches partial results. Simmel emphasizes the synthetic character of this kind of philosophy.

Human beings have always thought about the fact that they live in societies. Primitive peoples have created myths about the origin of their tribes to explain their structure. Greek thinkers like Plato and Aristotle have asked how a good and just society is made up, and within Christianity much thought about God and his relation to his creation concerns how he has made man fit for society and imposed social obligations on him. Out of such more or less speculative (and in this sense philosophical) endeavors the various social sciences have developed as methods were found to investigate social phenomena empirically and find the laws governing them. At the same time philosophers and social scientists have discussed these methods, their difference and likeness to those used in the natural sciences, and their presuppositions. This has become a recognized branch of philosophy called the philosophy of the social sciences. It is identical with what Simmel described as the philosophy "below" these sciences and could be considered part of social philosophy. Since that already has an identity and a name there is reason to reserve "social philosophy" for what Simmel described as "above" the social sciences, in addition to the prescientific speculations about social life hinted at earlier.

None of the individual social sciences can claim to deal with the totality of social life, and even together they are far from presenting a unified theory of society. Their results are always preliminary and fragmentary. However, they may be used to supplement and rectify our commonsense conception of what it means to live in a society. So social philosophy may be conceived as that branch of philosophy which uses the results of scientific investigations of social phenomena available at a certain time to build a coherent, synthetic theory of the basic traits in all social life, a theory from which its aspects and variations may be accounted for. Conceived in this way social philosophy is not a normative discipline like ethics or political philosophy, but in the same way as many social scientists try to derive normative conclusions from their descriptive and explanatory results, social philosophers in their work often have considerations about "the good life" in "a good and just society" in mind.

One may take what Talcott Parsons has called "the Hobbesian problem of order" as the focal point for such a social philosophy, or one may ask it to account for how rationality and irrationality combine in human social conduct. Questions about "nature and nurture" in social life also belong here. In any case, the fact that society consists of individuals who interact with and are dependent upon each other must form the starting point, and social philosophy has to face the problem of how to deal with the relationship between the individuals and the various kinds of social wholes (groups, organizations, mobs, societies) to which they belong. Concepts like "social norm," "social role," "rational choice," "community," "conflict," and "culture" are among those which must be used and clarified in a social philosophy.

References

Blegvad, Mogens. "What Is Social Philosophy?" *Rechtstheorie* 15 (1993), 421–440.

Feinberg, Joel. *Social Philosophy*. Englewood Cliffs NJ: Prentice-Hall, 1973.

Kempski, Jürgen von. "Sozialphilosophie" (Social Philosophy). *Handwörterbuch der sozialwissenschaften* 9 (1956), 527–532.

Nisbet, Robert. *The Social Philosophers*. London: Heinemann, 1974.

Parsons, Talcott. *The Structure of Social Action*. 1937. 2d ed. Glencoe IL: Free Press, 1949.
Simmel, Georg. *The Philosophy of Money*. 1900. Trans. T. Bottomore and David Frisby. London: Routledge and Kegan Paul, 1978.

Mogens Blegvad

See also ECONOMICS; POLITICAL PHILOSOPHY

Socialist Philosophy of Law

It is often supposed that law would be unnecessary in an ideal society. David Hume (1711–1776) argued that law arises only in "circumstances of justice," conditions of material scarcity, and human selfishness. For Hume, such circumstances were inevitable; the idea of a society without law was a mere theoretical abstraction. Socialists, however, have envisaged transcending these conditions and thus the need for law. The orthodoxy on this subject comes from Karl Marx (1818–1883) and Friedrich Engels (1820–1895), who contended that law serves three overlapping purposes under capitalism: first, law mediates the property relations of bourgeois egoists; second, law is an ideology which camouflages exploitation with the rhetoric of formal rights and freedoms; and third, law is the means by which the dominant class oppresses other classes. The task of the proletariat is to overthrow capitalism and thus to eliminate private property, individual selfishness, the exploitation of labor, and class divisions. In a socialist society of solidarity and fellow-feeling, law and state would "wither away," to be replaced by the mere "administration of things."

This doctrine was taken up, elaborated, and applied in the former Soviet Union. The early writings of the bolshevik jurist Evgeny Pashukanis (1891–1937), for example, identify law's source in commodity exchange. However, for all Pashukanis's "legal nihilism," he provides a sophisticated theory of law which represents, in effect, the first socialist jurisprudence. Pashukanis's orthodox position subsequently fell out of favor with state ideology, although it might be said that it was realized in practice. Stalinist legal theory abandoned the thesis that law mediates relations among bourgeois egoists, but retained the idea that law secures the power of the ruling class, with the rationale that class conflict and law would disappear with the full flowering of communism. Law therefore persisted simply as a club with which to beat down dissent, a far cry from the legal ideals of the rule of law and individual rights.

In the west, the socialist tradition has been more hospitable to the idea of socialist law. Center-socialists, such as the British fabians and their heirs in labor, and social democratic parties take it as given that socialism requires law to regulate and monitor economic relations. [There has been some debate as to whether such administrative law elides the formal principles of procedural justice, but such a criticism, espoused by conservatives like Friedrich von Hayek (1899–1992), relies on a rather narrow understanding of what is to count as law.] Support for socialist law often involves the antiutopian claim that law is necessary because selfish motivations are inevitable even among a socialist citizenry. Law is thus a remedial measure, a view not that unlike the presumption of the withering-away thesis (and Hume's circumstances of justice) that law is necessary under flawed social conditions. These more moderate socialists would concur with much of the marxist critique of law, however, arguing that access to legal redress too often depends on wealth and social standing, and that capitalist law favors the protection of private property rather than its redistribution.

More radical western socialists have sought to revise the marxist orthodoxy in a sympathetic way, without collapsing into the moderate position, to find a role for law in an ideal society. Their inquiries are organized around three main issues: the nature or sources of law, the rule of law, and rights. The most fundamental, perhaps, is the first. What is law? Socialists are likely to envisage legal institutions that are radically unlike those of the past or present; jurisprudential debates as to when a system of rules is a legal system thus have a special significance here. One position in the mainstream debates is natural law, which identifies law in terms of its conformity to universal moral values. As such, the natural law position seems particularly antithetical to marxist ideas about the historical context in which ideal phenomena, values, and principles are produced. Thus, where a case for socialist law and rights is made, it tends to be couched in terms diametrically opposed to natural law, such as those of legal positivism. Positivists maintain that the source of law lies in the particular institutional facts of the society in question. A classic example is the pro-law argument of the Austro-Marxist Karl Renner (1870–1950), the target of much of Pashukanis's early writings. For Renner, legal rules themselves are resistant to change, but the norms which these rules serve are capable of considerable development; with such a view, socialist deployment of capitalist law is possible precisely because of the formal nature of legality.

On the other hand, a positivist position that denies law any necessary normative content conflicts with the ideas of those socialists who urge a reappraisal of the classical marxist conception of law because legal institutions possess some intrinsic measure of justice. On this view, law ought to be defined with some reference to fairness, in which case stalinist law was not really law (recalling the debates over the legality of Nazi law). It is significant in this regard that recent interest in socialist law was sparked by the controversial claim of E.P. Thompson (1924–1993) that the rule of law is an "unqualified human good."

Notwithstanding the appeal of some kind of normative conception of law, it is likely to remain counter to socialist philosophy to prescribe the existence conditions for law in any detailed or substantive sense. The marxist insistence that socialism will evolve according to the social conditions in which it emerges is equally applicable to socialist legality. The idea of the rule of law, though, suggests that criteria, which are morally significant and yet formal and dynamic enough to allow for historical change, can be specified for the existence of law. Nevertheless, the rule of law is hardly a popular idea on the Left: first, because of the (erroneous) use of the term by authoritarian conservatives to refer to law and order; and second, and more important, the quasi-anarchist leanings of many marxists, which prompts them to reject "legalism" as an obstacle to more direct, spontaneous, and fraternal social relations. In a society where there is much greater scope for the public domain, the advantages of requiring of law that it be prospective, clear, general, consistent, and nonarbitrary would seem to far outweigh the loss of intimacy that a lawless society might promise.

Individual rights have always been the centerpiece of liberal legal and political theory and, as such, have aroused the suspicion of many a socialist. Rights are typically impugned on two grounds: first, for their roots in the idealist arguments of natural law, antithetical, as we have seen, to historical materialism; and second, for their excessive individualism, considered divisive in a society seeking solidarity and community. One way of countering the first criticism is to make an explicitly positivist argument for socialist rights. Tom Campbell (1938–), for example, maintains that the only rights a socialist theory can recognize are those instantiated in positive law. Yet it is worth recalling that the Left, broadly speaking, has in fact made use of natural rights arguments, be it in international campaigns for human rights under right-wing dictatorships, or in the west, in demands for social rights to health care or collective bargaining rights for trade unions. The idea that we have rights to fundamental freedoms or the satisfaction of basic needs, whether or not they are instantiated in positive law, is a powerful source of social criticism. It may be possible to conceive of individuals as the bearers of, not natural rights derived from a presocial state of nature, but human rights that reflect our evolving conception of human dignity.

That rights promote egoism is a less abstract and more obvious criticism, common not just to socialists, but to many conservatives as well. It is difficult to deny the charge that individual rights involve individuals making claims against each other and against society, although Campbell's argument for socialist rights as the rights of altruists seeks to avoid such a scenario. However, if we consider the myriad of legitimate, indeed valuable, individual interests to which rights might refer, then the view that rights serve selfish interests seems an oversimplification. Socialist rights could after all be individualistic without invoking Thomas Hobbes' conceptions of human nature as inherently antisocial.

The fate of the bolshevik project is difficult to evade in contemporary discussions of socialism. The Soviets' policy of legal nihilism spawned not just authoritarian politics, but ultimately a deep-seated hostility to the socialist ideal, which persists even after the authoritarian framework has been dismantled. However, the end of the Soviet chapter on socialist law may enable a more constructive approach. Law's role in rendering social life more predictable and fair, as well as assuring the individual a sphere of privacy and respect, are important ideals for socialists and nonsocialists alike. At the same time, law's capacity in a capitalist society to deliver on this emancipatory promise is severely restricted by unequal access to legal representation, the conservative proclivities of the judiciary, and structural constraints on egalitarian legislation. Irrespective of the viability of socialism itself, there is much to be learned from socialist critiques of capitalist law. Moreover, the morasses of traditional jurisprudence on such questions as the source of law, natural rights, or the import of the rule of law, also suggest the need for rejuvenation. Marxist theory's unique conception of social institutions as the product of human activity, which is at once materially instantiated, historically evolving, and purposeful and normative, might prove an important source for jurisprudential innovation, from which not just socialists might benefit.

References

Buchanan, Allen E. *Marx and Justice: The Radical Critique of Liberalism.* London: Methuen, 1982.

Campbell, Tom. *The Left and Rights: A Conceptual Analysis of the Idea of Socialist Rights.* London: Routledge and Kegan Paul, 1983.

Collins, Hugh. *Marxism and Law.* Oxford: Clarendon Press, 1982.

Marx, Karl. "On the Jewish Question" and "The Critique of the Gotha Programme." In *The Marx-Engels Reader,* ed. Robert Tucker. New York: Norton, 1978.

Pashukanis, Evgeny. *Selected Writings on Marxism and Law.* Ed. P. Beirne and R. Sharlet. London: Academic Press, 1970.

Renner, Karl. *The Institutions of Private Law and Their Social Functions.* Ed. O. Kahn Freund. Trans. Agnes Schwarzchild. London: Routledge and Kegan Paul, 1976.

Sypnowich, Christine. *The Concept of Socialist Law.* Oxford: Clarendon Press, 1990.

Thompson, E.P. *Whigs and Hunters: The Origins of the Black Act.* New York: Pantheon, 1975.

Christine Sypnowich

See also Marx, Karl; Marxist Philosophy of Law; Radical Class, Gender, and Race Theories: Positionality

Sociological Jurisprudence

The concept of sociological jurisprudence refers to a legal science discipline which examines law in the light of knowledge derived from disciplines other than law, in particular from the social sciences. This concept emerges with the growing momentum of antimetaphysical thought, beginning, as far as distinct legal theory is concerned, with the historicizing concepts of, among others, Friedrich Carl von Savigny (1779–1861). It finds its distinctive form in Europe, and in North America at the turn of the nineteenth and at the beginning of the twentieth century, and it fades into insignificance under pressure from a further differentiation of scientific approaches to law. Such pressures come, above all, from a theoretically and methodologically more elaborate sociology of law, as reflected in law and society theory, as well as in sociolegal research and research organizations beginning in the early 1960s, and from more politically motivated theory concepts of law provided, in North America, by the critical legal studies and feminist jurisprudence movements in the late 1960s and throughout the 1970s, and, in Europe, by postmarxist concepts of theories of communicative actions and structuralist discourse theories. However, the major tenet of sociological jurisprudence, that is, the need of a specialist sociological knowledge for lawyers, is generally accepted and responded to in all modern legal systems today.

The establishment of sociological jurisprudence as a special legal discipline reflects historically the digression of legal thought from exclusively normative concepts founded on customs, beliefs, and moral practice, and an opening of methodological approaches in order to arrive at a more empirically and pragmatically based conceptualization of the functions, effects, and outcomes of law and legal operations. Typically, Friedrich Carl von Savigny and G.W.F. Hegel (1770–1831) move the concept of legal dynamics away from the understanding of law as being part, or even the center, of an eternal, divine, and ultimately immutable order and toward an observation of the historical process of social change expressed in law. However, the resulting concepts of law only substitute assumed divine order by assumed historical order, now expressed as the "spirit of the people" or "the spirit of history," respectively. Karl Marx (1818–1883), disciple of both Savigny and Hegel, and wedded to their historicist theorizing, takes their antimetaphysical positions radically further to a fully developed materialist concept of social process. This concept locates the motor of social dynamics in human practice itself, namely, the relations between classes as defined by the economic power which they can exert. Importantly, such an understanding of social process attributes to law only a marginal, superstructural position of state law, which is doomed to, ultimately, "whither away." While sociological jurisprudence, as a discipline of lawyers for lawyers, insists, in its further development and against Marx, on a legal inward-looking focus on legal practice, rather than on human practice as a whole, it never falls back behind Marx on two essential counts. First, law is seen as a special form of human practice. Second, the explanation for and the understanding of legal operations are seen to be found not in law but only in the observation of human practice.

The concept of the "purpose of law" (*Zweck im Recht*) of Rudolf von Jhering (1818–1892) reflects this move of lawyers to accept the materialist position in order to arrive at a new assessment of the causes of legal operations while not questioning the traditional framework of law as a whole. However, his observations of how legal operations are dominated by mainly economic interests and how interests reveal in their conflictive containment by legal procedure the essence of law as a "struggle for law" (*Kampf ums Recht*) open the way to new methodological perspectives on legal theory and legal practice. His "jurisprudence of interests (*Interessenjurisprudenz*)", based on observation and analysis of legal events conducted by rational reasoning, challenges the dominant "jurisprudence of legal concepts" (*Begriffsjurisprudenz*), based on doctrinal analysis conducted by legal reasoning, prepares the ground for sociological jurisprudence in a highly influential manner. Similarly, Leon Petrazycki (1867–1931), sharing with Jhering the recognition of the reflection of economic structures in, predominantly, private law as the centerpiece of legal dynamics, contributes to the growing body of multidisciplinary jurisprudential approaches to law. Based on the impressive research record of contemporary, clinical psychology as a prototypical "exact" science, he introduces two essentially new concepts to jurisprudential thought. First, he stresses the importance of psychological processes within individuals that have been virtually ignored by legal doctrine. Second, he attempts, influenced by the research of Gabriel Tarde (1843–1904), to relate individual psychological events to collective behavior. Through his work, he gives law and legal operations a wider, as yet unconceptualized meaning, notably in the overlapping areas of legal norms, moral norms, and individual norms of consciousness and conscience. In a famous distinction, he arrives at the construct of an oppositional pair, which begins its incisive historical journey through sociological jurisprudence here. Petrazycki contrasts the "unofficial law," constituted by what individuals actually do, guided by a complex web of normative orientations, with the "official law," constituted by what legal officials think is achieved by law and legal operations. This concept of the nature, at least dual, of legal structure, which only as a whole accounts for the functioning of law and which cannot be decreed by legal officials on notions of legal doctrine alone, is the launching pad for a pragmatic, sociotechnical concept of sociological jurisprudence as a legal discipline. It forms the bridge between a European theoretical and academic jurisprudential approach, which concentrates, following the philosophical tradition of European-Continental law, on legislation and legal systemic development, and a North American pragmatic approach through legal practice, which concentrates, following the pragmatic tradition of common law, on judicial lawmaking and court actions. To a degree, this sociotechnical concept of sociological jurisprudence also softens the stereotypically perceived distinctions between European-Continental law and common law.

Eugen Ehrlich (1862–1922) is the foremost representative, and through his contributions in many respects the prototypical one, of a mature sociological jurisprudence. He consolidates the methodological opening of sociological jurisprudence by calling for a systematic sociology of law (1913, for the first time by this name), based on empirical research in the faculties of law under the guidance of established chairs in sociology of law and economics, and leads the way with his own research and a seminal monograph. Here, the oppositional pair of constructs on the nature of law are elaborated to confront a concept of "living law" (*lebendes Recht*) with the concept of an official law made up by the operations of legal professionals and state officials. In one of the most famous forewords in sociological jurisprudence literature, Ehrlich summarizes programmatically the tenet of his monograph, and of sociological jurisprudence, as the endeavor to demonstrate that "today as at all times" the center of gravity of law is not to be found in law itself but in society. Ehrlich avoids all psychological references in his theoretical concepts while keeping to the individualist notions of private law, and especially Roman law, as the empirical ground for his observations, which he promotes in both ethnographic and comparative approaches. While these are limited by the contemporary levels of development of social science theory and methodology, he projects a workable program of legal education that turns lawyers into methodologically conscious, sociological observers rather than doctrinal automats. However, Ehrlich's suggestions of an independent, critical, and observational role of lawyers, and especially of judges, deviate considerably from accepted contemporary European concepts of hierarchically ordered and statute-oriented legal decision making. This led to a general rejection of his concept of a pragmatic, critical, and science-based "free finding of law" (*Freirechtschule*), and with it of sociological jurisprudence in Europe, while finding more enthusiastic support in North America, especially through promotion by Roscoe Pound. However, similar programs of a "free" methodological opening of jurisprudence, as propagated by Ehrlich, were also developed in France, inspired by the momentous research of the sociologist Emile Durkheim (1858–1917). Here it is especially François Gény, who proposes a jurisprudence founded on "science and technology" that should integrate jurisprudential approaches to the recognition of physical, psychological, moral, economic, and political conditions of the operation of law in order to promote a rational development of positive law. While Gény's rationalist approach lacks a thorough sociological grounding, such a sociological positivist position is developed much more strongly by Léon Duguit, following Durkheim in accepting only an empirically grounded, observable reality for legal theory-building. This requires the exploration and development of methods that are not provided by doctrinal jurisprudence.

The jurisprudential tradition of common law lacks the strong accent on public law, which feeds into the development of concepts of a "better" lawmaking in European sociological jurisprudence, which is methodologically more open and more conscious. In contrast, common law jurisprudents utilize the strong pragmatist traditions of common law jurisprudence for a methodological opening, especially in the United States, with the seminal work of the members of the "Metaphysical Club," notably William James (1842–1910), Charles Sanders Peirce (1839–1914), and not least Oliver Wendell Holmes (1841–1935). Here it is above all Roscoe Pound (1870–1964), who also coins the term "sociological jurisprudence" for the new legal discipline and who integrates the common law pragmatist and European sociological traditions to form a coherent and definitive program of interdisciplinary research and legal theory as a basis for a projected "social engineering" through law. Pound's oppositional pair of constructs, namely, the "law in the books" versus the "law in action," decisively reformulates the structural notion of a dual (both overt and latent) nature of law, inherent in Ehrlich's concept of a "living law" and Petrazycki's concept of an "unofficial law," shifting the focus to a notion of only two sides of legal practice. In this practical sociotechnical, more jurisprudential than sociological reformulation, sociological jurisprudence and its inquiry into the working of law as a social instrument make their appearance in the teaching in law schools and to a lesser extent within legal argument in the common law world. The encyclopedic work of Julius Stone develops this instrumental aspect of sociological jurisprudence further and represents both the high-water mark and the end of the discipline of sociological jurisprudence in the meaning given to it by Pound. Stone observes clearly the tensions to which sociological jurisprudence is exposed in view of an unprecedented differentiation of methodologies and theoretical approaches to legal theory in the 1960s, when he notes approvingly "the tendency for Sociological Jurisprudence to take a wider and more theoretical view of its subject-matter than it did in its pioneering decades from the turn of the century." However, he also insists "that Sociological Jurisprudence should also strive to maintain its earlier courage and vigour in tackling numerous pockets of obvious conflict, distress, confusion and injustice which are thrown up constantly and urgently for practical handling."

Sociological jurisprudence today has finally succumbed to these tensions between, on one hand, a pragmatically and instrumentally conceived positivist understanding of law, which pits empirical research and practical solutions against social theory, and, on the other hand, the demands for methodological rigor and theoretical consistency exerted by the modern social sciences in view of a higher sensitivity for and a radical criticism of the ways in which a reliable knowledge base for the "working of law as a social instrument" can be ascertained. Here, a future for sociological jurisprudence, as a special legal science discipline of lawyers for lawyers, is only assured if, as is happening, the narrow confines of pragmatic, positivist concepts of the working of law in society are left behind, and lawyers are provided with the full scope of social theory and available research methodologies for the inquiry into societies and their laws.

References

Cotterrell, Roger. *The Sociology of Law*. London: Butterworth, 1984.

Ehrlich, Eugen. *Grundlegung der Soziologie des Rechts*. München/Leipzig, 1913. Engl. transl. as *Fundamental Principles of the Sociology of Law*. Intro. Roscoe Pound. Cambridge MA: Harvard University Press, 1936.

Petrazycki, Leon. *Teorija prava i gosudarstva*. St. Petersburg, 1909.

Pound, Roscoe. *Social Control Through Law*. New Haven: Yale University Press, 1942.

Stone, Julius. *Social Dimensions of Law and Justice*. Sydney: Maitland Publications, 1966.

Ziegert, Klaus A. "The Sociology behind Eugen Ehrlich's Sociology of Law." *International Journal of the Sociology of Law* 7 (1979), 27–73.

Klaus A. Ziegert

See also SOCIAL PHILOSOPHY; SOCIOLOGY OF LAW

Sociology of Law

In the 1960s, when the sociology of law was just conceived, Philip Selznick stated that the development of this branch of sociology could be divided into three periods: (1) discussions on main problems and issues, (2) development of empirical studies, and (3) attempts to formulate theories.

Basic Problems

The main ideas of sociology of law were articulated by Emile Durkheim (1858–1917), Max Weber (1864–1920), and Leon Petrazycki (1867–1931).

According to Durkheim, the main function of law (and morality) is to integrate society into a consistent body governed by the fundamental moral values. Law, according to him, is a phenomenon generated by society (perceived as something coming from above), which has the force to incline people to conform to the basic values of this society. Integration of society can be achieved in an "organic" way (when various elements of the society are "naturally" interrelated) or in a "mechanic" way (when various elements of the society are interrelated in an impersonal manner). Such pathological phenomena as crime, suicide, and divorce not only accentuate the fundamental norms of the society, but also serve as occurrences integrating society even more closely.

Max Weber regards law as one of the most important elements of social life that is able to structure and rationalize complicated processes that develop inside society. Various types of domination (traditional, charismatic, and legal-rational) mold social life in different ways, constantly pushing it toward more and more organizationally and institutionally elaborated forms. According to Weber, social and economic life is influenced by values not so much of an economic character, but mainly of an ethical and religious nature, including legal constructions. In fact, law generates bureaucracies, complicated structures that are built according to impersonal canons and solve the problems submitted to them impartially.

Leon Petrazycki, the unrecognized father of sociology of law, entered the field of legal policy at the end of the nineteenth century with a sharp critique of a new version of the German civil code. He showed convincingly that the institutions of Roman law had accumulated more wisdom of an unconscious type in their historical development, than specialists of civil law had been able to manifest. He regarded law as a phenomenon (officially conceived or habitually existing), which is formatted by mutuality of duties and claims. This phenomenon (1) motivates people to behave in a conformist way, (2) distributes goods and services according to predesigned patterns, and (3) forms people's behavior into organizational and institutional units. Through the "ingenious process of continuous adaptation," law tends to develop new forms of coordinated behavior that is eufunctional for individuals, social groups, and whole societies. Under various external or internal pressures, law may undergo regressive processes, if this law is used for the benefit of those who possess uncontrolled power (totalitarian law).

Empirical Research

After 1945 an enormous number of empirical studies started to penetrate various areas of social life. A group of scholars, mainly Scandinavian and Polish, with chairman Berl Kutchinsky, studied relations between "Knowledge, Opinions, Law." They found that these matters have to be studied on three levels (external declarations, motivations by accepted values, and actual behavior), and that law (with the exception of procedural norms) is generally well known (since usually legal norms coincide with the moral norms on which they are designed). Simultaneously, many investigations concerning *lege ferenda* (law giving) questions and unanticipated consequences of *lege lata* (law interpretation) have been studied empirically. Some of them are presented, as illustrations, in pell-mell fashion: private litigation (Galanter), punitiveness of legal systems (Jasinski), noncontractual relations in business (Stewart Macaulay), forms of mediation (Kawashima), conflict resolution (Vilhelm Aubert), judges' behavior (Fisher, Fairbanks), Watergate and legal order (Bickel), limits of law's effectiveness and types of deviance (Chambliss), average people's response to law, including "workers' courts" (Adam Podgórecki), legal and antilegal attitudes, and invisible factors (Podgórecki), class justice (Carlin, Howard), confidence game (Blumberg), economic legislation (Ball, Lawrence Friedman), "justice without trial" (Skolnick), divorce (Górecki) and attitudes toward divorce (Podgórecki), obedience to authority (Milgram), legal professions (Lewis, Haliday), legal attitudes of the whole population (Podgórecki, Los, Kurczewski, Kwasniewski), "does punishment deter crime?" (Tullock), law as an instrument of revolutionary change (Massell), jury system (Zeisel, Kalven), "society of captives" (Sykes), speeding and drinking (Campbell, Klette, Ross), legal evolution (Schwartz, Miller), "second life or hidden life" (Podgórecki), legal subcultures (Aubert, Schwartz), "second economy" (Los), public opinion and law (Kutchinski, Podgórecki), legal attitudes of recidivists (Kojder), social systems and legal systems (Podgórecki, Whelan, Khosla), death penalty and attitudes toward it (Bedau), lobbying (Ablard, Ehrlich), law versus social control (Kwasniewski), legal culture (Friedman, Chiba), ombudsman (Gellhorn), abolitionism (Hulsman), nomenclature (Zybertowicz), judges' trade unions (Renato Treves), law as an instrument of social macro changes (Massell), sentencing (Walker), informal legal order in queues (Kurczewski), "wetbacks" (Bustamante), totalitarian and posttotalitarian law (Podgórecki and Olgiatti).

Additionally it should be mentioned that Vincenzo Ferrari in *Developing Sociology of Law* edited a 930-page collection of research studies from many countries which have recently been conducted in the sociology of law. The variety of topics and methods used to investigate these topics indicate that researches were conducted in a spontaneous way, without a preconceived plan. This situation shows that a theory (or theories) trying to unify these investigations is (are) missing. Those studies very rarely try to examine or reject the theoretical concepts as they have been developed by classic studies.

Theories

In contrast to the enormous amount of empirical studies, there exist but few theories which try to synthesize existing factual material. According to Donald Black, "[L]aw is governmental social control," and "[L]aw is a quantitative variable." The quantity of law is indicated by the number and extent of prohibitions and obligations, and by the rate of legislation, litigation, and adjudication. The behavior of law can be observed and measured in the following areas: stratification, morphology, culture, organization, social control, and anarchy (communal and situational). The weak points of Black's very influential synthesis are that (1) although he understands law as governmental social control and excludes living law from this category, he still tests his propositions by references to anthropological data. As well, (2) he never operationalizes more closely the concept of "quantity of law." Does he understand by quantity the amount of rules, behaviorally accountable actions, amount of civil officers involved, institutions implicated, financial gravity of cases, or court level of trial? (3) Where in his theory is the humanistic element so needed in a society governed by reified patterns of behavior and impersonal institutions?

Niklas Luhmann stresses the role of expectations as the most important task of the law. Through expectations, law transmits the system of norms and roles into the fabric of society; expectations confirm predictability, reaffirm mutuality, support consistency of law with established norms, with interactions with other citizens, and with authorities; they also imply guarantees against coercive activities of state. Law is a system which has, in social life, a unique potential for autopoesis, that is, the ability to self-perpetuate (a concept introduced into jurisprudence by Hungarian jurist Barna Horvath). Since Luhmann does not try to confront his own thinking with social reality, his abstract synthesis makes it difficult to relate the generalizations to the existing empirical data.

Criticizing the emptiness of jurisprudence, Adam Podgórecki replaces it by empirically oriented sociology of law. Law operates through three basic cultures: that of whole society, that of the appropriate subculture, and through the psyche of an individual. Findings of sociology of law should provide the ground for legal policy (an essential branch of social engineering). Following ideas of Petrazycki, he understands law as interhuman schemes which provide mutually integrated relations inside the social system. Law is neutral; it may be used to integrate moral environments, but it could also serve tyrants. The order of a sovereign (quite often understood as law itself, as by John Austin) is nothing else but a subsidiary norm helping to strengthen the basic norm of duties and claims valid among parties.

Organization

Sociology of law was first established organizationally as the Polish Section of Sociology of Law in 1962 by Adam Podgórecki; also in 1962, a Research Committee of Sociology of Law of the International Sociological Association was founded by William M. Evan and Adam Podgórecki. The American Law and Society Association was installed in 1964. The activities of the Research Committee, with Renato Treves as its first president, stimulated the development of sociology of law in several European countries. The American, Italian, Polish, and Scandinavian centers are the most developed and have influenced many European and American universities.

References

Aubert, Vilhelm, ed. *Sociology of Law*. Harmondsworth: Penguin, 1969.

Bendix, Reinhard. *Max Weber*. Berkeley: University of California Press, 1977.

Black, Donald. *The Behavior of Law*. New York: Academic Press, 1976.

Evan, William, M., ed. *Law and Sociology: Exploratory Essays*. New York: Free Press, 1962.

Ferrari, Vincenzo, ed. *Developing Sociology of Law*. Milan: Giuffrè, 1990.

Friedman, Lawrence, and Stewart Macaulay. *Law and the Behavioral Sciences*. Indianapolis: Bobbs-Merrill, 1969.

Górecki, Jan, ed. *Sociology and Jurisprudence of Leon Petrazycki*. Urbana: Illinois University Press, 1975.

Luhmann, Niklas. *Theory of Sociology of Law*. London: Routledge and Kegan Paul, 1985.

Lukes, Steven. *Emile Durkheim*. London: Penguin, 1974.

Podgórecki, Adam. *A Sociological Theory of Law*. Milan: Giuffrè, 1991.

Rokumoto, Kahei. *Sociological Theories of Law*. Aldershot: Dartmouth, 1994.

Trevino, A. Javier. *The Sociology of Law*. New York: St. Martin's Press, 1996.

Adam Podgórecki

See also ECONOMICS; ECONOMICS AND LAW; SOCIOLOGICAL JURISPRUDENCE

Sodomy

The word "sodomy" derives from "Sodom," the name of the ancient city allegedly destroyed by God for its wickedness (Genesis 18–19; but see John Boswell and Richard Posner). In its broadest and vaguest sense, "sodomy" means unnatural sexual intercourse, according to the *Oxford English Dictionary*. As a crime, sodomy has medieval roots. The English jurist William Blackstone characterized sodomy in his *Commentaries on the Laws of England* as "the infamous crime against nature." The state of Mississippi still prohibits "the detestable and abominable crime against nature." Sodomy encompasses whatever sex acts are taken to be unnatural, which has varied widely by time and place even within western culture.

For example, if "natural" means *intraspecific* intercourse (that is, intercourse involving two or more human beings), then any intercourse between a human being and an animal (usually known as "bestiality") constitutes sodomy. If "natural" means *human heterosexual* intercourse, then sodomy includes homosexual intercourse of any kind as well as bestiality, according to *Webster's Third New International Dictionary*. If "natural" means *human procreative* intercourse (intercourse that either can produce or is intended to produce offspring), then sodomy includes both of the above as well as heterosexual fellatio, cunnilingus, and buggery (that is, oral and anal intercourse) (*Black's Law Dictionary*). Sometimes the word "sodomy" is used to refer only to *male homosexual* intercourse (fellatio and buggery), as noted in the *Oxford American Dictionary,* and even more narrowly to homosexual buggery. "Sodomy" has been used in all of these ways both in and out of the law; there is no canonical or univocal meaning.

The main philosophical issue concerning sodomy, besides clarification of the concept, is the justification (if any) of laws prohibiting and punishing the act. What follows refers only to consensual adult sodomy. Forcible or nonconsensual sodomy, or sodomy involving minors or other incompetents, is, like rape, widely held to be legitimately punishable on harm-prevention grounds, as is discussed by Richard Mohr. As of 1993, twenty-five states and the District of Columbia made sodomy (in one or more of its guises) a criminal offense. The question is whether the state, using the mechanism of the criminal law, may, consistently with morality, prohibit and punish private, consensual acts of oral or anal intercourse, whether heterosexual or homosexual.

The conservative argues that sodomy is morally wrong, that the inherent wrongness of an activity constitutes a sufficient reason to prohibit and punish it, and that sodomy may, therefore, be criminalized. An alternative conservative argument relies on the offensiveness or disgust allegedly felt by the majority of citizens toward acts of sodomy. The liberal rejects the conservative's normative principles, claiming that only harm or serious, *unavoidable* offense to others constitutes a reason to limit individual liberty through the mechanism of the criminal law. Since private, consensual sodomy neither harms nor seriously offends, it ought to be noncriminal. This is true even if one believes that sodomy is morally wrong (of course, not all liberals believe that it is). The liberal, qua liberal, draws a distinction between what is morally wrong (or thought to be morally wrong) and what may be prohibited and punished by law. These classes are logically disjoint.

The liberal position is reflected in England by the *Wolfenden Report* and in the United States by the *Model Penal Code,* both of which recommend the decriminalization of sodomy (which the latter denominates "deviate sexual intercourse" and defines as "sexual intercourse per os or per anum between human beings who are not husband and wife, and any form of sexual intercourse with an animal"). The *Model Penal Code* has significantly influenced state law in this as in other areas. Neither document, however, advocates the decriminalization of lewdness, public displays of homosexual affection, public indecency, solicitation of another for homosexual acts, or loitering for purposes of solicitation. The public-private dichotomy presupposed by both conservatives and liberals has recently been criticized by radicals, for example, Larry Backer, as an unjust suppression of "sexual nonconformity." These critics argue that the criminal law is being used to marginalize, stigmatize, oppress, and ultimately scapegoat those who engage in nonstandard sexual practices. A veneer of tolerance is said to hide an attitude of disgust and intolerance.

In jurisdictions where sodomy remains a criminal offense, various constitutional challenges have been mounted. In 1986 the United States Supreme Court ruled (in the case of *Bowers v. Hardwick,* 478 U.S. 186) that the Georgia antisodomy statute (which prohibits "perform[ing] or submit[ting] to any sexual act involving the sex organs of one person and the mouth or anus of another") does not violate the United States Constitution. The case involved two adult men who engaged in private, consensual fellatio. The Court's reasoning in *Bowers,* while celebrated by conservatives, has been widely criticized by both liberals and radicals.

The criticism of *Bowers* takes different forms. One objection is that the Court misframed the issue by asking whether there is a fundamental constitutional right to engage in homosexual sodomy, rather than whether there is a fundamental right to *privacy* that includes or entails a right to engage in private, consensual sex acts. Another is that the Court ignored or misinterpreted its own line of privacy precedent. A third is that the Court improperly assimilated consensual sodomy to crimes such as adultery and incest (which, unlike consensual sodomy, harm others). Finally, it has been argued that the Court relied on an unexamined and indefensible doctrine of legal moralism according to which the inherent immorality of a line of conduct (or the widespread *belief* that a line of conduct is inherently immoral) constitutes a reason for its criminalization.

Granted the constitutionality of statutes that criminalize sodomy, the range of punishment prescribed for the offense has been challenged as cruel and unusual, and therefore, under the Eighth Amendment of the United States Constitution, unconstitutional. Georgia's antisodomy statute, for example, allows a prison sentence of up to twenty years for a single offense. Justice Lewis F. Powell, concurring in the judgment in *Bowers,* suggested in dicta that a more promising line of argument (which, curiously, was not advanced on appeal, perhaps for strategic reasons) would focus on the Eighth Amendment. This argument is likely to be made in future cases in both state and federal courts.

Other philosophical issues raised by sodomy include (1) whether, for constitutional purposes, a distinction may be drawn between homosexual and heterosexual sodomy (some states, such as Texas, prohibit only homosexual sodomy; others, such as Georgia, nominally cover both homosexual and heterosexual sodomy); (2) whether it is morally permissible for unenforced antisodomy statutes to remain on the books, given that such laws can be selectively enforced by zealous police officers and prosecutors and are in fact used to impose civil disabilities (for example, disqualification for employment as a police officer or teacher) on those who are known to violate (or suspected of violating) them, and given that these statutes stigmatize and insult otherwise law-abiding citizens; and (3) whether laws designed to halt the spread of diseases, such as acquired immune deficiency syndrome (AIDS), but which have a disparate impact on homosexuals, are justified. Some of these issues stem from the vagueness and ambiguity of the term "sodomy." To avoid confusion and equivocation, one must specify its meaning before employing it in argument.

References

American Law Institute. *Model Penal Code and Commentaries.* Philadelphia: American Law Institute Press, 1985.

Backer, Larry Catá. "Exposing the Perversions of Toleration: The Decriminalization of Private Sexual Conduct, the Model Penal Code, and the Oxymoron of Liberal Toleration." *Florida Law Review* 45 (December 1993), 755–802.

Boswell, John. *Christianity, Social Tolerance, and Homosexuality: Gay People in Western Europe from the Beginning of the Christian Era to the Fourteenth Century.* Chicago: University of Chicago Press, 1980.

DeCew, Judith Wagner. "Constitutional Privacy, Judicial Interpretation, and *Bowers v. Hardwick.*" *Social Theory and Practice* 15 (Fall 1989), 285–303.

Devlin, Patrick. *The Enforcement of Morals.* London: Oxford University Press, 1965.

Dworkin, Ronald. *Taking Rights Seriously.* Cambridge: Harvard University Press, 1978.

Feinberg, Joel. *The Moral Limits of the Criminal Law.* 4 vols. New York: Oxford University Press, 1984–1988.

Goldstein, Anne B. "History, Homosexuality, and Political Values: Searching for the Hidden Determinants of *Bowers v. Hardwick.*" *Yale Law Journal* 97 (May 1988), 1073–1103.

Hart, H.L.A. *Law, Liberty, and Morality.* Stanford: Stanford University Press, 1963.

Mohr, Richard D. *Gays/Justice: A Study of Ethics, Society, and Law.* New York: Columbia University Press, 1988.

Posner, Richard A. *Sex and Reason.* Cambridge: Harvard University Press, 1992.

Keith Burgess-Jackson

See also CRIMINALIZATION; DRUGS; PATERNALISM; PROSTITUTION

Southern European Philosophy of Law

In southern Europe during recent decades, the philosophy of law has developed significantly in Italy and in Spain. These two countries are closely related in terms of language and in their social, economic, cultural, and political conditions; this is easy to see in both countries, from the profound influence exercised by the Catholic church to the prevalence of totalitarian political governments through much of this century. Courses in philosophy of law carry great weight in legal education, which runs quite aloof from legal practice. Numerous journals devoted to the discipline are published (*Rivista internazionale di filosofia del diritto*; *Ratio Juris*; *Analisi e diritto*; *Ars interpretandi*; *Anuario de Filosofía del Derecho*; *Anales de la Cátedra F. Suárez*; *Doxa*; *Derechos y libertades*). Publication of monographs in legal philosophy is plentiful, if uneven in quality, of course. These cover all the areas and theoretical orientations that can be identified: theory of law in the strict sense (theory of norms, of legal order, of interpretation), normative ethics, deontic logic, legal reasoning, legal semiotics, legal hermeneutics, legal epistemology, marxism and law, law and economics, critical legal theory, philosophy of criminal law, foundations of human rights, history of jurisprudence, postmodern jurisprudence, and others.

In Italy, this development began in the years immediately following World War II and is due especially to the extraordinary work of Norberto Bobbio, without doubt one of the greatest legal (as well as social and political) philosophers in the twentieth century. In Spain, development had to await the end of the dictatorship in 1975, when a veritable explosion occurred in legal philosophy. Its ground was laid in the late 1960s, largely mediated by the influence of Italian scholars. Bobbio could be considered as a "common teacher."

The same could be said, on a lesser scale, of Renato Treves, the "father" of Italian sociology of law. Italian legal marxism of the late 1960s and the 1970s also found considerable response in Spain, particularly the so-called *uso alternativo del diritto* (another way in law), a movement of legal scholars and practitioners that bore some similarity to critical legal studies and experienced some success in several Latin American countries during the 1980s and 1990s. Finally, the most open conceptions of natural law, such as Guido Fassò's, were influential over some Spanish natural lawyers such as Pérez Luño, who were able to break with the neothomism dominant within the "official culture" of the Franco regime, and were able to start dealing not only with the "duties" but also with the "rights" of human persons.

In fields such as analytical philosophy, Italian and Spanish philosophers of law to a large extent form nowadays a joint intellectual community, which has much less to do with French work (surely due to the more restricted development of philosophy of law in France) and nothing to do with the Greek (easily explained by the linguistic differences, among other reasons) or the Portuguese (which may seem strange, especially with regard to Spain; but the cultural isolation between these two countries on the Iberian peninsula is not peculiar to this domain).

Neither Italian nor Spanish philosophy of law today can be reduced to the analytical school, of course; but it is this tendency which can be considered as dominant, although more from the qualitative than the quantitative point of view. In Italy, as mentioned, the "analytical turn" inaugurated by Bobbio in an article of 1950 represented a radical path in view of the traditional metaphysical-naturalist and idealistic-historicist orientations. (The neohegelians Benedetto Croce and Giovanni Gentile were the two most influential philosophers also in the philosophy of law during the years between the wars.) Two other prominent authorities in what came to be called "the Italian school of analytical philosophy and general theory of law" are Uberto Scarpelli *(Il problema della definizione e il concetto di diritto,* The Problem of Definition and the Concept of Law) and Giovanni Tarello (*Diritto, enunciati, usi. Studi di teoria e metateoria del diritto,* (Law, Words, and Practice: Studies in the Theory and Metatheory of Law). Scarpelli initiated the analytical philosophy of law known as "linguistic analysis," while Bobbio's works belong more to the stream of analytical positivism or "analytical jurisprudence." Tarello wrote important works on the history of legal culture and on the interpretation of law. Now deceased, both began as did Bobbio, from a neo-illuminist secular ideology that lay between liberal and socialist positions. They defended a conception of law which can be characterized as positivist, in the broad sense of being contrary to the several currents of natural law represented by such authors as Giorgio Del Vecchio, Giuseppe Capograssi, Pietro Piovani, Enrico Opocher, Sergio Cotta, Fassò, and Lombardi Vallauri. In ethical theory they took a frankly noncognitivist stance. However, their approaches to law were different: Scarpelli's was basically a normativist approach, while Tarello's was rather a realist one; legal realism is also represented in Italy by an author such as Enrico Pattaro, a student of Fassò and of Bobbio. The difference between their approaches, which was not really that large, remains present in two of the principal groups to which the school gave rise: one in Milan, represented by authors such as Mario Jori and Anna Pintore (*Manuale di teoria generale del diritto*, Manual of Legal Theory), and the other in Genoa, to which belong Riccardo Guastini (*Dalle fonti alle norme*, Sources of Norms), Paolo Comanducci, and Tecla Mazzarese.

The "Bobbio school" is not exhausted with these, however. Others who also should be noted have operated basically in the field of deontic logic and, particularly, in the development of the theory of constitutive rules, such as Amedeo Conte and Gaetano Carcaterra. Still others have focused more on the study of legal argumentation, as has Letizia Gianformaggio. Mario Losano has done wide-ranging work and was a real pioneer in legal computer science in his country. Luigi Ferrajoli has recently published a *magnum opus*, titled *Diritto e ragione* (Law and Reason), in which he develops a complete theory of due process in criminal law (*garantismo penale*), which also involves a contribution of the first order in the field of legal epistemology, theory of law, and theory of justice.

In the case of Spain, the civil war (1936–1939) festered as a continuing trauma, not least from the cultural point of view. For a long time the philosophy of law remained dominated by natural law of a thomistic persuasion, in a clerical and profoundly antiliberal mold (nor was the Italian influence entirely absent here, either). One of the few exceptions was Luis Legaz y Lacambra, whose works represent a not so successful synthesis of Hans Kelsen's normativism (whose first translator into Spanish he was), Georges Gurvitch's sociology, and Catholic natural law (which became the dominant influence over the others). Another exception was Luis Recaséns Siches, a student of José Ortega y Gasset, who was exiled to Mexico after the civil war, and became a kind of precursor to the "New Rhetoric" of Chaïm Perelman. Above all, Felipe González Vicén's works, few but rigorous, feature negatively a critical attitude in the face of natural law and legal formalism, and positively the adoption of legal historicism and positivism (see *Estudios de filosofía del Derecho*, Studies in the Philosophy of Law).

The renewal of Spanish legal philosophy that began at the end of the sixties looked especially to Elías Díaz and Juan Ramón Capella. The first published *Estado de Derecho y sociedad democrática* in 1966, which had a strong influence in laying out the principles of democratic socialism. He followed this with an effort to recover the liberal and progressive Spanish thought which had preceded the civil war, the so-called Krausist philosophy, and in 1971, with his *Sociología y filosofía del Derecho* (Sociology and Philosophy of Law), which percolated through new generations of Spanish legal philosophers the possibility of "getting up to date" in their discipline. (The influence of Bobbio and H.L.A. Hart on this work is discernible, but Elías Díaz never was an analytical philosopher.) The publication in 1968 of *El Derecho como lenguaje* (Law as Language) by Juan Ramón Capella came to stand for the birth of a Spanish school of analytical philosophy of law. Capella later moved away, however, from an analytic paradigm; his later works basically drew their inspiration from marxism and in many instances focused on oblique criticism of the representative democratic state (see *Materiales para la crítica de la filosofía del Estado*, Materials for the Criticism of the Philosophy of the State). In addition to this "internal influence," the Spanish school of analytic philosophy of law (which has seen a vast expansion during the most recent twenty years) benefited much from the "external influence" coming from the Argentine analytical school, from writers such as Genaro Carrió, Ernesto Garzón Valdés, Carlos Alchourrón, Eugenio Bulygin, Roberto Vernengo, and Carlos Nino. The works of Francisco Laporta ("Sobre el concepto de derechos humanos," On the Concept of Human Rights), Juan Carlos Bayón (*La normatividad del Derecho. Deber jurídico y razones para la acción*, The Normativity of Law: Legal Duty and Reasons for Action), and Manuel Atienza with Juan Ruiz Manero (*Las piezas del Derecho; Teoría de los enunciados jurídicos*, The Compartments of Law: Theory of Legal Statements) could be considered as representing a movement too heterogeneous to be called a "school," and whose principal centers are in the Universidad Autónoma de Madrid, the Universidad Pompeu Fabra de Barcelona, and the Universidad de Alicante.

Both Italian and Spanish philosophers of law, particularly those of an analytical persuasion, should reflect on the fact that, notwithstanding their having produced a large number of works at a high level of technical sophistication, they have still failed to influence significantly the legal cultures in their respective countries, which remain much more set in paleopositivism than in postpositivism.

References

Ballesteros, Jesus. "Notas sobre la alteridad del derecho en la filosofia juridica italiana actual" (Notes on Otherness in Law in Contemporary Italian Legal Philosophy). *Anales de la cátedra F. Suárez* 13 (1973), 181–195.

Barberis, Mauro. *Introduzione allo studio della filosofia del diritto (cap. VII)* (Introduction to the Study of the Philosophy of Law (Ch. 7)). Bologna: Mulino, 1993.

Frosini, Vittorio. "Il dualismo tra diritto e società nell'Italia contemporanea" (The Dualism of Law and Society in Italy Today). *Rivista internazionale di filosofia del diritto* 52 (1975), 85–95.

Gil Cremades, Juan José. "Filosofía del Derecho en España" (Philosophy of Law in Spain). *Anales de la cátedra F. Suárez* 25 (1985), 225–243.

Maresca, Mariano. "Aportacion a una bibliografia del Krausismo espanol" (Contribution to a Bibliography of Spanish Krausismo). *Anales de la cátedra F. Suaréz* 11 (1971), 281–336.

Nicolacopoulos, Pantelis. "Law and Economics." In *Greek Studies in the Philosophy and History of Science,* ed. Petros Gemtos. Dordrecht: Kluwer, 1990.

Olivecrona, Karl. "On the Problem of Law and Force in Recent Literature." *Rivista internazionale di filosofia del diritto* 53 (1976), 548–552.

Saavedra, Modesto. "Bibliografia de la filosofia del derecho en España (1961–1971)" (Bibliography of the Philosophy of Law in Spain (1961–1971)). *Anales de la cátedra F. Suárez* 12 (1972), 161–200.

Sardina-Paramo, Juan Antonio. "Sobre la funcion de la filosofia del derecho en la realidad juridica espanola (1960–1974)" (On the Role of Legal Philosophy in Spanish Legal Reality). *Anales de la cátedra F. Suárez* 15 (1975), 429–445.

Scarpelli, Uberto. *Il problema della definizione e il concetto di diritto.* Milan: Nuvoletti, 1955.

Specht, Rainer. "Spanisches Naturrecht—Klassik und Gegenwart" (Spanish Natural Law—Classic and Present). *Zeitschrift für philosophisches Forschung* 41 (1987), 169–182.

Tarello, Giovanni. *Diritto, enunciati, usi. Studi di teoria e metateoria del diritto.* Bologna: Mulino, 1974.

Manuel Atienza

See also BOBBIO, NORBERTO; CENTRAL AND EASTERN EUROPEAN PHILOSOPHY OF LAW; NORTHERN EUROPEAN PHILOSOPHY OF LAW; WESTERN EUROPEAN LEGAL CULTURE IN THE TWENTIETH CENTURY

Sovereignty

Sovereignty is the term used to denote both the power and authority by which a state is governed. It is often thought of as the defining characteristic of a state. The individual or corporate entity wielding state power is called the "sovereign." Though the prerogatives attributed to sovereignty vary from theory to theory, positive law is always among them. Positive law is enacted by the sovereign and derives its moral authority and coercive force from sovereignty. Because sovereignty is synonymous with statehood on the world stage, it is a key element of international law. For these and other reasons sovereignty and the sovereign have been central to discussions in social and politicial philosophy, as well as philosophy of law and political science. The origin of sovereignty, its limits, and who should be sovereign are some of the key questions asked in all these disciplines.

Though the term "sovereignty" was not use until the 1300s, theories concerning state power have been around for some time. Popular sovereignty, now widely accepted, has its roots in classical Greece. Citizens often acted as sovereign in a popular assembly or delegated the power to a representative body. Plato accepted the notion of popular sovereignty within his overarching metaphysics, but specified a rigid selection and training process for those who held sovereign power. In Aristotle's state all the citizens would rule and be ruled in turn, but requirements for citizenship were extremely narrow. Natural law was generally thought to be the only limitation on sovereignty.

The Romans made liberal use of Greek traditions but were forced to change during the *Imperium.* Under the empire, *summa potestas* or supreme authority was derived from the citizens but was wielded by the emperor. The emperor had achieved hegemony among the citizens and thus held the sovereignty derived from them. In keeping with the natural law tradition, the emperor was supposed to work for the good of the citizens.

Medieval conceptions of sovereignty were formed by the ongoing power struggle between church and state. The spiritual and temporal realms were explicitly divided, with the church and monarch supreme in their respective domains. Sovereignty was derived from God. The church conveyed God's grant of temporal sovereignty to the monarch, giving the monarch authority to use his power. In return, the monarch recognized various church prerogatives. The church's ability to withdraw sovereign authority from the monarch gave the church a great deal of temporal power. The only recognized limit on sovereignty was the need to obey divine law.

Jean Bodin's model of the state was an idealized synthesis of the state structures existing at that time. Though sovereignty was "vested in a commonwealth," the prince was sovereign. Bodin specified a large number of limitations on sovereignty. Among other things, the sovereign must obey natural and divine law, keep oaths to other princes, keep covenants with subjects, and obey constitutional laws regarding the king's estate. Despite these limitations, Bodin repeatedly avowed the absolute supremacy of the sovereign, arguing that such limitations really did not affect the sovereign's power. These arguments hinged on the assumption that the limitation in question could be derived from natural law. It is to Bodin that we owe the clear equation of sovereignty and the state.

Thomas Hobbes derived sovereignty from the individual's submission to state authority. He believed that individuals submitted to state authority out of fear. People fear each other in the "state of nature" where the individual's freedoms are not constrained by state control; in a conquered state they fear the conqueror. In each case they submit to the will of some individual or group to reduce their fears. The individual or group submitted to becomes sovereign. Hobbes, like his predecessors, stressed the absolute nature of state power and authority. The sovereign was limited only by the need to maintain an appropriate balance of fear in which the subjects fear the sovereign's rule less than the alternatives.

Jean-Jacques Rousseau returned sovereign power to the citizenry, but unlike Aristotle he had a much more inclusive view of citizenship, requiring everyone in the state to participate. Sovereignty was derived from the people, who freely and unconditionally put themselves under the direction of the general will as part of a "social contract." The general will was the considered will of the people with respect to the common good. Though the people might submit to a sovereign to escape the depredations of Hobbes' state of nature or the fear of a conqueror, Rousseau argued that only a submission to the general will could truly work. Since submission to the general will was the best any person could hope for, it had absolute authority. There were no external limitations on the general will, since it was necessarily self-limiting. The people would never knowingly will anything contrary to their own good. Rousseau explicitly differentiated between the physical power and the moral authority of the sovereign. "Executive power" was the physical side of sovereignty delegated to the government, which was to act only as an agent of the sovereign. The people as sovereign were the moral authority, or "legislative power," under which the government acted.

Though sovereignty continued to be the subject of philosophical theories for decades after Rousseau, the word has almost disappeared from philosophy in recent years. This is because of the ambiguity of the term. Since "sovereignty" denotes both the moral authority by which states wield power and the power itself, any discussion using it is prone to confuse might and right. This crucial ambiguity arose for many reasons. The earliest theorists sometimes conflated power and authority. Later theorists were often more intent on description rather than prescription. The ambiguity has been propagated in part due to its usefulness in justifying otherwise questionable positions. Would-be sovereigns have cited their power over others as sovereignty and then cited their sovereignty to claim authority. Such abuses ensure the term's popularity in political discourse, necessitating its continued study by political scientists. It is in political science that we find the most philosophical examinations of sovereighty today.

Even without the troublesome ambiguity, study of sovereignty would have languished because of the tacit acceptance of popular sovereignty limited by human rights. The modern constitutional state assumes this framework and the modern theorist usually works within some version of it. This framework obviates the need to debate sovereignty per se, leaving only such questions as how to properly implement popular sovereignty and the nature and extent of the limitations imposed by human rights.

Recent developments ensure a renaissance of sovereignty theories or their cognates. New entities have been created, requiring new theories of sovereignty. The United Nations and the European Community are examples of organizations composed of "sovereign states," which may in fact or by agreement limit the sovereignty of their member states. Multinational corporations often have the power to influence or even dictate state policy; their very existence raises jurisdictional issues.

At the same time that new structures are arising, old ones are breaking down. The vague notion of popular sovereignty has been found lacking because of growing acceptance of multicultural views involving ideas like group rights. Racial, ethnic, and other groups are claiming a right to "self-determination," limiting state sovereignty over them, or are even asserting their own sovereignty. These groups usually justify such claims with reference to one or more of the following: past possession of sovereignty, commonality of interest within the group and its lack with other groups, distributive injustices, cultural preservation, and self-defense.

References

Bartelson, Jens. *A Genealogy of Sovereignty.* Cambridge: Press Syndicate of the University of Cambridge, 1995.

Hinsley, F.J. *Sovereignty*. New York: C.H. Watts, 1966. 2d ed. New York: Cambridge University Press, 1986.

Milward, Alan S. et al. *The Frontier of National Sovereignty: History and Theory, 1945–1992.* London: Routledge, 1993.

Morgan, Edmond Sears. *Inventing the People: The Rise of Popular Sovereignty in England and America.* New York: Norton, 1990.

Pennington, Kenneth. *The Prince and the Law, 1200–1600: Sovereignty and Rights in the Western Legal Tradition.* Berkeley: University of California Press, 1993.

Thurman Lee Hester, Jr.

See also AUTHORITY; CUSTOMARY LAW; STATE

Speech Acts

Speech acts, or performative utterances as they are sometimes called, were introduced by the late Oxford philosopher John Langshaw Austin in his famous essay, "Other Minds." Austin had noticed that there are certain sentences the uttering of which constitutes a certain kind of action. An example of such as sentence is "I now pronounce you husband and wife," said at the altar by a minister to a couple about to be married. Said in the first person, present tense, the very uttering of the sentence constitutes the act of marrying, an act that could hardly be performed (or performed as well) in any other way.

In calling our attention to performative utterances, Austin identified a class of sentences that are not, strictly speaking, true or false. They are, however, nonetheless meaningful. Influenced by logical positivism, ordinary language philosophers previously believed that only declarative sentences are cognitively meaningful; that is, statements whose purpose is to describe a state of affairs and which are either true or false. Performative utterances, by contrast, are neither true nor false since they are not statements at all. Their purpose, rather, is to perform an action. Compare the sentence "The pope is Polish" with the sentence "I'm sorry I missed our appointment." The first sentence, being declarative, is true if the pope is Polish and false if he is not. The second sentence is used to perform the act of apologizing, just as the sentence "I promise to return the favor" is used to perform the act of promising. Austin's insight, then, served to correct the tendency of philosophers to construe statements as the sole repository of cognitive meaning. As members of the class of actions generally, performative utterances were to be analyzed as such.

Austin listed six conditions that must be met for a locution to count as a performative utterance: (1) There must be an accepted conventional procedure having a certain conventional effect with that procedure including the uttering of certain words by certain persons in certain circumstances. (2) The particular persons and circumstances must be appropriate for the invocation of the procedure. (3) The procedure must be executed by all participants correctly and (4) completely. (5) Where the procedure is designed for use by people having certain thoughts and feelings or for the inauguration of certain consequential conduct on the part of the participant, the person must in fact have these thoughts or feelings and intend to conduct himself or herself appropriately. (6) The participant must conduct himself or herself appropriately.

If any of the first four conditions are violated, then the utterance "misfires" and the act is "aborted." If any of the last two conditions are violated, the utterance is "abused." Consider, in this light, "I now pronounce you husband and wife." If the locution is uttered incorrectly (violating 3), or the couple is not in a position to get married because they are already married (violating 2), or it is the caterer and not the minister who is conducting the ceremony (again violating 2), then the locution misfires and the procedure fails. If the bridegroom pledges fidelity only to go back on his pledge once the marriage has occurred (violating 6), then the formula succeeds but the utterance is "hollow." (A bad marriage is still a marriage and a broken promise is still a promise.)

Philosopher of law H.L.A. Hart has brought speech act analysis to bear on legal utterances. Hart has pointed out that it is speech acts that are used to confer or transfer property rights. If, for example, a father hands over his watch to his child, saying, "This is yours," the utterance of the sentence works to transfer property rights. The father is not declaring that he is transferring property rights, which analysis would have been made prior to Austin. Rather, the father is transferring the rights by the uttering of the sentence. Of course, the rights will vest only if the requisite conditions are met. If, for instance, the watch turns out not to be the father's but someone else's (violating 2), then the formula misfires and the rights do not transfer. If the father recalls the watch, having attached no prior conditions, then, though the child still owns the watch, the formula is abused.

The sentence "I pardon you" is another example of a speech act with significance for legal philosophy. When Gerald Ford said, "Now therefore I, Gerald Ford, President of the United States, pursuant to the pardon power conferred upon me by Article II, Section 2, of the Constitution, have granted and by these presents do grant a full, free, and absolute pardon unto Richard Nixon . . . ," he set in motion the legal machinery to ensure that Nixon would not be punished. Had Spiro Agnew uttered the same formula, or had Ford uttered a radically different one, the pardon would have failed to take effect.

What is perhaps the most interesting use of performative utterances in the domain of law concerns jury declarations. Given the presumption of innocence under the Fifth Amendment, it would appear that a criminal defendant is not guilty until such time as a jury declares him to be. What is required is that a jury utter "We find the defendant to be guilty as charged," or words to that effect. This is troubling, since we tend to believe juries find defendants guilty, not make them as such. However, if the formula is a speech act, then the defendant's guilt is something that is made. In a word, the formula construed as a speech act has an air of arbitrariness that it does not have when construed as a statement. The problem, however, is more illusory than real. For one thing, juries rarely know if it is true that a defendant did what he was accused of doing, and so construing the formula to be a statement would hardly remove the quandary. For another, the air of arbitrariness vanishes once we realize that there are procedures in place (namely, appeals) for correcting unsatisfactory utterances.

References

Austin, John Langshaw. *How to Do Things with Words*. Cambridge University Press, 1962.

———. "Other Minds." *Proceedings of the Aristotelian Society*, Supp. Vol. 20 (1946). Reprinted in *Logic and Language*, 2d ser., ed. A.C.N. Flew. Oxford University Press, 1953.

Haber, Joram Graf. *Forgiveness: A Philosophical Essay*. Lanham MD: Rowman and Littlefield, 1991.

Hart, H.L.A. "The Ascription of Responsibility and Rights." *Proceedings of the Aristotelian Society* 49 (1948–1949), 179.

Searle, John. *Speech Acts*. New York: Cambridge University Press, 1969.

Joram Graf Haber

See also JURY SYSTEM; JURY TRIALS; PERELMAN, CHAÏM; VOICE

Spencer, Herbert (1820–1903)

The British philosopher and sociologist once best known for developing and applying evolutionary theory to philosophy, psychology, and the study of society—his "synthetic philosophy"—Herbert Spencer is now remembered primarily as a critic of utilitarian positivism and as a defender of individual rights.

Born in Derby, England, on April 27, 1820, Spencer was the product of an undisciplined, private education and trained as a railway engineer. In his early twenties he turned to journalism and political writing. He was initially an advocate of many of the causes of philosophic radicalism, and some of his ideas (for example, his adoption of a version of the "greatest happiness principle") show similarities to utilitarianism.

Nevertheless, Spencer was a strong opponent of the legal positivism and the theory of government of Jeremy Bentham and J.L. Austin. He maintained that the arguments of the early utilitarians on the justification of law and authority and on the origin of rights were inconsistent—that they tacitly assumed the existence of claims or rights that have both moral and legal weight independently of the positive law. As well, Spencer rejected the utilitarian model of justice as resting on an egalitarianism that ignored desert (a basic principle of justice) and, more fundamentally, biological need and efficiency—though he did defend a "rational utilitarianism" of his own.

Spencer thought that social life was analogous to, if not an extension of, the life of a natural body, and that the development of biological and social "organisms" reflected common (Lamarckian) evolutionary principles or laws. All natural and social development could, therefore, be understood as reflecting "the universality of law." Accordingly, Spencer's social and legal philosophy depends on a theory of natural law. Beginning with the "laws of life," the conditions of social existence, and the recognition of life as a fundamental value, moral science can deduce what kinds of laws promote life and produce happiness. These latter principles are the laws of human conduct and constitute the basis of Spencer's account of social justice.

Yet, despite his "organic" view of society, Spencer was an individualist and argued for natural rights. In his view, the natural growth of an organism required "liberty." Spencer concluded, then, that everyone had basic rights to liberty "in virtue of their constitutions" as human beings, and such rights were essential to social progress. (These rights included rights to life, liberty, property, free speech, equal rights of women, universal suffrage, and the right "to ignore the state"—though Spencer reversed himself on some of these rights in his later writings.) He followed earlier liberalism in maintaining that law is a restriction of liberty and that the restriction of liberty, in itself, is evil and justified only where it is necessary to the preservation of liberty.

Rights, however, are not inherently moral, but become so by one's recognition that for them to be binding on others the rights of others must be binding on oneself. This reflects Spencer's other (though, he claimed, equally fundamental) principle of justice—"the law of equal freedom"—that the "liberty of each [be] limited by the like liberty of all." These arguments for natural rights and for the view that such rights constitute a limit on law and the state extend those of John Locke and are more systematically presented, but have often been challenged.

Spencer has a rights-based theory of the legitimacy of positive law. Law and public authority have, as their general purpose, the administration of justice (equated with freedom and the protection of rights). Moreover, Spencer maintained that government action requires individual consent, and his model for political association is that of a "joint stock company," where the "directors" can never act for a certain good except on the explicit wishes of its "shareholders." When parliament goes beyond the defense of rights to impose a "good" on a minority, Spencer suggested, it is no different from a tyranny and, in his later writings, he was a severe critic of existing "representative" governments, seeing them as exhibiting a virtual "divine right"—that is, claiming that "the majority in an assembly has power that has no bounds."

Spencer has been frequently accused of inconsistency, for one finds variations in his conclusions concerning land nationalization, the adoption of laissez-faire in economics, and the role of government. Much of this can, however, be accounted for by distinguishing his earlier from his later (post-1880) work, which is particularly concerned with making his political views consistent with his evolutionary theory.

In recent studies of Spencer's theory of social justice, there continues to be some debate whether justice is based primarily on desert or on entitlement, whether the "law of equal freedom" is a moral imperative or a descriptive natural law, and whether the law of equal freedom is grounded on rights, utility, or, ultimately, on "moral sense."

Spencer's influence was at its peak in the 1870s and early 1880s, but had declined dramatically by the time of his death. Parallels can be drawn between the recent work of Friedrich von Hayek and Robert Nozick and Spencer's defense of natural rights, of the spontaneous cooperation of individuals as fundamental to social development, and of laissez-faire capitalism, though there is no evidence that Spencer directly inspired either.

References

Francis, Mark. "Herbert Spencer and the Myth of Laissez-Faire." *Journal of the History of Ideas* 39 (1978), 317–328.

Gray, T.S. "Is Herbert Spencer's Law of Equal Freedom a Utilitarian or a Rights-based Theory of Justice?" *Journal of the History of Philosophy* 26 (1988), 259–278.

Spencer, Herbert. *Man versus the State*. 1884. Intro. A.J. Nock. Caldwell ID: Caxton, 1960.

———. *Social Statics*. London: Chapman, 1851.

Taylor, M.W. *Men versus the State: Herbert Spencer and Late Victorian Liberalism*. Oxford: Oxford University Press, 1992.

Wilbanks, Jan J. "On the Ontological Deduction of Natural Rights." *Pacific Philosophical Quarterly* 62 (1981), 293–301.

William Sweet

Spinoza, Baruch de (1632–1677)

Baruch de Spinoza was the first philosopher to suggest that human activity and social organization are rigorously determined by scientifically discernible laws. He thereby initiated the critique of dualistic theories in theology and philosophy, specifically those that distinguish between entities subject to the laws of nature, such as the human body, and those governed by free will, such as the human mind.

Spinoza was born in Amsterdam in 1632. He studied with distinguished Jewish scholars but eventually rejected orthodox belief. As a result, he was excommunicated from the Sephardic Jewish community for heresy in 1656 and expelled from Amsterdam four years later. The *Tractatus Theologico-Politicus* (Theological-Political Treatise), one of his two works of political and legal theory, was published anonymously in 1670. The publication was greeted by a storm of invective. The book was prohibited by the States-General of the Netherlands and placed on the Roman Catholic Index. Spinoza never permitted it to be published in the vernacular in his lifetime. He was offered a chair in philosophy at Heidelberg in 1673 but declined it. He died in 1677. Both his principal work, the *Ethics*, and his second work of political and legal theory, the unfinished *Political Treatise*, were published posthumously.

There are three essential elements to Spinoza's legal and political thought. First, Spinoza borrowed Thomas Hobbes' conception of natural right and the social compact, although he also criticized Hobbes' failure to draw the logical consequences from his own system. Spinoza accepted Hobbes' idea that individuals have the right to strive for self-preservation. Hobbes, however, denied the right to individuals who act out of misguided passion, while Spinoza accepted passion and vice as natural elements of the human condition and integrated them into his political theory. To do so, he proposed a conception of natural right that is totally independent of moral duty: the natural right, whether of a human being or a state, extends as far as its power.

Since, in the state of nature, individuals pursue exclusively their own interests, they are naturally enemies. However, the fear that results from the unrestrained exercise of natural powers also moves individuals to unite so that they might enjoy mutual assistance and security. The civil state they create is able to provide equality of rights and binding force to promises, benefits which were not available in the state of nature. Unlike Hobbes, however, Spinoza did not suggest that individuals are obligated to obey the state's commands. As individuals, they have little choice: they lose right to the extent the collectivity gains power. As a group, though they might have the power to disobey, they choose not to do so because they generally find that the advantages derived from the existence of political order far outweigh the inconvenience produced by ill-considered legislation.

Second, Spinoza continued the realist political tradition of Niccolò Machiavelli. Spinoza believed that the state is not bound by its promises or any other norm of civil law. Since the state has the right to do everything within its power, its right is limited only by the extent to which, as a practical matter, it has the ability to pursue its course. One of the limits is that the commonwealth can pursue only those actions that its citizens will accept, because of either fear, habit, complacency, or love for the state. The commonwealth's right is thus restrained by the possibility of rebellion.

Finally, Spinoza believed that the purpose of government is to secure freedom for its subjects. Freedom of thought provides a second limit to governmental action. Since the commonwealth has no power to command the thought of its citizens—even fear cannot cause an individual to love the state or to believe in God—the state has no right to intervene in this domain. Moreover, though the citizenry may temporarily be kept from rebellion by threat of punishment, Spinoza followed Seneca in the belief that no one can long retain a tyrant's rule. Commonwealths thus seek to convince their citizens that their laws promote peace and security, the ends that initially caused individuals to unite. In other words, human freedom (which, for Spinoza, meant obedience to law on the basis of reason) is not an obstacle to the realization of the state's objectives but rather a condition of its success. This reflection on freedom is one of Spinoza's most far-reaching contributions to political theory.

To contemporary theorists, Spinoza is also important for his explanation of the illusion of free will: human beings are conscious of the goals they pursue but unaware of the forces that cause them to pursue those goals. This insight has provided a basis for conceiving of the law as a form of ideology and also inspires skepticism about those jurisprudential theories that suggest that legal norms result exclusively from purposeful effort to resolve social problems.

References

Balibar, Etienne. *Spinoza and Politics*. Trans. P. Snowdon. London: Verso, 1998.

Hyland, Richard. "The Spinozist." *Iowa Law Review* 77 (1992), 805–835.

McShea, Robert J. *The Political Philosophy of Spinoza*. New York: Columbia University Press, 1968.

Negri, Antonio. *The Savage Anomaly*. Trans. M. Hardt. University of Minnesota Press, 1991.

Norris, Christopher. *Spinoza and the Origins of Modern Critical Theory*. Oxford: Blackwell, 1991.

Spinoza, Benedict de. *The Political Works*. Ed. and trans. A.G. Wernham. Oxford: Oxford University Press, corrected ed. 1965.

Vries, Theun de. *Baruch de Spinoza*. Reinbek: Rowohlt, 1970.

Richard Hyland

Standards

Standards are a means of according values to facts by reference to the ideas of reasonableness or normality. They are minimum, generally plausible requirements for ascribing rightness, correctness, goodness, or acceptability to behavior or a state of affairs. In that sense, one distinguishes technical, social, ethical, and legal standards. These classes correspond respectively to the mechanical, statistical, moral, and normative character of standards. When technical, standards express the current state of art, that is, a generalized use of certain technologies between the levels of the "past" and the "advanced." When social, they represent empirically ascertainable regularities of behavior in social groups. When ethical, they form a basic threshold of decency; one cannot go beyond them, without rejecting one's moral code. When legal, they function as the limits of permitted action by presupposing commonly expected criteria of right conduct. Understood in that way, standards always set down paths of permitted or promoted behavior, a kind of self-evident rule, which could or should have been followed. Legal standards are either discursive ("due process") or extradiscursive in kind ("due care," "high danger," "reasonable man," "interest of the child"). In extradiscursive standards, law incorporates technical, social, or ethical standards. The reception of extradiscursive standards in law is necessary, since legal norms are divided into formal and substantive rules and concepts. Formal elements of law require technical skill for their interpretation and application, because of requiring a specific legal rationality. Substantive rules and concepts can be used only by considering facts first, which are evaluated under evident postulates of practical reason or common sense.

At present there exists a tendency among Anglo-American and Scandinavian scholars to use the term "legal standards" to describe every legal provision. Legal norms being just sources of law, and judicial decisions being the law, every legal source becomes a "standard" for adjudication. Furthermore, legal principles, constitutional human rights, or even interpretive methods for legal statutes are called standards, as are general clauses of codified law, vague legal concepts, or legal values. This practice runs contrary to the tradition of the theoretical treatment of standards, which has been based on the specificity of standards as parts of the legal discourse, that is, on the distinction between rules, principles, policies, and standards.

The first to treat of legal standards as a specific category of legal thinking was Roscoe Pound. In his opinion, standards are legally defined measures of conduct, distinct from rules, principles, conceptions, and doctrines. In the course of their application by or under the direction of tribunals, they are closely linked to the ideas of intuition, reasonableness, and fairness. According to Pound, thinking about standards has a long tradition. Roman law already used certain standards, such as what an upright and diligent head of a family would do, or how a prudent husband would use his land. The fair conduct of a fiduciary was a standard worked out by English equity. The law of torts has been the genuine field for the formation of standards, like the behavior of a reasonable, prudent man under the circumstances. Legal standards possess three main characteristics. First, they take account of the facts of a particular case, so they are relative to times, places, and circumstances. For that reason, they are not formulated absolutely nor given an exact content. Their application, second, does not require exact legal knowledge, but common sense about common things, or trained intuition. This is why, finally, an average moral judgment is involved, when one has to find out whether a certain conduct comes up to the requirements of a standard. The political, economic, and sociological knowledge of the judge, just as his own trained intuition about things outside of common experience, becomes important for a legal judgment. The two poles between which standards have to function are legal security and judicial discretion: on one hand, the flexibility of the law in a changing society; on the other, the just outcome of a particular case.

In that sense, standards have also been important for the free law movement, which emphasized the predominance of the judge in setting the law by interpretation of rules or legal concepts. For Hermann Kantorowicz, standards are met under two forms. The first is as vague concepts, like *boni mores* (good morals), equity, the exigencies of life, the nature of things, and justice, which cannot be applied before having been filled up by substantive rules. Second, they are met as standards of valuation when a choice among opposite interests has to be made. A measure of that kind can be extralegal, that is, of an economic or sociological nature, or it can be legal. The legal standard consists in favoring that among the conflicting interests which is preferred and protected by the law itself.

The antiformalist character of legal standards and the possibilities of judicial discretion they offer have served French comparatists around Lambert, like Al-Sanhoury and M.O. Stati (*Le standard juridique,* The Legal Standard), as arguments against the positivism of the exegetical school. Unlike the common law tradition, continental judges were only supposed to interpret and not to create the law. Legal standards, defined as *mesures moyennes de conduite sociale correcte* (measures facilitating correct social conduct) lead to a free judicial decision, in the sense of a decision not directly related to a rigid legal provision. The standards of opportunity, rationality, morality, and normality as guiding elements of every judgment should replace the dogmatic thinking in concepts of codified law. Modern French theory insists, instead, on the connection between standards and the juridicalization of normality. Stephane Rials in *Le juge administratif français et le technique du standard* (The Judge in French Administrative Law and the Use of Standards) distinguishes between standards, directives, maxims, and principles; Rials then sets down a casuistic typology of legislative, judicial, and administrative standards. The normative character of standards arises with their integration into a positive rule.

The theory of standards in modern German jurisprudence has followed four paths. There is a topical, a sociological, and an analytical model of standards. Representative of the *topical* is Joseph Esser (*Grundsatz und Norm in der richterlichen Fortbildung des Privatrechts,* Principle and Norms in Lawyers' Development of the Private Law), who defines standards following Pound as legal norms which contain a reference to common sense and opinions or modes of normal behavior in a society. Standards differ from statutory rule, but also from principles, the blanket or general clauses, because they consist in a measure taken from the practice of valuing duty or care in vivo. They have in common with these last legal provisions that they are all applied in the same argumentative way: first, in a case- and not system-oriented rationality; relying, second, on wise opinion and not on logical strictness; and being guided, third, by consensus-building and not by apodeictic reason.

The *typical* model of standards is a hermeneutical one. Karl-Heinz Strache (*Das Denken in Standards,* Thinking with Standards), tries to distinguish between concepts, which can be used for interpretative logical subsumption, and standards, which correspond to the understanding of normal types of conduct. Thereby what is usual, prelegally, becomes a legal ought, which is recognizable only because it is self-evident to opinion that certain types are included. The *sociological* model of standards refers first of all to the use of empirical techniques, such as polls, for determining the existence of a standard. The intuition of a judge is no longer the medium for the recognition of standards. Further, this theory, developed by Gunther Teubner (*Standards und Direktiven in Generalklauseln,* Standards and Directives in General Stipulations), examines the use of standards as a phenomenon of modern legal culture, which shows the shift of responsibilities from the legislator to the judge. The *analytical* theory of Manfred Riedel (*Theorie der Menschenrechtsstandards*) conceives standards as guidelines for legal argumentation. Based on the theory of H.L.A. Hart, who examines standards as legislative and interpretive techniques within the framework of the open texture of the legal system and again in his chapters on rule-skepticism, Riedel also treats standards as socially typical, average criteria, to which one recurs when the positive legal system has no satisfactory solutions to offer. Standards exist either as internal elements of positive law, when incorporated into the text of concrete statutory rules and the more abstract blanket or constitutional norms, or as elements external to positive law, as meta-standards, when they act as maxims for legal interpretation. As their characteristics, standards display, first, an orientation by intuition and experience with reference to sane human reason; second, their casuistic nature; and third, their reference to collective value options.

Summarily, the connection between the concept of legal standard and the ideas of normality, averageness, and reasonableness needs stating. Standards are a technique of legislation permitting the law to remain flexible by conceding to the judge competencies overlapping his interpretive task. The obvious importance of legal standards for judicial discretion and for the theory of legal sources has been linked in various methodological approaches to the problem of incorporating extralegal practices into legal discourse.

References

Al-Sanhoury, Ahmed, and Stati, M.D. *Le standard juridique* (The Legal Standard). Paris: LGDJ, 1980.

Goebel, John P. "Rules and Standards: A Critique of Two Critical Theorists." *Duquesne Law Review* 31 (1992), 51.

Grondin, Joseph R. "Are Rules Really Better than Standards?" *Hastings Law Journal* 45 (1994), 569.

Hien, Kelly D. "The Rule of Law Is Dead, Long Live the Rule: An Essay in Legal Rules, Equitable Standards, and the Debate over Judicial Discretion." *SMU Law Review* 50 (1997), 1769.

Johnston, Jason Scott. "Bargaining under Rules versus Standards." *Journal of Law, Economics, and Organization* 11 (1995), 256.

Kantorowicz, Hermann. "Legal Science." *Columbia Law Review* 28 (1928), 679–707.

Pattaro, Enrico. "Ethical Aspects of the Concept of the Legal Standard." In *Prescriptive Formality and Normative Rationality in Modern Legal Systems* [Festschrift for Robert S. Summers], ed. W. Krawietz, N. MacCormick, and G.H. von Wright, 177–185. Berlin: Duncker und Humblot, 1994.

Pound, Roscoe. "The Administrative Application of Legal Standards." *Reports of the American Bar Association* 44 (1919), 445–465.

Schauer, Frederick. *Playing by the Rules: A Philosophical Examination of Rule-based Decision-Making in Law and in Life.* Oxford: Clarendon; New York: Oxford University Press, 1991.

Les standards dans les divers systèmes juridiques. Revue de la recherche juridique. Droit prospectif (Standards in Various Legal Systems. Preview of the Research. Legal Prospectus). Presses Universitaires d'Aix-Marseilles 4 (1988).

Sullivan, Kathleen M. "Foreword: The Justice of Rules and Standards." *Harvard Law Review* 106 (1992), 22.

Michel Paroussis

See also NORMS

Standing

Joseph Vining introduces his book on legal identity with the following: "Standing is a term of art that mesmerizes. It is part of a special language lawyers love to use and nonlawyers quiver on hearing. 'You can't get into court,' a lawyer says. 'Why not?' a nonlawyer asks. 'You have no standing,' the lawyer replies, much as if he were saying, 'You have no feet.'" While one finds the term *locus standi* in use in the nineteenth century in British legal and political proceedings, it is only in the twentieth century that the term "standing" has gained widespread use in American legal practice, suggesting that it is a recent term of jurisprudential practice.

The concept of standing is intertwined with a number of other legal terms and concepts and may not yet be fully articulated independent of those terms. The core idea of standing is whether it is appropriate for the individual or other entity to have an opportunity to be heard in a legal forum. Does the person have the right interests, credentials, characteristics, or other relevant features to qualify to make claims and arguments against others or the process itself? If not, the person is not to be heard in that legal forum, whatever the merit of the individual's complaint. Issues of standing range from private law to constitutional law to the more recently developed fields of administrative and public law. The growth in cases of standing reflects the growth in public and administrative law in the latter two thirds of the twentieth century and the inclination of the Congress to assign standing to citizens in new areas such as environmental law. Judge Patricia M. Wald of the D.C. Circuit states: "No plaintiff before our court can afford any longer to be unprepared to defend standing, and a defendant must be prepared in any case to explain why it was not raised. Last year we denied standing in about one-third of our published opinions on the issue."

Two large categories of issues surround the standing issue. One set addresses the question of whether the person bringing suit has the appropriate interest in the proceedings. Since decisions carry precedential weight, there needs to be an assurance that the plaintiff has enough of an interest in the issue that relevant matters will be effectively raised. Another set involves the appropriate role of the judiciary in relation to the other branches of government. What issues should the judiciary decide, and when do the courts have jurisdiction to accept and hear a case? One can see that the appropriateness of the plaintiff to bring suit and the appropriateness of the judiciary to hear a case could overlap and even on some occasions be confused. In fact, Kenneth Scott under the distinction of access decisions and jurisdiction decisions sees these as falling under a more general category of limiting the role of the judiciary.

The accepted wisdom characterizes the doctrine of standing as a function of constitutional and prudential considerations. The constitutional considerations find their basis in Article III of the U.S. Constitution's case and controversy doctrine. Prudential considerations relate to such issues as the ability of the court to fashion an effective remedy, or whether it is wise for the court to enter a particular domain at a particular time.

Standing doctrine intertwines with several other issues: for example, ripeness for decision, the political question doctrine, justiciability, mootness, jurisdiction, and exhaustion of other remedies.

Vining traces, in the American context, what he sees as the major change in standing doctrine from the "legal interest" test to the "injury in fact, economic or otherwise" doctrine. His view is that the attempt to develop standing doctrine in the area of administrative law drew heavily on the notion of property and economic interest in private law. Eventually, the inadequacy of that basis led to a revamping of the doctrine, associated most directly with the 1970 case of *Association of Data Processing Service Organization, Inc. v. Camp,* 397 U.S. 150. According to Vining:

> The Supreme Court did not purport in 1970 to leave American jurisprudence in a situation where it was necessary to reconstruct the role of the courts using only the most basic tools. The legal interest test was not simply abandoned. It was replaced by a new test, reaffirmed and repeated *in haec verba* [in just these terms] since: injury in fact to the challenger and demonstration that the interest the challenger is seeking to protect is arguably within the zone of interests to be protected or regulated by the statute or constitutional guarantee in question.

To the extent that one can find a common legal doctrine guiding the area of standing, it can be characterized as follows. The doctrine of injury in fact is cashed out to require for meeting the Article III test that (1) a plaintiff has in fact been injured, (2) that there is a causal connection between the injury and the actions complained about, and (3) that if the plaintiff is successful, there is available an effective judicial remedy. Further, the injury limitation must satisfy four conditions: it must involve a legally protected interest, it must be a particular interest of the plaintiff, the injury must be actual or highly likely to occur, and finally it must be imminent. The causation and redressability requirements frequently merge, since a clear, relevant cause is necessary if the court is to effectively redress the injury.

While a reasonable, clear doctrinal formula is asserted, there is considerable dissent regarding whether it guides decision making or simply covers decisions without a consistent rationale. Gene Nichol's comments on standing doctrine are an example of this skepticism:

> In fact the law of standing has become so disjointed that the danger now exists that the Court will come to accept it as a manipulable doctrine whose primary value lies in its ability to serve nonjurisdictional ends. Standing law is unsatisfactory in part, of course, because of unprincipled decisionmaking. More importantly, however, its shortcomings can also be traced to the weakness of its claimed foundation—injury in fact.

Considerable recent discussion has been directed at the decision in *Lujan v. Defenders of Wildlife,* 112 U.S. 2130 (1992), since it refused to give standing to individuals even though Congress had provided that individuals could sue on behalf of environmental concerns. Craig Gottlieb speculates this decision will contribute to continuing the process of narrowing the grounds upon which standing can be based.

Even the authors of *Federal Practice and Procedure,* an extensive review of the case law on standing, express a skepticism about their own effort to give an account of standing doctrine:

> The uncertainty of standing principles arises directly from doubts about the underlying problem of justiciability. At any time, judges, lawyers, and society at large divide on the proper role to be played by the courts in addressing large public issues. Over time, the balance of opinion shifts. These broad divisions are forced into the narrow terminology of standing. At the best, it would be extremely difficult to identify all the factors that have influenced a particular decision. At the worst, this difficulty is compounded by some measure of disingenuous dissembling.

While standing has evolved to the point where we have reasonably clear doctrine for guiding decisions, it is sometimes difficult to see consistency in the decisions. Continuing tension is to be expected between a desire for clear doctrine, and the broader and changing legal and political views that shape the extent to which citizens can expect relief through the judiciary for perceived injuries, particularly from the workings of public law.

References

Fletcher, William A. "Structure of Standing." *Yale Law Journal* 98 (1988), 221–291.

Gottlieb, Craig. R. "Comment: How Standing Has Fallen." *University of Pennsylvania Law Review* 142 (1994), 1063–1143.

Nichol, Gene R., Jr. "Justice Scalia, Standing, and Public Law Litigants." *Duke Law Journal* 42 (1993), 1141–1169.

———. "Rethinking Standing." *California Law Review* 72 (1984), 68–102.

Scott, Kenneth E. "Standing in the Supreme Court—A Functional Analysis." *Harvard Law Review* 86 (1973), 645–692.

Vining, Joseph. *Legal Identity*. New Haven: Yale University Press, 1978.

Wald, Patricia M. "The D.C. Circuit: Here and Now." *George Washington Law Review* 55 (1987), 718–728.

Wright, Charles Allen, Arthur R. Miller, and Edward H. Cooper, *Federal Practice and Procedure*. Vols. 13 and 13A. St. Paul MN: West, 1984.

Alan R. Mabe

See also JURISDICTION; STATUS

State

The state is the organized part of a sovereign political community, as opposed to society, the spontaneous and everyday activities of its masses of individuals. The word "state" comes from the Latin word *status,* which means "condition" or "way of existence," as in status quo, the way in which we exist. The state refers to a complex hierarchy of command and obedience by officials who usually govern a massive population and territory.

What Is the State?

There is no consensus on a general definition of the state, and skepticism about whether all states share a common set of features is warranted. As an abstract ideal, the state is a public good as opposed to the evil of open warfare and brute power. The modern nation-state involves a hierarchy of command and obedience that is commonly recognized as a legitimate means for ensuring both efficient cooperation and individual freedom. The state is nothing but *regulated force* supposed to be for the common good. This claim for the common good is the basis for most argument about the state.

A plausible definition of the modern nation-state, according to David Held et al., is "an impersonal and privileged legal or constitutional order with the capability of administering and controlling a given territory." A standard way of describing the three main features of the state is that it is, as noted by Alexander D'Entreves, (1) an organized force, or "a force outside the individual will, superior to it, and able not only to issue commands but to enforce them"; (2) a legal system, or "a power exercised in accordance with definite procedure, with rules that are known"; and (3) a supremacy, or a sovereignty, "an authority which is recognized as warranted and justified in practice."

However, legal discourse is plagued by ambiguity concerning the word "state," which is used as a morally regulative concept in ideal theory and also descriptively as a name for any sovereign power. We should distinguish *a state,* or any particular, existing, modern state from the more general concept of *the state,* which is used in arguments concerning justice, government, legitimacy, and sovereignty. The state is a regulative concept structuring certain forms of moral agency, or an abstraction; whereas a state is a historical institution erected by a particular group of persons. A *particular* state such as the United States of America is, in fact, as Robert Nozick labels it, "the dominant protective association" for the individuals who have lived in its territory after the American Revolution. Any particular state can be judged in terms of one or another general theory of the state, but there is a far greater degree of controversy regarding theories of the "Good State" than there is concerning how to describe the functions or features of particular states. There is very little consensus on the limits of state power, or the rights and responsibilities of states, and thus we must keep the positive, factual institution and its actual functions separate from the ideal theory of the state. The state refers ultimately to values or standards that must be developed in order to criticize or commend existing governments.

The state is not identical with the current governing group. In modern democracies, political groups compete for offices of the state, which they will hold until the next election. Just as a driver controls a car and remains subject to its performance limitations and the road conditions, so a political regime steers a particular state subject to constitutional limits on its power and the conditions of that state in the world. The usual system is that politicians occupying state offices must obey the rules and procedures developed throughout that state's history, but are also in a commanding position to reform those rules or propose new laws.

In western philosophy, two metaphors have dominated theories of the state. The *organic theory* compares the state to a natural organism, a living force that is more than merely the individuals who make it up (Plato, Aristotle, and others). This view holds that the state is part of the order of things and hence not in need of any further justification. The *social contract theory* compares the state to a machine, an artificial construction that individuals create through communication, agreement, and institutionalization (Thomas Hobbes, John Locke, and others). If all political ideas emerge through human endeavor, then the state is a social experiment as opposed to a chance occurrence or a divinely ordained condition. The state as an invention which we develop is more plausible than the organic theory that denies our responsibility in finding the best ways to live with each other. This second view holds that any state is always vulnerable to questions about its legitimacy, and this fits our experience better than the simplistic organic justification.

Since the sixteenth century, there has been a general evolution from tyranny to democracy, or from absolutist states where power is concentrated in an indivisible, ultimate authority to constitutional states with divisions of power that allow parts of the political system to act as checks on other parts, though totalitarian states continue to appear where democracy has never taken root or when it breaks down.

Some Definitions of the State

Western philosophers have defined the state in both positive and negative ways. John Locke (1632–1704) understood the state as guardian of rights for citizens who remain autonomous regarding their own interests and that it must be limited in order to ensure freedom. In 1690, Locke wrote: "Political power then I take to be a right of making laws with penalties of death, and consequently all less penalties, for the regulating and preserving of property, and of employing the force of the community, in the execution of such laws, and in the defence of the common-wealth from foreign injury, and all this only for the public good."

H.L.A. Hart also defines the state positively: "The expression 'a state' is not the name of some person or thing inherently or 'by nature' outside the law; it is a way of referring to two facts: first, that a population inhabiting a territory lives under that form of ordered government provided by a legal system with its characteristic structure of legislature, courts, and primary rules; and secondly, that the government enjoys a vaguely defined degree of independence." Liberal theorists who support the state as the only way to avoid anarchy and attain a reasonable rule of law have dominated twentieth-century debates concerning the state. The state has come to be regarded as necessary for any well-ordered society with decent opportunities for a good life, and we have lost all sense that there is any alternative form of political life for large, industrialized, and culturally complex populations.

Negative pictures of the state tend to emphasize its violence and oppressiveness. William Godwin (1756–1836) was an early critic of the state: "The object of government is the suppression of such violence, as well external as internal, as might destroy, or bring into jeopardy, the well being of the community or its members; and the means it employs are constraint and violence of a more regulated kind." Karl Marx and Friedrich Engels described the state as an instrument of ruling-class domination, but also believed that it could be used for emancipatory purposes.

Max Weber defined the state as "a human community that (successfully) claims the *monopoly of the legitimate use of physical force* within a given territory." This alleged monopoly on legitimate force does not capture the fact that though the state reserves judgment on violence within its territory, it can neither enforce the peace because of advances in technology and weapons nor keep the law of nonviolence without becoming violent itself. This contradiction between the nonviolent purposes of the state and its necessary violence and coercion for the sake of law and order is fatal to the benign self-image of the state.

Contemporary negative views focus on the state's role in punishment, administration, and propaganda. Theda Skocpol writes: "The state properly conceived . . . is a set of administrative, policing, and military organizations, headed, and more or less well coordinated by, an executive authority. Any state first and fundamentally extracts resources from society and deploys those to create and support coercive administrative organizations. . . ." Murray Bookchin warns that "the State is not merely a constellation of bureaucratic and coercive institutions. It is also a state of mind, an instilled mentality for ordering reality." This deeper distrust suggests, in contrast to the liberal focus on moral agency within a system of state offices accepted as legitimate themselves, that the state is problematic no matter how well its officials perform their duties because all states diminish individuality and self-government of reasonable persons.

Features of Existing States

Leslie Green argues that "the state is distinguished from other social institutions not by its functions, but by its authoritative means of acting, which are expressed primarily though not exclusively through law." The state's authority is supreme in that it preempts "all other authorities and it recognizes no appeal from its own authority to any other source."

This core self-image of supremacy in its own territory is combined with many other features that vary considerably in degree: size, stability, prosperity, homogeneity of population, industry, military power, and government responsibilities. The basic legal structure of a modern nation-state includes a written constitution, a legislative assembly, and an executive of elected and appointed officials, an independent judiciary, and regular elections that are all legitimized in terms of impersonal norms of democracy rather than as personal commands. The state has two main legal roles: it creates law by consulting the people as occasions require and it enforces existing law by prosecuting criminals, defending victims, settling disputes, and punishing. All states tax their populations in order to support police forces, prisons, public safety, the military, and their own bureaucratic apparatus.

Leading Philosophical Questions

Does the state have rights, and if so, how do they balance with individual rights? Nozick argues that states are abstractions and that only individuals have rights. Does the state have a right to execute convicted criminals? Do individuals have a right to life that makes any military draft illegitimate? These older questions have been joined by new issues recently: Does the state have the duty to provide health care for all citizens, or to protect the environment? Should the state be permitted to act covertly and to break its own law in pursuit of security and justice?

Another set of questions concerns the contrast between the Good State and illegitimate states. A well-ordered state has constitutionally limited powers, whereas other states manifest arbitrary power. When is a state legitimate? Ronald Dworkin says: "A state is legitimate if its constitutional structure and practices are such that its citizens have a general obligation to obey political decisions that purport to impose duties on them."

Can legitimate states keep secrets from their people and use spy agencies? With secret police forces and official secrets acts, states have decreased their accountability. Since the actions of officials cannot be judged unless they are known, wrongdoing can be cloaked by claims about national security. Through secrecy, officials are able to protect themselves from both legal charges and questions of political morality.

Do citizens have a general obligation to obey the state? Can the state advance its interests at the expense of some individuals? How can the state resolve differences about the common good? How can the state neutrally judge conflicts between itself and citizens?

Is the state necessary for the good life in the world as we know it? Peter Kropotkin argues that the state is intrinsically unfree: it is "the old machine, the old organism, slowly developed in the course of history to crush freedom, to crush the individual, to establish oppression on a legal basis, to create monopolists, to lead minds astray by accustoming them to servitude." The hope of those who refuse the state is that persons are better off without the state because its coercive machinery is redundant, as long as persons generally are reasonable.

In 1896, Kropotkin reviewed the history of the state as a "mutual alliance between the lord, the priest, the soldier, and the judge." If the state always involves a hierarchy of command and obedience, and those offices have never been open to all equally, then it is an exploitative apparatus. It does not follow that the state is necessarily evil, but this history of inequality shifts the burden of proof to those who support the state as an institution that is just because it improves the lives of the worst off classes. If the oppressive bureaucracy of the modern state is unavoidable in mass societies, then perhaps the very ideal of the Good State is illusory.

References

Bookchin, Murray. *The Ecology of Freedom: The Emergence and Dissolution of Hierarchy*. Rev. ed. Montreal: Black Rose, 1991.

D'Entreves, Alexander P. *The Notion of the State*. Oxford: Clarendon Press, 1967.

Dworkin, Ronald. *Law's Empire*. Cambridge: Harvard University Press, 1986.

Godwin, William. *An Enquiry Concerning Political Justice*. Harmondsworth: Penguin, 1976.

Green, Leslie. *The Authority of the State*. Oxford: Clarendon Press, 1988.

Hart, H.L.A. *A Concept of Law*. Oxford: Clarendon Press, 1961.

Held, David et al. *States and Societies*. Oxford: Martin Robertson, 1983.

Kropotkin, Peter. "The State: Its Historic Role." In *Fugitive Writings*. Montreal: Black Rose, 1993.

Nozick, Robert. *Anarchy, State, and Utopia*. New York: Basic Books, 1974.

Skocpol, Theda. *States and Social Revolutions: A Comparative Analysis of France, Russia and China*. Cambridge: Cambridge University Press, 1979.

Tony Couture

See also Anarchist Philosophy of Law; Authority; Constitutionalism; Public and Private Jurisdictions; State Action

State Action

The phrase "state action" is a term of art in American constitutional law that refers to the fact that the United States Constitution places duties almost exclusively upon, and creates rights almost exclusively against, governments (federal, state, and local). Thus, in almost every case, for one to make out a claim of constitutional violation, one must point to some act of the "state" that is so violative.

Questions about whether the requisite state action is present typically arise in two types of cases. The first type consists of those cases in which a private individual complains that an act of another private individual has infringed the constitutional interests of the former. In that type of case, the determination of whether there is sufficient state action to make out a violation of the Constitution turns on the relationship between the infringing private individual and the state. For instance, the private individual may be acting under contract with the state or with a subsidy from the state, or the state may in some other way be implicated in the private individual's act. The second type of state action case is one in which the infringing actor is a governmental employee who is acting beyond or against his or her legal authority. The question in this type of case is whether the state, which can only act through agents, should be deemed to be acting through this agent given the limits of the agent's authority.

The law surrounding state action is quite difficult and confused, largely because the state action inquiry usually fails to distinguish and thus conflates two entirely separate issues. The first issue is an issue about the constitutional merits: Does whatever action the state has taken violate constitutional rights?

The second issue is an issue about who should be sued and in what court. Sometimes a ruling that the defendant's act did not violate the plaintiff's constitutional rights means only that the state itself has acted constitutionally by proscribing and providing constitutionally adequate remedies for what the defendant has done. The plaintiff's mistake, therefore, may have been to sue the defendant for a constitutional violation in federal court rather than for a state law violation in state court.

How these two distinct issues become conflated in the state action inquiry can best be understood by appreciating that all private actions take place against a background of laws and have a legal status under those laws. Thus, private actions may be legally forbidden, legally required, or legally permitted. If they are legally permitted, moreover, that permission can be cashed out in terms of legal prohibitions and legal immunities. If one couples this fact about private actions—that they occur against a background of various legal duties and immunities, which background gives them their legal status—with another fact—that these various background legal duties and immunities are paradigmatic "state actions"—one comes to the conclusion that all private action implicates state action. Therefore, despite some case law that suggests otherwise, no case involving a constitutional challenge can be lacking in state action.

The foregoing argument makes a conceptual claim; one can grant the conceptual claim without yielding on any normative point, because nothing normative follows from the point that "there's always state action."

First, even if there is always state action, it does not follow that the party alleged to be acting wrongfully is a state actor subject to constitutional duties. For example, the law of defamation is state action, but this does not mean the defamed party invoking the law is a state actor.

Second, to say state action is omnipresent because all acts take place against a legal background and have some legal status raises a second conceptual issue: is it only "laws" that can be unconstitutional, or can acts that are not lawmaking acts, and perhaps even illegal acts, be unconstitutional as well? Consider, in this regard, acts of government officials that enforce unconstitutional laws, or acts of private citizens that invoke unconstitutional laws. In addition, consider acts that violate constitutionally valid laws and that could not be made legally permissible without the laws making them so being unconstitutional. Can these types of acts violate the Constitution, or can only lawmaking acts do so? How is the class of lawmaking acts defined so that it can be distinguished from other acts?

These conceptual issues regarding what kinds of acts—lawmaking, official or private, legal or illegal—can violate constitutional duties are interesting and difficult, but their practical import is less than one might expect. Their resolution theoretically affects neither whether a complainant should win his or her lawsuit nor what the remedy should be; their resolution only affects which court, state or federal, may hear the suit.

To illustrate: Consider again the governmental employee who violates nonconstitutional legal restrictions and infringes the plaintiff's constitutional interests. If the employee's acts are considered to be state action, then the state has acted unconstitutionally and can be sued in the federal courts as well as in the state courts. If those acts are not considered to be state action, then the state has not violated the plaintiff's constitutional rights if the state law remedies are constitutionally adequate. Even if the plaintiff may only sue for a nonconstitutional violation in state court, however, the remedy should be the same as for the constitutional violation. Otherwise the state would have violated the Constitution, not because of the employee's acts per se, but because it had failed to provide a constitutionally adequate set of laws restricting and remedying those acts.

Third, the ubiquity of state action as a conceptual matter does not affect the content of constitutional rights and duties. To say, for example, that the realm of the private is defined and buttressed by law—state action—is not to say that private choices within it are held to the same standards as the Constitution imposes on, for instance, the state police or welfare department. *Shelley v. Kraemer,* 334 U.S. 1 (1948), a Supreme Court case involving racially restrictive covenants, is both a source and an illustration of this confusion. *Shelley* is usually criticized for its finding of state action in the Missouri courts' enforcement of private covenants. On that point, however, *Shelley* was absolutely correct. The problem in *Shelley* was the Supreme Court's immediate jump from "judicial enforcement of private discriminatory covenants is state action" to "judicial enforcement of private discriminatory covenants is constitutionally tantamount to state discrimination." The latter simply does not follow from the former, and the Court never filled in the missing premises. State action stands behind private choices. However, state action permitting and enforcing private choices of a type the state would be constitutionally forbidden to make is not necessarily or even usually unconstitutional; the state has legitimate, often compelling, and sometimes constitutionally compelled reasons for permitting private actors to choose in ways that the state itself is constitutionally forbidden to choose. For example, the state may be constitutionally compelled to enforce a homeowner's exclusion of blacks from his or her property, even though the state could not exclude blacks from its property.

There are thus two distinct types of questions in the typical state action case. One type is substantive regarding whether the state laws are constitutional in permitting private conduct that the state itself is constitutionally debarred from undertaking. The second type is conceptual and asks whether, assuming the plaintiff's legal rights were violated, those rights are constitutional or nonconstitutional and whether the correct defendant has been sued.

References

Alexander, Larry, and Paul Horton. *Whom Does the Constitution Command?* Westport CT: Greenwood Press, 1988.

The Civil Rights Cases, 109 U.S. 3 (1883).

"Symposium on the Public/Private Distinction." *University of Pennsylvania Law Review* 130 (1982), 1289–1609.

"Symposium on the State Action Doctrine." *Constitutional Commentary* 10 (1993), 309–331.

Larry Alexander

See also DUE PROCESS; PUBLIC AND PRIVATE JURISDICTIONS; RULE OF LAW; STATE

Status

To have status under the law is to be recognizable in legal proceedings. For example, it is to be a subject of a right, to be any entity recognized in law as supporting such capacities as instituting and/or defending judicial proceedings.

Legal status and personhood are always something conferred, they are never merely the result of the act or acts of parties. Status also is not an inborn quality of humans. It may be said that the law raises those on whom it confers status from whatever natural associations they may enjoy with other entities to membership in a constituted society.

The idea of a legal person (indeed the term "person" itself) comes from the Romans. The Latin *persona* was originally limited to the theater, *dramatis persona*. Roman law appropriated the term to refer to anything that could act on either side of a legal dispute. In Roman law it was clearly understood that all legal persons are artifacts of the law itself. It was no concern of the law that legal persons may have an existence prior to or outside of the legal sphere. The biological status of a subject was not relevant, so it was not necessary to draw a clear distinction between real and artificial juristic persons. All are creations of law.

Roman law may be profitably thought of as identifying legal personhood with status. Status is not a question of fact so much as it is a matter of legal principle. That is, the characteristics anything must possess to have legal status are fixed by law, not given outside of it.

There is, of course, a significant difference between Roman law and the English common law on the interpretation of status. In English law status is conferred, as a matter of public law, only on exceptions to normality. Status was used to deal with exceptions to the paradigm cases of legal personhood. Status has been conferred on married women, illegitimate children, bankrupts, convicts, mental incompetents, and so forth. In English law, R.H. Graveson writes: "[S]tatus . . . is . . . applicable to any body in fact capable of sustaining any degree of legal personality." Its roots lie in Norman land tenure and in the *wergild* (restitution)-based codes of the Anglo-Saxons.

Status should be kept distinct from legal capacity, the possession of legal power. One is a legal state of being, the other a state of doing. "Capacity" refers to the legally permitted abilities one has to affect one's own rights and those of others. Status determines one's legal condition in the community. Of course, the terms have been used to define each other. Jeremy Bentham, for example, claimed that status is to have certain capacities, rights, and duties. John Austin defined it as "an aggregate of rights or duties with capacities residing in the individual as a member of a class."

For Roman law, on the other hand, to have legal status was, *eo ipso* (by that very fact), to be a normal legal person, an empowered citizen. Status distinguished the Roman law of persons from the law of things and embedded it in private law.

It is of special note that the Roman conception of the legal person when applied to corporate entities produced the fiction (or the grant or concession) theory. Justice Marshall in *The Trustees of Dartmouth College v. Woodward,* 17 U.S. (4 Wheat.) 518 (1819), provided perhaps the most famous American statement of the fiction theory: "A corporation is an artificial being, invisible, intangible, and existing only in contemplation of law."

Roman law recognized two types of organizations as having status, but only one of which had legal personhood. One, governed by contract, a *societas,* was such that its assets were owned by the contractors. The other, a *universitas,* was a legal entity separate from its members, capable of holding property and of possessing distinct rights and obligations. Personhood was conferred on the *universitas*, not the *societas*.

It is elemental in Roman law that legal personhood was always conceived as a privilege and not a matter of right. In 57 B.C. the *lex Juliae de collegiia* (Julian law on corporations) authorized corporations, but to be granted incorporation and so personhood an association had to show, as noted by Charles Sherman, that it would be "helpful to the state or beneficial to the public." The suggestion that apparently was not worked out in Roman jurisprudence is that all legal persons qua legal persons are extensions of the state. In the corporate cases this produced interesting legal results. Corporations, according to the fiction theory, can do only what the state permits them to do. So, as George Ellard notes, all of their actions become extended acts of government, and corporate officers are ultimately accountable to the state. The fiction theory must hold the state responsible for the supervision of the acts of all legal persons. It might be argued that the fiction theory, at least in its extreme forms, is grandly totalitarian. All rights, privileges, and duties are ultimately conferred by and through a central civil authority. In the corporate sphere the activities of freely associated humans are severely restricted, and the interests and wills of organizations are either interpreted as extensions of the state and always lawful or as reducible to the actions and attributes of the human membership.

In legal history the major rival of the fiction theory is the reality theory. The basic premise of the reality theory is that the law does not invent its subjects, it recognizes or conveys status on entities that have nonlegal existence as persons. The most influential versions of the reality theory were put forth by Otto von Gierke, J.N. Figgis, F.W. Maitland, and Ernst Freund. When applied to human persons, the reality theory draws few detractors, for it simply asserts that extralegal considerations regarding personhood dominate the issue of whether any human ought to be treated as a legal person. The law's task is to capture the players in the social game as its subjects. It does not create those players, though it attempts to regulate their play.

Gierke and the other realists, however, did not restrict the theory to human persons. In fact, humans were hardly their primary interest. In simplest terms, for the realist, corporations are persons regardless of the law's attitude toward them. They meet the conditions of personhood that are applied to any natural entity seeking admission to the legal sphere. In fact, they are natural persons. This point is clarified by Ellard's distinction (borrowed from Frederick Pollock and F.W. Maitland) between natural and physical persons. It was certainly the case, as he notes, that large classes or groups of physical persons, for example, Jews, monks, serfs in medieval Europe, minors, and mental incompetents in the United States, and so on, are or were not accorded the status of natural persons under law. Law, according to the reality theory, recognizes persons, it does not create them. It merely determines which societal facts are in conformity with its requirements. De facto personality precedes de jure personhood.

References

Austin, John. *Lectures on Jurisprudence.* London: J. Murray, 1885.

Ellard, George. "Constitutional Rights of the Corporate Person." *Yale Law Journal* 91.8 (July 1982).

Figgis, J.N. *Churches in the Modern State.* London: Russell and Russell, 1914.

French, Peter. "Law's Concept of Personhood." In *Responsibility Matters.* Lawrence: University Press of Kansas, 1992.

Freund, Ernst. *The Legal Nature of Corporations.* Chicago: University of Chicago Press, 1897.

Gierke, Otto von. *Das deutsche Genossenschaftrecht* (German Corporate Law). 1887. Reprinted Graz: Akademische Druck U. Verlageanstalt, 1954.

Graveson, R. *Status in the Common Law.* London: Athlone Press, 1953.

Maitland, F.W. *Collected Papers.* Vol. 3. Cambridge: Cambridge University Press, 1911.

Sherman, Charles P. *Roman Law in the Modern World.* Boston: Boston Book Company, 1917.

Peter A. French

See also PERSONS, IDENTITY OF; ROLE; STANDING

Strict Liability, Criminal

The criminal law holds someone strictly liable insofar as it rules out such excuses as "I didn't mean to," "I didn't know," and "I was careful." If conduct is faulty only insofar as it does wrong intentionally, knowingly, recklessly, or negligently, then strict liability is liability without fault.

Strict liability is an aspect of the definition of crime, not the standard of proof. Statutes that treat certain acts as prima facie or presumptively negligent, reckless, knowing, or intended do not impose strict liability (though they often have much the same effect as a strict liability statute). However, statutes that treat an act as criminal negligence, recklessness, or intentional wrongdoing per se (or otherwise create an "*unrebuttable* presumption" of fault) are probably best regarded as creating strict liability (though they preserve the language of fault).

Strict liability should not be confused with absolute liability (though critics of strict liability often use the terms interchangeably). A statute holds someone absolutely liable insofar as it rules out (in addition to excuses like those above) such excuses as "I didn't do that, it just happened," "Someone else physically moved my hand against my will," and "There was no way anyone in my place could have prevented it." If strict liability may be said to do away with "guilty mind" (mens rea) as a condition of criminal liability, absolute liability does away with the "guilty act" (actus reus) condition as well, leaving something like a mere event, reflex, or external cause. Vicarious liability, that is, criminal liability for another's wrongdoing (rather than for failure to exercise control), is absolute liability (in this sense), not strict liability.

Strict liability can be found in the criminal law as early as the mid-nineteenth century. It is now common in statutes concerning the sale of liquor, impure foods or drugs, financial instruments, and misbranded articles; acts affecting the safety, health, or general welfare of the community; serious crimes such as murder, bigamy, rape, and possession of narcotics; and traffic and other motor vehicle regulations.

In general, strict liability arises when a legislature omits words of fault from a criminal statute, and judges interpret that omission to imply liability without fault. Suppose, for example, M has this statute: "Any person who, being married and having a living spouse, marries or cohabits with another, shall be guilty of bigamy." Suppose too that a woman in M hears from her husband's shipmates that he was lost at sea, that she waits five years hoping he will return, and that she then marries another, believing her first husband dead. Last, suppose that her first husband returns a year after her second marriage (having been found marooned on an uncharted island by a freighter blown off course in a storm). Is this woman guilty of bigamy? Though she acted on the reasonable belief that her husband is dead, her conduct satisfies the terms of the statute. She is guilty of bigamy unless a judge reads into the statute a requirement of fault.

Whether a judge should read in such a requirement is, of course, dependent on such factors as precedent, the known or presumed intention of the legislature, general principles of justice, specific social policies, and other considerations typical of statutory interpretation.

Liability need not be strict with respect to every element of the offense. For example, the same court that found the woman above guilty of bigamy might not have found her so had she obtained a divorce before remarrying, even if her husband was later able to invalidate it on technical grounds. Her trust in an official court document might be treated with a respect that her reasonable belief concerning her husband's death was not.

The more severe the punishment for a crime, the less likely liability will be strict with respect to any of its elements. Thus, liability is strict for many elements of traffic offenses, while strict for few, if any, elements of such serious crimes as armed robbery or murder. This is, however, only a tendency. In some serious felonies, including capital crimes like felony-murder, liability can be strict with respect to many elements.

Strict liability is a good example of how divorced theory and practice can be. The American Law Institute's *Model Penal Code* sought to eliminate strict liability "whenever an offense carries a possibility of sentence of imprisonment." Though the *Code* allowed strict liability for minor offenses, that allowance was not an endorsement. No offense in the *Code* itself imposed strict liability. Most of this century's important legal theorists, including Jerome Hall, Glanville Williams, and H.L.A. Hart, have condemned strict liability. Of the few theorists defending it, most have expressed substantial reservations. Yet strict liability offenses have become more, not less, common and, indeed, today constitute a substantial part of the criminal law.

What objections do theorists have to strict liability in the criminal law? Though utilitarians and retributivists tend to answer this question differently, their answers are complementary rather than inconsistent. For both, the failure of an analogy with negligence is informative.

For utilitarians, justifying a law imposing criminal liability means showing (in part) that providing for punishment will prevent undesirable acts not to be prevented by less costly means (blame, civil liability, or the like). While some prevention may be by reform (the effect of punishment or forced treatment) or incapacitation (the effect of imprisonment or execution), most prevention is probably by (general) deterrence (threat). So, showing that punishment for a certain form of negligence should prevent certain undesirable outcomes is generally easy. The threat of punishment should encourage some people to exercise reasonable care whom mere civil liability would not. Insofar as punishment can deter negligence, punishing negligence should prevent crime much as punishing recklessness or intentional wrongdoing does. Hence, punishing negligence will produce similar benefits.

What about the cost of such benefits? (Not all prevention is worth the cost.) The cost of holding people criminally liable for negligence is not much different from the cost for intentional wrongdoing. The social cost of preventing intentional crime is primarily (1) the cost of punishing however many criminals are caught and (2) whatever opportunities potential criminals lose when the threat of punishment deters them. The social benefit of less crime generally repays this cost. The social cost of preventing crimes of *conscious* negligence (recklessness) is a bit higher, because it includes abstaining from acts known to be negligent. Only in crimes of mere (unknowing) negligence is the cost of prevention much higher than for intentional crimes. To prevent mere negligence, one must undertake an inquiry; one must find out whether what one is doing meets the standard of reasonable care. The cost of this inquiry can be substantial but cannot be unreasonable. Reasonable care is that level of care reasonable people, taking all costs into account, including the cost of finding out whether their conduct meets the standard, would ordinarily exercise. Exercising reasonable care is, by definition, a net good for society, not a net expense.

Here, then, is an important difference between crimes of negligence and crimes of strict liability. Strict liability holds people to a higher standard than reasonable care, what we might call "super care." Super care is that level of care necessary to prevent the harm the law forbids. The bigamist of our example could not exercise super care simply by taking reasonable precautions to make sure her husband is dead. She had to be right about his death (or refrain from remarrying). Insofar as we cannot know in advance what precautions are sufficient to prevent the harm in question (in this case, bigamy), super care is a backward-looking standard. We can know that we have failed to meet it (without negligence) only when the forbidden outcome has occurred.

Insofar as super care is a backward-looking standard, the criminal law cannot prevent failures of super care in the way it can prevent failures of reasonable care. Insofar as the criminal law can prevent failures of super care (failures, that is, that are not also negligence), it can do so only by encouraging people to exercise care *beyond* what a reasonable person in the circumstances would exercise. To avoid bigamy, for example, one might have to abstain from remarrying even when remarrying is reasonable.

Strict liability statutes are, then, by definition, either ineffective (unable to prevent crimes less drastic liability cannot prevent) or wasteful (preventing some crimes even liability for negligence does not but at an unreasonable cost). Hence (the utilitarian critics conclude), one way or another strict liability must fail the test of utility.

Retributivists object not to these *effects* but to the justice of demanding super care. For (most) retributivists, a law imposing criminal liability for negligence is justified, if it is, only because there is a *natural* duty of reasonable care. "Evil mind"—a mind not up to the standard of the ordinary reasonable mind—is still part of justifying punishment for negligent crime. The retributive objection to strict criminal liability is that no such natural duty exists for super care. Since failing to exercise super care is not failing in a natural duty, crimes of strict liability must (it is said) punish for failure to take unreasonable precautions, bad luck, or some other nonfault. No one can deserve punishment for that.

Utilitarian defenders of strict liability (Richard Wasserstrom, for example) generally respond to utilitarian criticism by finding unnoticed utility of one or more of at least three sorts:

First, there is the utility of *simplified procedures*. In some areas of the law, for example, traffic offenses, proof of fault is (it is said) too expensive for the protection such proof would provide. The penalty for a traffic offense is (generally) a small fine, a sum easily devoured in a few minutes of legal maneuver.

Second, there is the utility of *threats to justice*. For example, why require that a rapist be shown to have intended to rape his victim (that is, have intended to have sex against his victim's will), knew that he was raping her, or should have known that he was raping her? Why not define rape so that its proof requires only a showing that the rapist intended to have sex with his victim, knew that she objected over and over again, and went ahead anyway? His intention to have sex would ordinarily be obvious from what he said and did, as would his knowledge of her objections. His intention to rape her (as opposed to his intention to have consensual sex) is, in contrast, much harder to show. He may have had odd ideas about the way women act or may now find such odd ideas convenient. How are we to know? Requiring proof of negligence about consent (rather than intention) would make proof of rape easier, but not as easy as strict liability would. The proof of negligence would also have risks society should not run. In some matters, consent to sex being but one, juries (and judges) may have odd ideas about what assumptions are reasonable. Society may be better off if they are not given an opportunity to bring those ideas into a trial.

Third, there is the utility of *second thoughts*. In certain activities easily avoided, the primary effect of strict liability may not be to encourage people to exercise super care so much as to make sure that they exercise reasonable care. Consider a company packaging dangerous drugs. Strict liability for accurate labeling means that the company—and its responsible officers—know that, in case of error, they cannot hope to avoid criminal liability merely by showing that they had this or that procedure. The company therefore has an incentive to review procedures regularly. If such review is prohibitively expensive, or leaves the company uncomfortable about its ability to prevent labeling errors, the company *should* leave the field. A company that cannot afford procedures sufficient to make it reasonably sure its packaging is safe, is a company whose absence from the field would benefit society.

Response to retributive criticism of strict liability in the criminal law may be divided into two categories. Some theorists (Hyman Gross, for example) have argued that crimes of strict liability do impose liability for fault but for a fault less serious than negligence. So, for example, the woman of our example should be held strictly liable for bigamy, if she should remarry, because remarrying when any doubt remains about the termination of the first marriage is always objectionable. Where one's conduct exhibits that fault, the law may justly force one to act at one's own risk.

Other theorists (for example, Michael Davis) have argued instead that fault is not necessary for criminal punishment to be deserved. A statute imposing strict liability is morally justifiable if it prohibits a threat of harm (or loss of advantage) with which the law justly concerns itself, the threat cannot be controlled satisfactorily by any reasonable provision short of criminal prohibition but can be controlled satisfactorily by such prohibition, and strict liability does not impose an unfair burden (for example, by attaching to an activity not easily avoided).

We have so far been concerned with a question of *demarcation,* whether the criminal law should include any strict liability at all. Assuming it should, we reach a question of *proportion,* how much to punish those found strictly liable.

In practice, there seems to be general agreement that strict liability offenses, if punishable at all, should be punished less severely than the corresponding intentional, knowing, reckless, or negligent offense. Judges generally consider the actual degree of fault at sentencing, reserving the lightest penalties for those who acted without fault.

Yet both retributivists and utilitarians have trouble explaining lesser punishment for strict liability. For retributivists, the problem is that, while a lesser degree of fault clearly deserves less punishment, it is not obvious why no fault deserves any punishment. For utilitarians, on the other hand, the problem is explaining why strict liability offenses should not be punished *more* severely than others. Insofar as the purpose of punishment is to prevent crime (whether by deterrence, reform, or incapacitation), relative fault can only be relevant insofar as relevant to prevention. Insofar as strict liability demands more of people than even liability for negligence does (super care rather than reasonable care), deterring crimes of strict liability should, it seems, require higher, not lower, penalties than deterring the corresponding negligent crimes.

References

Alexander, Larry. "Reconsidering the Relationship Among Voluntary Acts, Strict Liability, and Negligence in Criminal Law." *Social Philosophy and Policy* 7 (1990), 84–104.

American Law Institute. *Model Penal Code and Commentaries.* Philadelphia: American Law Institute Press, 1985.

Davis, Michael. *To Make the Punishment Fit the Crime.* Boulder CO: Westview Press, 1992.

Gross, Hyman. *A Theory of Criminal Justice.* New York: Oxford University Press, 1979.

Hall, Jerome. *Principles of Criminal Law.* Indianapolis: Bobbs-Merrill, 1960.

Hart, H.L.A. *Punishment and Responsibility.* New York: Oxford University Press, 1968.

Sayre, Francis B. "Public Welfare Offenses." *Columbia Law Review* 33 (1933), 55–84.

Wasserstrom, Richard. "Strict Liability in the Criminal Law." *Stanford Law Review* 12 (1969), 731–745.

Williams, Glanville. *Criminal Law: The General Part.* London: Stevens, 1961.

Michael Davis

See also FAULT; INTENT; LIABILITY, CRIMINAL; MENS REA; NEGLIGENCE, CRIMINAL; PRIMA FACIE OBLIGATION

Successions

See INHERITANCE AND SUCCESSION

Suicide

See EUTHANASIA AND SUICIDE

Supererogation

Supererogation, literally action "above what is asked," is the name given to actions regarded as beyond what is required of duty. The category includes especially actions considered heroic or saintly. Supererogatory actions are those which are thought to be highly commendable morally but not morally mandatory. They are not duties, as duty is usually understood to comprise that which is expected of everyone and which if neglected earns the agent reproach or demerit. Supererogatory acts are not expected: they are ideals or aspirations. It is not shameful to fail to perform a heroic rescue, for example; rather, doing so earns one high praise. More precisely, an act is supererogatory if (1) it is not morally required, (2) performing it earns high praise for the agent, and (3) failure to perform does not subject the agent to legitimate rebuke. This distinguishes supererogatory acts from actions fulfilling ordinary duties, such as truth-telling and promise-keeping, which are obligatory rather than praiseworthy. These are defined by the contradictory of the three conditions mentioned: they are required of everyone, performing them does not earn one any special praise, and, since it is wrong not to do them, failure to perform earns one censure.

The fact that our conceptual scheme admits supererogatory acts is said to exhibit a shortcoming in "single principle" ethical systems such as utilitarianism and kantianism. According to single principle systems, actions which satisfy the principle are morally required, and all other actions are prohibited (or at best are morally indifferent). For example, according to utilitarianism, if among all the actions one might do at any given moment, there is one which produces more happiness than any other, then that action is required and all the other actions are prohibited; if several actions each would produce greatest happiness, then any one of these is required and all the others prohibited. There is evidently no place for a supererogatory act, that is, an action which is not morally required but is nonetheless morally commendable. Any morally commendable action according to utilitarianism must maximize happiness, but any action that did would be morally required. Similarly, in Kant's system, moral worth consists entirely in the desire to do one's duty, duty being determined by conformity to the categorical imperative; if neither doing nor refraining from an action violates the categorical imperative, it is a matter of moral indifference whether or not the action be done. This does not seem to allow for actions which are not required yet are morally good. According to Kant's principle, actions normally thought of as supererogatory would seem to be required: we could not will that everyone refrain from performing dangerous rescues, for example, so rescue would be mandatory.

Furthermore, supererogation seems to throw doubt on the general applicability of many principles said to be fundamental. According to utilitarianism, moral worth can only come from production of happiness, and the more happiness produced, the greater the worth of the action. However, it is far from clear that saintly or heroic acts are highly praiseworthy because of the good they do, or because of the happiness they produce; it is even less evident that they are praiseworthy because they do more good than simple duties such as promise-keeping. The basic idea of the supererogatory seems to be selflessness or sacrifice beyond what most people are willing or able to manage; putting the self out of the picture rather than doing good as such seems to be the principle that identifies supererogatory acts.

Additionally, the standard classification of actions as either prohibited, permitted, or required is inadequate if supererogatory acts are allowed, at least if permitted actions are regarded as morally indifferent, since supererogatory actions, though not required, are not morally indifferent but highly commendable and praiseworthy.

Supererogation was well studied by the classical theologians but was lost from view until recently in modern philosophy (the term is not listed in Flew's *Dictionary of Philosophy*), the current interest in the topic stemming from the 1958 essay by J.O. Urmson, who however does not use the term "supererogation." Thomas Aquinas argued that chastity, poverty, and renunciation of worldly success are not commanded nor for everyone, but earn special merit. The actions of the saints were recognized as a special category of morally commendable act; in doing more good than was obligatory, the saints stored up extra good in heaven, which could be drawn on by those suffering from moral deficits on earth (this was the theoretical basis of the system of indulgences which later figured in the Reformation). Even the commandment to love your enemies could be taken as supererogatory, such love being regarded as too difficult for most people and thus not a universal duty. Martin Luther and John Calvin, however, who vigorously disputed that God's word could be divided in obligatory commandments and optional exhortations and recommendations, supported moral perfectionism or rigorism, that we must always do our moral best. Immanuel Kant also holds that moral perfection is required of us by the moral law; however, his distinction between perfect and imperfect duties elsewhere reintroduces an element of choice in our moral constraints. Perfectionism may be also attributed to utilitarianism, according to which it is always a duty to produce the greatest good. In these views there can be no place for supererogation. However, it could be the case that we ought to strive to be perfect, yet not be at fault if we fail to reach perfection. So perfectionism may be regarded as a confusion between ideals and duties: even if we ought to aspire to be perfect, it cannot subject us to reproach should we fail.

It can be said that saints are not very nice people, since they tend to lack many ordinary virtues such as fellowship and a sense of humor, and that therefore we would not in fact want to live among them, so that sainthood is overrated. This view seems to assume that saints are people whose lives are dedicated to something, possibly to being moral, aiding the sick, intensifying spirituality, or upholding religious convictions. Such people might be thought of as one-sided, stuffy, and intimidating. But if we regard saints as people who lead lives of extraordinary morality, there is no reason to assume that saints cannot be perfectly good company, as well as good citizens, friends, parents, and fellow workers.

Supererogation, however, may seem to offer an easy excuse for not doing what is difficult. There seem to be situations in which we are called on to do what is heroic; failure to do so may subject the agent to justified reproach. A person who fails to effect a dangerous rescue may nonetheless be dishonored and suffer pangs of guilt for not doing what was not required. This is not irrational. Germans and others who during the Nazi period failed to help victims of Adolf Hitler should not be excused simply on the grounds that rendering assistance was dangerous and therefore would have been heroic. Though those who rescued earned special praise, those who failed to rescue are properly subject to rebuke. Thus there seems to be needed a third class of morally commendable actions in addition to ordinary duties and the supererogatory. These are actions which, like supererogation, earn for the agent special merit, but which are nonetheless morally mandatory; failure to perform them subjects agents to justified rebuke. These are defined by condition (2), not (1) and not (3). They may be called "heroic duties."

Supererogation enters the law notably with regard to the duty to assist or to rescue. Assisting strangers in distress is regarded by the (Anglo-American, though not generally European) law as supererogatory, but it is often argued that rescue should be made a legal duty, at least where it can be effectuated without "undue danger, inconvenience or expense" to the rescuer. Another currently supererogatory area is organ donation, but again, it could be held that, given the shortage of available organs for transplant, the law should recognize, perhaps through some form of implied consent scheme, a legal duty to donate healthy organs of the recently dead. These reforms are opposed by libertarians, who want to limit the sphere of the obligatory, and supererogationists, who think much of the moral value of good deeds would be lost if they were required by law.

References

Ellin, Joseph. "Saints, Heroes and Supererogation." In *Morality and the Meaning of Life*. Fort Worth TX: Harcourt Brace, 1995.

Heyd, David. *Supererogation: Its Status in Ethical Theory*. New York: Cambridge University Press, 1982.

Mellema, Gregory. *Beyond the Call of Duty: Supererogation, Obligation and Offence*. Albany: State University of New York Press, 1991.

Urmson, J.O. "Saints and Heroes." In *Essays in Moral Philosophy,* ed. A.I. Melden. Washington University Press, 1958.

Wolf, Susan. "Moral Saints." *Journal of Philosophy* 79 (August 1982).

Joseph Ellin

See also IMPERFECT OBLIGATION; MERCY AND FORGIVENESS; OMISSIONS; RESCUE IN TORT AND CRIMINAL LAW; VIRTUE

Superior Orders and Legitimate Authority

In a way, the distinction between superior orders and legitimate authority, in just war theory, tracks the distinction between *jus in bello* and *jus ad bellum*. One acts under superior orders (or fails to) in the field, during the act of war making. Thus, the notion of superior orders is one attached to justice in war, *jus in bello*. On the other hand, one acts under legitimate authority (or fails to) in the decision to wage war at all, that is, the justice of war, *jus ad bellum*.

At least one authority (James Childress) points out that legitimate authority to wage war is a prerequisite to all other criteria of *jus ad bellum*, for someone (a person or institution) must decide upon just cause, proportionality, and so forth, and that person or institution is picked out by the criterion of legitimate authority.

One can then imagine a soldier or even a newly conscripted citizen deciding whether the sovereign is legitimate and legitimately exercising its authority in taking the manner it wages its country's war. That is the *jus in bello* notion of superior orders—how a war is waged. The prima facie duty is to obey superior orders if they issue ultimately (through the ranks) from a legitimate authority. Note that the issue of superior orders and conscientious objection are closely related, for both involve either questioning the legitimacy of an authority or its order, an authority whose normative force comes originally from the sovereign.

There is, however, an important logical difference between legitimate authority and superior orders beyond that cited above. Legitimate authority is one of several necessary conditions, each of which must be satisfied for the decision to make war to be just. Others include just cause, proportion of good to evil, and the possibility of victory. Superior orders work somewhat differently. Superior orders are not necessary for the just waging of war, because many of the actions soldiers in the field perform are on their own initiative. Rather, superior orders is an affirmative defense or excuse for what otherwise might be immoral or illegal action. Let us return to the moral status and justification (to the extent any exists) for superior orders after considering the history of both notions.

These notions, like just war theory in general, can be traced back to early and medieval Christian thought. Augustine spoke of the Christian's obligation to the sovereign to fight in wars, anticipating the distinction between *jus ad bellum* and *jus in bello*. Thomas Aquinas has the logical space for questioning authority through his well-known distinction between human law and natural law and his distinction between legitimate rule and tyranny. However, it seems that so long as a prince is legitimate, he is the "minister of God" who should destroy those who do evil. This presumably includes other princes who are doing evil.

Early modern thinkers like Francisco de Vitoria and Hugo Grotius, seeing the space left by Thomas Aquinas and Christian doctrine as natural law thinkers themselves, maintained a moral position from which princely authority to wage war could be questioned. However, they sometimes seem to assume that, if a prince was legitimately a prince, his authority to wage war was ipso facto legitimate and unquestioned. (Grotius demurred from this view more clearly than the other two.)

Throughout this time, the issue of superior orders never really emerged as a separate issue from that of legitimate authority, although as early as Vitoria, the more general distinction between *jus in bello* and *jus ad bellum* was clear. Perhaps this was because it was simply assumed that a soldier in the field must obey his superior officer. Lines of authority and command responsibility were never too clear in medieval, that is, feudal, armies or in those made up of mercenaries in the early modern period. However, by the time of the rise of the professional, national army with Gustavus Adolphus in the seventeenth century, and Frederick the Great in the eighteenth, field discipline was unquestioned and unquestionable.

With the development of professional armies and the rise of the nation-state, the natural law of war that was part of the Roman Catholic tradition, as well as the work of Grotius and Emer de Vattel, went into eclipse. Positivism rose in its stead, claiming that the only restrictions on a nation-state were those of treaty or convention, and *raison d'état* (state necessity) overrode even that. So, if a state and its government were legitimate, no other question could be asked. The notion of *compétence de guerre* held, in the words of James Turner Johnson, "that if a prince could make war and get away with it, he had authority to do so." In addition, as Donald Wells explains, "No one ever imagined that laws of war would take precedence over the demands of national sovereignty." So, neither the notion of legitimate authority nor limitations on superior orders served as any moral or legal limitation upon the war making of states or the action of soldiers in the field.

Everything changed in 1910 when the major world powers signed the Hague Convention on the Laws of Land War. Now an authority above the sovereign could make *illegal* certain means of war waging a sovereign or its representatives might choose. Thus certain acts of war waging were illegitimate and certain (superior) orders were nonbinding, if they contravened that higher authority, that is, the convention. With the advent of the Covenant of the League of Nations, the Kellogg-Briand Pact, the Nuremberg Charter, and finally the United Nations Charter, the very waging of wars not in self-defense or the defense of alliance partners became illegal. So *jus ad bellum* considerations could render a legitimate sovereign's decision to wage war illegal and presumably morally illegitimate. Also, through the Nuremberg decisions, the defense of superior orders has been highly limited; it clearly will not justify or excuse crimes against humanity. Furthermore, most authorities believe superior orders will not excuse the more serious *jus ad bellum* offenses, such as the intentional killing of civilians or prisoners of war. This seems much more clear for those in immediate field command (even though acting under direct superior orders) than for rank-and-file troops, however.

The moral foundation of the legitimate authority doctrine traces directly back to the notion of the legitimacy of sovereign government in political theory. However, the moral foundations of the superior orders defense and its exceptions are more complicated. Michael Walzer believes that the defense must be based upon either ignorance or duress. The soldiers or officials might plead they did not know of the crimes being committed or know that the acts constituted crimes, or they might plead that they knew but that their own safety would have been compromised had they refused. This brings us to a famous moral conundrum: can individuals be required to refuse an order to kill, knowing they will be killed for refusing? Needless to say, authorities differ in a case where the choices are so stark.

References

Child, James W., and Donald Scherer. *Two Paths to Peace: Pacifism and Just War Theory*. Philadelphia: Temple University Press, 1992.

Childress, James F. *Moral Responsibility in Conflicts*. Baton Rouge: Louisiana State University Press, 1982.

Cooper, David. "Responsibility and the 'System'." In *Individual and Collective Responsibility: The Massacre at My Lai*, ed. Peter French, 83–100. Cambridge MA: Harvard University Press, 1972.

Johnson, James Turner. *Just War Tradition and the Restraint of War*. Princeton: Princeton University Press, 1981.

O'Brien, William V. *The Conduct of Just and Limited War*. New York: Praeger, 1981.

Taylor, Telford. *Nuremberg and Vietnam: An American Tragedy*. New York: Times Books, 1970.

Walzer, Michael. *Just and Unjust Wars*. New York: Basic Books, 1977.

Wells, Donald. *War Crimes and the Laws of War*. New York: University Press of America, 1984.

Weston, Burns H., Richard A. Falk, and Anthony D'Amato. *International Law and World Order*. 2d ed. St. Paul MN: West, 1990.

James W. Child

See also Civil Disobedience; Conscience; Conscientious Objection

Surrogacy

The typical case of commercial surrogacy involves a contracting couple paying a fee to a woman beyond her reasonable expenses to bear a child who will be raised by the couple and whose genetic father is the husband. A surrogate arrangement could involve as many as five parties, if the resulting child were the product of egg and sperm donations by two other parties. In such a case, neither the surrogate nor the contracting couple would be genetically related to the resulting child.

The moral issues are whether parties should be free to make such agreements and whether these agreements should be enforceable in law. Arguments for a negative answer to the first question are either deontological or utilitarian. The chief deontological arguments conclude that such agreements treat the resulting child and the surrogate's body as a mere means, commodifying the children and women's bodies. The utilitarian argument is that these agreements lead to the exploitation of surrogates and infertile couples.

That children are treated as mere means in such arrangements is the conclusion of those who believe the contract is for the sale of a baby. If it were a contract merely for the gestational services of the surrogate, the surrender of custody would not be required: the surrogate would have fulfilled the contract when she gave birth. Yet such agreements specify that the fee (over and above expenses) is to be paid only when custody has been surrendered.

One response to this argument is that the baby is not sold as a slave. Instead, only the right to rear the child is transferred. Unlike sales of inanimate objects that permit the buyers to destroy or mutilate the object, the right to rear the child is circumscribed by numerous duties, prohibiting child neglect and abuse.

It has been argued in response that commercial surrogacy contracts are for services with a particular outcome, not unlike the fee paid a plumber to repair a sink—to whom nothing would be paid for a failed attempt at repair. The transfer of custody rights might be viewed as one of the services called for in the contract. As might be expected, those opposed to commercial surrogacy on these grounds find that this response disguises the sale of a baby as a service.

An important assumption behind the argument that the child is sold is that the gestational mother has parental rights which she can surrender, or that the "real" mother of the child is the gestational mother. If this is correct, then it could happen that the gestational mother could surrender rights to a child to which only the contracting couple were related. We might suppose that the egg and sperm came from the contracting couple, or that their embryo is implanted in the surrogate. It seems odd that the couple must acquire parental rights from a surrogate to a child with their genes and none from the surrogate.

The other deontological objection to commercial surrogacy is that there are certain services that cannot be for sale without violating human dignity, one of which is reproductive service. Jones violates Smith's human dignity by buying Smith's reproductive services, much as Jones would violate Smith's dignity if Smith sold herself into slavery to Jones.

The response to this is that such agreements are (or can be) voluntary and do not involve the surrender of all freedom, as sale into slavery or indentured servitude would. So, short of some evidence of coercion or surrender of all autonomy, it does not appear that the surrogate becomes a mere means.

The utilitarian argument against surrogacy is that it leads to exploitation of surrogates and infertile couples by brokers, who will seek to maximize their return by paying as small a fee as possible to the surrogate and charge the contracting couple as much as possible. The fear is that women who are otherwise destitute will rent their wombs only with an eye to the fee. As with all utilitarian arguments, opposition to the practice depends on long-term consequences being favorable to the general happiness. An argument could be made that commercial surrogacy should be given a trial run to determine whether surrogates are often destitute.

Granting the force of some or all of these objections, surrogacy might still be allowed. So-called "altruistic surrogacy" where a sister or a mother acts as a surrogate would escape all these objections, because there would be no compensation for the acquisition of parental rights (over and above expenses). Commercial surrogacy might be permitted if the contract allowed the surrogate to keep the child and the entire fee until a specified time after birth. There might also be minimum incomes for surrogates to ensure that poor women are not exploited.

Where surrogacy contracts are permitted, the form enforcement of them should take would be problematic. Among the difficulties would be forcing the surrogate not to engage in conduct detrimental to the fetus during pregnancy, determining whether the contracting couple must accept a child born with serious defects and whether the surrogate can be forced to surrender parental rights should she choose not to do so. In all these cases, except perhaps the first, the argument can be made that the contracting couple takes its chances on the outcome. In this way, there would be little encroachment on the autonomy of the surrogate.

Some feminists have expressed concern about the eugenic implications of surrogacy in light of genetic research. The ability to manipulate the embryo in the laboratory may lead to women's increased loss of control over reproduction. One can envision, for example, mandatory genetic screening of all embryos for certain diseases and conditions, along with a requirement that, where possible, there be intrauterine surgery.

One can also envision, however, "made-to-order" babies, so skin color, gender, height, physical agility, and so on could be manipulated as the parents might wish. Far from loss of control, this scenario might afford parents a troubling amount of control over the characteristics of their children.

At present, however, the primary way of determining characteristics of the child is genetic testing followed by an abortion. Sex determination is accomplished this way, though other characteristics detectable by genetic testing could also be controlled in this manner.

As improvements are made, not only in such testing but in intrauterine corrective surgery, the basis for wrongful life suits may become more plausible. Though few jurisdictions allow children to recover damages for the defects which, for example, a physician or laboratory failed to discover, the basis for such suits is that the child's nonexistence is preferable to life with certain kinds of severe defects. Advances in the safety and sophistication in medical techniques for correcting such defects would permit children born with them to argue that the defects should have been corrected before birth.

References

Kornegay, R. Jo. "Is Commercial Surrogacy Babyselling?" *Journal of Applied Philosophy* 7 (1990), 45–50.

Moody-Adams, Michele. "On Surrogacy: Morality, Markets, and Motherhood." *Public Affairs Quarterly* 5 (1991), 175–190.

Page, Edgar. "Donation, Surrogacy, and Adoption." *Journal of Applied Philosophy* 2 (1985), 161–172.

Rae, Scott B. *The Ethics of Commercial Surrogate Motherhood.* Westport CT: Praeger, 1994.

Schedler, George. "Women's Reproductive Rights." *Journal of Legal Medicine* 7 (1986), 357–384.

Spallone, Patricia, and Deborah Lynn Steinberg. *Made to Order.* Oxford: Pergamon, 1987.

George E. Schedler

See also FEMINIST PHILOSOPHY OF LAW; LEGITIMATE OBJECT OF CONTRACT; SALE; SLAVERY

Symbols

See METAPHOR AND SYMBOL

Systems Theory

See LUHMANN, NICKLAS

T

Takings

See Eminent Domain and Takings

Taxation

How should we pay for the costs of government? Three answers come to mind. The government can print money, it can borrow money, or it can tax its citizens.

Most modern governments do all three. However, it is generally agreed that taxation is a superior mechanism. Both printing and borrowing stimulate inflation. Inflation is, in itself, a tax. Moreover, it is a tax whose burden is allocated unfairly among the citizens. Those citizens who are retired on fixed incomes bear a heavier burden from inflation than those who are still in the workforce.

The analysis of inflation suggests the major philosophical question which arises in the consideration of taxation: how should the burden of taxation be allocated among the populace? This question divides into two further issues: the proper tax base and the proper rate structure—progressive, regressive, or proportional.

Tax Base

A Head Tax

The simplest way to collect a tax would be to divide the government expenditure by the number of citizens and collect an equal amount from each citizen. Within recent memory, the figures for the United States might have been: Annual Government Expenditure / Number of people = $750 billion / 250 million = $3,000.

The problem is that not every citizen (some of whom are infants) can afford to pay $3,000 per year, and some can afford to pay much more. Therefore, it is appropriate to consider modes of taxation which levy different amounts on different people.

Benefit Tax

Benefit theory holds that the burden of taxation should be allocated according to the benefits of government services received. Consider a government-built turnpike. Those who drive on the turnpike pay for its construction and maintenance. The more miles they drive, the higher the toll. Those who do not use the turnpike do not pay for it. What could be more fair?

The problem is that not all services are as measureable as the use of a turnpike, and some which are cannot possibly be taxed to the recipients. How do we measure the benefits of national defense or a clean environment? Moreover, how can we tax welfare benefits, no matter how easily measured, to welfare recipients? Do we not confer welfare benefits precisely because the recipients cannot afford the necessities of life? What sense does it make to tax them?

Having rejected a benefit tax, one arrives at the principle of ability to pay. Those who are able to pay more should pay more in tax; those who are less able to pay should pay less. Now, how does one measure ability to pay? Three measurements have been suggested: income, spending, and wealth.

Income

Income is the major tax base in many western countries. Clearly, those with high incomes are generally better able to pay taxes. However, income alone will not work. Imagine a maharajah in his palace and a beggar at the palace gate. The maharajah has everything he could possibly desire already at hand. The beggar has nothing. However, neither has any income, according to Nicholas Kaldor. The maharajah clearly has more ability to pay, but the income tax does not distinguish him from the beggar. Either a spending tax or a wealth tax would do the trick.

Spending

As Thomas Hobbes asked, which makes more sense: taxing those who produced and contribute goods and services *into* the common pool or taxing those who take goods and services *out*? An income tax is levied on those who put things in; a spending tax is levied on those who take things out. All taxes unavoidably lessen the behavior taxed. Should we not encourage the production of income and discourage spending?

Should all spending be taxed? Should we exempt the poor family's porridge and tax the rich family's caviar at high rates? Note that, if we were to do this, rich people would acquire a new taste for porridge.

Wealth

An annual wealth tax would also distinguish the maharajah and the beggar. However, there are good arguments for exempting some items from a wealth tax. Do we really want to tax the poor person's home? Do we want to bother appraising the value of one's toothbrush in adding up one's wealth? Yet, as soon as we tax some wealth and exempt others, we generate complexity and avoidance, as noted previously.

Tax Structure

Definitions

When charting effective tax rates over the tax base, any line which has a positive slope is a *progressive* tax. Note that a progressive tax takes not only more dollars, but an increasing proportion of dollars, as the tax base increases.

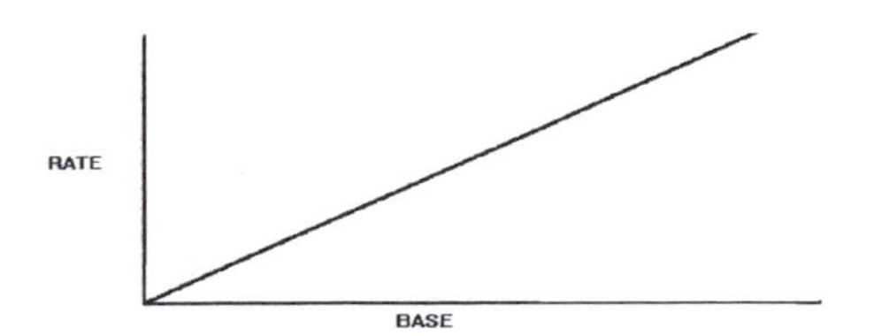

Any tax structure which produces a flat, horizontal line is called a *flat, or proportionate,* tax. A flat tax takes the same *proportion* of taxable base from the haves as from the have-nots, although it inevitably takes more *dollars* from the haves.

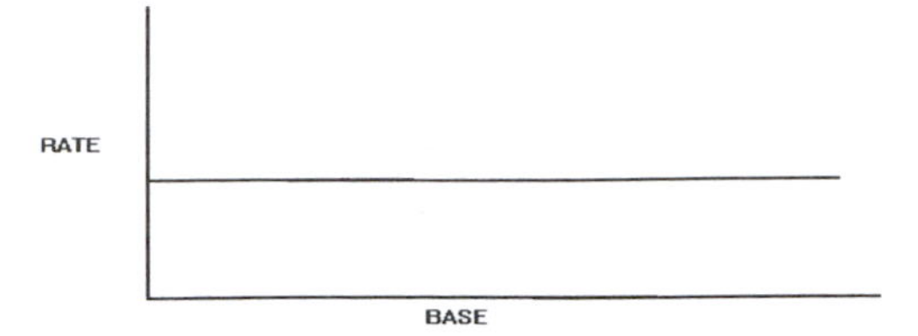

A *regressive* tax is a tax which produces a negative slope when effective rates are graphed against the tax base. In contrast to the flat and progressive taxes, a regressive tax takes both fewer dollars and a decreasing proportion of dollars as the tax base increases.

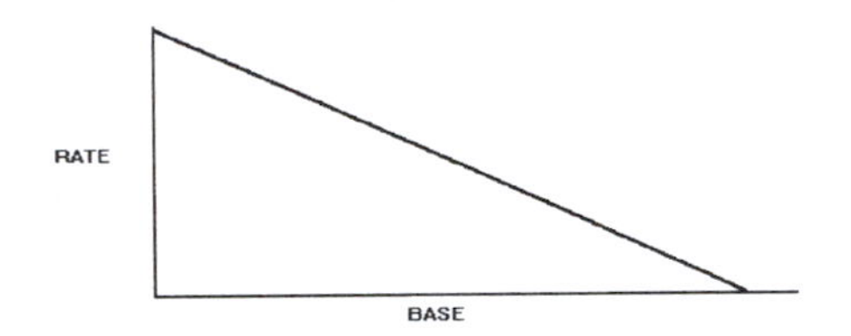

Arguments

Virtually no one argues for a regressive tax. Thus, the battle shifts to proportional taxes versus progressive taxes. Earlier arguments based on the goal of minimum aggregate sacrifice (John Stuart Mill) and the marginal utility of money (Walter Blum and Harry Kalven) have proved unworkable. The only viable argument for progressivity is that (1) there is too much inequality in the distribution of wealth and income in the society, (2) taxation is the best medium for redistribution, and (3) a progressive rate structure is the most effective way to make the tax system do this job.

In making this argument, one must face the undeniable fact that progressivity is an enormously complicating factor in a tax. Furthermore, progressivity, especially in an income tax, penalizes the very people who are contributing the most to the society, as measured by the marketplace. If these people produce less, then all of us are worse off.

Moreover, one must consider the difference between equality of income and wealth, and equality of opportunity. Equality of opportunity suggests that the race is not fair unless we all start from the same starting line. Equality of income suggests that we call off the race altogether. Is not equality of opportunity more easily justified than equality of income? This premise would suggest steeply progressive taxes on the transfer of wealth, and flat taxes on current income, spending, or wealth.

I would suggest that the current amount of progressivity in the United States is about right and that the mix of taxes in the European countries (which have somewhat more emphasis on spending taxes, through the value-added tax (VAT), and less on income than the United States) would be preferable.

References

Blum, Walter J., and Harry Kalven, Jr. *The Uneasy Case for Progressive Taxation.* Chicago: Phoenix Books, 1953.

Groves, Harold M. *Tax Philosophers*. Madison: University of Wisconsin Press, 1974.

Hobbes, Thomas. *The Leviathan*. Cambridge: Cambridge University Press, 1991.

Kaldor, Nicholas. *An Expenditure Tax*. London: Allen and Unwin, 1955.

Kay, J.A., and M.A. King. *The British Tax System*. 4th ed. Oxford: Oxford University Press, 1986.

Meade, J.E. *The Structure and Reform of Direct Taxation*. London: Allen and Unwin, 1978.

Mill, John Stuart. *Principles of Political Economy*. London: Longmans, Green, 1936.

Okun, Arthur. *Equality and Efficiency: The Big Tradeoff*. Washington DC: Brookings Institution, 1975.

Royal Commission on Taxation (Canada). *Report of the Royal Commission on Taxation*. Ottawa: Queen's Printer, 1966.

Smith, Adam. *An Inquiry into the Nature and Causes of the Wealth of Nations*. Chicago: University of Chicago Press, 1976.

Joel S. Newman

See also Distributive Justice; Economics; Efficiency; Inheritance and Succession

Terrorism

It is disheartening to acknowledge that terrorism is on the rise, globally, even while large-scale wars are becoming less commonplace. The inclusion of that topic in a work on philosophy of law is in itself somewhat contentious, since it implies that terrorism might be a form of activity that is, or should be, under the control of laws, by no means a universally agreed upon fact. The basic question is precisely what is terrorism: is it an (illegal) form of war? Is it simply a species of organized crime? Is it "mindless violence," as stated by Paul Gilbert? Jan Narveson, for instance, argues that "terrorism can be neither murder, which is purely private and has no political significance, nor war, which is entirely public and overt, but which the terrorist's party would be incapable of winning."

In essence, the terrorist does not engage in either civil war or revolution, although the results the terrorist advocates may be similar to both. As far as "random violence" is concerned, that which separates "terrorism" from either random activities, or even crime, is a political stance of a special kind, namely, one aimed at forcing a government hostile to the terrorist's territorial claims or freedom claims to change its position, by the strongest means possible, short of waging an actual war.

If that is the case, then all the ethical and political questions addressing what might be appropriate or permissible for those with strong "territorial" or "freedom" claims rest on a further metaphysical question. In other words, what is appropriate behavior for a political community rests on the underlying question of what *is* a political community. This question must be answered before deciding whether a "political community" might have some justification in their violent quest for self-affirmation or freedom from imposed (and unacceptable) governance. When viewed from this perspective it is not necessary for a political community to be oppressed before it could claim to be justified in repelling "foreign" governance. Paul Gilbert says that "the justification for removing discriminatory injustice by achieving independent government, is thus analogous to that for throwing off foreign occupation." What terrorist groups may want is to be treated like *political equals*, rather than simply to be "treated well." In fact, international terrorism is normally concerned primarily with either (1) territory or (2) political equality. Moreover (1), when it is in question, precludes the very possibility of (2): "A political community can only exist within a certain territory."

Hence the argument often advanced against terrorism, that these national groups ought to seek redress for their grievances by peaceful means, does not stand up to logical scrutiny. Democracy, at best, reflects only the will of the majority within *one* national state. In cases when this national state comprises two or more political communities, some of which may well be in the minority, any possibility of self-affirmation is precluded. Moreover, if the existence of a divided or fragmented political community extending across a state's national borders is a major cause of the political impotence of a community, this community, even if partially housed in a democratic state, will have no way to combine with others belonging to the same "community" beyond the state's borders.

In sum, terrorism appears to be more than crime or "mindless violence": it may support morally defensible positions that do not appear to be open to legal support, even less to peaceful implementation. On the other hand, even the most valuable points terrorists may attempt to make are lost in the immoral and unacceptable form taken by their attempts at self-affirmation.

There are several terrorist aims that may appear to be at least prima facie legitimate, or, at the very least, intelligible. First of all, terrorists present a communitarianism or a collectivism which is normally missing from the individualistic modern states. It might be represented by the aim to "free" (or restore previous territories to) a community which is presently denied equal consideration by a state's government. Second, reaffirming and restoring traditionally held values may also be viewed as a legitimate goal, particularly if these values have been depreciated or even repressed by the present rule. Either of these positions may appeal to a "vision" of a better society/community, in the future, after the objectionable or intolerable present conditions have been removed.

Such appeals appear based on consequentialist arguments, appealing to the end or results, to justify the means. Upon closer consideration, however, even the establishment of these worthy states, or utopias, cannot be defended on utilitarian grounds, and the "vision" itself remains problematic. Taking the last point first, we must admit that popular desire for the "vision," or consent to it, is not often researched or sought by terrorists; both are simply affirmed, without proof. Moreover, terrorists typically do not engage in feasibility studies, cost/benefit analyses, or social audits, to support their chosen goals. However, in order for any "vision" to be used to justify possible violence on its behalf, one would need strong evidence that (1) the "vision" will represent a clear improvement on the present system, with respect to justice, and that (2) there is strong evidence that present violent action will indeed serve to bring about the better state, in spite of human fallibility and incapacity to accurately assess long-term consequences (a common failing of utilitarianism in other contexts as well; see *An Environmental Proposal for Ethics* by L. Westra).

Utilitarian principles cannot be used by terrorists for another reason as well: the doctrine demands impartiality in the calculation of pleasure and pain which will result from our actions. The terrorists, on the contrary, claim they are justified in inflicting pain or death on innocents, because of their ultimate goal and because of the special kinship and communitarian ties they have to "their own." Yet one of the most significant differences between the terrorist and the "war wager," or the criminal, is precisely the claim made that the terrorist has a *principled* activity, that neither gain nor personal or group advantage motivates his violence. It is only intended to foster the achievement or recovery of the prized values of freedom, egalitarian respect, or justice from state institutions. Violence is undertaken as a "statement" or a "declaration of intent" to either initiate a dialogue with state institutions to modify their present interpretations of shared values, or to introduce new but defensible values which are not presently supported or even understood by these institutions.

Hence the terrorist's aim is deeply ethical and may be the expression of frustration and indignation, as well as the rejection of unacceptable institutional practices. Terrorist violence is therefore both *reactive and proactive* in its purpose, although terrorists are typically much clearer about its reactive role than they are about its proactive one. A major problem of terrorism is that the proactive role is seldom clearly and rationally set out and defended, although a view of what the state ought to be like plays a clear role in shaping the terrorist's conception of the prevailing situation as unjust.

If the proactive aspect of terrorism could be made explicit and defended, then some form of "self-defense" could be claimed to at least explain terrorist activity, within a somewhat kantian framework. In essence, principles of respect for personal, autonomously chosen values, strong enough to even supersede biological life, can be defended as such, although they certainly cannot support violence, using Immanuel Kant's doctrine.

Even if principles govern the terrorists, their practices are not acceptable for the most part, and the further question, which requires an urgent answer in that case, is what is the appropriate response on the part of the state and its institutions to the presence of terrorist activities, and what might be viewed as justifiable responses? If terrorism, as Paul Gilbert argues, "has the double character of war and crime," then the state must respond to it either as it would to a military threat (that is, with some form of state terrorism, since the terrorism is not a just war) or by enforcing the law against individuals, thus perhaps risking the maintenance of state security, which represents the state's major obligation.

This dilemma is far more complex than can be indicated at this time. It presents modern-day nations with radical questions about the efficacy and viability of both liberal democracy and the modern state itself, as ultimate center of legitimacy.

References

Barron, Bat-Ami. *Why Terrorism Is Morally Problematic in Feminist Ethics*. Lawrence: University Press of Kansas, 1991.

Frey, R., and C. Morris, eds. *Violence, Terrorism and Justice*. Cambridge: Cambridge University Press, 1991.

Gilbert, Paul. *Terrorism, Security and Nationality: An Introductory Study in Applied Political Philosophy*. London: Routledge, 1994.

Hare, R.M. "On Terrorism." *Journal of Value Inquiry* 13 (1979), 241–249.

Oruka, Odera H. "Legal Terrorism and Human Rights." *Praxis International* A (1982), 376–385.

Teichman, Jenny. "How to Define Terrorism." *Philosophy* 64 (1991), 505–517.

Westra, L. *An Environmental Proposal for Ethics: The Principle of Integrity*. Lanham MD: Rowman and Littlefield, 1994.

———. "Terrorism, Self-Defence and Whistleblowing." *Journal of Social Philosophy* 20 (1989), 46–58.

Laura Westra

See also REBELLION; REVOLUTION; SELF-DEFENSE; WAR AND WAR TRIALS

Testimony and Expert Evidence

The problem of expert evidence neatly resolves into problems to do with expertise and those to do with evidence. The evidence of the expert witness is that of testimony, and here the problem principally concerns epistemological status. Although the word of witnesses is deeply entrenched in legal practice as the primary form of evidence, the philosophical tradition has been distinctly wary of the probative status of human say-so.

Perhaps this is one more instance of the legendary remoteness of philosophical concerns from the domain of practice. Although we are nowadays familiar with a variety of apparently nonpersonal methods of proving conclusions and sifting evidence, ranging from DNA testing to ballistic investigations, courts still depend heavily upon the direct testimony of witnesses. For one thing, the vast majority of criminal convictions rest upon the accused's confession; for another, the evidence of victims and complainants must continue to play a central role in the courts. Moreover, reliance upon the word of others is entrenched in all our practical and cognitive practices, beginning in childhood and continuing in refined and more critical ways throughout adult life.

Most philosophers, who have reluctantly recognized the pervasive significance of reliance upon testimony, have sought to justify this by reductive strategies. Influenced by the individualist ideal of "autonomous knowledge" whereby (in John Locke's words), "the floating of other men's opinions in our brains makes us not one jot the more knowing, though they happen to be true. What in them was science is in us but opiniatrety," they have tried to show that our dependence upon the authoritative reports of others is something that each individual can justify personally by relying solely upon individual resources, such as personal observation. This reductive project seems to have ineradicable flaws. In particular, it tends to ignore the ways in which these individual resources are, directly or indirectly, permeated with the influence of testimony (frequently when we claim something as a matter of observation, it is the observation in whole or part of others), and it is blind to the fact that the personal checking of reports the project requires is not only impossibly extensive, but relies upon an understanding of the common language that already presupposes some degree of unchecked reliability on testimony.

In spite of this, the courts' reliance upon testimony has long been subjected to critique by empirical psychologists. A central thesis has been "the unreliability of testimony," though the critique is largely innocent of any understanding of the central role played by the word of others in our cognitive life. Consequently, its large claims are not really supported by the evidence gathered, a good deal of which itself suffers from faulty methodology. At best, what is established is that defects in testimony, perception, and memory long familiar to ordinary people can be even more dramatic in certain contexts than one might expect. In one experiment, for instance, subjects were shown a picture of a small white man involved in an altercation with a large black man on a subway train. Although the white man wielded a weapon in full view, a distressing number of subjects recalled the weapon as being used by the black man.

The broad epistemological background needs to be remembered when we turn to the expert witness. Ordinary lay testimony already involves cognitive and linguistic expertise, so the expert witness is in many respects simply a special case of the ordinary testifier. On top of the standard testifying skills, the expert brings those appropriate to the area that the court needs information about. Where we have grounds for suspicion about the ordinary witness, there will be similar grounds for suspicion about the expert, but there may also be circumstances peculiar to the expert that should occasion caution. Nonetheless, there is much controversy about expert testimony, and there appear to be three main reasons for this: doubts about the authenticity of the expertise, doubts about the value of "contests of experts," and concerns about the expert subverting the judicial role of the court. All of these are related to the central role played by the adversary system in courts influenced by the Anglo-American model, especially in jury trials.

As to the first, contestants in court inevitably seek the advantages of authority and push the limits of what is expertly known for such advantage. Yet there are more and less secure areas of human knowledge, and many areas that have little claim to security at all. The contestability of so much putative knowledge has driven some critics to suggest that separate boards should be set up to certify acceptable expertise for the courts. This proposal has disadvantages, chief among which is the likely conservatism of such boards, by seeking only the least controverted criteria, and it seems preferable to leave the question of the acceptability of the expert to the court itself, where the matter can be openly debated. What one thinks of the proposal for separate panels will depend somewhat upon what view one takes of the adversary system and the value of juries.

This is also true about the "disedifying" contests of experts. The spectacle of expert "hired guns" shooting it out tends to upset the picture of science as that of dispassionate superminds cooly dissecting or assembling the truth. But this picture, although it gestures toward an important ideal of objectivity, distorts the reality of scientific, or any other, form of inquiry. There are fissures and factions within the scientific community at its best, and all inquiry involves a degree of advocacy. Nonetheless, very strong versions of the adversary process can certainly make it harder to get at what truth the experts have to offer, and this may be a reason for re-examining the ways in which experts are paid for their appearances and how they conceive of their role. Lawyers and judges can usually understand and sift what experts have to say, but this is less clearly true of the average jury. Court-appointed experts would remove some of the problems associated with the experts becoming advocates for "their" side, but those who see a great value in the adversary process for finding truth or protecting rights will worry about the capacity of lawyers to challenge such experts without being able to call witnesses who can do it with more authority.

Finally, the worry about the expert subverting the role of the court arises most acutely where the expert evidence may be regarded as close to providing a verdict on the defendant's guilt or on the civil issue at trial. Psychiatric evidence on defendants' states of mind, for instance, may be directly addressed via mens rea to whether they are responsible for what they did, and hence such witnesses may see themselves (and even be seen) as presenting a verdict on guilt. If we think of the trial process as issuing in a judgment or verdict involving a moral element, we will be anxious that experts not usurp the role of judge and jury, precarious and fallible as the exercise of that role may often be.

References

Coady, C.A.J. *Testimony: A Philosophical Study*. Oxford: Clarendon Press, 1992.

Freckleton, Ian. *The Trial of the Expert*. 2d rev. ed. Melbourne: Oxford University Press, 1997.

Jasanoff, Sheila. *Science at the Bar.* Cambridge MA: Harvard University Press, 1995.

Jones, Carol. *Expert Witnesses*. Oxford: Oxford University Press, 1994.

Kenny, Anthony. "The Expert in Court." In *The Ivory Tower: Essays in Philosophy and Public Policy*. Oxford: B. Blackwell, 1985.

Locke, John. *An Essay on the Human Understanding*. Ed. John W. Yolton. London, 1961.

Wells, G.L., and Elizabeth F. Loftus, eds. *Eyewitness Testimony: Psychological Perspectives*. Cambridge: Cambridge University Press, 1984.

Wigmore, J.H. *A Treatise on the Anglo-American System of Evidence in Trials at Common Law.* 3d ed. Boston: Little, Brown, 1940.

C.A.J. Coady

See also CONFESSIONS; EMPIRICAL EVIDENCE; EVIDENCE; OATHS; RELEVANCE

Theft and Related Offenses

Theft, as the commentary to the *Model Penal Code*, Article 223, specified, is one of a group of the traditional acquisitive offenses. While it is possible to define theft (according to the particular legal system concerned), it is not possible to define the group, simply because there is unlikely to be agreement on the entire catalog of theft-like or even acquisitive offenses.

Theft, under the heading of larceny, is the oldest of the acquisitive offenses. Originally cast in terms of taking and carrying away movable property with intent permanently to deprive the owner thereof, it gradually extended into instances of deception in which the rogue came into possession of goods as a result of deception and made off with them, but the nature of the transaction was such that property did not pass from the owner. This was known historically as *larceny by a trick*. *Embezzlement* grew up to fill a hiatus caused by the requirement that the rogue have taken away property against the will of the owner. The essence of the offense was the subsequent conversion of property by one who took it with the owner's consent and for a particular purpose. Statute extended property offenses into obtaining property by *false pretenses* (available where property passed). Conversion of trust property by the lawful owner was made criminal by the offense of *fraudulent conversion*. The knowing acquisition of stolen goods, usually by purchase, became the crime of receiving stolen goods, and exceptional procedural provisions facilitated proof in the case of the professional receiver or fence.

Over and above these were crimes created to deal with an expanding commercial economy. In England and elsewhere in the Commonwealth the crime of *false accounting* facilitated prosecution when otherwise it would have been necessary to prove theft of a general balance. False accounting extended, however, to the falsification of documents used for an accounting purpose. Offenses concerning *misrepresentations* by company directors were provided for. So too was the acquisition of property by menaces, commonly called *blackmail*, and the use of deception to obtain transfers of valuable securities. In some jurisdictions check *kiting* was dealt with either as a specific offense or by adjustments to the burden of proof in deception offenses.

A further body of offenses involves theft taken with another element, for example, *robbery,* which, essentially, is theft facilitated by violence or threatened violence, *dacoity* under the *Indian Penal Code,* which is similarly defined, and *burglary*, the most important branch of which was *breaking and entering* premises with intent to steal, or stealing after having broken and entered when such intention could not be proved to have existed ab initio. The list of theft-like offenses is, however, not closely defined, nor can it readily be.

Certain common law systems retain codes that perpetuate many of the antique distinctions that applied in this field. The *Criminal Code of Canada* affords an example, and further examples may be found in those jurisdictions that drew inspiration from the *Indian Penal Code,* which, with local variations, perpetuates the law of England as it existed during the mid-nineteenth century. Other jurisdictions have endeavored by way of modern statute to extend the offenses the crime can reach. This was the impetus behind the *Model Penal Code,* whose provisions have been widely adopted in the United States, and the English Theft Act 1968, which has been adopted in certain Commonwealth jurisdictions and, notably, Victoria.

Modern statements of theft and related offenses seek for a unifying principle to bring together the provisions of theft and related offenses. The *Model Penal Code* found the underlying conception that unified larceny, embezzlement, obtaining property by false pretenses, cheating, blackmail, extortion, and receiving stolen property to be the involuntary acquisition of property. Nonetheless, the situations which these offenses deal with are distinct, and some differentiation between them is required if they are to be stated with sufficient particularity to satisfy the exigencies of other doctrines, such as that of legality and the values to which they relate, together with such values as fair notice to the accused of the charge being faced.

The scheme adopted by the *Model Penal Code* is to create a single offense of theft and then to specify in a series of articles different modes of theft, for example, theft by taking or disposition (art. 223.2), theft by deception (art. 223.3), theft by extortion (art. 223.4), theft of lost property (art. 223.5), receiving stolen property (art. 223.6), and theft of funds received (art. 223.7). Also dealt with in the same bundle are such offenses as taking and driving away a motor vehicle (art. 223.9). Other offenses concerning property are dealt with separately from theft, for example, the misuse of credit cards and passing bad checks.

The *Model Penal Code* reform thus consolidates theft but nonetheless specifies distinct modes in which the offense may be committed. It has the advantage of relative simplicity, but this entails a degree of prolixity in its provisions.

The English Theft Act 1968 represents an intellectually more adventurous approach, but one which poses, in some respects, considerable problems in practice. The Criminal Law Revision Committee's *Theft and Related Offences* recommended and the government accepted that the organizing concept in this part of the law ought to be appropriation rather than taking. Theft was thus cast in terms of appropriating property belonging to another, and in turn this was defined not in terms of appropriating a thing, but of appropriating the owner's rights or a right over the thing. The act then specified what property should be capable of being stolen (essentially excluding real property), how property should be defined, and to whom property rhould be taken to belong. The section covering the attribution of property assigned trust property, for example, to the beneficiary, or property received on terms to the one who passed it over on the understanding that it would be dealt with in a particular way. Next, property obtained by the transferor's mistake was attributed to the transferor to the extent that the transferee was subject to a restitutionary obligation in respect of the property. It is through this attribution provision that the consolidation of offenses is achieved. Finally, the baffling provisions of section 6 assimilate certain cases of temporary deprivation to permanent deprivation. The most common case, in the common law, is doubtlessly that of goods temporarily entrusted to another, who then pawns them under conditions for their return that may be impossible to fulfill.

The Theft Act 1968 contains a further bundle of offenses, not all of which can be brought under any organizing principle, either of appropriation or of involuntary transfer of property. Deception can, of course, be regarded as covered by appropriation if fraudulently obtained consent is set aside. So too, no doubt, can robbery. Receiving stolen goods is, however, replaced by handling, which can be committed by receiving, but also by different modes of assisting another to retain or dispose of the goods. False accounting, as before, does not require that goods be acquired. Furthermore, the Theft Act 1978 contains other deception offenses, which cover such topics as dishonestly failing to pay for goods and restaurant bilking. It is clear that considerations of convenience rather than principle dictate which crimes shall, in English law, be included in theft legislation.

This structure was criticized as being too indefinite and too sophisticated at the time of its enactment. Despite criticism by judges who have deplored the reception into theft of difficult doctrines of civil law, per Lord Roskill in *Morris*, A.C. 320 (1984), theft cases continue to attract such difficulties, if only because the Theft Act 1968 is itself cast in terms of property rights, and the law in respect of these is both uncertain and subject to mutation and growth (for example, restitutionary obligations). The choice of appropriation as an organizing principle means that theft can be committed without any physical movement of goods, and thus electronic transfers of balances may be comprehended within it. Although it was thought that theft and deception would have to remain distinct, courts have homologated the two by holding that references in theft to property belonging to another refer, essentially, to the state of property rights at the inception of a transaction and not to its effectiveness in passing property, as decided in *Gomez,* 3 W.L.R. 1067 (1992). In the result, only deception in respect of real property cannot be brought under theft. The degree of compression thus achieved makes the law difficult to work with, and it also engenders problems of jurisdiction. Certain traditional problems remain as well, notably those concerning mistake and the transferee's knowledge that the transferor acted in error.

The *Model Penal Code* (U.S.) and the Theft Act 1968 (U.K.) also differ in their specification of the mental element. The former specifies unlawful taking with a purpose to deprive (while, for example, conceding mistake-based defenses such as claim of right), while the latter requires dishonesty, a term with a wide residual meaning that originally caused confusion.

The English legislation contains no special provisions concerning the kiting of checks or the dishonest use of credit cards. These are brought under theft and deception.

Continental approaches to theft appear simpler. Theft and certain other offenses are regarded as crimes against patrimonial rights. As in common law systems, theft protects the property of a person other than the thief. Because, however, the criminal law concept of property corresponds to the civil law concept, only corporeal property can be the subject of theft, so that in German law, for example, theft is the abstraction of movable property with the intention to appropriate that property illicitly. It is fair to say, however, that theft is supplemented with a series of other offenses, which, it would seem, present problems.

It seems fair to say that there is no universal definition of theft, nor any universally conceded unifying principle, save that theft is as such understood as being an acquisitive crime, and, to a degree faithful to its origins, excludes immovables from its scope.

References

American Law Institute. *Model Penal Code and Commentaries*. Philadelphia: American Law Institute Press, 1985.

Criminal Law Revision Committee. *Theft and Related Offences*. 8th Report. Cnmd. 2977. 1966.

Fletcher, G.P. *Rethinking Criminal Law*. Boston: Little, Brown, 1978.

Hall, Jerome. *Theft, Law and Society*. 2d ed. Indianapolis: Bobbs-Merrill, 1952.

Seidman, R.R. *A Sourcebook of the Criminal Law of Africa*. London: Sweet and Maxwell; Lagos: African University Press, 1966.

Smith, A.T.H. *Property Offences*. 1995.

L.H. Leigh

See also OWNERSHIP; PROPERTY

Theology

See RELIGION AND THEOLOGY

Thomas Aquinas

See AQUINAS, THOMAS

Time and Imputation

"What is time? When no one asks me, I know; when someone asks me, however, I do not know." This is St. Augustine's famous puzzle in his *Confessions*, which apparently has not been solved, although his philosophical discovery of subjective time has inspired many philosophers, notably Henri Bergson, Edmund Husserl, Martin Heidegger, and Ludwig Wittgenstein, and has received special scholarly attention recently by K. Flasch. In the recent past, time has been dealt with in many branches of science and the humanities. By the mid-twentieth century, A.N. Prior established a logic of time ("tense logic"), continued most prominently by Nicholas Rescher.

In the philosophy of law, an early account is given by the German scholar Gerhart Husserl. On the basis of Edmund Husserl's phenomenological account in philosophy, he identified the three dimensions of time with adjudication (past), administration (present), and legislation (future), and tried to establish a priori the elements of law binding the legislator. This is a rather traditional attempt, which considers the speed and acceleration of change as essential elements of modern civilization, determining social and legal relations. These dynamics of time are difficult to grasp with commonsense categories. It seems that Karl Marx's famous Eleventh Thesis on Ludwig Feuerbach from 1845 must be inverted: it is not the change of the world that is lacking but the philosophical interpretation of that change. The historian Henry Adams, a leader in diagnosing lifeworld acceleration while examining the speedy progress in the American Gilded Age, studied the historic structure of time and formulated a "law of acceleration": the future continously shortens recourse to the experiences of the past, and history is no longer a reservoir of guidelines for action. Considering this speedy progress Adams' contemporary Oliver Wendell Holmes formulated a genuine American legal philosophy, the prediction theory of law.

In modern social science and philosophy, prominent scholars have taken their turn at contemplating time. Jürgen Habermas's discourse theory, as well as the system theory, of Niklas Luhmann, mirror specific aspects of time. However, most prominent in focusing on time are the so-called postmodernist, deconstructivist thinkers like Jacques Derrida. Most notably, Paul Virilio has analyzed the modern phenomenon of time and argued for resistance against a racing speed in favor of a "democratic speed." The common feature in all of these theories is a radical temporalization of formally metaphysical or ontological concepts, despite substantial conceptual differences in coping with it.

In law, time has traditionally played an important role with its *objective, quantitative element* that philosophically was conceived of by Aristotle as what is "counted," in his *Physics*. This is, for example, tangible in the field of time-limits or deadlines, time liabilities, or, in contract law, "time of the essence" clauses. Statutes of limitation put an outer limit on the time during which a legal action may be pursued. With respect to the legal force of statutes or of common law jurisdiction, the point at which something gets or loses effectiveness is important for due process rules based on the principle of fairness, for instance, the protection of individual trust in the case of unconstitutional ex post facto criminal laws (according to the Enlightenment principle of *nullum crimen sine lege praevia* (no crime without a prior law)). On the reverse side (and not unconstitutional), there are "sunset laws," that is, legislative acts subjected to a stipulation of time. Under certain common law doctrines, such as adverse possession and constructive easement, some practices that take place "openly and notoriously" over long periods of time (for example, twenty years) are endowed with legal status. Of course, there are more instances for the crucial role of quantitative time.

The philosophical approach to time and law, however, focuses primarily on the qualitative, normative aspects of time. In general, this means the status of time in imputation. In a broad sense, there is an internal coherence between time and law, since expectation gives time a structure: something is "right on time," "too late," and so on. An example is the *self-obliging* of parties to a contract permitting expectations and reliance by the other party. This can be well illustrated by Jewish history, namely the Covenant that gives a genuine time perspective for Jewish and Christian history. Stabilizing expectations, in Luhmann's theory, is the main function of the legal system. Referring to the normative aspect of self-commitment in human communication, discourse theory tries to establish criteria for legitimate expectations.

In the details of legal doctrine, the issue can best be treated in criminal law where *subjective imputation* is most sensitive to individual actors. The structure of criminal law's reaction concerning the time factor could be illustrated by almost each element of the penal imputation. Following are only some examples relevant to the advanced doctrinal discussion on the European continent.

An offense, first of all, requires an act. The concept requiring this act and dating back to the last century must come to terms with the element of accelerated change in a modern *risk society*, because it is dominated by the commonsense category of an acting substance. It is not adequate to face the potential damage of acts in the present time. For the causality criterion, the second element in the physical constitution of an offense, modern forms of damages (so-called proximate, distant, and long-term damages) have become familiar.

Furthermore, proving causal relations in *procedural* law is a difficult matter involving solutions that have been excluded from substantive law. In recent European criminal product liability cases, some high courts (as in Germany and Spain) have allowed the procedure of "eliminating alternative explanations." Although this black-box-like procedure leads to great difficulties in detail, it hardly can be repudiated in general, as noted by Lorenz Schulz.

Referring to the concept of *damage* itself, the issue of "consequential damages" is illustrative: these damages can be "too late to be imputed," as many AIDS cases show. So far, there is no convincing criterion to cope with these cases.

That time is a growing issue in *objective imputation*, as well as in *subjective mens rea*, is a result of a risk society characterized by permanent and even accelerating change. Although risks have always been permitted in legal history, the damage potential of the present society is substantially higher. Lifeworld change and acceleration, however, cannot themselves function as normative criteria for imputation, although in criminal law they probably should be considered as excusing elements for individual actors because they place a heavy burden on them. Such criteria supposedly may only be developed for specific spheres of action, due to the complexity of the diverse domains of legal regulation.

The prominence of time in modern society doubtlessly provokes *time-indefinite* solutions. One thinks of the procedure of trial and error connected with Karl Popper's falsificationism. As this model does not provide a criterion for the selection of probationary hypotheses, it was repudiated by philosophers of science. This deficiency is easy to understand in the domain of law, where hypotheses often violate constitutional rights and therefore must be justified. In criminal law, experimentation is justifiable only by statutory law and only when the experimentation has no retroactive effects. However, to prohibit sunset laws entirely goes too far, since they should generally be allowed *in bonam partem* (when beneficial). Moreover, in a certain manner, every law is an experiment, as Holmes' opinions say. At least in criminal law, this experiment must be conducted with specific care, because of the gravity of sanctions.

With respect to *sentencing*, the subjective and, therefore, normative element of the time factor is most tangible: the sanction of incapacitation is most relative to the personality each individual. Since law is only a crude instrument, equal punishment with respect to the individual experience of time is substantially limited.

References

Calabresi, Guido. *A Common Law for the Age of Statutes*. Cambridge MA: Harvard University Press, 1982.

Cornell, Drucilla. "The Relevance of Time to the Relationship Between the Philosophy of the Limit and Systems Theory." *Cardozo Law Review* 13 (1992), 1419 (symposium *Closed Systems and Open Justice: The Legal Sociology of Niklas Luhmann*), 1579–1603.

Habermas, Jürgen. *Faktizität und Geltung*. Frankfurt: Suhrkamp, 1992. Trans. W. Regh as *Between Facts and Norms*. Cambridge: MIT Press, 1996.

Holmes, O.W., dissents in *Abrams v. United States* 250 U.S. 616, 630 (1919), and *Truax v. Corrigan* 257 U.S. 312, 344 (1921).

Husak, Douglas, and Brain P. McLaughlin. "Time-Frames, Voluntary Acts, and Strict Liability." *Law and Philosophy* 12 (1993).

Husserl, Gerhart. *Recht und Zeit* (Law and Time). Frankfurt: V. Klostermann, 1955.

Mackaay, Ejan et al. "The Logic of Time in Law and Legal Expert Systems." *Ratio Juris* 3 (1990), 254–271.

Schulz, Lorenz. "Die Zeit drängt" (Time presses). In *Ökologie und Recht,* ed. L. Schulz, 127–164. Cologne: Heymann, 1991.

Virilio, Paul. *Rasender Stillstand* (Frantic Halt). Munich: Hauser, 1992.

Lorenz Schulz

See also Ex Post Facto Legislation; Legislation and Codification

Tolerance

Derived from the Latin *tolerantia*, the word "tolerance" was used by the writers of antiquity to denote the passive sense of suffering, submissive acceptance, and conformity in the face of pain and adversity. This is the definition assigned to this word in the 1694 first edition of the *Dictionnaire de l'Academie Française*, as being "condescension, indulgence before that which we cannot prevent."

During the sixteenth century, the word "tolerance" began to be used more with the sense of permission, particularly when granted by the government to ensure religious freedom. The core issue of theological thinking during the early days of the modern age within the context of divided Christianity after the Lutheran Reform centered on the discussion over whether or not it was *permitted* or *tolerable* for two or more religions to exist side by side in the same Christian country. However, this government permission did not mean approval or acceptance of the nonofficial religion, as the maxim of the 1555 *Pax Augsburg* was still much to the fore: *cujus regio, eius religio* (whose the rule, his the religion). The practice of tolerance arose within the context of Christianity where Roman Catholicism or Protestantism was the state religion and referred to the establishment of parallel relations at the civil level, prompted by the outbreak of religious wars that put the very survival of political society at risk.

The idea of tolerance with the meaning of "acceptance of the convictions of others" was first used within the context of theological discussion and then grew into a political issue when attempts were made to define religious pluralism within both the state and Christianity itself. This discussion took place among Christians who, although not united, did not abjure Christianity. Tolerance thus did not include the issue of relationships between Christian and non-Christian beliefs, since this basically involved Roman Catholics and Protestants.

The first text to express this viewpoint and which sought to systematize this question in a philosophical manner within a strictly Christian sphere was John Locke's *A Letter Concerning Toleration,* published in 1688, in which this British philosopher laid out the argument that tolerance was a permission which should benefit some Christians, although excluding Roman Catholics. Locke's arguments in favor of tolerance were founded on the idea of separation between the religious community/the church and the political community/the state, with tolerance being one of the civil rights of the individual guaranteed by the political community. The limits of tolerance were defined in the thinking of Locke by the civil courts and were established by institutional constraints on the practice of religion. This was the reason given by Locke for condemning the Inquisition, based on the empirical observation that repression was not an efficient policy: power could force a person to practice a religion but could not impose true belief. The Inquisition was rejected by Locke not for moral reasons, but rather through political expediency, since the outcome of repression would be mere civil hypocrisy. With an eye to the interests of the political community, Locke felt that tolerance should not be guaranteed to people whose convictions threatened institutions; the British philosopher urged that tolerance could not be extended to atheists because, not believing in God, they could not swear oaths before God, and anyone unable to swear could not enter into agreements, the basis of civil society. Locke even felt that Roman Catholics should not benefit from tolerance, as they owed allegiance not to the British Crown, but to a foreign potentate, the pope.

The argument developed by Pierre Bayle in his *Commentaire Philosophique*, first published in 1686, presented a theoretical defense of tolerance beyond the theological field. Bayle transferred this issue to the field of moral legislation, the fruit of fine-tuned, practical reasoning, independent of religious faith. This French thinker showed that disputes triggered by theological disagreements could well find a solution at the moral level, where reason speaks to all human beings. The thinking of Bayle attempted to construct a positive form of tolerance based on the relationship between opinion and the sincerity of people in defending their convictions. However, the error of the individual would not invoke ontological blame, as proclaimed by the Inquisition. Bayle thus established one of the mainstays of modern tolerance: the right to erroneous conscience, which consists of the inalienable right of the individual to profess doctrines that individual considers as true. Bayle identified freedom of conscience as the expression of the relations between humans and their Creator, viewing any attempt at clerical or public control as "a spiritual rape."

During this period, tolerance represented an attitude that was more intellectual than political, with a view to establishing peaceful cohabitation between Roman Catholics and Protestants. However, enlightened thinkers highlighted freedom of conscience as a political and constitutional cornerstone of the "liberal state." Tolerance in liberal thought became identified with a social virtue vital to the functioning of the liberal constitutional order.

It was John Stuart Mill who linked tolerance with freedom. Developing his own philosophical arguments that located this issue within the liberal stream of thinking, Mill was concerned with determining which are the rights that allow a person to conduct one's life freely, and found them to be those that originate in the exercise of individual autonomy. Mill saw the use of the principle of the autonomy of the individual vis-à-vis the state as being the keynote liberal argument in favor of tolerance.

The crisis in tolerance cresting at the close of the twentieth century should be referred back to Mill's interpretation of the democratization of the classic liberal state in pluralistic mass societies. Liberal tolerance seems drained, due to the debility of that liberal state. The appearance of new forms of intolerance among social groups and nations, prompted by ethnic, religious, and political factors, spotlights this conceptual crisis that is mirrored in the functioning of the political order. Contemporary history shows that there is a deep-rooted relationship not only in the links between tolerance and freedom, but principally between tolerance and religious, political, and cultural pluralism. In other words, an explicit link binds the appearance of pluralism to the practice of tolerance, with the consequent flowering of intolerance fostering the negation of pluralism.

Challenged by ethnic, religious, and political conflicts, philosophical reflection is striving to pinpoint a moral justification for the virtue of tolerance in contemporary society. The belief in a universal cure-all for moral and political quandaries has always resulted in the establishment of totalitarian societies and states where intolerance has been institutionally enshrined. Tolerance is thus undergoing a process of conceptual redefinition, similar to its evolution during the sixteenth and seventeenth centuries.

Philosophical discussion on this issue seeks to fill the gap that undermines expression, caused by relativism and lack of intellectual convictions in contemporary society, where tolerance has come to represent a type of leveling-down of all ideas and convictions, as though all were of the same value. Contemporary philosophical research has returned to the approach used by Bayle, seeking to base tolerance on respect for others in their convictions, as far as conviction is possible.

Some writers mention two sources for a "program of practical tolerance": the first is the principle of *abstention* or nonintervention, of laissez-faire so appropriate to the liberal state and characterized in its application by indifference to the exercise of the rights of others. The second source consists mainly of the principle of *admission* unknown in liberal formulations, whose outcome is respect for the rights of others. This is where tolerance can truly represent a virtue within a political and juridical order, based firmly on fairess and solidarity.

References

Bayle, Pierre. *De la tolérance. Commentaire Philosophique* (On Tolerance. A Philosophic Commentary). Intro. Jean-Michel Gros. Paris: Presses Pockets, 1992.

Berlin, Isaiah. *Four Essays on Liberty*. Oxford: Oxford University Press, 1969.

Dworkin, Ronald. *Taking Rights Seriously*. Cambridge: Harvard University Press, 1977.

Labrousse, Elizabeth. *Pierre Bayle*. 2 vols. The Hague: Martinus Nijhoff, 1963–1964.

Locke, John. "A Letter Concerning Toleration." 1823. In *The Works of John Locke*, vol. 4. Aalen: Scientia Verlag, 1963.

Mendus, Susan. *Toleration and the Limits of Liberalism*. Atlantic Highlands NJ: Humanities Press International, 1989.

Mill, John Stuart. *On Liberty*. Ed. Gertrude Himmelfarb. Harmondsworth: Penguin, 1978.

Nagel, Thomas. *Equality and Partiality*. Oxford: Oxford University Press, 1991.

Rawls, John. *A Theory of Justice*. Cambridge: Harvard University Press, 1972.

Ricoeur, Paul. *Lectures 1*. Paris: Editions du Seuil, 1991.

Wolff, Robert P. et al. *A Critique of Pure Tolerance*. Boston: Beacon Press, 1965.

Vicente De Paulo Barretto

See also AUTONOMY; LIBERTY; SELF-DETERMINATION, PERSONAL

Torts

Torts is that branch of the common law concerned with private liability for interpersonal harms, especially but not only physical harms to persons or property. Accordingly, it draws upon certain notions—including understandings of action, causation, and responsibility—that are of substantial philosophical interest and difficulty. In determining liability for harmful events, tort law raises to the attention of a philosopher of law the ample question of the relation among these separately puzzling matters. When, and with what justification, does an action that causes harm give rise to responsibility according to law? This question of the rationale and justification for tort liability has proven to be of significant difficulty and, indeed, remains unsettled, despite the efforts of advocates of the several competing accounts. This article will undertake to give a sense of the jurisprudential difficulty, its repercussions for tort doctrine, and its treatment in the various theoretical attempts to supply a justificatory rationale for tort law, as well as, in conclusion, an account of certain underlying philosophical issues on which that difficulty may shed light.

Doctrinal and theoretical attention in torts alternates between accounts that ground liability in *causation* alone (that is, in the succession of physical events in the world following on the actor's doing) and those that look also, in one way or another, to the actor's *intent* to bring about such effects. Starting from a causal basis of liability, which is for the most part unquestioned, tort doctrine and theory generally conceive of the problem for torts as that of accounting for the involvement of the will, or its lack, in intending the effect. Given this basis, the difficulty for tort law appears as lying in the fact that causation alone can seem too capacious or too arbitrary a ground for liability, as when catastrophic consequences can be traced to minor errors. However (the conception of the problem continues), if more is needed for liability than sheer causation, then by virtue of what other aspect of the relationship between actor and result is responsibility justified? The leading candidate for this additional justifying element is intent. Certainly, with some exceptions (such as business harms arising from normal competition), an actor is justifiably liable for those harms that one both caused and intended.

Harm intentionally caused does not, however, supply the bulk of the occasions for possible tort liability; rather, tort law has the peculiarity that, unlike the law of contracts or crime, with which it is sometimes compared, the situations arousing tort law's distinctive concern are those where the relation of human action to the world suffers a flaw. The actor's knowledge or control fails; the effects of one's action outstrip one's intentions; in short, *action miscarries*. It is such miscarried actions, rather than situations where action proceeds as intended, that constitute the core problem for tort law, as the centrality of negligence to modern tort doctrine suggests. Indeed, even for the so-called intentional torts, the party's intent regarding the harm he has caused may be highly attenuated, as when liability for battery lies for an unpermitted, intentional contact, made without intent to cause the harm that ensues.

This peculiarity of tort law—the fact that intent, such as might readily justify liability, is typically absent in the situations tort law confronts—only renders more acute the questions of action, causation, and responsibility that tort law faces. For, however justifiable liability may be for intentionally caused harms, that justification, premised on traditional understandings of responsibility as grounded in the willing of an action's effects, does not avail in holding a party liable for the harmful effects of his actions when those effects are unintended. Rather, in the absence or attenuation of intent, it becomes both more urgent and more difficult to establish just how the happening of untoward effects redounds to an actor, leaving him legally responsible. Indeed, so much more acute does the issue then become that some theories offering a justification of tort law sidestep this peculiarity, attempting to enclose torts within a treatment of intentional actions, where it fits only uneasily.

Tort Doctrine: The Poles of Causation and Intent

Tort doctrine may be seen to have developed in tacit response to this dilemma concerning its ground, as manifested in its alternation between the two poles of causation-based liability and intention-based liability. Thus, for example, intentional torts, privity requirements, assumption of risk doctrine, and economic treatments that understand a tortfeasor as a rational maximizer of utility all partake of the model of torts as matters of intent; strict liability for wild animals, blasting, or trespass, or for defectively manufactured products, liability for unforeseen harms or to unforeseen plaintiffs, and the rule that a tortfeasor "takes his victim as he finds him" all partake of the model of torts as matters of causation not dependent upon a showing of the tortfeasor's intent. The case of negligence doctrine is more complex, for the conflict is played out there in the very specification of the doctrine's content. The doctrine of negligence provides for liability in the event an actor's causation of damages is the result of his breach of a duty of care owed the plaintiff. Because such breach need not be intentional, negligence liability might be thought adequate to the adjudication of such errant harms as confront tort law. However, the doctrine has not proven easily capable of clear or definitive formulation, having instead been the object of a sustained series of attempts to isolate and formulate the standard of care, breach of which will then constitute negligence.

One recurring approach to giving substance to the negligence standard has been to look to standards already in place, such as those given by statute, or by custom, or by the dictates of economic efficiency, since those also govern the standard of care in negligence—an approach that provides a ready formulation, perhaps, but at the price of losing the distinctiveness of *negligence* as the ground of liability. Another approach has looked to a defendant's imposition of risk upon a plaintiff, or to the foreseeability of the resultant harm, as constitutive of a breach of the defendant's duty of care. When not conflated, these may be understood as alternative ways of moderating—without questioning—the causation and intent requirements of the underlying model that negligence liability was to have improved upon, by diluting, with probability, the certainty of the result, or the intent to bring it about, respectively. In an inchoate and unthematic way, such dilution may more closely describe the events at issue in tort law, where causation is uncertain and intent attenuated. As this dilution weakens these elements it must weaken as well their traditional justificatory force, further exacerbating the difficulty of grounding tort law's determination of liability.

Tort Theory: Economic Efficiency, Compensation, and Morality

In view of the ongoing irresolution concerning the *grounds* of tort liability, it cannot be surprising that there persist deep disagreements concerning its *justification* as well. Thus tort theory, the academic counterpart of tort law concerned with the elaboration and justification of tort liability, finds itself internally at odds, riven into discordant schools of thought over the nature and purposes of tort liability, its adequacy in meeting certain proffered justifications, and, in the end, the possibility of justifying it at all. The debate goes so deep that various theorists argue for the abandonment of different doctrines and contours presently part of tort law, or even of tort law itself, in the name of justificatory ends which it is seen to promote only imperfectly.

One may discern three main contemporary theoretical and justificatory accounts of tort law: (1) the economic school, which understands tort law to be premised on considerations of efficiency and interprets the aims and methods of tort law as providing for the bargaining, internalization, or deterrence of the costs of tortious action; (2) social compensation theory, which views the purpose and justification of tort law as lying in the systematic distribution and rationalization of the costs of accidents; and (3) a variety of moral theories, which look for the justification of tort law to a moral interpretation of such factors as the causation of harm, creation of disparate risk, or correction or annulment of harm caused. A fourth position may be seen to shadow these three, consisting in the conclusion of (4) the critical legal studies movement that law (here, tort law) is inherently indeterminate, and incapable of justification, because it consists only in the present configuration of accumulated power, which its decisions serve.

Although none of these accounts has won the day, the economic analysis of tort law is the most prominent approach within contemporary legal doctrine and academic discussion. Indeed, its fundamental premise is shared by the compensation account as well: that the matter with which the law is concerned is accessible to economic thought and methods. The object of analysis for tort law thus becomes the cost of accidents, and its efficient allocation; the incidence of accidents is relevant only insofar as it affects this cost. From this common starting point there develops both the account that rests tort law on a justification of efficient deterrence and that which aims at the social rationalization of costs.

Influenced by the work of Nobel economics laureate Ronald Coase, the first approach holds that tortious action, like any other, is inefficient, hence problematic, whenever its "social" cost (that is, its cost to any party) exceeds its benefit. Collecting and setting off the costs of accidents and of their prevention against the gains to be had by incurring them, the Coasian theory seeks to account for the behavior of rational actors under the tort law in terms of the parties' choice among, and opportunities to bargain over, such costs and benefits. The theory also draws implications for tort doctrine from the operation of deterrence and other incentives upon tortfeasors, for example, equating the standard of care under negligence doctrine with that given by considerations of efficiency. To be able to reach such conclusions, the Coasian economic account must deny that there is a distinctive character to the actions at issue in tort law, for it understands these as occasions for the operation of economic rationality—informed choice among sets of costs and benefits—rather than of error or inadvertence.

A second group, the cost-centered tort theorists, spurred both by empirical doubts as to the deterrability of accidents on the Coasian model of tort law and by concerns about its high administrative costs in practice, has moved in recent years to streamline and rationalize the tort system by supplanting it, in part or in whole, with systems of pure compensation. Conceiving of tort compensation as a matter of social welfare for which the appropriate mechanism is a system of social insurance, such proposals dispense with the adjudication of tort liability based on fault in favor of the administrative disbursement of funds to pay for the damage suffered. As with existing systems of loss administration (such as workers' compensation) which they resemble, the proposed programs' concern is triggered by the fact of loss, not by the nature of its genesis, which is seen as largely arbitrary and unimportant. As a result, however, the compensatory rationale provides no grounds for distinguishing tortious harm from any other misfortune. Since these grounds are seen to evaporate, so too does the sense in which the contemplated payments constitute compensation, as distinct from social welfare maintenance in general.

Thus the economic and the compensation accounts may be seen to suffer from mirror-image deficiencies, for the deterrence rationale offers no ground for the connection of tort damages with the victim; the compensatory rationale, none for the connection of compensation to the tortfeasor. Neither retains the distinctiveness of the occasion for tort law as residing in tortious action resulting in harm, but collapses it into general inefficiency, where no harm need transpire, or into general misfortune, where no action need bring it about.

A third group of tort theorists tries to preserve and explain the connections that these two variants of economic tort theory cannot, by turning from economic analysis to moral theory. The array of such theories currently includes proposals how to ground liability: in the imposition of "nonreciprocal" risk, from Professor George Fletcher; in direct physical causation, from Professor Richard Epstein; in the "annulment" of loss as by insurance payments, from Professor Jules Coleman; and in a restoration of formal equality undone through the exercise of will, from Professor Ernest Weinrib. Each of these distinct proposals has its considerable attractions, but none is without its difficulties, and none is widely seen as offering a satisfactory account of the moral foundations of tort law.

This dissension in moral tort theory is instructive because it is traceable to the persistent difficulty of tort law itself: finding a justificatory nexus between the causal eventuation of harm and the actor's involvement in bringing it about. The Coasian and compensation accounts each concern themselves with only one of these elements, and so can more easily account for "tort law"; in contrast, the moralists, though drawn at times to solutions resting on intent or causation, strive to resist either of these reductions. They thereby remain more faithful to the complexity of tortious events but are also more beset by the genuine difficulty of satisfactorily grounding liability for these events.

Indeed, even in those moral theories most attentive to the problem, the nexus of action and harm appears, finally, only as arbitrary juxtaposition. Yet it can only appear thus, for, as the disaccord within moral tort theory suggests, the problem is intractable, given the conventional understandings of action and responsibility from which tort theory begins. It is, accordingly, these understandings that the problem of tort law, viewed as a whole, may finally bring to the light of philosophical questioning.

Conclusion: Questions of Will and Obligation

The difficulty of accounting for tort liability may be seen, not merely as derivative of others familiar to philosophers (such as accounting for the relation of the will to events in the world, a problem inherited from René Descartes' dualism), but as philosophically novel, and even illuminating. In particular, in posing the problem of how events that exceed our intention and escape our will may nevertheless be laid to our charge, tort law calls into question traditional understandings holding that control by the will is foundational to action and responsibility. (Some flavor of this challenge already appears, at points, in recent inquiries into moral luck.)

Further, by attending to the recalcitrance of tort law's subject matter—accidents—despite the battery of theorizing efforts brought to bear against it, we may gain intimations of a vaster challenge, implicating our understanding both of law and of our relation to events in the world. Our confrontation with the accidental, as exemplified in the doctrinal and theoretical course of tort law, consists in repeated efforts of will, brought to bear against that which persistently escapes its control. Thus, in treating accidents at law, we resort, first, to intent as the ground and control of concrete accidental events; failing that, to systematic rationalization of their cost effects; and, finally and throughout, to theorizing—that is, to the project of encompassing, establishing, justifying, grounding, and so mastering—our responsibility for them. Perhaps in the recurrency of these efforts, and their shortfall, we may at last be brought to wonder why it is that we undertake to approach the law of accidents in this way, and how we must first understand accidents, and law, to think to do so.

Ultimately, the problem of grounding responsibility for accidents, when control by the will is unavailing, affords us an invitation to reconsider the relation of law to will and, in particular, prompts us to ask whether our understanding of law as a matter of willful rationalization does not impede our understanding of law as obligation. For in the stubborn escape of responsibility for accidents from our every effort at rationalization, justification, and control, we may discern a suggestive iteration of the utter alienness and opposition of obligation to will's demand for justificatory ground, an opposition which Immanuel Kant taught but which, it seems, still remains for us to grasp.

References

Abel, Richard L. "Torts." In *The Politics of Law: A Progressive Critique*, ed. David Kairys. New York: Pantheon Books, 1982.

Calabresi, Guido. *The Cost of Accidents: A Legal and Economic Analysis*. New Haven: Yale University Press, 1970.

Coleman, Jules L. "The Mixed Conception of Corrective Justice." *Iowa Law Review* 77 (1992), 427–444.

Epstein, Richard A. *A Theory of Strict Liability*. San Francisco: Cato Institute, 1980.

Fletcher, George P. "Fairness and Utility in Tort Theory." *Harvard Law Review* 85 (1972), 537–573.

Landes, William M., and Richard A. Posner. *The Economic Structure of Tort Law*. Cambridge MA: Harvard University Press, 1987.

Sugarman, Stephen D. "Doing Away With Tort Law." *California Law Review* 7 (1985), 559–664.

Weinrib, Ernest J. "Understanding Tort Law." *Valparaiso University Law Review* 23 (1989), 485–526.

Weston, Nancy A. "The Metaphysics of Modern Tort Theory." *Valparaiso University Law Review* 28 (1994), 919–1006.

Nancy A. Weston

See also EFFICIENCY; NEGLIGENCE, CRIMINAL; STRICT LIABILITY, CRIMINAL

Torture

In view of the tragic history of the use of torture throughout the world, not only to obtain confessions and information, but simply to inflict pain and/or terrorize enemies of the state, torture is today legally prohibited by all civilized nations and by numerous instruments of international law.

Article 1 of the *Covenant Against Torture and Other Cruel, Inhuman, or Degrading Treatment or Punishment* defines torture as

> any act by which severe pain or suffering, whether physical or mental, is intentionally inflicted on a person for such purposes as obtaining from him or a third person information or a confession, punishing him for an act he or a third person has committed or is suspected of having committed, or intimidating or coercing him or a third person, or for any reason based on discrimination of any kind, when such pain is inflicted by or at the instigation of or within the consent or acquiescence of . . . a public official. . . .

While the moral outrageousness of torture has been taken almost universally as a given, and justly so, there are a few philosophical questions that are still being explored.

Torture Employed to Obtain Confessions of Guilt

As Chief Justice Earl Warren of the Supreme Court of the United States observed in *Chamber v. Florida,* 309 U.S. 227 (1940):

> The testimony of centuries, in governments of varying kinds over populations of different races and beliefs, stood as proof that physical and mental torture and coercion had brought about the tragically unjust sacrifices of some who were the noblest and most useful of their generations. The rack, the thumbscrew, the

> wheel, solitary confinement, protracted questioning and cross-questioning, and other ingenious forms of entrapment of the helpless or unpopular had left their wake of mutilated bodies and shattered minds along the way to the cross, the guillotine, the stake, and the hangman's noose.

The claim has been made that some of the prohibited techniques of interrogation would not necessarily produce false confessions. Torture was permitted to obtain confessions in the thirteenth century in certain European states, according to John Langbein:

> Substantial safeguards were devised to govern the actual application of torture. These were rules designed to enhance the reliability of the resulting confession. Torture was not supposed to be used to elicit an abject, unsubstantiated confession of guilt. Rather, torture was supposed to be employed in such a way that the accused would disclose the factual detail of the crime—information which, in the words of a celebrated German statute, "no innocent person can know."

For a number of predictable reasons, such systems deteriorated into unconfined torture with resulting false confessions. As Henry Shue has suggested, even if there were a justification for limited torture, it could not be actually restrained: "[T]here is considerable evidence of all torture's metastatic capacity."

Torture Employed to Obtain Information

A sophisticated article by Shue asks: if killing is sometimes morally permissible, why is not torture, which is presumably a lesser harm? The matter is not simply a choice of evils. Shue derives, from the laws of war, the more general moral prohibition of doing violence to defenseless persons.

Is the evil of torture mitigated if the captive has within his power an act of compliance that would terminate the torture (for instance, giving information)? Here, Shue points out, that even if the torturers are not vengeful or sadistic, often victims have no way of persuading their torturers that they do not have the information or that they have disclosed all that they know.

Moreover, where compliance means betrayal of one's highest values, it is morally unacceptable to demand such self-abnegation. Succinctly put, it is the profoundly committed and the innocent who are most likely to be severely tortured.

If a government agent feels very strongly that the good to be produced by the use of torture far outweighs its evil in a particular case, that agent can engage in an act of civil disobedience, as long as he or she is willing to accept the punishment.

A. Jonson and L. Sagan have considered whether a very limited use of torture could be justified on utilitarian grounds—where it is the mildest method available to produce information necessary to save many lives. They reject torture even under this rule, on the ground of its uncertainty in application, uncertainty of the good effect, the difficulty of limiting it to terrorists, and the unlikelihood of avoiding its use for political or retaliatory reasons. Responding, Gary Jones argues that the points raised by Jonson and Sagan simply require refinement in application, and that abuse can be prevented by taking great care to prevent exceeding the limitation of inflicting minimal pain on terrorists necessary to bring substantial benefits. Finally, Jones argues that medical technology can assure that torture be as humane as possible, inflicting pain on certain centers of the brain without physical abuse or physical side effects. Jones closes with a classic hypothetical in this field: that is, a bomb is hidden in a city, set to kill 100,000 people, and the only way of learning its location is to torture a captured terrorist.

P.F. Brownsey, commenting on the Jones article, asks whether the deontological case against torture trumps any utilitarian argument in its favor. He acknowledges that many people feel deep revulsion at licensing torture, that it may be a wrong in itself, as to which it is profoundly immoral to weigh consequences, but contends that so asserting is not necessarily to provide a rationale for the revulsion. Brownsey acknowledges that respect for autonomy is flagrantly violated by torture, but feels unable to distinguish the situation of a hundred thousand people who will die if the state *fails* to administer the torture, arguing that permitting such deaths is also to deny respect for persons.

Jonson and Sagan have the better of the utilitarian argument, for they are connected to the virtually universal reality of historical experience with abuse of the power to inflict torture.

Regarding deontological moral prohibitions, morality often rests on widely shared, deeply rooted, emotional foundations. The deep-seated emotional revulsion against torture, with its active, personal destruction of physical and psychological integrity and its blatant subversion of human autonomy, is a sufficient explanation of the deontological prohibition of torture, whatever its arguable utilitarian consequences. "They torture in the name of justice, in the name of law and order, in the name of the country, and some go as far as pretending they torture in the name of God" (Omar Rivabella, *Requiem for a Woman's Soul*, 1986).

References

Brownsey, P.F. "Commentary." *Journal of Medical Ethics* 6 (1980), 14.

Inbau, Fred, John E. Reid, and Joseph P. Buckley. *Criminal Interrogation and Confessions*. 3d ed. Baltimore: William & Wilkins, 1986.

Jones, Gary E. "On the Permissibility of Torture." *Journal of Medical Ethics* 6 (1980), 11–15.

Jonsen, A., and L. Sagan. "Torture and the Ethics of Medicine." *Man and Medicine* 3 (1978), 1.

Langbein, John H. "Torture and Plea Bargaining." *University of Chicago Law Review* 46 (1978), 1–22.

Machan, Tibor R. "Exploring Extreme Violence (Torture)." *Journal of Social Philosophy* 21 (1990), 92–97.

Maran, Rita. "The Juncture of Law and Morality in Prohibitions Against Torture." *Journal of Value Inquiry* 24 (1990), 285–300.

Shue, Henry. "Torture." *Philosophy and Public Affairs* 7 (1978), 124–143.

Joel Jay Finer

See also CONFESSIONS; DUE PROCESS; NATURAL JUSTICE

Transfer

See ACQUISITION AND TRANSFER

Treason

Treason is crime against the external security of a political community or state by attacking its essence (independence, honor, territorial integrity). As a major political crime, treason focuses a philosophical debate concerning the mutual influences of law and politics. Both in ancient Rome and in feudal times treason was a public crime, while other injuries were considered as mere delicts or private crimes. Cicero considers that the obligation of fidelity goes first to fatherland and only after that to family. Patriotism comes always in first place, justifying sacrifice of life; so even recent laws of the European continental codification period punish treason with death.

Roman law contributed to the doctrine of treason one of its seven specialized courts, the court *de maiestate* (of sovereignty), proscribing the abuse of power and the betrayal of the people's sovereignty. Christianity contributed a profile of the traitor and sinner, the recurrent image of Judas's thirty pieces of blood money for having betrayed Christ.

During the middle ages, the most cruelly punished crime was treason, with the loss of peace and patrimonial confiscation. In earlier medieval times, that crime consisted in homicide of someone with whom a special fidelity relationship existed, at the earliest only the murder of a parent. Later it extended to people engaged in feudal bonds, journey companions, people related by ties of hospitality, and other close relatives.

Although first structured on the protection of concrete real privileges, fidelity became more formal. All rights protected earlier by municipal or local powers were gradually assumed by central institutions. In French Carolingian times, the state did not care to prosecute most crimes, but reserved to its jurisdiction treason, desertion, and coin falsification, three different branches in the expanding central power: political, military, and financial. In the Iberian ancient *fueros* (districts), when private revenge was tolerated, treason was one of the few crimes that involved all the community and did not admit composition or settlement (*calumnia*). This communitarian dimension was a sign of public interest in the crime.

Formalization of the idea of fidelity centered on the symbolic person of the king, the unique passive subject of this crime against all the community. Previous ties, spontaneous, natural, and even contractual, lost importance, and first place went to new rights or privileges conferred by the monarchs, as the monarchical institution changed from a conjugated power to an absolute one. Treason became a crime of *laesae majestatis* (diminished sovereignty), and this became the crime par excellence in a temporal order.

In the eighteenth century even humanitarian penalists favored public punishment as a manifestation of power and for general prevention. Punishment as show developed during the French Revolution. Many political trials were presented as questions of treason, from the French Terror to the Moscow trials.

In *Leviathan* Thomas Hobbes considers in the same category as *crimina laesae Majestatis* (crimes of offense to sovereignty) "all atempts upon the Representative of the Common-wealth, be it a Monarch or an Assembly; and all endeavours by word, or deed to diminish the Authority of the same, either in the present time, or in succession. . . ." Montesquieu in *De l'esprit des lois*, however, critisized Japanese traditional government for its abuse of the death penalty, imposed for almost all crimes, based precisely on the idea that any minor offense in society involved an attack (or some kind of a treason) on the emperor. Cesare Beccaria (*Dei delitti e delle pene*, XXVI) also considers that, even if all sorts of infractions are against society, only a few could destroy it immediately: only these he identifies with *crimina laesae Majestatis*.

Current penalistic doctrine limits treason. The sovereign is now constitutionally the people, so treason is no longer seen as a crime against a single person. Depersonalized, the crime once again is seen as a crime only against the community, but now against any single national community, committed by one of its members.

Often, however, the crime is judged in military courts, whose principles have a completely different logic than do civil cases. At question is a matter of security, but also of honor, both private and public, an aristocratic system of values very peculiar and difficult to understand in democratic societies. The trials at Nuremberg and Tokyo showed clearly that fidelity to *fides* (honor), as a compromise toward natural law, was much more important, in contemporary times, than blind obedience to the powers of one's own country (even if elected, in the case of Germany). What could be seen, legally, as treason, would be seen as a kind of tyrannicide, if it involved active conspiracy against a power deprived of legitimacy by its own wrongdoing, and as conscientious objection or civil disobedience, if carried out passively.

When political regimes change through war or secession, mutual accusations of treason arise. In political and philosophical terms, the validity of such accusations will always be debatable. However, to the legalist positivism of any *hic et nunc*, treason is what the legal code, here and now, says it is.

The "aporia" is not modern. Both outlaws and political persecutors always mimic true legal procedures. When Robin Hood sings "I love no man in all the worlde/ So well as I do my Kinge," is he an outlaw and a traitor or, on the contrary, a hero? That is the philosophical question.

References

Boveri, Margaret. *Treason in the 20th Century*. New York: Putnam, 1963.

Chapin, Bradley. *The American Law of Treason: Revolutionary and Early National Origins*. Seattle: University of Washington Press, 1964.

Chroust, Anton-Hermann. "Treason and Patriotism in Ancient Greece." *Journal of the History of Ideas* 15 (1954), 280–288.

Cuttler, S.H. *The Law of Treason and Treason Trials in Later Medieval France*. New York: Cambridge University Press, 1981.

Friedrich, Carl J. *The Pathology of Politics: Violence, Betrayal, Corruption, Secrecy, and Propaganda*. New York: Harper & Row, 1972.

Hurst, James Willard. *The Law of Treason in the United States: Collected Essays*. Westport CT: Greenwood, 1971.

Kelly, G.A. "From Lese-Majesté to Lese-Nation: Treason in Eighteenth Century France." *Journal of the History of Ideas* 42 (1981), 269–286.

Law Reform Commission of Canada. *Crimes Against the State*. Ottawa: Law Reform Commission of Canada, 1986.

Lear, Floyd Seywood. *Treason in Roman and Germanic Law*. Austin: University of Texas Press, 1965.

Paulo Ferreira da Cunha

See also CIVIL DISOBEDIENCE; CONSCIENTIOUS OBJECTION; MILITARY PHILOSOPHY OF LAW; REBELLION; REVOLUTION; WAR AND WAR TRIALS

Trusts

A trust is an obligation enforceable in equity under which a trustee holds property that he or she is bound to administer for the benefit of a beneficiary or beneficiaries (a private trust), or for the advancement of certain purposes (a purpose trust). The property may be of any kind. Trusts are established expressly by a settlor in a trust deed or a testator in a will (an express trust) or by implication (a resulting trust). They may also be established by operation of law (constructive trust). In the case of the express and resulting trust, the obligations of the trustee are voluntarily assumed; in the case of the constructive trust, they are imposed by courts. The trustee's primary duty is to act loyally and prudently in the administration of the trust property. The trustee's obligation is enforceable by the beneficiary, in the case of a private trust, and the attorney general or the Crown, in the case of a charitable purpose trust.

The trust originated in the middle ages in the conveyance to uses. The conveyance to uses was invented to circumvent the burdens of the feudal system of landholding, to create the possibility of willing land, and to simplify land transfer requirements. A conveyance to a feoffee "to the use of a religious house" or "to the use of the grantor, and on the grantor's death to whomever he should appoint," were, with the complicity of the Court of Chancery, employed to reform the feudal system from within, largely with fictions.

The trustee is said to be the legal owner of the property held in trust; the "equitable" owner, in the case of a private trust, is the beneficiary. The language of property is used to describe the interests of the trustee and beneficiary because their rights are said to be in rem, not merely personal or contractual. The legal title/equitable title nomenclature also reflects the fact that the trust was developed by courts of equity (as opposed to courts of common law). If the trustee conveys the trust property to a good faith purchaser for value, the beneficiary's title is, in most circumstances, extinguished. If the conveyance is made in breach of trust, the beneficiary has only a personal claim against the trustee.

The trustee's obligations in respect of the property may range from a simple duty to convey the property when requested to do so to a duty to administer it and distribute it in specified ways. The trust, thus, has a variety of uses in modern society. These include to benefit the future generations of a family through the establishment of successive equitable interests in property, to benefit employees through the holding of a company's shares or other assets in trust for their benefit, to hold funds for public investment (a mutual fund or unit trust), to carry on a business (a business trust or Massachusetts trust), to hold debt claims (and associated enforcement rights) for the benefit of a company's creditors (a debenture or trust for bondholders), to create rights of security, to hold the property of an unincorporated association, and to advance a charitable purpose. Trusts are also created legislatively for a variety of purposes.

The trust is to be distinguished from agency primarily by the fact that the legal title is conveyed to the trustee in the trust, but not to the agent in agency. Further, the trustee always contracts with third parties as principal, the agent does not. The trust is to be distinguished from bailment since the bailee also does not have legal title, nor, unlike the agent, does the bailee have the power to convey legal title to a good faith purchaser for value. Because the beneficiary has equitable title in the trust property, a trust obligation is also not the same as a debt: the beneficiary may always seek an accounting by the trustee of the use of trust property; the beneficiary may follow the trust property into the hands of a purchaser who is not in good faith and for value; and the beneficiary may claim its recovery in priority in the event of the trustee's own bankruptcy. Trust property is also protected against transformations in its form by equitable tracing rules. These allow the beneficiary of the trust to identify property unlawfully substituted for the trust property and to have it treated as the trust property. The trust in the common law tradition is also thought to be distinguishable from contract. The main internal evidence in favor of the thesis that the trust is not a contract is the fact that doctrinally the trust is said to be created prior to the trustee accepting the responsibility of trustee and the fact that the settlor of the trust has, at least historically, no standing to sue for its enforcement. Unlike a corporation, a trust is not a legal person and therefore does not by itself have any legal capacity to own property, to be the titulary of rights, or to sue in its own name.

Since the trust is an indigenous development of English law, it has had to be imported by statute or code into the civil law and other legal traditions. There were Roman law institutions that bore some of the characteristics of the trust. The *fideicommissum* (settlement) and *fiducia* (trust) recognized the possibility of splitting the benefits of property ownership among several persons over generations. These institutions, however, did not create a simultaneous ownership interest in the beneficiary and trustee: in the *fideicommissum* the interests were successive; in the *fiducia*, the beneficiary's interest was personal, not proprietary. Modern civilian institutions, likewise, serve many of the same functions as the trust: curatorship and tutorship require the faithful administration of property of incompetents and minors; the fiduciary substitution permits successive interests in property; the foundation (*fondation, Stiftung*) is equivalent in function to the charitable trust; and the stipulation for the benefit of another allows a third person to enforce a contract made between two others where the contract is meant to benefit him or her. In Islamic law, the *wakf* is equivalent in most of its effects to the charitable trust. The main difficulty in accommodating the trust in civil law jurisdictions is the incoherence, to civilians, of the concept of two simultaneous owners. This difficulty is especially problematic in jurisdictions influenced by the French Civil Code of 1804, wherein ownership is defined as absolute and therefore incapable of the division in interests required by the trust.

The historical origins of the trust in the English legal system, arising out of fictions intentionally created and judicially sanctioned, therefore lend it a peculiar aura. This is attested to by the fact that civilian systems have had a distinct aversion to it and a difficult experience receiving it. Much of the difficulty, however, is due to the trust's poor juridical conceptualization. The common law tradition maintains that the trust is not contractual, but proprietary. Yet, from the civilian perspective, most of what is accomplished in the trust could be accomplished by a contract for the benefit of another. The proprietary elements—in particular the beneficiary's bankruptcy priority to the assets still held in trust—is difficult to account for in a contract theory. One possible avenue of argument, only now being explored, is the theory of unjust enrichment. Although the dominant common law trend is to conceive of the trust as proprietary, many distinguished common lawyers—F.W. Maitland and F.H. Lawson, among them—have argued otherwise.

The constructive trust presents itself explicitly as a fiction. As such, it is malleable and has been used in some common law jurisdictions as a vehicle of legal development. Jurisdictions around the common law world express different views, but it is clear that several new legal ideas are emerging from this fiction. A notion of family property and the cause of action in unjust enrichment are the primary ones.

The charitable purpose trust, because it lacks a specific beneficiary, lacks an obvious enforcer. Traditionally, the Crown or attorney general stepped in to enforce these trusts. The involvement of a public entity in their enforcement, however, requires a public justification. There is, as a consequence, a well-developed jurisprudence on the meaning of charity and the necessity for public benefit. Economists have argued in favor of a public goods interpretation of this jurisprudence, specifically, that the concessions to charitable activity are justified because charities produce public goods. There is much doctrinal writing, but little philosophical study devoted to the issue of the nature of these trusts and the meaning of charity.

Trust law forms the most significant portion of a more general body of law called fiduciary law. Other fiduciaries include directors, agents, partners, and lawyers. Persons who receive confidential information from another person are in some jurisdictions also thought to be fiduciaries. The underlying notion is that one person, the fiduciary, has the legal power to affect the interests of the other and is legally obliged to exercise that power in a way that is loyal to (in the best interests of) the beneficiary and is prudent. Legal scholars disagree as to the nature of the fiduciary obligation, in particular whether it is imposed by law or voluntarily assumed.

The nature of "equity" is perhaps the most fundamental philosophical question in this area. For Jeremy Bentham, and in the English tradition in general, "equity" refers simply to the rules administered by a court of equity. In contrast, Aristotle employed the term in the sense of an overarching idea of fairness or justice to be applied by courts in cases where the law, due its nature as universal, failed to take proper account of the circumstances of particular cases. In a related conception, "equity" refers to a principle of statutory interpretation which requires the judge to have regard to the equity of the statute.

References

American Law Institute. *Restatement of the Law of Trusts, Second*. Washington DC: American Law Institute Press, 1957.

Elias, Gbolahan O.A. *Explaining Constructive Trusts*. Oxford: Clarendon Press, 1990.
Fratcher, William F. *Trust*. Vol. 6. *International Encyclopedia of Comparative Law*. Tübingen: J.C.B. Mohr (Paul Siebeck); New York: Oceana, 1973.
Langbein, John H. "The Contractarian Basis of the Law of Trusts." *Yale Law Review* 105 (1995), 625–675.
Maitland, Frederic W. *Equity: A Course of Lectures*. 2d rev. ed. Cambridge: Cambridge University Press, 1936.
Scott, Austin Wakeman. *The Law of Trusts*. 1987. 4th ed. Boston: Little, Brown, 1993.

David Stevens

See also AGENCY (MANDATE); ESTATE AND PATRIMONY; FRAGMENTATION OF OWNERSHIP; UNJUST ENRICHMENT AND RESTITUTION

Truth

Truth is an ideal that consists in the warranted assertibility of a thesis or set of theses. Problems relating to truth occur at two basic levels in the philosophy of law: at the level of philosophy and at the level of law. At the first level, the germane questions center on the ultimate posture and limitations of legal discourse and legal thought in every possible world. The focus lies, for example, on the necessary grounds or the absence of necessary grounds for true legal propositions. At the second level, the germane queries center on the force and meaning of particular components of some particular legal system(s). Propositions advanced at the second level are juristic propositions, rather than philosophical propositions about juristic propositions.

Various philosophical standpoints attempt to supply answers to the questions concerning truth that are raised at the first level. For example, some theorists argue that the attainment of truth in the many institutions of law will have ultimately rested on nothing firmer than the assumptions shared by competent participants in the institutions. Other theorists allow that nothing can be known about law except through interpretive frameworks of assumptions, but they maintain an agnostic attitude toward the existence of an independent reality with which our discourse and thought may or may not accord. Still other theorists maintain that an assumption-independent reality does indeed exist and that we can have sufficient knowledge of it to be able to affirm its existence. (Many other positions have likewise been adopted, of course.)

Such philosophic questions and answers, which require philosophic argumentation, are very different from the questions and answers that arise within the institutions of law. At this level, the problem of truth consists in attempting to ascertain the validity and significance of any of the countless materials that make up a legal system—materials such as judicial opinions, common law maxims, procedural rules, legislative statutes, administrative regulations, and commentators' assessments. At least implicitly, analysts have to decide whether specific texts and practices are indeed valid parts of a legal system, and they then have to determine the true meanings and scopes of those texts and practices. Here the determinations of truth proceed through interpretive inquiries, rather than through abstract argumentation detached from specific data. Officials have to make judgments about the correct ways in which they and their fellow officials should formulate and implement the law. Those judgments in turn receive scrutiny from other officials and from external analysts. Instead of attempting to postulate the ultimate grounds or the absence of any ultimate grounds for true legal propositions, the actors within a legal regime put forward (or seek to put forward) such propositions in relation to the specific components of their regime. They can agree on those propositions even while they disagree about the ultimate grounds therefor or even while they give no thought to what the ultimate grounds might be. They are making statements within a discourse rather than making statements about all conceivable discourses.

At times, legal scholars have unwisely run together these distinct levels of truth in their analyses of law. Ronald Dworkin has correctly upbraided some members of the critical legal studies movement for conflating philosophical skepticism ("external skepticism") and legal skepticism ("internal skepticism"). Critical legal theorists have oftentimes attempted to derive the second of the following two theses from the first: (1) There are no ultimate underpinnings—as opposed to contingent assumptions—from which true statements in legal interpretation derive their trueness. (2) Purportedly true statements about various doctrines and rules are in fact wholly arbitrary, because the truth about such matters is indeterminate within our Anglo-American legal systems. The first of these two theses is philosophical. It attempts to describe the general status, or part of the general status, of all conceivable propositions about law. By contrast, the second thesis occurs within the practice of legal interpretation. It points to the degree of settledness that characterizes the meanings which are associated with the diverse materials that constitute certain bodies of law. Neither the first thesis nor the second thesis entails the other. Anyone can accept that no ultimate foundations exist to underpin legal knowledge, while still maintaining that contingent assumptions are firm enough to yield substantial regularity and determinacy throughout the law; in a converse manner, anyone can insist that ultimate foundations are indeed available for legal knowledge, while still avowing that our current legal systems are rife with indeterminacy (because those systems have badly failed to adhere to their proper foundations).

With regard to each of the two levels of truth—the philosophical level and the juridical level—analysts have debated whether truth is desirable. For example, John Finnis has propounded arguments in which he aspires to show that truth in all its forms is an intrinsic good. Finnis contends that any skeptical argument against the inherent goodness of truth must be self-contradictory, since it will have put itself forward as a worthwhile truth. Finnis's discussion commits a number of serious errors, however. Finnis neglects the possibility of insincere skeptical statements that happen to be true; he fails to show that a commendation of truth on purely instrumental grounds must involve a commendation of truth as an inherent good; he likewise fails to demonstrate that a commendation of certain specific truths must involve a commendation of truths in general; and he overlooks the numerous situations in which self-deception can be better than undeceived misery.

Although Finnis is the most prominent legal scholar in recent years who has argued for the intrinsic goodness of truth, perspectives broadly similar to his have appeared in related fields (in the writings of Jürgen Habermas, for instance). All such arguments give insufficient heed to the variety of reasons that can prompt one's commitment to the utterance of certain truths as truths; such arguments therefore move too quickly in presuming that every such commitment is a commitment to the inherent goodness of truth. One ought not to infer, of course, that truth is never desirable or only rarely desirable. One should conclude, rather, that the goodness of truth cannot be established independently of the contexts in which truth emerges.

References

Dworkin, Ronald. *Law's Empire*. London: Fontana, 1986.

Finnis, John. *Natural Law and Natural Rights*. Oxford: Oxford University Press, 1980.

———. "Scepticism, Self-Refutation, and the Good of Truth." In *Law, Morality, and Society*, ed. P.M.S. Hacker and Joseph Raz, 246–267. Oxford: Oxford University Press, 1977.

Kirkham, Richard. *Theories of Truth*. Cambridge: MIT Press, 1992.

Kramer, Matthew. "What Good Is Truth?" *Canadian Journal of Law and Jurisprudence* 5 (1992), 309–319.

Rorty, Richard. *Philosophy and the Mirror of Nature*. Princeton: Princeton University Press, 1979.

Matthew H. Kramer

See also ERROR, DECEIT, AND ILLUSION; SKEPTICISM

U

Ulpian, Domitius (ca. A.D. 165/70–223/4) Domitius Ulpian was of a family from Tyre; he was killed in A.D. 223, or early in 224, when clearly at least middle-aged. At the time of his death, under Severus Alexander (A.D. 222–235), he was Praetorian Prefect, a post he held for about eighteen months. This office had acquired, under Septimius Severus (A.D. 193–211), unlimited criminal jurisdiction in Italy beyond 100 miles from Rome, as well as appellate jurisdiction, civil as well as criminal, on the emperor's behalf. Just before his Praetorian Prefecture he was Prefect of the Grain Supply (*praefectus annonae*). He almost certainly held the office *a libellis* (for petitions) under both Severus and his son Caracalla (A.D. 211–218), in which his duty was to compose—or supervise the composition of—the rescripts issued in the name of the emperor.

Ulpian was a prolific writer, the author of about a third of Justinian's *Digest*. His major works were his commentary on the Edict of the Urban Praetor in eighty-one books (a "book" in the ancient world was roughly what we would think of as a chapter), which takes up more than half of his preserved output, and the unfinished fifty-one books *ad Sabinum*. He also wrote two books on the edict of the *curule aediles* (Roman office responsible for public works and games, police, and the grain supply), also described as books 82–83 of the Edict, nineteen books on the duties of various magistrates and officials, fourteen on courts and appeals; six on tax law, five on the crime of adultery, thirty-two on specific aspects of private law, ten books of *Disputations*; and two elementary books of *Institutions*, as well as some annotations of other jurists. The *Opinions*, the *Pandects*, the *Regulae*, and perhaps the *Responsa*, too, are probably spurious or, at most, derived from authentic works.

Ulpian was not a systematizer; he made relatively few generalizations or deductions from principle. He was more concerned to find what was equitable or expedient for the individual case; he thus frequently recommended the use of actions *in factum*, policy actions. His style was lucid, if bland. He took a moderate line, balancing official rights and official powers. For example, the emperor was above the law (*legibus solutus est*) but he alone; even the empress was bound in theory. When Ulpian maintained that the emperor's will had the force of law, he went on immediately to explain that this was due to a sort of delegation of popular power. He did not, therefore, provide a model for the rule of law in a constitutional sense, although the Glossators could and did argue, on the base of this text, about whether the people had made an irrevocable surrender of sovereignty to the ruler by the *lex regia* (rules of sacral law attributed to ancient kings).

Ulpian was a very traditional jurist, holding to legal autonomy; even where an imperial enactment by rescript had decided a point, he cited the arguments of earlier jurists. He saw jurists as the priests of justice and wanted them to be held in the same high respect as philosophers. Roman jurists were, however, not normally "philosophical" in their approach to law. Thus, when a jurist does make an ideological point and this is not due to imperial moralizing, it is significant.

The texts on which Ulpian's reputation for legal philosophy chiefly rests are not particularly original; other jurists made similar points but were not selected for such prominence by Justinian's compilers of the *Digest*, nor taken into Justinian's *Institutes*. It was therefore Ulpian's division of law into public and private and his further division of private law into *ius civile* (civil law), *ius gentium* (law of the peoples), and *ius naturale* (natural law) which were preserved. The definition that law is the art of the good and the equitable is acknowledged to be a citation from the jurist Celsus. The famous sentences—"Justice is the constant and enduring will to give to each person his due right. The precepts of the law are to live honorably, not to injure others, and to render to each his own. Practical understanding of law means cognizance of divine and human affairs, knowledge of the just and the unjust."—are from the dubious *Regulae*. Nevertheless, Ulpian provided later generations of lawyers, medieval and modern, with a framework in which to systematize legal relationships, recognizable forms, and particular rules.

References

Bauman, R.A. "The Death of Ulpian, the Irresistible Force and the Immovable Object." *Zeitschrift Savigny-Stiftung (Romanistische Abteilung)* 112 (1995), 385–399.

Cleve, R.L. "Cassius Duo and Ulpian." *The Ancient History Bulletin* 2 (1988), 118.

Honoré, Tony. *Ulpian*. Oxford: Oxford University Press, 1982.

Nörr, D. "Iurisperitus sacerdos." In *Xenion, Festschrift für Pan. J. Zepos*, ed. E. von Caemmerer et al., 555–572. Athens: Ch. Katsikalis Verlag, 1973.

Ulpian. *Digest*. Ed. Alan Watson. Philadelphia: University of Pennsylvania Press, 1985.

Olivia F. Robinson

United States of America

See AMERICAN JURISTS, 1860–1960; FEDERAL JURISTS, 1800–1860, U.S.; FOUNDING JURISTS, 1760–1800, U.S.

Universal Rights

The view that some rights are universal holds that these rights are ethical norms, applicable to all human beings, everywhere, and at all times.

The claim to the normative universality of some fundamental rights does not deny the diversity of cultures, of conceptions of the good life, and of systems of authority. It also concedes that many cultural practices such as euthanasia, arranged marriages, genital mutilation, child labor, and various forms of censorship may be incompatible with the standards contained in the *Universal Declaration of Human Rights*. What the universalist position rejects, however, is the proposition held by epistemological relativists that the only absolute truth about cultures is that no culture can be proved to be morally superior.

In its most extreme form, universalists adopt what can be called a foundationalist view of human rights, defining them as resting on some general and enduring features of human beings. In this view, the notion of human rights as developed intellectually in the West would be rooted in an ontological attribute of human beings that is independent of culture and community. Their historical emergence in the West was presented in the eighteenth century as the discovery of the final truth of legitimate authority against the untruth of old scholastic justifications of authority.

This strong version of universalism usually takes direction from Immanuel Kant, grounding human rights on the essential autonomy of human beings that allows them to make moral choices. The main objectives of human rights standards, in this view, are either to oppose the regulation by the state of this autonomous sphere (and in some versions, to minimize regulations of the market) or to protect it against the encroachments of power.

Those engaged in struggles for human rights within unsympathetic cultures often adopt a robust dogmatic belief in a transhistorical foundation, but this view carries no conviction in an era struggling also to free itself from metaphysics and unquestionable truths.

A second view takes universality not as an ontological pre-given but as an end of history, as the necessary historical outcome of the relentless march toward planetary enlightenment and freedom. This view is skeptical about absolute claims to knowledge on the nature of human beings and offers, instead, a liberal neo-hegelian, eschatological view of history as a totalizing planetary process toward a community of free individuals. The end of ideologies of total state organization, represented dramatically by the fall of the Berlin wall and of racial supremacy with the end of apartheid in South Africa, led to speculations about the end of history.

This view of universalism assumes optimistically that interpretations of human rights will gradually converge and that a common conception of the good life will eventually prevail once all the world has been successfully colonized by a secular modernizing humanism. The nation-state is still the main obstacle for the achievement of a universe of free individuals—effective interventions of states in the way other states treat their own citizens are rare—yet it follows the same universalist logic. As a centralizing administrative unit, the modern state rationalizes and gradually destroys local instances and customs, and its laws address universal and equal subjects.

However, the spread of technology and of individualistic systems (free markets, modern systems of law) has been shown to be compatible with repressive practices and with different forms of state subjection. Disillusionment with a culture of neo-darwinian individualism, free markets, and media-driven electoral politics has generated a new interest in communitarianism at the end of the twentieth century. Some fear that this tendency might weaken the dominant ideological commitment to individual human rights.

A third view grounds universalism on an unstable *sensus communis* as defined by Kant in his philosophy of aesthetics (as exposed in his *Critique of Judgment*). A *sensus communis* in this sense is neither based on an objectively universal law nor produced by an empirically given consensus, but it is a subjectively universal commitment to a contingent normative ideal. This position asserts the historical fact that human rights have become the dominant common sense. Today, all human beings ought to agree that human rights are an ideal in the same way that everybody ought to agree that Shakespeare is a great writer.

In this view, the subjective yet universalist commitment to human rights stems from pessimism rather than from the belief in a common human foundation or from an optimistic belief in a climax of history. This pessimism is universalistic precisely because it is cynical about the self-justifications of power holders. It rejects a prescriptive relativism that preaches equal tolerance vis-à-vis all value systems, whether they themselves are tolerant or not.

This reticent universalism postulates a belief in a cross-cultural, hard core of principles such as those human rights that are generally considered as part of *ius cogens* (nonderogable international standards): the prohibition of genocide, racial discrimination, slavery, executions without trial, retrospective criminal laws, and, perhaps, torture (although the International Law Commission does not regard it as subject to universal jurisdiction).

This self-restrained universalism impregnates international human rights standards. These standards are minimal and only apply to a small number of areas of power. They can be used only against the state, not against private power. An additional weakness is that most human rights are derogable claims because the idea of human rights grew alongside the consolidation of the modern nation-state and its overriding doctrines of national security.

Standards are formulated in broad terms. This allows in practice what the European Court of Human Rights has called a margin of appreciation, that is, a latitude granted to power holders to use discretion and to interpret standards taking local conditions into account. This pragmatic universalism is compatible with a relativistic conception that subjects the implementation of human rights standards to local and historical conditions. It accepts that judicial decisions on competing claims (rights against rights and rights against communitarian concerns) are not dictated by general principles. Judicial positions on abortion, the death penalty, the prevalence of the right to privacy, the right to publish obscene or blasphemous materials, and so on, and decisions on the meaning of elastic notions (such as the prevention of disorder, the protection of national security or of morals, and so forth) are strongly influenced by culturally conditioned conceptions of the good life and even by contingent political views.

Views on whether a particular practice is compatible with human rights will not only vary between cultures but will also vary within cultures. The European Court of Human Rights has accepted this cultural dependence in many cases, investigating "evolutionary trends" in European countries on matters such as privacy.

Supporters of a strong universalism argue that this pragmatic universalism is in fact a relativism in disguise because it confuses the metaphysical being of human rights with their imperfect textual appearance. A pragmatic universalism is compatible with a position of ethical relativism in so far as both share a common ethos of respect for difference, pluralism, and diversity.

References

An-Na'im, Abdullahi A., ed. *Human Rights in Cross-Cultural Perspectives: A Quest for Consensus*. Philadelphia: University of Pennsylvania Press, 1992.

Donnelly, Jack. *Universal Human Rights in Theory and Practice*. Ithaca: Cornell University Press, 1989.

Gaete, Rolando. *Human Rights and the Limits of Critical Reason*. Aldershot: Dartmouth, 1993.

Pollis, Adamantia, and Peter Schwab, eds. *Human Rights: Cultural and Ideological Perspectives*. New York: Praeger, 1980.

Renteln, Alison Dundes. *International Human Rights: Universalism versus Relativism*. Newbury Park CA: Sage, 1990.

Teson, Fernando R. "International Human Rights and Cultural Relativism." *Virginia Journal of International Law* 25 (1985), 870.

Rolando E. Gaete

See also FUNDAMENTAL RIGHTS; HUMAN RIGHTS; TORTURE

Unjust Enrichment and Restitution

Major legal systems of the world strive to prevent people making gains through the losses of others. Gain made through another's loss is what an unjust (or unjustified) enrichment implies. Civilian jurisdictions including Germany, Japan, Russia, and Israel prohibit the phenomenon in general terms. Common law countries pursue the same objective less directly. By the award of suitable remedies, common law systems sanction unjust enrichments in many of the cases where they occur. Jurists in common law countries have asserted that remedies for the purpose are unified by an unwritten "principle against unjust enrichment." It is an area where property rights and personal obligations overlap and one where lawyers from both types of system share a common concern. Their attention is directed to the making of gains, as well as to the sources of those gains. Measurable profit of one should not derive from the measurable loss of another. Unjust enrichments should be reversed, despite the practices of the world. Such an ideal has influenced the development of the private law, and lately, the public law, in many ways.

To characterize an enrichment as "unjust" is to suggest an obvious remedy. The enrichment should be reversed. The exercise introduces an arithmetical standard into the complex web of human relations, with the potential to undo many otherwise valid legal transactions. Unjust enrichment is subversive of contract law, for example, or the law of binding gifts, and its competence has been contentious throughout the last century. Many otherwise valid contracts or benefactions involve enrichments derived at another's expense. In ancient Roman law, and each of the civilian jurisdictions dealt with in the following text, the unjust enrichment idea has been expressly limited in order to protect the integrity of the private law.

Philosophical Basis

The sense of (in)justice in an "unjust enrichment" is mostly a species of what Aristotle described in *Nicomachean Ethics* as rectificatory justice. Later philosophers have referred to this as commutative justice (for example, St. Thomas Aquinas in *Summa Theologiae,* Giorgio Del Vecchio in *Justice,* and John Finnis in *Natural Law and Natural Rights)*. The reference is to transactions and exchanges that are concluded in favor of the party enriched. Equal rights and reciprocity are denied to the party impoverished. It is what occurs where the claimant is denied recovery of mistaken payments, of transfers made without cause, or transfers caused by the other party's undue influence or duress. Justice in a different sense is applicable when the benefits and burdens of a common enterprise are unequally distributed. Then an enrichment may be "distributively" unjust instead of, or in addition to, being commutatively unjust. Claims to salvage awards, or the restitution of benefits conferred under frustrated contracts, are of this distributive type.

Unjust enrichment as an analytic category makes parasitic use of an existing regime of distributive justice and the set of established institutions in the private law. Contractual, tortious, or other matrices of an unjustly enriching event assume the existence of these things. The concept involves a judgment internal to a given structure of reciprocal rights and obligations. It is not a basis on which to found a radical critique of a legal system. H.L.A. Hart has suggested that unjust enrichment, like an entitlement to compensation, is derived from the moral conviction that those with whom the law is concerned have a right to mutual forbearance from certain kinds of harmful conduct. The unjust element in the term can be traced, more distantly, to denial of that equality between individuals which inspires the precept "Treat like cases alike and different cases differently."

Function of the Concept in Different Legal Systems

The notion of unjust enrichment emerged for the first time in ancient Rome, late in the life of its legal system in the first or second centuries A.D. Categories of redress in the Roman private law were organized around the remedies that the system afforded. Jurists analyzing results achieved with the remedy of *condictio*, like recovery of money not due (*condictio indebiti*) or for a purpose which failed (*condictio ob causam datorum*), saw them to amount to prevention of another party's unjust enrichment. See Justinian in *Digest*. This insight never became a rule of law and, except in the latest times, it remained subject to nonavailability of the *condictio* where there was no direct transfer of the enriching money or thing. Vitiated transfer, rather than wrongful enrichment, seems to have been the injustice attended to. The *actio de in rem verso* (action for recovery of an object wrongly transferred) was an exception to this, enabling persons to recover a limited class of enrichments conferred by third parties. Slave owners were liable to disgorge enrichments made through the dealings of their slaves.

Title 24 of the *German Commercial Code* of 1900 (the BGB) is devoted to unjust enrichment. Section 812 states the principle that "a person who, without legal justification, obtains anything from a person at his expense, whether by transfer or otherwise, is bound to give it up to him." German codification of unjust enrichment at the end of the nineteenth century followed Roman law fairly closely. A recoverable enrichment had to result from a direct transfer, not one from a third party, and be without justification by any other law, emphasizing the subordinate nature of the idea (see BGB 816).

The French *Civil Code* of 1804 contained express reference to the reversal of unjust enrichment only in the narrow categories of necessitous intervention (art. 1372–1375) and payments not due (art. 1376–1380). However, by analogy with the Roman *actio de in rem verso*, actions outside the code to reverse unjust enrichments have generally been allowed. The German requirement of direct enrichment by the claimant is not insisted upon. While French law would seem to allow many of the three-party restitutionary contests familiar to common lawyers, in fact it has its own way of preventing the incursions of unjust enrichment. A principle of subsidiarity is followed, which provides that an enrichment must be *sans cause légitime*, or not otherwise justified, with no other contractual, delictual, or other form of relief available. If an alternative remedy would have been available, but for an expired period of limitation or some other procedural bar, then the *actio de in rem verso* is also excluded. French positive law will never be outflanked by unjust enrichment recovery.

Common law systems in the United States, Britain, Canada, and Australia each endorse unjust enrichment as an organizing factor in the common law. Sometimes the term is used interchangeably with restitution, though restitution has other common law grounds as well. Orthodoxy in United States jurisdictions provides that prevention of and reparation for unjust enrichment is the basis of several remedies, the constructive trust in particular. Constructive trusts in Canada are similarly based. Britain, by contrast, still bases this remedy on the fiduciary relationship, on fraud, and the similacra of both. Australian private law uses the unconscionability idea to explicate the constructive trust, which resembles the U.S. approach. Unconscionability is instanced in Australia by insistence on an unjust outcome. Recovery in common law systems for mistaken transfers, ineffective contracts, discharge of another's liability, and breach of fiduciary obligation have all been explained by their restitutionary tendency. Relevant remedies, such as the constructive trust, the lien, the money counts, and subrogation, have each received restitutionary interpretations accordingly. Restitution as a cause of action on its own, though, the equivalent to the *actio de in rem verso* in French law, has had a slow reception. This is despite the observations of commentators in particular common law systems that the systems have "sufficiently matured" to allow an unjust enrichment cause of action to be allowed.

Character of the Concept

Whether as an ideal, a rule, a principle, or just a means of organizing remedies, unjust enrichment performs a particularly useful role. Much of the private law is taken up with procedure.

The unjust enrichment idea is concerned with results. As J.P. Dawson says, the doctrine points to the unjust outcome, the *excessive* gain in a bargain transaction, which are the things that may attract the doctrines of duress, undue influence, unfair competition, and breach of fiduciary relationship. The fairness is of a particularly commercial kind. Noncommercially, when a transaction is attacked because of one party's insanity or lack of capacity, unjust enrichment concentrates on its substantial merits, rather than what may be scarcely knowable states of mind. Unjust enrichment may alone be too naked, or crude, a concept on which to base judicial intervention. Together with an established right or doctrine of the distributive or antienrichment kind, however, unjust enrichment focuses judicial review on important aspects of transactions that other doctrines ignore.

There is a small practical difference between the reception of undue influence in civil and common law systems. Attitudes to the voluntary intervenor are not the same. Civil law doctrine rewards the gratuitous intervener who manages the affair of another. Benefits are thrust on people, as it were, behind their backs. Common law systems are more individualistic. Enrichment is defined as something that a party chooses, rather than is chosen by someone else. Respective formulations of unjust enrichment doctrine are otherwise in summary like this. Unjustly enriching transactions in civilian systems are abstractly prohibited and liable to be reversed unless the enrichment is indirectly conferred and/or justifiable and/or remediable by some other law. Unjustly enriching transactions in common law systems are liable to be reversed if some specific legal recovery or unjust ground is applicable to their instant facts.

References

Barry, Nicholas. *An Introduction to Roman Law*. Oxford: Clarendon Press, 1962.

Birks, Peter. *An Introduction to the Law of Restitution*. Rev. ed. Oxford: Clarendon Press, 1989.

Dawson, John P. *Unjust Enrichment*. Boston: Little, Brown, 1951.

Del Vecchio, G. *Justice*. Trans. Lady Guthrie. Ed. A.H. Campbell. New York: Philosophical Library, 1953.

Gutteridge, H.C., and J.A. David. "The Doctrine of Unjustified Enrichment." *Cambridge Law Journal* 5 (1935), 204–229.

Hart, H.L.A. *The Concept of Law*. 2d ed. Oxford: Clarendon Press, 1994.

Kaser, Max. *Roman Private Law*. Trans. R. Dannenbring. 3d ed. Durban: University of South Africa Press, 1965.

Zweigert, Konrad, and Hein Katz. *Introduction to Comparative Law*. Vol. 2. Trans. T. Weir. Oxford: Clarendon Press, 1987.

John Glover

See also AGENCY (MANDATE); LEGITIMATE OBJECT OF CONTRACT; TRUSTS

Utilitarianism

Utilitarianism is the normative theory which takes advancement of the general welfare as the ultimate aim of ethics and politics. Over the past two centuries utilitarianism has been the most influential ethical and political theory in western philosophy. Some scholars have attempted to trace its roots back to Epicurus, or even to Plato, but the distinctively utilitarian idea of equal consideration for everyone's welfare is foreign to Greek thought. The earliest intimations of an ethics grounded in utility appeared in the latter part of the seventeenth century, but it was only in the eighteenth century that utilitarianism began to achieve its ascendant status, especially in the empiricist tradition.

Its first great exponent was David Hume (1711–1776), for whom utility served as the foundation of all the social virtues (most notably benevolence and justice). However, it was mainly the work of Jeremy Bentham (1748–1832) which shaped the theory into what we recognize today as its modern form. Bentham equated utility with happiness or well-being and argued, or rather declared, that its maximization—promoting the "greatest happiness"—was the proper aim of ethics, politics, and law. Although Bentham devoted some attention to the question of how individuals should conduct their lives, his most lasting influence has been in the domain of legislation and public policy.

Through most of the nineteenth century utilitarianism was the dominant normative theory in the English-speaking world, overshadowing its intuitionist and perfectionist rivals. Its principal exponents during this period were John Stuart Mill (1806–1873), who refined and popularized Bentham's formulation of the theory, and Henry Sidgwick (1838–1900), whose work remains to this day the most systematic articulation and defense of a utilitarian ethics. Both Mill and Sidgwick preserved the identification of utility with happiness, though they attempted to refine Bentham's crude conception of happiness as the balance of pleasure over pain. They also had a subtler appreciation than Bentham of the complexities of ethical decision making and devoted much effort to reconciling utilitarianism with commonsense morality. Although Mill and Sidgwick both applied the theory to politics, neither expanded significantly on Bentham's treatment of the law.

The twentieth century opened with a robust defense of a (somewhat idiosyncratic) version of utilitarianism by G.E. Moore (1873–1958). However, since that time acceptance of the theory has declined considerably, at least within academic philosophy where it has been challenged by such rivals as intuitionism, deontology, rights theory, virtue theory, and social contract theory. During the latter part of the century it has also been one of the main targets of antitheorists in philosophy, who have argued that the very idea of an abstract and universal ethical theory understates the role of context and particularity in our moral thinking. As a result of these various critiques, only a minority of moral or political philosophers would nowadays count themselves utilitarians.

Perversely, however, the theory remains as prominent as ever in philosophical circles. It has its own journal (*Utilitas*) and scarcely an issue appears of any ethics journal from which it is entirely absent. Books are still regularly published discussing it, favorably or unfavorably. Its continuing influence no doubt results in part from the perennially appealing idea that actions and policies should be justified by the good they do, and that this good should somehow culminate in making people's lives go better. Even those who manage to resist this idea are seemingly unable to ignore the theory. Because of its long pedigree and high historical profile, utilitarianism remains the option against which rival traditions tend to be defined and defended. It is fair to say that during the twentieth century most of the best work on utilitarianism has been done, but by the theory's opponents. In reaction, the theory's supporters have continued to articulate it in new and more sophisticated forms. Whichever side one stands on, it is evident that this dialectic between utilitarians and their critics has engaged some of the deepest issues in ethical theory, which is another reason why it shows no sign of withering away. More than twenty years ago Bernard Williams, one of the most influential of the critics, wrote of utilitarianism: "The day cannot be too far off when we hear no more of it." That day still seems as far off as ever.

In order to understand what has been at issue in the debate concerning the merits of utilitarianism, it is best to decompose the theory into three key ideas, each of which has been controversial. First, utilitarianism is one variety of consequentialism, which begins by identifying certain basic or intrinsic values and then holds that whatever is susceptible to moral evaluation—actions, agents, policies, institutions, and so forth—should be assessed for its tendency to produce the best overall state of affairs, measured in terms of these values. As a form of consequentialism, utilitarianism requires agents to take an impartial, or impersonal, standpoint from which everyone's good matters equally—in Bentham's famous phrase, "Everybody to count for one, nobody for more than one." Critics have argued that attempting to practice this very demanding form of impartiality would be incompatible with pursuing our own projects, maintaining close personal relationships, and respecting constraints imposed by the rights of others. In response, utilitarians have stressed that while living the best life we can from the impersonal point of view should be our ultimate aim, it need not be the dominant consideration in our everyday moral thinking. Indeed, it is likely that the utilitarian aim is best pursued indirectly by often defecting from the impersonal standpoint so as to privilege our own position or that of particular others connected to us by bonds of friendship or obligation.

Utilitarianism departs from some other varieties of consequentialism by the method it uses for determining the best overall state of affairs. Its second constituent idea is aggregation, according to which the best state of affairs is the one which contains the greatest sum total of intrinsic value. By embracing aggregation, utilitarians reject the view that the distribution of intrinsic goods across individuals has any ethical significance in itself, though of course it may affect the overall total. Objections to utilitarian aggregation have typically taken the form of urging that an exclusive concern with the total good may require tolerating considerable inequality in the distribution of resources. Utilitarianism has therefore long been suspect as a theory of distributive justice.

Utilitarians have replied by pointing to the diminishing marginal utility of most resources, which tends to support a roughly equal distribution on grounds of efficiency.

Finally, varieties of consequentialism may also differ in what they regard as intrinsically valuable. Here utilitarianism endorses welfarism, the idea that the only thing of intrinsic value is individual welfare or well-being. Maximizing the sum total of well-being—the general welfare—thus becomes its sole ultimate standard for both ethics and politics. Welfarism has come under attack by ethical pluralists for its omission of other personal goods, such as rationality, self-development, or autonomy. Here the utilitarian's strongest response has been to agree that these other goods are valuable, while denying that they are valuable for their own sake; instead, they are worth promoting only to the extent that they make the lives of individuals go better. Utilitarians have also tried to neutralize the criticism somewhat by discarding inadequate accounts of the nature of well-being, such as Bentham's quantitative hedonism, which tend to be presupposed by their pluralist critics. The individualism inherent in welfarism has also been attacked by environmentalists who embrace holistic values, such as the preservation of species or the integrity of the ecosystem. In reply, utilitarians have contended that collectivities—groups, communities, species, ecosystems—are worth preserving only if they enrich the lives of their constituent members. They also remind their environmentalist critics that, alone among the traditional ethical theories in western philosophy, utilitarianism has extended its concern to all sentient beings, human and nonhuman alike.

Utilitarianism has always been advanced both as a personal ethic and as a political morality. It continues to thrive today in large part because of its appeal in the latter domain, as a normative standard for assessing social policies and social institutions, including the law. Despite its somewhat beleaguered status among philosophers, utilitarianism remains secure in the social sciences, and especially in economics where it serves as the normative underpinning of cost/benefit analysis and most debate concerning public policy. It is also arguably the implicit methodology of courts when, in the course of settling indeterminate areas of the law, they find themselves faced with the necessity of balancing conflicting social values.

Despite its historical role as a moral standard for legislatures and courts, utilitarianism is not itself a legal theory in the proper sense—that is, a theory about the nature of law or adjudication. In its earliest stages, especially in the work of Bentham and John Austin (1790–1859), it was closely associated with one such theory, namely, legal positivism. However, this association was always contingent (in principle, utilitarianism could be held in conjunction with any legal theory), and it has largely been dissolved. During the twentieth century the most influential legal positivists (Hans Kelsen, H.L.A. Hart, Joseph Raz) have not been utilitarians, and the best known utilitarians (such as Richard Brandt and R.M. Hare) have espoused no particular legal theory, indeed have shown little interest in the law as an institution.

References

Bentham, Jeremy. *An Introduction to the Principles of Morals and Legislation.* 1789. Eds. J.H. Burns and H.L.A. Hart. London: Athlone Press, 1970.

Brandt, Richard B. *A Theory of the Good and the Right.* Oxford: Clarendon Press, 1979.

Hare, R.M. *Moral Thinking: Its Levels, Method, and Point.* Oxford: Clarendon Press, 1981.

Hume, David. *An Enquiry Concerning the Principles of Morals.* 1751. 3d ed. Ed. L.A. Selby-Bigge and P.H. Nidditch. Oxford: Clarendon Press, 1975.

Mill, John Stuart. *Utilitarianism.* London, 1861. In *Essays on Ethics, Religion and Society*, ed. J.M. Robson. Toronto: University of Toronto Press; London: Routledge and Kegan Paul, 1969.

Moore, G.E. *Ethics.* London: Oxford University Press, 1912.

———. *Principia Ethica.* Cambridge: Cambridge University Press, 1903.

Sen, Amartya, and Bernard Williams, eds. *Utilitarianism and Beyond.* Cambridge: Cambridge University Press, 1982.

Sidgwick, Henry. *The Methods of Ethics.* 1874. 7th ed. London: Macmillan, 1907.

Smart, J.J.C., and Bernard Williams. *Utilitarianism: For and Against.* Cambridge: Cambridge University Press, 1973.

L. Wayne Sumner

See also LIBERAL PHILOSOPHY OF LAW; POSITIVISM, LEGAL

Vagueness
See INDETERMINACY

Validity
Validity is the qualifying label for the norms in law and the acts executed in the name of the law, according to and by the force of which the norms and acts in question are recognized as the norms and the acts, respectively, of the existing legal system. This concept of validity, defining membership within the system, is simultaneously completed by a concept of validity that selects and identifies the system itself. Accordingly, validity is also the qualifying label of the system itself, according to and by the force of which the system in question is recognized by the law and order of the international community as one of the national legal systems.

The concept of validity is only postulated analytically for the sake and within the frame of examination, but this does not have any reference in the outside world. The very fact that talking about "invalid law" would actually involve a *contradictio in adjectu* (oxymoron) clearly shows this point. The neo-kantian methodology, however, which conceives reality in terms of a rigid duality between the domains of "is" and "ought," treated validity as the property of ought projections. Therefore, it dedicated particular theories to it which should only be devoted to genuine problems of legal philosophy.

Validity can be both substantive and formal. Substantive validity is an early form of the concept of validity. When law was not yet formalized, not yet embodied in forms, anything that manifested itself as part of the enforced order could become valid. For instance, in arrangements based on open reasoning, and not yet using the selective criterion of formal relevance, like the *dikaion* (justness) type of Graeco-Roman jurisprudence, the *cadi* (Umayyad courts) jurisdiction in Islamic law, the rabbinic justice in Jewish law, the domain of the *li* (propriety) forming the main layer of Confucian law in China, or the *giri* (rites) in Japan, any consideration, argument, or reference could gain substantive validity, and could thereby become a component of law, inasmuch as it proved useful as a reference in the process of searching for the just solution. In the middle ages it was accepted that only the "good, old" law could get the legitimizing stamp of validity. Consequently, legal actors tried to measure against customs the dispositions of newly enthroned monarchs, and even the statutory products of reforming legislation, so that correspondence might be established between them. Thus, the time-honored practice proves its validity by itself; and, vice versa, ignoring the acceptance of a custom or breaking the application of it can grow into a force depriving it of validity (*desuetude*).

The formal concept of validity is the product of the *ius* (right) reduced to the *lex* (statute). Its development can be traced down from the Roman imperial era to the institutionalization of the modern formal law. Modern law provides that, independent of substantive criteria, any enactment can gain legal validity if issued (promulgated) by a certain authority through a certain procedure in a certain form; the enactment keeps its validity until the competent authority puts an end to it either expressly (for instance, through the repealing act of derogation) or implicitly (for instance, by counterregulation) through a formal procedure. Theoretical reconstruction names this as validity transfer and validity derivation within the system; it is ideal-typical, but is the only one acceptable in any normative justification or reference. In the continental law of Europe, Hans Kelsen's vision, described in his so-called theory of gradation, derives the origin of the legal order from the so-called basic norm, and this legal order has a hierarchical and pyramidal construction through its consistent derivation. In Anglo-American law, H.L.A. Hart distinguishes between primary and secondary rules, the former providing the genuine regulation, and the latter making and amending the former, that is, disposing of the conditions of their validity-granting and validity-ending.

Actually, law is a system which is both dynamic and open and, as opposed to any view suggesting a static closure, shows various possibilities of feedback for its internal mechanisms of validation. The vertical view of how validity originates hierarchically from the apex norm is complemented and eventually replaced by the practice of confirming validity horizontally, or upwardly, in a mutual and circular path between normative sources at similar and differing levels. According to Jerzy Wróblewski, the possibility that discrepancies or contradictions result from the dynamism of law in practice justifies the differentiation of formal validity into systemic validity reflecting the extension of the "law in books," and validity in force covering the domain of the "law in action."

Membership of a norm in the legal system and its actual enforceability are increasingly taken as a unity. According to Joseph Raz, the criterion of this unity must be expressed in the recognition that "the rules recognized and enforced in *s* are legally valid in accordance with *s* but are not thereby themselves part of the legal system *s*." This has regard to the foreign laws invoked by private international law, to the law of religious and ethnic groups, or to the rules of voluntary associations. These show that "validity according to law is broader than membership of the legal system."

Evidently, the legal quality of the system, that is, its validity, cannot be measured by a criterion from within the system. Validity requires completion by another standard, as well. Hans Kelsen stated:

> Although validity and efficacy are two entirely different concepts, there is nevertheless a very important relationship between the two. A norm is considered to be valid only on the condition that it belongs to a system of norms, to an order which, on the whole, is efficacious. Thus, efficacy is a condition of validity; a condition, not the reason of validity. A norm is valid because it is efficacious; it is valid if the order to which it belongs is, on the whole, efficacious.

In this double understanding of the concept of validity, the legal and the sociological, the normative and the real, the systemic and the factual finally meet, despite Kelsen's strict distinction between the domains of "is" and "ought." This means that the feasibility of any normative expectation can only be grounded by the prevailing factuality. Recognizing Ludwig Wittgenstein's fundamental ontological fact of language use, Hart writes: "No such question can arise as to the validity of the very rule of recognition which provides the criteria; it can neither be valid nor invalid but is simply accepted as appropriate for use in this way." As Raz formulated it: "Those ultimate rules of recognition are binding which are actually practiced and followed by the courts."

References

Eckhoff, Torstein. "Feedback in Legal Reasoning and Rule Systems." *Scandinavian Studies in Law* 22 (1976).

Fuchs, Albert. *Die Rechtsgeltung* (Legal Validity). Vienna, 1933.

Hart, H.L.A. *The Concept of Law*. Oxford: Clarendon Press, 1960.

Kelsen, Hans. *General Theory of Law and State*. Cambridge MA: Harvard University Press, 1945.

———. *Reine Rechtslehre* (Pure Theory of Law). Vienna: Deuticke, 1934.

Kern, Fritz. "Law." In *Kingship and Law in the Middle Ages*. 1919. Trans. S.B. Chrimes. Oxford: Blackwell, 1968.

Krawietz, Werner. "Die Lehre von Stufenbau des Rechts—eine säkularisierte politische Theologie?" (The Doctrine of Legal Order—A Secular Political Theology?) In *Rechtstheorie*. Beiheft 5: *Rechtssystem und gesellschaftliche Basis bei Hans Kelsen* (Legal System and Its Communal Basis in Hans Kelsen). Berlin: Duncker und Humblot, 1984.

Peczenik, Alexander. "The Concept 'Valid Law.'" *Scandinavian Studies in Law* 18 (1972).
Raz, Joseph. "Legal Validity." *Archiv für Rechts- und Sozialphilosophie* 63 (1977).
Wróblewski, Jerzy. "Three Concepts of Validity of Law." *Tidskrift utgiven av juridiska föreningen in Finland* 118 (1982).

Csaba Varga

See also AUTHORITY; LEGALITY; LEGITIMACY; ONTOLOGY LEGAL (METAPHYSICS)

Value

Philosophy of law, like all "philosophies of" (philosophy of mind, of art, of knowledge, of literature, of science, of history), has as one of its main issues the question of the nature of the entity being philosophized about. What is law? One simple way of thinking about the connection between law and values is to identify one value that figures directly or indirectly into all discussions about the nature of law: justice. Further, as we investigate this connection, we encounter another fundamental question as to the nature of value or what we mean by value.

Some illustrations of these observations serve both to clarify them and to establish the broad range of thinking about values in philosophizing about the law. This thinking, in addition to considering what law is, addresses topics ranging from the judicial decision, the enforcement of morality, and the justification of punishment to the rationale for an adversary system of justice and the conduct of attorneys within that system. Beginning with the nature of law, we find that adherents to some form of natural law theory believe that law is essentially connected with value. Thomas Aquinas endorses Augustine's famous adage that "that which is not just seems to be no law at all." In Aquinas's view, natural laws are part of a rational order which God has created, and their dictates, like do good and avoid evil, must be adhered to as we design rules to regulate society. Contemporary philosopher John Finnis identifies the value content with such basic human values as knowledge, play, and friendship. Lon Fuller thinks in terms of procedural values in his version of natural law theory. When our rules are contradictory, unintelligible, frequently changing, we fail to make law at all; when we succeed, we have adhered to values which stand in opposition to these procedural vices.

Other philosophers, the legal positivists, insist that the concept of law is value-neutral and that the moral evaluation of a law is a different issue from what a law is. Says John Austin, "The existence of law is one thing; its merit or demerit another." This approach makes matters of value no less important for legal philosophy than does the natural law approach but basically shifts the focus of when these matters become relevant. Once it becomes clear how values are important for these rival approaches, we can see that what remains is to determine which values are important. On this point all of the alternatives which we have already mentioned are relevant as are such alternatives as community or cultural values, religious values, civic values, and values connected with secular or reflective moralities, like kantianism (consistency and human worth) and utilitarianism (pleasure for the greatest number).

When looked at from the perspective of what we are trying to achieve with law, it is hard to imagine any discussion of the nature of law unfolding without some reference to human values. Thus, the American jurist Roscoe Pound depicts a legal system as a means for securing social interests like security and liberty. Benjamin Cardozo has us think about individual cases as being analogous to a scientist's experiments, with the rule of law which a case articulates as the counterpart to the scientist's working hypothesis. Looked at in this way, law becomes instrumentally valuable for solving social problems.

Turning to values and the judicial decision, we find Cardozo depicting justice and morals along with history, tradition, and social welfare as factors which bear on a judge's decision. Ronald Dworkin talks about moral rules as well as legal rules being relevant for the judge's decision in determining the right answer to a case. In cases where fundamental constitutional values are in conflict, we see a balancing test applied to arrive at a judicial decision.

Consider the matter of whether we should enforce morality with the law. Patrick Devlin, thinking that challenges to specific values in a society, such as prostitution and homosexuality, undermine the entire social fabric, argues for outlawing such practices. In a debate with Devlin, H.L.A. Hart rejects the notion that society as a whole is threatened by these victimless acts. This particular debate, like other thinking in this field about using the law to enforce morality, stems from John Stuart Mill's insight that we must identify harm to another person if we can justify restricting one's freedom and that restriction of freedom solely for one's own good is never sufficient. All of this thinking seems to suggest that we know what is good for the society and for the individual, that most people are seeking it, and that the only issue is whether we implement this good with the law. Other ways of thinking about law and morals suggest that the legal system be used to transform the fashion in which people think about values. Karl Marx, for example, used a dictatorship of the proletariat to abolish private property and presumably to instill the value of commonly held property, since, in his view, after the fall of this dictatorship, this value would endure.

Each justification for punishment can be seen as hinging on a value which is of considerable social importance. Retributivists like Immanuel Kant and C.S. Lewis see a system which confers on criminals what they deserve as the only way of achieving justice within the institution. When we promote the value of social utility, generally, and punish to deter, specifically, as do the utilitarians, we end up using the individual and treating the individual as an object. If we value wellness over disease, then, according to Karl Menninger and advocates of a humanitarian approach, we should adopt a treatment model for offenders, since they are sick and need help. If we accept such Christian teachings and values as doing no harm to others ("resist not evil") and loving and forgiving others, we reject punishment as an appropriate response to crime, as did Leo Tolstoy and Clarence Darrow.

Major approaches to settling disputes in society are the adversary and the inquisitorial systems. Their justifications identify how these approaches achieve or promote certain values. An inquisitorial system attaches paramount importance to the value of truth, with the judge becoming the active inquirer and the defense lawyers and prosecutors assisting the judge in this pursuit of truth. While defenders of an adversary approach affirm the value of truth and hypothesize that it emerges through a clash of adversaries at a trial, they emphasize that their approach allows the system to respect individuals in a way which an inquisitorial system cannot; the adversary approach allows each side to present its side in the best light and in doing so shows respect for individuals and their rights on each side of the case.

In their professional lives, lawyers can be seen as guided by some basic values which their codes of conduct promote. Thus, they strive for and place value on an independent professional judgment as they adhere to rules which prevent conflicts of interests, and they affirm the privacy of their clients as they keep confidential communications with their clients. Some commentators see that these values which lawyers affirm differ sufficiently from their counterpart in ordinary contexts and, for that reason, see aspects of legal ethics as irreducible to general or ordinary ethics. For example, lawyers have no choice about keeping confidential their conversations with their clients, and their clients need extract no special promise from the lawyer to rest assured that their conversations will be confidential. In ordinary contexts, on the other hand, we can make no assumption about our conversations with other people being held in confidence; here we recognize that we must extract a promise to keep the conversation a secret if we wish to rest assured that it will be regarded in that way by the other party. Other commentators assert that in both the ordinary context and in the legal context, our practices reflect a primary commitment to social utility or justice, and thus there is no essential difference between lawyers' values and those of ordinary people.

Debate over the status of legal ethics vis-à-vis general ethics narrowly focuses on two alternatives—that legal ethics is subsumable under general ethics, or that legal ethics is essentially different. This narrow focus masks an important observation: we all have something to learn from the way in which lawyers approach ethics. They routinely evaluate what they value and how they thereby conceive themselves; they build conceptions of themselves in an ongoing fashion and connect rules for their conduct to these conceptions. Thus, as they shifted from seeing themselves as people responding to a noble calling to seeing themselves, in part, as people in business, they relaxed their restrictions on advertising. Thinking of our roles in this developmental fashion, more in terms of creating them from our values than of simply occupying roles which other people defined for us, puts everyone as a role constructor under a common operational constraint: recognizing that we occupy a social world in which role modeling is a reality, we should only construct and live by roles which we are willing for others to use as a model for their conduct.

References

Cardozo, Benjamin. *The Nature of the Judicial Process*. New Haven: Yale University Press, 1921.

Darrow, Clarence. *Resist Not Evil*. Patterson Smith Reprint Series in Criminology, 1902.

Finnis, John. *Natural Law and Natural Rights*. Oxford: Clarendon Press, 1980.

Fuller, Lon. *The Morality of Law*. New Haven: Yale University Press, 1964.

Hart, H.L.A. *Law, Liberty, and Morality*. New York: Vintage Books, 1963.

Lewis, C.S. "The Humanitarian Theory of Punishment." In *God in the Dock*. London: Curtis Brown, 1970.

Luban, David. *Lawyers and Justice*. Princeton: Princeton University Press, 1988.

Luizzi, Vincent. *A Case for Legal Ethics: Legal Ethics as a Source for a Universal Ethic*. Albany: State University of New York Press, 1993.

Menninger, Karl. *The Crime of Punishment*. New York: Viking Press, 1968.

Tolstoy, Leo. *Resurrection*. New York: Grosset & Dunlap, 1899.

Vincent Luizzi

See also GOODNESS AND COHERENCE; VIRTUE

Vengeance

It has been suggested that the most fundamental purpose of imposing punishment under law is the attempt to domesticate and restrain the desire for vengeance. Other objectives are certainly recognized. In particular, the maintenance of order is important, and punishment that incapacitates, deters, or rehabilitates is imposed for the purpose of maintaining such order. Of course, these latter objectives achieve additional benefits. Society does not have to worry about the criminal who has been incapacitated and cannot engage in more crime. Deterrence, by treating the offender as an example for others, decreases the potential criminal population. Rehabilitation presumably transforms dangerous criminals into productive members of society either within or outside of prison. However, vengeance has certainly been, and, many would argue, continues to be, a primary focus.

When an individual is harmed by another, he or she usually wants revenge. This desire takes the form of wanting to respond to the perpetrator by harming him in return. Subsequently, some will identify with the first individual harmed. Others will have connections with the perpetrator and will desire to return the harm to the individual or individuals who harmed the perpetrator, even though the perpetrator is the one who instigated the harm. These latter individuals, emotionally connected to the perpetrator in one way or another, might be motivated by loyalty or love. In any case, it is clear that a series of responses are set in motion that are problematic for any society to countenance. Such responses, involving an escalating exchange of harms, are dangerously disruptive. A stable and orderly society cannot allow such responses to continue unchecked.

Aeschylus, in the *Oresteia*, dramatically presents this cycle of revenge. In order to be victorious in battle, Agamemnon, the father, sacrifices his daughter. Upon his return, Clytemnestra, his wife, kills him. Orestes, the son, avenging his father, kills his mother and her lover. At this point, the Furies, the goddesses of vengeance, pursue Orestes since he killed his mother. A court composed of deities tries Orestes, finds him not guilty, and Athena persuades the Furies to renounce their desire for vengeance. The Furies agree to live within the state and become the Eumenides, goddesses of the hearth. They will not pursue vengeance on any person who harms a family member and will have responsibility for protecting the hearth. Thus, the trilogy focuses on the transformation from a preoccupation with vengeance to a concern with justice.

Various societies, throughout history, have given a great deal of attention to the effort to accommodate the desire for vengeance within a framework of justice. There has been tension between legitimate and illegitimate expressions. The result has been a confusion between the notion of what constitutes vengeance and what constitutes justice. Many individuals find deeply disturbing the idea that the two might be the same. As a result, for those interested in advancing the idea that justice as retribution should be an objective of punishment, it is important to make the distinction between vengeance and retribution clear. Vengeance, after all, is often perceived to be prohibited by religion, or is viewed as too dark and menacing from the point of view of psychoanalytic thinking, or is regarded simply as unenlightened from the perspective of the objectives of punishment that would presumably be pursued by any civilized society.

In *Gregg v. Georgia*, 428 U.S. 153, 183 (1976), the United States Supreme Court reaffirmed the notion of an "instinct for retribution [as] part of the nature of man." The justices suggested that "channeling that instinct in the administration of criminal justice serves an important purpose in promoting the stability of a society governed by law." They viewed this desire as a perfectly acceptable "expression of society's moral outrage. . . ." Many argue, in response, that the Court is using of the word "retribution" as a synonym for "vengeance." What the justices describe, and claim to be a legitimate concern of the state, is the need on the part of human beings to satisfy a fundamental desire that erupts in reaction to a particularly egregious act.

As indicated above, many find this connection between justice as retribution and vengeance deeply troubling. Indeed, in the view of these individuals, the perspective of the U.S. Supreme Court, as expressed in *Gregg*, supports the claim that such a connection exists. The critical question, however, for the philosophy of law, independent of any particular court decision, is whether the two ideas can be distinguished conceptually. The answer, some would argue, is that a meaningful distinction can be made.

Retribution, as a form of justice, seeks to repay the perpetrator what he or she is due. Punishment would be imposed that is an appropriate response to the crime. Vengeance, on the other hand, is about satisfying the rage of the victim, the victim's family, or society. For retribution, again, as justice, it is claimed that the determination of what is owed is made on the basis of an objective perspective. Third parties (judge or jury) are involved. The focus involves attempting to identify what constitutes fair payment for the act committed, the intent with which the act was committed, and the damage that the act brought to the individual or individuals harmed. Rules are determined for conducting such proceedings. These include rules of evidence and due process. Vengeance, on the other hand, is guided by what will emotionally or psychologically satisfy the person harmed. No objective measure is applied. No impersonally conducted proceedings are held. The focus is on the outcome, as opposed to the means to judgment, and the outcome that is sought is the emotional satisfaction of the injured.

That the distinction between justice and vengeance can be made conceptually, of course, does not mean that, in any particular case, the state makes such a distinction in the punishment that it imposes. Indeed, it may, in some collective sense, often pursue ends more appropriately identified as vengeance, giving support, at least in terms of the state's observed behavior, to those individuals who claim not to see a distinction between retribution and vengeance. Furthermore, whether such practice, on the part of the state, contributes to the maintenance of order, or its dissolution, remains a question for serious debate.

References

Aeschylus. *The Oresteia*. Trans. H. Lloyd-Jones. Berkeley: University of California, 1993.

Altman, Andrew. *Critical Legal Studies: A Liberal Critique*. Princeton: Princeton University Press, 1990.

Belliotti, Raymond. *Justifying Law*. Philadelphia: Temple University Press, 1992.

Camus, Albert. *Resistance, Rebellion, and Death*. Trans. Justin O'Brien. New York: Knopf, 1961.

Gaylin, Willard. *The Killing of Bonnie Garland*. New York: Simon & Schuster, 1982.

Jacoby, Susan. *Wild Justice: The Evolution of Revenge*. New York: Harper & Row, 1983.

Pincoffs, Edmund. *The Rational of Legal Punishment*. Atlantic Highlands NJ: Humanities Press International, 1966.

Primoratz, Igor. *Justifying Legal Punishment*. Atlantic Highlands NJ: Humanities Press International, 1989.

Ten, C.L. *Crime, Guilt, and Punishment*. Oxford: Oxford University Press, 1987.

Mark Sheldon

See also DESERT; MERCY AND FORGIVENESS; RETRIBUTIVE RATIONALE

Vico, Giambattista (1668–1744)

For most of his academic life, Giambattista Vico was professor of rhetoric at the University of Naples (1699–1741), but his broader interests, which culminated in the doctrines of the various editions of his *New Science* (1725, 1730, 1744), lay in the development of a system of knowledge of the historical and social world, within which special emphasis was laid upon the nature and importance of law.

One of Vico's primary aims was to defend the legitimacy of historical systems of private law (*ius gentium*), which was threatened by claims that they were simply matters of convention (Carneades) or usefulness (Niccolò Machiavelli). Such a defense had already been attempted by Hugo Grotius, who had argued that a rational and eternal system of rights was contained in the law of all nations, but Vico criticized Grotius for failing to realize that legal systems, like all human institutions, undergo a process of historical development. If, as Vico agreed, actual systems of law were related to a universal and eternal system of natural rights, the contents of the latter must be modified by some equally necessary principles of historical development.

Vico's first thesis is that the individual cannot live outside society. Because human beings are by nature corrupt, however, societies require a countervailing legal structure. Such a structure cannot be based upon convention or contract, since the latter would have no force without legal support. It must therefore exist "by nature," that is, as part of the necessarily social character of human nature, and come into existence along with the customs which are natural to it.

Vico's second thesis is that the nature of the institutions of a nation, hence the structure and content of its legal system, must conform to its conception of its own nature. This changes according to a sequence of dominant modes of mind developed in a model which Vico calls the "ideal eternal history." The first mode is wholly imaginative and anthropomorphic, giving rise to a "poetic" or "theological" era in which man sees everything as god and in which the structure and content of the legal system will be determined by the belief that the laws are divine commands. The second era is a "heroic" period in which a nobility is believed to have descended from unions of gods and humans. Here the legal system will be an instrument for the protection of this nobility's vast private interests. Since the basic mode of mind is now becoming more rational, however, it can sustain a successful criticism of the heroes' claims to semidivine status and of their privileged legal status, which depends on this, leading to a period of class war between the heroes and the rest of the population. The third mode of mind is fully rational. The false conceptions of the previous eras have been overcome, and people understand that the true principle of law is that of equity for all. However, Vico does not believe that human rationality can overcome the natural corruption of individual humans and this era must decline into a new barbarism and the repeat of the nation's life cycle.

Vico's third thesis is that historical systems of positive law are rendered legitimate because they are always expressions of some stage of this developing idea of justice. The truth of this conception can be demonstrated philosophically and its regulative function in the past historically.

It may be wondered whether Vico is correct in claiming that the same rather than different developing conceptions of justice must underlie and vindicate historical systems of law. Even if he is incorrect in this view, three points remain of particular value in his philosophy of law. First, without a *natural* or nonconventional disposition toward law our life would never transcend a state of natural brutishness. Second, for a system of positive law to be legitimate it must rest upon a prior conception of what is fair or just. No system of positive law need be accepted simply because it has been willed by legislators. Third, changes in positive law are legitimate only in so far as they are dependent upon an understanding of higher standards of fairness and impartiality.

References

Bedani, Gino. *Vico Revisited.* Oxford: Berg, 1989.

Haddock, Bruce. *Vico's Political Thought.* Swansea: Mortlake Press, 1986.

Lilla, Mark. *G.B. Vico: The Making of an Anti-Modern.* Cambridge MA: Harvard University Press, 1993.

Pasini, Dino. *Diritto società e stato in vico* (Law, Society, and State in Vico). Naples: Jovene Napoli, 1970.

Pompa, Leon. *Vico: A Study of the "New Science."* 1975. 2d ed. Cambridge: Cambridge University Press, 1990.

Vico, Giambattista. *The New Science of Giambattista Vico (1744).* Ed. and trans.

Thomas Goddard Bergin and Max Harold Fisch. Ithaca: Cornell University Press, 1984.
———. *Opere giuridiche* (Works on Law). Ed. Paolo Cristofolini. Florence: Sansoni, 1974.

Leon Pompa

Villey, Michel (1914–1988)

Michel Villey, grandson of Emile Boutroux and son of Pierre Villey, the Montaigne scholar, taught Roman law, the history of law and, finally, the history of the philosophy of law, at Nancy, Saigon, Strasbourg, and at last Paris. Starting in 1961, he worked at reintroducing the philosophy of law as an academic discipline in France, first through his graduate courses at the University of Paris and later as the director of the *Archives de Philosophie du Droit*. His name is closely associated with a few major theses which he firmly and consistently espoused, all the while remaining sensitive to their subtleties.

The first theme is the rediscovery of natural law as the foundation of and necessary reference point for positive law. Villey only embraced what he called the "classical theory of natural law"—as opposed to "modern natural law"—which was developed by Aristotle in Book V of the *Nicomachean Ethics*, was first illustrated in the *Digest* and was adopted by St. Thomas Aquinas. Attacked by nominalism and neo-scholasticism, it gave way to modern natural law, some of whose chief representatives are Hugo Grotius, Samuel Pufendorf, Thomas Hobbes, and John Locke. The new theory's official monument is the French *Declaration of the Rights of Man and of the Citizen* of 1789.

A second major theme in Villey is tied to the re-evaluation of dialectics—whether it is the proper method for law and even for philosophy. He again traced back the theory and the practice of dialectics to Aristotle and Aquinas.

Aristotle broke both with the monological aspects of the demonstrations of the sophists and with the artificiality or mythical character of the platonic *Dialogues*. Aristotle was the first to have demonstrated that a jurist, like a philosopher, is a *zoon politicon* (political animal), and not a producer of systems or a solitary person. The jurist or the philosopher gives an opinion, resolves an issue only after having listened to the discordant voices that he has heard and after having given more importance to their weight than to their number; the decision, which is always provisional, tries to take into account everything that is true and just in each opinion without troubling itself with the rest. Villey called this method specific to law *concordia discordantium* (harmony in difference), used in the *Digest*, Gratian's *Decretum*, and Aquinas' *Summa Theologiae*. This dialectic, as opposed to the hegelian master/slave dialectic, makes possible the passage from the necessary but vague natural law to the relative but determinate positive law.

This leads to a third important topic found in Villey's work, legality and equality. One moves from general justice to particular justice, from justice as an overall virtue to justice as legality and equality. Legality is what binds a community in its journey toward its good and is what this community reads: *ligare* (to bind) and *legere* (to read).

Equality is what one expects from the judge and the law when one is concerned with the distribution of external goods of the community among its members. This equality of proportions supposes at least four elements: two people to share in the distribution and two things to distribute. This is a geometric equality because, far from distributing to everyone the same amount of goods, it distributes goods (a, b) to each and everyone (a′, b′) according to who they are: $a/a' = b/b'$. Equality is also concerned with exchanges that occur after the distribution. Accordingly, once sellers have parted with something which they owned, buyers must provide them with something of equivalent value so that the same distribution still exists after the exchange.

Other themes found in Villey's writings touch upon the specificity of law, its secular nature, and the rejection of individualism. Morality is concerned with the individual and internal aspect of a person, while law is concerned with the relations of humans with each other, *ad alterum*, and only with their external aspect. Religion is received within a church and is transmitted by theology, while law is received within the state and is within the particular competence of jurists. Individualism logically constrains one to make the subject the necessary and sufficient condition of law and transforms law into power over things or persons. Villey argues that law is a relation of people and things as parts of a whole; this relation is the point of equilibrium, and its stability is similar to the things themselves.

Villey's work is better known abroad than in France itself. It is an apology for jurisprudence as a profession with its greatness, its limits, and its demands, a defense and illustration of the specificity of legal language, a denunciation of the ravages of technology—like Jacques Ellul (1912–1994) and Martin Heidegger (1889–1976)—and a call for the voice of Themis (natural justice) to be heard anew in the courts.

References

Cabarillas, Renato Rabbi-Baldi. *La filosofia jurídica de Michel Villey* (The Philosophy of Law of Michel Villey). Pamplona: Ed. Universidad de Navarra, 1990.

Cunha, Paulo Ferreira da. "A Natural Natural Law." *Vera Lex* 11 (1991), 1–4.

Hatson, James H. "The Emergence of the Modern Concept of a Right in America: The Contribution of Michel Villey." *American Journal of Jurisprudence* 39 (1984), 185.

Niort, Jean-François, and Guillaume Vannier, eds. *Michel Villey et le droit naturel en question* (Michel Villey: The Natural Law in Question). Paris: L'Harmattan, 1994.

Rapp, Hans. "Michel Villey on Modern Natural Law." *Archiv für Rechts- und Sozialphilosophie* 65 (1979), 414–430.

van Overbeke, P.M. "Philosophie du droit" (Philosophy of Law). *Revue thomiste* 69 (1969), 435–462.

Villey, Michel. *Le droit romain* (Roman Law). 6th ed. Que sais-je? No. 195. Paris: PUF, 1972.

———. *La formation de la pensée juridique moderne* (The Foundation of Modern Legal Thought). 4th ed. Paris: Montchrétien, Paris, 1975.

———. *Philosophie du droit* (Philosophy of Law). Vol. 1, *Définition et fins du droit.* 4th ed. Paris: Dalloz, 1986. Vol. 2, *Les moyens du droit.* 2d ed. Paris: Dalloz, 1984.

———. *Réflexions sur la philosophie et le droit* (Reflections on Philosophy and Law). Paris: PUF, 1995.

———. *Seize essais de philosophie du droit* (Sixteen Essays in Philosophy of Law). Paris: Dalloz, 1969.

François Vallançon

Violence and Oppression

These two concepts have a particularly intimate relationship. Violence and threats of violence are perhaps the most direct and effective ways of causing oppression. In legal and political contexts, violence refers to (1) the use of force to cause physical harm, including death, or the destruction of property, and (2) practices, such as humiliation, deprivation, the use of threats, or the use of racial and religious slurs, which cause severe mental or emotional harm. Oppression, the condition of a person or persons being kept down, that is, being heavily burdened in body or mind, is not a necessary or inevitable result of violence, but is, nonetheless, a highly probable result. It is often the fear felt by victims or potential victims of violence which is the most significant factor in causing oppression. Oppression is an object of moral disapprobation because it severely undermines autonomy, a person's capacity to act and to choose, in short, to live as he or she sees fit.

Thomas Hobbes expounded a clear position on the relationship between violence, oppression, and the origins of law and the state. Without laws and the sovereign power to enforce them, in short, without government, the human condition would be wretched. Hobbes describes this oppressive condition as the "warre of every man against every man . . ." in which life is "solitary, poore, nasty, brutish, and short." Motivated by fear of violent death and guided by self-preservation, individuals covenant one with the other to give up their unlimited natural rights (excluding the right to self-defense) in order to institute a government to lay down laws binding on all and with power sufficient to enforce them. Stating that "[c]ovenants, without the Sword, are but mere words, and of no strength to secure a man at all," Hobbes emphasizes the necessity of strong government to provide individuals with the peace and security they seek. For each to protect himself or herself from others, as well as from common external enemies, all must transfer their individual use of violence to the state. Hobbes believes that in securing peace and safety, any government is better than no government at all, and he gives little consideration to the moral problems which concentration of power in the hands of the state presents. What follows is a discussion of several moral problems which arise when the relationship of violence and the state is considered.

Niccolò Machiavelli recognized the role that violence plays in history and in human affairs. It is through the creative use of violence that the prince, that is, the political leader, establishes and/or protects a political entity and its system of laws. In so doing, he carves out a social space for the development of nonpolitical pursuits, such as art or philosophy. Machiavelli believes that civilized life and the arts of peace we associate with it depend upon the art of war. In a number of his writings, he makes the point that good arms and good laws are mutually reinforcing. Good arms are necessary to protect good laws, and good laws are necessary to provide for good arms, that is, a strong, well-trained military. He also argues that the violence of the state used to defend against an external threat will often produce a degree of civic virtue and unity among citizens that is not usually found in peacetime.

The development of modern warfare in the twentieth century has rendered the relationship Machiavelli envisioned between warfare, good laws, and civic virtue morally problematic. The nature of modern total war, in which the distinction between combatants and noncombatants is blurred, fought with weapons of mass destruction, has led many to the conclusion that in war there can be no victors or salutary effects. The use of nuclear weapons by any state carries with it the possibility of escalation to the point of global destruction. Albert Camus has referred to the twentieth century as "the century of fear" and suggests that the specter of global destruction cuts humanity off from the future and represents a new form of oppression. The goal of preventing warfare has provided impetus for the development of international law as a response to this dangerous situation. Hobbes saw domestic law, and the sovereign power to enforce it, as the only remedy to unfettered violence among individuals. Many contemporary theorists see international law as the remedy to violence among states. This approach raises two related problems. First, the absence of enforcement mechanisms casts doubt on the efficacy of international law to prevent or stop interstate violence. Second, to the degree that efforts to enhance an international order, including enforcement power, are successful, it will be at the expense of the sovereignty of individual states. It has been argued that were sovereignty to be vitiated in this way, the sanctity and effectiveness of domestic law would be threatened.

A moral problem raised explicitly in Machiavelli's work involves what he sees as a tension or conflict between the morality of everyday life and the morality of political action. Political leaders must often violate ordinary morality to do what is necessary for political ends. Political action regularly demands intrigue, deceit, and violence, used both externally and internally. When the protection or greater good of the state is at stake, Machiavelli expects political leaders to breach ordinary morality if necessary. Thus, political morality is consequentialist, and political action must be guided by the ends of the state and not limited only to means conforming to ordinary morality. It has been argued, against Machiavelli, that political leaders should never violate ordinary morality to achieve a better political outcome. Michael Walzer claims that most of us would not choose to be governed by leaders unwilling to take immoral actions for political ends, particularly in a crisis. However, he also asserts that while such immoral actions may be excused, they can never be justified. Dennis Thompson suggests that the problem of political morality has special implications in a democracy. Because leaders govern with the consent of the people and are ultimately accountable to them, the people share responsibility for immoral actions taken on their behalf. Democracy embodies the values of human equality, universal human rights, and an open society. Given these values, we might consider whether democratic leaders have the same latitude in their actions as do leaders in nondemocracies. Are practices, such as political assassination, various covert actions, and the use or threatened use of nuclear weapons, consistent with fundamental democratic values? If not, are democracies at a strategic disadvantage vis-à-vis nondemocratic regimes?

Max Weber gives this definition of the state: "a human community that (successfully) claims the monopoly of the legitimate use of physical force within a given territory." He is correct in identifying violence as an essential part of the definition of the state, but fails to distinguish regimes which are legitimate in fact from those which are merely successful in getting claims of legitimacy accepted. The question of legitimacy is a pressing and important one. Violent and oppressive practices and institutions, such as slavery, colonialism, economic exploitation, or the subjugation of women and ethnic minorities, have not only been tacitly endorsed by states, they have often been actively supported and protected by the law. Entire political and social systems may be violent and oppressive, such as Nazi Germany or Stalinist Soviet Union. Such situations present another difficult moral problem: after a practice, institution, or entire state is determined to be illegitimate by some objective criteria, when, if ever, is violent opposition or revolt justified? This prompts the more theoretical questions of whether there are universal, objective standards for establishing legitimacy or illegitimacy, and how they are to be arrived at. If there are no such standards, the critical distinction between terrorists and freedom fighters is a subjective one and will depend upon which side of a conflict persons making the distinction find themselves. As stated previously, the relationship of violence to oppression is intimate, but so is the relationship of violence to law, politics, and the state.

References

Arendt, Hannah. *On Violence*. Hammondsworth: Penguin, 1969.

Camus, Albert. "Neither Victims Nor Executioners." Trans. Dwight Macdonald. *Politics* (July–August 1947).

Fanon, Frantz. *The Wretched of the Earth*. Trans. C. Farrington. London: Macgibbon and Kee, 1965.

Hobbes, Thomas. *Leviathan*. 1651. Hammondsworth: Penguin, 1972.

Macfarlane, L. *Violence and the State*. London: Nelson, 1974.

Machiavelli, Niccolò. *The Discourses*. 1517. Trans. Leslie Walker. Hammondsworth: Penguin, 1970.

———. *The Prince*. 1513. Trans. Robert Adams. New York: Norton, 1977.

Thompson, Dennis. *Political Ethics and Public Office*. Cambridge: Harvard University Press, 1987.

Walzer, Michael. "Political Action: The Problem of Dirty Hands." *Philosophy and Public Affairs* 2 (1973), 160–180.

Weber, Max. "Politics as a Vocation." In *From Max Weber: Essays in Sociology*, Ed. and trans. H.H. Gerth and C. Wright Mills. New York: Oxford University Press, 1976.

David T. Risser

See also PENAL LAW, PHILOSOPHY OF; REBELLION; REVOLUTION; SLAVERY; TORTURE; WAR AND WAR TRIALS

V

Virtue

The concept of virtue raises important issues in regard to legal normativity. Virtue concepts are aretaic as opposed to deontic, that is, they include notions like "excellent," "virtuous," "admirable," "(morally) good," and their opposites, in contradistinction to notions like "ought," "should," "right," "permissible," and "obligatory." Since aretaic notions seem "softer" and less "prescriptive" than deontic ones, it has been held that because virtue ethics is essentially based in such notions, it will of necessity lack the full normativity available to other theories of law and ethics and as such be inadequate as a grounding for our thinking about morality, politics, and the law.

In addition, it has been claimed that notions like virtue (virtuousness) make sense only derivatively and in relation to independently defined principles or goals of moral conduct. For kantians, virtue involves acting in accordance with previously understood moral and political principles or rules; for utilitarians, it is a matter of character traits or motives that are conducive to human or sentient happiness. Virtue ethics, however, treats virtue(s), admirable traits of character or motives, as the primary factor in morality, and the problem then arises whether we can make sense of such a crucial role for virtue or should content ourselves, rather, with understanding virtue and the virtues in relation to other, more important or basic, ethical factors.

Virtue ethics was the norm in ancient philosophy, and in recent years, virtue ethics, understood as a free-standing and total approach to ethical issues, has undergone something of a revival. However, the capacity of such approaches to do justice to the full range of individual and social morality depends on their ability to answer the sorts of questions raised just above. The following discussion will focus on this issue.

Is it true, for example, that virtue ethics lacks the capacity to make the sorts of strong or strict ethical judgments available to intuitionists, kantians, and others? That depends on just how strong aretaic judgments can be and on whether deontic judgments are as strong as they have been said to be. Taking the latter point first, it is worth noting that the kantian and intuitionist idea that moral prescriptions have a binding force and represent absolute and inescapable requirements is somewhat questionable in the light of recent discussions of the possibility of *moral dilemmas*, characterized as situations where a person cannot fulfill all his or her obligations, do everything he or she ought. The tragic situations of Agamemnon at Aulis and, more recently, of Sophie in *Sophie's Choice* reveal the possibility of having to choose an option that one may think of as morally horrible in order to make the best of a morally horrible situation. If such situations are genuine dilemmas, then the believed claim that it would be morally wrong to do something, that it is one's obligation not to do it, may not preclude doing it (perhaps even *having* to do it) in a situation where all other options are equally or more horrible. So it is not clear that deontic moral judgments have the inescapable action-guiding prescriptivity often attributed to them. (It is interesting in this connection that both Kant and traditional intuitionists deny or ignore the possibility of moral dilemma.)

In addition, Philippa Foot has pointed to the possibility of situations where individuals feel they must do something (they think of as) morally wrong in order to stave off disaster to themselves, their families, or their country. If such situations are understandable, the force of deontic moral claims may, again, be less absolute than kantians and intuitionists have held.

On the other side, aretaic judgments may actually have *more* force than is typically assumed. Is the claim that it would be morally bad to hurt someone really any weaker in moral terms than the claim that it would be morally wrong to do so? Does the latter prescribe or condemn in some way that the former does not? It is not clear that it does; and if that is true, then one may even argue that aretaic judgments sometimes entail, or allow the derivation, of deontic ones. Moving outside morality for the moment, why shouldn't we conclude from the assumption that something would be an aesthetically bad way to perform a certain dance routine that, aesthetically speaking, one *shouldn't* perform the routine that way? Similar derivations may be possible in morality proper, and aretaic judgments *may* be strong enough to allow virtue ethics to perform the ordinary and necessary tasks of ethics.

How could a virtue ethics ground any sort of political morality or notion of valid/just laws? Law and legality are deontic to the extent they entail the idea of legal permissibility (and legal rights). Is it possible to derive *such* deontic notions from purely aretaic ones? The answer in principle is yes, though once one sees how such a derivation is possible, one has to consider whether the kind of virtue theory in which it is embedded is as plausible as other approaches to morality and the law.

To illustrate this briefly, consider a (simplified) virtue ethics that takes its inspiration from the emphasis on sympathy and benevolence that one finds in British "moral sense" theory and, subsequently, in utilitarianism. This virtue ethics claims that benevolence is the morally highest motive and holds that acts are morally right or wrong depending on whether they come from benevolence or from some motive like selfishness or callousness that is morally inferior to benevolence. Such a theory treats the aretaic evaluation of motives as the foundation for other ethical judgments as well, and, for example, moral rules and principles are evaluated in relation to how well they express the motive of benevolence.

The theory also has the capacity to generate a view of social justice and the validity or justice of laws and legal penalties or privileges. A society can be said to count as just if the people in it are benevolent (which is somewhat different from the utilitarian criterion of a society's predictably producing the greatest happiness of the people living in it). Social customs, institutions, laws, privileges, and penalties can then be said to be just (or deserved) if they exhibit benevolence on the part of those responsible for them. Such a view treats the idea of desert not as the basis for understanding justice and other moral notions, but rather, in the manner of certain recent contractarians, as derivative from independent ideas about social justice. Unlike contractarianism, the view in question treats issues of justice, desert, and legal validity as ultimately grounded in admirable motivations, rather than in some kind of hypothetical situation of social contract. Whether any such virtue ethics can in the end be plausible and plausibly compete with other accounts of justice and law is an issue, however, that must be left to another forum.

References

Foot, Philippa. *Virtues and Vices*. Oxford: Blackwell, 1978.

Hutcheson, Francis. *An Inquiry into the Origin of Our Ideas of Beauty and Virtue.* 1725.
Scanlon, Thomas. "The Significance of Choice." In *The Tanner Lectures on Human Values.* Salt Lake City: University of Utah Press, 1988.
Slote, Michael. *From Morality to Virtue.* New York: Oxford, 1995.
Williams, Bernard. *Problems of the Self.* Cambridge: Cambridge University Press, 1973.

Michael Slote

See also CHARACTER; SUPEREROGATION

Voice

A concept found originally in classical Greek and Roman treatises on rhetoric and which served as a primary subdivision of the canon of delivery, voice emphasized rules for guiding a speaker's use of rhythm, volume, and tone as persuasive means of performatively coordinating the ethical, emotional, and logical or reasoned dimensions of a speech with both one another and the external constraints of time and place.

Classical Greece and Rome were inherently oral cultures that valorized the public performance and enactment of ethos or credibility. In such rhetorical cultures the management of voice through the imitation of natural or ordinary language was among the most important skills that an orator could master, for in so doing a public speaker could demonstrate sensitivity to the demands of propriety and decorum, and thus the capacity for phronesis or prudence, that is, practical wisdom, the key virtue of public and civic character. So it was, for example, that in ancient Athens litigants were required literally to speak on their own behalf before a jury as a means of giving public voice to their character, even though they could hire *logographers* or speechwriters to help them craft their actual words.

In contemporary times, the concept of voice has been appropriated by composition and literary studies when it refers loosely and often reductively to the power and controlling presence or persona of the implied author in a text. It is at the conjunction of these two perspectives—the performative and the textual—that voice has become an important site at which literary and philosophical modernists, poststructuralists, and postmodernists have contested the overlapping problems of meaning, authority, and identity in ways that bear special relevance to the agency of the law.

Interpretations of the meaning of the law rely on the ability to determine the voice or voices that are both present and absent in a particular legal text, whether contract, statute, court decision, or some other expression of the law. For modernists, who believe in a naturally autonomous or unitary "self," meaning comes from within an author, and voice is the public conduit of that meaning. Meaning is thus linked to authorial intention and authenticity. Although one can never access authorial intention with the certainty of scientific precision, analysis of the formal style, tone, and texture of a discursive utterance points to the author's controlling attitudes, values, and beliefs, and thus provides valuable evidence for decoding the presence or presumed, fixed meaning of a text.

Poststructuralists critique this perspective by denying the very possibility of an autonomous or unitary self, thus calling into question the root or source of the voice in a text. If the self is not unified but fragmented, not naturally authentic but socially constructed, they wonder, what then does it mean to talk about the author? If there is no unified or authentic author, then what becomes of voice as the controlling presence of meaning? What, for example, is the meaning of a decision handed down by a particular court, especially when there are competing majority and dissenting opinions? Is it determined by the voice of the individual justice or justices who compose the majority decision with no concern for the dissent? Or the voice of the journalists who report it to the mass public? Or the voice of subsequent courts that employ it as precedent in their own decision making? Or the voice of legislators and lobbyists who interpret it in their deliberations and negotiations? Or, for that matter, the voices of past generations leading to the present moment in history?

Postmodernists would be inclined to argue that the meaning of such a decision is chaotic, lacking any particular order, a seeming cacophony of all such voices, past and present, speaking at once. From this perspective the law is inherently multivocal or, in Mikhail Bakhtin's terms, heteroglossic: its meaning is not fixed but polymorphous, open to a wide range of competing and potentially legitimate interpretations, often simultaneously so; and more, it is dialogic, crafted in the crucible of public debate and discussion, perpetually subject to change as voices with different ideological accents come to the fore, interact, and produce more or less persuasive interpretations of its meaning. Of course, when the meaning of a legal text is decentered and destabilized this way, rooted in multivocality rather than univocity, we encounter questions about both the authority of the law and the possibilities for social and political agency within it.

In the Anglo-American, liberal-democratic tradition, the authority of the law is said to derive from the sovereignty of "the people": *vox populi vox Dei*, the voice of the people is the voice of God. Thus it is, for example, that the voice or authorial presence of the U.S. Constitution is identified in the opening sentence of its preamble, "We the people of the United States. . . ." The problem is in determining what counts as that voice in the enactment of the Constitution. How do we know it when we hear it? There are numerous problems here, but primary to the relationship between voice and authority is trying to identify the material embodiment of a collective self that lacks any corporeality. Inasmuch as the collective body of "the people" is a metaphorical abstraction, an anthropomorphizing of the body politic, so too must be its collective voice. Characterizing the voice of "the people" as a rhetorical construction has led to two very different critiques of the law's authorial presence, and thus its agency.

Some, following the contours of derridean deconstruction and the critique of logocentrism, argue that because "the people" is a purely linguistic phenomenon, its voice is indeterminate, at best a function of the sheer play of signification which denies any sense of authority or agency to "the people" as such. When political and legal advocates claim to speak for "the people," they are doing no more than attempting to colonize the authority of the law to legitimize their own ideological ends. Others, following the rhetorical pragmatism of James Boyd White, argue that the voice of "the people" is a function of the culture of argument that defines and constitutes a sociopolitical, legal community. A culture of argument consists of the inherited language, arguments, narratives, and symbolic usages that constitute the social system in and through which the law operates. Legal advocates thus give authorial presence to the law by creatively and persuasively performing its meaning in specific, contingent circumstances. From this perspective, the indeterminacy of "the people" is more a strength than a weakness of liberal democracy, for it opens up the possibilities for legal agency. To treat "the people" as indeterminate is to acknowledge that its identity must be negotiated from among the competing voices seeking to manage or control its authority, and within that process of negotiation resides the capacity for the law to adapt to the problems of a changing world.

References

Bakhtin, Mikhail. *Speech Genres and Other Late Essays*. Trans. Vern W. McGee. Austin: University of Texas Press, 1986.

Derrida, Jacques. *Of Grammatology*. Trans. Gayatri Chakravorty Spivak. Baltimore: Johns Hopkins University Press, 1974.

Elbow, Peter. "Introduction: About Voice and Writing." In *Landmark Essays on Voice and Writing*, ed. Peter Elbow, xi–xvii. Davis CA: Hermagoras Press, 1994.

Foucault, Michel. "What Is an Author?" In *Language, Counter-Memory, Practice: Selected Essays and Interviews by Michel Foucault,* ed. and trans. Donald F. Bouchard, 113–138. Ithaca: Cornell University Press, 1977.

McGee, Michael Calvin. "In Search of 'The People': A Rhetorical Alternative." *Quarterly Journal of Speech* 61 (1975), 235–249.

Ong, Walter. *Orality and Literacy: Technologizing the Word.* New York: Routledge, 1982.

Swearingen, C. Jan. "Ethos: Imitation, Impersonation, and Voice." In *Ethos: New Essays in Rhetorical and Critical Theory,* ed. James S. Baumlin and Tita French Baumlin, 115–149. Dallas: Southern Methodist University Press, 1994.

White, James Boyd. *Heracles' Bow: Essays on the Rhetoric and Poetics of the Law.* Madison: University of Wisconsin Press, 1985.

———. *When Words Lose Their Meaning: Constitutions and Reconstitutions of Language, Character, and Community.*

Chicago: University of Chicago Press, 1984.

John Louis Lucaites

See also INTERPRETATION; METAPHOR AND SYMBOL; POSTMODERN PHILOSOPHY OF LAW; SPEECH ACTS

Volenti

See CONSENT

Vote

See FRANCHISE AND REFERENDUM

War and War Trials

Dr. Samuel Johnson, England's greatest man of letters, best known for his first dictionary of the English language, published in 1755, defined war as involving "the exercise of violence under sovereign command." Elsewhere he refers to "violence, limited by authority." "Under sovereign command" and "limited by authority" obviously refer to civilian authority, the tradition of the military being subservient to the civilian authority, a tradition recognized in the western world. The most notable exception to this rule in the twentieth century was Adolf Hitler, who represented an amalgam of both the political and the military authority. The philosophy behind the foregoing is that the civilian authority would be more amenable to moral considerations, thus making war more humane than it probably would be if left solely to the military strategists and tacticians.

Hugo Grotius, the so-called father of international law, in his celebrated *De jure belli ac pacis*, laid down the rule that natural law is just as applicable to nations as to individuals. This ameliorative doctrine was given great impetus by Woodrow Wilson and accepted universally when war crimes as a concept was recognized and reached fruition in the Nuremberg War Crimes Trials. Preserving peace and preventing war must be worked at harder than ever. The wonderful title of General Dwight D. Eisenhower's book *Waging Peace* says it all. Peace has to be striven for; it has to be fought for; it has to be waged more resolutely and relentlessly even than war.

Literary alternatives to war, sans violence and albeit humorous, have been offered from time to time. Erich Maria Remarque had his soldiers suggest that a dispute between potential combatants be settled by the outcome of fisticuffs engaged in by their leaders. Thomas Carlyle counseled that the chiefs of state of adversaries sit together in a tent and smoke extra strong cigars and blow the smoke in each other's face until one passes out.

Surprise (or sneak) attacks should be outlawed by international law. There should be no more tricks with semantics played; a war should not be referred to as a "police action," and Article I, sec. 8, cls. 1 and 11 of the United States Constitution, and all that these provisions imply, should be rigorously observed: "The Congress shall have power . . . to declare war." War should be initiated only after the Congress declares same.

As to whether a war crimes trial should be held, the reactions of the four great victorious powers were very different. The question was met with apathy and disinterest by France. The United Kingdom and the Soviet Union agreed that summary execution of so-called German war criminals sans a trial would be the proper course to follow but disagreed as to the number to be shot, the former favoring approximately fifty (mainly civilian), the latter more nearly fifty thousand (principally military), almost five times the number of Polish officers the Soviet Union massacred at Katyn forest near Smolensk. The United States prevailed and proceeded to make a mockery and travesty out of the most notorious trial in history.

What could be as inconsistent as the United States, the only one of the four major victorious Allies really wanting and in fact insisting on trials in order to present the facade of legality to the punishment to be dispensed, but in the process violating its own organic law, its own highest secular law? The United

States was a signatory to the London Agreement, which was a treaty, and the Constitution of the United States proclaims a treaty "shall be the supreme law of the land," according to Article VI, sec. 2. The crimes specified in the Charter for the International Military Tribunal (IMT), promulgated pursuant to the London Agreement and after the fact, that is, after the acts were committed, were war crimes, crimes against peace, and crimes against humanity. These new crimes were applied retroactively to acts perpetrated before they were designated as criminal. The United States Constitution specifically prohibits an "ex post facto Law," according to Article I, sec. 9, cl. 3.

The IMT had no jury; the tribunal determined the facts as well as the law. The Constitution guarantees that "the trial of all crimes . . . shall be by jury," as stated in Article III, sec. 2, cl. 3. *Tu quoque* is a doctrine which can best be understood by explaining it in terms of the biblical statement "Let him who is without sin cast the first stone." Tu quoque was banned in toto by the IMT: defense counsel were forbidden from defending their individual or organizational clients by pleading that other individuals, organizations, or sovereign states committed the same acts with impunity. The IMT made a fatal mistake, however; it did not create an indispensable exception to its total prohibition of the tu quoque defense. It should have been receptive to the doctrine when the individual, organization, or state was one of the (or of one of the) plaintiff victorious Allies.

For example, Grand Admiral Erich Raeder, the commander-in-chief of the German Navy, was tried for, inter alia, the invasion of Norway when in fact it was a preemptive strike against a projected British invasion of Norway. In short, Grand Admiral Raeder was accused of the same act which Great Britain was planning to perpetrate. The planning to perpetrate was an attempted crime (a so-called war crime), but planning to commit a crime without more does not rise to an attempt to commit a crime; planning in addition requires an overt act in furtherance of the criminal enterprise. There was an overt act and the overt act consisted of the making of the tangible, physical plans in writing, the maps, the blueprints, the charts, the graphs, the diagrams of the projected Norwegian expedition in the files of the British Admiralty.

Further, for example, the German General Staff and the High Command were tried for, inter alia, the Katyn massacre, the murder of eleven thousand Polish officers in Katyn wood, which crime in fact was committed by the Russian Army. It was a study in hypocrisy to have banned the tu quoque defense in its entirety.

Any future international criminal trial could satisfy necessary criteria for justice using the same designated crimes and their respective definitions, plus the allowance of a jury and the limited tu quoque defense.

The IMT trials serve a salutary twofold purpose: (1) There is a new right (about fifty years old), and a fundamental right at that—the right to protection against war crimes. This is because (2) it is a matter of common knowledge that there will be redress of war crimes due to stare decisis, the binding force of legal precedent established by the IMT trials, providing the nation having the right to protection against war crimes is victorious.

Herbert Kraus, professor at the University of Göttingen and counsel for the defense of Dr. Hjalmar Schacht at the trials, wrote: "It would have been very desirable if German law (naturally not Nationalist Socialist sham law) had been applied instead of a law confusing not only to the defendants but to the defense counsels as well. . . . [I]t is particularly unfortunate that only representatives of the four great world powers sat on the bench." Karl Hänsel, professor at the University of Tübingen, wrote: ". . . the Tribunal consisted of neither a representative of the defeated Germany nor a representative of a neutral nation."

References

Hänsel, Karl. "The Nuremberg Trial Revisited." *De Paul Law Review* 13 (1967), 248.

Kraus, Herbert. "The Nuremberg Trial of the Major War Criminals: Reflections After Seventeen Years." *De Paul Law Review* 13 (1967), 233.

Howard Newcomb Morse

See also Conscientious Objection; Rebellion; Revolution

Weber, Max (1864–1920)

Rightly regarded as a key founder of the social-scientific study of the law, Max Weber

was born in Erfurt as the son of a lawyer and studied law at Heidelberg, Berlin, and Göttingen. He attained the status of *Referendar* (junior barrister) in 1886 and was granted his doctorate of laws in 1889 from Berlin with a dissertation on legal aspects of medieval trading companies. He was habilitated in 1891 with a thesis on Roman agrarian history and its significance in public and private law.

Weber studied with some of Germany's greatest legal scholars and historians (that is, Otto von Gierke, Evin Goldschmidt, Theodor Mommsen) and absorbed influences from several strands of German jurisprudence without becoming a disciple of any particular school. However, Stephen Turner and Regis Factor have argued persuasively that Max Weber's ideas about law were especially indebted to the school of historical jurisprudence centered on the work of Rudolph von Jhering. It was from Jhering that Weber derived his well-known definition of the state as the institution with a monopoly on the legitimate use of force to uphold a legal order.

Before his appointment to a professorship in political economy at Freiburg in 1895, Weber taught law courses at Berlin and considered a career practicing or teaching law. His turn toward political economy and eventually to sociology reflected his changing approach to the understanding of law and its relation to other institutions, especially the economy and the polity. He spent most of his career at Heidelberg and taught briefly at Vienna and Munich toward the end of his life.

Weber eschewed the philosophy of law, which he understood to be an ultimately *speculative* concern with such questions as the overall purpose of the law, in favor of the history and sociology of law. His concern with the history of law was an attempt to discern some pattern in the historical development of continental law from its Roman origins. Working with distinctions between irrational versus rational, and substantive versus formal rationality, he claimed that the course of occidental development was one of historical *rationalization*, associated with the decline of substantive values, coupled with an increase in rationality with respect to procedure. Modern institutions, especially law and the state, are thus characterized as increasingly *formally rational*. At the same time, Weber rejected theories of all-encompassing social evolution. He shared the historicist view that history lacked the systematic unity and linearity to sustain an evolutionary model. Historical patterns are uneven, contingent, and available only to hindsight.

Weber understood that his conception of modern *formal rationality* as the culmination of historical rationalization was more applicable to the development of continental law, than to English law. His views on the English exception to this development have been challenged by D. Sugarman, who has questioned whether English law is less rational than continental law.

Weber's sociology of law, presented in his major work, *Economy and Society*, is based on a distinction between the normative and the empirical *validity* of the law. *Normative* validity ("What is the [meaning of] the norm/law which applies to a specific case?") is the concern of the juridical perspective; *empirical* validity ("What is the probability that people in a certain situation will act in conformity with a certain norm?") is the focus of the sociological approach. In this respect Weber's approach countered that of Rudolf Stammler, a contemporary neo-kantian legal scholar, whom Weber critiqued for failing to make this distinction.

Sociologically, law, for Weber, is distinguished from both custom and convention. *Custom* is understood as the habituated patterns of conduct within a group or community. Whereas individuals can deviate from many customary patterns without fear of reprisals, both convention and law constitute social norms or rules, violation of which is likely to be sanctioned by the social environment. *Convention* is supported by sanctions of communal disapproval. In contrast to convention, *law* is coercively enforced by a *staff* of people responsible for enforcing compliance or avenging violation.

Although in modern societies the state has become the primary context of legal authority and coercion, Weber's conception of the law also accommodates the study of legal phenomena outside the sphere of the state (for instance, church and secular corporate bodies) as well as in premodern and non-western societies. Moreover, Weber believed that custom and convention continue to play key roles in patterning and regulating conduct, even in modern societies where legal institutions are highly developed, and, contrary to the expectations of evolutionary theories, are not displaced by the elaboration of law and the expansion of state legal institutions.

References

Kronman, A. *Max Weber*. Stanford: Stanford University Press, 1983.

Rehbinder, M. "Max Weber und die Rechtswissenschaft" (Max Weber and Legal Science). In *Max Weber als Soziologe* (Max Weber as Sociologist), ed. M. Rehbinder and K. P. Tieck. Berlin: Duncker und Humblot, 1987.

Rheinstein, M. "Introduction." In *Max Weber on Law in Economy and Society*, ed. M. Rheinstein. Cambridge: Harvard University Press, 1954.

Sugarman, D. "In the Spirit of Weber: Law, Modernity and the 'Peculiarities of the English.'" Madison WI: Institute for Legal Studies, 1987.

Turner, S., and R. Factor. *Max Weber: The Lawyer as Social Thinker*. London: Routledge, 1994.

Weber, M. *Critique of Stammler*. Trans. G. Oakes. New York: Free Press, 1977.

———. *Economy and Society: An Outline of Interpretive Sociology*. Ed. G. Roth and C. Wittich. 3 vols. Berkeley: University of California Press, 1978. [Translation of *Wirtschaft und Gesellschaft. Grundriss der verstehenden Soziologie*. 4th ed. Tübingen: J.C.B. Mohr (Paul Siebeck), 1956.]

John Drysdale

Western European Legal Culture in the Twentieth Century

The semantic distinction between the concepts of *culture* and *civilization* is necessary to reach a proper understanding of them. Today, the term "civilization" connotes mainly the technical rationality which encompasses the old European continent. Of course, the concept of civilization is usually included in the concept of culture, but it is only an element of it. The word "culture" has another and a broader meaning: it refers to judgments, memory, beliefs, norms, and values, and also to a strong creative liberty. Thus, culture opens the way to pluralism and relativity in time and space, by means of its spiritual dimension.

Western European culture, in the twentieth century, presents an authentic specificity in comparison with other cultures in the same period of time, such as eastern European cultures and Anglo-Saxon or Asian cultures. Nevertheless, in consideration of liberty, which is its most important component, western European culture is far from unilinear and homogeneous. Among its main characteristics, we can discern two major but antagonistic tendencies. The first one, dominant until the end of World War II, corresponds to a triumphant rationalism, inherited from the Enlightenment philosophy and the positivism of the nineteenth century. The second stream, which was almost imperceptible until the middle of this century, and which expressed much anxiety, was an irrationalist reaction, corresponding to an endemic crisis whose social, political, and ideological symptoms are at present pervasive.

The first half of the century was dominated by the *powers of rationality*: mathematics, the physical sciences, and technology achieved spectacular progress. Consequently, the idea of progress, inherited from eighteenth-century philosophy, was renewed and strengthened: comfort, well-being, and happiness increasingly became the chief preoccupation of people. The two terrible world wars greatly disturbed this progress. At the same time, however, both wars stimulated technical research and material progress. Further, since technical rationality is not the whole of culture, the wars brought social and ideological mutations with ethical and political consequences.

In order to understand these cultural transformations, we must understand their philosophical background. Because the kantian dichotomy between theoretical and practical reason had such an extraordinary success, the powers of reason are considered not only in a speculative and scientific perspective, but also in terms of social and moral views. Alongside the rapid development of positivist domination of man over nature, liberal and democratic ideas follow their own path. As heir to Enlightenment philosophy, modern thought values humanism: critical capacity and claims for autonomy are connected to a strong affirmation of the subject; being a vector of action, the subject also becomes an agent for the objective order of society. Individualism explains the growing hunger for property, the will for liberation of workers, the hope of women for independence, the aspirations of citizens for an active participation in political life, all of which express the freedom of the subject. This primacy of private interest, which is a characteristic of modern rationality, is the ground on which grow economical liberalism, the philosophy of human rights, and the spring of democratic ideas.

Of course, these general features do not have an absolute value. In a desacralized world, where laicization becomes a dogma, there are strong polemics and controversies about various conceptions of labor, equality, freedom, social contract, and political representation. Rationalization of society appears to be more problematic than the rational control of nature. So, just before World War II, signs of the European cultural crisis begin to rend and fragment the intellectual landscape.

Around the 1930s, the rise of national socialism was the most eloquent symptom of the uneasiness in culture. Soon, an *irrationalist movement* invaded western Europe. In its beginnings, the Nazi ideology was a reactive opposition to marxist materialism and, especially, to stalinist communism as well as to liberal democracy. However, it soon transformed itself to a pretended vitalism, more or less closed into irrationalist currents, which are said either to be impregnated by nietzschean philosophy or to borrow their inspiration from the myth of strength and power. Contrary to the philosophy of human rights, the Nazi ideology adopted "the right of the strongest" and developed a mystic of war, eugenics, ethnic purification, and the elimination of the Jewish race.

On one hand, the will to strength and power gave a formidable impulse to technology, but, in the war industry, all efforts led paradoxically to destruction and death. However, on the other hand, the misfortune and disaster of war gave rise to a certain solidarity among populations. Prewar individualistic habits were kept in the background, and the sense of community and mutual aid changed manners and ways of thinking. More than ever, the greatness of liberty became the ideal which was opposed to "the road of serfdom." With a striking intellectual lucidity, people became conscious of the analogies between totalitarianism, fascism, and communism. Gradually, these political systems appeared to be monstrous, since their archetypal regimes of a "closed society" were unforgivably offensive to human dignity. Thereafter the aspiration to freedom converted people to an imperative need for democracy, as if this type of regime could immediately bring the realization of all hopes. The ideal of "the open society" produced a new form of progress: democracy, human rights, constitutionalism, the idea of the "state of law," have gained a high prestige, since they symbolize the protection of citizens against the authority of power.

Despite its large consensus, this idea of open society led to an alarming drift: the image of the welfare state invaded social and political literature, producing frail but fascinating mirages of guaranteed security and well-being forever. Although Carl Schmitt and Hans Kelsen were enemies in their jurisprudence, they were radically opposed to this perspective. But, at the same time and despite Friedrich von Hayek's legal theory, the liberal idea of liberty was transformed into the libertarian idea of liberty. Progressively, the dream of an unconditional and absolute liberty took on the utopian guise of a sublime ideal: "If God does not exist, everything is permitted." In a climate defined as "postmodern," the libertarian vertigos, supported by the existentialist and vitalist or structuralist philosophies, dangerously inflated rights into a mass society without elites and hierarchy—but, if everything is right, nothing is right! So instrumental rationality and technology continued their development toward the "consumer society," rejecting traditional values, and provoking debate and confrontations, strikes and civil disobedience, legal transgressions, and even violence.

However, after the acute crisis of 1968, the malaise does not have the same tough figure today. From an *intellectual point of view*, a renewed rationalism, through practical and argumentative processes, takes the place of hypothetico-deductive rationalism and intemperate irrationalism. Chaïm Perelman in his "new rhetoric" introduced into legal and political spheres, for instance, the search for proofs to justify a thesis or a situation, the will to legitimate arguments or behaviors, the desire of consensus. Very often, tolerance is invoked in the name of universal reason and dignity. In the same constellation of ideas, and since the theme of universality had become quasi-obsessional, the appeal to a broadening conception of rights—either legitimately, such as women's rights, children's rights, patients' rights, or by aberration, such as animal rights, nature's rights, environmental rights—is put forth either unfinished or with solemnity but, in all cases, with dissonant tones. Even if ecological dogma expresses well-founded fears concerning the squandering of natural resources and the pollution of natural surroundings, the political pursuit of these ideas by various factions is often inappropriate, either by excess or by inefficiency.

From a *social point of view*, the will for democracy produces ambivalent and sometimes incoherent and contradictory manifestations. So, mass rule is evidently served by mass education, but this results from greater influence by mass media. Ideological indoctrination is facilitated by audiovisual communication, publicity, and electronic treatment of communication, for people are then reduced to the level of passive spectators. Similarly, while the level of life is generally higher, the number of unemployed is increasing; alongside the comfortable population, poverty is not negligible; while conditions of health are carefully controlled, the use of drugs and cases of AIDS are increasing.

Finally, from a *political point of view*, we can see the rise of nationalisms and regionalisms. More significant, however, is the "crisis of legitimation" of power. The gap is deeper and deeper between the aspirations of people and the degree of satisfaction offered by governments. If culture depicts one's values and liberty, western European culture is fragmented and anxious: unruliness, troubles, disorders, and financial corruption, even though sporadic, are signs that spiritual values are threatened.

During the twentieth century, western European culture, in which influences so different as the kantian or aristotelian or thomist also had place, appeared to be complicated and frail because of its multidimensional and conflictual character. Surely, that is due to its creative liberty, demonstrated in its science, arts, literature, and philosophy. Its differences in *space* (the plurality of nationalities, trade and connections with other cultures, intellectual relations between elites in sciences and arts, as well as immigration and the welcome to political refugees) and in *time* (the creative evolution of its thought, and the succession or the meeting of various philosophies) made European culture both vital and hazardous at once.

The long and rich history of old Europe is always sleeping behind the fortunes and misfortunes of the twentieth century. Consequently, it is difficult to imagine the decline or fall of western culture: it remains a source of spiritual values and, in spite of misadventures and in the face of dramas which tear our planet, it is surely the place where human dignity and liberty remain the most noble hope.

References

Bourgeois, Bernard. "Il destino francese dei 'Lineamenti di filosofia del diritto' di Hegel" (The French Appropriation of Hegel's "Outlines of Philosophy of Law"). *Giornale critica di filosofia italiana* 67 (1988), 321–347.

Buhr, Manfred, ed. *Vivarium: Das geistige Erbe Europas* (The Spiritual Heritage of Europe). Naples: Vivarium, 1994.

Gessner, Volkmar. "Global Legal Interaction and Legal Cultures." *Ratio Juris* 7 (1994), 132–145.

Gizbert-Studnicki, Tomas. "Conceptions of 'The Nature of Thing' in West German Philosophy of Law." *Etyka* 19 (1981), 133–155.

Goodhart, Arthur L. *English Contributions to the Philosophy of Law*. New York: Oxford University Press, 1949.

Hildendorf, Eric. "Rechtsphilosophie im vereinigten Deutschland" (Philosophy of Law in United Germany). *Philosophische Rundschau* 40 (1993), 1–33.

Jackson, Gilder D., IV. "Western Europe." *Journal of International Law and Practice* 1 (1992), 125.

Klami, Hannu Tapani. "Legal Philosophy in Finland: Trends in Past and Present." In *Man, Law and Modern Forms of Life*, ed. Eugenio Bulygin, 137–159. Dordrecht: Reidel, 1988.

Prott, L.V. "A Change of Style in French Appellate Judgments." *Logique et analyse* 21 (1978), 51–66.

Ward, Ian. "Kant and the Transnational Order: Towards a European Community Jurisprudence." *Ratio Juris* 8 (1995), 315–329.

Ziembinski, Zygmunt, ed. *Polish Contributions to the Theory and Philosophy of Law*. Amsterdam: Rodopi, 1987.

Simone Goyard-Fabre

Wittgenstein, Ludwig (1889–1951)

Ludwig Wittgenstein was the youngest of eight children born to Karl and Leopoldine Wittgenstein. As a young man, Wittgenstein studied mathematics, engineering, logic, and music. His philosophical views remain among the most-discussed in the twentieth century. How best to characterize what he said and wrote is subject to much dispute. He published one philosophical work in his lifetime, *Tractatus logico-philosophicus* (Logical-Philosophical Treatise). An English-language translation appeared in 1922. The work was not then understood. Equally

significant is *Philosophical Investigations*, published shortly after his death.

Although Wittgenstein only mentioned the law in passing, several aspects of his philosophical thought are worth serious consideration. His remarks on the philosophy of psychology are an antidote to the deleterious effects induced by "cognitive science" both in its pure form and its derivations in law. What Wittgenstein shows is that nothing that goes on in our brains can explain the meaning of what we say.

Of equal importance are Wittgenstein's remarks on practices, language games, and forms of life. Much has been written on these topics, both in the philosophical literature and elsewhere. The vast portion of this commentary is of questionable utility. In one field, literary theory, the work of Charles Altieri and John Ellis are exceptional in their understanding of the implications of Wittgenstein's thought for literature and literary theory.

Lawyers, particularly academic lawyers, have concentrated their attention on Wittgenstein's remarks on rule-following (see *Philosophical Investigations*, sec. 145–242). It is often said that Wittgenstein was a skeptic about rule-following, and that his remarks support the thesis that the law is "indeterminate." This view is mistaken. In fact, quite the opposite is the case: Wittgenstein showed that skepticism—relentless doubting—is itself little more than naked metaphysical assertion. Worse, careful consideration of Wittgenstein's remarks on rule-following show that the indeterminacy thesis itself is quite indefensible.

A related but distinct issue is the question of interpretation. It is often said, following Martin Heidegger, that all understanding is interpretation; that humans are by their nature "interpretive animals." In jurisprudence, it is now quite fashionable to assert that all understanding of the law is a matter of interpretation, as noted by Ronald Dworkin and Stanley Fish. This cannot be, however, and Wittgenstein showed why this is the case.

Wittgenstein addresses both rule-following and interpretation in sec. 201 of *Philosophical Investigations*. He states:

> This was our paradox: no course of action could be determined by a rule, because every course of action can be made out to accord with the rule. The answer was: if everything can be made out to accord with the rule, then it can also be made out to conflict with it. And so there would be neither accord nor conflict here.
>
> It can be seen that there is a misunderstanding here from the mere fact that in the course of our argument we give one interpretation after another; as if each one contented us at least for a moment, until we thought of yet another standing behind it. What this shews is that there is a way of grasping a rule which is not an interpretation, but which is exhibited in what we call "obeying the rule" and "going against it" in actual cases.
>
> Hence there is an inclination to say: every action according to the rule is an interpretation. But we ought to restrict the term "interpretation" to the substitution of one expression of the rule for another.

This section contains three paragraphs. The first paragraph states a (seeming) paradox. If everything can be made to accord with a rule, then the rule exercises no constraint on action. Thus, neither following the rule nor violating it is possible. In his much discussed reading of this passage, Saul Kripke argued that the paradox arises from a failure of our past intentions to constrain present dispositions.

As a possible solution to the paradox, the idea of "interpretation" is introduced. This occurs in the second paragraph, but the idea is immediately rejected because an interpretation of the rule itself would stand in need of interpretation. There being no way to stop this infinite regress, Wittgenstein suggests that there must be a way of grasping (*Auffassung*) the rule which is not an interpretation. Finally, in the third paragraph, Wittgenstein suggests that the use of the word "interpretation" ought to be restricted to those instances where understanding of the rule and what it requires breaks down.

Wittgenstein's theory of practices shows how the normative character of rule-following is a function of shared criteria for what counts as following and violating the rule. In jurisprudence, Philip Bobbitt has taken this insight the furthest, arguing that the truth of propositions of constitutional law is shown through the use of modalities of argument.

References

Altieri, Charles. *Act and Quality*. Amherst: University of Massachusetts Press, 1981.

Bobbitt, Philip. *Constitutional Interpetation*. London: Blackwell, 1991.

Ellis, John. *Against Deconstruction*. Princeton: Princeton University Press, 1989.
Kripke, Saul. *Wittgenstein on Rules and Private Language*. Cambridge MA: Harvard University Press, 1982.
Patterson, Dennis. *Law and Truth*. Oxford: Oxford University Press, 1996.
Schulte, Joachim. *Wittgenstein: An Introduction*. Trans. William H. Brenner and John F. Holley. Albany: State University of New York Press, 1992.
Wittgenstein, Ludwig. *Philosophical Investigations*. 3d ed. Trans. G.E.M. Anscombe. New York: Macmillan, 1958.
———. *Tractatus logico-philosophicus* (Logical-Philosophical Treatise). Trans. David Pears and Brian McGuinness. London: Routledge and Kegan Paul, 1961.

Dennis Patterson

Wróblewski, Jerzy (1926–1990)

Jerzy Wróblewski, after studies in law and philosophy at the University of Cracow, became an assistant in the chair of legal theory at its Faculty of Law, where he obtained the doctoral degree with a thesis on "Ethical Norms and Value Judgments" in 1949. Appointed assistant professor in the chair of legal theory at the University of Lodz in 1951, he remained active there as dean, 1955–1957 and 1962–1964, then rector, 1981–1983. He was a member of the Polish Academy of Science from 1983, president of the International Association for the Semiotics of Law, visitor at many institutions in Europe and America, and author of approximately eight hundred publications in several languages covering developments in all important trends of contemporary legal philosophy.

Initially influenced by Leon Petrazycki's psychological view of law, and the logical empiricism of the Vienna Circle and the Lvov-Warsaw philosophical school, he elaborated his own standpoint, which can be characterized as noncognitivistic and analytical, metatheoretical, and pluralistically relativistic. His main contributions belong to the domains of the theory of legislation, legal interpretation, and application of the law, as well as to the theory of legal systems and to general legal philosophical problems.

In the theory of legislation, his construction of a model of rational lawmaking includes the following stages: stating the goal in a way sufficiently precise to enable the choice of means serving its realization; stating the impact of potential means to the goal or projected state of affairs; stating which legal regulations are acceptable means in terms of their effectiveness, their concordance with the legislators' axiological choices, and their relation to other potential means; choosing appropriate legal means; and legal regulation in accord with this.

His theory of legal interpretation's semantic basis is that the intension of the norm is "the pattern of due behavior," while its extension is its fulfillment value and the normative direction of meaning. Legal interpretation is "operative interpretation," excluding cases of "directed understanding" of the norm. A distinction is made between normative and descriptive theories of legal interpretation.

There are four theoretical models to his theory of legal application: functional, informative, decisional, and procedural. His reconstruction of the types of ideologies in legal application include bound decision, free decision, and lawful-rational decision. He analyzed the role of value judgments in fixing the meaning of the norm, in validating decisions, in establishing facts of the case, and in determining legal consequences.

For Wróblewski, the completeness of a legal system is based on the assumption of the norm closing the system, on the norm of completeness in qualifying it, and on the general norm imposing a duty to decide cases. He distinguished the systems of "statutory," "logically expanded," "interpreted," "operative," and "postulative" law, and analyzed their relations to the models of dynamic, static, and mixed normative systems.

On general legal problems, Wróblewski studied the "levels" of law: linguistic, logical, psychological, sociological, and axiological. He analyzed multilevel and unilevel theories of law and preferred the pluralistic standpoint of the former. In analyzing law as a "normative science," he classified its ambiguities; for instance, "normative" can be taken to mean norm-creating, norm-evaluating, norm-describing, and normatively understanding. His work was to reconstruct the philosophical assumptions hidden in nonphilosophical theories of law. Gradually he shifted to a meta-theoretical standpoint, to consider the dependence of legal theories on their assumptions and their operational value relative to the kind of problems

under investigation. He affirmed or denied the scientific status of the study of law depending on the meta-scientific assumptions attached to a particular model of science.

References

Opałek, Kazimierz. "Philosophical-Methodological Considerations of Jerzy Wróblewski. Their Roots and Traits." Rivista Internazionale di Filosofia del Diritto 69 (1992), 321–337.

Ost, François. "L'oeuvre de Jerzy Wróblewski: Aux confins du paradigme analytique" (The Work of Jerzy Wróblewski: At the Limits of the Analytic Paradigm). *International Journal for the Semiotics of Law* 5 (1992), 115–130.

Wróblewski, Jerzy. *Contemporary Models of the Legal Sciences*. Wrocław: Ossolineum, 1989.

———. "The Problem of the Meaning of the Legal Norm." *Österreichische Zeitschrift für öffentliches Recht und Völkerrecht* 14 (1964), 253–266.

Kazimierz Opałek

Wrongdoing and Right Acting

To criminalize is to make an act a crime, that is, to pass a law that makes those who do the act liable to ordinary criminal penalties. Though the boundary between the criminal law and other parts of the law is not clear, it is clear enough for disputes about "criminalization." Such disputes generally turn on one or both of these questions: Is the act itself wrong? Should the criminal law seek to prevent it?

All crimes are (criminal) wrongdoing, by definition, but not all wrongdoing is criminal. There are legal wrongs that are noncriminal, for example, tort or breach of contract. There is also nonlegal wrongdoing: religious (cursing God), moral (betraying a friend), professional (violating the code of one's profession), social (belching at table), and even technical (misdiagnosing a patient). What, then, is the wrongdoing to be criminalized?

Wrongdoing is the opposite of doing right. For our purposes, an act is right in the strong sense ("*the* right thing to do") if, and only if, the appropriate standard requires it; but right in the weak sense ("all right") if the appropriate standard merely allows it. Thus, four is the "right" answer, in the strong sense, to the question How much is two plus two? But by train is only "all right" as an answer to the question How can I get from here to Detroit? Among the other (allowable) answers are by car and by plane.

While "right" has these two senses, "wrong" has only one: an act is wrong if, and only if, it is not all right. Wrongdoing is failing to satisfy the appropriate standard. Where there is more than one standard, an act can be both right and wrong. For example, what is right in a theatrical production, as judged by the standards of theatricality, may be wrong when judged by law, mathematics, or a child's view of things.

What, then, is the appropriate standard of right and wrong for criminalization? The common answer is morality. Criminalizing wrongdoing just means making criminal what is already morally wrong. This answer, though attractive in its simplicity, cannot be right. Hardly anyone appeals to morality to explain the main body of the criminal law. We generally explain the criminalization of, for example, random murder, theft, or disturbing the peace by the harm such acts do, not by their immorality (though they certainly are morally wrong). Something similar seems to be true of victimless crimes like tax evasion, failure to report a crime, or driving without a license. These crimes could be justified as punishing moral wrongs (for example, failure to do one's fair share). Instead, their defense is usually in terms of the practical benefits of having the law (for example, increasing the government's tax income).

If "criminalizing wrongdoing" means making *moral* wrongs crimes, the morality in question must be of a special sort. What sort? Crimes appearing most often in discussions of criminalizing wrongdoing can be divided into at least five (overlapping) classes:

Sexual Immorality

The most common wrongdoing under this heading today is same-sex intercourse. Less often mentioned are prostitution, adultery, premarital sex, nonstandard sexual practices (anal intercourse, for example), bigamy, and incest. Those involved must, of course, be consenting adults. Without consent, the acts in question would look much like ordinary crimes, such as battery.

Offensive Conduct

In this class belong such wrongs as public display of pornographic pictures, publicly soliciting sex, and desecrating an American flag (in the United States). Offense is similar to harm in being something unpleasant that one person does to another. Offense differs from (ordinary) harm insofar as offense depends on opinion. For example, sitting on an American flag is only offensive to those who think the flag is sacred.

Self-Abuse

"Self-abuse" is doing to oneself what morality forbids. Today the crimes most often defended (in part) as protecting people from self-abuse are those forbidding possession of certain recreational drugs ("drug abuse statutes"), though these can also be defended as protecting people from harming themselves.

Quasi-Persons

A quasi-person is a being that some people regard as sufficiently morally significant to deserve protection while others do not. Among quasi-persons today are the fetus, many animals such as whales and dogs, corpses, mountains, ecologies, and even the earth. Those who do not see the quasi-person in question as morally significant may complain that criminalizing harm to it is "legislating morality"; but those who see its moral significance will understand its protection as ordinary criminal law (that is, another instance of preventing harm to another).

Moral Pollution

Those who favor criminalizing striptease (in private clubs) or the discreet sale of pornography, as well as many of the acts already mentioned, sometimes appeal to the effect the acts in question have on the "moral atmosphere" of society. The analogy with ordinary pollution is that no single act does any (obvious) harm; it is (it is said) the pattern of action that causes "harm." The disanalogy is that the harm in question is not ordinary harm (as in ordinary pollution) but the "degeneration" of moral standards.

What do these five classes of wrongdoing have to do with morality? Philosophers often distinguish between "positive morality" and "critical morality." Positive morality consists of those practices actually in place in a given society that seem designed (however badly) to satisfy the requirements of critical morality. Positive morality is the standard of conduct that people generally attempt to follow and urge on others. More than mere custom, positive morality consists of actual practices everyone (more or less) wants everyone else to follow, even if that means having to do the same. Critical morality is a commentary on positive morality, seeking both understanding and improvement. Critical morality presupposes that, at their rational best, people would sometimes choose a standard of conduct different than they have in fact chosen.

What is striking about these five classes of "moral wrongdoing" is that they belong neither to positive nor to critical morality but to a hybrid category, what we might call "controversial morality." While a product of critical morality (however crude the reasoning), the judgment that such-and-such act (for example, homosexual sex) is morally wrong is presented as if positive morality plainly condemned it—when, in fact, the necessary social agreement either never existed or has ceased to exist.

While disputes about criminalizing "mere (moral) wrongdoing" now seem to arise only when the immorality of the wrongdoing is itself in question, such disputes might arise even about conduct everyone agreed to be immoral. Thomas Aquinas (1225–1274) long ago argued in sum that not all moral (or religious) wrongdoing ("vices") should be crimes because ordinary people, "being unable to bear such precepts, would break into yet greater evils." More recently, many writers, following John Stuart Mill (1806–1873), have argued for the "harm (or harm-to-others) principle": that the criminal law should punish only those acts doing or risking harm to others. Among recent writers who follow (something like) this tradition are Herbert Packer, Hyman Gross, and Douglas Husak, but Joel Feinberg is its best current representative.

The opposed tradition, though less articulate, has produced a few thoughtful defenses. Patrick Devlin (1950–1992) provides the best recent example.

References

Cranor, Carl. "Legal Moralism Reconsidered." *Ethics* 89 (1979), 147–164.

Devlin, Patrick. *The Enforcement of Morals.* London: Oxford University Press, 1965.

Dworkin, Ronald. "Moralism and Liberalism." In *Taking Rights Seriously*. Cambridge MA: Harvard University Press, 1977.

Feinberg, Joel. *Harmless Wrongdoing*. New York: Oxford University Press, 1988.

Gross, Hyman. *A Theory of Criminal Justice.* New York: Oxford University Press, 1979.
Hart, H.L.A. *Law, Liberty, and Morality.* New York: Vintage Books, 1963.
Husak, Douglas. *Drugs and Rights.* New York: Cambridge University Press, 1992.
Packer, Herbert L. *The Limits of the Criminal Sanction.* Stanford: Stanford University Press, 1968.
Schonsheck, Jonathan. *On Criminalization.* Dordrecht: Kluwer, 1994.
Schwartz, Louis B. "Moral Offenses and the Model Penal Code." *Columbia Law Review* 63 (1963), 670–182.

Michael Davis

See also PATERNALISM; PUNISHMENT; RESCUE IN TORT AND CRIMINAL LAW; RIGHTS AND LIBERTIES

Wrongful Life and Wrongful Death

In actions in tort for damages to compensate injured victims or their survivors for another's wrongful or negligent act, the jury must calculate the value of the difference between existence and nonexistence in the former and the value of the loss of existence of a deceased person in the latter

Wrongful life suits entail the claim by the infant that were it not for the physician's negligence, the infant would not have come into existence. The life itself constitutes the harm asserted because of the severe handicap or infirmity which characterizes the nature of the life. Most courts have rejected claims for wrongful life, recognizing that the law cannot calculate damages comparing existence in an impaired state to that of nonexistence because the damages enter the realm of speculation, contrary to well-established tort principles that require damages to be concrete and calculable. There is also difficulty in defining the injuries.

Competing rationales face courts in dealing with wrongful life suits. On one hand, children whose existence is allegedly due to the negligence of another should have a legal remedy. Conversely, the negligent parties have no actual liability for the handicaps of the children, for had the physician informed the parents of the possibility of bearing a severely handicapped or defective child, the child would not have been born, because the mother would have aborted the fetus.

Courts have difficulty quantifying the value of impaired life vis-à-vis nonlife and in dealing with the question of whether an impaired life is more burdensome than nonlife. The trend, therefore, is denial of a cause of action for wrongful life and a reaffirmation of the intrinsic value of life.

The wrongful life suit does not assert damages "cognizable at law." Early cases point out that there is no precedent for the recognition of a child's fundamental right to be born as a whole, functional human being, and the question of whether it is better never to have been born at all than to have been born with severe deficiencies is a proper question for philosophy and theology rather than law.

Four states, however, have recognized a wrongful life action: California, New Jersey, Washington, and Colorado. In the California appellate case that first dealt with the wrongful life cause of action, *Curlender v. Bio-Science Laboratories,* 106 Cal. App. 3d 811, 165 Cal. Rptr. 477 (1980), the court dismissed the philosophical aspects of the suit and upheld the wrongful life concept on public policy grounds. A subsequent California Supreme Court case, *Turpin v. Sortini,* 31 Cal. 3d 330, 182 Cal. Rptr. 377, 643 P.2d 952 (1982), realistically acknowledged that impaired life is not always preferable to nonlife, and that public policy has supported the rights of individuals to assess the value of their own lives—a determination that parents can make on behalf of their children. The court concluded that when parents are deprived of necessary information upon which to base a reasoned decision about the child's welfare, both parents and child are harmed. Courts have denied general damages (based on pain and suffering), but have awarded special damages (covering medical and other expenses) to the infant.

Collateral claims which have been recognized by most jurisdictions include wrongful birth actions, in which the parents are suing the caregiver for malpractice, alleging failure to provide adequate prenatal counseling or information (for example, timely warning of a potential problem in their child and the resultant failure to prevent the pregnancy or obtain an abortion), and "wrongful adoption" claims asserted by adoptive parents who sue agencies for money damages to defray the child's medical costs, asserting misrepresentation or withholding information about the biological family history that might affect the child later.

Wrongful death actions coupled with survival actions are prevalent in many states. Be-

cause there are then two causes of action, it is usually held that they may be pursued concurrently. Not recognized in the common law until mid-nineteenth century, there was no right of recovery for the death of one killed by the negligence or wrongful act of another. The family, therefore, was left without a remedy. While wrongful death statutes vary from state to state, their common purpose is to compensate the immediate dependent relatives for monetary losses caused by the death of the victim. Some states also permit recovery for deprivation of companionship, guidance, love, advice, and affection.

The wrongful death action is brought by the personal representative of the estate or the surviving spouse or next of kin seeking recovery for loss of support, consortium, and benefit to the survivors. The general measure of recovery is the value of the support, services, and contributions which the beneficiary might have expected to receive had death not intervened. Courts have also allowed consideration of a "hedonic" component of pecuniary loss, compensating for loss of the pleasure of living. Involving speculation to a greater or lesser degree, depending on matters such as life expectancy, income, character, habits, and health of the decedent and past contributions to his or her family, the jury is given wide discretion in assessing damages. This is especially true in cases involving the death of a minor child, where the course of the future is highly uncertain. Most states also permit prenatal wrongful death actions, at least after viability, to redress the wrong to the parents.

Survival statutes continue the decedent's cause of action; therefore, defenses such as contributory negligence, assumption of the risk, or consent may be asserted. The survival action is the estate's cause of action: the action which the decedent would have brought had he or she lived. Damages for pain and suffering, even if death was instantaneous, and medical and funeral expenses are included. Damages recovered by the estate are distributed according to the last will and testament of the decedent.

References

Botkin, Jeffrey R. "The Legal Concept of Wrongful Life." *Journal of the American Medical Association* 259 (1988), 1541–1545.

Peters, Philip G., Jr. "Rethinking Wrongful Life: Bridging the Boundary between Tort and Family Law." *Tulane Law Review* 67 (1992), 397–453.

Prosser, William L. *The Law of Torts*. 1941. 5th ed. with W. Page Keeton. *Prosser and Keeton on the Law of Torts*. St. Paul: West, 1984.

Smith, Stanley V. "Hedonic Damages in Wrongful Death Cases." *American Bar Association Journal* (September 1, 1988), 70–73.

Ulmer, Todd. "A Child's Claim of Wrongful Life: A Preference for Nonexistence." *Medical Trial Technique Quarterly* (1991), 225–239.

Marcia J. Weiss

See also ABORTION AND INFANTICIDE; PERSONAL INJURY; TORTS

Index of Names

The main entry for each topic is listed in **boldface.**

B

C

G

H

I

J

K

L

M

Q

R

S

Y

Z

Index of Cases

Index of Legislation and Legislative-Type Materials

Index of Topics

The main entry for each topic is listed in **boldface.**

A

B

C

D

E

F

G

H

J

K

L

M

N

O

P

Q

R

S

T

U

V

W